D1191196

IN THE EYE OF
THE BEHOLDER

IN THE EYE OF THE BEHOLDER

Contemporary Issues in Stereotyping

Edited by
Arthur G. Miller
Miami University

PRAEGER SPECIAL STUDIES • PRAEGER SCIENTIFIC

Library of Congress Cataloging in Publication Data
Main entry under title:

In the eye of the beholder.

Includes index.
1. Stereotype (Psychology)   2. Social
perception.   3. Social interaction.
I. Miller, Arthur G., 1940–
BF323   C5l48   305.5'6   81-11849
ISBN 0-03-051286-7   AACR2

Published in 1982 by Praeger Publishers
CBS Educational and Professional Publishing
a Division of CBS Inc.
521 Fifth Avenue, New York, New York 10175 U.S.A.

© 1982 by Praeger Publishers

3456789   052   98765432

Printed in the United States of America

PREFACE

The analysis of stereotyping has proved to be an issue of continuous importance and research interest to social scientists. Those with a social-problems or activist orientation have stressed the central position of stereotyping in prejudice, intergroup conflict, and hostility. Those with a laboratory orientation have emphasized the measurement of stereotypes and have been preoccupied with examining the information-processing and perceptual foundations of stereotyping. Stereotypes have been investigated from the perspectives of sociology and cultural anthropology as well as experimental cognitive psychology. Important contributions have been made within the disciplines of history, folklore, and political science, and students of literature, the media, religion, and psychiatry are also concerned with stereotypes. The topic has been, in essence, of extremely broad appeal.

The particular theme to be developed in this book is that stereotyping can be approached in two distinct ways. First, in the more narrow sense, stereotyping constitutes a manifestation of social perception. This perspective emphasizes the active role of the individual as he or she forms impressions of others, explains the behavior of others, and anticipates or predicts the actions of other people or groups. *In the Eye of the Beholder* was chosen as the title of this book to emphasize the central role of the perceiver or observer—the beholder or owner of stereotypes—in the process of stereotyping other people. This should not be misinterpreted, however, as implying that stereotypes are mirages or illusions, created in the mind and having no correspondence to the real stimulus world "out there." As will be developed more fully in the first chapter, this is not the intended message of the title. Yet, there is compelling evidence that it is all too easy to underplay the causal role of the observer in the process and product of social judgment, and to slip into the habitual belief that what is perceived is really out there, inside the person or group being judged. "In the eye of the beholder" should be understood as a sensitizer or correction factor, an important perspective—among several—to entertain in coming to grips with the elusive nature of stereotyping.

The second, broader approach recognizes the value of stereotyping as a conceptual unit of analysis regarding diverse aspects of social interaction. The emphasis here is upon the role of stereotyping in interpersonal relations—in prejudice, discrimination, intergroup conflict, and other arenas of social life. Because stereotyping involves people judging other people, it encompasses many related questions. It asks that we understand how people think about others, why people like or dislike others, and what it is that people find to be good or bad about others, for these are crucial elements in social outcomes—both for the target or victim of stereotypes as well as for the person owning them. Stereotypes force us to deal with other issues—with racism, sexism, and "isms" in general; with history, attitudes, and the media; with stigma, psychiatric diagnoses, and the labeling of deviance. One cannot isolate stereotyping from these concerns or appreciate the true significance of stereotyping without attending to these related factors. The task is thus a rather forbidding one in its scope. If this book succeeds in treating at least some of these matters in depth, and raising others to the reader's awareness, its mission will be achieved.

This book approaches stereotyping in terms of the scientific literatures that have developed around it. The first two chapters focus upon the basic conceptual dimensions of stereotyping. Chapter 1 outlines the major historical contributions to the study of stereotyping, raises the diverse and, at times, controversial aspects of the concept, and introduces the substantive chapters to follow. Chapter 2 discusses the process of stereotyping in terms of its social-perceptual and cognitive properties. The next seven chapters are concerned with stereotyping as manifested with respect to different social categories or target groups. The selection of these seven categories—racial and ethnic, anti-Semitism, sex, physical attractiveness, mental illness, aging, social class and poverty—was based on the extensive attention, in terms both of theory and of empirical research, that issues under these headings have received. While there are certain obvious parallels and similarities across these domains of stereotyping, there are important differences as well. The research literature reviewed in each chapter often can be quite accurately seen as homogeneous and distinct from the others. The final chapter considers additional illustrations of stereotyping and concludes with a review of certain issues yet to be resolved.

CONTENTS

IN THE EYE OF
THE BEHOLDER

1

HISTORICAL AND CONTEMPORARY PERSPECTIVES ON STEREOTYPING

Arthur G. Miller

INTRODUCTION

This book is about stereotypes. That very statement should prompt in the reader a variety of images about the likely nature of such a book. The word "stereotype" is so common in our vocabulary that it seems obvious what a book about stereotypes should be like. One thinks of stereotypes in terms of images, beliefs, prejudices, and bias—of caricatures, humor, and discrimination. One thinks of groups—of Jews, blacks, Puerto Ricans, and Poles. One thinks of conditions or stages of life—of the aged, the disabled, the mentally ill. There are stereotypes of occupations and hobbies—dumb "jocks," absent-minded professors, mild-mannered librarians, and crooked politicians. We stereotype nationalities and creeds—snobbish Englishmen, drunken Irish, Latin lovers, and lazy Mexicans. The list seems endless!

Alex Karras, a former star tackle with the Detroit Lions, was suspended for a year, in the middle of his career, on a gambling charge. In his autobiography he introduced this episode in his life with a passage that clearly illustrates ethnic stereotyping:

> All my life, even as a kid, I've known people who like to gamble. That doesn't make me unusual, because I'm Greek. If there's one trait a Greek has above all others, it must be his instinct to lay down a bet on just about anything that has odds attached to it. It's been part of our ethnic character for thousands of years. (1977, p. 152)

Notice the simplicity and plausibility of stereotyped reasoning, as well as the sheer usefulness of it. Karras seems to soften the personal taint of his gambling by "sharing the guilt" with his Greek compatriots.

The noted theologian James Parkes analyzed anti-Semitic stereotyping in a manner different in style but similar in substance to Karras's portrait:

> Antisemites never talk about "Jews" but always "*the* Jews." All are
> treated alike. If this is too glaringly absurd, then it will be insisted that
> any member of the minority who shows different characteristics is a rare
> exception. We all know the kind of remarks which begin with "some of
> my best friends are Jews but . . . ." . . . It could not be otherwise, for a
> "type" cannot have too subtle and complicated characteristics, or it
> would cease to be useful as a type. (1963, p. 12)

Parkes stresses the function or utility of stereotyping, addressing an issue
that has been raised by numerous theorists: the generalizations or oversim-
plifications in stereotyped imagery.

Illustrations of stereotyping span an enormous range, from reflections
on anti-Semitic stereotypes as a precursor of the Nazi Holocaust to the
humorous (for some, at least) sex stereotypes portrayed by Archie Bunker's
wife, Edith, and Archie himself. Humor, in fact, is intimately involved with
stereotyping, whether it be the "chicken soup" routines of Myron Cohen or
the ethnic hostility of Don Rickles or Richard Pryor. What seems funny to
some may not be to others. Consider Jack Olsen's commentary on the
Harlem Globetrotters:

> The old-style black athlete may still be seen . . . in the Harlem Globe-
> trotters, the white man's favorite black road show. The Trotters help to
> perpetuate the Negro stereotype. Running about the court emitting
> savage jungle yells, shouting in thick Southern accents ("Yassuh,
> yassuh!"), pulling sly larcenous tricks like walking with the ball when the
> (white) referee's back is turned, calling one another inane names like
> Sweetwater and Showboat, they come across as frivolous, mildly
> dishonest children, the white man's encapsulated view of the whole
> Negro race set to the bouncy rhythms of their theme song, *Sweet
> Georgia Brown.* Says Willie Worsley, a member of the University of
> Texas at El Paso national championship basketball team of 1966, "The
> Trotters are clowns and some of the young Negroes don't like it.
> . . . They're acting like white people think black people should act. If you
> turned the Harlem Globetrotters white overnight, they wouldn't draw
> the manager the next night. (Brigham & Weissbach, 1972, p. 28)

Others might focus instead on the athletic skill of the Globetrotters, the joy
in their interplay, the self-mocking aspect of their humor reflecting heightened self-esteem, their extraordinary salaries. Olsen's perception is instructive not because it is necessarily a valid interpretation, but simply because it
raises to our awareness an issue deserving of further thought. In this context
Daryl and Sandra Bem have described prejudice against women as "noncon-
scious ideology," as "a set of beliefs that we accept implicitly but of which we
are unaware because we cannot even conceive of alternative conceptions of
the world" (Aronson, 1980, p. 204). There is an overwhelming tendency to

habituate ourselves to the images we have of other people and to believe, casually and confidently, that "that's the way they are."

The subtlety of stereotypes is often crucial to their impact. At times it may be jolting to confront stereotypes when they are blatant and unexpected. When public figures "get caught" with their stereotypes, the media may justifiably regard them as "news." Such was the case with the well-publicized racial slurs by former Secretary of Agriculture Earl Butz, and remarks by former Chairman of the Joint Chiefs of Staff George S. Brown, who in a public speech referred to Jewish influence in Congress: ". . . it is so strong you wouldn't believe, now. . . . They own, you know, the banks in this country, the newspapers. Just look at where the Jewish money is" (*Newsweek*, Nov. 25, 1974, p. 39). Recall the saying "Sticks and stones may break your bones, but names can never hurt you." There would seem to be small comfort here to one on the receiving end of a stereotype.

Academic interest in the term "stereotype" is attributed historically to Walter Lippmann's book *Public Opinion*, published in 1922. Lippmann, a journalist, stressed the importance of understanding how people perceive and interpret the "facts" of social experience and events. As an analyst of public opinion, he felt it mandatory to appreciate the power and subtlety of subjective impressions. We shall shortly consider Lippmann's treatment, not only for its historical importance but also because it is a particularly convincing conceptualization of stereotyping. Although a host of disciplines have become involved with the concept, most of the theoretical analyses and research programs have been contributed by psychologists and sociologists. Those orientations, in particular that of social psychology, provide the general perspective of this book. To identify stereotyping with these disciplines should not, however, be taken as suggesting a coherent understanding of the term. There seems to be such an abundance of explicit as well as connotative substance to the concept that a consensus as to its conceptual nature has not been achieved. Yet, the complexities have been identified. The necessary and useful questions have been posed.

This chapter will review the historical landmarks as well as more contemporary developments in the literature on stereotyping. There is a coherence to this literature largely because of the impact of two works: Lippmann's conceptual analysis (1922), and Katz and Braly's (1933) research on the measurement of stereotypes. These will be reviewed, accordingly, in some detail. Various subsequent treatments of the stereotyping concept will then be examined. Although our goal is not to arrive at the true or even the best definition of stereotyping, there is a great deal to be learned by examining the efforts of others who have had this idea in mind. There is also an extensive network of issues and processes in which the stereotyping concept is embedded. The student of stereotyping must also be a student of social influence, attitudes, prejudice, intergroup relations, social perception, and other things. Yet despite the genuinely complex interactions with other phenomena, the stereotype concept has always seemed to have an intellectual appeal or intrigue of its own. It seems to constitute a pivotal issue or unifying theme amid a diversity of social phenomena.

WHAT IS A STEREOTYPE?

The derivation of the word is the Greek *stereos*, meaning solid, and *typos*, meaning the mark of a blow, impression, or model. The term was first used to describe a method of printing designed to duplicate pages of type. A metal plate, cast from a mold, was used instead of the original form. One link to contemporary usage was thus in the idea of duplication, that all products of the stereotype process would be identical. Another feature was rigidity or permanence. A dictionary of psychological terms has defined "stereotype" as:

> A relatively rigid and oversimplified or biased perception or conception of an aspect of reality, especially of persons or social groups, e.g., the perception of "bankers"—in general and without discrimination—as invariably cold-hearted in business dealings. (English & English, 1959, p. 523)

But what is meant, exactly, by the rigidity of stereotypes? What constitutes a legitimate simplification or generalization, as opposed to an oversimplification or overgeneralization? When is a perception biased, and when is it not? How might one tell whether a stereotype is true or accurate? These are reasonable questions to ask. Their answers have proved to be difficult. In pursuing them, let us first consider Walter Lippmann's remarkable treatment—the first of its kind—of stereotyping.

"PICTURES IN OUR HEADS"

Lippmann expanded on a theme that has become fundamental to contemporary thinking in social psychology: that people act not with respect to an objective or real environment, but in terms of their perception of that environment. In his opening chapter, entitled "Pictures in Our Heads," he voiced a phenomenological point of view: that to understand a person's behavior requires that we understand that person's view of his or her world. Lippmann advocated a cognitive view of behavior, specifying the link between thought and action:

> We must note . . . the insertion between man and his environment of a pseudo-environment. To that pseudo-environment his behavior is a response. But because it *is* behavior, the consequences . . . operate not in

the pseudo-environment where the behavior is stimulated, but in the real environment where action eventuates. (1922, p. 15)

What was the motivation for the construction of the "pseudo-environment"? Lippmann's answer was again predictive of contemporary thinking:

> For the real environment is altogether too big, too complex, and too fleeting for direct acquaintance. We are not equipped to deal with so much subtlety, so much variety, so many permutations and combinations. And although we have to act in that environment, we have to reconstruct it on a simpler model before we can manage with it. (1922, p. 16)

In order to bring the social world into more manageable dimensions, the individual imposes structure, seeking constancies or invariances. This is a major emphasis in contemporary attribution research (Schneider, Hastorf, & Ellsworth, 1979; see also Ch. 2 of this volume), where a central premise concerns our overwhelming tendency to view the actions of others as having causes and intentions. Social life seems to demand that we know the "why" of behavior. The gain, as we experience it, is a sense of control, of order, of predictability, of stability and meaning—hardly trivial outcomes for the seemingly simple act of perception. Indeed, the logic and apparent sanity in this mental imagery seem remote from the negative, antisocial connotations often associated with stereotyping. We shall reconsider this issue later in the chapter.

"Pictures in our heads" fittingly captured Lippmann's approach to public opinion, and led directly into an extensive discussion of stereotyping. Although not providing a formal definition of stereotyping, Lippmann used the term—as noun, verb, and adjective—to describe human perception and judgment in almost every conceivable way. It was hardly a lesson in conciseness, but it succeeded in launching the concept for generations of social scientists. Of no minor importance were the impressive style of his writing, the range of his intellect, the diversity of his illustrations, and the common sense of his arguments. He was in fact addressing common sense or "naive psychology," trying to make explicit the ways in which ordinary people explain, usually implicitly, their social worlds—a task Fritz Heider was to pursue some decades later (1958). We can best summarize Lippmann's analysis by listing a number of major themes and distinctions, most of which have become points of departure for subsequent research and theorizing.

Stereotypes as Constructive Mental Imagery

Lippmann referred to the active role of the observer in shaping his or her images of others: "An opinion is the joint product of the knower and known, in which the role of the observer is always selective and usually creative" (1922, p. 80). He suggested that people enter situations with preconceptions, and are likely to be most receptive to information that is consistent with these expectations. This observation bears directly on recent research emphasizing the individual's preference for information that confirms rather than negates his or her anticipations (Snyder, 1981, *a*).

Stereotypes as Simplifications in Perception

Stereotypes involved a deemphasis upon uniqueness and a premium on categorization: "We do not so much see this man and that sunset; rather we notice that the thing is man or sunset and then see chiefly what our mind is already full of on those subjects" (1922, p. 87). While it has become axiomatic that people react negatively to being typecast—"treat me as an individual" being the rallying cry for all who desire liberation—we see that the process of stereotyping epitomizes the loss of the individual case. Lippmann saw this process as inevitable and functional, but expressed admiration for those "whose consciousness is peopled thickly with persons rather than types, who know us rather than the classification into which we might fit" (1922, pp. 88–89). Perhaps on occasion there can be benefits in "getting lost" in a crowd of stereotyped targets. Consider the phrase "Black is Beautiful" as representing a kind of reverse stereotyping, in which a concerted effort is made to prize the category itself and to induce people to strive for group identification rather than be content with relatively individualized yet victimized status.

Are Stereotypes Good or Bad?

Although he has often been misinterpreted as championing a strictly negative view of stereotyping, Lippmann actually took an equivocal stand on this question. He emphasized the deficiencies of stereotyping in terms of its consequences, yet noted that "The abandonment of all stereotypes for a wholly innocent approach to experience would impoverish human life. What matters is the character of the stereotypes and the gullibility with which we employ them" (1922, p. 90). He thus made a sharp distinction between the process and the product of stereotyping, an insight that would often be rediscovered by later scholars (such as Fishman, 1956).

Our Awareness of Stereotyping

Lippmann felt that an effective antidote to stereotyping would consist in the simple recognition of its operation. Working against such recognition, however, were the subtlety of stereotyping, the quietness of its activation, and the illusion of its objectivity. A number of contemporary researchers have verified that individuals often lack conscious or verbalizable awareness of their own cognitive activity (Langer, 1978; Nisbett & Wilson, 1977a). Thus, an attractive photograph attached to a mediocre essay may result in that essay being judged as relatively high in quality (Landy & Sigall, 1974; also see Ch. 6 of this volume), although it is unlikely that raters would be able to verify that the photograph biased their judgments of the essay (Nisbett & Wilson, 1977b). (For a counterargument, however, see Ericsson & Simon, 1980.). This is not to say that individuals are unable to give an account of their perceptions but, rather, to suggest that such accounts may be inaccurate and imprecise in rather systematic ways. Lippmann pointed to the study of history as a strategy for sensitizing one to the simple fact that different people, at different times and places, perceive the world differently.

Stereotypes as a Defense

Lippmann conceived of stereotypes in emotional as well as cognitive terms:

> A pattern of stereotypes is not neutral. It is not merely a way of substituting order for the great blooming, buzzing confusion of reality. It is not merely a short cut. It is all these things and something more. It is the guarantee of our self-respect; it is the projection upon the world of our own sense of our own value, our own position, and our own rights. The stereotypes are . . . highly charged with the feelings that are attached to them. (1922, p. 96)

As Robert Zajonc (1980) has noted, it is impossible to think of social perception in strictly neutral terms, for the very substance of perception—trait images, for example—is inherently evaluative. Although many scholars have justifiably differentiated between the affective (such as prejudice and attitude) and cognitive (such as trait descriptions and images) dimensions of stereotyping (for example, Allport, 1954; Ehrlich, 1973), Zajonc's point is very pertinent. One's degree of liking or disliking for a person or group and one's stereotypes of that person or group, though useful to distinguish, are very intimately related.

In his use of the term "projection," Lippmann was suggesting that the individual's personality structure—needs, fears, habits—was a potential determinant of stereotyping. This was a perspective featured in research on authoritarianism (Adorno et al., 1950), where the association between stereotyping and individual differences in prejudice received its most pronounced statement (see also Ch. 4 of this volume). A similar emphasis appeared in the psychoanalytically oriented text on the dynamics of prejudice by Bettelheim and Janowitz (1950): In describing highly prejudiced soldiers (their research subjects), they noted:

> Their intolerance signified a much stronger underlying need for hostile discharge which had to be totally protected against possible disintegration through real experiences. In these cases the stereotype became their defense. . . .

> Any survey of those characteristics to which the members of the ingroup object in members of the outgroups is frequently a list of all those characteristics which they fear in themselves. (1950, pp. 34, 42)

Stereotypes served the classic anxiety-reduction function of defense mechanisms. In general, this orientation of relating stereotyping to individual differences in personality functioning was the prevailing point of view in the 1950s and 1960s. It remains an important perspective, although contemporary developments have approached stereotyping with a very different set of constructs and research goals.

Are Stereotypes True or False?

This question, a reasonable but difficult one, was given a measured, thoughtful answer by Lippmann:

> The myth is, then, not necessarily false. It might happen to be true. It may happen to be partly true. If it has affected human conduct a long time, it is almost certain to contain much that is profoundly and importantly true. What a myth never contains is the critical power to separate its truths from its errors. For that power comes only by realizing that no human opinion, whatever its supposed origin, is too exalted for the test of evidence, that every opinion is only somebody's opinion. (1922, p. 122)

He saw the difficulty of obtaining evidence that would bear on the accuracy of stereotypes, yet be independent of (or uninfluenced by) the stereotypes themselves, an observation similar to Allport's "traits due to victimization" (1954). He did not rule against the possible truth of stereotypes, but viewed this issue as less interesting than other kinds of questions, such as how the stereotype has come into existence, how the stereotype has affected human conduct, why the owner of the stereotype is in a poor position to assess its accuracy, and the possibility of stereotypes' becoming true even if initially false. The latter point forecast the influential "self-fulfilling prophecy" argument, a contemporary research problem in stereotyping (Snyder, 1981, *b*).

Stereotypes as Defective Cause-and-Effect Logic

Because stereotypes often take the form of personality attributions (such as lazy, stupid, submissive), it is important to understand how such images are sustained and how the individual finds support for such beliefs. Lippmann's insights again were prophetic (see Ch. 2 of this volume). Like later theorists (Nisbett & Ross, 1980), he portrayed the individual observer as a naive statistician: "The tendency of the casual mind is to pick out or stumble upon a sample which supports or defies its prejudices, and then to make it the representative of a whole class" (1922, p. 151). He referred to the ease with which the general (the poor are lazy, the beautiful are good) might be inferred from the specific individual case. Here Lippmann was critical, for he regarded stereotypes as too consequential to be based upon such minimally supportive evidence. Numerous theorists (Allport, 1954; Bettelheim & Janowitz, 1964) have suggested that when faced with an individual who does not manifest the stereotyped profile, the perceiver reacts to the individual as an exception that maintains rather than negates the rule.

Lippmann also commented upon linguistic features of stereotyping—for example, our dislike of qualifiers such as "maybe," "perhaps," "but," "in my opinion," or "some." Such words emphasize the "eye of the beholder," and could facilitate a more discriminating response to other individuals, in contrast with encompassing statements or beliefs about (all) members of social categories. He did not explain our lack of verbal modesty in this context, although one might suspect that the appearance of being in control, confident, and powerful is important to maintain. One would not want to appear indecisive or ambivalent by continuously qualifying or expressing hesitancy about one's social perceptions and images of others.

Summary of Lippmann's Contribution

Lippmann's conception of stereotyping involved describing how people think about others and why they do so. Stereotypes were viewed as relatively normal, and not the exclusive property of bigots. The process of stereotyping imposed control upon a potentially overwhelming array of social stimuli. In motivational terms, stereotypes helped to define one's status and to justify one's attitude or conduct toward others. Lippmann recognized the negative consequences of stereotyping, but also spoke to the implausibility of a cognitive system totally free of stereotypes. He noted the relationship between stereotyping and social behavior, commenting upon the individual's propensity to attend rather selectively to evidence that would be consistent with one's inferences. He was pessimistic as to the ability to monitor one's own stereotypes, although he felt this to be a useful corrective strategy. Although he considered various personal reasons for an individual to engage in stereotyping, his general treatment did not focus upon individual differences or variation in stereotyping.

Stereotyping, Lippmann asserted, is in all of us, as a reflection of our culture, our language, and (most critically) our manner of thinking. Lest we leave the impression that stereotyping is a relatively solitary or individualized, private experience, it is fitting to conclude our presentation of Lippmann's analysis with his comment on the role of stereotypes in intergroup conflict and interpersonal strife. This orientation has become a major contemporary perspective (as in Austin & Worchel, 1979), and Lippmann spoke directly to the matter:

> And since my moral system rests on my accepted version of the facts, he who denies either my moral judgments or my version of the fact is to me perverse, alien, dangerous. How shall I account for him? The opponent has always to be explained, and the last explanation that we ever look for is that he sees a different set of facts. . . . It is only when we are in the habit of recognizing our opinions as a partial experience seen through our stereotypes that we become truly tolerant of an opponent. Without that habit, we believe in the absolutism of our own vision, and consequently in the treacherous character of all opposition. For while men are willing to admit that there are two sides to a "question," they do not believe that there are two sides to what they regard as a "fact." (1922, p. 126)

Lippmann was the premier conceptualizer of stereotyping. Although he did not personally extend his ideas to research contexts, his work provided a stimulus for all subsequent developments. Perhaps it was his compelling metaphor "Pictures in our heads" that came to have the most lasting impact, specifically in its implications for the measurement of stereotypes. A case in point was the classic research of Katz and Braly (1933).

RACIAL STEREOTYPES OF 100 COLLEGE STUDENTS

Katz and Braly (1933) published one of the first research papers on stereotyping. It may well be the single most often cited reference in the literature. Their procedure was a simple one and related directly to the "pictures in our heads" analogy. They provided a list of 84 trait adjectives—negative (shrewd, lazy) as well as positive (intelligent, beautiful)—and asked research subjects to ". . . read through the list of words . . . and select those which seem to you typical of the Germans (etc.). Write as many of these words in the following space as you think are necessary to characterize these people adequately" (1933, p. 282).

The data were presented in tabular form, indicating the percentage of subjects endorsing each of the 12 most frequently assigned traits for each of 10 groups (Germans, Italians, blacks, Irish, English, Jews, Americans, Chinese, Japanese, and Turks). The basic research procedure was repeated at the same location (Princeton University) in 1951 (Gilbert, 1951) and in 1969 (Karlins, Coffman, & Walters, 1969). Table 1.1 presents a representative selection of the data from the original study and the two replications.

Katz and Braly calculated the degree of agreement among research subjects in terms of the least number of traits needed to account for 50 percent of all possible assignments. The original data were derived from each subject's five most preferred traits; thus perfect agreement among the 100 subjects would yield an index of 2.5, whereas perfect disagreement would be reflected by an index of 42 (that is, the entire list of 84 traits would be used with equal frequency). The investigators interpreted their data as indicating substantial agreement, in that the highest agreement, for blacks, was 4.6 and the lowest, for Turks, was 15.9. It should be noted here that the factor of interobserver agreement or consensus in trait endorsements has become a controversial problem. The degree to which consensus or agreement should be "built into" the conceptual definition of stereotyping has been a source of disagreement among researchers. This matter will be considered later in the chapter.

In a subsequent paper Katz and Braly (1935) analyzed the subjects' preference for the 10 groups in terms of social-distance rankings as well as the favorability of the traits assigned to each group. Diverse relationships among the measures were observed. The more a group was liked, for example, the more positive were the traits assigned to it—for instance, Americans and English were high on both measures, and blacks and Turks were lowest on both measures. However, while Turks were one of the most disliked groups, stereotypes were very low in agreement, suggesting that one could dislike or be prejudiced against a group in the absence of a well defined set of trait images of that group.

Katz and Braly linked their findings to the domain of prejudice. They interpreted stereotypes as the product of socialization, reasoning that their results could not reflect their subjects' actual interpersonal encounters with the various target groups. They took a decidedly moral stance, construing their results as proving the error involved in stereotyping:

> Stereotyped pictures of racial and national groups can arise only so long as individuals accept consciously or unconsciously the group fallacy attitude toward place of birth and skin color. To the realist, there are no racial or national groups which exist as entities and which determine the characteristics of the group members. It is true that certain behavior traits may be more frequently found among individuals of one nationality than those of another, but the overlapping is obviously very great. This can furnish no real basis for the race-entities which are ordinarily accepted and applied to foreigners (as well as to ourselves). (1933, p. 289)

TABLE 1.1
Percentage of Princeton Students Assigning Traits to Selected Groups: 1933, 1951, 1967

Trait	Checking Trait (%)			Trait	Checking Trait (%)		
	1933	1951	1967		1933	1951	1967
Germans				Blacks			
Scientifically minded	78	62	47	Superstitious	84	41	13
Industrious	65	50	59	Lazy	75	31	26
Stolid	44	10	9	Happy-go-lucky	38	17	27
Intelligent	32	32	19	Ignorant	38	24	11
Methodical	31	20	21	Musical	26	33	47
Extremely nationalistic	24	50	43	Ostentatious	26	11	25
Progressive	16	3	13	Very religious	24	17	8
Efficient	16	–	46	Stupid	22	10	4
Social	15	–	5	Physically dirty	17	–	3
Aggressive	–	27	30	Pleasure-loving	–	19	26
Arrogant	–	23	18				
Italians				Jews			
Artistic	53	28	30	Shrewd	79	47	30
Impulsive	44	19	28	Mercenary	49	28	15
Passionate	37	25	44	Industrious	48	29	33
Quick-tempered	35	15	28	Grasping	34	17	17
Musical	32	22	9	Intelligent	29	37	37
Imaginative	30	20	7	Ambitious	21	28	48
Very religious	21	33	25	Sly	20	14	7
Talkative	21	23	23	Loyal to family ties	15	19	19

Americans			
Revengeful	17	—	—
Pleasure-loving	—	28	33
Industrious	48	30	23
Intelligent	47	32	20
Materialistic	33	37	67
Ambitious	33	21	42
Progressive	27	5	17
Pleasure-loving	26	27	28
Alert	23	7	7
Efficient	21	9	15
Aggressive	20	8	15
Straightforward	19	—	9
Practical	19	—	12
Sportsmanlike	19	—	9
Individualistic	—	26	15
Conventional	—	—	17
Scientifically minded	—	—	15
Ostentatious	—	—	15

Chinese			
Persistent	13	—	9
Aggressive	12	—	23
Materialistic	—	—	46
Superstitious	34	18	8
Sly	29	4	6
Conservative	29	14	15
Tradition-loving	26	26	32
Loyal to family ties	22	35	50
Industrious	18	18	23
Meditative	19	—	21
Reserved	17	18	15
Very religious	15	—	6
Ignorant	15	—	7
Deceitful	14	—	5
Quiet	13	19	23
Courteous	—	—	20
Extremely nationalistic	—	—	19
Humorless	—	—	17
Artistic	—	—	15

Source: Adapted from Karlins, Coffman, & Walters (1969), Table 1, pp. 4–5, and Tedeschi & Lindskold (1976), Table 4.4, p. 165. Copyright 1969 by the American Psychological Association; 1976 by John Wiley & Sons, Inc. Reprinted by permission.

While many contemporary scholars (such as Campbell, 1967; Mackie, 1973) would take considerable issue with this statement, it still reflects a considerable amount of thinking to this date, and suggests the hesitation on the part of social scientists to attribute any sort of internal or genetic basis as a primary causal explanation for group differences. A contemporary illustration, of course, would be the heated controversy generated by Arthur Jensen's theory of racial differences in intelligence (1969).

Several features of the Katz and Braly procedure deserve emphasis. From a methodological point of view, their technique is simple and subjects seem to respond systematically to it. Critics have objected to the "demand for stereotyping" that seems inherent in the checklist instructions (Brigham, 1971). Subsequent replications of their study did note more frequent refusals to participate, even though subjects are actually allowed to select as many or as few traits as they wish. Some investigators (Ehrlich & Rinehart, 1965) have recommended the use of an open-ended or free-response format in which subjects do not check from a provided list of stereotypes, but enter their own descriptive adjectives. It is clear, however, that the standardized format has remained the more popular measurement approach.

Another problem concerns the transparency or obviousness of the technique. Subjects may be "on guard," suspicious that the researcher is studying their prejudice or stereotyping tendencies. In Gilbert's (1951) follow-up of the original, the data indicated more desirable trait responses, and these were attributed to a fading of the stereotypes themselves. Karlins et al. (1969) also noted a general increase in the positive tone of the stereotypes (with some exceptions, however), although the agreement among subjects was still substantial. One is left with the possibility that stereotypes have genuinely assumed a more liberalized character or that college students have become more cautious in expressing their (still) negative stereotypes in a research setting. These are not mutually exclusive possibilities, of course.

Sigall and Page (1971) tested the "on guard" hypothesis by comparing the checklist or rating scale format with a "bogus pipeline" procedure. The latter attaches the subjects to a lie-detector type of apparatus that is portrayed as an "infallible" indicator of true beliefs; the subject is then asked to predict what the machine is indicating. The goal is to obtain more genuinely held, deeper beliefs, assuming that under such circumstances the subject is pressured into being more revealing or candid. Their prediction was confirmed. Subjects were less positive in their stereotyping of blacks and more positive with respect to Americans when in the pipeline procedure than when using a rating scale. The pipeline technique has been criticized (Ostrom, 1973), but clearly the point has been made. There is a self-presentational bias that *may* distort stereotype responses. Of course, there is interest in the fact that subjects would feel obliged to "look good" in their responses even if these do not reflect innermost tolerance.

Another aspect of the Katz and Braly procedure that has been criticized concerns their not assessing the stereotypes held by individual subjects (see, for instance, Ashmore & Del Boca, 1981; Brigham, 1971; McCauley, Stitt, & Segal, 1980). A related point is that when subjects respond to the Katz and Braly procedure (or a variation thereof), they are indicating knowledge of the cultural stereotypes of the groups in question rather than their personal agreement with such trait patterns. These issues arc part of the more general problem of consensus or social sharedness of stereotypes, a problem that will be reconsidered later in this chapter.

The impact of the Katz and Braly paradigm has been profound. It is the prevailing technique for the direct assessment of stereotypes of all kinds of groups. Variations, of course, have been developed. It is now customary to use bipolar scales that assess degree or intensity of trait endorsement rather than the all-or-none approach (for example, *lazy*: 1 2 3 4 5 6 7: *industrious*). The statistical analysis of stereotype responses has also been refined—for example, in the use of factor analysis (Gardner, 1973) and scaling techniques (Rosenberg & Sedlak, 1972). These have permitted a greater understanding of the structure or organization of stereotype responses. Yet the central task confronting the research subject has remained basically the same. Stereotypes are cast in the language of personality traits, and subjects are asked to report on "the pictures in their heads."

One further point must be made concerning the issue of stereotype measurement. As will be shown in a number of the chapters of this book, many research investigations do not attempt direct measurement of the stereotypes at issue. The central measure might instead be the observers' evaluation of the target person, or their behavior toward the target person, or perhaps the amount of help extended to the person, or the degree of aggression directed against the person. The stereotype of the target person's group might constitute the crucial theoretical basis for a study, and yet the stereotypes per se might never be elicited. An advantage to this research strategy is that it may bypass the subject's awareness that his or her stereotypes are actually being investigated. The subjects may be quite unaware that their responses—such as judging the target's performance on a task, or degree of guilt for a crime—are influenced by stereotypes they hold of the target person. It may simply be the case, in addition, that the processes or behaviors to which stereotypes are related are of more theoretical interest or practical significance than are the stereotypes per se. In many circumstances we are very rarely asked point-blank to voice our stereotypes, but we are given countless opportunities to react to other persons in ways that reflect the covert operation of our stereotypes.

DEVELOPMENTS IN THE CONCEPTUALIZATION OF STEREOTYPES

The decades following the works of Lippmann, and of Katz and Braly, witnessed extensive research on problems of stereotyping and prejudice.

Racial conflict in the United States and the Nazi Holocaust were unquestionably the most influential "events" in directing the attention of social scientists to these concerns. There was a sense of moral as well as scientific urgency to the need to understand how one group could act in line with negative attitudes and ideology to cause the ultimate physical destruction of another group. Stereotyping was, from the outset, closely related to what had always been a primary focus in social psychology, the measurement and conceptualization of attitudes.

As we have noted in discussing Lippmann's notion of stereotypes as a defense, the spirit of the times, so to speak, in the 1940s and subsequent two decades was to regard stereotyping as a manifestation of the prejudiced personality. Freudian theory was either explicitly or implicitly applied. Strong links between stereotyping, prejudice, and hostility were made. The frustration-aggression hypothesis was at the height of its influence (Dollard et al., 1939), and such concepts as displacement and the scapegoat (Zawadski, 1942) were prominent. Research on the authoritarian personality (Adorno et al., 1950) epitomized this orientation. The fact that the latter project was funded by the American Jewish Committee indicated the close involvement of social action agencies with research bearing on matters of direct concern to them.

More recent developments in the analysis of stereotyping have assumed a different focus. There is less emphasis upon individual differences in stereotyping, and less preoccupation with viewing stereotyping as symptomatic of prejudice, frustration, or pathology. A consideration of several important published works will help chart the major lines of thinking that have characterized the more recent history of research on stereotyping. Four of these works will be summarized, and other citations will be indicated where appropriate.

Allport

Gordon Allport's influential text, *The Nature of Prejudice* (1954), was published at the time of the Supreme Court ruling against school segregation. It was an impassioned analysis with vivid depictions of the degrading effects of prejudice, particularly upon Jews and blacks. As Thomas Pettigrew (1979) has observed, it was traditional at that time to regard stereotypes as indicative of maladjustment, yet Allport's view was considerably broader. True, he saw prejudice and stereotyping as intimately related: "Ethnic prejudice is an antipathy based upon a faulty and inflexible generalization" (p. 10). However, in his second chapter, entitled "The Normality of Prejudgment," he spoke to the "ordinariness" of prejudice:

> Why do human beings slip so easily into ethnic prejudice? They do so
> because the two essential ingredients that we have discussed—erroneous

generalization and hostility—are natural and common capacities of the human mind. (p. 17)

Although Allport's book was a sweeping overview of prejudice, the one psychological issue that was stressed and that has come to be of particular contemporary significance was the concept of categorization (Taylor, 1981). Allport was struck by the extensive array of social groups that characterized human interaction—religious, athletic, social, political, ethnic, geographic, intellectual, and others. As did Lippmann, he saw this social complexity as presenting potentially severe adjustment problems. Categorization, in this context, was a type of psychological solution. It was an inevitable process, in Allport's view, but one likely to be misused or misapplied.

Allport described categorization in highly functional terms. It permitted planning, and served as a guide for behavior:

> When an angry looking dog charges down the street, we categorize him as a "mad dog" and avoid him. When we go to a physician with an ailment we expect him to behave in a certain way toward us. On these, and countless other occasions, we "type" a single event, place it within a familiar rubric, and act accordingly. (p. 19)

Categorization involved assimilating diverse instances into a compact, simplified strategy or summarization:

> It costs the Anglo employer less effort to guide his daily behavior by the generalization "Mexicans are lazy" than to individualize his workmen and learn the real reasons for their conduct. If I can lump thirteen million of my fellow citizens under a simple formula, "Negroes are stupid, dirty, and inferior," I simplify my life enormously. I simply avoid them one and all. What could be easier? (p. 20)

Allport described categorization as sometimes rational (for example, scientific laws), but often not so; and, in addition to having a substantive or explicit meaning, it involved emotionality and feeling. When categories would conflict with the evidence, the individual was likely to acknowledge the exception but stick with the rule—what Allport termed "re-fencing." He did admit that some (rare) individuals could adopt a style of "habitual open-mindedness," but that "plain self-interest" was likely to be the most effective antidote to erroneous categorization, as illustrated in this passage:

> He may think that Italians are primitive, ignorant, and loud until he falls in love with an Italian girl of a cultured family. Then he finds it greatly to his self-interest to modify his previous generalization and act thereafter on the more correct assumption that there are many, many kinds of Italians. (p. 24)

Allport noted that the process of categorization was facilitated by the presence of visible cues or marks. People simply look different from one another, and expectations of behavioral differences might be based on appearance factors. The problem was that "where visibility does exist, it is almost always thought to be linked with deeper lying traits than is in fact the case" (p. 130). Color was a case in point. While many white people desire darker skin—the "Florida tan phenomenon"—it is obvious that dark skin may also take on a repugnant significance. In the case of blacks, Allport suggests that this kind of reaction was "not because of their color but because of their lower status. Their skin implies more than pigmentation, it implies social inferiority" (p. 134). He noted that in Nazi Germany, because the criterion of visible distinctiveness could not be applied to Jews, they were forced to wear a yellow Star of David on outer garments. This mark—social rather than biological—would make all Jews immediately visible, and the star would prompt all observers to make the "proper" categorization about its wearer. Allport included an instructive reference to sex stereotypes based on this same idea: that differences in appearance are conducive to perceptual elaborations and inferences extending far beyond the observable aspects of the mark itself.

The concept of stereotype, per se, was defined by Allport as "an exaggerated belief associated with a category" (p. 187). He emphasized its power to rationalize or justify conduct toward its object. He devoted an entire chapter to "traits due to victimization," in which he discussed the diverse reactions to being the target of someone else's stereotypes. The process of the self-fulfilling prophecy received thoughtful attention. Although Allport recognized the kernel of truth of stereotypes, and endorsed the use of objectively derived group characteristics as a criterion to assess their accuracy, his discussion emphasized the falseness of stereotypes. He cited research documenting self-contradictory stereotypes in the same observers (Jews are clannish versus Jews overassimilate), concluding:

> The fact that prejudiced people so readily subscribe to self-contradictory stereotypes is one proof that genuine group traits are not the point at issue. The point at issue is rather that a dislike requires justification. (p. 191)

Allport spoke to biases in perception, a perspective that later would characterize a major development in the area of attribution theory (Hamilton, 1979). He linked stereotyping to the inclination to perceive the causes of behavior as personal rather than situational:

> While in reality our frustrations and ills are frequently due to impersonal causes—to altered economic conditions, to the tides of social and historical change—unless we fully realize this fact, we tend to slip into

the habit of blaming our lot upon identifiable human agents (scape-goats). (p. 166)

Allport stressed the ease with which trait labels are used to describe behavior, how convincing these labels seem to be, and how unlikely such explanations are to be refuted or publicly challenged. He noted the role of the mass media in sustaining stereotypes, particularly racial stereotypes involving deviance or criminality.

In summary, Allport's contribution was extensive, far more so than indicated here. He had a pronounced orientation to view behavior in terms of personality or individual differences, and recognized quite matter-of-factly that there are substantial limitations to a strictly psychological approach in terms of gaining a complete understanding of prejudice. His style, polished and literary, is similar to Lippmann's and, combined with a very orthodox research attitude, adds to the authority and credibility of his work. For our purposes, what was of lasting impact was his central theme: that a crucial dynamic in prejudice is human nature itself, the tendency to interpret—cognitively and emotionally—the social world.

Fishman

Joshua Fishman published the first major review of the stereotyping literature (1956). He first considered the factual inaccuracy of stereotypes, citing many researchers (Bogardus, Asch, Hayakawa) who had been convinced that error or misinformation was the crux of the matter. Fishman pointed to the role of social action agencies (such as the NAACP and the Anti-Defamation League of B'nai B'rith) in disseminating factually correct information to combat stereotyped images of minority groups held by the public. He suggested, however, that stereotypes need not be erroneous, at least in principle, and that more was likely involved than sheer misinformation. Fishman raised the "kernel of truth" problem, noting that however false they may seem to be, stereotypes must have a realistic basis in some manner. How, otherwise, could one account for the marked agreement among people on many stereotypes and the evidence that changes in stereotypes do occur in conjunction with real changes in political, economic, and social conditions?

How could one assess the accuracy of stereotypes? Fishman pointed to the need for validity data—data on the actual characteristics (personality, values, customs) of diverse ethnic groups and other social categories. His concept of a "criterion of truth" has become a popular one, and relates to such academic developments as the study of "national character" (Inkeles & Levinson, 1968) and cross-cultural psychology (Segall, 1979). Scientifically obtained evidence could serve as the standard against which to compare stereotypes. Many research programs, a number of them described in this volume, try to "debunk" stereotypes by proving their falseness through the use of objective data. Yet such data are often exceedingly difficult to obtain; even if they are available, there will be a marked lag in terms of their catching up with the stereotypes in question. Fishman suspected, as did Lippmann, that a more persuasive attack on the stereotyping problem required an examination of its perceptual basis.

Fishman considered the question of stereotypes as "inferior judgmental processes." He cited numerous researchers who endorsed Lippmann's views on the "economy of thought" in stereotyping:

> They are not only convenient and time-saving, but without them it would be necessary for us to interpret each new situation as if we had never met anything of the kind before. . . . Stereotypes have the virtue of efficiency but not of accuracy. (Newcomb & Charters, 1950, p. 214; cited in Fishman, 1956, p. 31)

The meaning of "inferior," thus related to the formation of expectancies on the basis of insufficient (at least in the researcher's view) information, is well captured in Hayakawa's description of stereotypes as "substitutes for observation" (1950). Yet Fishman denied that the process of stereotyping, with its shortcomings, necessarily resulted in an erroneous product or false image:

> We should no more expect all subjective and uncritical judgments (Asch's definition of stereotypes) to be wrong than we do all objective and critical judgments to be right. . . . Nor must we fear that we are overly dignifying stereotypes by admitting the possibility of their validity notwithstanding their questionable psycho-social parentage. (1956, p. 34)

Fishman stressed the minimal informational basis of stereotypes, focusing not on the false end product but, rather, on the individual's lack of searching for more precise, individuating information. He noted that although rigidity had traditionally been an assumed property of stereotypes, research evidence on this feature was simply nonexistent. The stability of stereotypes, over time and across different observers, was recognized but differentiated from rigidity. He noted the tenacity that certain individuals might display regarding their use of stereotypes or the emotionality that would accompany them, but these were interpreted as bearing on the personality of the observer rather than as constituting a crucial aspect of stereotypes per se. Recent research suggests, however, that rigidity may, in a sense, be characteristic of many stereotypes. Mark Snyder has observed that individuals are biased to seek as well as to accept information that confirms their expectations about others, even when disconfirming information is available (1981a). There are, then, cognitive processes that facilitate "sticking to our guns" in terms of perpetuating first impressions and the effects of labels, expectations, and other types of preconception.

Concerning the origin of stereotypes, Fishman acknowledged that some observers may have "really acute insight into the modal nature of certain groups" (p. 53), but he also emphasized that, once generated, stereotypes "come to lead an autonomous existence in that they *need* not face reality or be checked for 'goodness of fit' " (p. 54). He likened stereotypes to folklore, and cited Hayakawa's ideas concerning the cultural transmission of folk wisdom. Fishman touched upon a perspective that was to occupy much more attention in subsequent work: the intergroup-conflict approach (for example, Austin & Worchel, 1979; Campbell, 1967; Sherif & Sherif, 1969). The central premise here was that stereotypes reflect the practical concerns of interacting groups:

> If interaction is (or has been) such as to touch upon economic competi-
> tion, show of strength, or appreciation of non-tangible cultural elements,
> etc., then stereotypes will deal with shrewdness in business, stature and
> body type, education and sensitivity, etc. (p. 56)

In his concluding section, "Modifying Stereotyping Behavior," Fish-man argued for the strategy of inducing the observer to reperceive the target group in terms of dimensions and situations far removed from the stereotype itself. The opportunity must be created for observing other traits in the target group (or individuals from that category) than those constituting the original stereotype. Fishman recognized that because behavior is, in fact, often dependent upon situational conditions, the best technique for chang-ing the content of stereotypes is to alter the context of the observer-target interaction:

> Our problem is not that of eliminating social-stereotyping as a pheno-
> menon of human behavior . . . our problem, at least at first, is to replace
> socially disruptive stereotyping through more constructive group com-
> mitments. (p 58)

His thoughts on this matter were highly predictive of future research developments (including Aronson, Blaney, Stephan, Sikes, & Snapp, 1978; see also Chapter 3 in this volume).

Campbell

Donald Campbell's orientation to stereotyping reflects a blend of experimental psychology and cultural anthropology, the latter stemming from his collaboration with Robert LeVine. He construed stereotyping in basically perceptual terms, a response whose determinants emanate from the external stimulus world as well as the perceiver. An anti-Semitic stereotype would thus be a response (a verbal utterance, a thought) whose likelihood of occurrence would vary as a function of aspects of the perceiver (habits, reference groups, level of frustration) as well as of the target of the stereotype (behavior, observable degree of "Jewishness" in terms of cues, behaviors, or other criteria).

Campbell's central frame of reference concerns intergroup relations, with many of his research illustrations drawn from African intertribal perception (LeVine & Campbell, 1972). He argues that to the degree that groups differ in actual fact, this contrast will provide the stimulus for stereotyping. The accuracy of stereotypes—the degree to which they reflect real differences between the target and observer groups—should be greater with more frequent contact between the groups. The more remote the contact, the more projective—"in the eye of the beholder"—the stereotype content should be—and, in this respect, the less accurate or objectively based.

A particularly interesting aspect of Campbell's analysis is his direct assault on "social psychology's emphasis on the falseness of stereotypes." He notes that researchers in anthropology and sociology recognize that social groups differ in many (real) ways, and that such differences are a natural basis for the development of stereotype imagery between groups (tribes or subcultures, for instance). He also recognizes that inequality or domination in group interaction may result in what Allport termed "traits due to victimization": "the effects on personality, aspirations, achievement effort, and moral behavior caused by oppressed minority status" (Campbell 1967, p. 823). Psychology, however, particularly social and educational psychology, is centered on the premise that groups are very similar, "on the average identical"; thus "All stereotypes of group differences are false" (p. 823).

Campbell documents his charge against psychological interpretations of stereotyping. He suggests that the Katz and Braly (1933) findings, and a host of subsequent research, consider stereotypes to be false simply because they document stereotype responses among observers who have had no personal contact with the target group. For Campbell, lack of contact is an insufficient ground for assuming falsity. Other research is cited (LaPiere, 1936; Levinson & Sanford, 1944) that illustrates the self-contradictoriness of stereotypes (and hence their falseness) or the absence of stereotyped traits in a well-defined local community of Armenians (LaPiere's classic study). Campbell makes a simple but telling observation: that in the vast majority of cases, the necessary criteria—objective group characteristics to assess the falseness of stereotypes in a precise manner—were never obtained. Campbell not only is critical regarding the lack of empirical proof of falseness, but also seems to imply a reluctance on the part of investigators to admit even the need for or utility of such data, as if modern social psychology would be unable to address the unpleasant reality of certain stereotypes being proved true.

Campbell lists four specific errors that are involved in stereotyping but do not require the presumption that all groups are, on the average, equal or identical. First, there is the "phenomenal absolutism of the normal ingroup member's imagery of the minority group member." Here, Campbell points to the ease with which the observer becomes convinced that his or her perceptions are valid or descriptive of external reality. Campbell, as did Lippmann, emphasizes the observers' lack of awareness of their creative or projective role in the process of stereotyping. Second, the perceiver fails to appreciate the wide range of individual differences on a given trait (such as intelligence) in a given group and the large extent of overlap that is likely to describe both groups (the observers' ingroup and the outgroup). Campbell cites research on this illusion of within-group homogeneity. (Research bearing on this phenomenon, particularly that of Tajfel [1969], is considered in Chapters 2 and 3 of this book.) The third error involves "the erroneous causal perception of invoking racial rather than environmental causes for group differences." This point bears on one of the central hypotheses in research on social perception, namely the excessive readiness of observers to attribute dispositional causes in accounting for the actions of others. This perceptual phenomenon has received attention from numerous theorists in basic research on social judgment (e.g., Heider, 1958; Jones & Nisbett, 1972; Nisbett & Ross, 1980), as well as from those with a more activist or social-problems focus (Rothbart, 1976; Ryan, 1971).

Although not mentioned by Campbell, there is an important point to be made in this context. Note that stereotype images can describe behavior ("He acts aggressively") or explain behavior ("He fights because he is aggressive"). In this latter sense stereotypes constitute implicit theories, held by all of us, regarding why certain groups or kinds of people act as they do. As Campbell and many others have emphasized, however, there are many explanations for most behaviors, some more accurate than others. It thus becomes critical to understand our preference or bias for personal causality (personality or heredity, for instance) in accounting for the behavior of others. It is a perceptual strategy that "loads the gun," so to speak, for stereotyping activity. (This matter is considered by Russell Jones, in Chapter 2 of this volume, in the subsection "The Fundamental Attribution Error.")

The fourth kind of error considered by Campbell to be of particular importance again relates to a defect in the causal reasoning of the observer. Intuitively the perceiver tends to explain dislike for a group in terms of their characteristics. Thus, one might say, "The reason I hate Jews is that they are pushy, loud, and out to get you in business. If they weren't this way, I would like them." However, as Campbell argues, the social-science perspective is different:

> Causally, first is the hostility toward the outgrouper, generated perhaps
> by real threat, perhaps by ethnocentrism, perhaps by displacement. In
> the service of this hostility, all possible differences are opportunistically

> interpreted as despicable, and the most plausibly despicable traits are given most attention. (p. 825)

Here we note the importance of distinguishing between affect (liking) and trait imagery. From the observer's perspective, perceived traits cause the disliking; from Campbell's perspective, the disliking reaction is caused by other factors, but the individual adopts stereotypes instead because, as noted above, they seem to be perfectly acceptable and convincing explanations. An implication here is that efforts to modify stereotypes must address the issue of hostility first, rather than attack the stereotypes per se.

We have noted that Campbell emphasizes group differences—not differences in an intrinsic or hereditary sense, but differences based on patterns of social living, perhaps based on factors of climate, geography, child rearing, events of history, or economic competition for limited resources—as a stimulant of stereotypes. Yet he also notes that it is possible for two groups simply to interpret the behaviors of each other differently, though the behaviors could in fact be identical. In making this point he raises the important concept of ethnocentrism, described originally by Sumner in his *Folkways* (1906) as

> ... the technical name in which one's own group is the center of everything and all others are scaled and rated with reference to it. ... Each group nourishes its own pride and vanity, boasts itself superior, exalts in its own divinities, and looks with contempt on outsiders. (LeVine & Campbell, 1972, pp. 12–13)

Campbell documents the reciprocal or mirror-image aspect of many in-group/outgroup stereotypes, variations on Sumner's theme of "We are good—you are bad." (This perspective is considered further in Chapter 3 of this book.)

Brigham

John Brigham reviewed an extensive and diverse array of research on stereotyping, and considered matters from both conceptual and methodological approaches. Elaborating on a point made by Fishman (1956, pp. 53–54), he noted ambiguity in the meaning of the term "generalization." Generalizations can be incorrect in their directionality (for instance, "Most Greeks do not gamble" versus the stereotype "Greeks gamble") or in their magnitude ("Perhaps only 5 percent of Greeks gamble" versus assuming that all or most do). Why, then, are stereotypes undesirable? Brigham raises the important idea that part of the answer resides in the personal biases of the social scientist. He quotes Roger Brown:

> They [social scientists] think it is at least irrational and probably wicked to subscribe to them. ... Is it possible that the social psychologist has

used the word *stereotype* to stigmatize beliefs of which he disapproves but which he does not know to be false? Has he perverted his science to achieve a moral purpose? (pp. 364, 366)

Brown's point, similar to Campbell's, is that the investigator's values may influence the approach taken toward stereotyping. Mackie (1973) also has observed that "the liberal sympathies of social scientists discourage a test of ethnic accuracy" (p. 431). Although these analysts do not state precisely how these personal values or biases are to be defused or concealed, it is of obvious value simply to recognize their potential role and be sensitive to their influence.

Brigham points out that the responses of research subjects are obviously limited to the information given to them, and that often this information is quite sparse. Thus, if subjects are simply given the word or concept "Negro," various stereotypes will be elicited (for instance, Bayton, 1941). However, if the distinction is made between middle-class or upper-class Negro and lower-class Negro, for example, the resulting stereotypes may be markedly different (for example, Bayton, McAlister, & Hamer, 1956; Smedley & Bayton, 1978). By providing more information or more stimulus dimensions, one presents more realistic or generalizable circumstances to the subjects. Such research also allows the investigator to determine circumstances in which stereotyping does not occur, as well as when it does.

Brigham reviews the "kernel of truth" issue, raising a number of familiar points but some important new perspectives as well. He notes that the criterion for validating a stereotype, or establishing its falseness, is rarely present, in terms of objective (scientifically established) characteristics of the target. Even if a criterion *is* available, however, the issue can be complicated. Consider a study by Abate and Berrien (1967), which documented an agreement between a set of stereotypes held by observers and the self-ratings or self-stereotypes held by the target group. As Brigham points out, this constitutes one type of truth or validity, but in a limited sense. It was also found in the Abate and Berrien research that there was minimal agreement between the stereotypes and the actual personality characteristics of the target group as measured by a personality inventory. Thus, by one criterion (self-ratings) the stereotypes were valid, but by another (personality test scores) they were not. It then becomes an issue as to which criterion from among several is to be used to assess stereotype truth or accuracy.

Brigham reserves his sharpest criticisms for an analysis of the Katz and Braly method of stereotype assessment. Agreeing that their procedure elicits trait selections with a fair degree of consensus, he contends that their findings

do not prove of any value in elucidating what a stereotype is, how they are developed, or even how many people *hold* a stereotype. For example, how many subjects actually endorse (agree with) or *use* the generalization in behavior, and how many subjects are just reporting on their knowledge of the traits that persons in one's culture most commonly attribute to the given ethic group? ... we do not know whether the subject believes that a trait which is "typical" is found in 20%, 50%, 90%, or all of the members of an ethnic group. (pp. 29–30)

Although Brigham is accusing Katz and Braly's technique in terms of issues that the procedure was not designed to assess, his critique has been of value in redirecting research on stereotyping, in particular the process aspect itself (see Chapter 2 of this volume). Brigham notes that stereotypes have been relegated to the role of dependent variable—the object or end point of research—rather than used as predictors of social behavior. This is an important point, of course, and relates in part to the difficulties involved in establishing the relationship between attitudes and behavior (Wicker, 1969). As noted earlier, however, while there may be relatively few studies that explicitly examine linkages between stereotype trait responses and behavior, there are many illustrations of research that assesses differential reactions to social groups and categories in which the stereotypes are not explicitly measured but are presumed to play an important mediating role in the observed behaviors.

Brigham defines stereotyping as "a generalization made about an ethnic group, concerning a trait attribution, which is considered to be unjustified by an observer" (p. 31). He feels that previous research has not come to grips with the "unjustified" aspect. Others have, of course, been similarly disenchanted, yet Brigham fails to "come through" with a solution. He does not indicate, for example, what the precise consequence would be if it were established that the origin of a stereotype was firsthand acquaintance with members of the target group rather than hearsay. He does not clarify his apparent presumption that learning about a social group from others (would he include the study of history?) is less adequate or less "moral" than learning based upon personal interactions with a few individuals from a given group or social category. In essence, Brigham raises more questions than he answers—which is not, however, to detract from the substantive importance of his paper.

He concludes with a recommendation for more precise measurement of stereotypes, in particular the need for the measurement of individual stereotyping as contrasted with the Katz and Braly method, which calculates the amount of stereotyping that occurs within a defined group of research subjects. There have been advances along these lines (McCauley et al., 1980; see also Chapter 10 in this volume)—for example, within the context of individual differences in sex stereotyping (see Chapter 5 in this volume). Brigham advocates concern with the nuance or fine-grain aspects of stereotyping: questions such as the subject's commitment to his or her stereotypes, the certainty or confidence with which they are held, their centrality or salience in the individual's cognitive system, and the percentage of the target group presumed to exhibit the trait(s) from the observer's perspective.

Because Brigham is particularly impressed with the need to state, in an empirically rigorous manner, the relationship between stereotype responses and other types of responses and behaviors (for instance, measures of prejudice or social behavior), it is understandable that he urges greater precision in matters of assessment. His paper has been an important contribution to the literature, in particular standing as a kind of "turning point" between earlier conceptions and more recent research programs.

PERSPECTIVES ON STEREOTYPING: AN OVERVIEW

The history of the concept of stereotyping can usefully be partitioned into at least three major orientations (Ashmore & Del Boca, 1981). The sociological orientation emphasizes that stereotypes are ready-made for most of us—they are provided by our culture. We acquire them in the process of being socialized, and in expressing stereotypes, we are, in a sense, reinforcing them. Stereotypes constitute norms about how certain individuals and groups are to be treated. (As will be noted in Chapter 7, for example, stereotypes about the mentally ill generally result in an avoidance response. This can be interpreted as expressing the value that our culture places on being in control and independent—the value of not being mentally ill.)

Reflecting the Katz and Braly influence, a major research question in this tradition is the fundamental depiction of the stereotype itself. What *are* the images held about Jews, about the poor, about the blind, about other groups? There is also an emphasis upon the social channels responsible for the transmission of stereotypes. This issue receives considerable emphasis in most of the chapters of this volume. Another feature of the sociological orientation is the interpretation of changes in stereotype imagery in association with diverse cultural and social movements, such as economic crises, internation conflict, or the civil rights movement. An obvious feature of the sociological perspective is the wide agreement or consensus of people as to the stereotypes pertaining to various target groups.

The psychodynamic orientation emphasizes that stereotypes reflect inner drives or motivational needs of the observer or person holding the stereotypes. This was reflected in Lippmann's commentary on stereotypes as a "defense." Various psychoanalytic and related ego-defense theories suggest that individuals will project hostility upon innocent targets because of frustration and other unacceptable feelings. Stereotypes, in the form of negative attributions, represent displacement of aggression or projection. The most elaborated psychodynamic theory of prejudice is presented in *The Authoritarian Personality* (Adorno et al., 1950), which was designed to assess and explain individual differences in anti-democratic ideology. In this theory the role of stereotyping is based essentially on the premise that a person categorized as high in authoritarianism will be particularly intolerant of outgroups. Thus, the distinction between ingroup and outgroup—and, more specifically, a disposition to be harsh and punitive with respect to diverse minority and low-status groups—is linked to the general concept of stereotyping.

Individual differences in authoritarianism are important to recognize (for instance, Mitchell & Byrne, 1973; Bray & Noble, 1978), but the premise that stereotyping is characteristic of only "bad" (such as high authoritarian) people is clearly outdated. Perhaps the most significant contemporary development, reflecting (somewhat faintly) the psychodynamic tradition, is research on dehumanization and deindividuation. (As will be noted in Chapter 10, stereotypes appear to be fundamentally involved in acts of unrestrained aggression. This bears, at least indirectly, on the psychodynamic tradition that was forged in an effort to understand the atrocities and genocide perpetrated by the Nazis in World War II.)

The cognitive orientation, in conjunction with the sociological perspective, is a major theme of the present volume. As noted earlier in this chapter, and more extensively in Chapter 2, the "new look" in social cognition is to emphasize what Allport described as the "normality of prejudgment." People are conceived as having limited capacities to process information about the social world. Stereotypes are functional in the sense of reducing the complexity of this world. The phenomena associated with stereotyping are thus attributable to processes that are fundamental to human thought—categorization, concept formation, and judgmental inference, among others. The "badness" of stereotypes is retained, to an extent, in this seemingly neutral emphasis on cognition. But rather than emphasize individual differences—that certain kinds of people have defective cognition—the current approach is to emphasize that we are all susceptible to perceptual biases and distortions. Thus, as Jones indicates in Chapter 2 of this volume, we are all prone to commit the "fundamental attribution error," and to perceive personal causation in the acts of others even when the behavior is under situational constraint. In addition, we are all inclined to hold initial expectations or impressions with conviction, and to seek information that supports such images. These processes are fundamental to the contemporary cognitive perspective on stereotyping.

DEFINITIONS OF STEREOTYPING: A CONCEPTUAL SYNTHESIS

At first glance, definitions of stereotyping are as numerous and diverse as the scholars who have coined them, to their own satisfaction if not to many others'. All agree, however, that stereotyping involves an act of social perception or judgment on the part of an observer who assigns—overtly or in thought—a dispositional quality (trait, attitude, motive, intention) to another individual or group. The stimulus for the stereotype consists of some feature of the individual—in principle any feature, but typically a quality of the individual's physiological or biological identity (race, age, sex, physical appearance)—or an aspect of the individual's social or behavioral identity (religion, ethnicity, biographical history in terms of mental illness or imprisonment). Whatever the particular "trigger," stereotypes are viewed as embellishments, as extrapolations or miniature theories built around the categorical property or social identity at issue.

There are, however, at least two areas of disagreement. These include the questions of whether to emphasize the error or "badness" of stereotypes and whether to include agreement or social consensus in the definition. Considering both of these questions (bad? yes or no; consensus? yes or no) produces a fourfold typology, illustrations of which are presented below. In some instances the definitions are not used, in their original source, in a very precise or consistent manner. Still, their variety is instructive.

Definitions Incorporating Inferiority and Emphasizing Consensus

> A stereotype—by which is meant a fixed impression which conforms very little to the facts it pretends to represent and results from our defining first and observing second. . . . Even in the case of groups unknown personally to the students, characteristics were assigned with a high degree of consistency. (Katz & Braly, 1935, p. 181)

> A belief that is simple, inadequately grounded, at least partially inaccurate, and held with considerable assurance by many people is called a stereotype. (Harding, Proshansky, Kutner, & Chein, 1969, p. 4)

> Generally, the people of one nation—and the United States is no exception—harbor stereotyped images of other nations, starkly simple and exceedingly inaccurate. Yet these images are the basis upon which people feel for or against other nations . . . and judge what they themselves as a nation should do in relation to others. (Leighton, 1949, p. 102; cited in Buchanan & Cantril, 1953, pp. 45, 59)

Definitions That Include Inferiority but Do not Emphasize Consensus

> Stereotypes are not objectionable because they are generalizations about categories; such generalizations are valuable when they are true. Stereotypes are not objectionable because they are generalizations that have been proven false; for the most part we do not know whether they are true or false—in their probabilistic form. . . . What is objectionable about them? I think it is their ethnocentrism and the implications that important traits are inborn for large groups. (Brown, 1965, p. 181)

An ethnic stereotype is a generalization made about an ethnic group concerning a trait attribution, which is considered to be unjustified by an observer.... Although this consensus on attributed traits may be of interest from a sociological or statistical standpoint, it tells us very little about stereotypes or stereotyping. (Brigham, 1971, pp. 29, 31)

Definitions That Do not Include Inferiority but Emphasize Consensus

Stereotypes should properly be regarded as concept-systems, with positive as well as negative functions, having the same general kinds of properties as other concepts, and serving to organize experience as do other concepts.... the stereotype is defined in terms of the characteristics most often attributed to another group. Indeed, it is just this agreement which constitutes the phenomenon of stereotyping, and which raises the sorts of questions in which investigators are interested. (Vinacke, 1957, pp. 229, 231)

Stereotyping is a sociocultural phenomenon, in that it is a property characteristic of people sharing a common culture. People do three things in stereotyping: (1) they identify a category of persons (such as policemen or hippies), (2) they agree in attributing sets of traits or characteristics to the category of persons, and (3) they attribute the characteristic to any person belonging to the category. (Secord & Backman, 1974, p. 29)

A stereotype refers to those folk beliefs about the attributes characterizing a social category on which there is substantial agreement. (Mackie, 1973, p. 435)

Definitions That Do not Incorporate Inferiority or Consensus

Implicit personality theories are ... stereotypes we hold about other people.... To say warm people are imaginative (as did Asch's subjects) is a kind of stereotype that may involve the same sorts of processes as saying that English people are sportsmanlike (as did Katz and Braly's subjects). In each case, the perceiver infers something about the stimulus person that is not given directly by the information known about him. (Schneider, Hastorf, & Ellsworth, 1979, p. 172)

Stereotype ... the set of beliefs held by an individual regarding a social group ... the term "cultural stereotype" [should] be used to describe shared or community-wide patterns of beliefs ... it is essential that these concepts be distinguished. (Ashmore & Del Boca, 1981, p. 19)

What should one make of this barrage of definitions? The answer would hardly be to present yet another definition—clearly there are enough!

From the perspective of this book, a simple definition of stereotyping may be ill-advised. Several features or elements of the above-noted definitions would seem, however, to characterize the phenomen*a* (emphasize the plural) of stereotyping as they are considered in this book. First, from a psychological perspective, stereotyping is a process that occurs in the individual observer. It is a covert mental event, similar to other psychological constructs, such as memory, thinking, and attitude. It is not a group phenomenon similar, for example, to mob behavior, group decision behavior (jury behavior, parole board decisions), or group problem solving, although it may attain considerable impact in such social settings. In terms of strictly psychological processes, there is nothing evil, immoral, or inferior about stereotyping. Its central operating characteristics—categorization, inference, anticipatory thinking, and planning—are obviously adaptive, functional, and "good" (if that term is of any value).

Yet it is equally obvious, at least to this writer, that the term "stereotype," in the context of its usage, involves an element of negativism or displeasure on the part of some person (as Brigham pointed out)—whether it be the victim of the stereotyping, or the social scientist, or the analyst of the phenomena at issue. The psychological foundations of stereotyping can be abused and become critical factors in destructive social behavior, verbal as well as physical. This is more than the idle truism that people can misbehave. The social-perceptual, cognitive processes involved in stereotyping seem uniquely well-suited to undesirable ends—dehumanization, defensive rationalization for one's misconduct, blaming the victim rather than his or her environment, selectively responding to information consistent with one's expectations. Not recognizing these matters would seem to fall short of acquiring a full appreciation of the issues involved.

Finally, there is the issue of consensus or observer agreement. This is a matter central to any serious account of stereotyping. Although the individual is obviously the primary locus of stereotyping in terms of its fundamental judgmental properties, there is much more involved in the social reality of stereotyping. There are vital sociological and cultural factors that link individuals and create conditions for shared perceptions. The very learning of stereotypes, in the sense of being exposed to others—to one's parents, to the media—would seem to make this proposition self-evident. Were the images discussed in this book relegated to only a few individuals or seen to differ widely among observers, this book would be far different in substance. We have noted, of course, that individual differences in stereotyping are an important research question (Brigham, 1971). In a larger sense, however, stereotyping involves judgmental behaviors that are prevalent and are easy to study because of their availability. Stereotyping is, then, a complex psychological problem, but one that, at the same time, is inextricably bound to a much broader social matrix. There are, in short, large numbers of people involved in stereotyping—both on the observer side and on the target side.

INTRODUCING THE CHAPTERS

In Chapter 2, Russell Jones examines psychological research on the perceptual and cognitive foundations of stereotyping. The parallels between the developments in this chapter and Walter Lippmann's original treatment of stereotyping are striking. A central issue, discussed in this chapter, is the extreme readiness of perceivers to attribute personality traits to other people. It is as if we were "primed" or "wired" to stereotype. Indeed, much of this chapter is sympathetic to Allport's characterization of the "normality" of prejudgment, warning us not to equate the evils of prejudice and the undesirable consequences of stereotyping with the simplistic explanation that those who engage in these activities are inherently different from "the rest of us."

Chapter 3 focuses upon racial stereotyping. Walter Stephan and David Rosenfield point out diverse factors—historical, intergroup conflict, personality, and social-cognitive—contributing to racial stereotypes. They note the futility of examining stereotypes unless one appreciates historical factors. Their discussion brings to mind Alex Haley's *Roots*, and many influential theorists have more than once stressed the unique role of the institution of slavery in American history (Myrdal, 1962; Schaefer, 1979). A significant issue considered in this chapter is research designed to eliminate intergroup prejudice, and the orientation of this discussion relates strongly to Campbell's (1967) position. Although there is optimism in the conclusions of this research, one senses that racial stereotyping is very deeply entrenched in the social-psychological functioning of many Americans. The factor of skin color, per se, has been considered by some theorists to be of major importance (Gergen, 1967), and one cannot discuss racial stereotypes without bringing to mind social-class stereotypes as well (see Chapter 9 of this volume).

In Chapter 4 Robert Wuthnow reviews research on anti-Semitic stereotyping, essentially from a sociological orientation. His analysis focuses upon the phenomenon in relatively recent American society, although the problem itself belongs to world history. As slavery constitutes the hallmark of America's contribution to racism, certainly the Nazi Holocaust defines the epitome of anti-Semitism. Anti-Semitic stereotypes, for many Jews, are devastating in terms of raising to consciousness images and, for some, memories of the Holocaust. In terms of visible marks (skin color) and other factors (social status in many respects), one could not find two minority groups less alike than blacks and Jews, yet both have been the targets of stereotyping throughout American history, often from the same source (such as the Ku Klux Klan). The rift in black-Jewish relations, occasioned by the dismissal of Andrew Young as United Nations ambassador and the involvement of black leaders with the Palestine Liberation Organization, illustrates the sensitivity of intergroup relations to political and international events.

Wuthnow's chapter is particularly instructive in detailing the content of anti-Semitic stereotypes, and the many variables or factors influencing these data.

In Chapter 5, Diane Ruble and Thomas Ruble deal with sex stereotyping, perhaps the single most active research area on stereotyping in the 1970s. Empirical research has ranged from a concern with real differences, biological as well as psychological, between men and women, to the role of the media and social institutions in perpetuating sex stereotypes. Unlike stereotypes of blacks or Jews, stereotypes of the sexes are not a function of their minority status, at least in terms of numbers; but, as in the other illustrations, we are involved with stereotypes that have a very long history. The myth of the incompetent female may in fact be "older" than any other stereotype (Shields, 1975). Much of the research reported in this chapter has been performed by women—not surprising, perhaps, but of interest as yet another instance of "women's liberation." Male dominance in social research has, without question, been an undesirable characteristic of the past, and is now considerably less severe.

Although there are indications of the lessening of sex stereotypes, it should be noted that college students are very often the source of research subjects. This is true not only with respect to work on sex stereotypes, but in the other topical subareas as well. It is important to recognize that this population is not necessarily representative of the entire spectrum of American society, particularly in terms of educational and socioeconomic status (and associated values and reference groups). Generalizations made on the basis of data from college students, with respect to the fading of sex stereotypes, for example, may be inappropriately extended to other very considerable portions of the population.

In chapter 6, Gerald Adams reviews the literature on physical attractiveness as a determinant of stereotyping. Related aspects of physical appearance are also noted. Whether subtle or obvious, the fact is that we are all quite different in appearance, a difference that provides an immediate but lasting basis for differential first impressions and stereotypes. The "1 to 10" scale has become an American cliché, with "10" recently given dramatic meaning in a motion picture of that title. While it is perhaps strange to view the highly attractive and unattractive as minority groups, there is abundant research evidence to support such a position. The more general dimension of appearance, of course, is one that pertains to many other social categories and groups as well, for we can think of the elderly or the very young, blacks or whites, men or women, in terms of their "look" or their "social presentation" as well as in other terms.

Adams refers to Goffman's influential analysis of physical stigma, bringing to mind disability and physical disfigurement as additional instances of the attractiveness dimension. Research subjects might be expected to be less aware of this particular factor, or less sensitized to the possibility that their prejudices or judgmental biases are being investigated. Typical stimuli for research in this area are photographs previously scaled on the appearance variable, and experimenter assistants made up to appear attractive or unattractive. The cosmetic industry and the orthodontist are but two examples of the value our culture places on "looking good," a value not to be taken lightly, as shown in the research reviewed by Adams.

The stigma of mental illness is discussed by Amerigo Farina in Chapter 7. He brings the perspective of clinical psychology as well as experimental social psychology to his analysis of this problem area. At issue, of course, are individuals who have come to occupy the role of "sick person" in our culture. It might thus be expected that such individuals would elicit very positive images and behaviors on the part of observers, in view of the traditional values placed on extending sympathy and help to the ill. However, Farina's discussion centers on the negative images and avoidant behaviors that characterize many interactions between "normals" and the mentally ill. For the student of stereotyping, this raises the seemingly paradoxical fact that we are capable of disliking individuals who have, innocently and unintentionally, become victims—people who have had their identities spoiled, to use Goffman's classic reference to stigma. Farina points out the ambivalence that is likely to characterize the simultaneous experience of caring and revulsion toward the mentally ill.

An important theme concerns the fear that people may have of becoming mentally ill, and the consequences of this kind of threat in terms of images and beliefs about the mentally ill. Farina's opening discussion of how the mentally ill have been perceived throughout history is particularly informative. A rather special characteristic of the mentally ill as a target for stereotyping is the fact that there is a large group of professionals whose primary mission is to understand and treat such individuals. It is widely known that the diagnosis and treatment of mental illness has been a highly controversial, less-than-often successful, venture (for example, Rosenhan, 1973). Farina considers, in this context, the particularly interesting issue of the attitudes and stereotypes of professional mental health personnel toward their clients.

Kenneth Branco and John Williamson bring the perspective of gerontology to Chapter 8 in discussing stereotypes of the aged. In terms of contemporary interest and research funding, this area is a strong rival to that of sex stereotyping. The aged, as a social category, share a number of life conditions with other targets of stereotyping—they are different in appearance, and are generally in a numerical as well as social-status minority—but they also have some rather special characteristics. Becoming old is a prospect that confronts every human being. One may not wish to, or be able to, become Jewish, black, female, unattractive, or poor, but everyone, it seems, wants to become old—or wishes to live a long life, to phrase things more gently. Because of its proximity to death, old age is a social category with understandably negative associations. It is also a condition of life with important economic ramifications, for the elderly are often unemployed and physically under par—conditions that contribute to social dependency.

In American culture the aged may be accurately perceived as victims. This is not meant to suggest, of course, that all people over 65 lead the same kind of life. Yet in many instances their lives are relatively impoverished, and lend themselves to manifestation of behaviors and life-styles that are aversive to observers. These are, from a perceptual analysis, conditions ripe for stereotyping, with its attendant rationalizing attributions and avoidant behaviors. A particularly interesting feature of this content area is the socioeconomic institution of "retirement." Branco and Williamson discuss the rather provocative aspects of retirement as they address the question of the functional value of certain stereotypes of the aged.

Michael Morris and John Williamson, in Chapter 9, review the literature dealing with stereotypes in relation to social class and poverty. While there are certainly distinctive images characterizing the very rich and the middle class, the focus here is upon images of the poor. Their chapter, a blend of both psychological and sociological orientations, addresses problems explicitly bearing on political and economic concerns. The condition of poverty raises the classic attribution question "Why is this person like that?" Research points to the personal attribution (he or she is lazy) that is often given as an answer. The vicious cycle of poverty and lowered opportunities, as well as expectations, for success illustrates Allport's formulation of "traits due to victimization," noted here in terms of the "culture of poverty" doctrine.

The student of stereotyping must also recognize that many targets or objects of stereotyping are of a number of social categories. The classic illustration, of course, is the combination of race and social class; and it is naive, to say the least, to examine one thread of this complicated problem without appreciating the relevance of the other. Other intercategory stereotypes have been noted in the literature—for example, the relationships between sex stereotypes and mental illness, social class and mental illness, and sex stereotypes and physical attractiveness. In speaking to the reaction of many white, middle-class individuals confronting the racial and class problems of our society, Rothbart (1976) has emphasized factors contributing to the resistance of many people to social reforms. He does not emphasize prejudice but, rather, construes these reactions in terms of pragmatic, realistically based concerns held by many people regarding loss of jobs, reduced standards of living, inadequate schools, and fear of crime.

In this perspective the prospects appear minimal for substantial modifications in stereotypes relating to social-class distinctions. The "split city" phenomenon, in terms of race and social class, will be familiar to many, often assuming a kind of concrete reality that "will not go away." Yet, because social policies and legislation are based so strongly on the perceived causes of social problems (Caplan & Nelson, 1973), it is imperative to understand the determinants of social perception in this area.

In Chapter 10 a number of additional phenomena bearing on the concept of stereotyping that are of interest are described. These include stereotypes about the disabled, stereotypes of the outgroup in group decisions, the relationship between stereotyping and dehumanization, the role of stereotyping in judgments of responsibility, and developments in the measurement of stereotypes. The chapter concludes with a discussion of some central themes and problems for further research.

REFERENCES

Abate, M., & Berrien, F. K. Validation of stereotypes: Japanese versus American students. *Journal of Personality and Social Psychology*, 1967, 7, 435–438.

Adorno, T. W., Frenkel-Brunswik, E., Levinson, D. J., & Sanford, R. N. *The authoritarian personality*. New York: Harper & Row, 1950.

Allport, G. W. *The nature of prejudice*. Reading, Mass.: Addison-Wesley, 1954.

Aronson, E. *The social animal*. San Francisco: Freeman, 1980.

Aronson, E., Blaney, N., Stephan, C., Sikes, J., & Snapp, M. *The jig-saw classroom*. Beverly Hills, Calif.: Sage, 1978.

Ashmore, R. D., & Del Boca, F. K. Conceptual approaches to stereotypes and stereotyping. In D. L. Hamilton (ed.), *Cognitive processes in stereotyping and intergroup behavior*. Hillsdale, N.J.: Erlbaum, 1981.

Austin, W. G., & Worchel, S. (eds.). *The social psychology of intergroup relations*. Monterey, Calif.: Brooks/Cole, 1979.

Bayton, J. A. The racial stereotypes of Negro college students. *Journal of Abnormal and Social Psychology*, 1941, 36, 97–102.

Bayton, J. A., McAlister, L. B., & Hamer, J. Race-class stereotypes. *Journal of Negro Education*, 1956, 25, 75–78.

Bettelheim, B., & Janowitz, M. *The dynamics of prejudice*. New York: Harper & Row, 1950.

Bettelheim, B., & Janowitz, M. *Social change and prejudice*. New York: Free Press, 1964.

Bray, R. M., & Noble, A. M. Authoritarianism and decisions of mock juries: Evidence of jury bias and group polarization. *Journal of Personality and Social Psychology*, 1978, 36, 1424–1430.

Brigham, J. Ethnic stereotypes. *Psychological Bulletin*, 1971, 76, 15–38.

Brigham, J. C., & Weissbach, T. A. *Racial attitudes in America: Analyses and findings of social psychology*. New York: Harper & Row, 1972.

Brown, R. *Word and things*. Glencoe, Ill.: Free Press, 1958.

Brown, R. *Social psychology*. New York: Free Press, 1965.

Buchanan, W., & Cantril, H. *How nations see each other: A study in public opinion*. Urbana: University of Illinois Press, 1953.

Campbell, D. T. Stereotypes and the perception of group differences. *American Psychologist*, 1967, 22, 817–829.

Caplan, N., & Nelson, S. On being useful: The nature and consequences of psychological research on social problems. *American Psychologist*, 1973, 28, 199–211.

Dollard, J., Doob, L. W., Miller, N. E., Mowrer, O. H., & Sears, R. R. *Frustration and aggression.* New Haven: Yale University Press, 1939.

Ehrlich, H. J. *The social psychology of prejudice.* New York: Wiley, 1973.

Ehrlich, H. J., & Rinehart, J. W. A brief report on the methodology of stereotype research. *Social Forces,* 1965, *43,* 564–575.

English, H. B., & English, A. C. *A comprehensive dictionary of psychological and psychoanalytic terms.* New York: Longmans, Green, 1959.

Ericsson, K. A., & Simon, H. A. Verbal reports as data. *Psychological Review,* 1980, *87,* 215–251.

Fishman, J. A. An examination of the process and function of social stereotyping. *Journal of Social Psychology,* 1956, *43,* 27–64.

Gardner, R. C. Ethnic stereotypes: The traditional approach, a new look. *Canadian Psychologist,* 1973, *14,* 133–148.

Gergen, K. J. The significance of skin color in human relations. *Daedalus,* 1967, *96,* 390–407.

Gilbert, G. M. Stereotype persistence and change among college students. *Journal of Abnormal and Social Psychology,* 1951, *46,* 245–254.

Hamilton, D. L. A cognitive-attributional analysis of stereotyping. In L. Berkowitz (ed.), *Advances in experimental social psychology* (Vol. 12). New York: Academic Press, 1979.

Harding, J., Proshansky, H., Kutner, B., & Chein, I. Prejudice and ethnic relations. In G. Lindzey & E. Aronson (eds.), *Handbook of social psychology* (Vol. 5). Cambridge, Mass.: Addison-Wesley, 1969.

Hayakawa, S. I. Recognizing stereotypes as substitutes for thought. *Review of General Semantics,* 1950, *7,* 208–210.

Heider, F. *The psychology of interpersonal relations.* New York: Wiley, 1958.

Inkeles, A., & Levinson, D. J. National character: The study of modal personality and sociocultural system. In G. Lindzey & E. Aronson (eds.), *Handbook of social psychology* (Vol. 4). Reading, Mass.: Addison-Wesley, 1968.

Jensen, A. How much can we boost IQ and scholastic achievement? *Harvard Educational Review,* 1969, *39,* 1–123.

Jones, E. E., & Nisbett, R. E. The actor and the observer: Divergent perceptions of the causes of behavior. In E. E. Jones, D. E. Kanouse, H. H. Kelley, R. E. Nisbett, S. Valins, & B. Weiner (eds.), *Attribution: Perceiving the causes of behavior.* Morristown, N.J.: General Learning Press, 1972.

Karlins, M., Coffman, T. L., & Walters, G. On the fading of social stereotypes: Studies in three generations of college students. *Journal of Personality and Social Psychology,* 1969, *13,* 1–16.

Karras, A. *Even big guys cry.* New York: Holt, Rinehart, & Winston, 1977.

Katz, D., & Braly, K. Racial stereotypes in one hundred college students. *Journal of Abnormal and Social Psychology,* 1933, *28,* 280–290.

Katz, D., & Braly, K. Racial prejudice and racial stereotypes. *Journal of Abnormal and Social Psychology,* 1935, *30,* 175–193.

Landy, D., & Sigall, H. Beauty is talent: Task evaluation as a function of the performer's physical attractiveness. *Journal of Personality and Social Psychology,* 1974, *29,* 299–304.

Langer, E. J. Rethinking the role of thought in social interaction. In J. H. Harvey, W. J. Ickes, & R. F. Kidd (eds.), *New directions in attribution research* (Vol. 2). Potomac, Md.: Erlbaum, 1978.

LaPiere, R. T. Type-rationalizations of group antipathy. *Social Forces*, 1936, *15*, 232–237.

Leighton, A. H. *Human relations in a changing world.* New York: Dutton, 1949.

LeVine, R. A., & Campbell, D. T. *Ethnocentrism: Theories of conflict, ethnic attitudes, and group behavior.* New York: Wiley, 1972.

Levinson, D. J., & Sanford, R. N. A scale for the measurement of anti-Semitism. *Journal of Psychology*, 1944, *17*, 339–370.

Lippmann, W. *Public opinion.* New York: Harcourt, Brace, 1922.

Mackie, M. Arriving at "truth" by definition: The case of stereotype inaccuracy. *Social Problems*, 1973, *20*, 431–447.

McCauley, C., Stitt, C. L., & Segal, M. Stereotyping: From prejudice to prediction. *Psychological Bulletin*, 1980, *87*, 195–208.

Mitchell, H. E., & Byrne, D. The defendant's dilemma: Effects of jurors' attitudes and authoritarianism on judicial decisions. *Journal of Personality and Social Psychology*, 1973, *24*, 123–129.

Myrdal, G. *An American dilemma. The Negro problem and modern democracy.* New York: Harper & Row, 1962.

Newcomb, T. M., & Charters, W. W., Jr. *Social psychology.* New York: Dryden Press, 1950.

Newsweek. Nov. 25, 1974, p. 39.

Nisbett, R. E., & Ross, L. D. *Human inference: Strategies and shortcomings of social judgment.* Englewood Cliffs, N.J.: Prentice-Hall, 1980.

Nisbett, R. E., & Wilson, T. D. Telling more than we can know: Verbal reports on mental processes. *Psychological Review*, 1977, *84*, 231–259. (a)

Nisbett, R. E., & Wilson, T. D. The halo effect: Evidence for unconscious alteration of judgments. *Journal of Personality and Social Psychology*, 1977, *35*, 250–256. (b)

Olsen, J. *The Black athlete: A shameful story.* New York: Time-Life Books, 1968.

Ostrom, T. M. The bogus pipeline: A new *ignis fatuus*? *Psychological Bulletin*, 1973, *79*, 252–259.

Parkes, J. *Antisemitism.* Chicago: Quadrangle Books, 1963.

Pettigrew, T. The ultimate attribution error: Extending Allport's cognitive analysis of prejudice. *Personality and Social Psychology Bulletin*, 1979, *5*, 461–476.

Rosenberg, S., & Sedlak, A. Structural representation of implicit personality theory. In L. Berkowitz (ed.), *Advances in experimental social psychology* (Vol. 6). New York: Academic Press, 1972.

Rosenhan, D. L. On being sane in insane places. *Science*, 1973, *179*, 250–258.

Rothbart, M. Achieving racial equality: An analysis of resistance to social reform. In P. A. Katz (ed.), *Towards the elimination of racism.* New York: Pergamon Press, 1976. Ch. 10.

Ryan, W. *Blaming the victim.* New York: Pantheon, 1971.

Schaefer, R. T. *Racial and ethnic groups.* Boston: Little Brown, 1979.

Schneider, D. J., Hastorf, A. H., & Ellsworth, P. C. *Person perception* (2nd ed.). Reading, Mass.: Addison-Wesley, 1979.

Secord, P. F., & Backman, C. W. *Social psychology.* New York: McGraw-Hill, 1974.

Segall, M. *Cross-cultural psychology.* Monterey, Calif.: Brooks/Cole, 1979.

Sherif, M., & Sherif, C. W. *Social psychology.* New York: Harper & Row, 1969.

Shields, S. A. Functionalism, Darwinism, and the psychology of women. *American Psychologist*, 1975, *30*, 739–754.

Sigall, H., & Page, R. Current stereotypes: A little fading, a little faking. *Journal of Personality and Social Psychology*, 1971, *18*, 247–255.

Smedley, J. W., & Bayton, J. A. Evaluative, race-class stereotypes by race and perceived class of subjects. *Journal of Personality and Social Psychology*, 1978, *36*, 530–535.

Snyder, M. Seek, and ye shall find: Testing hypotheses about other people. In E. T. Higgins, C. P. Herman, & M. P. Zanna (eds.), *Social cognition: The Ontario symposium*, vol. 1. Hillsdale, N.J.: Erlbaum, 1981a.

Snyder, M. On the self-fulfilling nature of social stereotypes. In D.L. Hamilton (ed.), *Cognitive processes in stereotyping and intergroup behavior*. Hillsdale, N.J.: Erlbaum, 1981b.

Tajfel, H. Cognitive aspects of prejudice. *Journal of Social Issues*, 1969, *25*, 79–97.

Taylor, S. E. A categorization approach to stereotyping. In D. L. Hamilton (ed.), *Cognitive processes in stereotyping and intergroup behavior*. Hillsdale, N.J.: Erlbaum, 1981.

Tedeschi, J. T., & Lindskold, S. *Social psychology*. New York: Wiley-Interscience, 1976.

Vinacke, W. E. Stereotypes as social concepts. *Journal of Social Psychology*, 1957, *46*, 229–243.

Wicker, A. W. Attitudes versus actions: The relationship of verbal and overt behavioral responses to attitude objects. *Journal of Social Issues*, 1969, *25*, 41–78.

Zajonc, R. Feeling and thinking: Preferences need no inferences. *American Psychologist*, 1980, *35*, 151–175.

Zawadski, B. Limitations of the scapegoat theory of prejudice. *Journal of Abnormal and Social Psychology*, 1942, *43*, 127–141.

ADDITIONAL READINGS

Katz, P. (ed.). *Towards the elimination of racism*. New York: Pergamon Press, 1976.
An anthology dealing with diverse aspects of prejudice toward blacks. The emphasis is on conceptual and empirical approaches to attitude and behavioral change. Particularly recommended are chapters by Katz, focusing upon children; Ashmore and Del Boca, reviewing the psychology of prejudice; and Rothbart, analyzing resistance to social reform.

Kelley, H. H. Attribution theory in social psychology. In D. Levine (ed.), *Nebraska symposium on motivation*. Lincoln: University of Nebraska Press, 1967.
A very influential paper in the history of theory development in attribution research. A major emphasis is on the relationship between patterns of behavioral information and types of causal attributions associated with such input. Of particular relevance to the issue of stereotyping is the emphasis placed on consensus, essentially the idea that high agreement among perceivers leads to the impression that the target or object is the cause of the observed behavior.

Schaefer, R. T. *Racial and ethnic groups*. Boston: Little, Brown, 1979.
An important, sociologically oriented survey of racial and ethnic groups.

Particularly informative for the student of stereotyping is Schaefer's historical description, in which he emphasizes the complex of political, economic, psychological, and sociological factors contributing to the unique character of diverse groups and their interaction with other minorities as well as the majority. Groups included in his review are blacks, Indians, Chicanos, Puerto Ricans, Chinese Americans, Japanese Americans, Jews, and women.

Sherif, M., & Sherif, C. W. *Groups in harmony and tension.* New York: Harper & Row, 1953.
A classic analysis, conceptually as well as experimentally, of intergroup relations. The justifiably famous studies of campers—at war and at peace—are described in detail.

Wegner, D., & Vallacher, R. R. *Implicit psychology: An introduction to social cognition.* New York: Oxford University Press, 1977.
A very readable and stimulating analysis of the role of the perceiver in the construction of social reality. The authors draw an analogy between the individual's implicit theory construction and the scientist's explicit theoretical activity. This book provides a useful background for a number of the issues raised by Jones in Chapter 2 of the present volume.

2

PERCEIVING OTHER PEOPLE: STEREOTYPING AS A PROCESS OF SOCIAL COGNITION

Russell A. Jones

STEREOTYPES AND INFORMATION PROCESSING

Stereotypes are often claimed to be the result of illogical or faulty reasoning processes. It is seldom made clear exactly what and where the faults are, but the usual implication is that people who hold stereotypes are intellectually deficient. Archie Bunker, for example, with his myriad stereotypes of blacks, Jews, southerners, Californians, and almost every other group imaginable is clearly not too bright, and the revelations of his convoluted reasoning are filled with half-truths, inappropriate generalizations, malapropisms, and superstitions. Unfortunately, the Archie Bunkers of the world are not the only ones with stereotypes. We all have them, and it is very unlikely that increasing everyone's IQ by 20 or 30 points would change that fact. But is there any truth to the claim that stereotypes can result from faulty reasoning processes?

The purpose of this chapter is to examine some of the evidence bearing on that claim. In particular, we shall concern ourselves with evidence suggesting that stereotypes are in fact the normal result of certain flaws in the way in which we process information about other people. As we shall see, there are a number of imperfections in the ways in which we take in, manipulate, and try to make sense of the information about those we see and hear and interact with. However, far from being indications of abnormal or deficient functioning, these "imperfections" are in many cases information-processing shortcuts and procedures that usually serve us well and make our tasks easier.

I would like to thank Ron Dillehay, Joanne Scott, Jean Wiese, and Robin Welch for their comments on an earlier draft of this chapter.

For example, because of the tremendous amounts of information impinging on our eyes and ears in any given situation, we usually have to be quite selective about what we attend to. We simply cannot take it all in, so we pick out what we think are the most important aspects of a situation. But situations change, and our normal habits of attention may retard perception of those changes because we are looking elsewhere, at what we think is important. Similarly, once we have categorized another person in a particular way, we are likely to ignore the differences between that person and others who have been so categorized simply because categorization is, by definition, based on the perception of similarities. We tend to overgeneralize the bases of our categorizations and to act as if people categorized on the basis of similarity in one characteristic are likely to be similar in other respects, even when these "other respects" had no part in our initial categorization.

We shall explore these and a number of other information-processing biases in the pages to come. We begin with some basic issues in the perception of other people: how we go about attending to the behaviors of others, what sorts of things we are most likely to notice, and what is likely to happen once we make the leap from observation to categorization. We are seldom content with the simple perception of differences in behavior of different categories of people, however. We feel a need to explain those differences, to understand why they occurred. As we shall see, there is a fundamental error that we are likely to make in trying to explain why someone behaved as he or she did. We are likely to underestimate the extent to which that person's behavior was constrained by the situation, and to overestimate the extent to which it was due to his or her personal characteristics, to the sort of person he or she is.

Our explanations for behavior are also biased by several motivational forces. There is some evidence, for example, that we tend to blame victims for their misfortunes, even when the misfortune was entirely unpreventable. Such apparently irrational explanations serve to protect our sense of security. If we can convince ourselves that the victim failed to take certain precautions against disaster, all we have to do to prevent a similar disaster from occurring to us is to take those precautions. Once we have fleshed out our perceptual distinctions among people and groups with explanations for those differences, we are often in deep trouble, because we tend to rely on these internal representations. What we remember about a person or group becomes for us what they are, and what we can remember is often unrepresentative and distorted. We shall look at some of the reasons why this is so.

Finally, we shall examine some of the ways in which what we "remember" and what we have inferred about another person or group influence how we will behave toward that person or members of that group in the future. It appears that we often behave in ways that almost force a person or persons to conform to our expectations and stereotypes of how they will behave.

Before we begin, a caveat is in order. It should be kept in mind that stereotypes have many origins in addition to the sorts of information-processing biases we shall be discussing. Exposure to the mass media, to our parents' opinions and beliefs, to the opinions and beliefs of our peers, and to numerous other sources of both accurate and inaccurate information help to shape our views of other people and groups. The processes to be discussed below, however, are particularly important, because once we think we have seen something, it has a reality for us, a concreteness, that secondhand information lacks. The problem, as we shall see, is that what we think we see is often only partly a function of what is out there.

PERCEPTION OF OTHER PEOPLE

Perception has to do with the "taking in" of information. As Erdelyi (1974, pp. 13–14) puts it, "Broadly conceived, perceptual processes may be best thought of as spanning the full sequence of events associated with information intake and consolidation, beginning just after stimulus input and ending prior to permanent storage in long-term memory." Thus, perception includes a number of different processes: attention, the encoding or interpretation of what we have just seen or heard or felt or tasted, short-term memory, and rehearsal of what we have encoded. Our encodings or interpretations, as well as what we choose to attend to and all other aspects of perception, are, of course, partially determined by what we have previously stored in long-term memory. Someone with an extensive knowledge of herbs and spices, for example, may get a great deal more enjoyment out of a gourmet meal because he or she will be more likely to be able to distinguish and name and remember the various tastes than someone without such knowledge. Thus, to some extent it is artificial to discuss perception and memory separately, as we shall do here, because there is a continuous and reciprocal interplay between them. We separate them here only for convenience.

Segmenting the Stream of Behavior

If we want to find out what another person is like, one of the best ways to start is by simply observing that person: watching, listening, smelling, comparing what he or she does with what others do, and comparing what he or she does with what we would have done in the same situation. Our purpose in observing another's behavior is, first of all, to make sense of what the person appears to be doing. An intriguing line of research by Newtson and his colleagues has focused attention on the perceptual processes involved when we try to understand what another person is up to. The basic assumption behind Newtson's research is that the perceiver does not passively take in information about the behavior observed. Rather, the perceiver actively participates in the perceptual process by organizing the ongoing observed behavior into meaningful segments or actions. Thus, to a large extent the preceiver controls the amount and kind of information obtained when observing another's behavior, and may literally generate more or less information from a given behavioral sequence, depending on such factors as expectations and attentiveness.

In one of his first experiments, Newtson (1973) hypothesized that perceivers who break down an observed, ongoing behavior sequence into small units will subsequently be more confident of the validity of their impressions, and will have more differentiated impressions, than perceivers who break down the observed behavior sequence into larger segments. The idea is that when we break the behavior into small segments, we are attending to it more closely and, hence, obtain more information. The more information we have about another person, the more confident we are likely to be about our impression of the person and the more differentiated that impression is likely to be.

To check on this, Newtson asked first-year male students at the University of Wisconsin to observe a five-minute videotaped behavioral sequence. The subjects were furnished with a continuous event recorder, synchronized with the videotape, on which they were to mark off the behavior of the person on the videotape into meaningful segments. However, half the subjects were told to mark off the behavior into the largest units that seemed natural and meaningful, and half the subjects were told to mark off the behavior into the smallest units that seemed natural and meaningful. After watching the tape, subjects were asked to rate the observed person on a number of social and intellectual qualities, and to indicate how confident they were of their ratings.

Subjects instructed to use the smallest meaningful units did, in fact, divide the videotape into significantly more segments than those instructed to use the largest meaningful units (52.1 versus 21.3). As anticipated, subjects who broke the observed behavior into finer units—who attended more closely to what they saw—were more confident of their impressions. Further, the correlation between ratings of social and intellectual qualities was high and positive for subjects using large units, and virtually nonexistent for subjects using small units. In other words, subjects using small units had more differentiated impressions.

One other finding is of particular interest here. Following the confidence and impression ratings, subjects were asked to respond to four items, on each of which they were to imagine the person they had just observed on the videotape performing some additional action. For each of the items subjects were asked to choose between two explanations for the action: a dispositional explanation (he did that because of the type of person he is) and a situational explanation (he did that because of the situation he was in). Subjects who had broken down the videotaped behavior into small units made significantly more dispositional attributions on these items than did subjects who had employed grosser units and/or attended less closely to the behavior on the videotape. Thus, it appears that subjects who attend closely to another's behavior are more likely to perceive the other's subsequent behavior as personally caused—that is, as caused by traits, characteristics, and personality dispositions.

Additional research indicates at least one reservation is necessary with respect to this latter finding. Newtson (1976) reports that stronger personal attributions are made by fine-unit perceivers primarily when they are observing films or videotapes of actors and actresses performing "free" behavior sequences—that is, when they are moving about more or less on their own volition, and not when they are depicted performing a specific, limited task, such as putting together a model. "Free" behavior sequences are, of course, the kind we are more likely to see others performing in everyday life. Thus, the more closely we attend to such behavior, the more likely we are to perceive it as due to characteristics of the person performing the behavior and the less likely we are to perceive it as being due to the situation in which the person finds himself or herself. We are also likely to be quite confident about the validity of such impressions. But what sorts of things are likely to lead us to attend to another's behavior more or less closely?

In subsequent research Newtson, Engquist, and Bois (1977) have shown that observers segment the behaviors they are watching at break points, points in the ongoing stream of behavior where a noticeable change occurs in one or more of the features the observer is monitoring. Thus, the information we obtain from observing another's behavior is defined by changes. The unit of perception, as we have seen, is variable, and the observer has a great deal of choice in how the observed behavior is segmented. The usual purpose in observing another's behavior is, of course, to gain enough information to understand what the observed person is doing. As a sequence of behavior becomes predictable, Newtson has found, observers gradually begin to segment the behavior into larger and larger units. It is as if they feel they do not have to pay so much attention, because now they know what is going on. However, Newtson has also found that if an unexpected or unusual behavior occurs in the sequence being observed, perceivers quickly shift back to fine units and attend more closely to the person being observed, apparently in order to gain sufficient information about the person to reestablish predictability.

We attend most closely to the unusual in behavior, and we do so, apparently, in order to learn, to gain sufficient information about the person performing this unusual behavior so that we may anticipate how he or she is going to behave in the future. Further, one consequence of our focused attention is that we are more likely to see the behavior as being personally caused, as being due to some quality of the person we are observing, at least when the behavior is not constrained by a particular task. It should follow, then, that if there are certain situations in which particular people are unusual or salient, we are more likely to pay closer attention to them than to those around them and, perhaps, more likely to attribute their behaviors to their personality dispositions.

Tokens and Other Distinctive People

As noted above, in most situations there is simply more information available than we can handle. We are overwhelmed with sights, sounds, and smells, and have to select small portions of what is available to attend to and encode. The aspects of a situation that we choose to attend to are, of course, a function of many things, such as our interests and experience. There is some evidence, however, that in many situations we do not "choose" at all, at least not in a conscious, rational manner. Sometimes it seems as if situations "choose" for us by drawing our attention to certain of their features.

Consider the question of self-perception. There are literally thousands of things that each of us could tell another person if we were asked to describe ourselves. McGuire, McGuire, Child, and Fujioka (1978), however, suggest that what we notice about ourselves and what we choose to tell another person about ourselves are often those characteristics that are unusual in our customary environments. It follows that the only son of a couple who also have three daughters should be more conscious of his maleness than the son of a couple who also have one daughter. Similarly, a black child in a classroom with 29 white children should be more conscious of his or her identity as a black than would the same child in a classroom with 15 white and 14 other black children. Further, McGuire et al. argue that distinctiveness influences our conceptions of ourselves in two major ways: directly, in that we may define ourselves in terms of our distinctive or unusual features, and indirectly, in that others may perceive us and respond to us in terms of our distinctive attributes.

In support of the hypothesis that we define ourselves in terms of our distinctive attributes, McGuire et al. (1978) and McGuire, McGuire, and Winton (1979) report a study in which students in a predominantly white school system were interviewed and asked to describe themselves. Only 1 percent of the predominant white group spontaneously mentioned their ethnic group membership, while 17 percent of the black and 14 percent of the Hispanic students did so. Similarly, males were significantly more likely to mention being male when they came from households in which females were in the majority, and females were significantly more likely to mention being female when they came from households in which males were in the majority. Further, boys who came from homes where the father was absent were significantly more likely to mention being male than were boys who came from homes in which the father was present. Thus, there is some evidence that those characteristics we possess that are unusual in our normal environments are particularly salient in our self-perceptions.

It also seems to be the case that in perceiving other people, as in self-perception, we attend most closely to the unusual and the distinctive. Further, this focusing of attention on the distinctive has consequences for how we interpret what we have seen. "Distinctive" may, in fact, be too strong a word. In observing other people, we often seem to attend merely to whatever or whoever is easiest to attend to—the closest person, the person with the loudest (clearest) voice, the person we can see most easily. Taylor and Fiske (1975; 1978) prefer the term "salient" to "distinctive," and argue that, all too often, we unthinkingly devote the lion's share of our attention to whatever or whomever happens to be the most salient stimulus in our environment.

In a series of studies, Taylor and Fiske and their colleagues asked subjects to view simple interaction situations, such as a conversation between two people, and manipulated salience of the people conversing by varying the seating positions of the observers. Thus, some observers were seated so that they were looking directly at one of the two participants, but could see only the back and side of the second participant. Other observers were seated so that they were looking directly at the second participant, but could see only the back and side of the first participant. Still other observers were seated to the side of the participants, so that they could see both equally well. The two participants, actually confederates of the experimenters, carried on a five-minute conversation while being observed by groups of six who were seated as in Figure 2.1.

Following the conversation, observers were asked a number of questions about what they had heard, and were asked to rate the participants on a number of scales. The major result was that observers 1 and 2 (who were facing participant A) rated A as having been significantly more responsible for the nature and direction of the conversation, while observers 5 and 6 (who were facing participant B) rated B as having been significantly more responsible for the nature and direction of the conversation. Observers 3 and 4, who could see both participants equally well, rated them as having been about equally responsible for the tone and topics of conversation. As Taylor and Fiske (1975, p. 445) note, "Where one's attention is directed in one's environment influences what information is perceptually salient. Perceptually salient information is subsequently overrepresented when one imputes social or causal meaning to one's perceptual experience."

It is true, of course, that our impressions of others are usually grounded in a greater wealth of information than can be obtained by having observed them for five minutes while they sit in one position and converse

FIGURE 2.1

Seating Arrangement of Taylor and Fiske, in Which Two Participants Converse While Watched by Six Observers.

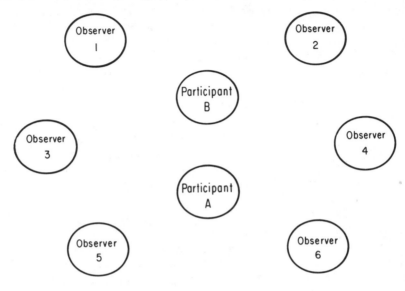

Source: Taylor & Fiske (1975), Fig. 1, p. 441. Copyright 1975 by the American Psychological Association. Reprinted by permission.

with one other person. We typically see those about whom we form impressions in various settings, conversing with various people, and doing various different things. Under these circumstances how likely is it that mere perceptual salience plays such an important role in our impressions? Surely, when we have more meaningful information about a person, the distinctive or novel feature that at first caught and held our attention is no longer the keystone of our impression. Unfortunately, some field research on the experiences of token women in predominantly male organizations suggests otherwise.

Kanter (1977) defines a "token" as someone identified by ascribed characteristics such as race or sex, who carries with him or her a set of assumptions about status or likely behavior, and who is a member of a group in which all of the other members differ from the token on one such ascribed characteristic. Thus, a white in a group of blacks or a male in a group of females would be a token. In order to study the experiences of token women in ongoing social interaction, Kanter gained access to the sales division of a large industrial corporation, a division consisting of over 300 men and only 20 women. Further, since the sales division was geographically decentralized into a number of field offices, the skewed ratio of men to women in the sales force meant that each field office had only one female, or at most two, on the sales staff. Kanter spent hundreds of hours interviewing both male and female members of the sales division, observing their interactions in training groups, sitting in on their sales meetings, and participating in their informal social gatherings.

On the basis of her observations, Kanter argues that the proportional rarity of tokens in such groups is associated with three perceptual phenomena: (1) visibility—because of their differentness, tokens capture a larger share of attention; (2) polarization—the presence of the token, who has characteristics different from those of the other group members, makes the others more aware of their similarities to each other and their differentness from the token; and (3) assimilation—the token's attributes tend to be distorted to fit preexisting beliefs about the token's "social type." Each of these perceptual phenomena has consequences for the token. Visibility, for example, creates demanding performance pressures, because everything the token says or does is closely attended to. He or she cannot just slip into the shadows and relax. Polarization leads to an exaggeration of the dominant majority culture within the group and isolation of the token. Assimilation results in the token's being forced into limited roles within the group.

According to Kanter, the interaction dynamics accompanying the presence of a token in a group are heightened and dramatized when the token's social category is physically obvious. While it is true that such physically obvious stimuli as another's age, sex, or race do influence much of our social interaction, it seems to be the case that most of the discriminations we make among people are not based on physically obvious stimuli. We group people in many different ways—in terms of their intelligence, or friendliness, or arrogance, or modesty. We make such categorizations for our own convenience, of course, since they lessen the volume of information we have to retain. Once we categorize another person as, say, intelligent, we anticipate how he or she will react in certain future situations, even though we may never have seen him or her perform in similar situations. However, the very act of categorization may induce distortions in what we think we know about another person, distortions that may underlie what Kanter refers to as the polarization and assimilation processes that occur in groups with a token member of a race or sex different from that of the majority.

Categorization

The number of ways in which people are perceived to differ is enormous and, with the possible exception of sex, each of these individual differences varies along a continuous dimension. People are not, for example, simply intelligent or unintelligent, but vary in their degree of intelligence. We all know that. For convenience, however, we often break up these individual-difference dimensions into categories—such as "dumb,"

"average," and "smart." Transforming the gradual and continuous variations in intelligence into these three clear-cut categories makes life easier for
us, in that it simplifies a tremendous amount of information and, for most
everyday uses, such gross distinctions may suffice. The danger is that once
we have classified two people or two groups into different categories, we may
exaggerate the differences between them and ignore their similarities—or,
conversely, once we have classified two people or two groups into the same
category, we may exaggerate their similarities and ignore their differences.
Some evidence that these are real and present dangers comes from the work
of Tajfel.

As a preliminary demonstration of these effects, Tajfel and Wilkes
(1963) asked subjects to make judgments of lengths of lines, each line being
presented on a separate cardboard background to subjects seated several feet
away. The eight lines presented varied in length from 16.2 centimeters to
22.9 centimeters, and all subjects were asked to make their judgments in
centimeters. Some subjects simply made the judgments a number of times,
the lines being presented in a different random order each time. However,
for other subjects the cardboard sheets on which the four shorter lines were
printed each had a large letter A drawn on them, and the sheets on which the
four longer lines were presented each had a large letter B on them. Thus, the
letters "A" and "B" provided a classification of the lines into two groups
(shorter and longer), even though the lines within each group still differed in
length. One of the more dramatic results from this experiment is presented in
Figure 2.2. As may be seen in the figure, the superimposed classification (A
versus B) that enabled subjects to divide the lines into two groups led them
to exaggerate the differences between the two classes—or, more precisely, to
exaggerate the difference between the longest line in the "short" class and the
shortest line in the "long" class.

Thus, while Tajfel and Wilkes's study provides some evidence that
classification of stimuli into categories leads to an exaggeration of intercategory differences, there is little evidence in the study for minimization of
intracategory differences. Tajfel, Sheikh, and Gardner (1964) attempted to
find some evidence for the latter by asking subjects to listen to interviews
with members of two different groups (Canadians and Indians), and then to
rate the interviewees on a number of scales. The two Indian interviewees
were rated significantly more similar than the Canadians on traits that had
previously been selected by other subjects as characterizing "people from
India." On the basis of this, Tajfel et al. (p. 199) conclude that ". . . it is clear
that stereotypes were operating . . . to reduce judged differences between
individuals within an ethnic group." Unfortunately, that conclusion is not
justified by the data, because, as far as we know, the two Indian interviewees
may in fact have appeared more unassuming, relaxed, and submissive (and
other traits said to characterize "people from India") than the two Canadian
interviewees.

FIGURE 2.2

Results of Tajfel and Wilkes Experiment, Showing Exaggeration of Differences in Classified Series

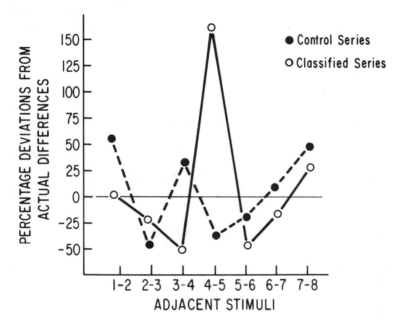

Source: Tajfel & Wilkes (1963), Fig. 3, p. 111. Reprinted by permission of Cambridge University Press and the British Psychological Society.

Another way to look at this question of whether categorization induces us to exaggerate intracategory similarities is in terms of confusion. That is, if we have categorized people on the basis of attribute A—say, sex or skin color—are we more likely to confuse their standings on some other characteristic or on some behavior? If we observe a group of three males and three females interacting, for example, and are later asked to recall who said what during the interaction, what sorts of errors are we likely to make? If we do not categorize people by sex, we should be as likely to err by attributing something that a female said to a male as to another female, and vice versa. However, if we do categorize by sex, then we should be more likely to err by attributing something that a female said to another female than to a male, and something that a male said to another male than to a female.

Taylor, Fiske, Etcoff, and Ruderman (1978) provide some evidence on this point. Harvard undergraduates were asked to listen to tape-recorded discussions in which either six men or three men and three women took part. A picture of each speaker was projected onto a wall as he or she spoke, and subjects who listened to the six men found that three were white and three were black. Following the tape-slide presentation, subjects were asked to identify the participants who had made each of a number of suggestions during the discussion. Subjects who had heard the six-man discussion were more likely to err by attributing suggestions made by blacks to other blacks and by attributing suggestions made by whites to other whites than they were to err by attributing suggestions made by blacks to whites or vice versa. That is, the errors in attribution were more often intraracial than interracial. Similarly, errors made by subjects who listened to the discussion carried on by three males and three females were more often intrasex than intersex. As Taylor et al. (1978, pp. 790–791) note, subjects do "indeed process information about social groups using race and sex as ways of categorizing the group members and organizing information about them. . . . As a result of the categorization process, within-group differences tended to be minimized, whereas between-group differences remained clearer."

To avoid this sort of intracategory confusion, Hayakawa (1963) suggests that we should develop the habit of indexing our ideas, particularly our abstractions and categorizations. That is, we should constantly remind ourselves that two items or people or events that we have placed in the same category are not, thereby, the same. When dealing with people, we may categorize two people as similar with respect to one or even a dozen attributes, but they may differ with respect to thousands of attributes and items of personal history, interests, attitudes, values, and plans for the future. The problem is that once we have categorized or labeled someone, we tend to reify the label, to treat the word as if it captures the true essence of all that person is, when in fact the label at best designates the person's standing on one of thousands of personal attributes.

Given the multiple ways in which we can classify people, are there any reasons to believe that some are more likely than others? In the perception of objects and events there is some evidence that certain shapes and colors seem to stand out and are perceived more easily than others (Rosch, 1973). In form perception, for example, circles, squares, and triangles are more readily learned, more easily recalled, and more precisely encoded than are variations on these basic shapes. Similarly, in person perception Gergen (1967) has argued that color differences are more perceptually salient than are differences on most other personal attributes. Sex differences are also more obvious than most other kinds of individual variations. Hence, it may be that perceptual salience contributes to the readiness with which certain categorizations are made. It is certainly true that race and sex stereotypes are among the most notorious and perennial. However, Hayakawa (1963), Pettigrew (1967), Tajfel (1970), Hamilton (1976), and a number of others have argued that the basic distinction we make among people is whether they are "like us," and that we can make this distinction on any of a number of different bases. As Tajfel (1970, p. 98) puts it, "Perhaps the most important principle of the subjective social order we construct for ourselves is the classification of groups as "we" and "they"—as ingroups (any number of them to which we happen to belong) and outgroups."

The problem is that we know so much more about ourselves and others than the mere fact(s) of group membership. During the course of our experience with others, we learn to expect certain characteristics to co-occur. Having made a distinction between "us" and "them" on the basis of one characteristic, we may infer that "they" possess additional characteristics for which we have no evidence.

IMPLICIT THEORIES OF PERSONALITY

Everyone has a set of beliefs about what people are like. Further, casual observation suggests that these expectations about others differ in some respects from person to person, even though there may be large areas of overlap between the belief systems of any two people. But what do these "belief systems" really entail? As Rosenberg and Jones (1972) point out, two things are involved: the categories we employ to describe the range of abilities, attitudes, interests, physical features, traits, and behaviors that we perceive in others, and the beliefs we hold concerning which of these perceived characteristics tend to go together and which do not. One way to sensitize people to the existence of such beliefs is to pose a question such as "What do you think of a wise, cruel man?"—a jarring inconsistency for most people. To most people, wise men are generally old, kindly—perhaps jaded—but never cruel. The categories into which we sort our perceptions of others and the beliefs about their associations constitute the rudiments of a theory of personality. Most people, however, are under little pressure to make explicit either the categories they employ or their beliefs about the relationships among categories—hence the term "implicit theories of personality."

The evidence for the existence of implicit theories of personality is relatively clear, and has been around for a long time. Asch (1946), for example, reported a study in which two groups of subjects were each read a list of characteristics that supposedly described a person. The two lists were identical except for one term. One group heard that the person was intelligent, skillful, industrious, warm, determined, practical, and cautious. The second group heard that the person was intelligent, skillful, industrious, cold, determined, practical, and cautious. Both groups of subjects were then asked to write brief sketches of the person described and to check (on a provided form) those additional qualities or characteristics that the described person would be likely to have. The resulting differences in impression were dramatic. Subjects for whom "warm" had been included on the list were much more likely to describe the stimulus person as generous, wise, happy, good-natured, humorous, sociable, popular, humane, altruistic, and imaginative.

Asch's basic demonstrations that we do infer additional qualities of a person from small initial amounts of information, and that changes in the initial information result in changes in the inferences made, have held up well through a series of replications. The next question one might ask about our implicit theories of personality, then, is whether there is any evidence that they influence the actual perception of other people—that is, whether they influence what we think we see other people doing and how we encode the behaviors of other people.

Some evidence on this comes from a study by Dornbusch, Hastorf, Richardson, Muzzy, and Vreeland (1965), in which information was solicited from boys and girls in summer camps. Each child was interviewed twice and, in each interview, was asked to describe two other children who shared his or her tent. A set of 69 categories was developed to code the various things mentioned about the children being described. The categories included a wide range of variables, from simple demographic descriptors, such as age and race, to personality attributes, such as generosity and cooperativeness. The verbal descriptions were reliably coded into these categories. Without exception there was greater overlap in category usage— that is, more of the same categories were used—when one child was describing two others than when two children were describing the same other child. This finding held up even when the two descriptions from a given child were elicited a week apart.

A related finding comes from a study by Rubin, Provenzano, and Luria (1974), in which the parents of newly born infants were asked to rate their young (less than 24 hours old) sons and daughters. Objective comparisons established that the male and female infants did not differ in weight, length, color, reflex irritability, or heart and respiration rates. Even so, the parents, especially the fathers, rated their sons as firmer, larger-featured, better coordinated, more alert, and hardier, and daughters as softer, finer-featured, more awkward, more inattentive, weaker, and more delicate. Thus it appears that the categories of our implicit theories and the interrelations among them may determine what we attend to and how we encode another person's behavior. Our implicit theories may play more of a role in our perception of others than the actual characteristics of the others, at least under some conditions.

What might some of those conditions be? One has to do with our own standing on the attribute in question. As an example of what is meant by this, consider a study by Benedetti and Hill (1960), in which students were selected, on the basis of test scores, as high, medium, or low in sociability. Each subject in each of these three groups was then asked to read a list of traits that were supposedly descriptive of another person, following which he or she selected from a list of 20 pairs the 20 traits that best fitted his or her impressions of the stimulus person. Half of the subjects in each of the sociability groups read the following list: "intelligent, skillful, industrious, sociable, determined, practical, cautious." The list read by the remaining subjects had "unsociable" substituted for "sociable." Of interest here is the finding that among those students who heard the person described as unsociable, those who were themselves low in sociability were more likely to attribute desirable charactcristics to the person than were those who were high in sociability.

Another condition in which our implicit theories of personality might be expected to play a large role in our impressions of others is working from memory, trying to formulate an impression based on bits and pieces of information about another that have been accumulated over time. In a reanalysis of some data originally reported by Newcomb (1929), Shweder (1975) has provided some evidence on this point. The original study was conducted at a summer camp for boys. Two groups of campers attended the camp for about three and one-half weeks each, and their day-to-day behaviors were recorded by six observers. The observers recorded every occurrence of each of 26 separate behaviors exhibited by the boys. Some examples of the behaviors recorded are the following:

Speaks with confidence of his own abilities,
Spends more than an hour of the day alone,
Painstaking in making up his bed,
Talks more than his share of the time, and
Gets into scraps with other boys. (Shweder, 1975, pp. 460–461)

These observations, recorded as soon as possible after they occurred, constitute the actual behavior of the boys. In addition, at the end of each three-and-one-half-week session, each of the six observers was asked to give an overall rating to each boy on each of the 26 behaviors. The latter ratings constitute what Shweder terms the rated behavior of the boys. These indexes of actual and rated behavior were both obtained by Newcomb in the 1920s.

In the early 1970s Shweder asked some graduate students at the University of Chicago to look at the 26 behaviors from Newcomb's study and, for each possible pair of those behaviors, to rate the conceptual similarity of the behaviors. These ratings constitute what Shweder refers to as the preexisting conceptual scheme—that is, the "believed-in" relationships among the behaviors themselves. Shweder then correlated the actual behaviors performed by the boys, the rated behaviors as judged by the observers at the end of camp, and the preexisting conceptual scheme of perceived similarities among the behaviors themselves. The results are shown in Figure 2.3. The numbers in the figure are correlation coefficients, and there are several points to note about the relationships depicted. First, the actual behavior of a group does *not* correspond very closely to the rated behavior.

FIGURE 2.3

The Relationships Among Subjects' Actual Behaviors, Rated Behaviors, and the Preexisting Conceptual Scheme

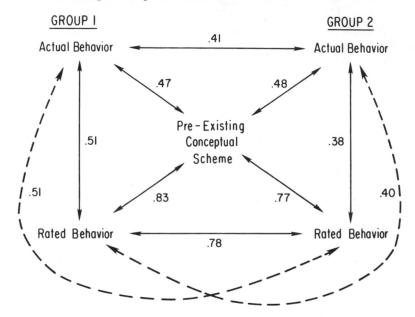

Source: Shweder (1975), Fig. 1, p. 462. Copyright 1975, Duke University Press (Durham, N.C.). Reprinted by permission.

Second, the preexisting conceptual scheme corresponds much more closely to the rated behavior than to the actual behavior. Thus, there appears to be a distortion in ratings of behavior, a distortion produced by conceptions of what-is-likely-to-be-related-to-what. Note also that the actual behavior of each group corresponds as closely to the rated behavior of the other group as it does to its own rated behavior. The actual behaviors of the two groups do not, however, correspond very closely.

Thus it appears that we do have implicit theories about what characteristics are likely to "go together" in other people; and once we have categorized another person on the basis of his or her standing on one attribute, we are likely to infer certain additional characteristics. It is important to note that such inferences are based on our beliefs about what characteristics are likely to be associated with the one that served as the basis for the initial categorization. The problem is that we then treat our inferences as facts, and believe that what we have inferred is the way things are (Nisbett & Ross, 1980). We shall return to the ways in which our implicit theories influence what we think we have seen.

But do we always behave in such an unscientific fashion? We often observe behavior for which we have no ready interpretation, and when we do, we may seek an explanation of why the person behaved as he or she did in what appears to be a relatively careful, analytic manner. There are several theoretical positions that assume we proceed in such a manner. But even when we honestly set out to understand why the person behaved in a certain way, there are traps for the unwary—traps that may induce and perpetuate stereotypical attributions.

EXPLANATIONS OF BEHAVIOR

In perceiving another's behavior, we tend to simplify as time passes. We start out observing discrete actions marked off by noticeable changes in the features we happen to be monitoring, and gradually organize these discrete actions into larger units. Zadny and Gerard (1974) have found that attributing a purpose or intent to an actor allows us to organize a behavioral sequence into larger units, and that, having done so, we tend to pay attention only to those aspects of the other's behavior that are relevant to the attributed purpose. If we are correct about our attributed intention, the accuracy of perception of the other's behavior will, of course, be enhanced. If we make a mistake, however, and attribute the wrong intention, the selectivity of our subsequent perceptions will make it quite difficult for us to realize the error. Even when we are correct about what the person is trying to do, we are rarely satisfied to stop at this point. We usually want to know why the person has a particular intention, why he or she is doing whatever we have observed.

Seeking the Causes of Behavior

Much of the research and theory on how we go about trying to pin down the cause of someone's behavior stems from the work of Heider (1958). The basic premise of Heider's work is that in order to understand the interpersonal world around us, we attempt to link the fleeting and variable interpersonal behaviors and events in which we find ourselves immersed to relatively unchanging underlying conditions or dispositional properties. According to Heider, any given behavior is dependent upon a combination of personal and situational forces. Further, the personal component can be broken down into ability and motivation. Heider's claim is that we tend to invoke these three general types of explanations (situation, ability, motivation), in varying degrees, whenever we want to understand why someone behaved in a particular way.

Building on Heider's basic premise, E. E. Jones and Davis (1965; also Jones, 1978) have developed a theory to explain some of the processes mediating the gap between observing someone perform a particular behavior and attributing a particular disposition to that person. The key to their conception is the idea that any given behavior represents a choice from among several that could have been performed, and that any effects of the behavior that are common to all of the alternatives could not be used to explain why the person behaved as he or she did. On the other hand, any consequences that are unique to a given behavior may provide some evidence on why the behavior was performed or why that particular course of action was chosen. Jones and Davis assume, as does Heider, that the more an act appears to be caused, or "called for," by the environment or situation, the less informative that act is about the person who performs it. Specifically, behaviors that are high in general social desirability, such as being polite, do not tell us much about a specific person because nearly everyone does these things.

In the attribution-theory tradition of Heider and E. E. Jones and Davis, Kelley (1967; 1973) has analyzed the problem of how we decide whether behavior in which we see someone engage is caused by the external environment or by an inner disposition of the person. According to Kelley, we need to consider four criteria to help us make this decision: distinctiveness, consistency over time, consistency over modality, and consensus. For example, McArthur (1972) asked subjects to read the responses that other people had made in certain situations, such as having laughed at a particular comedian, and then to decide the extent to which the responses were due to the person, the stimulus (in the example it would be the particular comedian), the circumstances, or some combination of these three. To help them make such decisions, subjects were given three additional items of information pertaining to variables Kelley had identified as important to the attribution process: consensus, distinctiveness, consistency over time.

Thus, to manipulate consensus information, some subjects read that almost everyone laughs at this comedian, while others read that hardly anyone laughs at this comedian. To manipulate distinctiveness, some subjects read that the person does not laugh at other comedians, while some subjects read that the person laughs at almost all comedians. To manipulate consistency, some subjects read that the person had in the past usually laughed at this comedian, while other subjects read that in the past the person usually had not laughed at this comedian. As anticipated, subjects were more likely to "explain" the responses by saying they were due to the characteristics or qualities of the people who made them when provided with low consensus information (hardly anyone laughs at this comedian), low distinctiveness information (the person laughs at most comedians), and high consistency information (the person has laughed at this comedian in the past).

Thus, attribution theory, as formulated by Heider, Jones and Davis, and Kelley, assumes that we behave in a fairly rational, scientific manner when we try to understand or explain why a person behaved as he or she did. There is evidence, as we have seen, that under certain conditions we are as rational as attribution theory postulates. In spite of such findings, it is one of the ironies of modern social psychology that the overwhelming message of research on attribution processes is that in seeking to understand and predict behavior, we often, even usually, do not behave in the rational, analytic manner postulated by attribution theory. For example, consider the distinction between an outcome that is determined by skill and one that is determined by chance. In principle, this distinction can be easily made. In skill situations one presumably can influence the outcome; in chance situations one cannot. This distinction is basic to attribution theory, because if we are going to explain why someone behaved in a particular way, we must be able to separate those outcomes that are due to the person's ability and motivation and those outcomes that are due to situational factors such as luck. According to Langer (1975), however, in our day-to-day experience this distinction is often blurred, if not totally ignored. People often act as if things that can influence only skill-related outcomes can also influence chance outcomes.

For example, in skill-related competitive situations, the more competent one's opponent, the more likely one is to lose. The less competent one's opponent, the more likely one is to win. But what if the outcome is determined by chance, by the toss of a coin or the luck of the draw? Then, of course, the competence of one's opponent is completely irrelevant. However, if people do confuse skill and luck situations, they may let the characteristics of their opponent influence their behavior even in the latter. To check on this, Langer recruited male undergraduates at Yale to play a simple card game in which they and another "subject" drew for high cards after placing bets between 0 and 25 cents. For some subjects the opponent was neatly dressed, clean, and apparently competent, while for others the opponent was awkward, shy, and apparently incompetent. The major dependent measure was the average amount bet. As anticipated, subjects bet significantly less when their opponent was neat, clean, and confident than when he appeared to be a "schnook."

Another problem that interferes with our rational evaluation of evidence when trying to explain why someone behaved as he or she did is that we are dealing with hindsight and, by definition, we have outcome knowledge. That is, we know what behavior was actually performed in response to the situation in which the person found himself or herself and, according to Fischhoff (1975), this information is likely to lead us to believe that that behavior was more inevitable than it really was. Fischhoff calls this effect "creeping determinism," and to demonstrate its existence, he asked groups of subjects to read brief descriptive passages concerning historical events or clinical case studies, each of which had four possible outcomes provided. Some subjects read the description and then rated the probability of each outcome. Other subjects read the descriptions, but before making their ratings were told that outcome 1 (or 2, 3, 4) had in fact "actually" occurred. All subjects were asked to rate the probability of each outcome ". . . in the light of the information appearing in the passage" (p. 289). The results for one of the case studies are given in Table 2.1. As may be seen in the table, knowledge that an outcome had occurred increases its perceived probability of occurrence.

Thus, in trying to understand the causes of behavior, we may some-times fail to distinguish between chance-determined and skill-determined situations as sharply as we should. Further, once we are aware of the outcome of a situation, we may not reconstruct the various possibilities inherent in the situation in the same way we would without such knowledge. Another issue concerns the *onset* of the attribution process. What factors— other than an experimenter making a formal request—are responsible for a person thinking about the causes of another's behavior and processing behavioral information in a deliberate, careful manner? Pyszczynski and Greenberg (1981) have suggested that people engage in more thorough attributional processing for behaviors which are unusual or unexpected. When expectancies *are* confirmed—as when a black person commits an act of aggression and the observer holds to a stereotype linking violence with blacks—one "may simply rely on the disposition prescribed by the stereo-type without even considering other possible causal factors" (p. 37). There are a number of other ways in which we depart from the ideal in our attempts to explain behavior, but there is one that is so pervasive that it has come to be called the fundamental attribution error (L. Ross, 1977).

The Fundamental Attribution Error

When we observe someone's behavior, we observe that behavior in a context. Only in science fiction movies are we ever likely to see people

TABLE 2.1
Mean Probabilities Assigned to Each Outcome in Fischhoff's Experiment

		Outcome Evaluated as Most Likely			
		1	2	3	4
No outcome provided		26.6	15.8	23.4	34.4
Outcome	1	43.1	13.9	17.3	25.8
	2	26.5	23.2	13.4	36.9
Provided	3	30.6	14.1	34.1	21.3
	4	21.2	10.2	22.6	46.1

Source: Fischhoff (1975), Table 1, Event C. p. 291. Copyright 1975 by the American Psychological Association. Reprinted by permission.

behaving in a featureless environment, and then only for very brief periods—until they climb back into the spacecraft. Behavior usually occurs in complex, many-faceted situations, and quite often it is constrained by the situation in which it occurs. But, as noted before, we simply cannot take in and process all of the information available to us at any given time, and so we are likely to focus on the most salient aspects. When observing another person in a particular setting, the most salient aspect is likely to be the behavior of that person. Heider (1958) referred to this phenomenon as "behavior engulfing the field." Subsequent research has documented the fact that in making attributions about the causes of behavior, we often do give undue weight to what a person says or does, and too little attention to the conditions surrounding the person's behavior. The result is that we tend to see others' behavior as being due to their personal characteristics, to the sort of person they are; this is what L. Ross (1977) has termed the fundamental attribution error—that is, the tendency to underestimate the impact of situational factors in producing another's behavior and to overestimate the role of dispositional or personality factors.

The fundamental attribution error has been well documented in various areas. For example, E. E. Jones and Harris (1967) found that after having heard an unpopular attitude position being defended by another person, observers attributed belief in that position to the person, even when they knew the person had been assigned to defend the position by the debating team adviser. But the fundamental attribution error is not a mere laboratory phenomenon. It apparently plays a major role in our understanding of history, for example. As children we are told of the exploits of heroes and heroines. We learn of Caesar, Columbus, Florence Nightingale, and Robin Hood, but seldom are we told of the complex social circumstances surrounding these figures. As Carr (1961) puts it:

> It is easier to call Communism "the brainchild of Karl Marx" . . . than to analyze its origin and character, to attribute the Bolshevik revolution to the stupidity of Nicholas II . . . than to study its profound social causes, and to see in the two world wars of this century the result of the individual wickedness of Wilhelm II and Hitler rather than of some deep-seated breakdown in the system of international relations. (p. 57)

This does not mean, of course, that there are not great men and women who play crucial roles in various settings. It does mean that the perception of history is biased by what Boring (1963) referred to as the principle of "focus and margin." We focus on the most prominent and easily identifiable features, which are usually individual men and women, and we relegate to marginal status the elaborate and complex web of events surrounding those people. In short, we commit the fundamental attribution error.

In a similar manner the roles that we play in our day-to-day life may make us appear to have qualities and characteristics that we do not really possess. Interpersonal encounters are typically constrained by roles such as teacher-student, policeman-traffic offender, lecturer-audience. And, as L. D. Ross, Amabile, and Steinmetz (1977) point out:

> Roles confer unequal control over the style, content, and conduct of an encounter; such social control, in turn, generally facilitates displays of knowledge, skill, insight, wit, or sensitivity, while permitting the concealment of deficiencies. Accurate social judgment, accordingly, depends upon the perceiver's ability to make adequate allowance for such role-conferred advantages and disadvantages in self-presentation. (p. 485)

Again the point is that in forming an impression of another, we may not give sufficient weight to the situation in which we observe the other's behavior.

As a demonstration of this, L.D. Ross et al. recruited male and female students at Stanford to participate in a quiz game. The students participated in pairs, with one assigned the role of questioner and the other assigned the role of contestant. The questioner for each pair of students assigned to the experimental condition was instructed to compose a set of difficult, but potentially answerable, questions to which he or she knew the answers; the contestant was to try to answer the questions. For the pairs of subjects assigned to the control condition, both questioner and contestant were informed that the questioner would simply ask questions prepared beforehand by someone else. During the actual quiz the questioners gave the contestants 30 seconds to answer, then indicated whether the given answer was correct, and supplied the correct answer if it was not. Immediately following the quiz, the subjects rated themselves and their partners on level of general knowledge. The results are shown in Table 2.2.

Contestants in the experimental condition, but not in the control condition, rated themselves as significantly less knowledgeable than their partners, even though the contestants knew the questioners had selected questions about isolated bits of knowledge that they happened to possess.

TABLE 2.2
Ratings of General Knowledge by Questioners and Contestants, Immediately Following the Quiz; in Experiment of Ross et al.

	Experimental Condition		Control Condition	
	Rating of Self	Rating of Partner	Rating of Self	Rating of Partner
Questioner	53.5	50.6	54.1	52.5
Contestant	41.3	66.8	47.0	50.3

Source: L.D. Ross et al. (1977), Table 1, p. 489. Copyright 1977 by the American Psychological Association. Reprinted by permission.

Had the roles of questioner and contestant been reversed, the new questioners could easily have composed questions that would have stumped their partners. Nevertheless, contestants apparently failed to consider the self-presentation advantage enjoyed by their questioners. In a subsequent experiment L. D. Ross et al. were able to demonstrate that observers who watched the quiz game and who also heard the instructions given the questioner made the same error as the contestant in the original experiment. That is, they estimated that the questioner had significantly more general knowledge than the contestant. The analogy between the Ross et al. results and the situation of minority group members in subservient roles is fairly straightforward. Seeing people behave in demeaning and obsequious ways, we may fail to recognize the extent to which the situation forces them into such behavior patterns. Consequently, we may too readily attribute their behavior to personality dispositions.

There is another twist here, however, that makes this sort of attribution error a particular problem in the context of stereotypes and the perception of group differences. Most of us tend to see our own choices and behavior as appropriate to the situations in which we find ourselves. We may not always do the best thing, but we do what seems best, given the circumstances, and assume that others would do the same in the same circumstances. L. Ross, Greene, and House (1977) point out that this, in effect, is a belief in a false consensus about the situational appropriateness of our own responses.

Whether false or simply untested, it follows that we are likely to judge the behavior of someone who behaves differently, as someone from a different cultural or ethnic background might well do, as revealing that person's stable dispositions. Our own behaviors and the behaviors of those who respond similarly, as people of similar backgrounds might be expected to do, are seen as being appropriate to or called for by the situation—and, hence, as less revealing about our personality dispositions. As support for the existence of the false consensus effect, L. Ross et al. (1977) report a study in which students were requested to wear a "sandwich board" sign of advertisements around campus. Those who agreed to do so estimated that 62 percent of their peers would do so, while those who refused to do so estimated that 67 percent of their peers would refuse. Further, those who agreed to wear the sign made more extreme inferences about the personality characteristics of those who refused, and those who refused made more extreme inferences about the personality characteristics of those who agreed.

The fundamental attribution error is a basic nonmotivational source of bias in our perception of others. It seems to stem largely from how we allot our attention when observing a person in a situation. The person's behavior is usually more salient, we focus on it, and, as L. Ross (1977) points out, whatever we "focus our attention on" is likely to be cited as a causal agent.

There are also motivational sources of bias in our perceptions of others—that is, sources of bias that stem from our needs to protect and enhance our self-esteem. The false consensus effect seems to be on the border between motivational and nonmotivational biases. It may be a function of the vested interest we have in preserving our view of what is appropriate, or it may be a selective exposure effect due to the fact most of our friends and associates are basically similar to us and, hence, are likely to respond as we do in any given situation.

Motivational Influences on Explanation

One of the more active areas of research on motivational influences has to do with the manner in which we explain successes and failures—both our own and others'. In an extension of some of Heider's ideas about personal and environmental forces, Weiner, Heckhausen, Meyer, and Cook (1972) point out that one may attribute the causes of success and failure on a task to four elements: ability, effort, task difficulty, and luck. Further, they argue that these four elements may be conceptualized as varying along two dimensions, which they refer to as stability and locus of control. Using these two dimensions, the four elements may be organized as depicted in Table 2.3.

As may be seen in the table, Weiner et al. postulate that we attribute the causes of success and/or failure on a task to either fixed or variable factors that may be internal or external to the person who has succeeded or failed. There is evidence that how we allocate responsibility for success or failure to these four elements has important consequences for future performance, if it is our behavior we are explaining, and important consequences for our impressions of others, if it is their behaviors we are explaining (R. A. Jones, 1977). Here, however, we shall focus on the issue of whether there is any evidence that our needs to protect and enhance our self-esteem make a difference in our explanations for success and failure. That is,

TABLE 2.3
The Four Elements That Weiner et al. Say Are Used to Explain Success and Failure, and the Two Attributional Dimensions: Stability and Locus of Control

		Locus of Control	
		Internal	External
Stability	Fixed	Ability	Task Difficulty
	Variable	Effort	Luck

Source: Weiner et al., (1972), Table 1, p. 240. Copyright 1972 by the American Psychological Association. Reprinted by permission.

are we likely to explain the successes and failures of others in the same ways that we explain our own?

According to Snyder, Stephan, and Rosenfield (1978), we are more likely to explain our own successes by appeal to internal factors of ability and effort, and to explain our failures with external factors such as task difficulty and luck. They define these tendencies as "egotism," and say that egotism may also include the obverse phenomena when we are explaining someone else's success or failure—that is, we are more likely to explain others' successes by appeals to luck and low levels of task difficulty, and their failures by lack of ability and/or effort.

In a demonstration of such self-serving biases in the interpretation of one's own behavior, Miller (1976) administered a bogus test of social perceptiveness to subjects. After taking the test, some subjects learned it was a well-established and valid test that gave quite accurate results, while others were led to believe that the test was just being developed and did not seem to be very accurate.* This information was intended to make it important for the first group of subjects (high involvement) to have done well on the test, assuming they would like to think of themselves as socially perceptive, intelligent, and sensitive individuals. For the subjects who learned that the test was not very accurate (low involvement), doing well or poorly on it should have fewer implications for the maintenance of their self-esteem.

After taking the test and hearing that it was either valid or invalid, each subject's test was ostensibly "scored." Some subjects in each condition learned that they had done quite well, while others learned that they had done quite poorly. All subjects then answered a number of questions about the test and about their performance. Analyses of their answers revealed that high-involvement subjects who "failed" attributed more responsibility for their failure to luck and less responsibility to their lack of ability than did low-involvement subjects. Conversely, high-involvement subjects who "succeeded" gave more credit to their own ability than did low-involvement subjects who succeeded. As Miller (1976, p. 905) points out, ". . . the perception that external factors played a larger role under high- than low-involvement failure would certainly seem to indicate a motivationally based attributional distortion."

Suppose, however, that the one who has failed is someone else. Are we as generous in explaining that person's failure? Do we also invoke external agents like luck and task difficulty to protect their self-esteem? As Wortman (1976) has pointed out, one of the main reasons we make causal attributions at all is to enhance our feelings of being in control of our fate. If some disaster befalls another person and we attribute it to luck, we are, in effect, acknowledging that we ourselves are in grave danger. It could have hap-

---

*Note that this information was given *after* subjects had taken the test. Hence, it could not have made a difference in how hard they tried on the test itself.

pened to us. On the other hand, if we can find some flaw in the person's character or behavior that might possibly explain why he or she was singled out for nature's backhanded slap, then we can proceed about our own business with relative calm and assurance. All we have to do to avoid a similar disaster is try harder, or sharpen our skills, or be a better person (whatever that means).

As Lerner (1970) puts it, we have a need to believe in a just world where good things happen to good people and bad things happen only to bad people. If we seriously believed otherwise, it would be more difficult to continue to work and struggle to make our way in the world. At any moment it might all be made meaningless—a bolt of lightning, a flood, cancer, or any of another thousand disasters could strike. Because our need to believe in a just world is so strong, we construct explanations that place blame on the victims of such unfortunate events (he shouldn't have been on the golf course during a storm, they should have built their house on higher ground, she should have stopped smoking). In an intriguing series of studies, Lerner (1980) and his colleagues (Lerner and Matthews, 1967; Lerner, Miller, and Holmes, 1976) have found that not only do we see others as responsible for their suffering, when objectively they are not, but we also derogate people whom we see suffering. We apparently derogate them for no reason other than the fact that they are suffering. Our belief in a just world is maintained by assuming that if they are suffering, they must deserve it.

Thus, there is some evidence that we tend to explain our successes and failures in ways that enhance and protect our self-esteem. When explaining the successes and failures of others, we are not so protective or so generous (M. Ross and Sicoly, 1979). We blame them for their shortcomings, which we see as being due to their lack of ability and/or effort, and we give them less than adequate credit for their achievements. Further, Miller, Norman, and Wright (1978) suggest that our tendency to attribute "explanatory" dispositions to others is likely to be enhanced if we anticipate having to interact with them, rather than just observing and rating them, for example. Specifically, Miller et al. postulate that we have a need for effective control, a need to convince ourselves that we will be able to handle interactions with others in ways that allow us to achieve our goals. The best way we can do this, of course, is to convince ourselves that we understand what another person is like. When we understand what another person is like, we can predict how he or she will react.

To demonstrate that our needs for effective control will induce us to attribute personality dispositions to others, Miller et al. set up a four-condition experiment. In one condition subjects actively participated via an electronic setup in a competitive game with another—the "other's" behavior, or moves in the game, being simulated by the experimenter. In a second condition subjects passively overheard the game being played. In a third, pre-expectant passive, condition subjects passively overheard the game but anticipated that in a second session they would have to play the "player" whose moves were being simulated by the experimenter, Player A. In a fourth, post-expectant passive, condition subjects passively overheard the game being played but were not told until afterward that they would play Player A in a second session.

Miller et al. reasoned that if the observers under the various conditions differ in the extent to which they draw inferences about the personality of Player A because they process information about A differently, then the post-expectant observers should not differ from true passive observers. Subjects in both of these treatments observed the game under the same conditions—that is, with no anticipation of interacting with Player A. If, however, the anticipation of interacting with someone arouses a need for us to convince ourselves that we understand another—a need for effective control—post-expectant observers should draw stronger inferences about the personality of Player A than passive observers. That is precisely what happened. As Miller et al. (1978) point out, the results indicate that not only are people sometimes motivated to distort the amount of information about another's personality that is reflected in that person's behavior, but they may distort information that they have already encoded and stored in memory.

We began this section on explaining the causes of behavior with a discussion of attribution theory and, as we saw, the common view of attribution theories is that we behave as rational, analytic information processors when we try to sort out why someone behaved in a certain way. Research on attribution processes, however, has revealed that we are not so rational after all. We have difficulty distinguishing skill- and chance-determined situations. We let outcome knowledge distort our estimates of other possible outcomes. We are subject to the fundamental attribution error, the false consensus effect, and various motivational biases. As if that were not enough, there was even the final suggestion by Miller et al. (1978) that we may distort information that we have already tucked away in memory. When dealing with stereotypes of groups or impressions of individuals, we are, in fact, usually working from memory. Hence, we need to pursue this suggestion that memory is malleable.

RECONSTRUCTING THE PAST

We all know that memory is fallible. We forget a tremendous amount of information, and there are many reasons why this is so. Much of what we say we have "forgotten," of course, we never really learned. Much of what we do learn may cloud our memory for previously learned information (retroactive interference), or learning something at time 1 may make learning at time 2 more difficult (proactive interference). Both proactive and retroactive interference are more likely, the greater the similarity between the two sets of material. These, and related phenomena, are important topics, but they are not the focus of our concern here. Rather, we shall concern ourselves with distortions and fabrications in memory. Specifically, are there systematic biases in memory that may be implicated in the perpetuation of stereotypes?

Availability

Tversky and Kahneman (1973) point out that memory-based judgments of the frequencies with which various classes of events have occurred are common, and the basis for many such judgments appears to be a simple law of repetition—the more frequently an event has occurred, the stronger the associative links to that event. Strength of association is later used as an aid or clue in making judgments of the event's frequency. The ease with which instances of a particular class of events can be brought to mind has been termed "availability." Generally, availability is a valid clue for frequency judgments because frequent events are usually easier to recall or imagine than infrequent ones.

There are things other than repetition, however, that affect the availability of a particular class of events. Anything that makes a particular class more salient or distinctive than related classes will make that class more available in memory. Bias occurs when the frequencies of related classes do not correspond to the ease with which those classes can be retrieved from memory. As one of several demonstrations of this bias, Tversky and Kahneman (1973) asked subjects to make a number of estimates, such as whether the letter "R" occurs more often as the first or third letter in words. In response to this question, most subjects said that "R" occurs more often in the first position. When asked why they said so, they reported having tried to think of a few examples of words in each class—that is, words with "R" in the first position and words with "R" in the third position—and they could think of more examples of the former. In fact, "R" occurs more often as the third than as the first letter in words in English. However, we usually do not store words according to which letter is in the third position, and this makes it difficult to think of examples of such words.

There is some evidence that relying on availability may bias what we think we know about others. For example, Hamilton and Gifford (1976) suggest that the overattribution of undesirable behaviors to members of minority groups may stem from the statistical infrequency of minority group members and the nonnormativeness of undesirable behavior combining to make the performance of an undesirable behavior by a minority-group member particularly salient. Subsequently, if asked to estimate the relative frequencies of desirable and undesirable behavior performed by majority-group and minority-group members, examples of the "minority group-undesirable" class will be more easily brought to mind—that is, more available—and the frequency of that class is likely to be overestimated.

To test this idea, R. A. Jones, Scott, Solernou, Noble, Fiala, and Miller (1977) and R. A. Jones and Scott (1979) asked subjects to view a series of 42 slides on each of which a desirable or an undesirable personality trait was attributed to a member of one of two groups. The traits were distributed so that the proportions of desirable and undesirable traits were the same for the two groups, but one group had more members. Thus, on 20 slides a desirable personality trait was attributed to a member of the larger group and on eight slides an undesirable trait was attributed to a member of this group. On ten slides a desirable trait was attributed to a member of the smaller group, and on four slides an undesirable trait was attributed to a member of this group.

After the slide presentation, subjects were given a list of the 42 traits; for each they were to indicate the group membership of the person to whom that trait had been attributed in the slide set. The results of this measure are depicted in Figure 2.4, where it may be seen that subjects were most accurate in recognition of undesirable traits that had been attributed to members of the minority group.

On another measure, subjects were asked to estimate the frequency with which undesirable traits had been attributed to members of each of the two groups. For the larger group they were fairly accurate, but they significantly overestimated the frequency of undesirable traits that had been attributed to members of the smaller group. Thus, it appears that the salience or distinctiveness of a particular class of events may make examples of that class more available to memory (the recognition measure) and, as a result, the frequency of that class will be overestimated (See also Hamilton & Rose, 1980).

Research by Rothbart, Fulero, Jensen, Howard, and Birrell (1978) indicates that availability may bias our memories about group members in other ways. Suppose that you observe four members of some group and, by chance, two of these people are behaving in a socially desirable manner and two are not. Further suppose that the next day you see the latter two again, and again they are behaving in an undesirable manner. If you organize your impression of the group around individual members, then the proportion of group members who exhibit undesirable behavior is .50—that is, two of four members exhibit undesirable behavior. If you organize your impression around the group as a whole, then .67 of the times you have observed representatives of the group, they have been performing undesirable behaviors. That is, you have seen members of the group six times, and four of those times undesirable behaviors were being performed. In this case, of course, your impression of the group is likely to be more negative. But the question is when are we likely to organize our impressions around groups as opposed to individual members of those groups?

FIGURE 2.4

Proportion of Correct Recognition Above Chance, as a Function of Trait Desirability and Group Membership

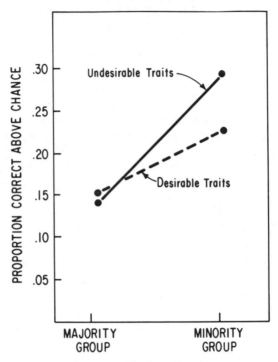

Source: R. A. Jones & Scott (1979) Fig. 1, p. 15.

Rothbart et al. (1978) suggest that we will organize our impressions around individual members when we have only a little information about the group and/or know only a few members—that is, when there is little demand on memory. On the other hand, when there is a heavy demand on memory—when we have a great deal of information about the group and/or know many members—we are likely to organize our impression around the group as a whole. In the latter case it simply becomes too difficult to keep track of the characteristics of each individual white or black, or southerner or Catholic or Jew, that we have ever known.

To test these ideas, Rothbart et al. presented subjects with either 16 (low memory load) or 64 (high memory load) sentences of the form "Frank is stubborn," and varied the ratio of desirable and undesirable traits within the 16 or 64 sentences. In addition, for some subjects each trait was presented with a different person's name, while for other subjects a given trait always appeared with the same name. Following the presentation of the sentences, subjects estimated the proportion of desirable and undesirable persons in the group, and rated the attractiveness of the group as a whole.

As anticipated, when overwhelmed with information (high memory load), subjects treat multiple presentations of the same group members as if each presentation were new information about the group. That is, seeing the sentence "Fred is stubborn" four times had about the same effect on their impression of the general "stubbornness" of the group of which Fred was a member as seeing that group members Fred, Bob, Frank, and Jim are stubborn. On the other hand, under low memory load, subjects were able to make more adequate adjustment for multiple presentations of the same group members. Thus, if we know many members of a group, but see only a few of them very frequently, the characteristics of the latter are likely to have an undue influence on our impressions of the group as a whole, simply because they will be more available to memory.

In subsequent research Rothbart et al. (1978) were able to demonstrate that the presence in a group of one or two individuals who are extreme on some characteristic may also bias memory of the group. As they put it, "Extreme individuals, by virtue of their being novel, infrequent, or particularly dramatic, should be more salient or available in memory and, if availability is a cue to frequency, overestimated when we judge their prevalence in a group" (p. 250). For example, subjects who knew there were a few extremely tall individuals in a group overestimated the number of group members who were over six feet tall. Similarly, subjects who knew that a few individuals in a group had committed serious criminal offenses overestimated the number of criminals in the group as compared with subjects who knew that a few individuals in the group had committed less serious criminal offenses.

It appears, then, that one of the major ways in which memory can deceive us is by serving up a biased sample of what we know. What we are likely to recall about a group, say, is the novel, the unusual, the most easily available—and that information may not be representative of the group or even of what we know about the group. Unfortunately, it does not stop there. As we have already seen, our implicit theories of personality may influence both how we perceive others and what we remember about them, but we need to look at the directive influence of our implicit theories on memory a little more closely.

Stereotypes and Memory

From our earlier discussion of implicit theories of personality, it follows that stereotypes of various groups are simply aspects of our more general implicit theories. A stereotype is nothing more than a set of interrelated characteristics we impute to a given group and its members. In a sense a stereotype is a mental prototype of what representatives of a category of people are "like." With respect to stereotypes and memory, a question of interest is the extent to which we are selective in what we remember about group members. That is, are we more likely to remember behaviors of individuals that are consistent with our stereotype of their group?

To check on this, Cohen (1977) asked students to rate each of 90 life-style characteristics in terms of whether a waitress or a librarian would be more likely to exhibit it. A number of the items clearly differentiated the two. For example, a waitress was seen as being very likely to wear a uniform, not to wear glasses, to eat hamburger, and not to eat roast beef. Librarians, on the other hand were seen as being likely not to wear a uniform, to wear glasses, not to eat hamburger, and to eat roast beef. On the basis of these and similar items, Cohen constructed a script for a 20-minute videotape of a woman and her husband eating dinner and talking. The tape was produced so that it contained a number of behaviors that had previously been rated as being typical of a waitress *and* a number of behaviors typical of librarians.

Some new subjects were then recruited and asked to look at the tape and answer a few questions about it. However, prior to seeing the tape, half of the subjects were told that the woman they would be viewing on the tape was a waitress, and half were told that the woman they would be viewing was a librarian. As anticipated, subjects who thought they were watching a waitress were subsequently more accurate in remembering stereotypical waitress behaviors than stereotypical librarian behaviors. Subjects who thought they were watching a librarian were subsequently more accurate in remembering stereotypical librarian behaviors than stereotypical waitress behaviors.

It may be that Cohen's subjects simply paid more attention to behavior consistent with their ideas about a waitress or a librarian, or even that they were actively looking for such stereotype-confirming behavior. Hence, they should indeed remember such behavior better when it does occur. A more rigorous test of the effects of stereotypes on memory would be to see if subjects recall stereotype-consistent behaviors as having been exhibited when in fact they were not. Some pertinent data on this point are reported in an experiment by Cantor and Mischel (1977), in which subjects were presented with material describing four fictional characters. On the basis of previously obtained ratings, the descriptions were constructed so that one was made up of six adjectives moderately related to extroversion and four adjectives unrelated to extroversion. A second was made up of six adjectives moderately related to introversion and four adjectives unrelated to introversion. Two additional "control" descriptions, each of ten adjectives unrelated to extroversion or introversion, were constructed.

Each of the descriptive items was presented, on an individual slide, in a simple sentence of the form "Laura is energetic." Following the slide presentations of the descriptions, subjects were given a 62-item recognition test and were asked to rate their confidence that each of the items had appeared in the descriptions they had just seen. Some of the items had indeed appeared in the descriptions, but others had not. Of the latter, some were related to extroversion, some were related to introversion, and some were unrelated to either. As anticipated, subjects were more confident that they had seen nonpresented items that were conceptually related to extroversion and introversion than nonpresented items that were neutral. As Cantor and Mischel (1977) put it, subjects ". . . exhibited a clear memory bias consistent with the trait prototypes, expressing greater confidence that they had seen nonpresented but conceptually related material as opposed to nonpresented, unrelated material" (p. 45).

Thus, we are likely to infer additional stereotype-consistent attributes for which we have no evidence once we have labeled someone as "waitress" or "librarian," or "extrovert" or "introvert," or any of the other thousands of categories for which we have sets of interrelated expectations. Further, once we have classified someone in a particular way, our memory of the behavior or features that led us to invoke that particular classification may be lost. We may be able to recall only the label we used, and that can get us into trouble. Doob and Kirshenbaum (1973), for example, report a police case in which one witness coded the criminal only as "good-looking." When confronted with a police lineup some time later, she incorrectly identified the best-looking* individual in the lineup as being the criminal. It appears, then, that when we have categorized someone in a certain way, we are more likely to attend to and remember his or her actual behaviors that are consistent with the categorization (Cohen, 1977); we are more likely to fill in gaps in our memory with attributes for which we have no evidence but that are consistent with our stereotype (Cantor and Mischel, 1977); and we may even remember only the label we used and forget the specific features that led us to use the label (Doob and Kirshenbaum, 1973).

There is another way in which stereotypes influence what we think we know about someone. Suppose that after having known someone for years, you discover that he or she is homosexual. Note that this is different from the situation investigated by Cohen (1977), in which subjects were told that the person was a waitress or librarian *before* they observed the person's behavior. Here the question is what you are likely to remember about a person if you have a lot of information about him or her, and *then* find out that he or she belongs to a category of people about whom you have a definite stereotype.

Snyder and Uranowitz (1978) hypothesized that when we learn something new about a person that leads us to categorize him or her in a certain way, we may selectively review or recall what we already know about the person and, in essence, reconstruct our image of him or her. To test this idea, they asked subjects to read a narrative of events in the life of a woman. After having read the narrative, some subjects learned that the woman was

---

*As determined by photo ratings of noninvolved students.

currently leading a lesbian life-style, other subjects learned that she was currently leading a heterosexual life-style, and still other subjects were given no information about her current sexual preference. All subjects were then asked to answer a series of multiple-choice questions about information contained in the narrative life history they had read earlier.

The multiple-choice questions were constructed so that some of them had alternatives that raters had previously indicated were relevant to stereotypical images of lesbian and heterosexual women, as well as alternatives that were neutral with respect to these images. On these items it was found that subjects who had learned the woman was living a lesbian life-style recalled the events of her life in a manner more consistent with stereotypical views of lesbians than did subjects who learned the woman was currently heterosexual or subjects who had not learned of her current sexual preference.

Further, Snyder and Uranowitz were able to demonstrate that these results were due to both differential errors of recognition and differential accuracy of recognition. That is, when subjects made an error, it was more likely to be by selecting an alternative conceptually related to the stereotypical image (lesbian or heterosexual) that they believed to apply to the woman. Conversely, they were most accurate when the correct alternative was also conceptually related to the information they had been given about the woman's sexual preference. As Snyder and Uranowitz (1978, p. 948) put it: ". . . current beliefs can and do exert powerful channeling effects on attempts to remember the past." Current beliefs and information may in fact be incorporated into such attempts, so that we end up with "memories" of things that never were and events that never happened. To see how this occurs, we first need to make the nature of memory explicit.

Manufacturing Memories

For many years memory was considered to be analogous to a large, multidrawer filing cabinet. If you wanted to remember a fact, you just looked it up. Of course, it was never quite clear how you would know where to look if you did not know the fact you wanted to remember, but this problem was usually finessed by assuming that we "cross-file" things in a number of ways. By pursuing a chain of associations we would, sooner or later, stumble across the information. Or, to keep strictly to the analogy, the information would suddenly reappear, falling out of a file drawer.

This file-cabinet view of memory has gradually been replaced by a view of memory as a constructive, problem-solving activity. As an example of what this means, consider how you would respond if someone were to ask you what you had for dinner a week ago last Thursday. Your first response might well be "I don't remember," but if pressed, you might go through a sequence such as, "Well, a week ago last Thursday? Let's see—that was the

24th of May. School was already over—was it? Yes, school was over on the 16th. I started work on the project on the 17th. My nights to cook are Monday and Wednesday—so, I did not cook. We did not eat out that week because we were broke. Was that the night of the concert? No, that was the 25th. So, the night before the concert. Thursday is Karen's night to cook. For the last three weeks she has been trying a new dish each time. Last week it was that awful stuff with tuna and peanut butter. So, the week before that she cooked. . . . Oh, Yeah, a week ago last Thursday I had oriental tuna casserole, salad, and pineapple upside-down cake!"

Such sequences are typical when we try to recall meaningful material. We go through a constructive process very similar to the process we go through in trying to solve a novel problem. We piece together evidence, try out alternatives, encounter blind alleys, bring up irrelevant items, test hypotheses, and choose the most likely possibility as the solution or "memory." This constructive, problem-solving approach to specific memories is not random, of course. It is guided by our acquired knowledge, by our expectations, by our desires, by statistical probability, and by the way we have encoded specific items of information.

One of the major ways in which this construction process is likely to err is, in fact, a function of the way in which we encode or categorize material when it is first presented. For example, if we are told that some abstract figure we are viewing is a portrait of a man, when we are subsequently asked to reproduce the figure, the reproduction is likely to look quite a bit more like a man than the original figure did (see Figure 2.5).

As Bartlett (1967, p. 178) puts it: ". . . whenever material visually presented purports to be representative of some common object, but contains certain features which are unfamiliar . . . these features invariably suffer transformation in the direction of the familiar." In a series of experiments in which individual subjects were asked to reproduce stories and figures repeatedly, or one individual was asked to reproduce material for a second, who reproduced it for a third, and so on, Bartlett was able to isolate a number of other transformations that are likely to occur in memory. One of particular importance is that memories are likely to be more coherent or rational than the actual event they supposedly reflect. It is as if we overdo it in our attempts to make sense out of what we know, tending to make all the details fit together even when they do not. This is of particular importance for the perpetuation of stereotypes, since, as Tajfel (1969) points out, most social behaviors and situations contain many ambiguous elements that can be retrospectively molded into consistency with stereotyped beliefs.

Perhaps even more distressing, however, is evidence that we actively add elements to our memories of situations, elements that were not a part of the original situations. One of the factors that can produce such manufactured memories is a question containing a presupposition about the nature of the situation to be recalled. For example, Loftus (1975) asked students at the University of Washington to view a brief videotape of an automobile

FIGURE 2.5

Result of Bartlett's Experiment Involving Sequential Reproduction of Abstract Figure from Memory by Five Different Subjects

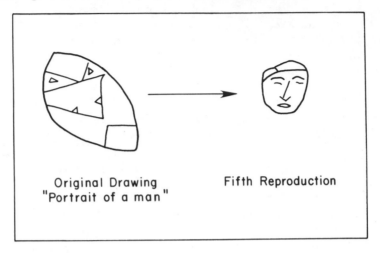

Original Drawing
"Portrait of a man"

Fifth Reproduction

Source: Bartlett (1932), p. 178.

accident involving a white sports car traveling along a country road. After viewing the tape, subjects were asked a number of questions about it. Among these questions, some subjects were asked how fast the car was going when it passed the barn, and others were simply asked how fast the car was going. There was in fact no barn seen on the tape. A week later, without seeing the tape again, all subjects were asked, "Did you see a barn?" Over six times as many subjects who had earlier been asked how fast the car was going when it passed the barn reported having actually seen a barn as did subjects who had earlier been asked simply how fast the car was going. As Loftus points out, it appears that merely asking about a nonexistent object can increase the tendency to report the existence of that object at some later time.

To account for such results, Loftus proposes what she refers to as a "construction hypothesis." That is, when asked a question containing a false presupposition (such as the existence of the barn in the above experiment), we try to "visualize" or "reconstruct" that portion of our experience that we need to answer the question. In doing so, we may try "fitting in" the presupposition to see if it looks familiar. Later, when asked about the existence of the presupposed object or incident, we respond with the altered or imagined version of the actual incident. We may then "see" the object or incident that we in fact constructed in our attempt to remember if it were part of the original scene. As Loftus puts it:

... information acquired during a complex experience is apparently integrated into some overall memory representation. Subsequent information about that event—for example, that introduced via questions containing true or false presuppositions—is also integrated, and can alter the initial representation. When the person is later queried about the original experience, he forms a regenerated image based on the altered memorial representation, and bases his response on that image (1975, p. 571)

Our memories of interactions and events involving individuals who are members of groups about which we have stereotypes are likely to be particularly susceptible to the sort of bias identified by Loftus (e.g. Cohen, 1981; Rothbart, et al. 1979). Our beliefs about the interrelationships among personality dispositions are, in effect, presuppositions that may induce similar sorts of insertions and additions into our memories of the behaviors we observe those individuals perform. The result of such memory construction, of course, is the repeated pseudo confirmation of the validity of our stereotypes. The insidious effects of stereotypes are not limited, however, to such rewritings of the past. They also play an important part in scripting the future. How we behave toward other people is, as we shall see, partially determined by what we think we know about them.

SHAPING THE FUTURE

We have already seen, in the sub-section "Categorization," that the act of categorizing a person has certain definite cognitive consequences. We tend to exaggerate the similarities between people placed in the same category and the differences between people placed in different categories. These processes have consequences for the future, of course, but categorization of others may have even more direct and immediate consequences on how we behave toward them.

Ignoring New Information

One of the major ways in which stereotypes and categorization may shape our interpersonal futures is by interfering with appropriate utilization of new information about others. We often act as if the label we have applied to someone or our first impression of that person, which is usually based on quite superficial information, is all there is to the person. As a demonstration of this, Dailey (1952) asked subjects to read autobiographical sketches written by other people, and then to predict how those people would respond to specific items on a personality inventory. The criterion in each case was how the person had actually responded. Some subjects made predictions after reading half an autobiography and again after reading all of it. Other subjects made predictions only after reading an entire autobiography. The latter subjects were significantly more accurate in their predictions of how the stimulus person in each case would respond to the items on the inventory.

As Dailey points out, the premature decisions made after reading only half of an autobiography apparently prevented the subjects from fully profiting from the additional information in the second half of the autobiography. In subsequent research Dailey manipulated the importance of the material on which premature conclusions were based and, as expected, premature decisions were most detrimental when based on unimportant information. Also, simply allowing subjects to pause after reading some information (and think about it) had a biasing effect similar to asking for personality predictions on the basis of only a small amount of information. The decisions that subjects apparently made during the pause seemed, in effect, to close their minds to new information.

There is some evidence that we will continue to seek new information about another person for a longer time if the initial information we have received is ambivalent. Nidorf and Crockett (1964), for example, prepared booklets in which various stimulus persons were described; subjects were to read only as much of each booklet as necessary for them to infer whether the person described had certain additional characteristics. In some of the booklets the persons being described were depicted as possessing a series of uniformly desirable attributes. In other booklets the descriptions were of uniformly undesirable attributes. In still other booklets the descriptions contained a mixture of desirable and undesirable attributes. As anticipated, subjects sought more information about a stimulus person when what they had already received was ambivalent. Nidorf and Crockett also found that both male and female subjects sought less information about female stimulus persons than male stimulus persons, suggesting that females may be categorized more quickly. In addition, male subjects who received ambivalent information about female stimulus persons formed much more negative impressions than others* who received ambivalent information.

The problems posed by premature conclusions about another person are complicated tremendously when the initial impression turns out to be negative—and, as we all know, many stereotypes are predominantly negative. One of the major things that differentiates negative from positive initial impressions is that negative impressions seem much more difficult to change. Briscoe, Woodyard, and Shaw (1967), for example, asked subjects to read a favorable and an unfavorable paragraph about a person, and to rate the person on a number of scales after reading each paragraph. When the unfavorable paragraph was read first, the changes from first to second

---

*Females reading ambivalent information about female stimulus persons and males and females reading ambivalent information about male stimulus persons.

ratings were significantly less than when the favorable paragraph was the basis of the initial impression.

Not only are negative first impressions likely to be more difficult to change, they are likely to result in less opportunity for change. According to Fishbein and Ajzen (1975), the beliefs we have about a person or group partially determine our affective orientation to that person or group. Our affective orientation, in turn, is the main determinant of our intentions about how to behave toward the person or group. When dealing with a group, of course, our beliefs about the group and its members are part of our stereotype, and our affective orientation, particularly if it is negative, is referred to as prejudice toward the group. Technically, "prejudice" can refer to positive or negative orientations, but in the realm of intergroup relations, it has come to mean, almost exclusively, a negative orientation. If a person has strong negative affect toward any ethnic group, it seems reasonable to suppose that exposure to that group might be avoided whenever possible. Such avoidance might explain why "All those (whites, blacks, Chinese) look alike" to the prejudiced person. He or she simply avoids them at every opportunity and, hence, never pays sufficient sustained attention to them to distinguish among them. There is, in fact, evidence (Malpass & Kravitz, 1969; Luce, 1974) that we recognize and remember faces of members of our own race better than faces of members of other social groups. Whites, for example, recognize and remember white faces better than black faces.

Taking this one step further, Sensenig, Jones, and Varney (1973) attempted to relate white subjects' levels of prejudice toward blacks to their avoidance of black faces in a photo-inspection task. Prejudiced and nonprejudiced white subjects, who had been selected from a larger group on the basis of their responses to two measures of prejudice, were contacted individually and asked to participate in a yearbook evaluation. As part of the study they were to inspect a series of 50 pictures taken from various yearbooks and rate each picture. Some of the pictures were of whites and some were of blacks, and the main dependent measure was the amount of time spent inspecting white versus black pictures.

As anticipated, nonprejudiced subjects spent approximately the same amount of time inspecting white and black pictures. In contrast, prejudiced subjects spent significantly less time looking at black pictures than at white pictures. While it may be that prejudiced subjects were actively avoiding exposure to blacks by looking at their pictures less, it is also possible that prejudiced subjects simply found pictures of blacks easier to rate than pictures of whites. That is, prejudiced subjects may simply believe that less variation exists among black faces and, as a consequence, that black faces can be rated more quickly. Such twin beliefs are self-reinforcing, of course. Belief in less variation leads to less inspection time, and less inspection time results in the actual perception of less variation.

Initial impressions and decisions about others, then, are likely to interfere with our ability to make intelligent use of subsequent information about those others. Further, if the initial impression we have of someone is negative, not only will it be relatively more resistant to change in response to new information, but it may make it quite likely that we will simply avoid obtaining additional information. We may just avoid further interaction with those about whom we have negative impressions. But what happens when circumstances dictate that we must interact with those about whom we have definite expectations and stereotypes? Is there any reason to believe that we behave in ways that increase the likelihood of having our expectations confirmed?

Behavioral Confirmation

There is evidence from various areas that we behave in ways that induce others to confirm our expectations of them. For example, as we shall see in Chapter 6, many people have definite stereotypes about the physically attractive. Dion, Berscheid, and Walster (1972) have found that people attribute desirable personality characteristics to physically attractive others, and expect physically attractive others to lead better and more interesting lives than the unattractive. Of interest here is the possibility that because we believe attractive others have certain additional characteristics, we may behave toward them in ways that lead them to behave as we expect. That is, if we believe certain people have a number of socially desirable characteristics, we may treat them with more than average esteem and respect. When people are treated in such a manner, of course, they are more likely to behave in socially desirable ways. By giving the physically attractive the benefit of the doubt about their additional characteristics, we make it easier for them to be socially rewarding to us. Hence we confirm our initial assumption that they are more pleasant to interact with than the physically unattractive.

Snyder, Tanke, and Berscheid (1977) use the term "behavioral confirmation" to refer to how we may unknowingly induce others to treat us in such a way that our initial impressions of them are confirmed. For example, if we believe certain people are cold and hostile, we may be less friendly than if we believe them to be warm and generous. They, in turn, may be mildly offended by our coolness, and reciprocate in kind. Thus, our initial impression of their lack of warmth is confirmed, although the confirmation is brought about by our own behavior.

To see whether this sort of self-fulfilling prophecy occurs with stereotypes of the physically attractive, Snyder et al. designed an experiment in which male college students were to try to get acquainted with a female student over the telephone. The male-female pairs who participated in the research were not allowed to see each other prior to the telephone conversation. However, each male student was given some information about the woman he would be talking with and was shown a photograph that supposedly had just been taken with a Polaroid camera. All of the information furnished the males, except the photograph, was supplied by the actual person they were to talk with. The photographs were selected from one of two sets that had previously been rated as attractive or unattractive. After receiving this information, the male students indicated their initial impressions of their partners. Those who had just seen an attractive photo expected their partners to be, for example, more poised, more humorous, and more sociable than those who had just seen an unattractive photo.

Each male-female pair then engaged in a 10-minute phone conversation. The conversations were recorded with the male and female voices on separate tracks, and raters were later asked to listen to the tape tracks containing the female voices and answer a number of questions about the females. For example, they rated each female participant on a number of bipolar scales and answered questions such as "How much is she enjoying herself?" and "How animated and enthusiastic is this person?" Note that these raters heard only the females, who were just being themselves, but who were believed to be either attractive or unattractive by the person to whom they were talking. As anticipated, the females whose partners thought they were attractive were rated as sounding more poised, more humorous, more sociable, and generally more socially adept than the females whose partners thought they were unattractive. Data from another group of raters who listened to only the male voices revealed that those males who thought they were talking to an attractive female were themselves warmer, more sociable, and more interesting. It appears, then, that the beliefs of the males changed their behavior, which in turn induced changes in the behavior of the females.

In subsequent research Snyder and Swann (1978) addressed the question of the conditions under which such behavioral confirmation effects will persist. Attribution theory suggests that if one is induced to behave in a particular way, and believes that the behavior was primarily a function of the situation, the behavior should cease as soon as the situation changes. On the other hand, if one is induced to behave in a particular way, and believes that the behavior reflects a personality disposition, the behavior is more likely to continue even when the situation changes. To test these ideas, Snyder and Swann recruited groups of three subjects to compete on a reaction-time task. One subject in each group was assigned the role of "target," one was assigned the role of "labeling perceiver," and one was assigned the role of "naive perceiver." The task was structured so that the target and labeling perceiver were to compete against each other first; whether they won or lost was to be determined by their respective reaction times and the use of a "noise weapon" to disrupt each other's performance. The noise weapon could be set at several levels of intensity, and changed hands every three trials. First, the labeling perceiver used it, then the target, then the labeling perceiver, and so on.

Prior to the first trial, however, the labeling perceiver was given information about the target's personality. Some labeling perceivers were led to believe the target was generally a hostile person, while others were led to believe the target was generally nonhostile. Also prior to the first trial, the target was given information that encouraged him or her to regard how the noise weapon was used as reflecting "personal characteristics" (dispositional attribution) or to depend more on treatment by specific opponents (situational attribution).

The target and labeling perceiver then competed for 24 trials over the reaction-time task, with the labeling perceiver having access to the noise weapon first. After the 24 trials the labeling perceiver answered a number of questions about the target and the target began a new series of trials against a new opponent, the "naive perceiver." In this second interaction the target had access to the noise weapon first, and the naive perceiver had been given no information about whether the target was usually hostile or nonhostile.

The results, in terms of intensity of noise used and perceived aggressiveness of the target, are depicted in Table 2.4. As may be seen in the table, during the first interaction, targets who were believed to be hostile did indeed set the noise weapon at more intense levels than targets who were believed to be nonhostile (row 1). Further, this was reflected in the labeling perceivers' final impressions of them as being more aggressive (row 2). This greater aggressiveness of the targets who had been labeled as "hostile" prior to the interaction was, however, brought about by the behavior of the

TABLE 2.4
Results of Snyder and Swann's Reaction-Time Task Experiment

	Dispositional Attribution		Situational Attribution	
	Hostile Label	Non-Hostile Label	Hostile Label	Non-Hostile Label
Behavioral confirmation of hostility: first interaction	4.12*	3.17	3.92	3.02
Labeling perceiver's final impressions of targets	3.83**	2.64	3.39	2.83
Preservation of behavioral confirmation: second interaction	4.30*	2.70	3.35	3.77
Naive perceivers' final impressions of targets	3.66**	2.75	3.12	3.34

*The higher the number, the greater the behavioral display of hostility, as assessed by intensity of "noise weapon" usage.

**The higher the number, the greater the perceived aggressiveness.

Source: Snyder & Swann (1978), Table 1, p. 155. Reprinted by permission of Academic Press.

labeling perceivers. When the noise weapon was available to them, over 60 percent of the labeling perceivers who anticipated hostile opponents used intensities in the higher half of the intensity range. Less than 30 percent of those who anticipated nonhostile opponents did so. In the second interaction, only those targets who had been labeled as hostile and who had been encouraged to believe their use of the noise weapon reflected a basic personality disposition continued to behave in a hostile manner (row 3) and to be perceived as aggressive (row 4). Thus, it again appears that perceivers may induce the very behaviors they anticipate in others, and that these behaviors may persist if those who perform them are given reason to believe they reflect enduring personality dispositions.

Such interpersonal self-fulfilling prophecies are a pervasive part of our daily existence, and they play a major role in the perpetuation of stereotypes. Once we have a set of expectations about what members of a particular group are like and how they are likely to behave, we often induce those very behaviors. Rubovits and Maehr (1973), for example, note that many white, middle-class teachers expect lower-class blacks to perform poorly in academic subjects. To examine the effects of this expectation, they asked 66 white females enrolled in a teacher-training course to teach a brief lesson on television to groups of four seventh and eighth graders. In each group of four, two students were white and two were black. During the sessions an observer sat behind the students and coded the teachers' behaviors in terms of the amounts of attention, elaboration, encouragement, ignoring, praise, and criticism directed toward the individual students. Unfortunately, it was not possible to keep the observer blind as to the race of the student, and this may have biased the results. Even so, it is of interest that white students received significantly more attention than black students. Further, fewer statements were requested of black students, more statements of the black students were ignored, and black students were praised less and criticized more. All of these behaviors on the part of the teachers will, of course, eventually result in confirmation of their stereotype of poor academic performance by blacks.

An individual's behavior can be understood only as part of a system, a system that includes the behaviors of others and the expectations that those others hold about how the individual is going to behave. The ways in which such interpersonal expectancies and stereotypes can be communicated to the individual are manifold, running the gamut of verbal behaviors, nonverbal behaviors, and situational arrangements (Darley & Fazio, 1980). From mutual glances to avoidance of eye contact, from name dropping to name calling, from cooperation to competition—almost all aspects of behavior can be employed to let someone know what we expect from him or her. All too often the result is that we will have defined the situation so that the other person has little choice but to behave as expected and, thereby, confirm our stereotypes of him or her.

SUMMARY

We began this chapter by calling attention to the possibility that the existence of stereotypes may be in part a function of imperfections in the way we process information about others. In exploring that possibility we started by examining some data on how we perceive others' behaviors, and found that we do not passively take in information about behavior. Rather, we organize the observed behavior into meaningful segments. We also noted that the smaller the units we use, the more differentiated our impressions are likely to be, and under some conditions, the more likely we are to make dispositional attributions about the person we are observing. We also seem to attend more closely to the unusual, to that which is different.

This, of course, has implications for what we notice about ourselves and others. We saw that in groups, those members who are in the minority ("tokens") by virtue of some irrelevant, but highly visible, difference from the other group members are more constantly "visible" and, hence, under greater performance pressure. They also seem to produce polarization within the group and an exaggeration of the dominant majority culture. The token's own characteristics are likely to be distorted to fit preexisting beliefs about his or her "social type." The latter was seen to be an example of certain basic perceptual processes that accompany categorization—that is, we tend to exaggerate the similarities between objects or people placed in the same category, and to exaggerate the differences between objects or people placed in different categories.

Once we have categorized someone in a particular way, we often infer additional characteristics for which we have no evidence. Such inferences stem from our preexisting implicit theories of personality—the categories we employ to encode the various features and behaviors of others and the beliefs we hold concerning which of these categories tend to go together and which do not. We saw that our implicit theories influence how we encode another's behavior, and introduce a systematic distortion into what we remember about another's behavior. We are likely to "remember" that categories of behavior we believe to be associated both occurred, when in fact only one of them may have.

We usually are not satisfied with simple observation, however. We want to know why someone behaved as he or she did. We seek to explain behavior and, according to attribution theories, we do so in a relatively logical, rational manner. We seem to understand that behavior can be a function of ability, effort, situational factors, or any combination of these. We employ a covariation principle in our search for explanations—that is, we look for things that are present when the behavior is present and absent when the behavior is absent. Research on attribution processes, however, has found that we are not quite so rational as the theorists paint us. We confuse chance-determined and skill-determined outcomes. Once we know which of several possible outcomes did occur, we see it as being more inevitable than it really was. We are subject to the fundamental attribution error—that is, we tend to underestimate the power of situational constraints on behavior and to overestimate the role of dispositional factors. We are subject to a false consensus effect of seeing our own responses as typical and different responses as more revealing of the actor's personality quirks. We are also subject to egotism in explaining behavior. We give ourselves more credit for success and less blame for failure than we accord others. We apparently have a need to convince ourselves that we understand others when we anticipate having to interact with them, a need for effective control that again leads us to infer that we know more about them than we really do.

Next we turned to a consideration of what we are likely to remember about others. Our memories may mislead us by serving up what is most available, most easily recalled—and what is most available may be severely biased. We are likely to recall the unusual and the bizarre most easily and, as a result, they may have an undue influence on our impressions of others. It also appears that when we have categorized someone in a certain way, we are more likely to attend to and remember actual behaviors consistent with the categorization and to fill in memory gaps with attributes for which we have no evidence (but are consistent with the initial categorization). We may even remember only the categorization itself, and forget the features that prompted us to make it. Perhaps most insidious of all is the fact that we may distort or selectively recall what we already know about someone to make it consistent with new information we obtain about the person. We construct memories via a process very similar to problem solving, and in doing so we may add items that never existed.

Finally, we looked at how our beliefs about others may constrain future behavior toward them, and may even determine their own behavior. Once we have an impression of someone, we are less open to new information about that person. Our expectations may even lead us to behave in certain ways that have the effect of eliciting from others the very behaviors that will confirm our expectations.

REFERENCES

Asch, S. E. Forming impressions of personality. *Journal of Abnormal and Social Psychology*, 1946, *41*, 258–290.

Bartlett, F. C. *Remembering: A study in experimental and social psychology.* Cambridge: The University Press, 1932.

Benedetti, D. T., & Hill, J. G. A determiner of the centrality of a trait in impression formation. *Journal of Abnormal and Social Psychology*, 1960, *60*, 278–280.

Boring, E. G. *History, psychology, and science.* New York: Wiley, 1963.

Briscoe, M. E., Woodyard, H. D., & Shaw, M. E. Personality impression change as a function of the favorableness of first impressions. *Journal of Personality*, 1967, *35*, 343–357.

Cantor, N., & Mischel, W. Traits as prototypes: Effects on recognition memory. *Journal of Personality and Social Psychology*, 1977, *35*, 38–48.

Carr, E. H. *What is history?* New York: Vintage, 1961.

Cohen, C. E. Cognitive basis of stereotyping. Paper presented at the 85th annual convention of the American Psychological Association, San Francisco, 1977.

Cohen, C. E. Person categories and social perception: Testing some boundaries of the processing effects of prior knowledge. *Journal of Personality and Social Psychology*, 1981, *40*, 441–452.

Dailey, C. A. The effects of premature conclusions upon the acquisition of under-standing of a person. *Journal of Psychology*, 1952, *33*, 133–152.

Darley, J. M., & Fazio, R. H. Expectancy confirmation processes arising in the social interaction sequence. *American Psychologist*, 1980, *35*, 867–881.

Dion, K. K., Berscheid, E., & Walster, E. What is beautiful is good. *Journal of Personality and Social Psychology*, 1972, *24*, 285–290.

Doob, A., & Kirshenbaum, H. Bias in police line-ups—partial remembering. *Journal of Police Science and Administration*, 1973, *1*, 287–293.

Dornbusch, S. M., Hastorf, A. H., Richardson, S. A., Muzzy, R. E., & Vreeland, R. S. The perceiver and the perceived: Their relative influence on the categories of interpersonal perception. *Journal of Personality and Social Psychology*, 1965, *1*, 434–440.

Erdelyi, M. H. A new look at the new look: Perceptual defense and vigilance. *Psychological Review*, 1974, *81*, 1–25.

Fischhoff, B. Hindsight/Foresight: The effect of outcome knowledge on judgment under uncertainty. *Journal of Experimental Psychology: Human Perception and Performance*, 1975, *1*, 288–299.

Fishbein, M., & Ajzen, I. *Belief, attitude, intention and behavior: An introduction to theory and research.* Reading, Mass.: Addison-Wesley, 1975.

Gergen, K. J. The significance of skin color in human relations. *Daedalus*, 1967, *96*, 390–406.

Hamilton, D. L. Cognitive biases in the perception of social groups. In J. S. Carroll and J. W. Payne (eds.), *Cognition and social behavior.* Hillsdale, N.J.: Erlbaum, 1976.

Hamilton, D. L., & Gifford, R. K. Illusory correlation in interpersonal perception: A cognitive basis of stereotypic judgments. *Journal of Experimental Social Psychology*, 1976, *12*, 392–407.

Hamilton, D. L., & Rose, T. L. Illusory correlation and the maintenance of stereotypic beliefs. *Journal of Personality and Social Psychology*, 1980, *39*, 832–845.

Hayakawa, S. I. *Symbol, status, and personality.* New York: Harcourt, Brace, & World, 1963.

Heider, F. *The psychology of interpersonal relations.* New York: Wiley, 1958.

Jones, E. E. Update of "From acts to dispositions: The attribution process in person perception." In L. Berkowitz (ed.), *Cognitive theories in social psychology.* New York: Academic Press, 1978.

Jones, E. E., & Davis, K. E. From acts to dispositions: The attribution process in person perception. In L. Berkowitz (ed.), *Advances in experimental social psychology* (Vol. 2). New York: Academic Press, 1965.

Jones, E. E., & Harris, V. A. The attribution of attitudes. *Journal of Experimental*

Social Psychology, 1967, *3,* 1–24.

Jones, R. A. *Self-fulfilling prophecies: Social, psychological, and physiological effects of expectancies.* Hillsdale, N.J.: Erlbaum, 1977.

Jones, R. A., & Scott, J. V. Availability and the Pollyanna effect in memory for the characteristics of group members. Unpublished manuscript, University of Kentucky, 1979.

Jones, R. A., Scott, J., Solernou, J., Noble, A., Fiala, J., & Miller, K. Availability and formation of stereotypes. *Perceptual and Motor Skills,* 1977, *44,* 631–638.

Kanter, R. M. Some effects of proportion on group life: Skewed sex ratios and responses to token women. *American Journal of Sociology,* 1977, *82,* 965–990.

Kelley, H. H. Attribution theory in social psychology. In D. Levine (ed.), *Nebraska symposium on motivation* (Vol. 15). Lincoln: University of Nebraska Press, 1967.

Kelley, H. H. The processes of causal attribution. *American Psychologist,* 1973, *28,* 107–128.

Langer, E. J. The illusion of control. *Journal of Personality and Social Psychology,* 1975, *32,* 311–328.

Lerner, M. J. The desire for justice and reactions to victims. In J. Macaulay and L. Berkowitz (eds.), *Altruism and helping behavior.* New York: Academic Press, 1970.

Lerner, M. J. *The belief in a just world: A fundamental delusion.* New York: Plenum Press, 1980.

Lerner, M. J., & Matthews, G. Reactions to suffering of others under conditions of indirect responsibility. *Journal of Personality and Social Psychology,* 1967, *5,* 319–325.

Lerner, M. J., Miller, D. T., & Holmes, J. G. Deserving and the emergence of forms of justice. In L. Berkowitz and E. Walster (eds.), *Advances in experimental social psychology* (Vol. 9). New York: Academic Press, 1976.

Loftus, E. F. Leading questions and the eyewitness report. *Cognitive Psychology,* 1975, *7,* 560–572.

Luce, T. S. Blacks, Whites, Yellows: They all look alike to me. *Psychology Today,* Nov. 1974, *8,* 105–108.

McArthur, L. A. The how and what of why: Some determinants and consequences of causal attribution. *Journal of Personality and Social Psychology,* 1972, *22,* 171–193.

McGuire, W. J., McGuire, C. V., Child, P., & Fujioka, T. Salience of ethnicity in the spontaneous self-concept as a function of one's ethnic distinctiveness in the social environment. *Journal of Personality and Social Psychology,* 1978, *36,* 511–520.

McGuire, W. J., McGuire, C. V., & Winton, W. Effects of household sex composition on the salience of one's gender in the spontaneous self-concept. *Journal of Experimental Social Psychology,* 1979, *15,* 77–90.

Malpass, R. S., & Kravitz, J. Recognition for faces of own and other race. *Journal of Personality and Social Psychology,* 1969, *13,* 330–334.

Miller, D. T. Ego involvement and attributions for success and failure. *Journal of Personality and Social Psychology,* 1976, *34,* 901–906.

Miller, D. T., Norman, S. A., & Wright, E. Distortion in person perception as a consequence of the need for effective control. *Journal of Personality and*

Social Psychology, 1978, *36*, 598–607.

Newcomb, T. M. The consistency of certain extrovert-introvert behavior patterns in 51 problem boys. *Teachers College contributions to education* (no. 382). New York: Teachers College, 1929.

Newtson, D. Attribution and the unit of perception of ongoing behavior. *Journal of Personality and Social Psychology*, 1973, *28*, 28–38.

Newtson, D. Foundations of attribution: The perception of ongoing behavior. In J. H. Harvey, W. J. Ickes, and R. F. Kidd (eds.), *New directions in attribution research* (Vol. 1). Hillsdale, N.J.: Erlbaum, 1976.

Newtson, D., Engquist, G., & Bois, J. The objective basis of behavior units. *Journal of Personality and Social Psychology*, 1977, *35*, 847–863.

Nidorf, L. J., & Crockett, W. H. Some factors affecting the amount of information sought about others. *Journal of Abnormal and Social Psychology*, 1964, *69*, 98–101.

Nisbett, R., & Ross, L. *Human inference: Strategies and shortcomings of social judgment*. Englewood Cliffs, N.J.: Prentice-Hall, 1980.

Pettigrew, T. F. Social evaluation theory: Convergences and applications. In D. Levine (ed.), *Nebraska symposium on motivation* (Vol. 15). Lincoln: University of Nebraska Press, 1967.

Pyszczynski, T. A., & Greenberg, J. Role of disconfirmed expectancies in the instigation of attributional processing. *Journal of Personality and Social Psychology*, 1981, *40*, 31–38.

Rosch, E. H. Natural categories. *Cognitive Psychology*, 1973, *4*, 328–350.

Rosenberg, S., & Jones, R. A. A method for investigating and representing a person's implicit theory of personality: Theodore Dreiser's view of people. *Journal of Personality and Social Psychology*, 1972, *22*, 372–386.

Ross, L. The intuitive psychologist and his shortcomings: Distortions in the attribution process. In L. Berkowitz (ed.), *Advances in experimental social psychology*, (Vol. 10). New York: Academic Press, 1977.

Ross, L., Greene, D., & House, P. The "False consensus effect": An egocentric bias in social perception and attribution processes. *Journal of Experimental Social Psychology*, 1977, *13*, 279–301.

Ross, L. D., Amabile, T. M., & Steinmetz, J. L. Social roles, social control, and biases in social-perception processes. *Journal of Personality and Social Psychology*, 1977, *35*, 485–494.

Ross, M., & Sicoly, F. Egocentric biases in availability and attribution. *Journal of Personality and Social Psychology*, 1979, *37*, 322–336.

Rothbart, M., Evans, M., & Fulero, S. Recall for confirming events: Memory processes and the maintenance of social stereotypes. *Journal of Experimental Social Psychology*, 1979, *15*, 343–355.

Rothbart, M., Fulero, S., Jensen, C., Howard, J., & Birrell, P. From individual to group impressions: Availability heuristics in stereotype formation. *Journal of Experimental Social Psychology*, 1978, *14*, 237–255.

Rubin, J., Provenzano, F., & Luria, Z. The eye of the beholder: Parent's views on sex of newborns. *American Journal of Orthopsychiatry*, 1974, *44*, 512–519.

Rubovits, P. C., & Maehr, M. L. Pygmalion black and white. *Journal of Personality and Social Psychology*, 1973, *25*, 210–218.

Sensenig, J., Jones, R. A., & Varney, L. Inspection of faces of own and other race as a function of subjects' prejudice. *Representative Research in Social Psychol-*

ogy, 1973, *4*, 85–92.

Shweder, R. A. How relevant is an individual difference theory of personality? *Journal of Personality*, 1975, *43*, 455–484.

Snyder, M., & Swann, W. B., Jr. Behavioral confirmation in social interaction: From social perception to social reality. *Journal of Experimental Social Psychology*, 1978, *14*, 148–162.

Snyder, M., Tanke, E. D., & Berscheid, E. Social perception and interpersonal behavior: On the self-fulfilling nature of social stereotypes. *Journal of Personality and Social Psychology*, 1977, *35*, 656–666.

Snyder, M., & Uranowitz, S. W. Reconstructing the past: Some cognitive consequences of person perception. *Journal of Personality and Social Psychology*, 1978, *36*, 941–950.

Snyder, M. L., Stephan, W. G., & Rosenfield, D. Attributional egotism. In J. H. Harvey, W. Ickes, and R. F. Kidd (eds.), *New directions in attribution research* (Vol. 2). Hillsdale, N.J.: Erlbaum, 1978.

Tajfel, H. Cognitive aspects of prejudice. *Journal of Social Issues*, 1969, *25*, 79–97.

Tajfel, H. Experiments in intergroup discrimination. *Scientific American*, 1970, *223*, 96–102.

Tajfel, H., Sheikh, A. A., & Gardner, R. Content of stereotypes and the inference of similarity between members of stereotyped groups. *Acta Psychologica*, 1964, *22*, 191–201.

Tajfel, H., & Wilkes, A. L. Classification and quantitative judgment. *British Journal of Psychology*, 1963, *54*, 101–114.

Taylor, S. E., & Fiske, S. T. Point of view and perceptions of causality. *Journal of Personality and Social Psychology*, 1975, *32*, 439–445.

Taylor, S. E., & Fiske, S. T. Salience, attention and attribution: Top of the head phenomena. In L. Berkowitz (ed.), *Advances in experimental social psychology* (Vol. 11). New York: Academic Press, 1978.

Taylor, S. E., Fiske, S. T., Etcoff, N. L., & Ruderman, A. J. Categorical and contextual bases of person memory and stereotyping. *Journal of Personality and Social Psychology*, 1978, *36*, 778–793.

Tversky, A., & Kahneman, D. Availability: A heuristic for judging frequency and probability. *Cognitive Psychology*, 1973, *5*, 207–232.

Weiner, B., Heckhausen, H., Meyer, W. V., & Cook, R. E. Causal ascriptions and achievement behavior: A conceptual analysis of effort and reanalysis of locus of control. *Journal of Personality and Social Psychology*, 1972, *21*, 239–248.

Wortman, C. B. Causal attributions and personal control. In J. H. Harvey, W. J. Ickes, and R. F. Kidd (eds.), *New directions in attribution research* (Vol. 1), Hillsdale, N.J.: Erlbaum, 1976.

Zadny, J., & Gerard, H. B. Attributed intentions and informational selectivity. *Journal of Experimental Social Psychology*, 1974, *10*, 34–52.

ADDITIONAL READINGS

Becker, H. S. *Outsiders: Studies in the sociology of deviance* (rev. ed.). New York: Free Press, 1973.

An eminently readable introduction to labeling theory. Using examples from various sources, Becker develops the position that there is more to deviance than the behaviors of a "deviant" individual. Many social rules, for example, are only selectively enforced. If the rule breaker has status or power in the community, he or she is relatively unlikely to be labeled as deviant. Others, who may break precisely the same rules, but who are without such resources, are likely to be labeled as deviant, ostracized, and punished in other ways.

Berkowitz, L. (ed.). *Cognitive theories in social psychology.* New York: Academic Press, 1978.

A collection of important chapters related to information processing in social contexts. Each chapter originally appeared in *Advances in Experimental Social Psychology,* edited by Berkowitz, and is reprinted here with a short, updated "progress since publication" addendum. Topics include cognitive algebra, congruity, dissonance, self-perception, attribution, labeling bodily states, and self-awareness.

Carroll, J. S., and Payne, J. W. (eds.). *Cognition and social behavior.* Hillsdale, N.J.: Erlbaum, 1976.

This volume consists of the papers presented at a symposium on cognition held at Carnegie-Mellon University. The purpose of the symposium was to bring representatives of the fields of cognitive psychology and social psychology together to explore areas of mutual concern. The 16 chapters, one by Nobel laureate Herbert Simon, cover topics such as inference processes, stereotypes, decision making, risk taking, personnel selection, and attribution. The individual contributions are a mix of basic theory and applications to such areas as consumer information-seeking about products, parole decision making, and selection of college students.

Clifford, B. R., and Bull, R. *The psychology of person identification.* London: Routledge & Kegan Paul, 1978.

An examination and review of psychological research that has implications for the identification of criminals by police and by witnesses. Topics include the influence of stereotypes on identification, memory distortions, language influences on memory for persons and events, and individual differences in cognitive style. The book is of interest both from an applied point of view—for those interested in the criminal justice system—and from a basic psychological research point of view. One of the major messages is that perceptions and memory are limited, fallible, and biased.

Elstein, A. S., Shulman, L. S., and Sprafka, S. A. *Medical problem solving: An analysis of clinical reasoning.* Cambridge, Mass.: Harvard University Press, 1978.

The report of a research program in which the diagnostic problem solving of experienced physicians was analyzed. Successful diagnosticians apparently generate hypotheses about possible problems and/or diseases quite early in an encounter with a patient, and then progressively "home in" on the most likely by selectively seeking certain types of information. Common errors in this problem-solving approach are explored in detail.

Hamilton, D. L. (ed.). *Cognitive processes in stereotyping and intergroup behavior.* Hillsdale, N.J.: Erlbaum, 1981.

An extensive treatment of the social-perceptual and cognitive foundations of stereotyping. This volume includes chapters by specialists in the areas of memory (Rothbart), categorization (S. E. Taylor), intergroup perception (Wilder), and illusory correlation (Hamilton).

Harvey, J., Ickes, W., and Kidd, R. F. (eds.). *New directions in attribution research* (Vols. 1 and 2). Hillsdale, N.J.: Erlbaum, 1976, 1978.
The chapters in these volumes constitute current reports of ongoing research and theoretical developments in attribution. The range of topics covered is quite diverse—from how we segment observed behavior to the questionable role of thought in social interaction. Included in Volume 1 is an interview with Fritz Heider, and Volume 2 has a combined interview with E. E. Jones and H. H. Kelley. One of the major strengths of the volumes is that they convey the robustness and diversity of research on attribution and related processes.

Neisser, U. *Cognition and reality: Principles and implications of cognitive psychology*. San Francisco: Freeman, 1976.
An introduction to cognitive processes, with specific emphasis on naturalistic and developmental perspectives. Neisser develops an information-processing and pickup view of perception, attention, memory, and related topics. Of particular interest is the discussion of cognitive structures, termed schemata, that serve the perceiver by facilitating the acquisition of certain kinds of information from the environment, information that most closely "fits" the preexisting schemata.

3

RACIAL AND ETHNIC STEREOTYPES

Walter G. Stephan
David Rosenfield

INTRODUCTION

Defining Stereotypes

Social psychology, like the automobile, is primarily a product of the twentieth century. If a car is classified as an antique after 25 years, how, then, should social psychologists regard a concept that has existed for more than 50 years? Stereotyping might be considered to be a Model T among social psychological concepts. Just as it would be impossible to understand today's Ford without knowing something of the history of cars, an understanding of the present state of knowledge regarding stereotypes must necessarily be built on a grasp of the changes that the concept has undergone.

We define a stereotype as the set of traits that is used to explain and predict the behavior of members of a socially defined group. This definition differs from many earlier ones in two respects: it is nonevaluative, and it emphasizes the cognitive functions served by stereotypes. We agree with Vinacke (1957) that "Stereotypes should properly be regarded as concept-systems, with positive as well as negative functions, having the same general kinds of properties as other concepts, and serving to organize experience as do other concepts" (p. 229). We tend to disagree with researchers who regard incorrectness, irrationality, and rigidity as defining features of stereotypes and with those who think of them as morally wrong (see Brigham, 1971a, for a review of these approaches). This is not to say that we view stereotypes positively, but that we feel that these presumed defining features are absent from many stereotypes. Thus, such definitions make it more difficult to understand the origins and functions of stereotypes.

Our primary focus will be on racial and ethnic stereotypes, which tend to be characterized as incorrect (in the sense that they are overgeneralizations), irrational, and rigid more often than other stereotypes, such as those applying to age, political association, religion, sexual preference, physical disability, sex, and social class. Age provides an illustrative case. Our stereotypes of age are acquired from direct experience, informal socialization by parents and peers, the mass media, and formal teaching. The generalizations formed through these processes will be overgeneralizations in some cases—not all infants are cute—but in other cases they will not be— all babies are helpless and dependent. Age stereotypes may also be rigid, but they clearly are not necessarily unchangeable, as indicated by our changing views of older people (the Gray Panthers).

Stereotypes may be incorrect, irrational, and rigid; and when they are, they are rightly condemned as morally wrong. But when stereotypes are none of these things, they are still explanations and predictions of behavior based on categorical distinctions among people. Our reason for stressing this fact is that it frees us, to some extent, from the highly evaluative nature of most discussions of racial and ethnic stereotyping. A parallel point can be made about the content of stereotypes. The sets of traits of which stereotypes are composed are rarely all negative or all positive; thus, stereotypes are distinct from prejudice. In fact, there is considerable evidence that stereotypes and prejudice are not always highly correlated (Gardner, 1973; Brigham, 1973).

Stereotypes and prejudice can be considered to be two different types of attitudes. Most psychologists believe that attitudes have three components: cognitive, affective, and behavioral (Kiesler, Collins, & Miller, 1969). For prejudice, the emphasis is on the affective component of attitudes, since prejudice is characterized by negative evaluations. In contrast, stereotypes emphasize the cognitive component of attitudes, since they are sets of beliefs about the traits that characterize a given group. Neither prejudice nor stereotyping has any necessary relationship to discrimination, the behavioral expression of racial and ethnic attitudes. While prejudice may predispose people to respond in negative ways toward members of the negatively evaluated group, the factors that determine whether this predisposition will result in discrimination are complex, including such things as situational constraints that may inhibit discriminatory behavior and the importance of racial and ethnic attitudes in the individual's value system.

People use stereotypes to predict how others will behave. As we will see shortly, this can affect their behavior toward others. However, because stereotypes typically consist of some positive as well as negative traits, a positive, a negative, or no predisposition to behave may be elicited, depending on the situation. Before we consider these and other effects of stereotyping, it may be helpful to discuss the ways in which stereotypes are measured.

How Stereotypes are Measured

In 1933, D. Katz and Braly conducted the first study of ethnic stereotypes. The technique they used provided the foundation for most of the later investigations of stereotypes. In their study, subjects were given a list of 84 traits. The subjects were then asked to select from this list the traits that they thought were typical of the particular ethnic group they were rating. Later, the subjects were asked to reexamine the traits they had selected and to "star" the five that seemed to be the most typical of each ethnic group. Katz and Braly examined these starred traits to determine which ones had been selected most frequently as being typical of a given ethnic group. The traits selected most frequently were considered to constitute the stereotype of that group. The stereotype of "Negroes" included "superstitious," starred by 84 percent of the subjects, and that of Jews included "shrewd," starred by 79 percent of the subjects. Stereotypes measured in this way consist of traits that most people feel are typical of the ethnic group.

Although the Katz and Braly technique has been employed for years, researchers (such as Brigham, 1971a; McCauley & Stitt, 1978; McCauley, Stitt, & Segal, 1980) have noted problems with this measure. The primary problem is that the Katz and Braly technique provides no measure of the degree to which a particular individual stereotypes a given ethnic group. Several more recent techniques provide such measures. Brigham (1971a; 1973) has measured stereotypes by asking subjects to indicate the percentage of the outgroup that possesses each trait. The traits that most subjects attribute to a large percentage of the group constitute the social stereotype of that group. The individual's stereotype can be obtained by examining the traits attributed to a large proportion of the group.

McCauley and Stitt (1978) have developed a slightly different way of assessing individual stereotypes. First, subjects indicate the percentage of the ethnic group that possesses each trait. Then they indicate the percentage of all people who possess that trait. Their measure of stereotyping is the "diagnostic ratio," which consists of the first percentage divided by the second percentage. The diagnostic ratio indicates the extent to which an individual perceives that a given group differs from all other groups on a trait. One advantage of the diagnostic ratio is that it prevents traits that characterize all groups (such as ethnocentrism) from being included in the stereotype.

A technique used by Broverman, Vogel, Broverman, Clarkson, and Rosenkrantz (1972) is an interesting combination of the Katz and Braly technique and the diagnostic ratio. Broverman et al. asked subjects to indicate the extent to which certain traits characterized males and females. Then they examined the percentage of people who agreed that a trait was more characteristic of males than of females, and vice versa. Only traits that were considered to be more characteristic of one sex than of the other by at least 75 percent of the subjects were included in the stereotype. Thus, this method yields traits that distinguish females from males (as does the diagnostic ratio), but only traits on which most people agree that males and females are different. The Broverman technique has additional advantages over the Katz and Braly method, in that it can be used as an individual measure of stereotyping, and it does not force people to stereotype. Its only major drawback is that it does not lend itself to quantification as easily as the diagnostic ratio does.

One final technique for assessing stereotypes is the bogus pipeline (Sigall & Page, 1971). In studies employing the bogus pipeline, subjects are attached to an electromyograph, which they are told measures "implicit muscular response tendencies"—and, hence, ostensibly measures their true responses to questions asked of them. Subjects are asked to accurately predict their reactions to certain questions in order to determine whether they are in touch with their true feelings. Sigall and Page suggest that subjects will tend to answer questions more honestly under these conditions because they want to appear to know their own feelings. The results showed that subjects tended to give significantly more negative evaluations of blacks in the bogus pipeline condition than in a condition without the bogus pipeline.

In a later study Brigham, Bloom, Gunn, and Torok (1974) found that the bogus pipeline only rarely yielded answers that were substantially different from those derived from anonymous questionnaires. Given the difficulty of administering the bogus pipeline, we agree with Jones and Sigall (1973) that "The bogus pipeline should only be used when important theoretical issues are involved, when subjects are otherwise likely to resist disclosure of their attitudes, or when the experimenter is interested in tapping different attitudinal components" (p. 261).

The Functions of Stereotypes

The major function of attaching labels to different racial and ethnic groups is to impose order on a chaotic social environment. We use categorical labels to divide the social world into intelligible units. This division is accomplished by learning or creating criteria for defining group membership. The criteria used are potentially as infinite as the differences among people, but in practice some criteria are more easily applied than others, and thus facilitate the process of organizing and clarifying our position with respect to other people. The simplest and most widely used criteria are those that are immediately apprehended, such as skin color, size (for some age stereotypes), facial features, body shape, nonverbal behavior, and language. We will call these aspects of group membership defining features, after a distinction made by Smith, Shoben, and Rips (1974).

The link between racial and ethnic group labels and the defining features of group membership has been documented in a study by Gardner and Taylor (1969) on the stereotypes of English and French Canadians. The subjects in their study were asked to free-associate to the words "English Canadian" and "French Canadian." The words that were most frequently associated with these ethnic labels were then tabulated. For English Canadians these words included "England," "Ontario," "Protestant," "queen," and "white"; and for French Canadians the words included "Montreal," "Quebec," "language," "Catholic," "separatists," and "bilingual." Gardner and Taylor concluded that "The associations appear to reflect major identifying characteristics of the groups" (p. 190).

In addition to being associated with the defining features of group membership, group labels are associated with a second set of features consisting of personality traits. We will call these sets of traits characteristic features, again relying on a distinction made by Smith et al. (1974). It is these traits that people commonly think of as stereotypes, but as the Canadian results indicate, we must include defining features in any comprehensive definition of stereotypes. The characteristic features associated with a given group are not random. They arise from the nature of the historical contacts between the ingroup and the outgroup, the actual cultural traits possessed by both groups, and the psychological consequences of identification with the ingroup. Together, the characteristic features arising from these sources constitute the cultural equivalent of an implicit personality theory (Bruner & Taguiri, 1954) about the ways that members of a given group can be expected to behave. This implicit theory generally is internally consistent and is unlikely to contain sharply contradictory traits.

More recent evidence suggests that group labels and characteristic features are associated together in semantic memory (Thompson, Stephan, & Schvaneveldt, 1980). Identifying a person by use of a group label facilitates access to the traits that are associated with the group label. If this other person is a stranger, it is likely that the person will be thought to possess the characteristics of a prototypical member of the group (Cantor & Mischel, 1979; Rosch, 1973).

To summarize briefly, the process we have just described consists of two stages. First, the defining features of stereotyped categories of people are used to identify the group (or groups) to which an individual belongs. Second, the group label elicits the associated characteristic features of the group.

The primary function of the characteristic features associated with group labels is to provide predictions and explanations of behavior. To understand the importance of these predictions, it is necessary to briefly consider the nature of the interaction process. Social interaction is premised on the assumptions and expectations each individual brings to the social context. The assumptions often include a shared system of verbal communication, a shared system for interpreting nonverbal behavior, and a shared system of cultural norms relating to the conduct of interactions. Without making some of these basic assumptions, interaction would be impossible. These assumptions set up a broad and rather ill-defined set of expectancies for how the other party to the interaction will respond. In addition to these basic assumptions, the situational context provides information concerning appropriate normative conduct. Combined with the implicit assumptions that are made, these situational cues serve to reduce our uncertainty about how to behave.

Nonetheless, substantial uncertainty remains. It is to further reduce this uncertainty that stereotypes are so readily called into play in social settings. The presumed characteristic features of a stereotyped group provide us with information about how others will behave toward us and about how we should behave toward them. To the extent that the stereotypes are valid, the task of interacting with unknown others is facilitated. Correspondingly, to the extent that the stereotypes are inaccurate, or to the degree that a particular individual does not fit the group prototype, the stereotyping process can hinder interaction. Ordinarily we acquire information about particular others through our experiences with them. These experiences help us to determine the extent of similarity in our meaning systems and to make inferences about the attributes they possess. For the people using them, stereotypes seem to provide a shortcut to this knowledge. The advantage of stereotypes is that they allow people to believe they have a basis for interaction; the disadvantage is that they may be wrong.

ORIGINS OF STEREOTYPES

Historical Intergroup Relations

Stereotyping is a generic process applicable to any socially defined group. The content of stereotypes depends in part on basic principles of categorization, and in part on factors unique to the relations between the groups in question. We will consider some of these unique factors first, concentrating particularly on historical aspects of contact between blacks and whites in America. Then we will discuss the psychological implications of categorization.

The nature of the contact between groups is one crucial determinant of how each group will view the other. While this is especially true of the initial contact between the groups, contact continues to shape intergroup perceptions by modifying or reinforcing them. In the United States the history of intergroup contact is especially rich. With the exception of native Americans, it is a nation of immigrants—a sometimes seething, sometimes gently bubbling cauldron of peoples. The role of intergroup contact in the distillation of stereotypes from this ethnic stew is well summarized by LeVine and Campbell (1972):

> Institutionalized role relations constitute the most repeated and socially reinforced context for interaction and observation between groups. . . . This context acts to *sensitize* persons to the role-relevant attributes of those groups, thus limiting the basis for stereotype content. (p. 158)

In the United States this process is exemplified by the relations between whites and blacks. Many aspects of the stereotypes of both groups can be traced to the role relationships involved in the plantation system and its successors in the South. The plantation evolved on the frontiers of America as a way of organizing agriculture for the production of commercial staple crops. In order to have a stable resident labor force where land was plentiful but labor was scarce, the planters turned to forced labor, first by indentured servants and later by slaves. Within this context the concept of race developed as a justification for slavery. According to E. T. Thompson (1975):

> The conception that certain people coming from the same general territory overseas and possessing similar physical traits were innately and immutably "different," almost different enough to constitute a separate species, powerfully reinforced the position of slavery in America and especially in the South. . . . The idea of race in the South has been no mere academic concept; it was generated out of the interaction of men of different physical marks and it functioned as a part of the plantation situation itself. (p. 95)

The concept of race and the stereotypes associated with it enabled the dominant group to view members of the subordinate group as inferior beings, and to treat them accordingly. Whites attempted to divest blacks of their traditions and languages under the plantation system. This means that the stereotypes of blacks and whites were determined by the nature of the contact between the groups to a greater degree than was the case for ethnic groups in America that retained more of their traditions. The economic roles that blacks performed and the conditions under which they were forced to live became prime determinants of how they were viewed by the dominant group. It was "inherent in a system of forced labor" that slaves would be regarded as lazy, because there were few positive incentives for work (Franklin, 1974, p. 144). Because their maintenance was provided for in the most minimal manner, slaves were seen as slovenly and dirty. The education of slaves was actually illegal in nearly every state in the South (Weinberg, 1977). This fact, combined with the limited exposure blacks had to the wider white society, led to their being regarded as ignorant.

The almost total dependence of the subordinate group, together with the paternalistic attitude of the dominant group, led blacks to be viewed as if they were in a state of perpetual childhood (the use of the word "boy" is a symbol of this relationship). The result was that blacks were characterized as pleasure loving and happy-go-lucky. The reluctance of blacks to display anger and resentment toward members of the dominant group, for fear of being punished, reinforced the view that blacks were happy with their lot. But whites were not wholly unaware of the hostility their treatment of blacks engendered, and they were suspicious and fearful of blacks. This fear of blacks contributed to the almost unbridgeable chasm of assumed and actual differences that the historical relations between blacks and whites created.

Although there are some relatively unusual features of the historical relationship between blacks and whites in America, the stereotypes that emerged can be largely understood in terms of transcultural principles of stereotyping. LeVine and Campbell (1972) have outlined two of the most important dimensions of intergroup contact and the consequences of each for stereotyping. First, urban groups tend to see rural groups as unsophisticated, guileless, gullible, and ignorant, whereas rural groups view urban groups as sophisticated, urbane, avaricious, dishonest, and immoral. Second, manual laborers are seen as strong, stupid, pleasure loving and improvident, whereas businessmen are thought of as grasping, haughty, cunning, and domineering. A third dimension, also mentioned by LeVine and Campbell, and studied by Bayton (Bayton, McAlister, & Hamer, 1956; Smedley & Bayton, 1978) concerns social class stereotypes. Upper-class people are viewed as intelligent, ambitious, progressive, and neat, whereas lower-class people are thought of as ignorant, lazy, loud, dirty, and happy-go-lucky.

An inspection of the stereotypes for blacks and whites (Table 3.1) shows a remarkable fit between the characteristic features proposed by LeVine and Campbell and by Bayton, and the descriptive traits most frequently chosen for blacks and whites.* Blacks are stereotyped by whites as musical, superstitious, ignorant, dumb, dirty, lazy, loud, happy-go-lucky, and pleasure loving, whereas whites are stereotyped by blacks as industrious, deceitful, sly, treacherous, and intelligent.

Thus, while some characteristic features of the stereotypes of whites and blacks may be attributable to unique aspects of the historical relationships between the groups, especially the institution of slavery, most aspects

---

*These lists come from a number of different reviews and studies of stereotypes done since 1935 (Bayton, 1941; Brigham, 1974; Hartsough & Fontana, 1970; Karlins, Coffman, & Walters, 1969; Krantz & Foley, 1976; Samuels, 1973). All of the stereotype traits for blacks appear in more than two studies, with the exception of "proud" and "militant," which appeared only in Samuels (1973) and Thompson, Stephan, and Schvaneveldt (1980). Since the stereotypes of whites by blacks and blacks by blacks have been studied less, these stereotypes are based on only two or three studies.

TABLE 3.1
Blacks' and Whites' Views of Themselves and Each Other

Blacks' view of

Blacks	Whites
Intelligent	deceitful
Very religious	sly
Musical	intelligent
Sportsmanlike	treacherous
Loud	dirty
Pleasure-loving	industrious
Athletic	lazy
Sense of rhythm	cruel
Lazy	selfish
Superstitious	nervous
	conceited

Whites' view of

Blacks	Whites
Lazy	industrious
Superstitious	intelligent
Ignorant	materialistic
Loud	ambitious
Musical	pleasure-loving
Materialistic	progressive
Poor	efficient
Stupid	individualistic
Dirty	neat
Peace-loving	clean
Happy-go-lucky	good manners
Very religious	
Feel inferior	
Pleasure-loving	
Militant	
Proud	

of the stereotypes can be understood in terms of urban or rural residence, and occupational and social class differences. An additional example of the effects of the relationships between groups on stereotyping is the case of Chicanos, who for decades have worked primarily as manual laborers in rural areas of America. A survey of undergraduates at a southwestern university revealed the following characteristic features for the Chicano stereotype: lazy, religious, clannish, radical, dirty, ignorant, dumb, traditional, revengeful, bitter, and unreliable (G. Thompson et al., 1980). Again, many of these stereotype traits can be explained in terms of the universal characteristics associated with place of residence, occupation, and social class.

The stereotypes of blacks and whites have undergone gradual changes since the early part of the twentieth century (Gilbert, 1951; Karlins, Coffman, & Walters, 1969; Samuels, 1973), but they have not changed nearly as much as relations between the two groups. The trends toward integration and equal rights, combined with the increased visibility of minority groups in the media and more thorough presentations of minority culture and history in the school system, have increased direct and vicarious contact between blacks and whites. Amazingly, the legacy of stereotypical perceptions that remains from earlier relations between the races exists in the face of all of these forces for change. This suggests that there are powerful mechanisms that serve to maintain stereotypes. These forces include categorization processes and the psychological consequences of identification with the ingroup. Our discussion of these two facets of the stereotyping process will demonstrate that stereotypes need not arise slowly out of a prolonged historical process of interaction like the one we have just described regarding blacks and whites in America. As a prelude to this discussion, we will consider an example of the rapid polarization of ethnic group perceptions in an African nation.

Rwanda is a small (pop. 4,460,000) republic in central Africa. Before independence was granted by Belgium in 1961, a minority tribe, the Tutsi, was economically dominant over a much larger tribe, the Hutu. During the four years before and after independence, peaceful relations between these groups degenerated into genocidal massacre. This process of rapid polarization was facilitated by a spiral of increasingly negative intergroup perceptions. Tracing this process will provide insights into how quickly stereotypes can emerge and into the conditions that promote their emergence.

In the years immediately prior to independence, two political organizations existed in Rwanda, one dominated by the Tutsi and one dominated by the Hutu. Both organizations were ideologically moderate. A Hutu manifesto published in 1957 declared that, while the principal problem of the country was the domination of one group by the other, both groups shared a common ancestry and in this sense were brothers. The Tutsi-dominated party (UNAR), although elitist in its defense of Tutsi privilege, expressed a commitment to the fight against racial hatred. Thus, in the initial phases of preindependence political consciousness, ethnic differences were downplayed and conciliatory stances were adopted. As independence approached, ethnically based political tension escalated. Increasingly the common ground between the two groups was eliminated, and a polarization occurred in which group differences were accentuated. In 1959 the president of UNAR called for a war without mercy against all traitors. The use of repression by the dominant minority led to a fear of aggressive retaliation by the subordinate majority. The aggressiveness imputed to the subordinate group was then used to justify the repression.

The spark that ignited this highly flammable mixture was the beating and rumored murder of a Hutu subchief in 1959. The response was a peasant uprising during which Hutu tribesmen burned thousands of Tutsi huts and killed some Tutsi tribesmen. Tutsi authorities responded on a more massive scale. The reprisals consisted of the summary arrest, torture, and execution of Hutu leaders. The stage was now set for the greater violence that followed independence. Fear and suspicion gripped the country. Each group increasingly perceived the other group in a dehumanized manner, as bloodthirsty barbarians. Each group held the other to be collectively responsible for aggression against its members, and ultimately this made indiscriminate killing of members of the other group seem justifiable.

Elections before independence and in 1962 raised the majority Hutu to power. Tutsi were removed from positions of authority, many were executed, and UNAR was eradicated. The Tutsi responded by mounting military raids against the Hutu, who countered with massive reprisals. According to de Heusch (1964), "From then on every Tutsi, in the interior as well as the exterior, whether or not supportive of these military adventures . . . [was] considered an enemy of the country" (cited in Kuper, 1977, p. 193). The categorical process was complete. All differentiation among the Tutsi was obliterated. The final atrocity was committed by the Hutu in response to an invasion mounted by the Tutsi from neighboring Burundi in 1963. "Hutu, armed with clubs, pangas and spears, methodically began to exterminate all Tutsi in sight, men, women and children" (Kuper, 1975, p. 196). An estimated 10,000 to 12,000 people were slaughtered before the massacre ended.

This descent into genocidal murder illustrates the speed with which a society can become polarized along ethnic lines. The intergroup perceptions changed from an initial stance of some common goals, tempered by expressions of reservation and suspicion, to attributions of hostility and aggressive intent, then perceptions of outgroup members as hated barbarians, and finally to a view that justified an attempt by one group to exterminate the other.

This example demonstrates the fact that the changing nature of intergroup relations can lead to enormous alterations in intergroup perceptions in a relatively short period of time. As the Rwanda example makes clear, negative stereotypes can be created rapidly. But as we have noted in the case of blacks and whites in America, the dissolution of stereotypes appears to occur much more slowly. The reason is that there are several processes, in addition to the nature of the contact between the groups, that operate to maintain stereotypes in intergroup perception.

Social Categorization

One of the basic processes by which stereotypes are created and maintained is the categorization of the social world into distinct racial and ethnic groups. Fundamentally, the formation of racial and ethnic concepts is the same as the formation of any concept. According to Bourne (1966), "A concept exists whenever two or more distinguishable objects or events have been grouped or classified together and sit apart from other objects on the basis of some common feature" (p. 1). The important aspect of this definition with respect to ethnic concepts is that it suggests that perceived similarity is essential in the formation of such concepts. This similarity is often perceived where, in fact, considerable diversity exists. For instance, skin color is a continuous dimension that is broken down into color categories such as white, black, red, yellow, and brown. The use of such labels implies a similarity among people who are assigned a given label. Typically, the amount of similarity that is perceived is greater than what actually exists. This process is referred to as assimilation, and it is accompanied by a second process that serves to highlight the differences between groups (Allport, 1954; Campbell, 1967; Tajfel, 1969; Billig, 1976). The exaggeration of differences between groups is referred to as a contrast effect.

When a stereotyped trait is associated with a group, the members of that group are perceived to be relatively homogeneous with respect to the trait (Tajfel, Sheikh, & Gardner, 1964) and as being different from members of other groups on this trait. The polarization of the mutual perceptions of the Tutsi and Hutu illustrates these processes. Table 3.1 indicates that whites view themselves as intelligent and they view blacks as unintelligent. The enormous overlap between the two groups on this trait tends to be minimized by people subscribing to this facet of the stereotypes.

When the social world is divided into groups, any given person will be a member of some groups and a nonmember of others. Each of us derives important aspects of our self-concepts from our identification with various groups, such as those based on sex, age, race, nationality, religion, and social class. Most of us have a desire to maintain a positive self-image. One way of achieving this goal is to evaluate our ingroup membership favorably. Typically, we do this by thinking of the ingroup as being superior to other groups. Thus, a positive ingroup identity is achieved at the cost of rejecting outgroups. Assimilation and contrast go hand in hand with this process of ingroup-outgroup evaluative bias. People tend to perceive and accentuate differences between groups on dimensions on which ingroup members feel they can make a favorable comparison. Brewer (1979) has noted that when ingroup members cannot easily think of themselves as superior on a certain dimension, differences between groups on this dimension will tend to be minimized or ignored in the formation of ingroup-outgroup stereotypes.

The effect of the tendency to identify with and positively value ingroups is so basic to social existence that even the creation of arbitrary groups can lead to ingroup-outgroup bias. This has been demonstrated by Tajfel and his colleagues (Tajfel, 1970; Billig & Tajfel, 1973; Tajfel & Billig, 1974). In one experiment, high school students performed a perceptual task in which they guessed the number of dots projected on a screen. The experimenters then told the students that they consistently overestimated or underestimated the number of dots. Later, when given an opportunity to allocate rewards to other students, the subjects gave more rewards to students who performed as they had than to members of the other performance group (Tajfel, 1970). The distinction between overestimators and underestimators is obviously a meaningless one, yet it led to ingroup-outgroup bias.

Ethnocentrism

By making an additional assumption, it will be possible to understand how ingroup-outgroup bias contributes to the specific content of stereotypes. This assumption is that there is a substantial number of real differences between groups in their norms and characteristic behaviors. While this assumption would be readily accepted by most anthropologists and sociologists, many psychologists have chosen to emphasize the similarities between groups. For instance, in referring to blacks and whites, one psychologist has argued that "Race is not a relevant variable for studies of personality" (Edwards, 1974, p. 48).

The principal reason that many psychologists have tended to deny the importance of racial and ethnic differences is the continued controversy over the existence of, and meaning of, differences in intelligence, achievement, and self-esteem. Low scores on these dimensions frequently have been interpreted as an indication of pathology (Adam, 1978), in spite of the fact that many social scientists have explained group differences on these dimensions in terms of other variables, such as social class or cultural biases in testing instruments (Klineberg, 1975). To counteract the explosive implications of viewing low-scoring groups in negative terms, some social scientists have argued that all groups are essentially the same.

The problem created by stressing the similarities between groups is that it leads to a deemphasis on the important role played by race and ethnicity in determining people's identities and interpersonal relationships (Stephan & Rosenfield, 1979). It is our position that race and ethnicity constitute such an integral part of our social identities that the processes of ingroup-outgroup bias operate with special force in this domain. Racial and ethnic group members tend to identify with and to favor the ethnic ingroup, and they tend to reject outgroups. This tendency is so basic that it appears to be universal among ethnic groups around the world (Campbell, 1967; LeVine & Campbell, 1972; Brewer, 1979).

Egocentrism is the tendency to view the world only from our own perspective, with a corresponding inability to see the world as others see it. Egocentrism is paralleled on the group level by ethnocentrism, the "view of things in which one's own group is the center of everything, and all others are scaled or rated with reference to it" (Sumner, 1906, p. 13). The relevance of ethnocentrism to the formation of stereotypes is that it biases the way the behaviors of ingroup and outgroup members are labeled. Campbell (1967) has outlined some of the basic rules concerning the effect of ethnocentric biases on stereotypes:

1. The greater the real differences between groups on any particular custom, detail of physical appearance, or item of material culture, the more likely it is that the feature will appear in the stereotyped imagery each group has of the other.

2. Those trait differences involved in intergroup interaction will be most strongly and accurately represented in mutual stereotypes.

3. Those traits which have well-established rejection responses associated with them for within group usage will be most apt to be perceived in outgroup stereotypes.

4. Differences between the ingroup and outgroup, if sufficient to be noted, will be exaggerated in the mutual stereotypes each hold of the other.

5. There is a "tendency to perceive racial rather than environmental causes for group differences." (adapted from pp. 821–825)

Ethnocentric biases affect both the labeling of traits on which two groups differ, and the labeling of traits that they share. First, let us consider how these biases affect the labeling of traits on which two groups differ. Americans (at least white, Anglo-Saxon Protestants) tend to view themselves as friendly and outgoing. The English, in referring to the same behavior on the part of Americans, label it intrusive and forward. For their part, the English consider themselves to be reserved and as respecting the rights of others, whereas Americans label these behaviors snobbish and cold (Campbell, 1967). Here we have an example of acknowledged differences between groups in norms for interpersonal relations that are labeled in favorable terms by ingroup members, but are labeled negatively by outgroup members.

A similar ethnocentric bias operates in the labeling of behavior patterns that are shared by the ingroup and the outgroup. One characteristic shared by all groups is ethnocentrism. In the ingroup, people use the terms "loyalty" and "patriotism" when referring to this ethnocentrism. However, when referring to the same behavior in the outgroup, it is likely to be labeled negatively as clannishness, favoritism, or unfriendliness. Several studies have explored ethnocentric biases in the way we view similar behavior in the ingroup and the outgroup. These studies have shown that there is a tendency to attribute positive behavior by ingroup members to underlying traits, whereas the same behavior by an outgroup member is perceived to have been caused by external constraints in the situation.

The opposite pattern occurs for negative behaviors; in this case ingroup members tend not to be blamed, whereas the same behavior performed by outgroup members is attributed to their negative traits (Mann & Taylor, 1974; Stephan, 1977; Greenberg & Rosenfield, 1979). For example, in one study it was found that white students tended to believe that if a white student worked hard on a project, it was because the student was industrious, but black students believed it was because somebody made the white student work hard (Stephan, 1977). This process creates a perception of ingroup members as possessing positive traits and of outgroup members as possessing negative traits, even though members of both groups have behaved in exactly the same way (cf. Pettigrew, 1979).

Psychodynamic Factors

In addition to these ethnocentric biases, there are various psychodynamic factors that *may* contribute to the formation of stereotypes. We say "may contribute" because the evidence for these factors is more intuitively compelling than empirically validated. One of the factors is projection, which refers to the perception by an individual that others possess traits that he or she possesses but that he or she represses or rejects. At the group level the operation of projection can be seen in the belief that it is the outgroup that is hostile toward the ingroup, not the ingroup that is hostile toward the outgroup. Because it is generally the case that ingroup members, except in times of war, would prefer to see themselves as peace-loving, the easiest way to justify their antipathy toward the outgroup is to view the cause of ingroup hostility as the hatred the outgroup bears toward the ingroup (Campbell, 1967). Schofield (in press) has provided an example of this type of projection from interviews she conducted in a desegregated junior high school. A black student was quoted as saying, "A whole lot of Black kids think that everybody that's White hates them. So, they'll hate White people back" (p. 34).

A second psychodynamic mechanism involved in stereotyping is scapegoating, the tendency to blame others for our problems. At the group level, scapegoating consists of perceiving the outgroup as the cause of the difficulties and frustrations of the ingroup. Because people generally have favorable attitudes toward the ingroup, they rarely blame their problems on ingroup characteristics. Outgroups, particularly powerless ones, constitute a convenient scapegoat. In the dominant group, scapegoating can lead to a perception of the subordinate group as unreliable, incompetent, and lazy (the dominant group perceives that it would be more economically successful, but for the subordinate group's incompetence). For the subordinate group, scapegoating can lead to the perception of the dominant group as domineering, exploitative, and oppressive (the subordinate group perceives that life would be better, but for the actions of the dominant group). Thus, scapegoating leads to a perception of outgroup members as either subhuman or inhumane (LeVine & Campbell, 1972). In either case, blaming the outgroup helps to justify hostility toward it.

Black and White Stereotypes Reconsidered

Let us now examine the stereotypes of blacks and whites for evidence of the operation of these factors (see Table 3.1). This is a speculative exercise only; we cannot be certain of the exact origins of any of the traits in these stereotypes. Nonetheless, speculating on the origins of stereotypes can help us to understand how stereotyping works. The ethnocentrism of both groups is exemplified in the relative proportions of positive and negative traits assigned to the ingroup and outgroup. The differential labeling of the traits assigned to whites by both blacks and whites can be seen in the whites' view of themselves as individualistic and aggressive and the blacks' view of whites as selfish and cruel. The stereotype lists provide no clear examples of the differential labeling of the traits of blacks by the two groups.

Blacks and whites believe that they share several traits, and when they perceive this similarity, they often label these traits in identical terms. This occurs for whites' perceptions of themselves and blacks as materialistic and pleasure loving, and for the blacks' views of themselves and whites as intelligent. From the perspective of McCauley and Stitt (1978), traits for which there is this type of agreement should not be included as characteristic features of the stereotype, since all people (or at least these two centrally important groups) are perceived to have them.

There do appear to be some similar traits in the black-white stereotypes that are differentially labeled. While blacks view whites as intelligent, they also view them as sly and deceitful, both of which are negative traits related to intelligence. These traits may, therefore, reflect the operation of the tendency to label shared traits negatively in the outgroup. It is also possible that there is a bias operating in the whites' view of themselves as aggressive, a trait they may evaluate positively, and their view of blacks as militant, a similar but negatively valued trait.

Evidence for the operation of projection exists when there is a direct contradiction in the ingroup and outgroup stereotype, with the ingroup perceiving that the outgroup possesses the negative trait. For instance, blacks view whites as dirty, but whites view themselves as clean. One interpretation of the fact that whites view blacks as dirty is that whites reject and repress any signs of dirtiness among the ingroup and project this trait onto blacks (the high value that whites place on cleanliness is illustrated by the saying "Cleanliness is next to godliness"). Scapegoating of the subordinate group by the dominant group may account for the whites' perception of blacks as lazy, stupid, and ignorant, while scapegoating of the dominant group by the subordinate group may account for the blacks' perceptions of whites as cruel, treacherous, sly, and deceitful.

Taken together with the contribution made to black and white stereotypes by the historical relations between the groups, and social class, occupational, and residential differences, these psychodynamic factors and ethnocentric biases can account for a substantial number of the traits included in the black and white stereotypes. Thus, the origins of stereotypes are often explicable, and are not necessarily irrational or even incorrect. Another way to examine the origin of stereotypes is to discuss their development in children.

DEVELOPMENTAL ASPECTS OF STEREOTYPING

There appear to be relatively few studies that have directly examined the development of stereotyping in children. An exception is Brigham (1974), who found that by the fourth grade, children have clearly assimilated many of the characteristic features of the cultural stereotypes held by adults in our society. A number of studies have examined developmental aspects of other dimensions of racial and ethnic attitudes, and some of these studies provide information that is relevant to stereotyping. In particular, considerable effort has gone into determining when children learn to categorize social groups and when evaluative connotations become associated with these categories. In addition, research on the self-images of blacks and whites provides some information on stereotyping in children. We will consider these studies first.

Racial Attitudes in Children

Since the 1930s researchers have presented black and white dolls, pictures, and animals to children and asked them questions about these stimuli. Among the questions that are most frequently asked are "Which of the dolls is the nice doll?" "Which doll looks bad?" and "Which doll looks pretty?" While these questions may not tap characteristic features that are central to the reported stereotypes of adult blacks and whites, they do touch on the dimensions of physical attractiveness and perceived appropriateness of behavior that appear in children's and adolescents' stereotypes (Brigham, 1974; Lerner & Knapp, 1976). For whites these studies have found that preschool and early-school-age children most frequently choose the white doll as looking nice and the black doll as looking bad (Asher & Allen, 1969; Fox & Jordan, 1973; Greenwald & Oppenheim, 1968; Gregor & McPherson, 1966; Hraba & Grant, 1970).

For blacks the results are more complex. Some studies have found that blacks also most frequently choose the white doll as looking nice and the black doll as looking bad (Asher & Allen, 1969; Clark & Clark, 1947; Greenwald & Oppenheim, 1968; and for preschoolers, but not for early-school-age children, Hraba & Grant, 1970). Other studies have found that blacks choose the black doll as looking nice slightly more frequently than the white doll, and choose the white doll as looking bad considerably more frequently than the black doll (Fox & Jordan, 1973; and for early-school-age children, Hraba & Grant, 1970). In the studies that include blacks and whites, it is typically the case that whites choose the white doll as looking nice and the black doll as looking bad more frequently than do blacks. Since the procedure requires the children to attribute traits to the dolls, one way to view these results is as an indication that children of both groups stereotype blacks as being not nice and bad, although the whites do so to a greater degree than blacks.

This way of interpreting these results can also be applied to the Preschool Racial Attitude Measure (PRAM) developed by J. E. Williams and Morland (1976). This instrument uses stories and pictures of blacks and whites to assess the racial attitudes of children. After hearing a story, the child chooses a white or black person as the protagonist. A number of the 24 adjectives that are used to describe the protagonists—such as clean, nice, smart, dirty, mean, stupid, bad, ugly, naughty, cruel, and selfish—are related to characteristic features of the black or white stereotype. In scoring this measure, the frequency with which positive adjectives are attributed to whites and negative adjectives are attributed to blacks is tabulated. High scores indicate that positive adjectives apply to whites and negative adjectives apply to blacks.

Across a wide variety of subject populations, Williams and Morland have found that white and black children attribute more positive traits and fewer negative traits to whites than to blacks, although whites do this to a greater degree than blacks. There is also evidence indicating that this pro-white bias decreases from grade 1 to grade 4 (J. E. Williams, Best, & Boswell, 1975). Because the adjectives employed in this measure draw on a substantial number of characteristic features of black and white stereotypes, the scores reflect both the cognitive and the evaluative components of racial attitudes. Thus, high scores may be as much an index of knowledge of cultural stereotypes as they are of the evaluative preferences of the children. This is not the explanation that is preferred by Williams and Morland. They explain the pro-white bias on their measure in terms of transcultural tendencies to evaluate members of dominant groups favorably and to evaluate light colors more favorably than dark ones.

Black Self-Rejection

The idea that blacks acknowledge their inferior social position in their choice of black and white figures echoes a refrain from the doll-study literature. The most common interpretation of the findings from the numerous doll studies is that whites reject and negatively evaluate blacks, and that blacks reject and negatively evaluate themselves. These conclusions are based not only on the questions concerning which doll looks nice or bad, but also on questions concerning which doll the children would like to play with and which doll looks like them.

This interpretation of the doll studies has been questioned by Banks (1976). According to Banks, most of the doll studies dealing with black children indicate that they have no preferences between whites and blacks. Thus, the results should be taken as an indication of a lack of bias on the part of blacks rather than as an index of self-rejection. Banks regards the pro-white choices of white children as an indication that they are ethnocentric.

Another reason for believing that the results of the doll studies do not constitute evidence of self-rejection among blacks comes from studies that have directly examined the self-esteem of blacks. The issue of black self-rejection is an important one, because a central argument of the social scientists who testified in the *Brown* v. *Board of Education* trials was that school segregation led to low self-esteem among blacks. The doll studies were cited as evidence for this argument. Basically, this interpretation of the doll studies rests on an inferential chain that has three links. First, it is assumed that the black and white dolls represent black people and white people to the children. Second, it is assumed that choosing the white doll implies a rejection of the black doll, and thus a rejection of black people. Third, it is inferred that this rejection of black people is associated with self-rejection.

One more recent study supports the third inference that underlies the reasoning for the doll studies. In this study it was found that blacks who had low self-esteem did tend to reject their own group, as indicated by more negative evaluations of blacks on a set of ten adjectives (Stephan & Rosenfield, 1979). There was no relationship between self-esteem and evaluations of the ingroup by whites or Mexican-Americans. The correlational nature of the results for blacks makes it impossible to determine whether it was the rejection of the ingroup that led to low self-esteem or the low self-esteem that led to ingroup rejection. However, in this study, and in the majority of studies employing questionnaire measures of the self-esteem of blacks and whites in segregated schools, blacks were not found to have lower self-esteem than whites (Edwards, 1974; Engle, 1948; Hodgkins & Stakenas, 1969; McDonald & Gynther, 1965; Powell & Fuller, 1970; Stephan & Kennedy, 1975; Stephan & Rosenfield, 1978, 1979). Only a few studies have found that segregated blacks have lower self-esteem than whites (Deutsch, 1960; Gerard & Miller, 1975; Williams & Byars, 1968). Thus, while there is some evidence to indicate that rejection of blacks is associated with self-rejection among blacks, the results of the studies using direct measures of self-esteem indicate that blacks are not generally lower than whites in self-esteem.

Racial Categorization in Children

The doll studies and other studies of identification and preference provide information on the development of racial categorization and ethnocentrism. Although the results vary somewhat from study to study, generally it has been found that racial classification begins to emerge as early as age three, and becomes reasonably well established about the time children enter school. For instance, Clark and Clark (1947) found that 77 percent of their white and black samples correctly responded to the request "Give me the doll that looks like a colored (white) person." For five-year-olds the percentage correct in both groups was 94 percent, and by seven years of age it was 100 percent. Using a procedure requiring 10 of 12 correct classifications, J. E. Williams and Morland (1976) report that only 16 percent of black three-year-olds and 23 percent of white three-year-olds correctly classified racial pictures, whereas 59 percent of black five-year-olds and 87 percent of white five-year-olds made correct classifications.

The development of evaluative preferences is thought to occur at a later age than the development of racial categories (Goodman, 1952). The actual data on racial preferences, particularly in relation to the development of ethnocentrism, are mixed. J. E. Williams and Morland (1976) concluded that "There is little relationship between degree of racial awareness and the children's affective response to Euro- and Afro-American persons" (p. 236). In a large sample of children, they reported that among those high in racial classification abilities, 67 percent of the blacks and 89 percent of the whites said they would prefer a white playmate. Among children low in racial classification abilities, 59 percent of the blacks and 75 percent of the whites said they would prefer a white playmate. The similarity of the percentages for children who were high and low in racial classification abilities suggests that racial preference is independent of classification abilities. These results also suggest that whites are ethnocentric, but that blacks tend to prefer whites over blacks.

Other studies show some indications of ethnocentrism in both groups. In a summary of 10 studies dealing with willingness to play with ingroup and outgroup members, J. E. Williams and Morland (1976) report a greater willingness among young school-age children to play with ingroup members than outgroup members. Preschool children in these studies showed no differences in willingness to play with ingroup and outgroup members. These studies indicate that ethnocentric tendencies, like categorization abilities, start to emerge in the early school years for blacks as well as whites. A series of studies using a measure of racial preference points to the existence of a developmental trend toward ethnocentrism among blacks. In one study of preferences between blacks and whites, only 30 percent of preschool black children preferred blacks over whites, but among children of school age, 58 percent preferred blacks (J. E. Williams & Morland, 1976, p. 177). Results of three studies using the doll technique are consistent with the notion that there are developmental trends toward ethnocentrism among both blacks and whites. Ethnocentrism emerged only after children entered school, and in these studies there was less ethnocentrism among blacks than whites in the early school years (Greenwald & Oppenheim, 1968; Gregor & McPherson, 1966; Fox & Jordan, 1973). Several studies have found that by the fifth grade, both blacks and whites have ethnocentric attitudes and are ethnocentric in their behavior (Stephan & Rosenfield, 1978; 1979).

Taken together, these studies point to several conclusions. First, whites show evidence of ethnocentrism earlier than blacks, but both groups are ethnocentric within a year or two after entering school. Second, these racial preferences are not closely tied to racial classification abilities, which suggests that there are two different processes involved. In these studies the finding that is most difficult to understand is the lack of ethnocentrism among preschool blacks. J. E. Williams and Morland (1976) argue that children of both groups evaluate the color white positively and the color black negatively, in accordance with transcultural symbolism denoting white as good and black as bad. These culturally acquired evaluations of colors are then associated with light-skinned and dark-skinned people. For blacks ethnocentrism does not begin to counteract this more basic learned symbolism until the early school years.

It would appear that the clear developmental sequence outlined by theorists such as Goodman (1952) does not exist. The results of the studies reported here do not support the existence of a transition from awareness of ethnic categories, through the development of evaluations of ethnic groups, to the emergence of integrated ethnic attitudes. Instead, children appear to be simultaneously exposed to various parallel inputs regarding race and ethnicity (P. A. Katz, 1976). They acquire information about cultural stereotypes at an early age, primarily from their families, other socializing agents, and television. This information, while necessarily applying to specific groups, is available to children before, during, and after they acquire the ability to distinguish between groups.

Thus, information about the characteristic features of different groups can be acquired before or after the child becomes adept at using the defining features to distinguish between groups. The acquisition of information about the defining and characteristic features of groups may initially be independent of evaluative reactions and preferences for racial and ethnic groups. The norm of ethnocentrism begins to emerge in the early school years, and eventually results in a loose consistency among the cognitive, affective, and behavioral components of racial and ethnic attitudes. One reason that the correlations among these components of racial and ethnic attitudes is not extremely high, even in adulthood, may be that they are independently acquired during childhood.

NEGATIVE EFFECTS OF STEREOTYPING

The preceding discussion has been an analysis of the functions and origins of stereotypes. We have attempted to present stereotypes in a value-free manner because we feel that it facilitates a basic understanding of why they exist. However, even in this discussion we have referred to negative effects of stereotyping, such as projection, scapegoating, and genocide. In this section we would like to discuss some additional negative consequences of stereotyping for intergroup interactions. First, we will explore the effects of stereotypes on behavioral intentions toward outgroup members. Next, we will consider the consequences of treating individuals in terms of their membership in specific groups. This discussion will conclude with a consideration of the problems caused by behavioral expectancies that are based on stereotypes.

Assumed Dissimilarity

Stereotypes give ingroup members the impression that they possess considerable information about the traits of outgroup members. While there may be some overlap in the traits ascribed to the ingroup and the outgroup, there are likely to be more differences than similarities due to the operation of ethnocentric biases, assimilation and contrast, projection, and scapegoating. These presumed dissimilarities may lead to or reinforce negative attitudes and behavior toward the outgroup (Byrne & Wong, 1962). In the area of race relations, various types of similarity, such as similarity of general beliefs, similarity of beliefs concerning race-related issues, and similarity of personality traits, have been compared with similarity of race as determinants of behavioral intentions.

In experimental studies of these factors, usually only one type of belief similarity is contrasted with race as a determinant of behavioral intentions. This has given rise to the race-versus-belief similarity controversy, in which it has been argued that one factor or the other is more important. The major problem with conceptualizing the issue in this way is that race affects behavioral intentions primarily because it leads people to perceive that they differ from outgroup members. Thus, race-versus-belief is a false dichotomy, since race differences are already associated with assumed differences in personality traits and beliefs. The question that is actually being examined in such studies is whether the particular beliefs or traits being manipulated are more important than the dissimilarities that are associated with racial differences.

A careful consideration of ecological validity (or the degree to which the findings can be generalized to nonresearch contexts) is absent from most of these studies. It may be the case that when we know beforehand that we share many beliefs or many personality characteristics with another individual, his or her group membership is of diminished importance as a consideration in our decisions regarding whether to interact with this person. But we rarely have this kind of detailed information on the beliefs and traits of strangers. What we do know immediately is information concerning many of the defining features of groups. Age, sex, race, accent, dress style, and nonverbal behavior patterns are transmitted even in the absence of information concerning beliefs and specific personality traits. In fact, there is some evidence to suggest that in forming first impressions, a person's traits, as displayed in behavior, will be discounted in favor of the information carried by the characteristic features associated with membership in stereotyped groups (Taylor & Gardner, 1969).

Research varying different types of similarity in a questionnaire format suggests that when similarity information is available, personality similarity is the most important determinant of behavioral intentions, race is next, and belief similarity is least important (Goldstein & Davis, 1972; Davis & Goldstein, 1974). Race becomes more important, relative to other types of similarity information, as the intimacy of the interaction situation increases. Thus, race is a more important determinant of behavioral intentions regarding dating partners than of work partners. A study by Johnson (1979) has provided information on the crucial link between behavioral intentions in interracial settings and actual behavior. The behavior studied was racial discrimination by managers of apartments. Johnson found that behavioral intentions and beliefs concerning the norms for renting to a black were the best predictors of actual discrimination. This study is useful because it documents the fact that behavioral intentions are related to interracial behavior (the correlation was .43). Thus, one reason that it is important to study the causes of behavioral intentions is that they ultimately contribute to discriminatory behavior.

Although the majority of studies on the race-versus-belief issue have been concerned only with behavioral intentions, several studies have examined behavior with actual consequences. One of these studies found that belief similarity was a more important determinant of choice of work partners than was race (Rokeach & Mezei, 1966), and a second found that belief similarity was more important than race in choice of college roommates (Silverman, 1974). The Silverman study also found that race was a more important determinant of choice of roommates when the students thought they were choosing their actual roommates than when they thought their choices were purely hypothetical. This supports the idea that race is a major determinant of behavior when the consequences of the behavior are important.

Considered in their entirety, the 20 or so studies in this area do not yield clear conclusions. There appear to be various reasons for this confusion. As Silverman (1974) has shown, behavioral intentions are affected by perceived social pressure, a factor that has not usually been included in these studies, but that may have influenced the subjects' choices differentially, depending on the experimental context in which the choice was made and the type of situations for which the subjects were making choices. Also, the particular traits and beliefs employed vary widely from study to study. This makes it difficult to compare across studies because it is impossible to determine how central or important the traits or beliefs are to the subjects. If the manipulations involve unimportant traits or beliefs, then race may emerge as a major determinant of choice; but when the traits or beliefs are important, similarity on these factors may supersede racial similarity as a determinant of choice.

To summarize briefly, in interaction with strangers, it is likely that people use whatever information is available to them in determining their behavioral intentions. This information almost always includes group membership and the norms governing behavior in the settings in which the interaction occurs. In some cases it also includes information on the beliefs and personality of the other person. Stereotypes generally lead ingroup members to perceive that outgroup members possess a number of negatively evaluated personality traits, and to believe that they are very different from ingroup members. These assumed dissimilarities are likely to lead to negative attitudes toward outgroups and to a reluctance to interact with outgroup members unless they are counterbalanced by information on similarity or situational norms favoring interracial interaction.

The conceptual model underlying our analysis is similar to a general model of behavioral intentions proposed by Fishbein and Ajzen (1975). Our model specifies three types of factors that may influence behavioral intentions. They are diagramed in Figure 3.1. One factor consists of the information the ingroup member possesses about the outgroup member, including the various types of similarity information. The second factor refers to the attitudes, stereotypes, and personality traits of the ingroup member. The third factor concerns aspects of the situation, especially the norms for conduct in that situation and pressures that may exist, due to the presence of others, to behave in certain ways.

Overgeneralization

One of the most unfortunate aspects of stereotypes is that the characteristic features are viewed as being possessed by many members of the stereotyped group. This overgeneralization of the characteristic features of stereotypes can be traced to assimilation and contrast effects, lack of exposure to real differences among outgroup members, and to the functional value of stereotypes in reducing the complexity of the social environment. Evidence for the operation of overgeneralization has been obtained by

FIGURE 3.1

Factors Influencing Behavioral Intentions

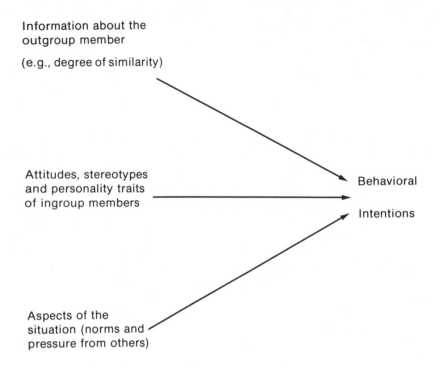

Secord (1959), who systematically varied the defining features of a group of blacks by selecting stimuli that differed along a continuum of negroidness. When subjects were asked to rate the photographs on characteristic features of the black stereotype, the same set of characteristic features was assigned to any stimulus person who was categorized as a black.

Thus, the same stereotyped traits were attributed to all of the members of the stereotyped group included in the study. The stereotyped traits assigned to a given group may actually characterize the group in general, or they may be distorted perceptions. Regardless of their validity, overgeneralization is a problem because it means that individuals are treated as group members who possess a given set of traits rather than as individuals to be judged on their own merits.

Expectancy Confirmation

Another problem created by stereotyping is that the characteristic features of the stereotype set up expectancies for behavior. These expectancies have two potentially negative effects. First, they influence the behavior of the ingroup member, and second, they influence how the behavior of outgroup members will be interpreted. An experiment by Duncan (1976) is a classic illustration. He asked people to observe a videotape of a discussion between two subjects (experimenter assistants). The discussion evolved into a heated argument, with one of the subjects mildly shoving the other. Duncan varied the race of the discussants (both black or white, or one black and the other white). Observers were asked to code the behavior and to attribute causality to the act of shoving. When a black shoved a white, 75 percent of the observers (who were white) labeled it as violent; when a black shoved a black, 69 percent termed it as violent. However, when a white shoved a black, only 17 percent coded the act as violent; when a white shoved a white, only 13 percent saw the act as violent. Thus when whites were in the role of transgressor, the act was interpreted more leniently—as playing around, dramatizing, or being aggressive. The term *violent*, as distinct from and more deprecatory than aggression, was far more readily applied to the same act when the actor was black. Less than 10 percent of observers saw a black's act of shoving as playing around or dramatizing. Furthermore, when the act was committed by a black, the observers attributed causality more to the person than to the situation. When the act was performed by a white, attributions were higher for situational than for personal causality. The essential features of this experiment have been replicated by Sagar and Schofield (1980), who found in white *and black* children the same tendency to interpret ambiguously aggressive acts as more mean and threatening when committed by a black than when committed by a white actor.

Perhaps the best-known demonstration of the effect of expectancies on behavior is a study by Rosenthal and Jacobson (1968). In this study teachers were led to believe, on the basis of bogus test results, that some of their students would "bloom" intellectually during the school year. The results indicated that the randomly chosen students who were expected to "bloom" actually showed significant increases on IQ tests at the end of the school year.

Subsequent research has indicated that these expectancy effects are mediated by four factors. The first mediator is classroom climate, especially teacher warmth as expressed in smiling, head nodding, and eye contact. The second mediator is teacher input, which refers to the fact that teachers may try to teach more material and more difficult material to students whom they expect to do well. The third mediator, the output factor, concerns the fact that teachers encourage greater responsiveness from students who are expected to do well. The final mediator, teacher feedback, refers to the finding that teachers give clearer and more consistent feedback to high-ability students than to low-ability students (Taylor, 1979). A study confirming the existence of these consequences of expectancies in the treatment of white and black students was done by Rubovits and Maehr (1973). This research suggests that expectancies can have a wide range of effects on the behavior of the people holding them.

Word, Zanna, and Cooper (1974) have explored the operation of the expectancy confirmation effect in an interracial situation. In the first of their two studies, white subjects interviewed white and black confederates as potential teammates for a competitive decision-making task. The subjects' nonverbal behavior during these interviews was then examined. It was found that the interviewers displayed more immediacy toward the white than toward the black confederate, as indicated by their sitting closer, talking longer, and making fewer speech errors.

In a second study Word et al. attempted to determine whether these differences in an interviewer's behavior would affect the behavior of interviewees. In this study the interviewer was a confederate who displayed the same high or low immediacy behaviors shown by the subjects who served as interviewers in the first study. The low-immediacy behavior of the interviewer (confederate) in the second study was reciprocated by the subjects who were interviewed, as indicated by more speech errors, less forward body lean and eye contact, a less direct angle of shoulder orientation, and a preference for sitting further from the interviewer. Independent judges also rated the subjects' performances as being less adequate in the low-immediacy condition. In addition, subjects in the low-immediacy condition liked the interviewer less than subjects in the high-immediacy condition.

This study, then, puts all of the components of the expectancy confirmation effect together. If whites hold negative attitudes toward blacks and this affects their behavior, their negative behavioral responses will lead the blacks to dislike them and to a reciprocation of these negative behaviors on the part of the blacks with whom the whites are interacting. This negative response by the blacks will, in turn, lead to a negative evaluation of the blacks by the whites, thus confirming their original negative attitudes. Further research employing the physical attractiveness stereotype has confirmed this sequence of events (Snyder, Tanke, & Berscheid, 1977).

When applied to stereotypes, this line of research suggests that group labels set up expectancies that modify behavior toward outgroup members, and consequently affect the behavior of outgroup members in a way that leads them to confirm the expectancies (cf. Snyder & Swann, 1978). Schofield (in press) cited an example of the self-confirming effects of expectancies in a recently desegregated school. In this school whites had a stereotyped view of blacks as aggressive.

> Many [of the white students] are so afraid of blacks that they do not stand up for themselves even in very unthreatening encounters. This lack of willingness to assert themselves and to protect their own rights when interacting with blacks makes whites attractive targets [for harassment by blacks] since their behavior also reinforces attempts to dominate them. (p. 40)

Thus, the whites' expectancy that blacks would behave aggressively led the whites to engage in behavior that made the prophecy come true.

Even when the expectancies are not fulfilled in outgroup behavior, they still can influence interpretation of outgroup behavior. The reason is that people tend to see behavior that confirms their expectancies even when it is absent (Cooper & Fazio, 1979). Another example from Schofield's study illustrates this process. Blacks viewed whites in this school as prejudiced and conceited. Whites viewed themselves as unprejudiced, and occasionally extended offers of help to black students:

> Black students often see such offers of help as yet another indication of white feelings of superiority and conceit. White students who do not perceive themselves as conceited feel mystified and angry when what to them seem to be friendly and helpful overtures are rejected. (p. 37)

In this example the blacks perceived the whites' behavior as confirming their stereotype even though the white students' intentions were just the opposite. Because so many characteristic features of outgroup stereotypes are negative, the behaviors to which they lead on the part of ingroup and outgroup members are unlikely to promote positive interactions.

Another bias in the interpretation of outgroup behavior occurs when behavior that is inconsistent with expectancies is attributed to external factors (Regan, Straus, & Fazio, 1974; Hayden & Mischel, 1976; Rosenfield & Stephan, 1977). In addition, when stereotypes set up expectations for behavior, disconfirming evidence tends to be ignored but confirming evidence tends to be remembered (Rothbart, Evans, & Fulero, 1979). This may be one of the reasons that stereotypes typically change at such a glacial rate. In the realm of individual behavior, it means that outgroup members will have considerable difficulty being viewed in nonstereotyped ways.

Stereotypes set up expectancies that may be confirmed because of the effects of the expectancies on the behavior of ingroup and outgroup members, or the expectancies may be perceived as having been confirmed even when they have not been. In both cases people probably feel secure in attributing the stereotyped trait to the other person. This circular attribution process is completed when the group label that generated the original expectancy is used as the ultimate explanation of the behavior of the outgroup member. For instance, if a white person is expected to, and does, act in an exploitative manner, then the explanation will be that he or she behaved that way because he or she is white. Thus, both group labels and the characteristic features of stereotypes furnish causal explanations for behavior.

The process we have just described may be presented as a sequence of events. (See Figure 3.2.) When an ingroup member identifies another person as an outgroup member, this identification elicits the associated stereotype. The stereotype leads the ingroup member to expect given behaviors and to

FIGURE 3.2

Stereotypes as Predictions and Explanations of Behavior

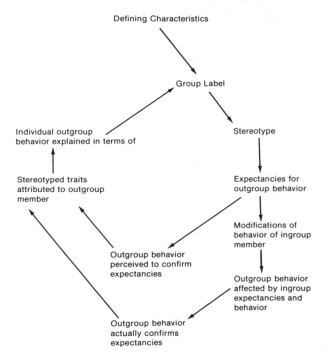

behave in such a way as to increase the chances that the outgroup member will fulfill his or her expectancies. Regardless of how the outgroup member actually behaves, the ingroup member tends to perceive that outgroup member as having acted in accordance with his or her expectancies. Next, the behavior is attributed to personality traits that are consistent with the stereotype. And finally, the stereotype leads to perception of the behavior as being inherent in membership in a given group.

THE ELIMINATION OF ETHNIC STEREOTYPES

Interethnic Contact—No Simple Panacea

If asked, most people would probably say that the solution to the problems created by stereotyping is simply to encourage contact between ethnic groups. This idea was behind the social scientists' hopes that school desegregation would put an end to interethnic hostility in American society. Unfortunately, simple desegregation in the schools has done little to solve these problems. A review of 18 studies of the effects of school desegregation on prejudice indicates that desegregation has increased interethnic hostility more often than it has decreased it (Stephan, 1978). Similar results have been found by Amir, Sharon, Bizman, Rivner, and Ben-Ari (1978) in a study of the intergroup attitudes of Middle Eastern and Western Jews in Israel. These findings indicate that simple contact is not sufficient to counteract the deeply ingrained stereotypes that many people possess.

For years social scientists have discussed the conditions that must be met if intergroup contact is to succeed in destroying negative stereotypes (Allport, 1954; Cook, 1957; Amir, 1969). First the contact between the groups should be intimate and varied, rather than superficial or merely frequent. Only when there is close contact can people find out that many of the assumed dissimilarities between the groups are unfounded. Second, the contact should involve people who are of approximately equal status. When status is unequal, contact may reinforce preexisting stereotypes. For example, contact between whites and enslaved blacks in the South prior to the Civil War did not eliminate the whites' stereotypes, partially because it tended to confirm the whites' stereotypes rather than to contradict them. Third, the contact should be cooperative, since competition increases interpersonal antagonism and independence does little to reduce hostility (Sherif et al., 1961). Fourth, relevant authority figures must lend their support to the interethnic contact if it is to be successful. For instance, when public officials, such as those in Boston during the period from 1966 to 1975, indicate that if desegregation causes enough problems, there is hope of returning to segregation, they encourage those who are opposed to desegregation to create problems.

School Desegregation

One way to illustrate the importance of these conditions is to discuss one contact situation in detail. The example we will discuss is the intergroup contact that occurs in desegregated schools. The reason for choosing this as our example is that school desegregation has been more extensively studied than any other contact situation. Many desegregation plans are initiated under circumstances that do not fulfill the conditions for reducing stereotyping and prejudice. Intergroup contact in desegregated schools is often minimized because of resegregation that takes place within the school. The assignment of students to different "tracks" based on test scores leads to the separation of blacks and whites when the two groups differ in test scores. In addition, considerable segregation occurs in desegregated schools due to ethnocentric choices in the selection of friends and the existence of ingroup friendship cliques (Gottlieb & Ten Houten, 1965; Schofield, in press; Schofield & Sagar, 1977).

The intergroup contact that does occur in desegregated schools is usually not between students who are equal in status. The primary reason is that lower-class blacks, who are lower in academic achievement than whites, are often placed in desegregated schools with middle-class whites (Coleman et al., 1966). This type of desegregation tends to reinforce status differentials that exist outside the school. Differences in social class and academic achievement create another problem in desegregated schools. Two studies have found that the greater the differences between minority groups and whites on social class and academic achievement, the greater the tendency for whites to avoid establishing friendships with members of these minority groups (St. John & Lewis, 1976; Rosenfield, Sheehan, Marcus, & Stephan, 1981). Thus, status differences between blacks and whites not only prevent equal status contact from becoming a reality in many desegregated schools, but they also limit the amount of interethnic contact that occurs in these schools.

An additional problem that exists in the vast majority of desegregated schools is that most classrooms are structured in such a way that competition among students is encouraged, but cooperation is not. In traditional classrooms students compete for the teacher's attention and social leadership, as well as for grades. Finally, opposition to school desegregation by school boards, community leaders, school administrators, teachers, and parents often means that there is little support from authority figures for the contact occurring between whites and blacks in desegregated schools.

Cooperative Learning Groups

In the 1970s considerable research was conducted in an attempt to examine the conditions under which intergroup contact in desegregated schools can promote better relations between groups. Research on cooperative learning experiences indicates that it is possible to undermine intergroup hostilities in the classroom (Blaney, Stephan, Rosenfield, Aronson, & Sikes, 1977; Cohen, 1980; DeVries, Edwards, & Slavin, 1978; Slavin, 1977; Weigel, Wiser, & Cook, 1975). One example of these techniques is the "interdependent classroom" (Aronson & Osherow, 1980; Blaney et al., 1977). In this technique each class is broken down into small, interethnic groups. Each group member is given one portion of the material to be covered. This member then teaches the material, which no other member has seen, to the rest of the students in the group. The students are later tested individually over the material learned in the cooperative groups.

In all of the cooperative techniques, the possibility of informal contact is greater than in traditional classrooms. Typically these techniques are introduced with the enthusiastic support of teachers and administrators. The results show various effects suggesting that these techniques can reduce stereotyping. Cross-ethnic helping and friendship increase under these conditions (Weigel, Wiser, & Cook, 1975; DeVries & Slavin, 1974; DeVries et al., 1978; Slavin, 1977). The students like other students and school more as a result of participating in the cooperative groups (Blaney et al., 1977), and their ability to empathize with other students increases (Bridgeman, 1977). These effects appear to occur without losses in academic achievement (Lucker, Rosenfield, Aronson, & Sikes, 1977).

Various influences converge to cause the generally positive outcomes that result from participation in cooperative groups. Worchel (1979) has suggested that one of the principal mechanisms by which cooperation influences intergroup relations is through reducing the salience of intergroup distinctions. Experience with members of other ethnic groups in cooperative interactions may negate stereotype-based expectancies by repeatedly providing contradictory evidence. Also, as Katz (1976) has argued, simply being able to differentiate between outgroup members destroys some of the "we-they" distinctions that ingroup members make, and reduces the tendency to generalize negative characteristics to all of the members of the group. Thus, varied experiences with different members of the outgroup should increase the complexity of one's perceptions of the outgroup and undermine any belief that most members of the outgroup fit one stereotype.

One issue that must be dealt with in cooperative groups is the problem of status inequalities within the group. As noted previously, blacks and whites often enter desegregated schools unequal with respect to social class and academic skills. Do these status inequalities affect the outcomes of cooperative learning? There are two reasons for believing that they do. The first is that instead of counteracting negative stereotype-based expectancies, status inequalities may reinforce stereotypes. Second, some studies suggest that when the work of another group member hinders an individual's performance, that group member will be disliked (Rosenfield, Stephan, & Lucker, 1980; Rosenfield & Roberts, 1980).

This outcome could occur in many forms of cooperative learning. For example, if a student does not do an effective job of teaching his or her material to the other members of the group, then the other members may become hostile because the incompetence of this group member may cause them to receive lower grades. Indeed, Rosenfield, Stephan, and Lucker (1979) found that in the interdependent classroom, low-competence group members were increasingly disliked over the course of a six-week cooperative learning experience, whereas low-competence students in traditional competitive classrooms were not increasingly disliked. Cooperative experiences like the interdependent classroom are likely to be most successful when group members cooperate on tasks on which they have approximately equal skills, or when they cooperate on tasks that will not be critically evaluated.

In some cooperative techniques the poor students are unlikely to hinder the outcomes of the better students. In Teams-Games-Tournaments (TGT) and Student Teams Achievement Divisions (STAD), poor students often can substantially aid the good students (DeVries et al., 1978; Slavin, 1977). TGT and STAD involve students studying together in multiethnic teams. Their performances on tests are not compared with the class as a whole, but with other students in their "achievement division." Thus, if poor students do better than the other students in their achievement division, they can help the grades of their group mates as much as the best students can.

One cooperative technique was designed explicitly to overcome status problems. This procedure was developed by Cohen (1980) and is based on expectation status theory (Berger, Canner, & Fisek, 1974). Expectation status theory suggests that people develop expectations about the competence of other people on the basis of diffuse status characteristics such as race and sex. The effects of status characteristics have been used to explain the finding that blacks in biracial groups make fewer proposals than whites, tend to accept the whites' suggestions uncritically, and display inhibition and subordination to the white group members (Berger, Cohen, & Zeldick, 1972). These results are obtained even when the blacks and the whites in the group are matched on intelligence. (It is interesting to note that these findings are consistent with predictions that would be made from our earlier discussion of the impact of stereotypes on self-fulfilling prophecies.)

Cohen suggests that the "interracial interaction disability" that results from diffuse status characteristics can be deactivated by specific status characteristics, such as competence on a task. However, it is not sufficient for the blacks merely to have competence equal to that of the whites. Rather, the competence of the blacks must be superior to that of the whites before interracial interaction disability can be overcome. Cohen and Roper (1972) were able to eliminate this disability when they pretrained blacks on a complex and highly technical mechanical task, and then had the blacks teach whites how to perform the task. Thus, it seems necessary to reverse the stereotype before blacks and whites can work together as equals in interracial groups.

Another factor that is important to the success of cooperative groups in desegregated schools is the outcome of the cooperative interaction. Outcomes can be based on at least three different criteria in settings where students work together in cooperative groups. The outcomes may be based on the total group effort or productivity, in which case the students are not only task-interdependent but goal-interdependent as well. This appears to have been the nature of the feedback in the cooperative technique developed by Weigel et al. (1975). Under these conditions success should lead to high ingroup cohesiveness. This cohesiveness could result from attributing the group's success to the skills of the group members (Streufert & Streufert, 1969) or from a generalization to other group members of the positive affect generated by success (Blanchard, Adelman, & Cook, 1975). At the same time, hostility toward other teams may be created by ingroup success because of the competitive relationships between teams and as a consequence of the ingroup's comparing favorably with other groups. Failure under these conditions could easily lead to low ingroup cohesion, if the cause of the failure is attributed to other group members, or to high outgroup hostility, if the cause is attributed to the other teams.

The second criterion that can be used to give feedback in cooperative groups is to give feedback to each member individually, regardless of the performance of the group. In this case the members are task-interdependent but goal-independent. This is the type of feedback given in the cooperative technique developed by Aronson and his colleagues (Aronson, Blaney, Stephan, Sikes, & Snapp, 1978). Under these conditions the positive affect generated by success should generalize to other group members, since they are responsible for teaching the individual most of what he or she has learned. Failure should have the opposite effect. Attitudes toward members of other teams should not be greatly influenced by the nature of the outcome.

The third feedback criterion is a mixture of team and individual outcome feedback. In this type of feedback, each individual's contribution to the group's level of productivity is charted, then added to the other members' productivity to arrive at a group total that is compared with the totals achieved by other groups. Successful outcomes under these circumstances may create hostility toward other groups and cohesion within groups, although the latter effect may be mitigated for individuals who are perceived to have contributed very little to the group's success. This could occur in TGT for students who do poorly with respect to their achievement division.

Failure would be likely to create low levels of ingroup cohesion and considerable outgroup hostility, depending on the attributions that are made for the causes of the failure. Thus, the outcome feedback provided in cooperative groups is likely to differentially affect interpersonal relations within and between teams, depending on the criteria that are employed in providing feedback. In general, it would appear to be desirable to provide success feedback under conditions where team competition is minimized. However, given the difficulty of ensuring success in academic settings, the outcome-feedback issue may pose major obstacles to the successful use of cooperative groups. One solution is to adopt a mastery approach to learning so that all students can potentially do well (Miller, 1980).

A third difficult issue associated with the use of cooperative groups in desegregated schools is the attitude of school personnel toward academic skills. In order to remove interracial interaction disability, Cohen (1980) suggests that the school atmosphere must stress that competence is multidimensional, and that most people are good at some things but less good at others. With this type of atmosphere, minority students are less likely to expect whites to be more competent than blacks on all dimensions, and hence whites are less likely to be allowed to dominate interracial groups. However, in classes where the teachers and students treat competence as if it were unidimensional, the minority students are more likely to allow whites to dominate interethnic groups. The reason is that the minority students will presume that the whites are more competent because whites are better at the single most important type of schoolwork outside the group.

The ethnic composition and curriculum of the school also play an important role in determining how blacks and whites will interact in desegregated schools. Cohen (1980) has noted that if the class and school reflect the traditional power structure of whites dominating blacks, it will be difficult to change stereotypes. Iadicola (1979) has found that white children are most likely to dominate minority students on collective tasks as the percentage of whites in the school increases, when there is a low percentage of minority teachers in the school, and when the school does not have a multicultural curriculum. The results of this study suggest that cooperative learning techniques may be most effective in eliminating interracial interaction disability and negative stereotypes when they are used in schools that support interracial contact.

Our discussion of the use of different types of cooperative learning groups points up some of the complex issues involved in reducing stereotyping, even in situations that would appear to be close to optimal. The history of race relations in American society, the powerful biases created by ethnocentrism, the functions served by stereotypes, and the effects of stereotyping on expectancies and behavior all operate to maintain stereotypes. The conditions required for the reduction of stereotyping can, with careful consideration, be created within the microcosm of the school, but they are much more difficult to create in other settings. If we are to move toward a pluralistic society in which invidious stereotyping is minimized, continued efforts toward equal rights in education, housing, and employment are essential. It is possible to create some of the conditions that lead to reductions in stereotyping even in situations where it is impossible to create all of them. The gains under these circumstances may not be large, but the losses incurred by maintaining the status quo are potentially much greater.

FUTURE DIRECTIONS FOR RESEARCH

We share with many researchers the belief that basic research and applied research are mutually beneficial. In the field of basic research, the cognitive emphasis that is emerging in social psychology shows great promise of making major contributions to our knowledge of the acquisition and nature of stereotypes. Much of the research we have covered can be understood within the context of the cognitive approach, although we have not always attempted to present it within this framework. For instance, the roles of outcomes, competence of group members, and intergroup relations in the mediation of the effects of cooperative groups reflect the operation of complex information processing related to forming impressions and encoding feedback. In a similar vein, assimilation and contrast, and ingroup-outgroup bias, are essentially cognitive in nature. Likewise, the crucial question of when race and ethnic categories are salient, and therefore likely to affect our expectancies and behavior, is primarily a problem in information processing.

Concepts that are currently being developed in cognitive psychology, such as schemata, scripts, prototypes, and various information-processing biases, offer a rich source of new insights into stereotyping. Further research into the acquisition, organization, and storage of information about racial and ethnic groups is needed to provide a more comprehensive understanding of how this information affects behavior. The knowledge obtained from basic research exploring these cognitive processes will almost certainly suggest new ways of attempting to modify racial and ethnic attitudes. But attempts to introduce changes based on this knowledge will just as surely suggest new questions for basic research.

SUMMARY

In this chapter stereotypes are defined as the sets of traits that are used to explain and predict the behavior of members of socially defined groups. A cognitive emphasis is given to stereotypes in an attempt to eliminate the highly evaluative nature of many discussions of stereotypes. The techniques for measuring stereotypes developed by D. Katz and Braly (1933), Brigham (1971a), McCauley and Stitt (1978), and Broverman et al. (1972) are reviewed and their relative merits are compared. Following this, the functions of stereotypes are analyzed. It is suggested that the labels given to racial and ethnic groups impose order on an otherwise chaotic social environment. The use of these labels is predicated on sets of criteria for defining membership in these groups. The labels are also associated with sets of traits thought to be characteristic of members of the group. These characteristic features of stereotypes are used to predict and explain the behavior of group members.

Stereotypes have their origins in the nature of the historical contacts between groups, in basic perceptual processes of categorization, and in the consequences of identification with the ingroup. The primary aspects of the historical contact between groups that leads to stereotyping are the institutionalized role relationships that exist between the groups, whether they are urban or rural residents, the types of jobs they perform (particularly whether they are manual laborers or businessmen), and the social class positions they occupy. The stereotypes of blacks and whites in America are used to illustrate these processes.

The basic categorization processes of assimilation and contrast operate to minimize the perceived differences within groups and to accentuate the differences perceived between groups. The tendency to identify with the groups to which one belongs and the universal propensity toward ethnocentrism in evaluating ingroup and outgroup behaviors contribute to the effects of assimilation and contrast. When differences are perceived to exist between groups, the traits of the outgroups tend to be negatively evaluated, whereas the traits of the ingroup tend to be positively evaluated. Ethnocentrism also influences the labeling of traits the groups are thought to share. Positive traits are used to describe ingroup behavior (such as loyalty), but negative traits are used to describe the same behavior in outgroup members (such as clannishness). In addition, the psychodynamic factors of projection and scapegoating contribute to the formation of stereotypes. Projection occurs when unfavorable traits in the ingroup are imputed to the outgroup (such as hostility). Scapegoating occurs when the outgroup is blamed for the problems of the ingroup.

Children acquire stereotypes through a set of parallel processes. They learn to categorize members of social groups beginning at about the age of three. Simultaneously they learn the traits that are imputed to the groups. Initially the acquisition of stereotypes appears to be relatively independent of preferences for different groups, but by the early elementary school years children become ethnocentric in both attitudes and behavior. While there appears to be some tendency for young black children to reject blacks, this tendency is typically reversed before the end of the elementary school years.

Stereotyping has various negative effects on interpersonal interaction. Because members of ethnic outgroups are assumed to differ from ingroup members on a number of dimensions, ingroup members may be reluctant to interact with them, and may have negative attitudes toward them. The overgeneralized nature of these assumed dissimilarities means that members of other groups typically will not be regarded as individuals, but instead will have the traits of the group attributed to them. The traits that are attributed to outgroup members set up expectancies for how they will behave. These expectancies affect the behavior of both the ingroup and the outgroup members in ways that increase the chances that the expectancy will be confirmed. However, even if an outgroup member's behavior does not confirm the expectancy, it is likely to be perceived as doing so. The actual or perceived confirmation of the expectancy leads to a firm attribution of the trait to the outgroup member, and ultimately this can lead to the inference that the outgroup member behaved this way because he or she is a member of the outgroup.

The elimination of stereotypes through intergroup contact is considered in the final section of the chapter. It is suggested that contact that is intimate, equal-status, cooperative, and sanctioned by authority promotes favorable relations between groups. The specific situation of school desegregation is analyzed as an illustrative case. The use of cooperative learning groups shows some promise of reducing stereotyping under certain conditions. It appears that in schools where the ethnic composition is not too imbalanced and intergroup relations are promoted, cooperative groups that experience success on tasks at which the minority group is initially superior to the majority group have the best chance of reducing stereotyping.

REFERENCES

Adam, B. D. Inferiorization and "self esteem." *Social Psychology*, 1978, *1*, 47–53.

Allport, G. W. *The nature of prejudice*. Reading, Mass.: Addison-Wesley, 1954.

Amir, Y. Contact hypothesis in ethnic relations. *Psychological Bulletin*, 1969, *71*, 319–342.

Amir, Y., Sharon, S., Bizman, A., Rivner, M., & Ben-Ari, R. Attitude change in desegregated Israeli high schools. *Journal of Educational Psychology*, 1978, *70*, 129–136.

Aronson, E., Blaney, N., Stephan, C., Sikes, J., & Snapp, M. *The jigsaw classroom*. Beverly Hills, Calif.: Sage, 1978.

Aronson, E., & Osherow, N. Cooperation, prosocial behavior, and academic performance: Experiments in the desegregated classroom. In L. Bickman (ed.), *Applied social psychology annual. Vol. 1*. Beverly Hills: Sage Publications, 1980. Pp. 163–196.

Asher, S., & Allen, V. Racial preference and social comparison processes. *Journal of Social Issues*, 1969, *25*, 157–166.

Banks, W. C. White preference in blacks: A paradigm in search of a phenomenon. *Psychological Bulletin*, 1976, *83*, 1179–1186.

Bayton, J. A. Racial stereotypes of Negro college students. *Journal of Abnormal and Social Psychology*, 1941, *36*, 97–102.

Bayton, J. A., McAlister, L. N., & Hamer, J. Race-class stereotypes. *Journal of Negro Education*, 1956, *41*, 76–78.

Berger, J., Canner, T. L., & Fisek, M. H. *Expectation states theory: A theoretical research program*. Cambridge, Mass.: Winthrop, 1974.

Berger, J., Cohen, B., & Zeldick, M. Status conceptions and social interactions. *American Sociological Review*, 1972, *37*, 241–255.

Billig, M. *Social psychology and intergroup relations*. London: Academic Press, 1976.

Billig, M., & Tajfel, H. Social categorization and similarity in intergroup behavior. *European Journal of Social Psychology*, 1973, *3*, 27–52.

Blanchard, F. A., Adelman, L., & Cook, S. W. The effect of group success and failure upon interpersonal attraction in cooperating interracial groups. *Journal of Personality and Social Psychology*, 1975, *31*, 1020–1030.

Blaney, N., Stephan, C., Rosenfield, D., Aronson, E., & Sikes, J. Interdependence in the classroom: A field study. *Journal of Educational Psychology*, 1977, *69*, 121–128.

Bourne, L. E., Jr. *Human conceptual behavior*. Boston: Allyn & Bacon, 1966.

Bourne, L. E., Jr. Knowing and using concepts. *Psychological Review*, 1970, *77*, 546–556.

Brewer, M. The role of ethnocentrism in intergroup conflict. In W. G. Austin and S. Worchel (eds.), *The social psychology of intergroup relations*. Monterey, Calif.: Brooks/Cole, 1979.

Bridgeman, D. L. The influence of cooperative interdependent learning on role-taking and moral reasoning: A theoretical and empirical field study with fifth grade students. Ph.D. dissertation, University of California at Santa Cruz, 1977.

Brigham, J. C. Ethnic Stereotypes. *Psychological Bulletin*, 1971a, *76*, 15–38.

Brigham, J. C. Racial stereotypes, attitudes, and evaluations of and behavioral intentions toward Negroes and whites. *Sociometry*, 1971b, *34*, 360–380.

Brigham, J. C. Ethnic stereotypes and attitudes: A different mode of analysis. *Journal of Personality*, 1973, *41*, 206–233.

Brigham, J. C. Views of black and white children concerning the distribution of personality characteristics. *Journal of Personality*, 1974, *42*, 144–158.

Brigham, J. C., Bloom, L. M., Gunn, S. P., & Torok, T. Attitude measurement via the bogus pipeline: A dry well? *Representative Research in Social Psychology*, 1974, *5*, 97–114.

Broverman, I. K., Vogel, S. R., Broverman, D., Clarkson, F. E., & Rosenkrantz, P. S. Sex-role stereotypes: Current appraisal. *Journal of Social Issues*, 1972, *28*, 59-78.

Bruner, J. S., & Taguiri, R. The perception of people. In G. Lindzey (ed.), *The handbook of social psychology*. Reading, Mass.: Addison-Wesley, 1954.

Byrne, D., & Wong, T. J. Racial prejudice, interpersonal attraction and assumed dissimilarity of attitudes. *Journal of Abnormal and Social Psychology*, 1962, *65*, 246–253.

Campbell, D. T. Stereotypes and the perception of group differences. *American Psychologist*, 1967, *22*, 817–829.

Cantor, N., & Mischel, W. Prototypicality and personality: Effects on free recall and personality impressions. *Journal of Research in Personality*, 1979, *13*, 187–205.

Clark, K. B., & Clark, M. P. Racial identification and preference in Negro children. In T. M. Newcomb & E. L. Hartley (eds.), *Readings in Social Psychology*. New York: Henry Holt, 1947.

Cohen, E. G. Design and redesign of the desegregated school: Problems of status, power, and conflict. In W. G. Stephan and J. R. Feagin (eds.), *Desegregation: Past, present and future*. New York: Plenum Press, 1980.

Cohen, E., & Roper, S. Modification of interracial interaction disability: An application of status characteristic theory. *American Sociological Review*, 1972, *37*, 643–657.

Coleman, J. S., Campbell, E. Q., Hobson, M., Mood, A. M., Weinfield, F. D., & York, R. L. *Equality of educational opportunity*. Washington, D.C.: U.S. Government Printing Office, 1966.

Cook, S. W. Desegregation: A psychological analysis. *The American Psychologist*, 1957, *12*, 1–13.

Cooper, J., & Fazio, R. H. The formation and persistence of attitudes that support intergroup conflict. In W. G. Austin and S. Worchel (eds.), *The social psychology of intergroup relations*. Monterey, Calif.: Brooks/Cole, 1979.

Davis, E. E., & Goldstein, M. Attributions of race, belief and personality characteristics as determinants of behavioral intentions. Paper presented at the American Psychological Association convention, New Orleans, 1974.

de Heusch, L. Massacres collectif au Rwanda? *Synthesis*, 1964, *19*, 416–426. Cited in L. Kuper, *The pity of it all*. Minneapolis: University of Minnesota Press, 1977.

Deutsch, M. Minority group and class status as related to social and personality factors in scholastic achievement. *Society for Applied Anthropology Monographs*, 1960, *2*.

DeVries, D. L., & Edwards, K. J. Student teams and learning games: Their effects on cross-race and cross-sex interaction. *Journal of Educational Psychology*, 1974, *66*, 741–749.

DeVries, D. L., Edwards, K. J., & Slavin, R. E. Biracial learning teams and race relations in the classroom: Four field experiments using Teams-Games-Tournament. *Journal of Educational Psychology*, 1978, *70*, 356–362.

Duncan, B. L. Differential social perception and attribution of intergroup violence: Testing the lower limits of stereotyping of blacks. *Journal of Personality and Social Psychology*, 1976, *34*, 590–598.

Edwards, D. W. Black versus white: When is race a relevant variable? *Journal of Personality and Social Psychology*, 1974, *29*, 39–49.

Engle, T. L. Personality adjustments of children belonging to two minority groups. *Journal of Educational Psychology*, 1948, *36*, 543–560.

Fishbein, M., & Ajzen, I. *Belief, attitude, intention and behavior: An introduction to theory and research.* Reading, Mass.: Addison-Wesley, 1975.

Fox, D. J., & Jordan, V. B. Racial preferences and identification of black, American Chinese, and white children. *Genetic Psychology Monographs*, 1973, *88*, 229–286.

Franklin, J. H. *From slavery to freedom: A history of Negro Americans.* New York: Knopf, 1974.

Gardner, R. C. Ethnic stereotypes: The traditional approach, a new look. *Canadian Psychologist*, 1973, *14*, 133–148.

Gardner, R. C., & Taylor, D. M. Ethnic stereotypes: Meaningfulness in ethnic group labels. *Canadian Journal of Behavioral Science*, 1969, *1*, 182–192.

Gerard, H. B., & Miller, N. *School desegregation: A long term study.* New York: Plenum Press, 1975.

Gilbert, G. M. Stereotype persistence and change among college students. *Journal of Abnormal and Social Psychology*, 1951, *46*, 245–254.

Goldstein, M., & Davis, E. E. Race and belief: A further analysis of the social determinants of behavioral intentions. *Journal of Personality and Social Psychology*, 1972, *22*, 346–355.

Goodman, M. E. *Race awareness in young children.* Cambridge, Mass.: Addison-Wesley, 1952.

Gottlieb, D., & Ten Houten, W. D. Racial composition and the social system of three high schools. *Journal of Marriage and the Family*, 1965, *27*, 204–212.

Greenberg, J., & Rosenfield, D. Whites' ethnocentrism and their attributions for the behavior of blacks. *Journal of Personality*, 1979, *47*, 643–657.

Greenwald, H., & Oppenheim, D. Reported magnitude of self-misidentification among Negro children—artifact? *Journal of Personality and Social Psychology*, 1968, *8*, 49–52.

Gregor, A. J., & McPherson, D. A. Racial attitudes among white and Negro children in a deep-south standard metropolitan area. *Journal of Social Psychology*, 1966, *68*, 95–106.

Hartsough, W. R., & Fontana, A. F. Persistence of ethnic stereotypes and the relative importance of positive and negative stereotyping for association preferences. *Psychological Reports*, 1970, *27*, 723–731.

Hayden, T., & Mischel, W. Maintaining trait consistency in the resolution of behavioral inconsistency: The wolf in sheep's clothing? *Journal of Personality*, 1976, *44*, 109–132.

Hodgkins, B. J., & Stakenas, R. G. A study of self-concepts of Negro and white youths in segregated environments. *Journal of Negro Education*, 1969, *38*, 370–377.

Hraba, J., & Grant, J. Black is beautiful: A re-examination of racial preference and identification. *Journal of Personality and Social Psychology*, 1970, *16*, 398–402.

Iadicola, P. Schooling and social power: A presentation of a Weberian conflict model of the school. Ph.D. dissertation, University of California at Riverside, 1979.

Jones, E. E., & Sigall, H. Where there is *ignis*, there may be fire. *Psychological Bulletin*, 1973, *79*, 260–262.

Johnson, D. A. Racial discrimination and attitude-behavior consistency. Unpublished manuscript, Interaction Research Corporation, Stanton, Calif., 1979.

Karlins, M., Coffman, T. L., & Walters, G. On the fading of social stereotypes: Studies in three generations of college students. *Journal of Personality and Social Psychology*, 1969, *13*, 1–16.

Katz, D., & Braly, K. Racial stereotypes in one hundred college students. *Journal of Abnormal and Social Psychology*, 1933, *28*, 280–290.

Katz, P. A. The acquisition of racial attitudes in children. In P. A. Katz (ed.), *Toward the elimination of racism*. New York: Pergamon, 1976. Pp. 125–156.

Kiesler, C. A., Collins, B. E., & Miller, N. *Attitude change: A critical analysis of theoretical approaches*. New York: Wiley, 1969.

Klineberg, O. Race and psychology: The problem of genetic differences. In L. Kuper (ed.), *Race, science and society* (rev. ed.). New York: Columbia University Press UNESCO, 1975.

Krantz, P. L., & Foley, L. A. Black stereotypes of whites. Paper presented at the Southeastern Psychological Association, New Orleans, 1976.

Kuper, L. *The pity of it all*. Minneapolis: University of Minnesota Press, 1977.

Lerner, R. M., & Knapp, J. R. The structure of racial attitudes in children. *Journal of Youth and Adolescence*, 1976, *5*, 283–300.

LeVine, R. A., & Campbell, D. T. *Ethnocentrism*. New York: John Wiley & Sons, 1972.

Lucker, G. W., Rosenfield, D., Aronson, E., & Sikes, J. Performance in the interdependent classroom. *American Educational Research Journal*, 1977, *13*, 115–123.

Mann, J. F., & Taylor, D. M. Attribution of causality: Role of ethnicity and social class. *Journal of Social Psychology*, 1974, *94*, 3–13.

McCauley, C., & Stitt, C. L. An individual and quantitative measure of stereotypes. *Journal of Personality and Social Psychology*, 1978, *36*, 929–940.

McCauley, C., Stitt, C. L., & Segal, M. Stereotyping: From prejudice to prediction. *Psychological Bulletin*, 1980, *87*, 195–208.

McDonald, R. L., & Gynther, M. D. Relationship of self and ideal-self descriptions with sex, race, and class in southern adolescents. *Journal of Personality and Social Psychology*, 1965, *1*, 85–88.

Miller, N. Making school desegregation work. In W. G. Stephan and J. R. Feagin (eds.), *School desegregation: Past, present, and future*. New York: Plenum Press, 1980.

Pettigrew, T. F. The ultimate attribution error: Extending Allport's cognitive analysis of prejudice. *Personality and Social Psychology Bulletin*, 1979, *5*, 461–476.

Powell, G. J., & Fuller, M. Self-concept and school desegregation. *Journal of Orthopsychiatry*, 1970, *40*, 303–304.

Regan, D. T., Straus, E., & Fazio, R. Liking and the attribution process. *Journal of Experimental Social Psychology*, 1974, *10*, 385–397.

Rokeach, M., & Mezei, L. Race and shared belief as factors in social choice. *Science*, 1966, *151*, 167–172.

Rosch, E. H. On the internal structure of perceptual and semantic categories. In T. E. Moore (ed.), *Cognitive development and the acquisition of language*. New York: Academic Press, 1973.

Rosenfield, D., & Roberts, W. R. The effects of success and failure upon liking for competent and incompetent members of cooperative and competitive groups. Unpublished manuscript, Southern Methodist University, 1979.

Rosenfield, D., Sheehan, D. S., Marcus, M., & Stephan, W. G. Classroom structure and prejudice in desegregated schools. *Journal of Educational Psychology*, 1981, *73*, 27–32.

Rosenfield, D., & Stephan, W. G. When discounting fails: An unexpected finding. *Memory and Cognition*, 1977, *5*, 97–102.

Rosenfield, D., Stephan, W. G., & Lucker, G. W. Attraction to competent and incompetent members of cooperative and competitive groups. Unpublished manuscript, Southern Methodist University, 1979.

Rosenthal, R., & Jacobson, L. *Pygmalion in the classroom*. New York: Holt, Rinehart, & Winston, 1968.

Rothbart, M., Evans, M., & Fulero, S. Recall for confirming events: Memory processes and the maintenance of social stereotypes. *Journal of Experimental Social Psychology*, 1979, *15*, 343–355.

Rubovits, P. C., & Maehr, M. L. Pygmalion black and white. *Journal of Personality and Social Psychology*, 1973, *25*, 210–218.

Sagar, H. A., & Schofield, J. W. Racial and behavioral cues in black and white children's perceptions of ambiguously aggressive acts. *Journal of Personality and Social Psychology*, 1980, *39*, 590–598.

Samuels, F. *Group images*. New Haven: College & University Press, 1973.

Schofield, J. W. Complementary and conflicting identities: Images and interaction in an interracial school. In S. Asher and J. Gottman (eds.), *The development of friendship: Description and intervention*. Cambridge: Cambridge University Press, in press.

Schofield, J. W., & Sagar, H. A. Peer interaction patterns in an integrated middle school. *Sociometry*, 1977, *40*, 130–138.

Secord, P. F. Stereotyping and favorableness in the perception of Negro faces. *Journal of Abnormal and Social Psychology*, 1959, *59*, 309–314.

Sherif, M., Harvey, O. J., White, B. J., Hood, W. E., & Sherif, C. W. *Intergroup conflict and cooperation: The Robber's Cave experiment*. Norman: University of Oklahoma Book Exchange, 1961.

Sigall, H., & Page, R. Current stereotypes: A little fading, a little faking. *Journal of Personality and Social Psychology*, 1971, *18*, 247–255.

Silverman, B. I. Consequences, racial discrimination, and the principle of belief congruence. *Journal of Personality and Social Psychology*, 1974, *29*, 497–508.

Slavin, R. E. Effects of biracial learning teams on cross-racial friendship and interaction. Unpublished manuscript, Johns Hopkins University, 1977. (Report no. 240, Center for the Social Organization of Schools.)

Smedley, J. W., & Bayton, J. A. Evaluative race-class stereotypes by race and perceived class of subjects. *Journal of Personality and Social Psychology*, 1978, *36*, 530–535.

Smith, E. E., Shoben, E. J., & Rips, L. J. Structure and processes in semantic memory: A featural model for semantic decisions. *Psychological Review*, 1974, *81*, 214–241.

Snyder, M., & Swann, W. B., Jr. Hypothesis testing processes in social interaction. *Journal of Personality and Social Psychology*, 1978, *36*, 1202–1212.

Snyder, M., Tanke, E. D., & Berscheid, E. Social perception and interpersonal behavior: On the self-fulfilling nature of social stereotypes. *Journal of Personality and Social Psychology*, 1977, *35*, 656–666.

Stephan, W. G. Stereotyping: The role of ingroup-outgroup differences in causal attribution. *Journal of Social Psychology*, 1977, *101*, 255–266.

Stephan, W. G. School desegregation: An evaluation of prediction made in *Brown v. the Board of Education*. *Psychological Bulletin*, 1978, *85*, 217–238.

Stephan, W. G., & Kennedy, J. C. An experimental study of inter-ethnic competition in segregated schools. *Journal of School Psychology*, 1975, *13*, 234–247.

Stephan, W. G., & Rosenfield, D. Black self-rejection: Another look. *Journal of Educational Psychology*, 1979, *71*, 708–716.

Stephan, W. G., & Rosenfield, D. Effects of desegregation on race relations and self-esteem. *Journal of Educational Psychology*, 1978, *70*, 670–679.

St. John, N. H., & Lewis, R. G. Race and the social structure of the elementary classroom. *Sociology of Education*, 1976, *48*, 346–368.

Streufert, S., & Streufert, S. C. Effects of conceptual structure, failure, and success on attribution of causality and interpersonal attitudes. *Journal of Personality and Social Psychology*, 1969, *11*, 138–147.

Sumner, W. G. *Folkway*. New York: Ginn, 1906.

Tajfel, H. Social and cultural factors in perception. In G. Lindzey & E. Aronson (eds.), *The handbook of social psychology* (2nd ed.). Reading, Mass.: Addison-Wesley, 1969.

Tajfel, H. Experiments in intergroup discrimination. *Scientific American*, 1970, *223*, 96–102.

Tajfel, H., & Billig, M. Familiarity and categorization in intergroup behavior. *Journal of Experimental Social Psychology*, 1974, *10*, 159–170.

Tajfel, H., Sheikh, A. A., & Gardner, R. C. Content of stereotypes and the inference of similarity between members of stereotyped groups. *Acta Psychologica*, 1964, *22*, 191–201.

Taylor, D. M., & Gardner, R. C. Ethnic stereotypes: Their effects on the perception of communicators of varying credibility. *Canadian Journal of Psychology*, 1969, *23*, 161–173.

Taylor, M. C. Race, sex, and the expression of self-fulfilling prophecies in a laboratory teaching situation. *Journal of Personality and Social Psychology*, 1979, *37*, 897–912.

Thompson, E. T. *Plantation societies, race relations, and the South: The regimentation of populations*. Durham, N.C.: Duke University Press, 1975.

Thompson, G., Stephan, W. G., & Schvaneveldt, R. The organization of stereotypes in semantic memory. Paper presented at Southwestern Psychological Association, Oklahoma City, 1980.

Vinacke, W. E. Stereotypes as social concepts. *Journal of Social Psychology*, 1957, *46*, 229–243.

Weigel, R. H., Wiser, P. L., & Cook, S. W. The impact of cooperative learning experiences on cross-ethnic relations and helping. *Journal of Social Issues*, 1975, *31*, 219–244.

Weinberg, M. *A chance to learn.* Cambridge: Cambridge University Press, 1977.

Williams, J. E., Best, D. L., & Boswell, D. A. The measurement of children's racial attitudes in the early school years. *Child Development,* 1975, *46,* 494–500.

Williams, J. E., & Morland, K. J. *Race, color and the young child.* Chapel Hill: University of North Carolina Press, 1976.

Williams, R. L., & Byars, H. Negro self-esteem in a transitional society: Tennessee self-concept scale. *Personnel and Guidance Journal,* 1968, *47,* 120–125.

Worchel, S. Cooperation and the reduction of intergroup conflict: Some determining factors. In W. G. Austin and S. Worchel (eds.), *The social psychology of intergroup relations.* Monterey, Calif.: Brooks/Cole, 1979.

Word, C. O., Zanna, M. P., & Cooper, J. The nonverbal mediation of self-fulfilling prophecies in interracial interaction. *Journal of Experimental Social Psychology,* 1974, *10,* 102–120.

ADDITIONAL READINGS

Austin, W. G., & Worchel, S. (eds.). *The social psychology of intergroup relations.* Monterey, Calif.: Brooks/Cole, 1979.
This book is a compilation of 21 articles, the majority of them written specifically for it, on intergroup relations. Most articles are high-level theoretical and empirical reviews of literature on specific approaches to intergroup relations, and are written by acknowledged experts in the area.

Bagley, C., & Verma, G. K. *Racial prejudice, the individual, and society.* Bagley, C., Verma, G. K., Mallick, K., & Young, L. *Personality, self-esteem, and prejudice.* (two volumes). Westmead, England: Saxon House, 1979.
A comprehensive analysis of prejudice in Britain. Included in this work are research findings from the perspectives of personality, social systems, and culture. The study of prejudice in a culture other than America will be instructive for American readers.

Billig, M. *Social psychology and intergroup relations.* London: Academic Press, 1976.
Billig reviews theories of intergroup relations with a special emphasis on the social categorization approach. His analysis is broader than that of most American social psychologists, and includes extensive discussion of ideology and political movements.

Franklin, J. H. *From slavery to freedom* (4th ed.). New York: Alfred A. Knopf, 1974.
A classical analysis of the history of blacks in America.

LeVine, R. A., & Campbell, D. T. *Ethnocentrism,* New York: John Wiley & Sons, 1972.
A comprehensive review of theories concerning the origins and effects of ethnocentrism. The authors discuss the following theories: realistic group conflict, social-structural, reference group, evolutionary, frustration-aggression, psychoanalytic, attribution cognitive congruity, and reinforcement.

Stephan, W. G., & Feagin, J. R. *School desegregation: Past, present and future*. New York: Plenum Press, 1980.
A look at the *Brown* decision and its effects 25 years afterward. Includes analyses of school desegregation by lawyers, sociologists, political scientists, psychologists, and educators.

Williams, J. E., & Morland, J. K. *Race, color and the young child*. Chapel Hill: University of North Carolina Press, 1976.
The authors critically analyze 40 years of research on racial attitudes and their development in children. They chart race differences and trends in preference and identification.

4

ANTI-SEMITISM AND
STEREOTYPING

Robert Wuthnow

In the years during and immediately following Hitler's dictatorship in Europe, the problem of anti-Semitism seemed both obvious and important to students of human behavior. Today other problems such as racism, sexism, inflation, and crime have come to appear far more urgent. Discussions of anti-Semitism, rather than seeming relevant, are likely to be regarded as vaguely outdated and perhaps only of academic curiosity. Isn't it the case, after all, that Jews have become highly successful in the professions, in business, and in the arts? How often does one hear of a synagogue being desecrated? In comparison with other minority groups, how frequently are Jews the subject of distasteful jokes or ethnic slurs?

But even a moment's reflection will suffice to indicate the current importance of discussing and understanding anti-Semitism. One reason is that much can be learned about the dynamics of prejudice toward minority groups in general from the literature on anti-Semitism. There are deep similarities among the various kinds of prejudice. Racial stereotyping, for example, although quite different in content, may be very similar to anti-Semitism in terms of its underlying cognitive assumptions. The particular value of the literature on anti-Semitism for understanding other kinds of prejudice is that it now constitutes a highly developed body of research.

Beginning in the 1940s and early 1950s, in response to the Nazi atrocities, a number of studies attempting to explain anti-Semitism were initiated, of which by far the most famous was that resulting in the volume entitled *The Authoritarian Personality* (1950), by T. W. Adorno and his colleagues. Following the publication of this volume, hundreds of subsequent studies were conducted to further explore the psychological components of anti-Semitism. Another early volume that guided much of this research was Gordon Allport's *The Nature of Prejudice* (1954). In the 1960s, following an alarming recurrence of anti-Semitic incidents, another large-scale study of anti-Semitism was begun. Using survey research techniques, researchers at the University of California at Berkeley examined the nature and causes of anti-Semitism in the general public, the churches, the schools, the mass media, and politics. In addition to this research, dozens of public opinion polls and hundreds of smaller research projects have focused on anti-Semitism. As a result of this research, a great deal of evidence has accumulated that is useful for understanding both anti-Semitism and other kinds of prejudice.

A second reason for acquiring an understanding of anti-Semitism is that it has occupied an important place in the history of modern culture. It can even be argued that a full understanding of the nature of Western civilization requires some familiarity with the role that anti-Semitism has played in the development of this civilization. This argument may not seem as obvious as it once did, now that the atrocities of World War II are beginning to recede from public consciousness. But in the long view of history, these atrocities remain very much a part of the contemporary period. History also shows that anti-Semitism has been subject to recurrent cycles of ebb and flow. Because it currently appears to be neither particularly visible nor virulent, it cannot be assumed that anti-Semitism is strictly a problem of the past that will not erupt again in America or in some other part of the world.

Finally, there is substantial evidence that anti-Semitism continues to be characteristic of at least a sizable minority of the American public. The time-worn stereotypes that have served as rationalizations for discrimination and hostility toward Jews over the centuries have by no means been eradicated. As we shall see presently, the most recent studies show that there are still many Americans who cling to these traditional stereotypes and who overtly express negative feelings about Jews. These attitudes and feelings generally have not resulted in blatant aggression. But American Nazi marches in Jewish neighborhoods, swastikas and anti-Jewish graffiti painted on synagogue walls, social club discrimination, and slanderous remarks made by people in the public eye all attest to the fact that open anti-Semitism is not entirely a thing of the past. In somewhat subtler ways prejudice against Jews also tends to recur. The accomplishments of Jewish people continue to elicit resentment and accusations of dishonesty and egotism. The "Jewish lobby" is accused of manipulating foreign policy. A "Jewish conspiracy" is suspected of controlling the media. "Liberal" Jewish intellectuals are accused of subverting traditional morality. For example, the Rev. Dan C. Fore, head of the New York Chapter of Moral Majority, was quoted as follows: "I love the Jewish people deeply. God has given them talents He has not given others. They are His chosen people. Jews have a God-given ability to make money, almost a supernatural ability to make money. They control the media, they control this city" (New York *Times*, Feb. 5, 1981, p. B4).

For each of these reasons it is useful to understand the nature and causes of contemporary anti-Semitism. This chapter reviews evidence on the extent and nature of contemporary anti-Semitism in America, indicates what the trends in anti-Semitism have been in recent years, identifies those sectors of the population that are most likely to register anti-Semitic attitudes and feelings, discusses the main theories that have been offered to explain why people cling to anti-Semitic beliefs, and briefly considers some of the proposals that have been suggested for combating anti-Semitism.

CONTEMPORARY IMAGES OF JEWS

Various polls and surveys in the late 1970s included questions aimed at measuring the public's attitudes and feelings toward Jews. Most of the questions were asked in response to particular events, rather than being part of any comprehensive effort to study anti-Semitism. Accordingly, it is impossible to address many of the questions that would have to be addressed if a complete portrait of contemporary attitudes toward Jews were to be developed. However, there is one fortuitous consequence of having to rely on these scattered bits of information: it forces us to abandon many of the conceptual crutches that have guided past research and to reconsider from the ground up, so to speak, the nature and meaning of the public's perceptions of Jews.

Perceptions of Jewish Power

The fear of overweening power groups runs deep in American culture. Citizens like to think they have a voice in running the government, not that the government is run for the benefit of a privileged few. The problem, of course, is that it takes big institutions to manage a modern society, and over the past few decades these institutions have grown bigger and bigger. As they have, alienation has risen proportionately, particularly from big government and big business. Over the centuries Jews have been implicated in both. "Power hungry," "monied," "aggressive," "devious"—these have been among the traditional epithets. Far out of proportion to their actual influence, Jews have been regarded as behind-the-scenes manipulators of political and economic policy. In studying current political opinions, therefore, pollsters have often asked questions about the public's perceptions of Jewish power.

According to the available polls, a small but not insignificant minority of the American public is persuaded that Jewish people have too much power and influence, though the exact percentages vary from survey to survey. For example, a Yankelovich survey conducted in January 1976 asked, "In general, do you feel that American Jews have too much power in the United States?" and found that 26 percent of those polled said "yes." A year earlier the same question had elicited an affirmative response from 37 percent of the public. The Center for Political Studies at the University of Michigan has used a somewhat more refined question in its national surveys, asking whether particular groups have "too much," "too little," or "about the [right] amount of influence" *they deserve*. In 1976, 17 percent of the public said they thought Jews had too much influence; 47 percent said about the right amount; 10 percent said too little; and 26 percent answered "don't know."

Is one in six, or even one in four, a significant proportion? Some perspective can be gained by comparing the response pertaining to Jewish power with responses pertaining to the power of other groups. As can be seen in Table 4.1, "American Jews" ranked near the bottom of the list of groups identified in the Yankelovich surveys as having too much power in the United States.

The Michigan study is helpful because it includes a more extensive list of groups, many of which make no pretense of manipulating power. As Table 4.2 shows, Jews rank exactly in the middle of the list, in terms of the percentages of the public regarding each group as having too much influence. The groups heading the list include business and labor, which genuinely exert large shares of influence; pressure groups such as black militants; and the "downtrodden," such as people on welfare, who are perceived as having more power than they deserve. At the bottom of the list are groups that are often characterized as not getting a fair deal in American society, such as older people and workingmen. Jews most resemble groups in the middle of the list about which there is either no clear imagery (such as "whites") or a division of opinion depending on one's own position (such as

TABLE 4.1
Perceptions of Jewish Power, 1975 and 1976

"In general, do you feel that _____ have too much power in the United States?" (percent of national sample answering "yes")

	1975	1976
Oil companies	80	79
Big business	78	76
Organized labor	60	63
Media	50	50
CIA	42	45
Arab interests	37	40
AMERICAN JEWS	37	26
Zionist organizations	22	21
Church interests	23	17

Source: Yankelovich, Skelly, & White, Inc., New York. 1975, 1976 Survey Data.

TABLE 4.2
Influence Ratings of Selected Groups, 1976

"Some people think that certain groups have too much influence in American life and politics, while other people feel that certain groups don't have as much influence as they deserve. Here are three statements about how much influence a group might have. For each group I read to you, just tell me the number of the statement that best says how you feel."

	In 1976, percentages saying		
	Too Much	About Right	Too Little
Big business	77	14	3
Labor unions	64	25	5
Black militants	50	25	8
Businessmen	33	48	11
People on welfare	33	29	28
Blacks	31	36	25
Women's lib	25	47	14
Men	22	65	6
Liberals	21	47	8
Republicans	18	55	14
Democrats	18	65	6
JEWS	17	47	10
Whites	14	64	15
Young people	12	48	33
Conservatives	11	51	17
Catholics	10	61	7
Chicanos	8	32	32
Southerners	7	56	19
Poor people	7	20	68
Women	6	54	34
Workingmen	4	38	53
Protestants	4	70	7
Middle-class people	3	49	43
Older people	2	26	68

Source: 1976 Center for Political Studies. National Election Survey, University of Michigan.

"Republicans" and "Democrats"). However, it should be observed that in comparison with other religious faiths, Jews rank higher (than Catholics and Protestants) in terms of the number of people who think they have too much influence. In short, only a minority of Americans think Jews have too much influence, but the matter of how significant this minority may be is not a question that lends itself to easy interpretation. The complexity of the issue is even more apparent in light of other evidence.

For example, some information is available on the kinds of influence

Jews are suspected of having. Depending on the kind of influence asked about, the proportions saying that Jews have too much power sometimes are quite large. As an example, there appears to be a large share of the public who, for one reason or another, believes Jews wield too much power in defining certain kinds of foreign policy. In the 1976 Yankelovich survey, for instance, 49 percent of those polled felt that Jews had "too much influence over our country's policies in the Middle East." On matters where Jewish interests are clearly defined, therefore, the amount of concern over Jewish influence is substantially higher than when Jewish influence is discussed in the abstract. Still, if there is a feeling that Jews have too much influence on American policy, there is an even greater feeling that Arab interests have too much influence. For example, Table 4.1 shows that in 1976, 40 percent of the public thought Arab interests had too much power in the United States, in comparison with the 26 percent who felt this way about American Jews.

Another kind of influence on which the polls give evidence is the public's perception of Jewish power over the economy. Here again there is evidence that a fairly sizable minority of the public feels that Jews somehow have more power than they should. In 1977, for example, a survey conducted in Los Angeles County found that 47 percent of those questioned thought Jews had too much economic power. By comparison, one in three thought Catholics had too much economic power and all but a few thought that blacks and Chicanos had too *little* economic power.

A poll conducted by Louis Harris and Associates in 1974 affords some further detail on the economic sectors that Jews are suspected of controlling. As shown in Table 4.3, banking, entertainment, and the media are the main industries that Jews are thought to control. Nearly half of the public thinks Jews either control or play an important role in these industries. It is also worth observing that 43 percent of the public regards Jews as having a heavy influence on "major American corporations" in general.

The Question of Jewish Loyalty

A second tenet of traditional anti-Semitic ideology has been the idea that Jews are less loyal to their country than other citizens. In the past Jews have been accused of being traitors and conspirators, and more recently, Communists and socialist sympathizers. Like members of other ethnic groups, there have been Jews who have fit these characterizations. The vast majority have not. Nor have these anti-Semitic accusations kept political leaders from routinely including Jews among their most respected advisers.

Since the founding of Israel in 1948, the question of Jewish loyalty has typically involved accusations that Jews are more loyal to Israel than to the United States. The recurrent conflicts in the Middle East, as well as Israel's dependence on support and aid from Jews (and non-Jews) in the United States, have made it seem apparent to some that Jews might indeed be more

TABLE 4.3
Perceptions of Jewish Power in Specific Areas, 1974

"Now I would like to ask you about some different groups and organizations. For each one would you tell me, to the best of your knowledge, if it is controlled by Jews, if Jews play an important role in it but don't control it, if Jews play only a minor role in it, or if they have no role in it at all?"

	Control	Important Role	Minor/No Role
Movie industry	18	31	51
Big New York banks	14	30	56
National TV networks	10	29	61
Major American corporations	9	34	57
Major East Coast newspapers	7	22	71
Big labor unions	4	13	83
U.S. Senate	2	12	86

Source: Harris and Associates, New York. 1974 Harris Survey.

loyal to Israel than to the United States. For example, a Harris poll conducted in 1978 found that 29 percent of the public agreed that "Jews are more loyal to Israel than to America" (42 percent disagreed and 29 percent said they weren't sure). Other polls using differently worded questions have also suggested that about a third of the public may suspect Jews of being more loyal to Israel than to the United States. In five polls conducted by the Yankelovich organization between April 1974 and January 1976, for instance, the proportion of the public who subscribed to the idea that Jews "feel closer" to Israel than to the United States ranged between 26 percent and 34 percent. Another 4 to 8 percent said "both" (Israel and the United States), and between 17 and 24 percent in each poll said they were unsure. In only one of the five surveys did a majority say they thought Jews felt closer to the United States than to Israel.

Stereotypes

In addition to the public's perceptions of Jewish power and Jewish loyalty, information exists on several other kinds of perceptions. These deal with what have usually been labeled "stereotypes" in the literature on anti-Semitism. They include notions about Jews being clannish, pushy, and dishonest. Besides these, some data are also available on positive stereotypes of Jews.

The 1974 Harris poll asked respondents (non-Jews) to volunteer things they liked and disliked about Jews. About 70 percent of respondents refused to say anything bad at all about Jews: 56 percent said they couldn't think of anything they disliked about Jews, 7 percent said they wouldn't generalize, 6 percent said they didn't know enough about Jews to say anything. Among those who did volunteer some negative comments about Jews, the following perceptions tended to dominate: too aggressive, pushy, shrewd, arrogant, or snobbish (10 percent); greedy, selfish, money-mad, control too much with their money (8 percent); and too clannish or cliquish (6 percent). Three percent said Jews were unethical in business, and 2 percent said they disliked the Jewish religion for its rejection of Christ.

The things that people in the Harris study liked about Jews included sticking together, supporting each other, and having strong family ties (22 percent); being hard-working, industrious, and good in business (19 percent); being friendly, considerate, and honest (18 percent); being religious' and having high moral standards (11 percent); and being intelligent (9 percent).

The Harris study also presented people with preformulated statements about Jews to see which stereotypes would elicit agreement and which would elicit disagreement (see Table 4.4). The results again showed that positive stereotypes are subscribed to with much greater frequency than negative stereotypes. Fewer than one-third of the respondents in the study agreed with statements about Jews feeling superior, being aggressive, clannish, or dishonest in business, whereas half to two-thirds of the respondents disagreed with these stereotypes. By comparison, a majority agreed that Jews are disciplined, honest, and charitable, and that Jews have contributed much to the cultural life of America. Fewer than one in five disagreed with these positive images.

A more recent Harris poll (conducted in 1978) shows a pattern of responses similar to the 1974 results. For example, only 27 percent of the persons surveyed agreed that "Jews are irritating because they are too aggressive," whereas 55 percent disagreed. Similarly, only 20 percent agreed that "Most of the slumlords are Jewish," while 36 percent disagreed. The statement "When it comes to choosing between people and money, Jews will choose money" also elicited less agreement (34 percent) than disagreement (42 percent). In contrast, a more positive statement such as "Jews have suffered from persecution through the centuries" elicited agreement from 75 percent of those polled and disagreement from only 15 percent.

In drawing conclusions from these kinds of figures, it is important to seek a balance, so to speak, between the "good news" and the "bad news." The good news is that, on the whole, Jews tend to be favorably perceived in American culture. If anything, they are admired for their high standards in work and in ethics. The bad news is that there is also a substantial amount of negative stereotyping. Between one-fourth and one-third of the American public still subscribes to traditional stereotypes about Jews being aggressive, clannish, and dishonest. And a smaller proportion, perhaps one in six, denies the positive characteristics that others attribute to Jews.

TABLE 4.4
Stereotypes of Jews, 1974

	Percent Who		
	Agree	Disagree	Not Sure
Jews raise their children to accomplish something in the world	85	3	12
Jews have suffered from persecution through the centuries	85	9	6
Jews are as honest as other businessmen	69	18	13
Jews give money away to good causes	58	15	27
Jews have contributed much to the cultural life of America	58	17	25
Jews are more a race than a religion	49	36	15
Jews are in the professions more because they study harder in school	47	32	21
Jews are richer than other people	46	43	11
Jews have supported rights for minority groups more than other white people	36	31	33
When it comes to choosing between people and money, Jews will choose money	34	41	25
Jews have to work harder because they are discriminated against in so many places	34	49	17
Jews are more loyal to Israel than to America	33	42	25
Jews feel superior to other groups	33	45	22
Jews are irritating because they are too aggressive	31	51	18
Jews always stick to their own and never give an outsider a break	27	56	17
Most of the slum owners are Jewish	21	38	41
Jewish businessmen will usually try to pull a shady deal on you	21	61	18
Jews are too ambitious for their own good	18	66	16

Source: Harris and Associates, New York. 1974 Harris Survey.

Feelings About Jews

Besides evidence on cognitive kinds of perceptions, some measurements have been made of the public's feelings toward Jews. Evidence of this kind tells nothing about the substantive content of the public's perceptions, but it provides a useful barometer of the degree of affect held by the public at different times toward various groups. For this reason, polling agencies periodically ask questions about how the public feels toward various ethnic, racial, political, and religious groups.

The two measuring devices that have been used most extensively are the "feeling thermometer," a drawing of a thermometer on which are printed numbers from 0 to 100 and labels indicating that scores below 50 represent "cool" or negative feelings while scores above 50 represent "warm" or positive feelings (50 means "no feelings"), and the "scalometer," which consists of ten boxes arranged vertically, the top five being white and labeled with positive numbers (+1 through +5) to represent degrees of "liking" and the bottom five being black and labeled with negative numbers (-1 through -5) to indicate degrees of "dislike." The "feeling thermometer" is employed periodically by the Center for Political Studies (CPS) at the University of Michigan in its national election surveys, and is used for a wide variety of target groups. The "scalometer" has been used by the Gallup poll, usually to measure feelings toward religious groups.

According to the 1976 Michigan election survey (the most recent survey in which the "feeling thermometer" was applied to Jews), 10 percent of the non-Jewish American public indicated that they held negative feelings toward Jews, 37 percent said they had positive feelings, 43 percent indicated no feelings, and 10 percent said they weren't sure what their feelings were. Only 3.4 percent expressed strongly negative feelings (scores from 0 through 15), while 11.5 percent expressed strongly positive feelings (scores from 85 through 100). The Gallup "scalometer" for the same year showed that 12 percent of the public held negative feelings about Jews, 70 percent expressed positive feelings, and 18 percent said "don't know." Extreme negative responses (-5) were given by only 3 percent of the public, while extreme positive responses (+5) were given by 23 percent of the public.

It is instructive to consider the similarities and differences between the two sets of results. Although the two measuring devices are worded differently and provide different kinds of response options, they yield roughly equivalent estimates of the proportion of the public that dislikes Jews: between 12.5 and 10 percent. By both estimates it also appears that only a tiny fraction (about 3 percent) of the public harbors deeply negative feelings about Jews. The similarities end there. The Michigan study suggests that only a minority of the public holds positive feelings about Jews, whereas the Gallup poll places the figure at 70 percent. The discrepancy is not difficult to resolve, however, once differences in the wording of the two measures are taken into account. The Gallup "scalometer" offers respondents no possibility of giving a neutral response. Not having this option, a few apparently choose to give no answer (hence, the higher percentage of "don't knows" than on the Michigan "feeling thermometer"), while the remainder give a mildly positive response. Overall, 36 percent give answers ranging from +1 to +3 (almost as many as the 43 percent who give neutral responses on the "feeling thermometer"), while 34 percent give answers of +4 or +5 (compared with the 37 percent who give positive responses on the "feeling thermometer").

How do the public's feelings about Jews compare with its feelings about other groups? Judging from average (mean) scores on the CPS "feeling thermometer," Jews tend to be less positively perceived than many groups in American society. Of the 29 groups for which feelings were asked in the CPS study, Jews ranked nineteenth (see Table 4.5). The groups heading the list in terms of overall levels of positive affect accorded them tended to represent large, noncontroversial demographic divisions in the society—older people and young people, women and men, middle-class persons and working-men. At the bottom of the list were groups representing controversial interests, such as black militants, pot smokers, labor unions, and big business. In the middle were groups of ethnic, religious, or regional origin (blacks, Catholics, southerners) or political factions (Democrats and Republicans, liberals and conservatives). Jews ranked about the same as Chicanos and slightly below Protestants, Catholics, southerners, and blacks.

These rankings paint a rather gloomy picture of the public's feelings about Jews. They seem to suggest that even though only a small fraction of the public overtly claims to dislike Jews, this fraction is not small when compared with feelings about other groups. Given the amount of ill-feeling that has often been observed in American culture toward blacks, for example, it is not encouraging to see that Jews rank below blacks on these scores. In dealing with statistics such as these, however, it is always wise to be cautious. Averages often hide much of the important information. In the present case a more accurate interpretation of the public's feelings about Jews needs to be obtained by looking carefully at the similarities and differences between these feelings and feelings about some of the other groups on the list with comparable rankings, rather than relying on mean scores (see Table 4.6).

A detailed comparison of the public's feelings about Jews and about blacks shows that a significantly larger proportion of the public expresses negative feelings about blacks than about Jews. The reason blacks come out ahead of Jews in the overall rankings is that more people also express positive feelings about blacks than about Jews. Put differently, the public is much more likely to say they have no feelings at all about Jews than about blacks. This may be understandable, since Jews constitute a much smaller

TABLE 4.5
"Feeling Thermometer" Ratings, 1976

Group	Mean Score
Older people	82.1
Women	78.7
Workingmen	76.6
Middle-class people	74.0
Young people	73.9
Men	73.4
Whites	73.2
Poor people	71.1
Policemen	71.1
Military	67.5
Protestants	65.8
Catholics	62.9
Democrats	62.7
Businessmen	62.5
Southerners	62.0
Blacks	60.6
Conservatives	58.9
Republicans	57.4
JEWS	57.2
Chicanos	55.4
Women's liberation	52.6
Liberals	52.3
People on welfare	52.0
Civil rights leaders	49.5
Big business	48.3
Labor unions	46.7
Pot smokers	32.3
Radical students	30.1
Black militants	24.5

Source: 1976 Center for Political Studies. National Election Survey, University of Michigan.

proportion of the population than do blacks. It is probably the case that many people simply have no occasion to develop feelings about Jews. It also seems likely that relations between Jews and non-Jews have ceased to command as much attention in the media and in the schools as relations between blacks and whites.

In comparison with feelings about Catholics, the public's attitude toward Jews appears low even on closer inspection. Jews receive significantly more negative responses and significantly fewer positive responses (with self-ratings among both groups removed). The ratio of extreme negative to extreme positive feelings is also much higher for Jews than for Catholics.

TABLE 4.6
Detailed "Feeling Thermometer" Responses, Self-Ratings Removed, 1976

	Percent Negative	Percent Neutral	Percent Positive	Percent Don't Know
Jews	9.78	43.13	37.36	9.71
Blacks	13.94	29.32	52.76	3.25
Catholics	5.67	41.91	42.03	10.56
Chicanos	11.51	39.95	34.20	14.60

Source: 1976 Center for Political Studies. National Election Survey, University of Michigan.

The group that turns out to be most similar to Jews on the "feeling thermometer" (one that probably would not have come to mind in advance) is Chicanos. Mean scores for the two groups (with self-ratings removed) are almost identical. About the same proportions of the public express neutral feelings or give "don't know" responses to each group. Roughly the same percentages (within ranges of sampling error) give positive ratings and negative ratings to the two groups. And the percentages giving extreme negative responses to each group are almost identical. The only noticeable difference is that a slightly larger percentage of the public expresses mildly negative feelings about Chicanos than about Jews, while Jews receive somewhat more mildly positive responses than Chicanos.

Some comparisons of a different sort are made possible by the results of the Gallup "scalometer," since it has been used with reference to a number of religious groups. Of the 12 religious groups asked about in the 1976 Gallup study (see Table 4.7), Jews ranked sixth in terms of the proportions of the public expressing positive feelings toward each group. Specifically, they ranked between Presbyterians and Southern Baptists. The groups that ranked higher tend to be mainline Protestant denominations, while the groups that ranked lower tend to be sectarian groups such as Seventh-Day Adventists and Unitarians. As on the "feeling thermometer," Jews ranked lower than Catholics. These rankings pertain only to positive sentiment.

As to negative feelings, Jews ranked among the least-liked religious groups. Only Mormons and Seventh-Day Adventists were accorded more dislike. Catholics, Quakers, Unitarians, and all the Protestant groups received smaller percentages of dislike.

To summarize, both the "feeling thermometer" and the scalometer show that a small minority of the public (about one-tenth) claims to dislike Jews at least mildly. This is probably a conservative estimate, since the Harris survey findings indicated that about 30 percent of the public will mention things they dislike about Jews if asked to do so. At the same time, these negative feelings have to be considered in light of the facts that only about one-third of the people who express dislike for Jews express strong or extreme negative feelings; close to three (or four) times as many people

TABLE 4.7
"Scalometer" Ratings, 1976

	Percent Positive	Percent Negative	Percent Don't Know
Methodists*	81	3	16
Baptists*	78	6	16
Catholics*	78	10	12
Lutherans*	74	4	22
Presbyterians*	74	4	22
JEWS*	70	12	18
Southern Baptists	69	9	22
Episcopalians	66	6	28
Quakers	56	10	34
Mormons	18	18	64
Seventh-Day Adventists	15	18	67
Unitarians	12	10	78

*Self-ratings removed.
Source: 1976 Gallup Poll. American Institute of Public Opinion, Princeton, N.J.

express positive feelings as express negative feelings; a large proportion of the public appears to have no feelings one way or the other about Jews; and when these people are pushed to express feelings, their feelings tend to be in a positive direction.

Discriminatory Attitudes

In 1974 the Harris organization asked a national sample of American Jews to say whether they had ever experienced discrimination. Thirty-six percent said they had, 62 percent said they hadn't, and 2 percent said they were not sure. Those who felt they had been discriminated against were asked what kind of discrimination they had experienced. Work-related discrimination, such as being turned down for a job or not getting a promotion because one was Jewish, was most frequently mentioned. Fifty-one percent of those who felt they had been discriminated against mentioned problems of this kind. The kind mentioned next most frequently (by 25 percent of those who felt they had been discriminated against) consisted of jokes and negative remarks about Jews. Social club discrimination was mentioned by about half as many (12 percent), as was discrimination in school (11 percent) and in housing (10 percent).

In the same survey a national sample of non-Jews was asked, "As an individual, what do you think it feels like to be discriminated against as a Jew here in this country? What do you think it does to Jewish people as individuals?" The responses are interesting, both in light of the fact that the question was worded in a rather "leading" manner, and in comparison with the large number of Jews who said they had experienced discrimination. In the first place, 15 percent of the sample said they didn't think Jews were discriminated against. What is of greater interest, though, is that about half of those who thought Jews had been discriminated against mentioned things like having one's feelings hurt or being made to feel like a second-class citizen, but the remainder (42 percent of those who gave answers that could be categorized) mentioned undesirable traits of the victims themselves as the main consequences of discrimination (such as becoming clannish or acting hostile and resentful) or suggested that discrimination doesn't bother Jews.

Data on the extent to which Americans actually subscribe to discriminatory attitudes toward Jews are limited (as far as recent polls are concerned) largely to three issues: intermarriage, political office, and some questions about persecution. As such, the data scarcely afford an adequate summary of what the public's views may be. Nonetheless, they shed some additional light that will prove useful in trying to arrive at an overall interpretation of the information discussed thus far.

The Gallup poll has periodically included questions aimed at measuring approval or disapproval of marriages between Jews and non-Jews. The most recent poll (conducted in mid-1978) showed that 69 percent of the public indicated approval, 14 percent expressed disapproval, and 17 percent said they had no opinion on the subject. By comparison, the poll also found that approval of marriages between Protestants and Catholics ran slightly higher (73 percent), while disapproval was almost the same (13 percent).

The second issue—attitudes toward Jews holding political office—also appears to elicit little overt disapproval, although the matter is not entirely straightforward. The question of a Jewish president has been asked about in various polls over a number of years, the most recent being in 1978, at which time 82 percent of the public expressed willingness to vote for an otherwise qualified presidential candidate who was Jewish. Surveys have also consistently found that there tends to be greater support for a Jewish president than for a black president, and somewhat greater support for a Jewish president than for a woman president.

In view of these results, the responses to the following question, asked of a national sample in 1974 by the Yankelovich poll, are instructive: "Considering the state of the country and the world today, would you consider it good for the country or not good for the country to have a President who was a Jew?" Far from receiving overwhelming approval, the idea of a Jewish president being good for the country was subscribed to by only 42 percent of those polled. Nearly as many (32 percent) said it would not be good for the country to have a Jewish president. And 24 percent said they weren't sure. The wording of the question (making reference to the state of the world) and the fact that it was asked among other questions dealing largely with the Middle East, during a period of considerable uncertainty in that region, probably caused the negative responses to be inflated. Even so, it is noteworthy that the negative responses ran higher on this question than they did on an identical question asking about a black president (46 percent thought a black president would be good for the country; 29 percent thought it would not be good for the country).

Finally, some evidence also exists on the issue of persecution: Would Americans condone or participate in the persecution of Jews? This issue has recently been raised anew, both by the resurgence of interest in the Holocaust and by the results of various laboratory experiments showing marked tendencies of subjects to engage in violent and inhumane acts (presumably) against other human beings if provided with sufficient prodding and legitimation.

According to the polls, most Americans do not consider the idea of overt persecution of American Jews a likely possibility in the foreseeable future. But a large number do believe that a hardened minority exists who would probably condone such behavior. In a poll conducted by Response Analysis in 1978, for example, only 4 percent of the public said they felt that "most people" or "a large number of people" would think it was all right to persecute Jews in the United States. But 56 percent thought "a small number of people" would think this all right. Only 28 percent felt that "nobody" would approve.

To summarize, the evidence on discriminatory attitudes, though sparse, appears by and large to be consistent with the other evidence on attitudes toward Jews. As with stereotypes and feelings, there appears to be a small core of the public that shows some willingness to engage in or to condone discrimination. Where comparisons exist between attitudes toward Jews and attitudes toward other groups, it appears that Jews are responded to somewhat more negatively than Catholics, and in one instance Jews seem to fare about the same in public opinion as Americans of Hispanic origin. The comparisons with attitudes toward blacks tend to show that there are certain kinds of issues for which Jews elicit as much (or nearly as much) attitudinal resistance as blacks. Whether these observations would apply to issues other than intermarriage and political office is a question that must be left open. Given that many Jews say they have experienced discrimination in the work place, it is particularly unfortunate that no evidence is available on these kinds of discriminatory attitudes.

A Note on the Holocaust

Contemporary attitudes toward Jews can scarcely be summarized adequately without some consideration of the Holocaust. This period (during which approximately 6 million Jews were killed) has occupied such a central role in modern Jewish history that Americans' understandings of it can hardly be isolated from their attitudes and feelings about Jews. By many indications the public's interest in the Holocaust has risen dramatically in recent years. Books about it have been on the best-seller list, dozens of conferences are held each year to commemorate it, and schools have increasingly incorporated discussions of it into their curricula. Young people who were born after the end of World War II appear to have become particularly interested in learning what the Holocaust was all about and what moral implications it has.

An occasion to examine perceptions and understandings of the Holocaust was provided in 1978, when the NBC-TV network aired a nine-hour, four-part miniseries entitled "Holocaust." More than 120 million Americans watched the program as it graphically portrayed the Nazis' atrocities through the experiences of a fictional Jewish family. Several weeks after the program the American Jewish Committee (AJC) conducted a national poll of viewers and nonviewers to assess generally the public's understandings of the Holocaust and to determine what effects the television broadcast may have had on these understandings.

The AJC study showed that "Holocaust" viewers were deeply disturbed by the atrocities portrayed, but also regarded the program as a valuable learning experience. Sixty percent said the program had given them a better understanding of Hitler's treatment of Jews (71 percent among viewers under age 30). About 40 percent said their feelings about Jews had been affected by the program (virtually all in a positive direction). Almost half (46 percent) said they had found parts of the program difficult or disturbing to watch. But the vast majority (68 percent) said they thought the program had been a "good idea," mostly because it had made people more aware of what could happen. And 71 percent said they considered it "a good idea to teach children about things like what the Nazis did." (Representative national polls conducted in Austria and Germany after the program had been aired in those countries found that 87 percent and 75 percent of the viewers in the two countries, respectively, described their reactions as "enthusiastic and satisfied.")

Judging from the AJC study, Americans consider themselves to be relatively well-informed about the Holocaust. Whether or not they had watched the television program, about 70 percent said they were "very well" or "fairly well" informed about Hitler's treatment of the Jews. Young people, however, were considerably less likely to say they were well informed. A large percentage of the public also appears to hold sympathetic attitudes toward Jews because of their experience in Nazi Germany. For example, persons who said the Jews' treatment had "not been their fault" outnumbered those who said it was "mostly or partly their fault" by a ratio of nearly three to one. Those who had watched the program were also significantly more likely than those who hadn't watched to say they were sympathetic with Israel and felt that American Jews' support of Israel "makes good sense."

RECENT TRENDS IN ATTITUDES TOWARD JEWS

Some perspective on contemporary attitudes toward Jews can be gained by comparing them with evidence from earlier surveys and polls. Information from national polls, although of varying comparability, has been available since the advent of public opinion polling in the late 1930s. This material affords some assessments of trends in attitudes toward Jews over a period of four decades.

It will simplify the examination of these trends if the period for which evidence is available is divided into two parts: from the late 1930s until the early 1960s, and from the early 1960s to the present. Trends in attitudes toward Jews during the first period were relatively unambiguous, and have been discussed in detail in Charles Herbert Stember's book *Jews in the Mind of America* (1966). The trends during the second period are less clear, and require a more careful examination of what the polls have shown.

The First Period: Trends Through the Early 1960s

Because of the events in Europe, a number of public opinion surveys in the United States conducted between 1938 and the end of World War II included questions aimed at measuring public attitudes toward Jews. In 1962, Stember replicated many of these earlier questions in a national survey, making it possible to examine any changes that might have occurred. As shown in Table 4.8, the comparisons revealed that a consistent and dramatic reduction in negative attitudes and feelings about Jews had taken place.

TABLE 4.8
Trends in Attitudes Toward Jews, 1938–1962

	Percent
Jewish power	
Do you think Jews have too much power in the United States?	
(percent "yes")	
1938–1946 (average of 14 polls)	47
1962	17
Jews have too much power in finance.	
1938–1944 (average of 4 polls)	21
1962	3
Jewish loyalty	
In your opinion, what nationality, religious or racial groups in	
this country are a menace to America? ("Jews")	
1940–1946 (average of 9 polls)	19
1962	1

Do you think Jews tend to be more radical in politics than other people?

1938–1940 (average of 6 polls)	28
1962	17

Stereotypes and feelings
Percent who said Jews have objectionable qualities

1940	63
1962	22

Percent who regarded Jews as a race

1946	42
1962	23

Jewish businessmen are less honest than other businessmen.

1938–1939 (average of 4 polls)	46
1962	18

Discriminatory attitudes
Would you vote for a Jew for president who was well qualified for the position? (percent "yes")

1937	49
1959	72

If a candidate for Congress should declare himself as being against the Jews, would this influence you to vote for him or to vote against him? (against)

1945	31
1964 (Selznick & Steinberg)	58

I definitely would not marry a Jew.

1950	57
1962	37

Percent saying it would make a difference to them if a prospective employee were Jewish

1940	43
1962	6

Source: Adapted from *Jews in the Mind of America* by Charles Herbert Stember, tables on pp. 50–209. © 1966 by the American Jewish Committee. Published by Basic Books, Inc., New York. Reprinted by permission.

In the late 1930s close to 50 percent of the public felt that Jews had too much power in the United States, but by the early 1960s this figure had dropped 30 percentage points. In the earlier period nearly a quarter of the public suspected Jews of controlling finance. By the latter date hardly anyone held this view. As to Jewish loyalty, questions were not asked, as they have been more recently, about Jewish ties with Israel, but some efforts were made to determine whether the public believed Jews to be involved in international conspiracies of a radical or Communist nature. This view had been widely disseminated in Nazi propaganda, and occasionally had been advanced by the media in the United States in connection with several highly publicized conspiracy cases. In the late 1930s about a fourth of the public held this view of Jews. By the early 1960s these attitudes had not disappeared entirely, but hardly anyone still believed that Jews were a threat to the country, and fewer than one in five thought Jews were more involved in radical politics than non-Jews.

Equally dramatic declines in anti-Semitism between the late 1930s and early 1960s were evidenced in data on stereotypes and negative feelings. For example, a survey in 1940 showed that nearly two-thirds of the sample mentioned characteristics of Jews that were regarded as objectionable. In the 1962 poll, by comparison, only 22 percent mentioned objectionable qualities. A replication of an earlier question asking about the honesty of Jewish businessmen also demonstrated a dramatic shift in the proportion of the public subscribing to this view, from nearly half to less than one-fifth.

Stember's comparisons also show consistent reductions in the proportion of the public favoring discriminatory attitudes toward Jews. For example, the proportion of the public saying it would vote for someone who was Jewish for president increased from about half to nearly three-quarters. Increases also occurred in the number of people who said they would vote against someone who was a self-declared anti-Semite. Other questions having to do with intermarriage, employment, housing, and college admissions also showed declining support for discrimination. While the proportion disapproving of intermarriage between Jews and non-Jews was still sizable, support for discrimination in hiring, housing, and college admissions had shrunk virtually to nothing.

The Second Period: Trends Since the Early 1960s

The trends in attitudes and feelings toward Jews since the early 1960s are more difficult to assess. In part this is because no survey such as Stember's has been done to replicate earlier polls exactly and, thereby, to provide reliable indicators of trends. A number of polls have asked questions about attitudes toward Jews, but often the wording of the questions is sufficiently different to make precise comparisons impossible. The other difficulty is that even the most reliable evidence does not point uniformly toward a single trend, as did the data for the period prior to the 1960s. Table 4.9 summarizes the results of questions asked since the early 1960s that give some basis for drawing inferences about trends in attitudes toward Jews.

The issue of Jewish power has been raised in at least seven polls since 1962. The wording of the questions has varied, from ones that ask straightforwardly whether people think Jews have too much power in the United States to ones that ask whether various groups have too much, too little, or about the right amount of power. Even those that have been worded exactly the same do not yield estimates of trends that are beyond dispute. For example, the 1962 and 1964 questions were worded identically, yet the

TABLE 4.9
Trends in Attitudes Toward Jews, 1962–78

	Percent
Jewish power	
Do you think Jews have too much power (influence) in the United States? (percent "yes")	
1962 (Stember)	17
1964 (Selznick & Steinberg, 1969)	11
1972 (CPS)	13
1975 (Yankelovich)	37
1976 (Yankelovich)	26
1976 (CPS)	17
1978 (Response Analysis)	12
Jewish loyalty	
Jews are more loyal to Israel than to the United States. (percent "yes")	
1964 (Selznick & Steinberg)	30
1974 (Harris)	33
1974–1976 (average of 5 Yankelovich polls)	29
1976 (Harris)	30
1978 (Harris)	29
Stereotypes	
Jews have objectionable qualities. (percent "yes")	
1962 (Stember)	22
1974 (Harris)	31
Jewish businessmen are not as honest as other businessmen. (percent "yes")	
1962 (Stember)	18
1964 (Selznick & Steinberg, 1969)	28
1974 (Harris)	18
Feelings	
"Feeling thermometer" scores indicating dislike	
1964 (CPS)	9
1968 (CPS)	8
1972 (CPS)	5
1976 (CPS)	10
Discriminatory attitudes	
Would vote for a Jew for President	
1967 (Gallup)	82
1978 (Gallup)	82
Do you approve or disapprove of marriage between Jews and non-Jews? (percent approving)	
1968 (Gallup)	59
1972 (Gallup)	67
1978 (Gallup)	69

results suggest that a dramatic reduction in negative sentiment somehow took place during this two-year period. The 1975 and 1976 Yankelovich questions were also worded identically but show widely differing results. Some caution must be exercised, therefore, in drawing inferences about trends.

The results seem to indicate the following: if anything, there was a modest *increase* in the proportion of the public that felt Jews have too much power between the early 1960s and the mid-1970s. This conclusion is evident from comparing the 1962/64 results with the Yankelovich results of the mid-1970s (these are the questions that were worded most comparably). Allowing for the fact that the Yankelovich figures may have been inflated by virtue of having been obtained from a question that also asked about the power of a number of groups other than Jews, the differences suggest a significant increase between the earlier and the later years. The average of the 1962 and 1964 figures is 14 percent, while the average of the 1975 and 1976 figures is 32 percent. The CPS figures are from differently worded questions. They indicate that absolute levels of negative sentiment about Jewish power may not have been as high as the Yankelovich figures would suggest. But these figures also indicate a relative increase in anti-Jewish sentiment for the period 1972–1976 (from 13 percent to 17 percent). Even a comparison between the 1976 CPS figure and the average of the 1962/64 figures suggests a modest rise in negative sentiment (from 14 percent to 17 percent).

The main finding that does not support the idea of an increase is the 1978 Response Analysis figure. It is possible that suspicion of Jewish power declined substantially between 1976 and 1978. But a more likely explanation of the discrepancy between the 1978 and the 1976 figures concerns the Response Analysis survey itself. Whereas the other surveys were drawn from carefully designed samples of the U.S. population, the Response Analysis study was drawn from telephone directories and conducted by telephone without the usual attempts to reach nonrespondents. It is quite likely, in other words, that the study contained sampling biases. More important, it was done shortly after the telecast of "Holocaust" and most of the questions asked were about the Holocaust. The question about Jewish power (which followed these other questions) probably elicited fewer negative responses than it might have under other conditions.

If the balance of evidence on attitudes toward Jewish power points to an upward trend in negative sentiment, the same cannot be said about attitudes toward Jewish loyalty. Here the evidence is remarkable for the stability it reveals. Both in 1964 and in various studies conducted between 1974 and 1978, the proportion agreeing that Jews are more loyal to Israel than to the United States has stood at about 30 percent. The reason this stability seems remarkable is that attitudes toward Israel itself have fluctuated dramatically with changing political conditions in the Middle East. The two facts taken together suggest that views of Jewish loyalty may be only weakly associated with opinions of Israel.

Information on other stereotypes has been less abundant than might be expected. Two questions that provide comparisons over time are Stember's 1962 question about objectionable qualities of Jews and Harris's similarly worded question in 1974. Judging strictly by the percentages mentioning negative qualities, it appears that there may have been an increase in negative stereotyping. But care must be exercised in drawing this conclusion, because the two questions were not worded exactly the same. Nor is it clear how much the responses may have been affected by interviewer probing or related questions. A comparison of the specific kinds of qualities mentioned (such as aggressiveness and clannishness) suggests that the content of anti-Jewish stereotyping may have remained much the same. The evidence, therefore, gives no indication that volunteered stereotypes have declined or become less negative since the early 1960s, but it is difficult to know with certainty whether they have become more negative, as the data may suggest at first glance.

The only stereotype question that was worded exactly the same in two studies is the one about Jewish businessmen being less honest than other businessmen. In both the Selznick and Steinberg study in 1964 and the Harris study in 1974, respondents expressed this stereotype by disagreeing with a statement denying any differences between the ethics of Jewish businessmen and other businessmen. The results indicate a substantial decline in the proportions disagreeing. The Stember study in 1962 included a related question that asked people whether they thought Jewish businessmen were "more honest or less honest" than other businessmen, and found fewer who thought they were less honest than in the Selznick and Steinberg study. But even the Stember figure suggests that there has, at least, been no increase in the prevalence of this stereotype.

The evidence on trends in feelings toward Jews presents an interesting contrast to the trends in stereotypes. This evidence is limited to that obtained from the CPS national election survey's "feeling thermometer," since the Gallup "scalometer" has not been used over any substantial period of time. The evidence, therefore, is subject to the limitations that were discussed earlier with respect to the "feeling thermometer." Nonetheless, the "feeling thermometer" is one of the few surveys to include questions about Jews that have been worded identically each time they have been asked. The data show that the proportions of the public who said they disliked Jews declined between 1964 and 1972. But between 1972 and 1976 these proportions increased, such that the percentage expressing dislike for Jews in 1976 was even somewhat higher than it had been in 1964.

A more detailed examination of these changes (see Figure 4.1) shows that there was also a substantial decline between 1972 and 1976 in the frequency of positive feelings toward Jews. This proportion was smaller in

FIGURE 4.1

**"Feeling Thermometer" Ratings of Jews, 1964–76
(national sample, age 21 and over, non-Jews only)**

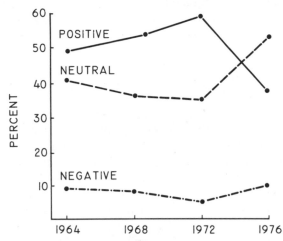

Source: Adapted from Center for Political Studies. National Election Surveys 1964–1976, University of Michigan.

1976 than it had been in 1964. The largest increase between 1972 and 1976 was in the proportion expressing no feelings toward Jews either way.

What may have caused this shift in feelings between 1972 and 1976 is a question that needs to be addressed in further research. The shift itself must be treated with some caution, however, since it is based on responses to a single survey question. If it is a meaningful shift, it suggests that the salience of Jews as a target for public sentiment of any kind may be declining. In other words, a larger proportion of the public now than previously feels it is acceptable to have no feelings about Jews one way or the other. There continues to be a small proportion of the public that dislikes Jews. But the prevailing shift has been toward no feelings rather than feelings of warmth.

There is also some limited evidence on changes in discriminatory attitudes toward Jews during the 1970s (see Table 4.9). Gallup questions on willingness to vote for a Jew for president show that current attitudes are more tolerant than they were in 1959 (82 percent favorable versus 72 percent). The current figure, though, is no higher than it was in 1967. In other words, political tolerance toward Jews appears to have risen steadily until about 1967, but has not risen further since that time. The evidence on tolerance of intermarriage between Jews and non-Jews shows a somewhat similar, though slightly later, pattern of change. Between 1968 and 1972 attitudes toward intermarriage appeared to be getting more liberal, but since 1972 they have stayed virtually the same. In other words, both kinds of attitudes showed little change in the 1970s, although there had been trends toward increasing tolerance through the mid-1960s to late-1960s.

A Closer Look at the 1970s

Overall, judging from the various sorts of available evidence, it appears that the 1960s marked a continuation of earlier trends away from negative attitudes and feelings about Jews. The two exceptions to these trends appear to have been an increase in negative sentiments about Jewish power and relative constancy in attitudes about Jewish loyalty toward Israel. But specific stereotypes, general feelings, and discriminatory attitudes all appeared to decline as far as negative sentiments were concerned. The trends during the 1970s suggest that anti-Semitic feelings may no longer be on the decline, and may have increased. Discriminatory attitudes and opinions of Jewish loyalty appear to have remained about the same during the 1970s, while opinions of Jewish power and feelings about Jews appear to be tinged with more suspicion and dislike at the end of the 1970s than they were in the early 1970s.

A somewhat more detailed picture of these trends is provided by data from three Harris surveys (conducted in 1974, 1976, and 1978) that asked several identically worded questions about attitudes toward Jews (see Table 4.10). The data show that there was little change in overtly negative beliefs about Jews between 1974 and 1978. The largest change was a 4 percent decline in the proportion who subscribed to the idea that "Jews are irritating because they are too aggressive." But this change is within the range of differences that might be due to sampling error. And another negative stereotype ("When it comes to choosing between people and money, Jews will choose money") showed identical responses in 1978 and in 1974. The main trend manifested in the data was a shift away from positive attitudes toward Jews. There was an 8 percent decline in the tendency to subscribe to the idea that "Jews have to work harder because they've been discriminated against in so many places," a 7 percent decline in the view that "Jews have supported rights for minority groups more than other white people," and a 10 percent decline in the idea that "Jews have suffered from persecution through the centuries."

Summary: Three Profiles

It is too soon to determine whether the trends in attitudes toward Jews during the 1970s represent something appreciably new or simply the culmination of longer-range trends. The longer-range trends are easier to evaluate. Since the late 1930s there has been a dramatic reorientation of public opinion toward Jews. Perhaps the best way of summarizing the force

TABLE 4.10
Trends in Stereotypes, 1974–78
"Do you tend to agree or disagree with the
following statements made about Jews?"
(percent agreeing)

	1974	1976	1978
Jews are irritating because they are too aggressive.	31	29	27
When it comes to choosing between people and money, Jews will choose money.	34	30	34
Most of the slumlords are Jewish.	21	20	20
Jews have to work harder because they've been discriminated against in so many places.	34	35	26
Jews have supported rights for minority groups more than other white people.	36	36	29
Jews have suffered from persecution through the centuries.	85	87	75

Source: Harris and Associates, 1978.

of this reorientation is to compare three composite profiles of public opinion toward Jews—in the late 1930s, in the early 1960s, and in the late 1970s.

In the late 1930s there were many who manifested no hostility or prejudice toward Jews. But at most they represented only about half the American public. The other half opposed hiring Jewish employees, thought Jewish businessmen were dishonest, regarded Jews as having too much power, said they would not vote for a Jew for president, and considered the persecution Jews were experiencing in Europe as being their own fault. Up to two-thirds of the public were against allowing more Jewish exiles to emigrate to America, said they would object to their son or daughter marrying a Jew, and regarded Jews as having objectionable traits. One in every five Americans considered Jews a menace to American society. About one-fourth expected there would be a widespread campaign against Jews in the United States; one in eight said they would support such a campaign.

By the early 1960s the picture had altered considerably. The dominant view was now one of tolerance rather than bigotry. Only one-third said they would object to marrying a Jew, and less than one-fourth thought Jews were dishonest, had objectionable traits, or had too much power. Virtually no one supported discrimination against Jews as far as housing, hiring, or college admissions was concerned, and hardly anyone still held the view that Jews were a menace to society. The only negative stereotypes that still received acceptance by large minorities of the public had to do with Jewish aggressiveness and clannishness.

As of the mid-1970s to late-1970s, public attitudes toward Jews continued to be overwhelmingly favorable in comparison with the attitudes of several decades before. Whereas the majority view during World War II had been to regard Jews as a race that had brought persecution on itself, the vast majority in the 1970s were aware of the history of Jewish persecution and only a few blamed it on the Jews themselves. The majority also regarded Jews as being honest, philanthropic, talented, and intelligent. Only about one-fourth of the public held negative attitudes about Jewish clannishness and Jewish aggressiveness. Over 80 percent said they would vote for someone who was Jewish for president, if that person was qualified. The core of consistently negative opinion and overt dislike toward Jews had shrunk to only about 10 percent of the population. Still, there were larger numbers—between one in four and one in three—who questioned the power and loyalty of Jews, who disapproved of intermarriage between Jews and non-Jews, and who subscribed to mildly negative stereotypes about Jews.

The Question of Interpretation

Once the factual evidence on trends and contemporary attitudes and feelings toward Jews has been considered, difficult questions of interpretation remain. First, there is the question of truth content. If a large number of Jews say they would support Israel even if this meant opposing U.S. policy, does saying that Jews are more loyal to Israel than to the United States necessarily constitute anti-Semitism? Or is it anti-Semitic to say that Jews are clannish when historically their very survival has required their sticking together? Consider the following. A study of prejudice among high school students in several schools containing large numbers of Jewish students found that non-Jewish students tended to regard their Jewish counterparts as clannish. But the study also found that Jewish students were indeed more likely to associate with Jews than with non-Jews, and that their parents put pressure on them to date Jews rather than non-Jews (as did Christians' parents to date Christians; Glock et al., 1975). Were the non-Jewish students responding to fact or displaying prejudice?

An argument used frequently in justification of considering attitudes like the above as signs of anti-Semitism is to say that these attitudes are stereotypes. A stereotype is an overgeneralization that attributes to an entire group characteristics that may be true only of some of its members. To say that "Jews" are clannish fails to recognize that some are and some aren't. To say that "Jews" are more loyal to Israel than to the United States denies the fact that a majority may be more loyal to the United States than to Israel, or may hold dual loyalties. Frequently stereotypic thinking develops in the absence of true information. One hears an anecdote about Jews being clannish or disloyal, and jumps to the conclusion that all Jews are this way. Evidence to the contrary may be dismissed as the exception proving the rule.

Unfortunately, the kind of evidence supplied by public opinion polls is seldom detailed enough to tell whether a person is genuinely manifesting stereotypic thinking by subscribing to a statement about Jews. Faced with the choice of having to agree or disagree with a statement about Jews (such as "Jews are more loyal to Israel than to the United States"), a person who knows that *some* Jews are like this may agree rather than imply by disagreeing that *no* Jews are like this (or earn the interviewer's displeasure by refusing to answer). What such a person means to say is that there is a probability of Jews being as the statement says, and, although this probability may not be high, it is perhaps higher than among non-Jews. Survey questions seldom provide for this degree of complexity. If the statement in question contains an element of truth, respondents are forced to deny this element of truth in order to avoid appearing prejudiced.

It is also the case, though, that the kinds of statements used to measure prejudice are typically more than mere probabilistic statements of fact. Usually they reflect an extreme view or one with clearly negative connotations. For example, the statement that Jews are more loyal to Israel than to the United States carries deeper connotations than one that merely describes Jews as willing to support Israel in opposition to official U.S. policy. Some of the survey questions typically employed also ask for evaluations to be made, rather than for mere agreement or disagreement (for example, Jews having *too much* power or *disapproving* of intermarriage with Jews). Questions phrased in these ways presumably tap into sentiments that are genuinely anti-Semitic. Yet there is no guarantee that even such questions provide infallible indicators of anti-Semitism.

Because any single survey question is likely to fall short of capturing the complexity of the public's views, careful studies of prejudice have generally been on scales that combine responses to a number of questions to measure anti-Semitism. In their study *The Tenacity of Prejudice* (1969), for example, Selznick and Steinberg combined responses to 11 stereotype questions to form an index of anti-Semitism. Such a measure makes it possible to arrange people along a continuum on which persons subscribing to most or all of the statements used to construct the scale are regarded as having a higher likelihood of actually being anti-Semitic than persons subscribing to none or to only a few of the items. A scale gives no firm criteria for classifying particular individuals as anti-Semitic or as not anti-Semitic, but it allows comparisons to be made between persons with higher and lower probabilities of being anti-Semitic.

Having a scale to measure anti-Semitism also makes it easier to assess the meaning of particular survey questions. For example, Selznick and Steinberg found that people who thought Jews were more loyal to Israel than to the United States were also more likely to agree that Jews have irritating faults, are dishonest, wield too much power, and so on. In other words, some who question Jewish loyalty are responding simply to the element of truth contained in the statement, but the overriding tendency is for this view to go along with other negative ideas about Jews. Among those in the study who subscribed to the other 10 stereotypes about Jews, 90 percent thought Jews were more loyal to Israel than to the United States, whereas on the average only 30 percent held this view. However, some of those who manifested no other signs of anti-Semitism still questioned Jewish loyalty (among persons agreeing with none of the other 10 items, for example, 5 percent agreed with the statement about Jewish loyalty). In short, some persons agreed with the statement, presumably because it bore an element of truth, even though they held no negative sentiments about Jews.

What can be inferred, then, from the survey evidence we have reviewed? Some assistance may be obtained from the Selznick and Steinberg study. In their sample (based on a national poll conducted in 1964) about three-quarters of those who held the view that Jews are more loyal to Israel than to the United States seemed to be persons who could be classified as anti-Semitic, judging from all the various questions the authors had at their disposal. The other one-quarter were not. If the meaning of this item has stayed roughly the same, these figures suggest that a reasonable inference to draw from the fact that 29 percent of the public now subscribes to this view would be that no more than about 21 percent could be classified as anti-Semitic if more extensive information were available.

Extrapolating in the same manner from other questions in the Selznick and Steinberg study suggests that about 24 percent of the public may be responding in an anti-Semitic way when they deny that Jewish businessmen are as honest as other businessmen; between 15 percent and 24 percent may be reflecting anti-Semitism in responses to questions about Jews having too much power (depending on which poll is used). These figures seem consistent with the findings (discussed earlier) showing that between one-fourth and one-third of the public volunteered things they disliked about Jews when asked to do so in the 1974 poll. They are higher, however, than the proportion (10–12 percent) that characterizes its overall feelings toward Jews as dislike.

Whether these particular extrapolations are accurate can be questioned. The general point worth remembering is that everyone who agrees with a particular survey question cannot be classified as anti-Semitic, especially if the question contains an element of truth. At the same time, responses to stereotype questions cannot be discounted simply because they contain a factual dimension.

A second question of interpretation is illustrated by the "fully-only" problem. The question is basically whether the 10 percent who say they dislike Jews (or the 25 percent who say things that may reflect negative attitudes toward Jews) constitutes a significant enough number to elicit concern ("fully 10 percent") or whether it is such a small proportion as to be negligible ("only 10 percent"). A satisfactory answer to a question such as this requires a great deal of knowledge about the history and character of prejudice, social conditions, and the role of prejudice in social life. Even those who claim such knowledge may arrive at different assessments. At minimum, the answer given will depend on several considerations.

First, what is being evaluated. A statistic showing that 10 percent of the public has cancer will be taken more seriously than one showing that 10 percent has sore throats. If "dislike Jews" conjures up images of concentration camps, pogroms, and synagogue burnings (actual or potential), any porportion clearly will be regarded more seriously than if "dislike Jews" is considered bland, natural, or inconsequential.

Second, what implicit comparisons are being made. Four options are possible: comparisons with the past, comparisons with other social groups, comparisons with an idealized state of affairs, and comparisons with what is considered reasonably attainable. Comparisons with the past typically lead to inferences that current levels of anti-Semitism are relatively benign. Comparisons with other social groups are more difficult to make, since various such comparisons are possible. As the survey evidence has shown, Jews tend to elicit more dislike than Protestants or Catholics, but less dislike (generally) than blacks. Comparisons with an idealized state of affairs are most likely to inflate the seriousness with which anti-Semitism is regarded. Many who have studied it have likened it to a disease that should be eradicated completely. As long as 10 percent of the population is afflicted, there is cause for concern. Comparisons with what is reasonably attainable tend to produce mixed evaluations.

Those making these comparisons readily admit the unlikelihood of eliminating prejudice completely, but hold to the conviction that it probably can still be reduced. Present levels of anti-Semitism, in their view, may not be high, but are perhaps higher than necessary. There is no reason why one, rather than all, of these comparisons should not be made. Knowing and using all the available options is likely to produce the most balanced assessment.

Third, who is doing the evaluating. Admittedly this is a touchy question, but it is one that must be confronted openly. An investigator who has devoted years of his or her life to the study of prejudice may be more inclined to emphasize, rather than minimize, the seriousness of the problem. The same may be said of a funding agency that has poured thousands of dollars into studying the problem. By the same token, someone who belongs to an ethnic group or social stratum accused of being prejudiced may discount the seriousness of the problem altogether. The victims of prejudice are also likely to be deeply divided over its importance: some will wish to ignore it entirely, while others will exaggerate its effects. Perhaps the main thing to be said is that both caution and introspection need to be exercised in interpreting statistics on anti-Semitism.

A third question concerns the balance between positive and negative stereotypes. What is the significance of the fact that positive images of Jews are subscribed to by a ratio of two to one, compared with negative images? This question can be addressed from three quite different perspectives. The first suggests that the positive images serve as a counterbalance to the negative images. The second says the positive images provide no counterbalance, and may even be detrimental. The third stresses the ambivalence illustrated by the joint presence of the two. Those who adopt the first view readily admit the truth content of stereotypes. They recognize that Jews, like any group, have likable and unlikable qualities. They are less concerned about the public's criticism of the latter as long as it also acknowledges the former. The second view tends more to regard stereotyping of all kinds as faulty thinking. From this perspective, negative images are problematic independently of whatever positive images may be held, and the positive images reflect a simplistic tendency to see Jews as a monolithic category rather than a heterogeneous population. The third view derives from the observation that negative and positive stereotypes often resemble each other, differing only in the evaluation attached to a perceived characteristic, such as Jewish ambition or the Jewish presence in business. According to this view, simultaneous but discrepant evaluations indicate an ambivalent orientation toward Jews. Ambivalence is an unstable attitude based on an exaggerated, if not irrational, assessment of desirable and undesirable qualities. When fear and fascination are present, unpredictable behavioral responses, including hostility and discrimination, can result.

Of the three views, the last has been least supported empirically. Those who hold negative images of Jews usually are not the same persons who hold positive images. If there is any ambivalence, therefore, it is at the cultural level rather than at the individual level. The second view has been emphasized in many empirical studies. These have shown the undesirable consequences of negative stereotypes, particularly at the interpersonal level when hostility or avoidance is manifested. The effects of positive stereotypes have been largely ignored in these studies. The first view gives perhaps the most balanced overall assessment of the relation between stereotypes and the larger position of Jews in the society. It is clear that positive as well as negative relations have been cultivated between non-Jews and Jews.

Finally, there is the question of what moral significance should be attached to stereotypes and negative feelings. Here again, different positions have been taken and it is difficult to determine which is more appropriate, since the arguments rest more on conceptions of value and propriety than on observations of fact. One argument holds that people have the right to think and feel what they please, as long as their thoughts and feelings do not infringe on the rights and freedoms of others. According to this view, prejudice does not afford cause for particular concern unless it results in discrimination. In the case of anti-Semitism, the relatively privileged status that Jews have acquired in American society is pointed to as evidence that prejudice should not be considered a problem of moral significance.

An opposing argument—and this is probably the most commonly shared view among social scientists who have studied prejudice—is that stereotypes and ill-feelings are intrinsically subject to moral reproach. According to this view all expressions of disapproval should be eradicated, and a culturally relative attitude of tolerance and acceptance should be engendered even toward groups whose life-styles and values may be radically different from prevailing cultural standards. Falling somewhere in between these opposing views is the argument that social criticism should be upheld and encouraged, even toward minority groups, as long as the criticisms stem from thoughtfully held value positions, are applied justly, and are not in violation of civil liberties.

The three views are well illustrated in the different arguments that have been presented concerning the right of openly prejudiced groups, such as the American Nazi party, to hold demonstrations. According to one view, these groups need not elicit serious concern because their activities (thus far) have not resulted in any overt aggression toward Jews or other minorities. According to a second view, the open display of prejudice is itself damaging, and should be actively opposed. Others hold the view that these groups' rights to speak out should be protected, but that their arguments should be scrutinized to determine if they are accurate and fair.

It should be fully apparent from these many views and considerations that the facts alone do not yield definitive inferences about the nature and extent of contemporary anti-Semitism. The evidence from polls and surveys provides a basis for interpretation, but the interpretation itself depends on additional considerations of perspective and evaluation. It is possible to lay out the main perspectives from which some choice must be made, but not to dictate what that choice should be. What social scientists have attempted to do is provide evidence on the relative magnitude of stereotypes and feelings that may serve as crude indicators of anti-Semitism, and to develop theories explaining variations in the occurrence of these stereotypes and feelings. Once this evidence has been provided, the problem of interpretation remains, but presumably can be addressed from a more informed perspective.

THE SOCIAL LOCATION OF NEGATIVE ATTITUDES

As a first step toward explaining why people hold negative attitudes toward Jews, social scientists have attempted to learn who these people are and how they differ from people who do not harbor hostility toward Jews. Research has generally focused on the following social distinctions: education, occupation, age cohort, religion, and race.

Education

Of all the social differences that appear to distinguish people who hold negative images of Jews and people who reject such images, educational differences appear to have the most decided effect. Quinley and Glock (1979) write in their overview of the Berkeley research, for example, that education is the "key factor" in explaining anti-Semitism. The higher a person's level of education, the less likely that person is to express negative attitudes or feelings toward Jews. In Selznick and Steinberg's national survey in 1964, for example, 52 percent of those who had received only grade school education scored "high" on the study's index of anti-Semitic stereotypes; by comparison, only 15 percent of those who had graduated from college scored high on the index. The only major exception to this pattern in the Selznick and Steinberg study was that the college-educated were more likely than the less educated to defend social club discrimination against Jews. Overall, the effect of education appeared to be one of increasing tolerance and sophistication as far as attitudes toward Jews were concerned.

Whether education is as strongly associated with attitudes toward Jews in the late 1970s as it was in the mid-1960s was examined in an unpublished report by Lipset and Schneider (1979). Using data from the 1974 Harris poll, they constructed an index of anti-Semitic stereotyping that, though containing questions different from those asked in the Selznick and Steinberg study, would classify respondents according to relative degrees of stereotyping in a manner comparable with the earlier research. This index, it turns out, is related just as strongly to education as Selznick and Steinberg's index had been. Lipset and Schneider concluded that education is still one of the most powerful factors affecting anti-Semitism, and that the rise in overall levels of education in the United States constitutes a significant reason for the reduction of anti-Semitic stereotyping that has occurred over the past several decades.

These conclusions pertain to anti-Semitic stereotyping. The relationships between education and other perceptions of Jews are less simple. For example, Lipset and Schneider show that persons with college and postgraduate degrees are more likely than persons with high school educations to say that Jews have too much power. They suggest that persons with higher levels of education may have more contact with Jews or may be more aware of the kinds of power that Jews actually have than persons with lower levels of education.

The relationships between education and feelings about Jews also differ from the relationships between education and stereotypes. The ratio of negative to positive feelings on the CPS "feeling thermometer" was higher among persons with lower levels of education than among persons with higher levels in both 1964 and 1976. But the differences between the less-educated and the more-educated were significantly smaller in 1976 than in

1964 (see Figure 4.2). This was due to the fact that feelings among the grade-school-educated had remained virtually unchanged while feelings among the college-educated had become substantially less positive than they had been in 1964. These changes suggest that the power of education as a force against prejudice may have diminished somewhat as the numbers of persons obtaining higher levels of education have increased. This is a relative decline. Overall, education remains strongly associated with the tendency to reject negative images of Jews.

Occupation and Income

Since levels of education are closely associated with differences in occupation and income, investigators have sought to discover whether anti-Semitism also varies according to occupation and level of income, and whether it is these differences or the differences in education that are actually responsible for differences in anti-Semitism. Studies such as those of Selznick and Steinberg and Lipset and Schneider have generally shown that

FIGURE 4.2

**Anti-Jewish Feeling by Education, 1964 and 1976
(ratio of negative to positive "feeling thermometer" scores on a log scale)**

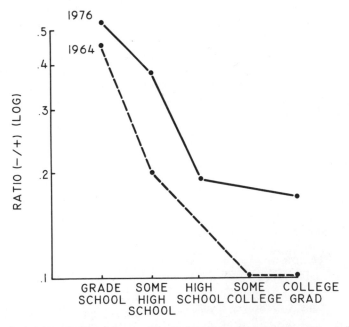

Source: Adapted from Center for Political Studies. National Election Surveys 1964–1976, University of Michigan.

anti-Semitism is lower among white-collar workers than among blue-collar workers, and that it decreases with rising levels of income. However, these differences usually disappear or are substantially reduced when level of education is controlled. Accordingly, most investigators have come to regard characteristics intrinsically associated with education, such as greater cognitive sophistication or different cultural values and tastes, as the principal factors leading to a reduction of anti-Semitism, rather than the sheer fact that educated people may have higher incomes or more secure jobs.

Age Cohort

Age differences have been of particular interest to researchers investigating anti-Semitism, since lower levels of prejudice among the young would provide further evidence that anti-Semitism was declining, whereas any substantial tendency for the young to hold higher levels of anti-Semitism might signal a trend toward increasing anti-Semitism. Judging from the trends that have been examined already, we would expect the young to be less prejudiced than the old. This is generally what studies have shown. In Selznick and Steinberg's study, for example, 59 percent of those in the survey who were 55 or older scored high on the anti-Semitism index, compared with 31 percent of those 35 or younger. Since levels of education tend to be higher among the young than among the old, Selznick and Steinberg also controlled for education, and found that the differences attributable to age, though reduced, were still significant. Lipset and Schneider found that similar differences were evident among white respondents in the 1974 Harris data.

Another use that has come increasingly to be made of data on age differences concerns the role of cohorts. Social scientists have suggested that a cohort of people born during roughly the same interval of time may respond to events in a way that differs from that of another cohort born at a different time. In the case of anti-Semitism, the cohort of people who were young during World War II, for example, might well be expected to have different attitudes toward Jews than a cohort of people who had matured before the war or another cohort that was not born until after the war.

Cohorts become particularly useful for studying changes in attitudes. Lacking data on changes in particular individuals' attitudes over a period of time, it is possible to make estimates of such changes by comparing the attitudes of a "birth cohort" (that is, a group of people born during a particular period) at one time period with the attitudes of that same birth cohort at a later time. For example, it would be possible to compare the "feeling thermometer" scores given in 1964 by people who had been born between 1900 and 1919 with those given in 1976 by people born during that period. The differences would provide an estimate of how much the attitudes of this particular cohort of people had changed between 1964 and 1976. By examining changes in the attitudes of cohorts, it is possible to determine whether trends have occurred because people's attitudes have actually changed over time, or simply because older people have died and have been replaced by new cohorts of younger people.

An illustration of a cohort analysis is shown in Table 4.11, which compares the "feeling thermometer" responses of four cohorts of people given in 1964 and again in 1976. They are a "prewar" cohort who had reached maturity before the start of World War II, a "World War II" cohort who matured during the war, a "Cold War" cohort who matured after World War II, and a "Sixties" cohort who matured during the countercultural unrest of that decade. It will be recalled that the overall trend in "feeling thermometer" scores between 1964 and 1976 was one of increasing negativity toward Jews. The data in Table 4.11 reveal more clearly how that change came about. The prewar cohort showed virtually no change in its feelings toward Jews. In both 1964 and 1976 it was the most negative of all the cohorts. The feelings of this group, it appears, had developed at a time when anti-Semitism ran high in American culture, and even at these later points these feelings remained relatively negative.

In comparison, the cohort that matured during World War II was least disposed to hold negative feelings toward Jews in 1964, but its feelings became markedly more negative by 1976. The Cold War cohort (which matured immediately following World War II) scored almost as low on negative feelings in 1964 as the World War II cohort. But by 1976 its feelings had become considerably more negative. Indeed, its feelings had become slightly more negative even than those of the prewar cohort. What appears

TABLE 4.11
Feelings Toward Jews by Cohort, 1964-76

| Cohort | Birth Year | Ratio of Negative to Positive Feelings | | |
		1964	1976	1976 ÷ 1964
Pre-World War II	1900–1919	.25	.28	1.12
		(406)	(560)	
World War II	1920–1927	.09	.18	2.00
		(250)	(258)	
Cold War	1928–1939	.13	.30	2.31
		(346)	(353)	
Sixties	1940–1943	.16	.19	1.19
		(101)	(172)	

Source: Center for Political Studies. National Election Surveys 1964–1976, University of Michigan.

to have happened in these two cohorts was that increasing distance from World War II led to an increase in anti-Semitism. Having been socialized during or immediately following the war, these cohorts probably were keenly aware of the effects of anti-Semitism, and may have adopted artificially positive feelings toward Jews. With age and with the declining salience of anti-Semitism as an issue in American culture, however, these cohorts gradually abandoned their positive feelings toward Jews and became neutral or negative.

Finally, the cohort that matured during the 1960s showed relatively low levels of negative sentiment, and these levels remained virtually constant between 1964 and 1976. It is impossible to know precisely why its feelings remained relatively constant, but the turbulence of the 1960s (including the civil rights movement) may have been an important factor. This cohort's feelings probably were rooted less in the memory of World War II than those of the older cohorts and, therefore, may have been less subject to change with increasing distance from the war. Instead, the strong sentiments against racial prejudice and in support of other civil rights and libertarian attitudes to which this cohort was exposed as it matured during the 1960s may have prevented its feelings toward Jews from shifting in a negative direction.

Religion

Research on the relationship between religion and attitudes toward Jews has shown that negative attitudes generally are more likely to be found among Protestants than among Catholics, among members of conservative or evangelical churches and sects than among members of theologically liberal denominations, and among persons firmly committed to traditional religious beliefs than among persons less committed to such beliefs.

The differences between Catholics and Protestants, while relatively small, have been documented consistently by virtually every major study of anti-Semitism. For example, the Selznick and Steinberg survey in the mid-1960s found that 36 percent of the Protestants scored "high" on anti-Semitism, compared with 32 percent of the Catholics. Stember found similar differences in his review of the earlier polls on anti-Semitism.

Comparisons between Catholics and Protestants are not entirely meaningful, though, since there are many different Protestant denominations. The more conservative of these denominations tend to manifest considerably more readiness than the more liberal denominations to subscribe to negative attitudes toward Jews. For example, Selznick and Steinberg distinguished Unitarians, Congregationalists, and Episcopalians from other denominations, and found that the former scored significantly lower on their measure of anti-Semitism than the latter, even when differences in education were controlled. Lipset and Schneider's analysis of the

1974 Harris data found much the same denominational patterns, with Episcopalians scoring lowest on anti-Semitism and Baptists and sects scoring highest (correcting for differences in education).

Denominational differences of this sort have led to speculation that persons more committed to their religious beliefs and practices might be more negative toward Jews than the less religiously committed. One of the most careful examinations of the relationship between religiosity and attitudes toward Jews was conducted in the mid-1960s by Charles Y. Glock (published under the title *Christian Beliefs and Anti-Semitism*) as part of the Berkeley project on anti-Semitism in America. The study showed that orthodox religious belief is not necessarily a source of anti-Semitism. But orthodoxy does tend to nurture three kinds of orientations that produce anti-Semitism: particularism—the view that only Christians are saved; historic anti-Semitism—the tendency to blame Jews for the death of Christ; and religious hostility—the idea that Jews belong to a false religion and will reap God's punishment as long as they do. These orientations reinforce one another, and lead those who hold them to adopt negative attitudes of a more secular nature about Jews.

Race

A final background factor that has been included routinely in research on the social sources of anti-Semitism is race, particularly differences between the attitudes of blacks and whites. Given the fact that prejudice tends to occur more among persons with lower levels of education, it might be assumed that blacks, on the whole, would be more prejudiced toward Jews than whites would be, since average levels of education among blacks are lower than among whites. This assumption has been confirmed only for certain kinds of anti-Semitism. Most research has found that blacks are somewhat more inclined than whites to agree with stereotypes about the economic characteristics of Jews. For example, Selznick and Steinberg found that 40 percent of the blacks in their sample thought Jews control international banking, compared with only 28 percent of the whites. They found similar differences on stereotypes dealing with aggressiveness and dishonesty in business. The same patterns were evident in the 1974 Harris survey. Forty-eight percent of the blacks, compared with 34 percent of the whites, agreed with the statement "When it comes to choosing between people and money, Jews will choose money." Blacks were also more likely to agree that "Most of the slum owners are Jewish" (37 percent versus 20 percent) and that "Jewish businessmen will usually try to pull a shady deal on you" (33 percent versus 19 percent).

On stereotypes of a less economic character, blacks are usually no more inclined to agree than whites are. In the Selznick and Steinberg study, for example, there were virtually no differences between blacks and whites on agreement with stereotypes about Jews sticking together too much or having too much power. Similarly, in the Harris study blacks were no more likely than whites to say that Jews feel superior to other groups, are irritating, or are too ambitious.

The difference between blacks and whites on economic stereotypes appears to be primarily a function of economic contact between blacks and Jews. Selznick and Steinberg were able to demonstrate this fact by showing that high scores on an index of economic anti-Semitism were much higher among blacks than among whites, among those who had contact with Jews in their work, whereas there were relatively small differences among blacks and whites who had no work contact with Jews. The effect of work contact was to increase economic anti-Semitism among blacks but to reduce it among whites. For noneconomic anti-Semitism, work contact produced a reduction among both blacks and whites.

Summary

Research has located anti-Semitism primarily among the lower classes, particularly among those with lower levels of education. The effects of other social variables on anti-Semitism, in comparison with the effects of education, tend to be small and partly a function of educational differences. There is also an overlap between the kinds of people who have been found to be more anti-Semitic according to other variables and the less well-educated. Members of religiously conservative denominations and older people, for example, also tend to be people with lower levels of education. In sum, education looms as an important factor for explaining and understanding variations in anti-Semitism.

But what is it about education that causes differences in prejudice? Is it that the educated have values that militate against prejudice? Are they taught not to be prejudiced? Or do they have more opportunities and fewer frustrations, so that they can afford not to be prejudiced? These questions require an examination of the theories that have been put forth to explain anti-Semitism and the evidence that has been gathered to test these theories.

THEORIES OF ANTI-SEMITISM

The main theories that have been advanced to explain why some people are more inclined than others to exhibit anti-Semitic stereotypes and feelings include contact, authoritarianism, cultural values, and cognitive sophistication. These theories have enjoyed different degrees of success when subjected to actual research tests.

Contact

One of the earliest and simplest theories of anti-Semitism stresses lack of contact as the principal cause of ill-feelings between Jews and non-Jews. Since Jews constitute slightly less than 3 percent of the U. S. population and are concentrated largely in a few urban areas, it has seemed reasonable to believe that absence of contact might be a factor in explaining anti-Semitism. This theory rests on the assumption that the more people interact, the more they will come to like one another. For many years this generalization was proclaimed as one of social science's basic "laws" of human behavior. Not only did it seem to be supported by a great deal of evidence, but it also squared intuitively with ideas about people fearing the unknown and favoring that with which they are familiar.

Like most "laws" of human behavior, this generalization has had to be severely qualified in light of closer attention to the facts. As social scientists began to examine the relationship between contact and feelings more carefully, they rediscovered the wisdom of another ancient maxim: familiarity breeds contempt. Sometimes conflict and hatred, rather than good-feeling, result from social interaction. Thus a modified "law" was formulated: the more people interact with one another, the more they will come to like one another, *unless* they come to hate one another!

This important stipulation must be applied to the contact theory of anti-Semitism. Most research has verified the assumption that contact between Jews and non-Jews is associated more with positive feelings than with negative feelings. But there are some important exceptions. As noted earlier, for example, contact between blacks and Jews seems to contribute to negative stereotypes about Jewish economic characteristics. This fact is consonant with the results of studies examining the effects of contact between blacks and whites on racial prejudice. When contact occurs between equals, as among friends, it usually reduces prejudice; but when it occurs between persons of unequal status, as between employers and employees or between persons of discrepant socioeconomic standing, it is likely to increase levels of prejudice, especially on the part of the subordinates.

A second qualification that must be made as far as the contact theory of anti-Semitism is concerned is that the interaction has to be relatively close. It is not sufficient merely to be in the same context with Jews. Being in the same context can actually increase prejudice. This is because of the "truth content" problem discussed earlier. No ethnic group is entirely free of unlikable qualities. Persons casually acquainted with its members are more likely to be aware of this than anyone else. If they do not cultivate personal friendships across ethnic lines, their perceptions are likely to remain at the level of generalizations and criticisms.

This is clearly illustrated in Glock et al., *Adolescent Prejudice* (1975). The study included teen-agers from three high schools. In the first nearly half the students were Jewish. In the second about one-fourth were Jewish. In the third there were virtually no Jews. The anticipated result was that anti-Semitism among non-Jewish students would be lowest in the first school because of greater contact and familiarity with Jews, and highest in the third school, where such contact was precluded. The study found just the opposite to be the case. Anti-Semitism among non-Jews was highest in the school with the most Jewish students, next highest in the second school, and lowest in the school with virtually no Jews. In all three communities, however, students who listed Jews among their close friends were, as expected, less likely to harbor negative stereotypes than students who did not cultivate such friendships.

Why were ill-feelings greater in the contexts with larger numbers of Jewish students? The reasons were difficult to establish precisely, but two factors seemed to be at work. One was that non-Jews seemed to be envious of the academic success of the Jewish students. In the settings with larger numbers of Jews, accordingly, stereotypes about Jewish aggressiveness and conceit were espoused with greater frequency. Second, both Jewish and non-Jewish parents in these settings put more pressure on their children not to date outside their own religious group, because dating of this sort was a clear possibility. This pressure was associated not only with anti-Semitism on the part of the teen-agers in general but also with perceptions of Jewish clannishness.

Authoritarianism

A second theory that has been advanced to explain differences in prejudice, and in anti-Semitism particularly, stresses personality factors. The research conducted by T. W. Adorno and his colleagues in the late 1940s, leading to the publication of *The Authoritarian Personality*, was heavily influenced by Freudian psychoanalytic theory and sought to explain anti-Semitism as a product of impaired psychological functioning. Anti-Semitism was held to be but one element in a complex of attitudes that the authors characterized as "authoritarian" and attempted to measure with the "F-scale" (F for fascism). The attitudes constituting this authoritarian orientation included rigid adherence to conventional, middle-class values; submissive, uncritical attitudes toward idealized moral authorities; a tendency to condemn and reject violators of conventional values; opposition to the subjective and imaginative; superstition and stereotypic thinking; a preoccupation with power relations, strength, and toughness; generalized hostility; a tendency to believe that wild and dangerous things go on in the world; and an exaggerated concern with sexuality.

In simplest terms, the authoritarian personality theory attributes anti-Semitism and other forms of prejudice to a particular style of psychological functioning. Frustration, anxiety, ambivalence, and rigidity combine to produce aggressive behavior and stereotyped attitudes toward Jews, minority groups, or other convenient scapegoats. Prejudice and discrimination provide an emotional outlet for the pent-up anxieties that the authoritarian person cannot otherwise express.

The Selznick and Steinberg study paid careful attention to the relationship between the F-scale and anti-Semitism. They had assumed, in fact, that this relationship would prove important, both as an explanation of anti-Semitism in its own right and as an explanation for the greater preponderance of anti-Semitism among members of the lower classes, who, it might be supposed, would be more subject to frustration and anxiety, and therefore more likely to vent aggression through prejudice and discrimination. What they found was that authoritarianism seemed not to be rooted in childhood upbringing or frustrating relationships with parents, as the initial theory had suggested, but in factors associated more with the subject's own style of cognitive functioning. Using various pieces of evidence showing the importance of differences in values and styles of thinking, Selznick and Steinberg argued that authoritarianism should not be regarded as a personality style produced by repressed childhood training or subsequent frustration, but that it should be regarded more as a measure of rigid, simplistic thinking.

The study of adolescent prejudice by Charles Y. Glock and his colleagues also explored various measures of authoritarianism, frustration, and anxiety to determine whether these factors might be important to the understanding of anti-Semitism among teen-agers. Their findings were even more damaging to the authoritarian personality explanation than those of Selznick and Steinberg. Using a measure of authoritarianism that had been extensively tested in previous research to ensure against response-set bias and other difficulties of interpretation, they found no relationship at all between authoritarianism and anti-Semitism. Nor did they find any relationship between anti-Semitism and other personality scales designed to measure frustration or lack of self-esteem. Although the investigators cautioned that the lack of relationships may have been due to unseen flaws in the scales themselves, they suggested that there seemed to be little support for the idea that anti-Semitism among teen-agers is rooted in frustration or impaired psychological functioning.

It is important not to misinterpret what researchers have concluded about the overall value of the authoritarian personality theory. They have not argued that authoritarianism doesn't exist or that it has no bearing on prejudice. At least some of the research has shown positive relationships between measures of authoritarianism and measures of anti-Semitism. What researchers have taken issue with primarily is the idea that prejudice is a response to deep frustrations and anxieties in the emotional or motivational makeup of individual personalities. They have suggested, instead, that authoritarianism is a way of thinking, a cognitive style, that people learn, not because it is needed to cope with psychological problems but because people are exposed to a subculture in which these ways of thinking predominate.

Cultural Values

A third theoretical approach has attempted to explain prejudice as a product of creeds, values, and ideologies. This approach regards anti-Semitism as but one element of a broader cultural ethos composed of unenlightened values. It claims that people are anti-Semitic because they are exposed to a subculture in which prejudice, bigotry, and anti-democratic values flourish. Anti-Semitism, therefore, need not satisfy deep-seated psychological anxieties to be adopted; it is passed on from one generation to another as part of a normal outlook on life, and will be perpetuated unless other values are introduced to combat it.

In the Selznick and Steinberg study, cultural values loomed as one of the most powerful predictors of variation in anti-Semitism. Another indication that anti-Semitism is rooted in a general climate of intolerance is the fact that persons who are anti-Semitic tend to hold intolerant attitudes toward other minority groups as well. In the Selznick and Steinberg study, anti-Semitic respondents also tended to score high on measures of racial prejudice and anti-Catholic prejudice. In the 1976 CPS "feeling thermometer" responses the same patterns were evident. Among persons who disliked Catholics, 35 percent also disliked Jews, whereas only 9 percent of those who said they liked Catholics disliked Jews. And among those who disliked blacks, 25 percent disliked Jews, while only 6 percent of those who said they liked blacks disliked Jews.

The general point is that anti-Semitism is not an isolated form of intolerance, but is part of a larger subculture of anti-democratic values. To understand why people are anti-Semitic, therefore, one must understand the mechanisms by which this general anti-democratic subculture is maintained.

One such mechanism is parental influence. Within an intolerant subculture it is only natural for parents to pass along intolerant values to their children, and for their children to learn these values as part of their childhood socialization. Research has shown that children pick up prejudiced language from their parents at an early age. Some research also suggests that parents may communicate intolerant values with increasing frequency as children grow older. For example, prejudiced teen-agers in the adolescent prejudice study were likely to say that their parents had put pressure on them to date and to associate only with members of their own race and religion. This tendency appeared to increase as teen-agers matured, apparently because parents become more concerned that their children might enter into interracial or interreligious romances.

Another mechanism by which an intolerant subculture is maintained is peer pressure. A characteristic of all subcultures is that persons holding similar values interact with one another, thereby maintaining and mutually reinforcing the values of their subculture. The effect of such interaction on anti-Semitism was also documented in the adolescent prejudice study.

A third mechanism that reinforces intolerant values is what social scientists have termed "localism." Localism refers to the degree to which persons' interests are oriented to their family, immediate friends, and local community. It contrasts with cosmopolitan interests of a more national or international scope. Social researchers have investigated the effects of localism and cosmopolitanism on prejudice and other forms of intolerance. In a study of North Carolina church members, for example, Wade Clark Roof (1978) showed that "locals" were significantly more anti-Semitic, racially prejudiced, and politically conservative than "cosmopolitans," even when differences in education were taken into account.

Roof's study also demonstrated that part of the relationship between traditional religious commitment and intolerance was attributable to the fact that religiously committed persons also tended to be locally oriented, and that religious participation reinforced intolerance when people were locally oriented, but not when their outlooks were cosmopolitan. The effect of localism, it appears, is to shield people from the influence of the larger culture. It serves, in effect, as a protective cognitive barrier around the traditional folk cultures in which intolerance flourishes.

The primary factor that weakens commitment to a subculture of intolerant values appears to be education. It exposes people to democratic ideals that they may not have learned from their parents or peers, and broadens their interests so that they come to be more tolerant of cultural diversity. As levels of education have risen, tolerance and civil libertarian values have also become more prevalent. The extent of the change has been documented by a replication of Samuel Stouffer's study *Communism, Conformity, and Civil Liberties*. In 1954, Stouffer found that 89 percent of the public thought an admitted Communist should not be allowed to teach in a college or university. By 1977 this figure had dropped to 57 percent. Other comparisons showed that support for removing a book by a Communist from the public library had dropped from 66 percent to 42 percent, willingness to deny the right of speech to a Communist had declined from 68 percent to 42 percent, and intolerance of atheists on each of these measures had also declined (from 84 to 39 percent for teaching; from 60 to 39 percent for books; and from 60 to 37 percent for speaking). In short, not only anti-Semitism but also the subculture of intolerance in general has eroded significantly over the past several decades.

The other main body of research concerning anti-Semitism and values has been that focused on the effects of political ideology. A major study by Lipset and Raab, *The Politics of Unreason* (1970), examined the role that right-wing extremism has played in American politics and its effects on attitudes toward Jews and other minority groups. The study showed that not only has there been an anti-democratic subculture in the United States, but that its fears and prejudices have been exploited repeatedly by arch-conservative political groups. Anti-Semitism has been nourished as part of the ideologies of such groups. People who have found themselves dispossessed by social change (the "once-hads") have been particularly susceptible to these appeals. These movements have emerged periodically in response to economic and political upheavals. Their successes have been limited as far as mainstream politics is concerned, but they have been an important force in the periodic rekindling of anti-Semitism.

Extremist left-wing movements have traditionally avoided anti-Semitism as part of their ideologies. However, Lipset and Schneider (1979) note that anti-Semitism appears to be gaining ground among younger political liberals. Young people (under 40) who voted for George McGovern in the 1972 presidential election, for example, were as anti-Semitic in the 1974 Harris survey as younger people who voted for Richard Nixon. They also expressed more sentiment against Israel. By comparison, older people who voted for McGovern were significantly less anti-Semitic than older people who voted for Nixon.

Lipset and Schneider suggest that two developments, in particular, have probably contributed to the new mood of anti-Jewish feeling among younger liberals. The first was the Black Power movement, which separated the more militant left, among both young blacks and young whites, from the more moderate liberals who had supported the civil rights movement. Jews had been associated with the latter, and therefore came under attack from the former. The anti-Jewish sentiments held by younger blacks have already been discussed. The second appears to have been Israel. Although liberals have generally expressed greater support for Israel in public opinion polls than conservatives have, these differences have been small (and sometimes reversed) among younger people. The reason has been a feeling, especially on the part of younger liberals and radicals, that Israel has exploited Palestinians and that the United States has used Israel to advance imperialist objectives against Arab countries.

Both of these ideologies are of recent origin, and may be of limited duration. But they illustrate a more general point about the relationship between values and anti-Semitism: its volatility. While there has been a general erosion of anti-democratic values in American culture, attitudes toward Jews are influenced by other values and interests. These have been subject to greater fluctuation that depends on short-term political and economic events.

Cognitive Sophistication

The leading theory of prejudice that has been advanced on the basis of recent research views anti-Semitism as a function of differences in levels of cognitive sophistication. Anti-Semitism, according to this theory, consists principally of faulty habits of thought. These habits are characterized by simplism, overgeneralization, and fallacies of logic. They reflect early childhood training and inadequate exposure to the educational process. Education, if effective, arms individuals against simplistic thinking and reduces their inclination to accept anti-Semitism and other stereotypes. It also exposes individuals to the historical, social, and cultural sources of differences between minority and majority groups, and teaches about the harmful effects of prejudice and discrimination.

The cognitive perspective on prejudice contrasts sharply with that represented by the authoritarian personality research. The two begin by raising different questions about prejudice. The authoritarian personality theory asks why people *adopt* prejudice, and suggests that they do so because they have deep-seated psychological needs that must be fulfilled. Cognitive theory asks why people *abandon* prejudice, and suggests that they will do so only if they are exposed to educational influences that jar them out of traditional habits of thought. In other words, cognitive theory assumes that prejudice is sufficiently prevalent to be learned naturally, and to become a natural way of thinking without having to fulfill any particular personality needs.

Cognitive theory also contrasts with theories stressing cultural values, although this distinction is less pronounced. In some respects, cognitive theory subsumes theories emphasizing cultural values, since exposure to enlightened, libertarian values presupposes a certain degree of cognitive sophistication. The difference is primarily one of emphasis. Those who stress the importance of cultural values emphasize the importance of specific ideas, such as democracy and liberalism, in inhibiting prejudice. Those who stress the importance of cognitive sophistication attach more emphasis to the style or form of one's thought, apart from its specific content. Thus, sophisticated modes of thought inhibit tendencies to overgeneralize, help one to make more accurate social distinctions, and lend themselves to more complex views of history and of society, which in turn reduce tendencies to engage in anti-Semitic stereotyping.

The effectiveness of cognitive theory for explaining variations in anti-Semitism has been demonstrated in various research studies. For example, the Selznick and Steinberg study found a strong relationship between a scale measuring "simplism" (tendencies to reduce complex social problems to simple solutions) and anti-Semitism. Similarly, the adolescent prejudice research found strong relationships between anti-Semitism and various cognitive measures, including simplism, intellectual orientations, and academic achievement. Other studies that have focused on different variables have also tended to stress the importance of cognitive sophistication. For example, Lipset and Raab's study of political extremism found that "monism" (seeing things through a single perspective) was a common theme in many extremist movements. Or, to take another example, Roof's study of the effects of localism stresses that localism is essentially a narrowed perspective that prevents persons from recognizing the complexity of social life.

Rethinking Anti-Semitism

The finding that anti-Semitism appears primarily to reflect a style of thinking rather than a need-induced personality formation has led social scientists to reexamine the cognitive components of prejudice. This work has resulted in some important modifications in the way prejudice is defined. These modifications suggest ways to overcome some of the difficulties of interpretation that were discussed earlier. They are also aimed at providing more effective means of combating prejudice. Essentially they revolve around a distinction between the perceptual and the explanatory components of attitudes toward Jews.

The perceptual component refers to the attitudes that are perceived as being characteristic of Jews. It refers particularly to perceptions of differences between Jews and non-Jews. For example, Jews may be perceived as being relatively powerful, intelligent, ambitious, wealthy, dishonest, clannish, pushy, religious, hard-working, greedy, and so on. Both positive and negative characteristics are likely to be perceived. Perceptions of this nature are to be evaluated primarily in terms of truth content. Research might show, for example, that there is some truth to the idea that Jews are relatively wealthy compared with other minority groups; it might show that the idea of Jews being relatively dishonest is completely false. Stereotyping, therefore, may be defined as a perception that is either untrue or overexaggerated. A group difference, for example, may in fact exist, but not exist to the extent or as universally as it is perceived.

The explanatory component of anti-Semitism refers to the fact that people generally not only perceive group differences, but also adopt implicit or explicit explanations to account for these differences. A perception of Jewish clannishness, for example, can be explained as a racial quirk, or it can be explained as a product of historical circumstances. The importance of the explanatory component, apart from perceptions, should be evident from this example. An explanation stressing racial quirks is likely to lead to quite different feelings and actions than one stressing historical conditions.

In attempting to explain why people harbor negative feelings toward Jews or engage in discriminatory acts toward them, both perceptions and explanations are likely to be important. A false or overexaggerated perception of some negative characteristic is likely to reinforce ill-feeling and discrimination. So is an explanation that focuses on racial, genetic, or other immutable group traits rather than on broader social forces. Even a mistaken perception of Jewish characteristics is less likely to lead to hostility or hatred if it is properly explained. All the more so for negative characteristics that may in fact exist: ill-feelings can perhaps be avoided simply by denying the existence of these characteristics, but a more effective means of avoiding ill-feelings would probably to be acknowledge their existence and to seek an accurate explanation.

PROPOSALS FOR COMBATING ANTI-SEMITISM

How can anti-Semitism be curtailed, eliminated, or at least prevented from increasing? Different proposals have been put forth, including programs involving the schools, the churches, the media, and the courts. Not everyone agrees on the most effective methods of fighting anti-Semitism. Nor is there consensus that the problem is serious enough to warrant special attention. Those who have studied the problem most carefully, however, agree that it should continue to be monitored, and that the results of existing knowledge about the sources of anti-Semitism should be applied in whatever ways possible to combat it. This knowledge, as we have seen, points primarily to methods involving cognitive skills.

One of the most recent, and perhaps the most thorough, reviews of the state of current knowledge about anti-Semitism is Quinley and Glock's *Anti-Semitism in America* (1979). In the final chapter of their volume they set forth the following recommendations:

1. People should be taught to recognize anti-Semitism in themselves and in others.

2. People should be taught that prejudice is morally wrong.

3. Instruction should be given in principles of equality, democracy, freedom of speech, freedom of religion, and other civil liberties.

4. The social and cultural differences both among Jews and between Jews and non-Jews should be openly discussed, and efforts made to teach about the historical reasons for these differences.

5. Instruction in the use of rules of logic and inference should be provided, especially with reference to understanding social phenomena.

Proposals of the kind set forth by Quinley and Glock place special emphasis on the role that schools could play in combating anti-Semitism. Many schools, in fact, have initiated courses to teach about prejudice, discrimination, and minority groups, or have included segments on these topics within social studies curricula. Still, there is evidence that schools have often placed instruction about prejudice among their lowest educational priorities or have failed to examine carefully what the most effective ways of teaching about prejudice might be. It is clear that more experimentation is needed to develop effective instructional packages. It is also clear, however, that the schools should continue to provide instruction about prejudice even in the absence of such experimentation.

SUMMARY

The main points of this chapter may be summarized as follows:

1. The latest public opinion polls indicate that at least one-fifth, and perhaps as much as one-third, of the American public harbors negative attitudes and feelings about Jews.

2. When compared over time, the polls show dramatic reductions in anti-Semitic stereotypes and feelings since the 1940s.

3. Research on the social location of anti-Semitism has found it to be relatively more common among the uneducated than among the educated; among the old more than among the young; among Protestants, members of theologically conservative denominations, and the religiously committed more than among Catholics, members of liberal denominations, and the less committed; and among blacks more than among whites, but only on stereotypes about economic characteristics of Jews.

4. Theories seeking to explain anti-Semitism have focused on contact, authoritarianism, cultural values, and cognitive sophistication. The leading theoretical approach to anti-Semitism in recent years has stressed the role of cognitive functioning. According to this approach, anti-Semitism is rooted principally in faulty habits of thought. These consist of simplism, overgeneralization, and fallacies of logic. They are strongly influenced by the extent of exposure one has had to the educational process.

5. The importance of cognitive factors as determinants of proclivities to engage in anti-Semitism has produced an interest in specifying more carefully the cognitive components of prejudice. A useful distinction is that between the manner in which group differences between Jews and non-Jews are perceived and the manner in which these differences are explained.

6. The main proposals that have been put forth for combating prejudice have focused in recent years on cognitive skills; churches, community groups, volunteer associations, the performing arts, and particularly the schools have been urged (with some success) to reexamine the content of their programs and teaching with an eye to eradicating stereotypes about Jews.

REFERENCES

Adorno, T. W., Frenkel-Brunswick, E., Levinson, D. J., & Sanford, R. N. *The authoritarian personality.* New York: Harper & Row, 1950.

Allport, G. W. *The nature of prejudice* (abridged ed.). Garden City, N.Y.: Doubleday, 1954.

American Jewish Committee. *Americans confront the Holocaust: A study of reactions to NBC-TV's four-part drama on the Nazi era.* New York: American Jewish Committee, Institute of Human Relations, 1979.

Brown, R. *Social psychology*. New York: Free Press, 1965. Chapter 10.

Christie, R., & Jahoda, M. (eds.). *Studies in the scope and method of "The Authoritarian Personality."* Glencoe, Ill.: Free Press, 1954.

Glock, C. Y., & Piazza, T. Exploring reality structures. *Society*, 1978, *15*, 53–59.

Glock, C. Y., & Stark, R. *Christian beliefs and anti-Semitism*. New York: Harper & Row, 1966.

Glock, C. Y., Wuthnow, R., Piliavin, J. A., & Spencer, M. *Adolescent prejudice*. New York: Harper & Row, 1975.

Harris, L., & Associates, Inc. *A study of attitudes toward racial and religious minorities and toward women*. New York: National Conference of Christians and Jews, 1978.

Kelly, J. R. The spirit of ecumenism: How wide, how deep, how mindful of truth? *Review of Religious Research*, 1979, *20*, 180–194.

Kirscht, J. P., & Dillehay, R. C. *Dimensions of authoritarianism: A review of research and theory*. Lexington: University of Kentucky Press, 1967.

Lipset, S. M., & Raab, E. *The politics of unreason: Right-wing extremism in America, 1790–1970*. New York: Harper & Row, 1970.

Lipset, S. M., & Schneider, W. Anti-Semitism and Israel: A report on American public opinion. Unpublished manuscript. Stanford University, Department of Sociology, 1979.

New York *Times*. Moral Majority establishes a beachhead in New York. February 5, 1981, p. B4. (Article written by J. Purnick)

Quinley, H. E., & Glock, C. Y. *Anti-Semitism in America*. New York: Free Press, 1979.

Roof, W. C. *Community and commitment: Religious plausibility in a liberal Protestant church*. New York: Elsevier, 1978.

Selznick, G. J., & Steinberg, S. *The tenacity of prejudice*. New York: Harper & Row, 1969.

Stark, R., Foster, B., Glock, C. Y., & Quinley, H. E. *Wayward shepherds: Prejudice and the Protestant clergy*. New York: Harper & Row, 1971.

Stember, C. H. *Jews in the mind of America*. New York: Basic Books, 1966.

Stouffer, S. A. *Communism, conformity, and civil liberties*. New York: John Wiley, 1955.

Wuthnow, R. *The consciousness reformation*. Berkeley and Los Angeles: University of California Press, 1976.

ADDITIONAL READINGS

Allport, G. W. *The nature of prejudice* (abridged ed.). Garden City, N.Y.: Doubleday, 1954.

A classic, and still useful, discussion of the nature of prejudice and of the factors that contribute to prejudice. This lively and highly readable book pays special attention to the problem of anti-Semitism. It discusses the psychological, social, and historical conditions that have perpetuated anti-Semitism.

Glock, C. Y., Wuthnow, R., Piliavin, J. A., & Spencer, M. *Adolescent prejudice*. New York: Harper & Row, 1975.

One of the most thorough studies ever conducted on anti-Semitism among high school students. Presents evidence on the prevalence of the problem in the schools studied, and examines various theories to account for anti-Semitism. Also discusses racial prejudice. Has been used widely by school systems and teacher organizations in designing curricula to combat prejudice among teenagers.

Kesten, A. H., Ellerin, M., & Kaufer, S. *Anti-Semitism in America: A balance sheet.* New York: The American Jewish Committee, 1981.
A review of anti-Semitic incidents in America in 1980–1981. The emergence of anti-Semitic activities by the Ku Klux Klan is discussed, as is the relationship between Jews and certain evangelical groups which have acquired political influence in the 1980s.

Meltzer, M. *Never to forget: The Jews of the Holocaust.* New York: Dell, 1977.
Describes in an emotionally moving and unforgettable way the effects of anti-Semitism in bringing about the Nazi Holocaust against European Jews during World War II. Makes clear the necessity of understanding the danger of prejudice.

Quinley, H. E., & Glock, C. Y. *Anti-Semitism in America.* New York: Free Press, 1979.
A comprehensive summary of nearly 20 years of research on the nature and causes of anti-Semitism. Discusses the extent of anti-Semitism in the United States and the manner in which churches, schools, and other organizations can contribute to the reduction of anti-Semitism. Summarizes research conclusions in clear, nontechnical language.

Selznick, G. J., & Steinberg, S. *The tenacity of prejudice.* New York: Harper & Row, 1969.
A careful examination of the nature and causes of anti-Semitism in the United States, using data from an extensive national survey. Especially valuable discussions of the content of anti-Semitic stereotypes currently espoused by the American public, of the strengths and weaknesses of the authoritarian personality theory, and of the role of cognitive factors in maintaining or reducing prejudice.

5

SEX STEREOTYPES

Diane N. Ruble
Thomas L. Ruble

According to Plato, "All the pursuits of men are the pursuits of women also, but in all of them a woman is inferior to a man." Of course, this rather extreme statement would not be endorsed by most Americans today. Certainly our current society has a more enlightened view of the abilities of men and women. But, while beliefs in the general inferiority of women probably are rare, there are a number of situations in which women are considered deficient. As this chapter was being written, the following report appeared on the front page of the *Wall Street Journal* (July 10, 1979):

SERIOUS ABOUT CAREERS?
Many male executives still think women aren't.

So says Youngs, Walker & Co., a Chicago-based management consulting firm, after surveying 280 male executives in six cities. Fully 75% of the members—mostly vice presidents and presidents of banks—believe women don't take their careers as seriously as men. Typical comments: "Women don't have men's drive for success" and "Women still put more emphasis on 'exterior' rather than career goals."

Asked to pinpoint problems in helping women become managers, 32% specified high risk of pregnancy or "male attachment" that could result in wasted training. The male managers polled were taking part in seminars on how to work more effectively with women in their organizations.

Preparation of this chapter was supported by a grant from the National Science Foundation, NSF-RANN, Apr. 77-16278, AO1. We thank Eugene Borgida, Irene Frieze, Anne Locksley, and Jacquelynne Parsons for many helpful comments on an earlier draft, and Linda Worcel for bibliographic assistance.

Thus, even though a number of significant changes have occurred in our society, stereotypes of the sexes continue in various forms.

Stereotypes of the sexes have been with us for a long time, but systematic and comprehensive research is a relatively recent phenomenon. Despite the recency of the research, however, the amount of relevant literature has become staggering. For example, in 1965 *Psychological Abstracts* reported only 50 studies related to sex roles; by 1975 that number had jumped to 500 (Wesley & Wesley, 1977).

This chapter represents a selective review of the literature. In the first section we take a brief look at the origins of our beliefs about men and women. In the second section we try to identify the current status of sex stereotypes: the beliefs that seem prevalent in our society, and some basic limitations of current research on sex stereotypes. The third section is concerned with consequences of sex stereotyping. To narrow the scope of this very broad topic, we focus on the potential effects of sex stereotypes on employment and career opportunities. As we shall see, sex stereotypes may lead to biases at many stages in the employment process. These biases are particularly likely to affect career opportunities for women aspiring to nontraditional occupations. Having documented the potential effects of sex stereotypes, we shift our attention in the fourth section to the acquisition of sex stereotypes. A major concern of this section is the development of sex stereotypes in children. As we shall see, sex stereotypes apparently are acquired very early in life, and are a strong component of an individual's identity. Thus, we would expect sex stereotypes to be deeply ingrained in adults and, probably, very difficult to change. In the final section we consider prospects for change and future trends in the study of sex stereotypes.

ORIGINS OF SEX STEREOTYPES

Interest in and beliefs concerning sex differences date back to ancient times. According to Aristotle:

> Woman is more compassionate than man and has a greater propensity to tears. She is, also, more envious, more querulous, more slanderous and more contentious. Farther still, the female is more dispirited, more despondent, more impudent and more given to falsehood than the male. . . . But the male . . . is more disposed to give assistance in danger, and is more courageous than the female. (Book IX, Chapter 1; cited in Miles, 1935, p. 700)

Throughout history, opinions concerning the fundamental differences between the sexes have been voiced in poetry and literature. Taylor Caldwell depicts the views of masculine and feminine traits prevalent around the time of the birth of Christ in her best-selling novel *Dear and Glorious Physician*:

Republics are masculine, and so they beget the sciences and the arts; they are prideful, heroic and virile. They emphasize God, and glorify Him. But Rome has decayed into a confused democracy, and has acquired feminine traits, such as materialism, greed, the lust for power, and expediency. Masculinity in nations and men is demonstrated by law, idealism, justice and poetry, femininity by materialism, dependency on others, gross emotionalism, and absence of genius. Masculinity seeks what is right; femininity seeks what is immediately satisfying. Masculinity is vision; femininity ridicules vision. A masculine nation produces philosophers, and has a respect for the individual; a feminine nation has an insensate desire to control and dominate. . . . Rome has become feminine, Priscus. And feminine nations and feminine men inevitably die or are destroyed by masculine people. (Caldwell, 1959)

They also appear in religion and philosophy (see Table 5.1).

It is interesting to note that discussions of sex differences have tended to focus on the nature of women rather than of men. In part this is probably because most records were kept by men (Bullough, 1973), and a man's perspective on this issue is likely to be oriented toward how the other group (women) differs from his own (men). Thus, in current social psychological terminology, speculation about the nature of sex differences has represented an analysis by an ingroup (male) of an outgroup (female). According to recent research the likely result of this kind of analysis is that members of the outgroup will be described in less favorable and more stereotypic terms than members of the ingroup (Quattrone & Jones, 1980).

Major Themes

Throughout history influential writers have speculated about the "true" nature of the sexes. Recent reviews of these historical beliefs and myths have identified several central themes or images about women (Bullough, 1973; Gould, 1976; Hunter, 1976; Hyde & Rosenberg, 1976; Whitbeck, 1976; Tavris & Offir, 1977; Williams, 1977). Although there are many different labels and connotations attached to these images, depending upon the writer and the period of history being examined, the themes can be grouped into two extremes, which Tavris and Offir (1977) have labeled the "pedestal-gutter syndrome" (p. 3) and which Williams (1977) categorizes as "idealization and disparagement" (p. 244). These range from the positive pole, in which women are regarded as love goddesses and wholesome mother figures, to the extreme negative view of women as inferior and evil (Bullough, 1973).

The "gutter" pole is manifested in several images. Woman is viewed as a partial man, deficient both in sexual capacity and in quality of mind (Whitbeck, 1976). With Eve as her representative, she is both an afterthought (an inferior being) and an evil temptress (Hunter, 1976; Tavris &

TABLE 5.1
Some Views of Men and Women in Major Religions

Christian Heritage: Old Testament
> And God said, Let us make man in our image. . . . So God created man in his own image. (Genesis 1)

> And the Lord God said, It is not good that the man should be alone; I will make him a help mate . . . she shall be called Woman because she was taken out of Man. (Genesis 2)

> And the Lord God said unto the woman, what is this that thou hast done? And the woman said, the serpent beguiled me. . . . Unto the woman [the Lord God] said, I will greatly multiply thy sorrow . . . and thy desire shall be to thy husband and he shall rule over thee. (Genesis 3)

Christian Heritage: New Testament
> For a man . . . is the image and glory of God: but the woman is the glory of the man. For the man is not of the woman; but the woman of the man. Neither was the man created for the woman, but the woman for the man. (I Corinthians 11)

> Let your women keep silence in the churches: for it is not permitted unto them to speak; but they are commanded to be under obedience. . . . And if they will learn anything, let them ask their husbands at home: for it is a shame for women to speak in the church (I Corinthians 14)

> Let the woman learn in silence with all subjugation. But, I suffer not a woman to teach, nor to usurp authority over the man, but to be in silence. For Adam was first formed, then Eve. And Adam was not deceived but the woman being deceived was in the transgression. (I Timothy)

Jewish Heritage*
> Blessed art Thou, O Lord our God, King of the Universe, that I was not born a gentile.

> Blessed art Thou, O Lord our God, King of the Universe, that I was not born a slave.

> Blessed art Thou, O Lord our God, King of the Universe, that I was not born a woman.

Islamic Heritage*
> Men are superior to women on account of the qualities in which God has given them preeminence.

---

*These passages are from Bem and Bem (1970), p. 97. Reprinted by permission of Wadsworth Publishing Company.

Offir, 1977). The belief in the inferiority of woman has been persistent throughout history. According to Hesiod, a major figure in Greek literature, a young man should start out by getting himself "a house, an ox, and a woman, but make sure it is slave woman who will work" (cited in Hunter, 1976). Napoleon Bonaparte has been credited with saying that "Nature intended women to be our slaves . . . they are our property" (Morgan, 1970). One additional aspect of woman's inferiority is her uncleanliness, as represented by menstrual beliefs and taboos (D. N. Ruble & Brooks-Gunn,

1979; Tavris & Offir, 1977). For example, it has been suggested that a menstruating woman could cause fruit to fall from trees, sour new wine, or wither green grass.

The view of women as evil is illustrated by the two forces of nature in Chinese mythology, Yin and Yang. The Yin, the feminine side, represents evil and darkness (Hyde & Rosenberg, 1976). The woman is the sexual temptress, the cause of man's downfall. The story of Samson and Delilah represents the common theme in religious writings that being seduced by a woman can drain a man of his strength (Williams, 1977).

The contrasting view of woman portrays her as meant to be worshipped. She has been the fertility goddess, the mother of all; and she has also been seen as the goddess of sexual love and as virtue incarnate (Bullough, 1973; Gould, 1976; Hyde & Rosenberg, 1976; Williams, 1977). The tradition of chivalry, which placed women on a pedestal, epitomizes this image (Hunter, 1976; Yorburg, 1974). However, as many historians have noted, there is even ambivalence about the side of woman's nature that is worshipped. Passionate love brought wretchedness along with ecstasy; and placing woman on a pedestal confined her to an essentially passive and powerless role (Hunter, 1976; Williams, 1977). Thus, both the positive and negative images have been used to justify oppression of women. As Bullough (1973) suggests, ". . . history has been written to emphasize that the proper role of woman is to be subordinate to man" (p. 4).

This brief discussion of historical images of men and women should not be considered as an exhaustive review of how sex differences have been perceived. Beliefs about the sexes have varied considerably throughout time, just as they continue to vary cross-culturally (cf. Tavris & Offir, 1977). However, the important points are that across time and history, women and men have been perceived as fundamentally different; these differences have been perceived as important; and they have been closely linked to the roles of the sexes in society. Moreover, assumptions that differences in the roles of men and women can be explained by inherent personality differences between the sexes have often led to flagrant contradictions difficult to justify as objective science (Eagly, 1978; Shields, 1975).

For example, Shields (1975) traces ideas about the "real" source of intellect in the brain. In the mid-nineteenth century it was generally believed that the frontal lobes of the brain (rather than the parietal lobes) were the seat of higher mental capacities. Many researchers at that time reported finding larger and more developed frontal lobes in males, compared with females. At the turn of the century the parietal lobes (rather than the frontal lobes) came to be regarded as more important in intellectual functioning. Then, researchers began to report that the frontal region was larger, relatively, in women but the parietal region was somewhat smaller.

Exactly why perceptions of sex differences persist remains a question of considerable scientific debate (Eagly, 1978; Frieze et al., 1978). What is clear, however, is that once such beliefs are formed, they may continue even in the face of contradictory evidence (Borgida, Locksley, & Brekke, 1981; Chapman & Chapman, 1969).

New Directions

The late 1960s saw some important changes in gender-related research. In part the dramatic increase in research was probably related to the rise of the women's liberation movement. Clearly the research has been influenced by personal and political concerns (for instance, Bem, 1978), in that much of the research of the 1970s was oriented toward debunking ideas about the inferior nature of women and toward understanding why women's roles and achievements were typically of lower status. More recently questions about men, masculinity, and restrictions associated with the male role have appeared in the literature (Brannon, 1976; Pleck, 1976; Pleck & Brannon, 1978). Currently additional directions appear to be emerging in the sex-role literature as a result of psychologists' heightened interest in cognitive processes. The sex role (with its associated stereotypes) has been recognized as an important and interesting category of cognitions about the self and the world. This impending merger between empirical research on sex roles and theoretical formulations about cognitive processes appears to offer some promising new approaches to both disciplines (for example, Ashmore & Del Boca, 1979; Borgida et al., 1981). In the remainder of this chapter we will selectively explore the substance and implications of this recent research.

CURRENT STATUS OF SEX STEREOTYPES

The increased research of the 1970s can be characterized by its diversity of concerns, of concepts, and of methodological approaches. This diversity has added a great deal to our understanding of the nature and effects of sex stereotypes. However, the steady growth in research has been accompanied by a number of conceptual and methodological difficulties. We feel that it is useful to identify some of these difficulties before examining the current status of sex stereotypes.

Conceptual and Methodological Limitations of Research on Sex Stereotypes

With different researchers using different methods to study different problems, the emerging body of knowledge lacks consistency and comparability. As a result there are often problems in interpreting and reconciling diverse results (see Brannon, 1978, for a more detailed discussion of these problems). We hope that identifying some of the conceptual and methodological difficulties in advance will alert the reader to potential limitations in the available data.

Ambiguous Concepts

To date, most of the available research on stereotypes concerning men and women has applied the label of "sex-role stereotypes" to explain the results. A number of reviews of the literature have objected to the addition of the word "role" (Ashmore & Del Boca, 1979; Brannon, 1978; Terborg, 1977). In general these authors argue that role is a separate concept, referring to beliefs about the appropriate behavior for men and women in a given situation. In contrast, other stereotypes reflect beliefs about the personal characteristics possessed by men and women. Ashmore and Del Boca use the term "sex stereotypes" to refer to sets of beliefs about the personal attributes of men and women. In this chapter we will adopt their terminology to distinguish between the two bases for stereotyping. Unfortunately the failure of many studies to distinguish between sex-role stereotypes and sex stereotypes may have created confusion and inconsistency in the literature.

Bipolar Assumptions

When conducting research, one's a priori assumptions about the nature of a phenomenon will influence the search for data and the interpretation of results. In research on sex stereotypes, one of the assumptions inhibiting progress was the assumption that sex characteristics were bipolar (opposite ends of a single continuum). This assumption suggests that a person possesses characteristics that are associated either with males (masculine) or with females (feminine), but not both. The result is a reinforcement of the notion of the "opposite" sex rather than a less polarized notion.

The bipolar assumption has been criticized by a number of researchers in the field (Bem, 1974; Constantinople, 1973; Heilbrun, 1976; Spence & Helmreich, 1978). The current view seems to be that a person can possess characteristics that are *both* masculine and feminine. Bem has applied the term "androgynous" to the person who possesses both types of characteristics (such as assertive and tender). Spence and Helmreich prefer to use the term "dualistic" as a more general way of referring to the idea that masculinity and femininity are two relatively separate dimensions of personality that may develop independently.

Despite the evidence supporting the dualistic model, the bipolar model cannot be dismissed easily. A study by Foushee, Helmreich, and Spence (1979) found that a person's perceptions of others may be based on a bipolar view. That is, perceiving that an individual possesses one set of characteristics (such as masculine) may lead to the inference that the other set (feminine) is absent. Other research has shown more mixed results, depending, for example, on the nature of the characteristics being rated (Deaux, 1981; Major, Carnevale, and Deaux, in press). Thus, although it is clearly useful for research purposes to question old assumptions, a dualistic model may not, in fact, reflect the reality of most people's perceptions. Further research is needed in this area to determine whether stereotypes tend to reflect the bipolar or dualistic model.

Further Dimensions in Masculinity and Femininity

In the dualistic model masculinity and femininity (M-F) are viewed as separate and relatively independent dimensions. The next question to ask is whether the separate dimensions are composed of relatively unitary or multidimensional characteristics. As Constantinople (1973) has pointed out, if the M-F characteristic is multidimensional, a single summary score that ignores variations in the subtraits would seem to be less appropriate than a profile of scores on subtraits themselves (p. 391). Thus, an overall score on M or F might be like adding the proverbial apples and oranges.

Brannon (1978) has noted that research progress is inhibited if different measuring instruments are treated as though they all measured the same constructs (that is, M or F) when, in fact, the measures are based on different factors (clusters of items). For example, assume that the stereotype of masculinity is composed of two relatively independent factors such as "power" and "wisdom." Further assume that we have two instruments that purport to measure masculinity. One instrument has ten items related to the power factor and five items related to the wisdom factor. The other instrument has five power items and ten wisdom items. If overall scores are obtained simply by summing items, then we essentially have a power-dominated instrument versus a wisdom-dominated instrument. It would be misleading to assume that equal scores on the two instruments were equivalent measures of masculinity. Masculinity measured by the first instrument would emphasize power, and masculinity measured by the second instrument would emphasize wisdom.

The Search for "Relative" Differences

The study of "sex-typed" characteristics implies the search for characteristics that are primarily associated with one sex or the other. In most studies the emphasis has been on identifying stereotypes of the relative differences between the sexes rather than stereotypes of the typical man or typical woman. Thus, a characteristic may be identified as more typical of one sex even though it is considered typical of both sexes. For example, the characteristic "active" has been classified as a masculine attribute (Spence, Helmreich, & Stapp, 1975), although it is considered to be typical of women as well (Ruble, unpublished data). In addition, a characteristic may be associated more with one sex than the other even though it is not strongly associated with either sex. This latter point is exemplified by the inclusion of "gullible" as a feminine characteristic on the Bem Sex-Role Inventory (Bem, 1974). Although gullibility was not seen as particularly desirable for a woman, it was viewed as more desirable for a woman than for a man.

Unfortunately the search for relative differences tends to deemphasize or understate the similarities of men and women, and further reinforces the notion of the "opposite" sex. Partly because of such problems, it has been suggested that the structure of sex stereotypes may be better understood in terms of prototypes than in terms of relative differences (Locksley & Colten, 1979). A prototype represents a category (such as woman) by identifying a cluster of images and beliefs that tend to define the category. These images and beliefs may include, but are not limited to, personal characteristics. Thus, the prototype approach is not based on a search for differences but, rather, on a search for characteristics that define men and women as separate categories of individuals.

The Search for "Absolute" Frequencies

One way of conceptualizing a stereotype is to think of it as a widely shared (consensual) belief about certain people. Working under this definition, we might ask about the characteristics believed to be typical of a certain target group, such as "men" or "women." We would then select some absolute frequency of endorsement (such as 60 percent or 70 percent) as a criterion for determining the consensual basis for the stereotype. For example, in one study (Rosenkrantz, Vogel, Bee, Broverman, & Broverman, 1968), a 75 percent level of agreement was used to identify sex stereotypes. However, one technical issue here is where to draw the line. There is no theoretical basis for choosing any particular level of agreement as the criterion. Thus, the choice is arbitrary. Moreover, if the level of agreement differs from study to study, it becomes difficult to compare results across different samples.

A more fundamental problem with the search for absolute frequencies is the use of consensus as a basis for defining stereotypes. Ashmore and Del Boca (1979) suggest that we distinguish between "cultural stereotypes" and "personal stereotypes." Cultural stereotypes are beliefs based on a consensus (widely shared), while personal stereotypes reflect one individual's beliefs about a target group. Ashmore and Del Boca suggest that we will gain a greater understanding of the psychological processes involved in stereotyping if we focus our research on personal stereotypes.

Problems of Measurement

Currently there appear to be four major approaches to measuring sex stereotypes: open-ended, adjective checklist, bipolar ratings, and multi-point, one-dimensional ratings (the "Likert"-type scale). Unfortunately the results from using these different measures may vary considerably (Brannon, 1978; Cicone & Ruble, 1978). The open-ended format seems to generate fewer stereotypic responses than the others (Frieze, 1974; Cowan and Stewart, 1977). For example, the study by Cowan and Stewart compared the open-ended, adjective checklist, and bipolar formats. They found that the open-ended format elicited no stereotypic items, while both of the others elicited stereotypes of females as being more emotional than males. However, the nature of the emotional stereotype differed somewhat, even though the two instruments were very similar in content. The stereotype elicited by the checklist format tended to emphasize more positive aspects of emotionality (such as cheerful, kind, warm), while the bipolar format elicited a stereotype emphasizing more negative emotions (such as cries very easily, very excitable in a minor crisis). The authors concluded that instrumentation made a difference, and more work is needed to assess the response biases of different formats.

The Failure to Measure

While the measurement of stereotypes has created some inconsistencies, an even greater problem may be the failure to measure stereotypes in many studies. Numerous studies have found that men and women are treated differently. However, this does not mean that the concept of a "stereotype" is required to explain the differential treatment. Men and women are different biologically, and are further differentiated by the socialization process. Thus, sex differences become confounded with various other factors that may lead to differential treatment (see Lockheed & Hall, 1976, for an example of how sex and status are confounded). Terborg (1977) has noted that many studies fail to provide an independent assessment of alleged stereotypes. Thus, even though the evidence may be consistent with a stereotype explanation, no firm conclusions can be reached.

In summary, we have a very large, but somewhat imperfect, data base to review. To keep the presentation manageable, we cannot include a methodological critique of all the studies. We urge the reader to accept the results as tentative rather than final answers regarding the nature and effects of sex stereotypes.

Stereotypes of Men and Women

A number of studies have identified characteristics that may be considered stereotypes of men and women (Bem, 1974; Broverman, Vogel, Broverman, Clarkson, & Rosenkrantz, 1972; Heilbrun, 1976; McKee & Sherriffs, 1957; Rosenkrantz et al., 1968; Spence, Helmreich, & Stapp, 1974; 1975). Despite the conceptual and methodological difficulties, there is some degree of consensus concerning the types of characteristics associated with one sex versus the other.

Rather than trying to compile an extensive list of the characteristics that have been identified as stereotypic, we will focus our discussion on a set of characteristics that have been studied periodically since the late 1960s. In this way we can identify current stereotypes as well as assess the degree of change in recent years.

In 1968, Rosenkrantz et al. developed a questionnaire to measure perceptions of characteristics associated with the typical adult male and adult female. They started with a list of 122 bipolar items (for example, not at all aggressive—very aggressive) and asked approximately 150 college students to rate the extent to which each item was characteristic of the adult male and adult female. A particular item was considered "stereotypic" if at least 75 percent of the male raters and female raters rated one pole as more typical of one sex than the other. Of course, selecting 75 percent agreement as sufficient to indicate consensus was an arbitrary choice. Using this criterion, 41 items were designated as stereotypic. Another 48 items also differentiated males from females (at $p < .05$) but did not reach a 75 percent level of consensus.

In 1972, Broverman et al. summarized the results of several studies based on the 1968 questionnaire. They offered the following conclusions:

> 1. A strong consensus about the differing characteristics of men and women exists across groups which differ in sex, age, religion, marital status, and educational level.
> 2. Characteristics ascribed to men are positively valued more often than characteristics ascribed to women. The positively valued masculine traits form a cluster of related behaviors which entail competence, rationality, and assertion; the positively-valued feminine traits form a cluster which reflects warmth and expressiveness. (1972, p. 61)

Of course, these conclusions reflect both the mode of thought at the time (1968–1972) and the nature of the measuring instrument. In order to evaluate the current status of those conclusions, we will first consider the refinement of the original sex-role questionnaire and then present some recent research.

The 1968 questionnaire was refined in 1974 by Spence, Helmreich, and Stapp. A study using the new instrument, called the Personal Attributes Questionnaire (PAQ), appeared a year later (Spence, Helmreich, & Stapp, 1975). Following the general procedure used by Rosenkrantz et al., Spence, Helmreich, and Stapp had one group of college students rate the typical adult male and female on 138 bipolar items (the original 122 items plus 16 more items). Another group rated the ideal male and female. From the ratings of the typical male and female, 55 items were identified as "stereotypic" on the basis of significant differences in the ratings. In refining the instrument, the original 75 percent agreement criterion was not applied, resulting in a larger number of trait adjectives being identified as stereotypic.

From the ratings of the ideal male and female, it was possible to identify whether the "masculine" pole (such as aggressive) was valued more or less than the "feminine" pole (such as not at all aggressive). For 23 of the items, ratings for both ideal males and ideal females were higher on the masculine side of the scale. These characteristics were classified as "male-valued." For 18 of the items, ratings for both ideal males and ideal females were higher on the feminine side of the scale. These characteristics were classified as "female-valued." For 13 of the items, ratings for the ideal male were higher on the masculine side and ratings for the ideal female were higher on the feminine side. These items were classified as "sex-specific." One item of the 55 could not be classified, so it was dropped, leaving 54 items to form the PAQ. These items are shown in Table 5.2. A short form of the PAQ is also available (see Spence, Helmreich, & Stapp, 1974).

Since the development of the PAQ, various changes (social and political) may have led to changes in the stereotypes (see Kravetz, 1976). However, the results of a more recent study (T. L. Ruble, in press) suggest that there has been little change in the stereotypes since the original study by Rosenkrantz et al. in 1968. Ruble asked 128 students to rate a typical man or typical woman on the 54 characteristics of the PAQ. Rather than using the bipolar rating format, a unidimensional, six-point Likert scale was used. For 53 of the 54 items, the stereotypes were still present. The only item that did not show a significant difference for males versus females was "intellectual." Thus, the nature of stereotypes about men and women, as measured by the PAQ, apparently remained remarkably stable in the 1970s despite the increased concern with women's liberation and equal rights. It is possible, however, that the measurements were unable to detect subtle changes in the degree of stereotyping (Borgida et al., 1981).

Dimensions in Masculinity and Femininity

As noted earlier, the dualistic view seems to be replacing the bipolar view of masculinity and femininity. The dualistic view suggests two basic dimensions (or clusters of attributes) that may coexist, at least to some degree, in every person. The two basic dimensions seem to reflect Bakan's (1966) concepts of agency and communion. Agency is directed toward self-accomplishment, achievement, and assertiveness (a task orientation), while communion is directed toward others, a desire to get along with others, and sensitivity (a socioemotional orientation). Of course, Bakan and others have associated agency with masculinity and communion with femininity.

The next step seems to be the extension of the dualistic model into a multidimensional view. That is, the two basic dimensions are being analyzed to determine whether they are further composed of subfactors. For example, Brannon (1976) and Cicone and Ruble (1978) have attempted to distill some "core concepts" of masculinity. Brannon identified four main

TABLE 5.2
Personal Attributes Questionnaire Items Classified as Male-Valued,
Female-Valued, and Sex-Specific

	Male-Valued	
Independent	Adventurous	Self-confident
Not easily influenced	Outspoken	Feels superior
Good at sports	Interested in sex	Takes a stand
Not excitable, minor crisis	Makes decisions easily	Ambitious
Active	Not give up easily	Stands up under pressure
Competitive	Outgoing	Forward
Skilled in business	Acts as leader	Not timid
Knows ways of world	Intellectual	

	Female-Valued	
Emotional	Strong conscience	Creative
Not hide emotions	Gentle	Understanding
Considerate	Helpful to others	Warm to others
Grateful	Kind	Likes children
Devotes self to others	Aware, others' feelings	Enjoys art and music
Tactful	Neat	Expresses tender feelings

	Sex-Specific
Male	**Female**
Aggressive	Cries easily
Dominant	Excitable, major crisis
Likes math and science	Feelings hurt
Loud	Home-oriented
Mechanical aptitude	Needs approval
Sees self running show	Needs security
	Religious

Source: Spence, Helmreich, & Stapp (1975), Table 1, p. 31. Copyright 1975 by the American Psychological Association. Reprinted by permission.

themes applicable to the male sex-role: "no sissy stuff"—the stigma of anything feminine; "the big wheel"—the attainment of success and status; "the sturdy oak"—strength, confidence, and independence; and "give 'em hell"—aggression, violence, and daring. Cicone and Ruble proposed a threefold categorization: how a man handles his life (active and achievement oriented), how a man handles others (dominant), and how a man handles his psyche (level-headed). Unfortunately these two classification schemes represent a conceptual analysis of the literature rather than a direct empirical attempt to isolate the underlying dimensions.

There have been a few attempts to identify empirically the underlying dimensions of masculinity and femininity. One group of studies has applied factor-analytic techniques to self-ratings on the Bem Sex-Role Inventory (Gaudreau, 1977; Pedhazur & Tetenbaum, 1979; Whetton & Swindells, 1977). Briefly, these studies suggest that self-ratings of masculinity and femininity may be multidimensional. For example, Pedhazur and Tetenbaum found that both males and females tended to use four underlying factors in rating themselves. The four factors appear to reflect assertiveness, social sensitivity, self-sufficiency, and gender identity. However, we must be cautious in applying these results to our analysis of sex stereotypes. The dimensions underlying self-ratings of masculinity and femininity may not be identical to dimensions operating in stereotypes of masculinity and femininity. As noted previously, Foushee, Helmreich, and Spence (1979) found that perceptions of masculinity and femininity in others may reflect a bipolar view.

The research by Ashmore and his colleagues (see Ashmore & Del Boca, 1979) offers a promising new approach to the study of sex stereotypes. In one study they used a multidimensional scaling technique to analyze the patterns of traits that raters attributed to people they knew. The results suggested that a two-dimensional configuration of traits provided an adequate representation of the ratings. They labeled these two relatively independent dimensions "social desirability" and "potency." Interestingly, these two dimensions seem very similar to the two dimensions of connotative meaning, "evaluative" and "dynamism," often found in semantic differential research on interpersonal perceptions (Osgood, Suci, & Tannenbaum, 1957).

The current direction of research seems to be toward a multidimensional view of the traits associated with men and women. The dualistic view suggests that masculinity and femininity are at least two relatively independent dimensions. Yet, these two dimensions may be composed of subdimensions. Research is under way to disentangle the complex stereotypes people may associate with men and women. In the meantime, stereotypes seem to have remained relatively stable over the 1970s. In the next section we will examine some of the effects of these stereotypes.

SOME CONSEQUENCES OF SEX STEREOTYPES

Sex stereotypes have a pervasive influence on our lives. They affect our self-image, views of what is good or bad in others, whom we marry, the careers we pursue, our leisure-time interests, how we raise children, and so on. To review all the possible effects of sex stereotypes would be an immense undertaking, and beyond the limitations of this chapter. Thus, to highlight the various effects of sex stereotypes, we are going to organize this section around an important concern in adult life: occupations or careers.

Careers serve as a useful focal point for discussion for at least two reasons: they are a principle around which people organize their lives (Van Maanen & Schein, 1977), and they are important elements of a person's self-concept or individual identity.

There has been an increasing interest in the potential effects of sex stereotypes on employment and career opportunities. Most of this interest has focused on the barriers encountered by women in their attempts to achieve equal employment opportunities. More women are attending college and many are planning on careers outside the home (see, for instance, Parsons, Frieze, & Ruble, 1978). There has been a steady increase in the participation of women in the labor force, yet women are paid much less than men, even when they have equal qualifications (Levitin, Quinn, & Staines, 1973). And the entry of women into traditionally masculine occupations has encountered noticeable resistance (see, for instance, Gordon & Strober, 1975).

As we shall see, both men and women experience discrimination in the pursuit of careers. However, men seem to have a decided advantage in gaining entry to higher-paying, more prestigious careers. Thus, the emphasis in this section will be on the role of sex stereotypes in creating barriers for women interested in nontraditional careers. The available research suggests that sex stereotypes affect the choice of a career, entry into a career, and advancement within a career.

Occupational Sex Typing and Career Choice

Just as we develop stereotypes about men and women, we develop stereotypes about jobs. For example, can you describe a typical "truck-driver" or a typical "secretary"? The chances are that your descriptions would include more masculine characteristics for the former and more feminine characteristics for the latter. A sex-typed occupation is one that has become strongly associated (psychologically) with one sex. Below is an example.

> A father and his son were driving along the highway when the father suddenly lost control of the car and crashed into a telephone pole. The father was killed instantly and his son was badly injured. The boy was rushed to the local hospital where it was found that he was suffering from serious internal injuries. A prominent surgeon was immediately summoned. When the surgeon arrived and went to the operating room to examine the boy, a loud gasp was heard. "I can't operate on this boy," the surgeon said. "He is my son."
>
> Can you solve this riddle? The father is dead; how could the boy be the surgeon's son?
>
> The answer, of course, is quite straightforward: the surgeon is a woman and also the boy's mother. If you were unable to provide it, though, don't be too upset. In a recent study (Goldberg, 1974), only 3

out of 26 males and 4 out of 24 females who had not heard the story before were able to answer correctly. Not too surprisingly, when this riddle is modified slightly so that the surgeon is described as bursting into tears and becoming hysterical upon seeing the boy, many more subjects are able to solve it correctly (Gorkin, 1972). Apparently, these extra clues, which are consistent with widely held stereotypes concerning women, are sufficient to suggest the correct answer.

This riddle, and many others like it, point to two important facts about our views concerning women. First, our inability to solve them derives, in part, from the stereotyped expectancies we hold for females, regardless of their individual skills, occupation, or training. And second, such stereotyping of women is not restricted to a few "chauvinistic male pigs"; rather, it is shared by many men and women alike. (Baron & Byrne, 1977)

To identify the level of sex typing associated with various occupations, Shinar (1975) asked college students to rate 129 occupations in terms of their masculinity versus femininity. The representative occupations listed in Table 5.3 fell in the top 20 percent for men or women based on Shinar's sample. Note that the masculine jobs seem to involve strength, wisdom, or leadership ability, while the feminine jobs seem to involve a supportive orientation.

The sex typing of occupations does not simply serve to define jobs as men's work or women's work, but also seems related to perceptions of the characteristics considered necessary for success in the career. Schein's research on "requisite management characteristics" (1973; 1975) found that both male and female middle managers tended to perceive "successful managers" in predominantly masculine terms, a finding replicated by Massengill and Di Marco (1979). In addition, Powell and Butterfield (1979)

TABLE 5.3
Representative Sex-Typed Occupations

Masculine	Feminine
Miner	Manicurist
Heavy equipment operator	Nurse
U.S. Supreme Court justice	Receptionist
Construction worker	Private secretary
Auto mechanic	Dental hygienist
District attorney	Head librarian
Company president	Elementary school teacher
Top labor official	Bank teller
University president	Social worker
High government official	X-ray technician

Source: Shinar (1975), Table 1, pp. 104–106. Copyright 1975 by Academic Press, Inc. Reprinted by permission.

found that both male and female business students considered a "good manager" as predominantly masculine (as opposed to androgynous). In these cases the occupational stereotype includes ideas about the type of characteristics deemed appropriate for the job.

Research by Krefting, Berger, and Wallace (1978) suggests that the major determinant of occupational sex typing is the current distribution of males versus females in the job category. And the current distribution seems to become defined as the "appropriate" distribution. Krefting et al. asked college students to indicate which sex would be "better suited" for various jobs. The results indicated that the current ratio of males to females in a job seemed to create the impression that the "majority" sex was the "appropriate" sex for a given occupation.

Given the general notion that certain jobs are "better suited" for one sex than the other, Shinar (1978) examined college students' perceptions of people in sex-appropriate, sex-inappropriate, and neutral occupations. She found that the sex typing of the occupation was an important determinant of one's perception of a jobholder. Individuals in masculine occupations were seen as more leaderlike and less socially sensitive than individuals in feminine occupations. The sex of the jobholder also had an effect, with males in a feminine field (such as male nurse, male secretary) being considered as having the fewest leadership qualities, being the least active, least well-adjusted, and least likable compared with females in a feminine field and with both males and females in masculine fields. In this particular study, women in masculine jobs were rated the same as men in masculine jobs. Thus, when work involved engaging in sex-inappropriate behavior, it would seem that men were "penalized" more than women.

The studies by Shinar and by Krefting et al. suggest that the sex typing of occupations seems to influence the careers considered appropriate for men and women. The next question is how the sex typing of occupations affects career choice. Other things being equal, individuals should be most likely to apply for, be selected for, and be accepted in jobs appropriate for their gender (Krefting et al., 1978). Of course, other things are not equal. For example, high-prestige jobs should also be attractive. And, most high-prestige jobs are held by men. Thus, women aspiring to such jobs are likely to experience some conflict and some resistance due to their interest in sex-inappropriate occupations.

In addition to gender, we would also expect self-concept to be related to career preferences (Korman, 1970). This relationship seems to exist in choices of sex-appropriate versus sex-inappropriate careers. For example, college students majoring in sex-appropriate fields seem to be more likely to rate themselves in a sex-typed manner and to endorse sex stereotypes of others. In one study, women majoring in engineering, men majoring in engineering, and women majoring in home economics completed the Bem Sex Role Inventory (Yanico, Hardin, & McLaughlin, 1978). Women in engineering scored in a more androgynous direction, men in engineering scored in a masculine direction, and women in home economics scored in a feminine direction. A study by Crawford (1978) found that women in sex-appropriate majors were more likely to endorse sex stereotypes than women in sex-inappropriate majors. Wertheim, Widom, and Wortzel (1978) found that male and female graduate students in traditionally female fields (education and social work) scored higher on the femininity scale of the PAQ than did men and women majoring in traditionally male fields (management and law). On the masculinity scale of the PAQ, management and education majors scored highest, social work students scored lowest, and law students fell in the middle.

Wertheim et al. concluded that differences in sex-typed self-ratings were greater between career fields (for instance, social work versus management) than differences between the sexes within careers. In short, individuals "locked in" to traditional sex-role stereotypes seem to be locked in to limited career preferences as well. Of course, just because a person has a larger set of preferences (such as nontraditional occupations) does not automatically mean that he or she can pursue the career of his or her choice—at least not without barriers to overcome. The presence of numerous constraints is taken up in the next two sections.

Career Entry: Evaluation of Job Candidates

A number of studies have attempted to determine the effects of sex stereotypes on the evaluation of job applicants. These studies usually present subjects with résumés of job candidates. About half of the studies reviewed in this section were based on student ratings, and half were drawn from samples of professional recruiters or other nonstudents. Surprisingly, there is very little difference between "role-playing" students and "real-world" decision makers when it comes to the evaluation of job applicants. Apparently the factors underlying the evaluations are very pervasive.

All of the studies compared evaluations of male versus female candidates. In most of the studies, the jobs to be filled were traditionally masculine. The results indicate that, in most cases, candidates were evaluated higher for sex-appropriate positions. That is, males were favored over females for masculine-typed jobs and females were favored over males for feminine-typed jobs (Cash, Gillen, & Burns, 1977; Cohen & Bunker, 1975; Dipboye, Arvey, & Terpstra, 1977; Dipboye, Fromkin, & Wiback, 1975; Fidell, 1970; Haefner, 1977; Rose & Andiappan, 1978; Shaw, 1972; Zikmund, Hitt, & Pickens, 1978). A study by Heneman (1977) failed to find a general bias favoring male candidates for a traditionally masculine occupation. However, when comparing evaluations of candidates who achieved high scores on a job-related placement test, Heneman found that males were considered more suitable for the job than equally high-scoring females. Two studies showed mixed results that basically failed to confirm the presence of an overall bias in the comparison of male versus female candidates (Muchinsky & Harris, 1977; Renwick & Tosi, 1978). On balance, the evidence suggests the presence of bias in the evaluation of job candidates.

Studies by Dipboye and Wiley (1977; 1978) also failed to find a general bias favoring male or female applicants for sex-appropriate positions. In the two studies college recruiters and students watched videotaped "interviews" of candidates for the positions of editorial assistant or supervisor in a retail store. Results indicated that moderately aggressive candidates were favored over passive candidates for the position of supervisor, while the reverse was true for the position of editorial assistant. For both positions the sex of the candidate did not affect the evaluations.

Despite the equal evaluations of male and female candidates in these two studies, the results suggest some rather subtle biases that may operate to favor the average male compared with the average female. In particular, aggressiveness is considered to be a desirable characteristic for men but not for women (Bem, 1974; Spence et al., 1974). Moreover, we expect men to display that characteristic to a greater extent than women (Spence et al., 1974). On the average, then, we would find a bias toward males for the higher-prestige position of supervisor and a bias toward females for the lower-prestige job of editorial assistant.

On the whole, evaluations of job candidates seem to conform closely to the matching of sex stereotypes and occupational sex typing. Because the higher-paying and more prestigious jobs tend to be typed as masculine, these results suggest that women face continuing barriers to equality in employment and career opportunities.

Career Advancement: Evaluations of Performance and Potential

Once people gain entry to occupations, the major issue becomes the manner in which their behavior is evaluated. Performance evaluations provide a basis for decisions about pay increases, promotions, assignments to routine versus demanding jobs, and opportunities for further growth and development. In short, the allocation of occupational rewards is based, substantially, on evaluations of a person's performance and potential.

Evaluations of Personal Achievements

A number of studies investigating possible discrimination have focused on the evaluation of literary and artistic achievements of men and women. In one of the early, oft-cited studies, Goldberg (1968) asked college women to judge the quality of several short articles. Half of the women were given articles signed by male authors and half received the same articles signed by female authors. The women consistently gave higher ratings to the articles attributed to a male author. The biased evaluations even extended to articles on dietetics, a traditionally feminine field. Goldberg concluded that women were generally prejudiced against women.

In a follow-up study Pheterson, Kiesler, and Goldberg (1971) found that paintings thought to be entries in a contest were evaluated by college women as the articles had been evaluated in the original study. That is, paintings attributed to males were rated higher than paintings attributed to women. However, when the paintings were thought to be winners in a contest, there were no differences in the evaluations of male versus female products. Thus, the work of women was not devalued by college women in all circumstances.

Unfortunately, neither of these studies included evaluations by male subjects. Since males are currently dominant in the prestige occupations, it is important to see whether their biases parallel the biases of women. To examine this issue, Cline, Holmes, and Werner (1977) compared ratings by male and female subjects, and found that males discriminate against the intellectual products of women. Contrary to previous results, females tended to discriminate against the products of men. Thus, in this study both male and female subjects displayed a "chauvinistic" orientation.

Another study utilizing a similar format yielded slightly different results. H. Mischel (1974) found that high school and college students of both sexes favored the work of male authors in traditionally masculine fields, but rated the work of female authors higher in traditionally feminine fields. Thus, ratings in this study conformed more to occupational sex typing rather than reflecting a general bias against women or a chauvinistic bias.

Most of the studies building on the Goldberg paradigm suggest that biases may be present, particularly against women working in nontraditional fields. In these cases the evaluations are likely to be made by men and, it would seem, reflect criteria based on masculine standards. Before accepting this conclusion, however, we must examine a number of studies focusing on performance evaluations in traditionally masculine fields. These studies suggest that the mechanisms underlying discrimination may be more complex than originally suspected.

Evaluations of Potential

Two early studies conducted in a business/management context by Rosen and Jerdee (1974a; 1974b) used an "in-basket" technique to study responses of actual managers to situations involving hypothetical male and female subordinates. The in-basket technique asks a subject to "role-play" a manager faced with a series of incidents requiring a decision. Rosen and Jerdee found that managers held rather consistent biases against women in promotions to managerial positions, assignments to demanding jobs, and selection for participation in supervisory training.

Two more recent in-basket studies drawn from college student samples have reported mixed results. Terborg and Ilgen (1975) found that women were assigned to more routine tasks, but no significant differences between men and women were found in ratings of performance and promotability. However, despite the equality of ratings of performance and promotability, males were granted a larger percentage increase in pay, which widened the gap in salary differences between men and women. Gutek and Stevens (1979) reported some differential treatment of male versus female employees but, generally, no significant differences were found. Finally, an attempt to replicate the Rosen and Jerdee studies with college student subjects failed to find similar biases in personnel decisions (Hunady & Wahrman, 1977).

Do these more recent results suggest that equal employment opportunities for women are becoming a reality? Certainly change is under way. However, one should be cautious in drawing conclusions from studies that fail to find significant differences. Any number of cues (demand characteristics) could have indicated to the subjects that their sexism or prejudice was being measured. If such cues were salient, the subjects may have minimized the expression of their biases. Thus, the lack of differences in recent studies may simply indicate that college students and managers are becoming less likely to express their biases overtly. If such is the case, we need to examine more subtle expressions of sex stereotypes.

Personality Characteristics and Management Potential

Research by Schein (1973; 1975) on perceptions of "requisite" management characteristics seems to deal with a more subtle form of bias. This line of research suggests that it is not one's sex alone that is used to infer management potential, but also possession of the proper masculine characteristics. This kind of stereotype involves more subtle forms of bias because, unlike one's sex, "personality" characteristics are not immediately obvious and cannot be verified easily.

To apply Schein's research to the evaluation of job incumbents, T. L. Ruble (1979) developed an exercise that asked individuals to rank eight candidates for promotion to middle management. All candidates were described as having "very good" performance records as lower managers. The candidates were also described with masculine, feminine, or neutral sex-typed characteristics. Two forms were used to present the candidates so that on one form a particular candidate would be identified as a male (for instance, Joe Block—ambitious, willing to take risks) and on the other form as a female (Joanne Block—ambitious, willing to take risks). When the exercise was used in the classroom, college students tended to recommend the promotion of men compared with women. In contrast, participants in a conference on women in management recommended women over men. However, in both settings, raters recommended candidates with masculine characteristics over those with feminine characteristics.

Subsequent research indicated that when the characteristics used to describe the candidates were rated separately, the masculine characteristics (such as ambitious) were generally considered as less desirable for a manager than feminine characteristics (such as ability to get along with others). Yet, in both studies the ratings indicate that less desirable masculine characteristics had been considered as more promotable than feminine characteristics. Thus, occupational sex typing, coupled with sex stereotyping, would seem to create biases against women aspiring to managerial careers. As Schein (1973) has argued, if it is generally believed that managers need to possess certain characteristics, and it is also believed that men are more likely than women to possess the "requisite" characteristics, then the probability of a man being selected for a managerial position is greater than the probability of a woman being selected. Of course, the validity of the belief that masculine characteristics are required for success is certainly open to question (Putnam & Heinen, 1976).

Evaluations of Performance: The Role of Objective Evidence

Most of the studies evaluating management potential have provided minimal information on the actual performance or behavior of the candidate. Borgida et al. (1981) suggests that stereotypes are unlikely to affect social judgments and predictions when specific behavioral information about a target person is provided. To test this hypothesis, subjects were provided with information indicating that a male or female target had previously behaved in an assertive way. Subjects then rated the target's personality and predicted the target's behavior in a novel situation. An analysis of the ratings indicated no differences in the impressions of male versus female targets. These findings suggest that "target-case" information about a particular male or female may, in many situations, outweigh "base-rate" information in forming impressions. The target-case information emphasizes the individual's behavior, while the base-rate information reflects stereotypic expectations for a class of individuals.

A study by Hall and Hall (1976) obtained results consistent with the reasoning outlined by Borgida et al. In a laboratory study students were given a case description of a situation in which a male or female manager performed successfully. Ratings of the manager's performance found no difference in the evaluation of males versus females. The authors suggest that biases may be reduced when objective behavioral data are provided to the rater.

In contrast with the results obtained by Hall and Hall, other studies have found sex biases in performance evaluation even when ratings are based on objective performance measures. In two studies of performance on a traditionally masculine task, female workers were rated higher than equally productive male workers (Bigoness, 1976; Hamner, Kim, Baird, & Bigoness, 1974). Similarly, additional research by Taynor and Deaux (1973;

1975) showed that women performing well on a masculine task were rated as more deserving of a reward than equally performing males.

These results, seemingly inconsistent with reports of bias against women performing masculine tasks, may be interpreted as an undervaluation of the male performance, an overvaluation of the female performance, or some combination of the two. For example, on certain (masculine) tasks we probably expect men to do better than women. And, when men and women perform equally, we may undervalue the men's achievement because they had a larger discrepancy between expected and actual performance. Alternatively, we might view certain (masculine) tasks as requiring more effort from women to achieve equal levels of performance. In this case we may give greater credit to the women for harder work. This latter interpretation seems to be preferred by Taynor and Deaux, as well as by Rose (Rose, 1978; Rose & Stone, 1978). In any event, the results of these studies suggest that the sex typing of the task interacts with the sex of the worker to influence evaluations.

A study by Feldman-Summers and Kiesler (1974) indicates that both under- and overvaluation might occur, depending on the sex of the rater. In this study subjects were asked to make causal attributions for the success of a physician. Each subject evaluated one stimulus person, who was identified as a male or female physician in surgery or pediatrics. Results indicated that both male and female subjects attributed greater motivation to the female physician, but male subjects also saw her as less able and having an easier task than the male physician. In contrast, female subjects saw the female physician as having a harder task. Because we are dealing here with attributions, and not performance evaluations, it is impossible to determine how occupational rewards would have been allocated. However, it does seem that female subjects would have been disposed toward overvaluing the female's performance, since the task was perceived as something of a barrier. Male subjects, on the other hand, did not seem to perceive the task as a barrier, and may have undervalued the female's performance.

In summary, when objective information was available, evaluations of performance on a specific task often failed to show bias, or were biased in favor of females performing well in masculine activities. However, the study by Feldman-Summers and Kiesler raises an important question about the effects of objective information on evaluations of performance versus evaluations of potential. A favorable evaluation of short-term or task-specific performance does not necessarily lead to a favorable evaluation of long-term potential or general ability. Feldman-Summers and Kiesler found that males rated a successful female physician as more motivated but less able than a successful male physician. Thus, rewarding a woman for successful performance on a specific masculine task does not mean that the woman would be recommended for promotion. Unfortunately, most studies of the effects of objective performance information have failed to consider the long-range implications of the task-specific evaluations. However, it is important to distinguish between short-term performance and long-term potential. This distinction is crucial because estimates of potential and decisions concerning promotion and advancement have the more profound effect on the careers of men and women.

A Model of Performance Evaluations

The studies reviewed in the last few pages suggest that the process of performance evaluation involves a complex interaction of factors that may result in negative biases concerning women's potential. Four major factors are identified in Figure 5.1: the evaluator's prior set of beliefs, the observed performance, the evaluator's causal explanations for the observed performance, and the consequences of the process.

The evaluator approaches the process with a set of beliefs and expectations based on sex stereotypes and occupational stereotypes. Research by Feather (Feather, 1975; Feather & Simon, 1976) indicates how these expectations might influence performance evaluations. In his 1975 study, college students were likely to judge males as being happier than females with success, and unhappier with failure, for jobs that were male-dominated. In contrast, females were judged as happier than males with success, and unhappier with failure, when the jobs were female-dominated. Thus, we would probably expect greater motivation and effort by individuals in relation to sex-appropriate jobs compared with sex-inappropriate

FIGURE 5.1

A "Process" Model of Performance Evaluation

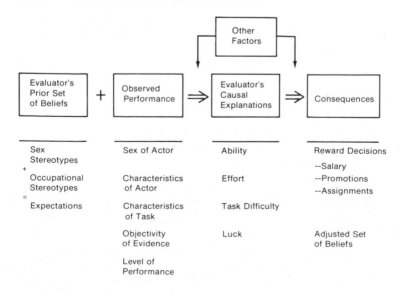

jobs. These expectations would then serve as standards for later judgments of performance.

In the next step in the evaluation process, behavior is observed along with other salient aspects of the actor or task. We have seen that the sex of the actor, the sex typing of the task, and objective performance measures seem to affect evaluations. Most studies we have reviewed tend to emphasize one or more of these factors, and then immediately assess the effect of the factor or factors on decisions. However, the model suggests that causal attributions may serve as a key link between observed performance and decisions. The study by Feldman-Summers and Kiesler indicated that performance of males and females may be explained differently. Other attributional research (such as Deaux, 1976; 1979; Frieze et al., 1978) confirms these differences. For example, male successes tend to be attributed to stable, personal qualities of the actor (that is, ability), while female successes tend to be attributed to unstable causes, such as effort or luck.

These gender-related attributional patterns are thought to be due to differential assumptions concerning the capacities of males versus females. That is, if males are expected to be competent, their successes are consistent with expectations, and are therefore attributed to something stable about them (Deaux, 1976). In contrast, if a woman is expected to do poorly on a masculine task, her success is attributed to a temporary cause, such as unusual effort, thereby leading to uncertainties about her future promise and to a closer scrutiny of her qualifications. The slow progress women seem to be making into the upper levels of most fields may be due, in part, to very subtle cognitive processes such as these.

A laboratory study by Heilman and Guzzo (1978) indicates that attributional processes may mediate reward allocations (pay raises and promotions) in organizations. Most important, attributing performance success to ability led to higher perceptions of the appropriateness of a promotion than did attributing performance to effort, task difficulty, or luck. This tendency occurred regardless of the sex of the employee. Thus, sex differences per se did not account for differential treatment; rather, attributions mediated rewards. This does not mean that biases would be reduced, since attributions to ability tend to be more associated with male success, while nonability attributions are associated with female success. Thus, the reward allocations found by Heilman and Guzzo, coupled with the attributional biases identified by Deaux, suggest that women would probably receive fewer important rewards (such as promotions) for equal performance.

Some Conclusions

There seem to be a number of biases in the evaluation process that favor males over females: the preference for masculine characteristics, higher initial expectations for males, and attributional biases. These biases are particularly relevant to women pursuing nontraditional occupations. Thus, equality in the pursuit of a career may not be as close as one might hope. Moreover, the subtlety of some of the factors involved means that change may occur slowly.

Further consideration of the bias favoring male characteristics in managers suggests that this form of stereotyping has important implications for men as well as women. The issue concerns the extent to which both men and women must live up to the higher-valued masculine image. For men the problem involves what Bem (1975a) has called the "tight-pants" model of humanity. This model suggests that adherence to rigid sex roles limits the full expression of human characteristics and emphasizes the "either-or" concept of sex-role behavior rather than an androgynous concept. Although more recent research suggests that male sex roles are changing (Pleck, 1976; Tavris, 1977) or may have been overstated (Cicone & Ruble, 1978), it would appear that traditionally masculine occupations may require males to avoid exhibiting behavior considered characteristic of females. As Bem (1975a) has suggested, the result may be that males experience reduced effectiveness in situations requiring a wide range of behaviors.

For a woman the preference for masculine characteristics involves the problem of meeting expectations that she remain "feminine" in a "masculine" world. Thus, the woman faces a potential dilemma of dual-role conflict (Darley, 1976). A simple answer to this dilemma of course, is that she could express both masculine and feminine characteristics. However, as Powell and Butterfield (1979) have shown, masculine managers were preferred to androgynous managers. Moreover, encouraging a woman to exhibit contradictory behaviors may lead to the classic "double bind." For example, Kristal, Sanders, Spence, and Helmreich (1975) found that "competent" women with "masculine" vocational interests and "feminine" personality characteristics were well-liked, but rated lower on various achievement-related attributes (such as success-oriented) than similarly competent women with both masculine vocational interests and masculine personality characteristics. Thus, until our sex-role stereotypes change, it would appear that both men and women must face biases that limit the full expression of their human potential. These issues will be considered further in the final section of the chapter.

THE DEVELOPMENT OF SEX-STEREOTYPIC KNOWLEDGE AND BEHAVIOR

We have seen that sex stereotypes are a deeply ingrained element in our society, and that they have subtle yet profound effects on the day-to-day lives of men and women. We turn now to a developmental analysis of these processes. There is considerable evidence, as detailed below, that knowledge of both sex stereotypes and sex-typed behavior is acquired by preschool children. Thus, children may become essentially restricted toward a sex-linked way of viewing and behaving in the world (and flexibility of choice may be concomitantly reduced) at a strikingly early age. As Mussen (1969) suggests, an individual's sex role may be the most salient and important of his or her many social roles. "No other social role directs more of an individual's overt behavior, emotional reactions, cognitive functioning, covert attitudes, and general psychological and social adjustment" (p. 707). It becomes extremely important, then, to analyze the early determinants of sex-role acquisition.

It is not possible in this chapter to review in detail the voluminous literature relevant to sex-role acquisition. Instead, in keeping with the general theme of the chapter, we will focus on the role of sex-stereotypic knowledge in determining sex-typed interests and behaviors. Current conceptions of sex-role acquisition are dominated by two theoretical orientations. First, according to social learning theory, children are assumed to develop sex-appropriate behaviors by the same learning processes that are involved in the acquisition of all patterns of behavior—that is, reinforcement and modeling (Bandura, 1969; W. Mischel, 1966; 1970). In contrast, according to the cognitive-developmental perspective, the child's active cognitive structuring of his or her social world is viewed as the major factor involved in sex-role development (Kohlberg, 1966; Kohlberg & Ullian, 1974). Although these two theoretical positions differ considerably in their hypotheses concerning how (and even when) the important components of sex roles are acquired, in both the presence of cultural stereotypes is a central determinant of children's emerging sex-role differentiation.

For stereotyping to serve as a determinant of sex-role behavior, it is necessary to posit a mechanism that leads children to behave in accordance with cultural guidelines for sex-appropriate behavior. There are several ways this transferral may take place: socializing agents may differentially respond to boys and girls because of their sex-typed expectations; children may be differentially exposed to same-sex models who are behaving in accordance with cultural stereotypes; and children may be motivated to seek out the "rules" of appropriate sex-typed behaviors.

The first two possibilities represent the major assumptions of social learning theory. A feature of note is that the child may take a relatively passive role in acquiring behaviors consistent with sex stereotypes; no prerequisite knowledge of stereotyping is necessary. In contrast, the third possibility assumes that children actively seek sex-role information and are motivated to behave appropriately. This approach is most consistent with the cognitive-developmental analysis. As we will see in the following review of research, neither theory is sufficient to account for all of the data. Instead, there is evidence that both active and passive processes operate in determining the relationship between stereotyping and behavior, though the two processes seem to be differentially important at different stages of development. We will first review the literature concerning the development of two types of sex-role knowledge: stereotypes and gender labeling and identity. Second, we will analyze the relationship between these two kinds of sex-role knowledge and behavior, and discuss the implications of this analysis for theoretical accounts of sex-role development.

Developing Sex-Role Awareness and Knowledge

Stereotyping

Studies concerned with the development of children's sex stereotypes have examined both perceptions about children (their characteristics, playthings, and activities) and about adults (their characteristics and activities). In these studies the major issues concern when children become aware of sex stereotypes, the content of those perceptions, and age-related differences in the strength of stereotypes. It is difficult to draw definitive conclusions about these issues because of the small number of studies and because each uses a different set of stimuli, questions, mode of response, and age range of subjects. Nevertheless, some consistent trends seem to emerge.

In general, the available research suggests that, on most dimensions, children's knowledge of sex stereotypes develops at an early age. Preschool and kindergarten-aged children make few "errors" in assigning sex-stereotypic labels to activities, occupations, and playthings (Edelbrock & Sugawara, 1978; Fauls & Smith, 1956; Garrett, Ein, & Tremaine, 1977; Guttentag & Longfellow, 1977; Hartley, 1960; Masters & Wilkinson, 1976; Nadelman, 1970; 1974; Papalia & Tennent, 1975). Indeed, stereotyping of objects has been shown in children as young as 24 months of age (Thompson, 1975). In contrast, recent research examining sex-typed traits suggests that this kind of knowledge develops somewhat later. For example, in one study, five-, eight-, and eleven-year-old children were asked which of two silhouette pictures (male or female) was best characterized by each of several traits presented in the form of brief stories (such as who gets into fights, who cries a lot) (Best, Williams, Cloud, Davis, Robertson, Edwards, Giles, & Fowles, 1977). Only 14 of the 60 five-year-olds responded above a chance level, compared with 60 of the 88 eight-year-olds and 47 of the 48 eleven-year-olds. Thus, it appears that children are typically aware of differential sex roles before they learn about sex-stereotypic personality characteristics.

These data, as well as implications of other findings, suggest that the degree of familiarity of the items and/or extent to which they have a concrete referent may determine, in part, the degree of stereotyping shown at young ages. For example, with regard to traits, young children generally agree that males are aggressive and strong, and that females are soft-hearted and emotional; traits with less obvious referents to physical behaviors (such as logical, fussy) are not perceived to be differentiated by sex (Best et al., 1977; Williams, Bennett, & Best, 1975). Furthermore, children are more likely to show sex-typing of characteristics for peers than for adults (Gold & St. Ange, 1974). Finally, even among concrete stimuli, it appears that items with which children are most familiar—namely, playthings—are the easiest for them to label in stereotypic terms (Hartley & Hardesty, 1964).

Most studies show that the strength of stereotyping changes with age, but there are inconsistencies in the nature of the changes reported. All theories of sex-role development would predict an increase in stereotyping with age in very young children, consistent with increased experience and cognitive skills; and, as expected, young children do seem to demonstrate increasing knowledge at least through the kindergarten level (Edelbrock & Sugawara, 1978; Flerx, Fidler, & Rogers, 1976; Thompson, 1975; Vener & Snyder, 1966; Urberg, 1979b). After this age, however, there are mixed developmental trends. Many studies show a sharp increase in knowledge between five and eight years of age, with some leveling off after that (Best et al., 1977; Masters & Wilkinson, 1976; Nadelman, 1974; Williams et al., 1975). In contrast, other research suggests linear decreases (for example, Garrett et al., 1977) or wavelike increases and decreases in stereotyping with increasing age (for instance, Guttentag & Longfellow, 1977; Ullian, 1976; Urberg, 1979a).

There are several possible ways of resolving these apparent contradictions. The first concerns the response measure employed. Specifically, measures that require a forced choice between males and females tend to show an increase in stereotyping during the early years of school (Best et al., 1977; Masters & Wilkinson, 1976; Nadelman, 1974; Williams et al., 1975), while those that allow for a "both" or "neither" response typically show a decrease during these years (Garrett et al., 1977; Guttentag & Longfellow, 1977; Urberg, 1979b). This pattern of results suggests that while the older children may have more complete knowledge about what kinds of activities and characteristics are stereotypically associated with males or females, they may also apply such stereotypes more flexibly or with finer discriminations (Masters & Wilkinson, 1976). This conclusion is consistent with reports of an increase with age in androgynous ("both") responses (Garrett et al., 1977; Urberg, 1979b).

A second possible explanation of inconsistent age effects is that sex stereotypes consist of various dimensions that are differentially salient and important according to age level. Clearly, the sex-role-related concerns of children in early elementary school differ considerably from those of adolescents, and thus one might predict peaks in the strength of stereotyping corresponding to the interests at different age levels. Indeed, it is frequently suggested that the nature of sex-typing changes during adolescence (Katz, 1979; W. Mischel, 1970; Newman & Newman, 1979), in accordance with a newly emerging identity as a sexual being and strong peer pressures, and may actually result in stronger adherence to sex stereotypes (cf. Frieze et al., 1978; Urberg & Labouvie-Vief, 1976).

For example, as Lamb and Urberg (1978) have noted, the insecurities associated with the sudden changes in and importance of physical appearance during adolescence may lead to a new commitment to traditional sex roles. Indeed, some research has reported a heightened degree of stereotyping in adolescence relative to middle elementary school (Guttentag & Longfellow, 1977; Stein & Smithells, 1969; Urberg, 1979a). In addition, the results of a large interview study suggested a pattern of alternating acceptance and rejection of sex-role norms, based on age-related changes in the perceived bases (for instance, biological versus social) of sex differences (Ullian, 1976).

In summary, a descriptive analysis of the development of sex stereotypes suggests that by the age of five, children have a reasonably well defined set of stereotypes about the more concrete aspects of sex roles—specific activities, playthings, and occupations. More abstract aspects of sex roles (that is, traits) are acquired somewhat later. In general, knowledge of stereotypes increases asymptotically with age, as shown by studies that require forced-choice responding. However, when other response options are provided, stereotypic versus egalitarian perceptions show fluctuations with age, depending on the nature of the stereotypes being assessed and the age range of the sample included in the study.

Gender Labeling and Identity

A crucial construct in the development of sex-role knowledge is the ability of children to apply accurate gender labels (boy or girl) to themselves and others. This categorization skill is an obvious prerequisite for sex stereotyping to serve as a basis for sex-typed evaluations and behavior.

Unfortunately, defining and operationalizing this construct is not as straightforward as it might initially appear; and there are wide variations in the age at which this skill is acquired, depending upon which measure is used. One measure consists of categorizing people according to common noun labels (such as "boy," "mommy"). Children's ability to distinguish between the sexes is first established on the basis of superficial physical characteristics (hair style, clothing, body type), with genitals acquiring increasing importance with age (Kohlberg, 1966; Thompson & Bentler, 1971). Several studies have shown that children are able to identify both their own sex and the sex of others by four years of age (Brown, 1956; Rabban, 1950). A more recent study has shown that this skill emerges at a surprisingly young age; 24-month-olds accurately applied gender labels to pictures of others, and by 30 months of age, the children were accurately applying such labels to themselves (Thompson, 1975).

Other research, however, suggests that this simple classification represents only a rudimentary understanding of gender. Specifically, children do not appear to understand that gender is a stable and consistent aspect of identity until several years after they can accurately label males and females (De Vries, 1969; Emmerich, Goldman, Kirsh, & Sharabany, 1977; Kohlberg, 1966; Marcus & Overton, 1978; Slaby & Frey, 1975). According to cognitive-developmental theory (Kohlberg, 1966), this concept of gender-identity constancy is the critical aspect of gender labeling, because it "can provide a stable organizer of the child's psychosexual attitudes only when the child is categorically certain of its unchangeability" (p. 95).

Gender constancy refers to the consistent labeling of oneself and others as male or female in spite of superficial transformations, such as hair style, clothing, or changes in toy interest. In one study (Slaby & Frey, 1975) this concept was measured by a series of questions and counterquestions, grouped into three aspects of gender constancy: identity (such as, Is this a woman or a man? Is this a [opposite sex of subject's first response]?), stability (such as "When you grow up, will you be a mommy or a daddy?"), and consistency (such as "If you played [opposite sex of subject] games, would you be a boy or a girl?"). Identity was the easiest, and was mastered by four years of age; stability and consistency were understood by four and a half to five years of age (see Table 5.4).

Other studies have used similar questions, but with additional features that have made the task more difficult and apparently have resulted in a later grasp of gender constancy. For example, when the measures use perceptual transformations (such as clothes or hair on dolls or live models) to accompany the questions, the development of gender constancy is closely associated with the development of the ability to perform accurately on Piagetian measures of the constancy of physical objects—that is, at approximately five to seven years of age in middle-class children (De Vries, 1969; Kohlberg, 1966; Marcus & Overton, 1978).

Thus, in summary, there is some debate about when gender constancy develops, though it clearly develops later than simple gender labeling and some aspects of sex-role stereotyping. The developmental timing of this concept is important because it is central to understanding the nature of the relationships between different kinds of sex-role knowledge and sex-typed behavior.

Relationship Between Developing Sex-Role Knowledge and Behavior

In this section we consider the extent to which the evidence suggests that children's knowledge of sex stereotypes plays a role in producing sex-typed behavior. Is the initial acquisition of sex-role behavior dependent on a prior knowledge of stereotypes, or at least a prior knowledge of gender labeling? Do stereotypes serve as guidelines by which children learn new behaviors or monitor the appropriateness of current activities? Direct

TABLE 5.4
Results from Gender Constancy Scale, Based on Three Question Sets

	Question Set			Percent of Children (total = 100)			Age (months)	
Type	Gender Iden-tity	Gender Stabil-ity	Gender Consis-tency	Boys	Girls	Com-bined	Mean	Range
Stage:								
1	−	−	−	9	16	13	34	26–39
2	+	−	−	26	16	20	47	35–62
3	+	+	−	17	31	25	53	36–68
4	+	+	+	48	34	40	55	41–67

Note: Failure to sum to 100% reflects error in rounding.
Source: Slaby & Frey (1975), Table 2, p. 852. Copyright 1975 by the Child Development Publications, Inc. Reprinted by permission.

evidence on these important questions is scarce, and definitive conclusions are impossible. However, it is possible to begin to examine these issues by means of an analysis of two aspects of the available evidence: developmental parallels across studies of different kinds of knowledge and behavior, and the nature of the relationships shown within single studies among the various components of sex roles.

Initial Acquisition of Sex Roles

The two major theories of sex-role development—social learning and cognitive-developmental—emphasize different types of determinants of early sex-typed values and behaviors. According to social learning theory (W. Mischel, 1966; 1970), differential reinforcement for sex-typed behavior begins early, and children begin to apply gender labels and stereotypes on the basis of this differential reinforcement. The ample availability of same-sex models at home and in the media provides a major source of information during the sex-differentiation process (Maccoby & Jacklin, 1974). In contrast, according to cognitive-developmental theory (Kohlberg, 1966; Kohlberg & Ullian, 1974), structural cognitive changes that allow children to perceive constancy of gender serve as the organizer of sex-role behaviors. Thus, children are hypothesized to become interested in same-sex models and to perceive sex-appropriate behaviors as reinforcing *because* of the newly acquired concept of inevitability of their gender.

What does the empirical evidence suggest concerning the first appearance of preferences and behaviors? Recent reviews of the literature suggest that some aspects of sex typing are evident as early as three to four years (Brooks-Gunn & Matthews, 1979; Constantinople, 1979; Edelbrock & Sugawara, 1978; Frieze et al., 1978; Maccoby & Jacklin, 1974). Although there are physiological differences between the sexes (such as height, weight, metabolic rate) during the first two years of life, there do not appear to be consistent sex differences at this age in sensory or attentional skills, temperament, or play (Frieze et al., 1978; Lewis & Weinraub, 1979; Maccoby & Jacklin, 1974). However, by preschool age, children indicate preferences for sex-stereotypic toys (for example, Fling & Manosevitz, 1972), there is sex differentiation in play activities (for instance, Cramer & Hogan, 1975; Fagot & Patterson, 1969), and boys tend to be somewhat more physically aggressive and active than girls (cf. Maccoby & Jacklin, 1974).

These findings are consistent with a social learning perspective on the role of stereotyping in the sex-role learning process. Although there is debate about the strength of evidence showing early same-sex modeling and sex-related shaping of behavior (Block, 1977; Lewis and Weinraub, 1979; Maccoby & Jacklin, 1974), there are some consistent suggestions of differential socialization. A number of studies have shown that adults have very clear expectations about the characteristics and behaviors of young girls versus boys. That is, people have been shown to differentially perceive and differentially evaluate the same behaviors, depending on whether the child is labeled as a girl or a boy (Condry & Condry, 1976; Gurwitz & Dodge, 1975; Haugh, Hoffman, & Cowan, 1980; Meyer & Sobieszek, 1972). One study showed that even among newborns, girls were described as softer, smaller, and cuter than boys, in spite of the fact that there were no objective height and weight differences between the infant boys and girls in the study (Rubin, Provenzano, & Luria, 1974).

It would be surprising if such expectations had no effect on interactions with the two sexes; and, indeed, there is evidence suggesting that people do respond differently to the same child, according to whether it is perceived to be a male or a female (Brooks-Gunn & Matthews, 1979; Seavey, Katz, & Zlak, 1975; Smith & Lloyd, 1978; Will, Self, & Datan, 1976). In addition, there is reasonably consistent evidence that boys are handled more roughly from infancy on (cf. Lewis & Weinraub, 1979; Maccoby & Jacklin, 1974), and that parents provide different toys for their sons than for their daughters (Cairns, 1979; Maccoby & Jacklin, 1974; Rheingold & Cook, 1975). Thus, although the evidence of social learning during early childhood is far from definitive, there are some suggestions that adults' sex-role stereotypes may lead to early differential socialization of the two sexes in subtle but potentially significant ways.

There are also indications that processes related to cognitive-developmental theory may partially explain early sex-role acquisition. The evidence presented in the preceding sections indicates that some aspects of sex-role knowledge are present by three years of age—specifically, gender labeling and stereotyping of some objects and activities—even though gender constancy does not develop until later. Perhaps these early types of knowledge exert some organizing influence on children's preferences and activities, which in turn helps lead to progressive cognitive awareness and differentiation. That is, the impact of children's growing knowledge about gender and stereotyping may have a gradual and reciprocal influence on sex-typed behavior prior to achieving gender constancy. Indeed, several theoretical analyses have similarly concluded that categorizing processes based on sex-role knowledge probably play an important role in guiding children's activities long before gender constancy is achieved (Constantinople, 1979; Frieze et al., 1978; Pleck, 1975).

In summary, several components of sex-role knowledge and sex-typed behavior become evident at an early point during development—three to four years of age—and appear to be influenced by subtle elements of both social learning and cognitive-developmental processes. These processes may be particularly powerful when their interactive effects are considered. For example, a child's ability to label herself as a girl, in combination with parents' providing sex-typed toys, may promote the ability to discriminate among toys on a stereotypic basis. This increased knowledge, in combination with external encouragement to engage in sex-appropriate activities, should, in turn, lead to increased sex-typed behavior.

The Influence of Stereotypes at Later Points in Development

The literature reviewed earlier suggests that there are substantial developmental changes in sex-role knowledge. What is the impact of these later changes on sex-typed behavior? Of particular interest is the acquisition of the concept of gender constancy, since it is a central construct in cognitive developmental theory. Although sex-typed behavior is clearly present prior to five years of age, is there any evidence that the attainment of gender constancy has a major impact on sex-role development?

According to Kohlberg (1966), once children develop a conception of a constant, categorical gender identity, they become motivated to learn what behavior is appropriate for their gender and to act accordingly. "Basic self-categorizations determine basic valuings. . . . After masculine-feminine values are acquired, the child tends to identify with like-sex figures" (pp. 164–165). Thus, it is at this point in development that children should actively begin to seek information about their own gender and to preferentially attend to and imitate same-sex models.

Interestingly, the lag in time between the emergence of sex-typed behavior and gender constancy seems to be perceived as more of a problem for cognitive-developmental theory in subsequent analyses of the theory (for instance, Lewis & Weinraub, 1979) than for the way the theory was originally stated by Kohlberg. Kohlberg readily acknowledges the importance of environmental influences on early sex-typed preferences (p. 112). However, one of the problems with Kohlberg's (1966) formulation is that he is not entirely consistent about the timing of and relationship among the various sex-role variables.

For example, early in the chapter he links gender constancy to Money, Hampson, and Hampson's (1957) research on a critical period for gender identity and estimates its timing at about five years of age. However, later in the chapter he discusses the relationship of gender constancy to conservation of the properties of physical objects, and places the timing of its development at six to seven years. Similarly, in some places he suggests that gender constancy precedes the development of masculine and feminine stereotypes and values (pp. 88–89, 107). For example, he states, "Once the boy has stably categorized himself as male, he then values positively those objects and acts consistent with his gender identity" (p. 89). Elsewhere, however, he states that children have acquired appropriate sex identity and relatively generalized sex-typed preferences and stereotypes by age four (p. 130).

Only a few studies are relevant to whether attention to same-sex models varies as a function of gender constancy. Grusec and Brinker (1972) found that children at the age associated with gender constancy (five- and seven-year-old children) recalled more of the behaviors of the same-sex models portrayed in a film, though no specific assessment of this cognitive construct was made. In a more directly relevant study, Slaby and Frey (1975) found, consistent with cognitive-developmental theory, that preschool boys at advanced stages of gender constancy spent more time selectively attending to a same-sex model in a movie than boys at lower stages, even with age controlled.

In contrast, Bryan and Luria (1978) failed to find differential attention to slides of males or females in children aged five to six years and nine to ten years. However, it is not clear that their results seriously question the validity of the hypothesis. Because the stimuli were relatively simple and only a single model was presented at a time, there was no need to selectively focus attention, as there was in the above two studies where male and female models were presented simultaneously. Furthermore, there was evidence in the Bryan and Luria (1978) study of greater recall of same-sex tasks and preference for same-sex models, suggesting the presence of sex-specific active information processing.

The idea that children show increased attention to information regarding sex appropriateness once they recognize the constancy of gender also leads to the hypothesis that children will show a heightened susceptibility at this time to gender labels of toys or activities. Unfortunately, this hypothesis has not been tested. Numerous studies have shown that the performance and evaluation of an activity by children in early elementary school are affected by whether the activity is labeled as male- or female-appropriate (Helper & Quinlivan, 1973; Liebert, McCall, & Hanratty, 1971; Montemayor, 1974; White, 1978). Although these findings are consistent with the prediction, sex-typed labels have been shown to affect the preferences of children as young as three years of age (Thompson, 1975). Thus, future research needs to examine more directly the relationship between cognitive-developmental level, gender constancy, and responses to sex-typed labeling.

There is also little directly relevant information concerning the association between gender constancy and sex-specific behavior. Only a few of the many studies of modeling show that children differentially imitate same-sex models (Barkley, Ullman, Otto, & Brecht, 1977; Maccoby & Jacklin, 1974; Perry & Bussey, 1979). However, most studies of same-sex modeling examined preschool children, who presumably had not yet attained gender constancy. Furthermore, in most of the studies including older children, developmental changes were not examined, and none of the studies included a measure of gender constancy. In the only study that divided children into age levels, same-sex imitation was found for those aged seven to eight, but not for the younger children, which is consistent with the cognitive-developmental hypothesis (Ward, 1969).

One study showed a direct relationship between gender constancy and differential modeling. In the middle of a cartoon, preschool and kindergarten children were shown a toy commercial in which either two boys or two girls played with a toy pretested to be perceived as equally appropriate for girls and boys. Among children who had achieved a high level of gender constancy, those who viewed same-sex children in the commercial subsequently played with that toy significantly longer than children who had seen opposite-sex children in the commercial. In contrast, there was no difference in playing time across conditions for children who were at a low level of gender constancy (D. N. Ruble, Balaban, & Cooper, 1981).

Thus, there is tentative support for the idea that once children's concepts of themselves as boys or girls have become fixed and stable, they are more attuned to same-sex behavior and more responsive to same-sex models. A somewhat different picture emerges, however, when another measure of sex-role behavior is examined: preferences for sex-appropriate activities. According to Kohlberg (1966), children's increasing awareness of the unchangeability of their gender is accompanied by increasing preferences for same-sex activities. However, the evidence is, at best, equivocal on this point.

For example, one study has specifically examined the relationship between gender constancy and sex-role preferences. Kindergartners, first-grade and second-grade children were asked about their preferences for games, television characters, and peers. Although there were some age-related changes in same-sex preferences, there was no relationship between their measure of gender constancy and sex-role preference (Marcus & Overton, 1978). As explanation of their failure to support the cognitive-developmental predictions, the authors suggest that neutral or opposite-sex activities may be less threatening, once children understand that their gender will not change regardless of their sex-role preferences. However, the previously described findings of an increase associated with gender constancy in children's attention to (Slaby & Frey, 1975) and imitation of (D. N. Ruble et al., 1981) same-sex models suggest that there is validity to the original hypothesis. It may be, instead, that a current-preferences measure is relatively insensitive to children's increased interest in gender-related information, because some sex differentiation of activities is readily acknowledged to be present prior to a child's stable identification as a boy or girl (Kohlberg, 1966).

Behavioral preferences in early childhood probably are multiply determined by such factors as patterns of reinforcement from socializing agents and what playthings are available. However, such preferences are assumed to represent specific interest differences, not an awareness of general masculinity/femininity values or categories. Thus, for example, a five-year-old boy might state his own or another child's preference for a truck "because I have a toy like it at home," whereas, a seven-year-old would say, "A boy . . . wouldn't want to play with dolls" (Kohlberg, 1966, p. 115). That is, the older child has greater awareness of his or her appearance, activities, or possessions as being appropriate (or inappropriate) for a boy or girl. Thus, according to the cognitive-developmental position, it is the reasoning that is changing between the ages of four and seven, not necessarily the behavior. Also, the greater attention to gender-related information associated with the attainment of gender constancy may not have much impact on play habits, especially when the information received is not likely to deviate much from stereotypic patterns already formed.

In summary, there is some evidence that children's changing awareness of the constancy of their gender is associated with heightened susceptibility to information from same-sex models. From this conclusion we can draw the potentially important inference that this stage of development may represent a point where change in sex-stereotypic behavior would be possible, if children encountered behavioral flexibility from same-sex models during this time of information-seeking. Several of the studies reviewed earlier indicate that the nature and strength of stereotypes may undergo a fairly dramatic change during adolescence, suggesting that there may be other important development shifts in information seeking. Indeed, some papers have suggested that a developmental analysis of the relationship between different kinds of sex-role knowledge and behavior at several key points in the lifespan would likely provide important insight concerning the role of stereotyping in the acquisition of sex-typed behavior (Emmerich, 1973; Huston-Stein & Higgins-Trenk, 1978; Katz, 1979).

Differential Evaluations of Maleness and Femaleness

A final but very important aspect of the influence of cultural stereotypes on sex-role development concerns the value placed on male versus female roles and characteristics. Although at young ages both boys and girls positively evaluate their own sex and prefer same-sex activities, there are various indications that males and maleness become preferred with increasing age. Girls' preference for same-sex activities seem to peak at about four years of age, while boys become increasingly sex-typed (cf. Edelbrock & Sugawara, 1978; Maccoby & Jacklin, 1974). Children perceive adult males (particularly fathers) as more competent and powerful (cf. Kohlberg, 1966). Finally, there is evidence that with age, both boys and girls increasingly view male characteristics as more desirable (Smith, 1939). Thus, although there are a few exceptions (for instance, Parish & Bryant, 1978), the bulk of the evidence seems to support the conclusion that "Attraction or preference for the female role appears to *decrease* during the elementary and adolescent years" (Huston-Stein & Higgins-Trenk, 1978, p. 260).

Exactly *why* children should begin to value the male role differentially is not clear. Kohlberg (1966) has hypothesized that the almost universal assignment of higher-status roles to males is indicative of a biological basis for these findings. Specifically, he suggests that children's perceptions of the greater size and strength of males leads them to attribute greater status to males (that is, bigger is better). Although there is little evidence concerning this or any other hypothesis about reasons underlying the development of differential evaluations, the potential importance of such findings cannot be overemphasized. Sex differences in self-esteem (for example, Loeb & Horst, 1978) or in expectations for success, discussed in the next section, may well be related to the perception of this fundamental difference between the sexes.

Summary and Conclusions

A considerable range and number of studies demonstrate that sex stereotypes exert a powerful influence on the course of children's development. Sex stereotypes affect the way socializing agents interact with boys versus girls from birth on. Furthermore, children themselves have learned most sex stereotypes by early elementary school, and show evidence of monitoring their own behavior in terms of these cultural expectations by this time.

Is it inevitable that children will learn sex stereotypes? What if a family prefers not to let sex stereotypes direct their children's values, interests, and behaviors? The ample availability of such stereotypes on television, in books and magazines, at school, and generally throughout the culture (Brooks-Gunn & Matthews, 1979; Frieze et al., 1978) creates large problems for an individual family who wants to raise their child in an egalitarian way. As previously discussed, it appears that children after the age of five to seven are highly responsive to sex-stereotyping information available from many sources—not just parents. Thus, in the present culture the development of sex stereotypes and concomitant behaviors by eight years of age may indeed be inevitable.

Nevertheless, individuals may, of course, vary considerably in the extent to which they stereotype others or behave in accordance with sex stereotypes. For example, family and peer group values may modulate the degree to which an individual is influenced by sex stereotypes (Frieze et al., 1978).

PROSPECTS FOR THE FUTURE

Much of the recent literature on sex roles and stereotypes has been stimulated by or has led to the conclusion that gender-related differentiation has become dysfunctional for modern society. The biological sex differences often assumed to be responsible for sex-role differentiation historically—greater male strength and female restrictions due to pregnancy and nursing—are no longer relevant to most societal functions (Hoffman, 1977). Furthermore, numerous negative implications of conforming to cultural standards of masculinity and femininity have been identified. With regard to women it has been noted that, as a group, they constitute a largely untapped national resource (Keller, 1975). As we have seen, they lack ready access to occupational positions of prestige and authority, and tend to be restricted to less-valued roles. In addition, traditional femininity has been associated with mental health problems, such as depression and low self-esteem, and with deficits in certain areas of skill and competence (cf. Frieze et al., 1978; Sherman, 1976).

Similarly, much of what is culturally defined as "masculine" is virtually unattainable by the majority of males, and many men and boys see themselves as faced from the start with what can only be a losing battle. For example, as part of an investigation of the personality traits that lead to popularity in elementary school, Tuddenham (1951) suggests that athletic skill is central to boys' constellation of values. Since athletic skill is largely based on factors that are partly inherited, such as size, motor coordination, and physical maturity, a boy's ability to live up to this standard may be beyond his control.

In addition, pressure to achieve is especially great on males in our culture. A study by Feather and Simon (1975) found that successful males are judged more positively by others than are successful females, but unsuccessful males receive less positive ratings than do unsuccessful females. One possible outcome of such pressure is physical malfunctioning; and one can, indeed, put together a rather alarming list of ailments, ranging from coronaries to suicide, from which males are statistically more likely than females to die (Kaye, 1974).

For these reasons one important current line of research is how to change traditional notions of masculinity and femininity (Newland, 1979; D. N. Ruble, Croke, Frieze, & Parsons, 1975; D. N. Ruble, Frieze, & Parsons, 1976). This point of view is well illustrated by the concluding statement of an article by Jessie Bernard (1976):

> Changing sex-specialized norms and sex-typed behavior is not a take-it-or-leave-it option. It is a fundamental imperative. The question is not whether to do it but rather how to do it. (p. 222)

In this section we will discuss changes in sex roles and stereotypes, barriers to change, and current theoretical constructs that go beyond sex stereotypes.

Changes in Sex Roles and Stereotypes

There are numerous indications of quite dramatic changes in sex roles. These changes are especially pronounced for women. Since World War II women have entered the labor force and higher education in increasing numbers, with concomitant decreases in the amount of time devoted to homemaking and motherhood (Frieze et al., 1978; Giele, 1979; Hoffman, 1977; Huston-Stein & Higgins-Trenk, 1978; Schlesinger, 1977; Van Dusen & Sheldon, 1976). The figures on percent of married women employed are striking, shifting from 15 percent in 1940 to 43 percent in 1974 (Van Dusen & Sheldon, 1976). Also impressive are the large increases in the percent of women entering medical and law schools (Colwill & Roos, 1978; Van Dusen & Sheldon, 1976). Finally, there have been measurable changes in women's sex-role attitudes (Frieze et al., 1978; Huston-Stein & Higgins-Trenk, 1978; Mason, Czajka, & Arber, 1976); women are less likely to perceive that their role options are limited to wife and mother.

Changes in men's roles have been less obvious, but there are indications that they may be forthcoming. Although there have been relatively few changes in men's occupational and family roles (Pleck, 1976; Tavris, 1973), there is increasing concern with how men will adapt to changing women's roles (Bear, Berger, & Wright, 1979; Newland, 1979). In addition, recent research suggests that men may be responding to working wives by increasing, albeit slightly, their participation in home and child care tasks (cf. Hoffman, 1977).

Interestingly, changes in roles do not seem to be accompanied by changes in the sex stereotypes that are often perceived to be the basis for gender differentiation (cf. Huston-Stein & Higgins-Trenk, 1978). In a content analysis of women's magazines, only one change was found in stereotypes about personality differences (the belief that women should be sheltered and protected) between 1955–1965 and 1966–1976 (Geise, 1979). Similarly, the portrayal of women in print advertisements between 1958 and 1972 was found to improve marginally, at best (Belkaoui & Belkaoui, 1976).

More direct analyses of changes over time in individual sex stereotypes show a similar pattern. In a comparison between beliefs in 1970 and beliefs reported by two studies in the 1950s, Neufeld, Langmeyer, and Seeman (1974) found very few differences over the 20-year period, and many of those differences seemed to reflect more extreme opinions about sex differences in the recent sample. A more recent study (Petro & Putnam, 1979) did report fewer stereotypes in a current sample as compared with the Rosenkrantz et al. (1968) study. However, Petro and Putnam used a different type of sample and a different criterion for designating differences, so it is not clear how to interpret these findings. Thus, in general, as Huston-Stein and Higgins-Trenk (1978) conclude, "Despite the changes in women's employment, achievement patterns, and expectations, stereotypes of females as incompetent, emotional, unable to handle high level jobs, and generally inferior persist to a remarkable degree" (p. 268).

Barriers to Change

Various factors present in the immediate social situations of men and women may act to maintain the status quo with regard to roles and stereotypes. For example, the existence of certain social institutions, such as day care centers, may serve to facilitate or inhibit variations in role choices (Zellman, 1976). In this section three types of maintenance factors will be discussed as illustrations: the mass media, cognitive processes affecting how people evaluate themselves and others, and social pressures to conform to expectations operating in a particular role situation. More detailed discussions of these and other factors may be found in Frieze et al. (1978), Huston-Stein and Higgins-Trenk (1978), and D. N. Ruble et al. (1976).

Mass Media

One potentially important contributor to the maintenance of the status quo in sex stereotyping is the mass media. As previously discussed, theories of sex-role development suggest that early learning of sex stereotypes and standards is based, in large part, on modeling and/or active information seeking from a wide range of sources in the environment. Furthermore, other research indicates that older children and adults are also attentive to and influenced by same-sex models and cultural norms portrayed in the media (Maccoby & Wilson, 1957; Maccoby, Wilson, & Burton, 1958; Perloff, Brown, & Miller, 1978; Wolf, 1975; Wood, 1971). Thus, it may be argued that the mass media play a key role in both the formation and the maintenance of gender-related beliefs and behavior.

What can people learn about sex roles from the media? Numerous studies have suggested that the portrayal of males and females in books, magazines, music, movies, and television is overwhelmingly consistent with sex stereotypes (cf. Perloff et al., 1978; Tuchman, 1979). On television males are predominantly portrayed as leading characters, especially in cartoons (Stein & Friedrich, 1975). In addition, males are shown as more aggressive, constructive, powerful, expert, and autonomous, while females are represented as more deferential, often defined in relationship to someone else (McArthur & Eisen, 1976; Sternglanz & Serbin, 1974).

The values regarding appropriate sex roles are well exemplified by one study that analyzed the achievement orientation of women depicted on television and the happiness of their social situations (Manes & Melnyk, 1974). They found that women who were depicted as having careers were either unmarried or portrayed as unsuccessfully married. On the other hand, 95 percent of all women who were not employed were portrayed as being happily married. Only women whose employment was at the lowest status levels were portrayed as having happy and successful relationships with men. The message seems clear. At least as depicted on television, women cannot have domestic happiness and a fulfilling career. By contrast, men were allowed to be seen as successful in both domains. Similar unrealistic and stereotyped portrayals of males and females have been shown in content analyses of music, magazines, cartoons, radio, and children's books (for example, Freudiger & Almquist, 1978; Geise, 1979; Mills, 1974; Streicher, 1974; Weitzman, Eifler, Hokada, & Ross, 1972).

Attention to the mass media, then, can provide information about the stereotyped behavior of men and women, boys and girls. Since children have been reported to watch three to four hours of television alone per day (Lyle

& Hoffman, 1972), the effects of exposure to the mass media attain immense significance. Indeed, an association between television watching and sex-role attitudes has been reported in one study: The more television a child watches, the more traditional are his or her sex-role attitudes (Frueh & McGhee, 1975).

A number of investigators have considered the possibility that the mass media may serve as an effective agent of change as well as a powerful factor in maintaining sex stereotypes. The logic underlying this line of research is as follows: If children learn sex stereotypes from the media, then showing characters engaged in nontraditional roles (as on the television show "Police Woman") should lead to a decrease in stereotyping. In four separate studies, evidence consistent with this hypothesis was reported (Flerx, Fidler, & Rogers, 1976; Miller & Reeves, 1976; O'Bryant & Corder-Bolz, 1978; Pingree, 1978). For example, children exposed to commercials portraying women in traditionally male roles (such as welder or butcher) were more likely to perceive such occupations as appropriate for females than children viewing women in traditionally female roles (such as file clerk or manicurist). In addition, comparable differences were found for the girls' own preferences for traditionally male versus female occupations (O'Bryant & Corder-Bolz, 1978). Finally, the potential of the media to stimulate change even in adults is shown by the results of a field study in Finland. From 1966 to 1970, Finland produced a planned media campaign emphasizing women's equality. Pre-test and post-test changes in egalitarian attitudes showed a shift from 50 percent of the sample to 80–90 percent of the sample favoring equality for women (Haavio-Manila, 1972).

Cognitive Processes

This book has emphasized that people's interpretations of their own and others' activities influence various subsequent responses. We have already indicated how cognitive processes might operate to influence evaluations of others' performance. In addition, cognitive processes shape one's own achievement behavior. For example, there are rather consistent findings that males hold higher expectations for personal success and higher self-evaluations of ability than do females (for instance, Crandall, 1969; Deaux, 1979; Frieze, 1975; Stein & Bailey, 1973). Interestingly, males are expected to outperform women in virtually every area of achievement, even those traditionally associated with females (Feldman-Summers & Kiesler, 1974). Such differences have been found in children first entering school (Parsons & Ruble, 1977; Parsons, Ruble, Hodges, & Small, 1976), and the origins of the differences have been related both to children's growing awareness of stereotypes concerning sex differences in competence corresponding to the attainment of gender constancy (Frey & Smythe, 1976) and to differential reinforcement, especially from teachers (Dweck & Goetz, 1978).

The important point about these differences in self-confidence is that people with high expectations for success have been shown to actually perform better—that is, to put forth more effort or persist longer—such that high expectations become a self-fulfilling prophecy resulting in a higher likelihood of success (Crandall, 1969; Frieze, 1975; R. A. Jones, 1977). Thus, for example, a man is more likely than a woman to enter a novel situation expecting to succeed, which in turn makes success more likely, and thereby helps maintain the stereotype of greater male competence and inhibits women from entering new achievement-related roles.

Social Pressures to Conform

Social situations involve a set of norms and expectations that serve as guidelines for appropriate behaviors by individuals in those situations. Sex-role demands are explicitly or implicitly part of a wide variety of social situations, and people tend to conform to such demands in order to avoid real or imagined sanctions for role deviations (Darley, 1976; Spence & Helmreich, 1978). For example, the often-cited fear-of-success explanations for women's failures to achieve at levels commensurate with their capacity (Horner, 1972) may be viewed as an avoidance of negative consequences accruing to women if they appear to be fulfilling a masculine role—that is, an orientation toward competitive achievement (Condry & Dyer, 1976; Darley, 1976). Similarly, as Darley (1976) points out, ". . . men will choose not to display behaviors that would, in a particular situation, be generally expected of women. This hypothesis suggests that men would not competitively or aggressively clean house and that as a rule women would not competitively or aggressively discuss sports" (p. 86).

The potent impact of situational factors on individuals' inclinations to display sex-appropriate behavior is shown in a clever study by Zanna and Pack (1975). College women who anticipated interacting with an attractive male portrayed themselves as more stereotypically feminine when they believed the man held traditional, as opposed to nontraditional, views. There were no differences between the two groups of women when they believed they would be interacting with an unattractive male. Thus, if women on occasion pretend to be less competent and more dependent than they actually are, these behaviors may be viewed as responses to situational demands that act most often to maintain the status quo (Spence & Helmreich, 1978).

Put in a broader context, such findings imply that sex stereotypes may be maintained, in part, because of the different roles men and women typically fulfill (Eagly, 1978). For example, inherent in the role of nursery school teacher is a situational demand for high nurturance. The fact that this role is filled almost exclusively by women means that they may be perceived as more nurturant than men—not necessarily because of any real sex difference in personality but, rather, because of differences in the demands of situations in which men and women are most often found.

Some research has actually demonstrated that sanctions are applied when individuals deviate from traditional sex stereotypes. In a series of three studies, subjects were asked to evaluate men and women who were behaving either consistently or inconsistently with sex stereotypes. The results showed negative effects on both popularity ratings and perceived psychological adjustment of passive men and assertive women (Costrich, Feinstein, Kidder, Marecek, & Pascale, 1975). More recent articles have also referred to more anecdotal evidence of overt hostility and ridicule applied to men who deviate from tradition by, for example, following a wife when she has to move to take a new position (Bear et al., 1979).

Changing sex-role norms that operate in social situations is obviously an extremely difficult endeavor. Situational forces toward maintaining traditional roles operate in very subtle ways—as seen, for example, in the nonverbal communication of dominance versus deference according to the ways men and women sit or stand (Frieze & Ramsey, 1976; Parlee, 1979). Other research, however, suggests that subtle manipulations may modify the way social situations are perceived, thereby allowing greater behavioral flexibility (for example, Lockheed & Hall, 1976; D. N. Ruble & Higgins, 1976).

For instance, college students' descriptions of themselves in terms of stereotypically masculine versus feminine traits were dramatically influenced by the sex composition of the group. Males described themselves as more feminine (for instance, introverted) and females described themselves as more masculine (for instance, competitive) when they were the lone member of their sex in a group of four (D. N. Ruble & Higgins, 1976). Such findings suggest one important way that affirmative action programs may contribute significantly to change: even small alterations in the sex composition of a decision-making group may have a radical effect on the basic nature of the group and the way it is perceived in terms of sex-role norms.

Beyond Sex Stereotypes: Current Theoretical Constructs

An orientation toward changing sex stereotypes is reflected in theoretical constructs concerning sex identity, the extent to which individuals view themselves as behaving in accordance with sex stereotypes. Early research in this area viewed masculinity and femininity as representing a bipolar continuum on a single scale, and implied that positive mental health was associated with a high degree of sex typing. That is, implicit in the approach to research was the question of how to promote healthy males and females by helping them acquire appropriately sex-typed attitudes, interests, and traits (for example, Biller, 1971; Brown, 1957; Kagan, 1964).

Currently, however, it is widely recognized that masculinity and femininity may be conceptualized as two independent dimensions, as discussed in the section on stereotyping. Of particular relevance to the current section is the additional assumption that a sex identity that incorporates both masculine and feminine traits (that is, androgyny or duality) may be associated with better psychological adjustment than a traditional sex-typed identity (Bem, 1974; 1975b, 1978; Heilbrun, 1976; Spence & Helm-reich, 1978). Thus, this approach complements indications that change is occurring, at least in some areas; furthermore, it examines the implications of such changes, generally assuming that they are positive. In this section we will briefly describe these new formulations, their correlates with indexes of mental health, and some of the issues currently being raised.

Two-Dimensional Models of Masculinity and Femininity

Central to these new formulations is the idea that a given individual may be both assertive (masculine) and sensitive to the needs of others (feminine), yet still function effectively. To study the effects of individual differences in sex identity, several self-report instruments have been developed. Individuals indicate the extent to which they personally exhibit each of a series of characteristics, some of which are stereotypically masculine and some stereotypically feminine (see, for example, the traits used in the Spence and Helmreich [1978] Personal Attributes Questionnaire [PAQ], presented in Table 5.2). The procedural and scoring details of the scales have been extensively discussed elsewhere (Bem, 1974; Heilbrun, 1976; Kelly & Worell, 1977; Spence & Helmreich, 1978), so our discussion here will be brief.

The Bem Sex-Role Inventory (BSRI) consists of a set of masculine, feminine, and neutral items, and individuals rate the extent to which each trait is "true" for them. The sex-typed traits represent standards of desirable behavior for men and women, based on ratings obtained from an independent sample. Masculine items are defined as characteristics rated significantly more socially desirable for men than for women (such as independent, forceful, ambitious), while feminine items are defined as characteristics rated significantly more socially desirable for women than for men (such as helpful, gentle, understanding). In most of her studies, Bem grouped individuals into three major categories, according to their self-ratings: feminine (high feminine-low masculine), masculine (low feminine-high masculine), and androgynous (no significant difference between the masculine and feminine scores). After extensive criticism of this procedure, Bem (1977) has revised her scoring procedure and has divided the third category into two: androgynous (both high) and undifferentiated (both low).

The Spence and Helmreich PAQ was discussed earlier in this chapter. Scores on the PAQ are grouped into four categories currently used by Bem, as described above. While the difference between what is considered desirable and what is considered typical may be minor, those small differences might lead to inconsistent results between studies using one instrument or the other (Spence & Helmreich, 1979). For example, Gilbert, Deutsch, and Strahan (1978) found that characteristics considered desirable for men or for women were generally related to the rater's concept of what was "ideal" rather than what was "typical" of the sexes, though this distinction did not apply to females rating women targets.

Correlates of Sex Orientation with Mental Health

The underlying question of the research based on these new formulations of sex identity is whether androgynous individuals are more behaviorally adaptive and psychologically healthy than individuals who are rigidly sex-typed. Although there have been some inconsistencies across studies, the answer to this question has generally been affirmative. Several studies have reported that androgynous individuals score high on measures of self-esteem and personal adjustment, and that undifferentiated subjects are particularly low on such measures (Bem, 1977; Orlofsky & Windle, 1978; Spence, Helmreich, & Stapp, 1975; Helmreich, Spence, & Holahan, 1979).

Other research has supported the hypothesis that androgynous individuals exhibit greater adaptability to the situation than sex-typed individuals. With regard to stereotypically masculine behavior, androgynous as well as masculine-typed individuals were found to conform less frequently to peer pressure for conformity than did feminine-typed subjects (Bem, 1975b). Similarly, androgynous females used more direct power strategies than feminine-typed females (Falbo, 1977). With regard to stereotypically feminine behavior, androgynous males exhibited higher levels of playful and nurturant behaviors than masculine males (Bem, 1975b; Bem, Martyna, & Watson, 1976); and for both sexes, androgynous individuals were found to be more interpersonally responsive than their sex-typed counterparts (Bem et al., 1976). Finally, masculine males and feminine females were found to make more stereotyped behavior choices and to be more uncomfortable performing cross-sex activities than androgynous or sex-reversed subjects (Bem & Lenney, 1976).

Thus, the results of validation studies generally support the usefulness of distinguishing between androgynous and other sex-related identifications. However, there is a noteworthy limitation to the conclusion that androgyny represents the preferred orientation. Several studies have reported weak or no differences between androgynous-typed and masculine-typed individuals. Indeed, most studies of self-esteem have failed to differentiate between these two groups; instead, they have found that they were both higher than feminine-typed and/or undifferentiated groups (Bem, 1977; Heilbrun, 1976; Orlofsky, 1977). Similarly, in some of her behavioral studies Bem (1975b) and her colleagues (1976) found that feminine-identified individuals performed relatively poorly on all activities, even stereotypically feminine ones. Furthermore, some research has suggested that flexibility and adjustment are more associated with masculinity than with androgyny for adults

(W. Jones, Chernovetz, & Hansson, 1978; Lubinski, Tellegen, & Butcher, 1981), and for children (Hall & Halberstadt, 1980). Finally, research by Helmreich et al. (1979) led them to suggest that the PAQ and the BSRI are measures of instrumental and expressive attributes, and are only indirectly related to more general sex-role behaviors. Instead, they suggest that the positive relationships observed may be mediated by self-esteem. These findings have led some to question the meaning of positive correlations between an androgynous orientation and socially valued behaviors (Locksley & Colten, 1979; Pedhazur & Tetenbaum, 1979). For example, Kelly and Worell (1977) suggest that "While androgynous persons possess approximately equal *numbers* of masculine and feminine characteristics, it may be principally the masculine-typed behaviors (assertiveness, instrumentality, dominance, etc.) that have greater potential for leading to social reinforcements in our society" (p. 1113). It seems possible that the socially undesirable characteristics (such as childlike, gullible) included on the feminine-typed, but not the masculine-typed, scales of the BSRI (Pedhazur & Tetenbaum, 1979) may partially explain these results, but at present this remains an untested hypothesis.

Current and Future Issues

To date the focal concerns of research looking beyond traditional bipolar conceptions of masculinity and femininity have been developing and validating new measurement instruments. It is, therefore, not surprising that a high proportion of articles in this area have addressed some kind of methodological or statistical issue (for example, Downing, 1979; Kelly & Worell, 1977; Orlofsky, Aslin, & Ginsberg, 1977; Strahan, 1975). Currently, however, there are indications of a shift in the nature of the questions being asked, such that the issue of whether androgyny or duality is "better" is no longer the central concern. Instead, there appears to be a growing desire to reconceptualize research on sex roles and stereotypes in a way that allows for possibility (considering what a future ideal might be) as well as reality (understanding what is happening now).

One such question is concerned with what types of changes in personal orientation will maximize psychological well-being for all individuals. For example, Garnets and Pleck (1979) suggest that there is unlikely to be the simple one-to-one relationship between sex-role orientation and psychological adjustment implicit in the androgyny formulation. Instead, they argue that this relationship is mediated by two other variables, and that failure to take these into account may have contributed to contradictory findings in early research and may lead to uneven effects of sex-role changes on different subgroups in society. To illustrate, they suggest that an androgynous orientation can be associated with good adjustment only when the individual's same-sex ideal is androgyny.

A corresponding postulate is that cultural change toward an androgynous ideal may be dysfunctional for subgroups with masculine or feminine real self-concepts. Thus, one important mediating variable is the real-ideal self discrepancy. A second mediating variable is sex-role salience, the degree to which individuals organize and characterize traits and behaviors in terms of masculinity and femininity. Sex-role strain is less likely to occur in individuals who are low in sex-role salience because, for example, an emotional man simply perceives himself as being emotional, not as being "unmasculine." A key implication of this variable is that it suggests that reducing sex-role salience (not just increasing androgyny) is the optimal way of achieving change across different sectors of society.

A second new question concerns developing alternative conceptions to androgyny as to what is ideal for the individual in terms of sex roles (for instance, Locksley & Colten, 1979; Spence & Helmreich, 1979). For example, according to one formulation, in the ideal state an individual does not represent just a combination of masculine and feminine attributes (androgyny) but, rather, has moved beyond or "transcended" sex roles altogether (Rebecca, Hefner, & Oleshansky, 1976). The concept of sex-role transcendence is viewed as the third stage in a developmental model of sex-role development in which the second stage, "polarized sex roles," represents the end point of most other developmental models. According to Rebecca et al. (1976), the key point is that "The concept of transcendence includes but often goes beyond situational flexibility, since very often situations demand responses that would compromise the personal integrity of the individual" (p. 204). They illustrate this point by referring to the competitive and aggressive styles often required to "get ahead" in present-day society. The concept of transcendence would allow for changes in the requirements of the role as an alternative to changes in personal styles as a way of achieving fit between the individual and the role demands.

These few examples represent a more general mood in the sex-stereotyping literature that individual and societal change is necessary, and that new paradigms and models must be developed not only to study change but also to promote it. Unfortunately, at present investigators have barely begun to operationalize such new concepts (Garnets & Pleck, 1979) or to consider how to test for differences across concepts, such as androgyny versus transcendence (Wolff & Taylor, 1979). Nevertheless, it seems that theoretical analyses about changing sex roles and stereotypes are now progressing at a faster pace than the actual societal change they are analyzing.

SUMMARY

The study of sex stereotypes represents one of the most rapidly growing and productive areas in the study of stereotyping today. This chapter represented a selective review of this voluminous literature, and focused on five aspects of sex stereotypes.

The first section consisted of a historical perspective on the origins of sex stereotypes. Descriptions of differences between the sexes appear throughout history, and several central themes or images were identified.

The second section was concerned with describing the nature of current beliefs about men and women in our society, and with discussing problems of conducting and interpreting research on sex stereotypes. There appears to be a reasonably high level of agreement across studies in the content of people's beliefs about the sexes, and such stereotypes have remained remarkably stable over time. However, several methodological and conceptual problems were identified that suggest the need to be cautious about drawing definite conclusions from these studies. An important trend in recent research is toward a multidimensional view of sex-related traits and away from a bipolar conception of such traits.

In the third section we discussed the consequences of sex stereotyping with a particular emphasis on employment and career opportunities. Sex stereotypes appear to create several types of limitations on career choice and advancement, and such barriers seem particularly severe for women interested in nontraditional careers. First, occupational sex-typing has been shown to create constraints on choice of careers. Not only does sex-typing of occupations serve to define jobs as men's work or women's work, but it also seems related to perceptions of personal characteristics considered necessary for success in a career. Second, several studies suggest that sex stereotypes lead to bias in the evaluation of job candidates. The implication of these findings is that hiring preferences are likely to conform closely to the matching of sex stereotypes and occupational sex-typing. Finally, on-the-job evaluations, important for crucial decisions regarding pay increases and career advancement, are subject to sex-related bias. There seem to be a number of subtle biases in the evaluation process that favor males over females: preference for masculine characteristics, higher initial expectations for males, and attributional biases. However, it is important to note that many studies in this area show mixed results, and there are a number of mediating factors that preclude simple conclusions. The complex interaction of factors believed to result in negative biases concerning women's potential were integrated into a proposed working model in Figure 5.1.

The fourth section represented a description and analysis of developmental processes in the acquisition of sex stereotypes. The development of two kinds of sex-role knowledge (stereotypes and gender identity) were briefly described. The evidence suggests that by the age of five, children have a reasonably well-defined set of stereotypes about the more concrete aspects of sex roles (specific activities, playthings, and occupations). More abstract aspects of sex roles, such as traits, are acquired somewhat later. Although there is some debate about when children develop a stable concept of gender identity, it clearly develops later than simple gender labeling and some aspects of sex stereotyping. Second, the relationship between these two kinds of sex-role knowledge and behavior was analyzed, and the implications of this analysis for theoretical accounts of sex-role development were discussed. The evidence indicated that several components of sex-typed behavior become evident at an early point during development (three to four years of age), prior to many types of sex-role knowledge. Traditional views of the two major theories of sex-role acquisition (social learning theory and cognitive-developmental theory) suggest that they have difficulty explaining this early acquisition. However, recent reconceptualizations of these theories indicate that subtle elements of both social learning and cognitive-developmental processes may lead to early behavioral differentiation along sex-stereotyped lines.

The fifth and final section concerned the prospects for change in sex stereotypes and possible future directions in this area of research. The results of recent studies on sex stereotypes suggest that surprisingly few changes have occurred in spite of attention to the women's movement and some obvious changes in women's roles in the work force. Thus, the question turned to why change might be a slow process, and three factors that serve to maintain the status quo were briefly discussed: mass media, cognitive processes affecting how people evaluate themselves and others, and social pressure to conform to expectations operating in a particular role situation. Finally, illustrations of new formulations of sex-stereotyping research were presented. Some current issues involve considerations of what an "ideal" conception of gender might consist of and what the implications of such possibilities would be for maximizing psychological well-being for all individuals.

REFERENCES

Ashmore, R. D., & Del Boca, F. K. Sex stereotypes and implicit personality theory: Toward a cognitive-social psychological conceptualization. *Sex Roles*, 1979, *5*, 219–248.

Bakan, D. *The duality of human existence.* Chicago: Rand McNally, 1966.

Bandura, A. Social learning theory of identificatory processes. In R. A. Goslin (ed.), *Handbook of socialization theory and research.* Chicago: Rand McNally, 1969.

Barkley, R. A., Ullman, D. G., Otto, L., & Brecht, J. M. The effects of sex typing and sex appropriateness of modeled behavior on children's imitation. *Child Development*, 1977, *48*, 721–725.

Baron, R. A., & Byrne, D. *Social psychology.* Boston: Allyn and Bacon, 1977.

Bear, S., Berger, M., & Wright, L. Even cowboys sing the blues: Difficulties experienced by men trying to adopt non-traditional sex roles and how clinicians can help them. *Sex Roles*, 1979, *5*, 191–198.

Belkaoui, A., & Belkaoui, J. M. A comparative analysis of the roles portrayed by women in print advertisements, 1958, 1970, 1972. *Journal of Market Research*, 1976, *13*, 168–172.

Bem, S. L. The measurement of psychological androgyny. *Journal of Consulting and Clinical Psychology*, 1974, *42*, 155–162.

Bem, S. L. Fluffy women and chesty men. *Psychology Today*, September, 1975, pp. 58–62. (a)

Bem, S. L. Sex role adaptability: One consequence of psychological androgyny. *Journal of Personality and Social Psychology*, 1975, *31*, 634–643. (b)

Bem, S. L. On the utility of alternative procedures for assessing psychological androgyny. *Journal of Consulting and Clinical Psychology*, 1977, *45*, 196–205.

Bem, S. L. Beyond androgyny: Some presumptuous prescriptions for a liberated sexual identity. In J. Sherman & F. Denmark (eds.), *Psychology of Women: Future directions in research*. New York: Psychological Dimensions, Inc., 1978.

Bem, S. L., & Bem, D. J. Training the woman to know her place. In D. J. Bem (ed.), *Beliefs, attitudes and human affairs*. Belmont, Calif.: Brooks/Cole, 1970.

Bem, S. L., & Lenney, E. Sex typing and the avoidance of cross-sex behavior. *Journal of Personality and Social Psychology*, 1976, *33*, 48–54.

Bem, S. L., Martyna, W., & Watson, C. Sex typing and androgyny: Further explorations of the expressive domain. *Journal of Personality and Social Psychology*, 1976, *34*, 1016–1023.

Bernard, J. Change and stability in sex-role norms and behavior. *Journal of Social Issues*, 1976, *32* (3), 207–223.

Best, D. L., Williams, J. E., Cloud, J. M., Davis, S. W., Robertson, L. S., Edwards, J. R., Giles, H., & Fowles, J. Development of sex-trait stereotypes among young children in the United States, England, and Ireland. *Child Development*, 1977, *48*, 1375–1384.

Bigoness, W. J. Effect of applicant's sex, race, and performance on employer's performance ratings: Some additional findings. *Journal of Applied Psychology*, 1976, *61*, 80–84.

Biller, H. B. *Father, child, and sex role: Paternal determinants of personality development*. Lexington, Mass.: Heath Lexington Books, 1971.

Block, R. N. Criteria in sex discrimination grievances. *Arbitration Journal*, 1977, *32*, 241–255.

Borgida, E., Locksley, A., & Brekke, N. Social stereotypes and social judgment. In N. Cantor & J. Kihlstrom (eds.), *Personality, cognition, and social interaction*. Hillsdale, N.J.: Erlbaum, 1981.

Brannon, R. The male sex role: Our culture's blueprint of manhood, and what it's done for us lately. In D. David and R. Brannon (eds.), *The forty-nine percent majority: The male sex role*. Reading, Mass.: Addison-Wesley, 1976.

Brannon, R. Measuring attitudes (toward women, and otherwise): A methodological critique. In J. Sherman & F. Denmark, (eds.), *Psychology of women: Future directions in research*. New York: Psychological Dimensions, Inc., 1978.

Brooks-Gunn, J., & Matthews, W. S. *He and she*. Englewood Cliffs, N.J.: Prentice-Hall, 1979.

Broverman, I. K., Vogel, S. R., Broverman, D. M., Clarkson, F. E., & Rosenkrantz, P. S. Sex role stereotypes: A current appraisal. *Journal of Social Issues*, 1972, *28* (2), 59–79.

Brown, D. G. Sex-role preference in young children. *Psychological Monographs*, 1956, *70*, no. 14, entire issue.

Brown, D. G. Masculinity-femininity development in children. *Journal of Consulting Psychology*, 1957, *21*, 197–205.

Bryan, J. W., & Luria, Z. Sex-role learning: A test of the selective attention hypothesis. *Child Development*, 1978, *49*, 13–23.

Bullough, V. L. *The subordinate sex*. Urbana: University of Illinois Press, 1973.

Cairns, R. B. *Social development: The origins and plasticity of interchanges*. San Francisco: Freeman, 1979.

Caldwell, T. *Dear and glorious physician*. New York: Bantam Books, 1959.

Cash, T. F., Gillen, B., & Burns, D. S. Sexism and beautyism in personnel consultant decision making. *Journal of Applied Psychology*, 1977, *62*, 301–310.

Chapman, L. J., & Chapman, J. P. Illusory correlation as an obstacle to the use of valid psychodiagnostic signs. *Journal of Abnormal Psychology*, 1969, *74*, 271–280.

Cicone, M. V., & Ruble, D. N. Beliefs about males. *Journal of Social Issues*, 1978, *34* (1), 5–16.

Cline, M. E., Holmes, D. S., & Werner, J. C. Evaluations of the works of men and women as a function of the sex of the judge and type of work. *Journal of Applied Social Psychology*, 1977, *7*, 89–93.

Cohen, S. L., & Bunker, K. A. Subtle effects of sex role stereotypes on recruiters' hiring decisions. *Journal of Applied Psychology*, 1975, *60*, 566–572.

Colwill, N. L., & Roos, N. P. Debunking a stereotype: The female medical student. *Sex Roles*, 1978, *4*, 717–722.

Condry, J., & Condry, S. Sex differences: A study of the eye of the beholder. *Child Development*, 1976, *47*, 812–819.

Condry, J., & Dyer, S. Fear of success: Attribution of cause to the victim. *Journal of Social Issues*, 1976, *32* (3), 63–83.

Constantinople, A. Masculinity-femininity: An exception to the famous dictum? *Psychological Bulletin*, 1973, *80*, 389–407.

Constantinople, A. Sex-role acquisition: In search of the elephant. *Sex Roles*, 1979, *5*, 121–134.

Costrich, N., Feinstein, J., Kidder, L., Marecek, J., & Pascale, L. When stereotypes hurt: Three studies of penalties for sex-role reversals. *Journal of Experimental Social Psychology*, 1975, *11*, 520–530.

Cowan, M. L., & Stewart, B. J. A methodological study of sex stereotypes. *Sex Roles*, 1977, *3*, 205–216.

Cramer, P., & Hogan, K. Sex differences in verbal and play fantasy. *Developmental Psychology*, 1975, *11*, 145–154.

Crandall, V. C. Sex differences in expectancy of intellectual and academic reinforcement. In C. P. Smith (ed.), *Achievement-related motives in children*. New York: Russell Sage Foundation, 1969.

Crawford, J. D. Career development and career choice in pioneer and traditional women. *Journal of Vocational Behavior*, 1978, *12*, 129–139.

Darley, S. Big-time careers for the little woman: A dual-role dilemma. *Journal of Social Issues*, 1976, *32* (3), 85–98.

Deaux, K. *The behavior of women and men*. Monterey, Calif.: Brooks/Cole, 1976.

Deaux, K. Self-evaluations of male and female managers. *Sex Roles*, 1979, *5*, 571–580.

Deaux, K. *Sex roles, stereotypes, and behaviors.* Invited address presented at the Eastern Psychological Association, New York, 1981.

De Vries, R. Constancy of generic identity in the years three to six. *Monographs of the Society for Research in Child Development,* 1969, *34* (3), Serial no. 127.

Dipboye, R. L., Arvey, R. D., & Terpstra, D. E. Sex and physical attractiveness of raters and applicants as determinants of resume evaluations. *Journal of Applied Psychology,* 1977, *62,* 288 294.

Dipboye, R. L., Fromkin, H. L., & Wiback, K. Relative importance of applicant sex, attractiveness, and scholastic standing in evaluation of job applicant resumes. *Journal of Applied Psychology,* 1975, *60,* 39–43.

Dipboye, R. L., & Wiley, J. W. Reactions of college recruiters to interviewee sex and self-presentation style. *Journal of Vocational Behavior,* 1977, *10,* 1–12.

Dipboye, R. L., & Wiley, J. W. Reactions of male raters to interviewee self-presentation style and sex: Extensions of previous research. *Journal of Vocational Behavior,* 1978, *13,* 192–203.

Downing, N. E. Theoretical and operational conceptualizations of psychological androgyny: Implications for measurement. *Psychology of Women Quarterly,* 1979, *3,* 284–292.

Dweck, C. S., & Goetz, T. Attributions and learned helplessness. In J. H. Harvey, W. Ickes, and R. F. Kidd (eds.), *New Directions in Attribution Research* (Vol. 2). Hillsdale, N.J.: Erlbaum, 1978.

Eagly, A. H. Sex differences in influenceability. *Psychological Bulletin,* 1978, *85,* 86–116.

Edelbrock, C., & Sugawara, A. I. Acquisition of sex-typed preferences in preschool aged children. *Developmental Psychology,* 1978, *14,* 614–623.

Emmerich, W. Socialization and sex-role development. In P. B. Baltes and K. W. Schaie (eds.), *Life-span developmental psychology: Personality and socialization.* New York: Academic Press, 1973.

Emmerich, W., Goldman, K. S., Kirsh, B., & Sharabany, R. Evidence for a transitional phase in the development of gender constancy. *Child Development,* 1977, *48,* 930–936.

Fagot, B. I., & Patterson, G. R. An in vivo analysis of reinforcing contingencies for sex-role behaviors in the preschool child. *Developmental Psychology,* 1969, *1,* 563–568.

Falbo, T. Relationship between sex, sex-role, and social influence. *Psychology of Women Quarterly,* 1977, *2,* 62–72.

Fauls, L., & Smith, W. Sex-role learning of five-year-olds. *Journal of Genetic Psychology,* 1956, *89,* 105–117.

Feather, N. T. Positive and negative reactions to male and female success and failure in relation to the perceived status and sex-typed appropriateness of occupations. *Journal of Personality and Social Psychology,* 1975, *31,* 536–548.

Feather, N. T., & Simon, J. G. Reactions to male and female success and failure in sex-linked occupations: Impressions of personality, causal attributions, and perceived likelihood of different consequences. *Journal of Personality and Social Psychology,* 1975, *31,* 20–31.

Feather, N. T., & Simon, J. G. Stereotypes about male and female success and failure at sex-linked occupations. *Journal of Personality,* 1976, *44,* 16–37.

Feldman-Summers, S., & Kiesler, S. B. Those who are number two try harder: The effect of sex on attributions of causality. *Journal of Personality and Social*

Psychology, 1974, *30*, 846–855.

Fidell, L. S. Empirical verification of sex discrimination in hiring practices in psychology. *American Psychologist*, 1970, *25*, 1094–1097.

Flerx, V. C., Fidler, D. S., & Rogers, R. W. Sex role stereotypes: Developmental aspects and early intervention. *Child Development*, 1976, *47*, 998–1007.

Fling, S., & Manosevitz, M. Sex typing in nursery school children's play interests. *Developmental Psychology*, 1972, *7*, 146–152.

Foushee, H. C., Helmreich, R. L., & Spence, J. T. Implicit theories of masculinity and femininity: Dualistic or bipolar? *Psychology of Women Quarterly*, 1979, *3*, 259–269.

Freudiger, P., & Almquist, E. M. Male and female roles in the lyrics of three genres of contemporary music. *Sex Roles*, 1978, *4*, 51–66.

Frey, K., & Smythe, L. Differential effects of sex role concepts on boys' and girls' achievement expectation. Paper presented at meeting of the Western Psychological Association, San Fernando, Calif., March, 1976.

Frieze, I. H. Changing self images and sex-role stereotypes in college women. Paper presented at the meeting of the American Psychological Association, New Orleans, 1974.

Frieze, I. H. Women's expectations for and causal attributions of success and failure. In M. T. S. Mednick, S. S. Tangri, & L. W. Hoffman (eds.), *Women and achievement: Social and motivational analyses.* Washington, D.C.: Hemisphere, 1975.

Frieze, I. H., Parsons, J. E., Johnson, P. B., Ruble, D. N., & Zellman, G. L. *Women and sex roles: A social psychological perspective.* New York: W. W. Norton, 1978.

Frieze, I. H., Parsons, J. E., & Ruble, D. N. Some determinants of career aspirations in college women. Paper presented at the symposium on sex roles and sex differences, University of California, Los Angeles, 1972.

Frieze, I. H., & Ramsey, S. J. Nonverbal maintenance of traditional sex roles. *Journal of Social Issues*, 1976, *32* (3), 133–141.

Frueh, T., & McGhee, P. E. Traditional sex role development and amount of time spent watching television. *Developmental Psychology*, 1975, *11*, 109.

Garnets, L., & Pleck, J. H. Sex role identity, androgyny and sex role transcendence: A sex role strain analysis. *Psychology of Women Quarterly*, 1979, *3*, 270–283.

Garrett, C. S., Ein, P. L., & Tremaine, L. The development of gender stereotyping of adult occupations in elementary school children. *Child Development*, 1977, *48*, 507–512.

Gaudreau, P. Factor analysis of the Bem sex-role inventory. *Journal of Consulting and Clinical Psychology*, 1977, *45*, 299–302.

Geise, L. A. The female role in middle class women's magazines from 1955 to 1976: A content analysis of nonfiction selections. *Sex Roles*, 1979, *5*, 51–61.

Geile, J. Z. Changing sex roles and family structure. *Social Policy*, 1979, *9* (4), 32–43.

Gilbert, L. A., Deutsch, C. J., & Strahan, R. F. Feminine and masculine dimensions of the typical, desirable, and ideal woman and man. *Sex Roles*, 1978, *4*, 767–778.

Gold, A. R., & St. Ange, M. C. Development of sex-role stereotypes in black and white elementary school girls. *Developmental Psychology*, 1974, *10*, 461.

Goldberg, P. Are women prejudiced against women? *Trans-action*, 1968, *5* (5), 28–30.

Gordon, F. E., & Strober, M. H. *Bringing women into management.* New York: McGraw-Hill, 1975.

Gould, C. C. Philosophy of liberation and the liberation of philosophy. In C. C. Gould & M. W. Wartofsky (eds.), *Women and philosophy: Toward a theory of liberation.* New York: G. P. Putnam, 1976.

Grusec, J. E., & Brinker, D. B. Reinforcement for imitation as a social learning determinant with implications for sex-role development. *Journal of Personality and Social Psychology,* 1972, *21,* 149–158.

Gurwitz, S. B., & Dodge, K. A. Adults' evaluations of a child as a function of sex of adult and sex of child. *Journal of Personality and Social Psychology,* 1975, *32,* 822–828.

Gutek, B. A., & Stevens, D. A. Effects of sex of subject, sex of stimulus cue, and androgyny level on evaluations in work situations which evoke sex role stereotypes. *Journal of Vocational Behavior,* 1979, *14,* 23–32.

Guttentag, M., & Longfellow, C. Children's social attributions: Development and change. In C. B. Keasey (ed.), *Nebraska symposium on motivation.* Lincoln: University of Nebraska Press, 1977.

Haavio-Manila, E. Sex-role attitudes in Finland, 1966-1970. *Journal of Social Issues,* 1972, *28* (2), 93–110.

Haefner, James E. Race, age, sex, and competence as factors in employer selection of the disadvantaged. *Journal of Applied Psychology,* 1977, *62,* 199–202.

Hall, Francine S., & Hall, Douglas T. Effects of job incumbents' race and sex on evaluations of management performance. *Academy of Management Journal,* 1976, *19,* 476–481.

Hall, J. A., & Halberstadt, A. G. Masculinity and femininity in children: Development of the Children's Personal Attributes Questionnaire, *Developmental Psychology,* 1980, *16,* 270–280.

Hamner, W. C., Kim, J. S., Baird, L., & Bigoness, W. J. Race and sex as determinants of ratings by potential employers in a simulated work-sampling task. *Journal of Applied Psychology,* 1974, *59,* 705–711.

Hartley, R. Children's concepts of male and female roles. *Merrill-Palmer Quarterly,* 1960, *6,* 83, 91.

Hartley, R. E., & Hardesty, F. Children's perceptions of sex-roles in childhood. *Journal of Genetic Psychology,* 1964, *105,* 43–51.

Haugh, S. S., Hoffman, C. D., & Cowan, G. The eye of the very young beholder: Sex-typing of infants by young children. *Child Development,* 1980, *51,* 598–600.

Heilbrun, A. B., Jr. Measurement of masculine and feminine sex role identities as independent dimensions. *Journal of Consulting and Clinical Psychology,* 1976, *44,* 183–190.

Heilman, M. E., & Guzzo, R. A. The perceived cause of work success as a mediator of sex discrimination in organizations. *Organizational Behavior and Human Performance,* 1978, *21,* 346–357.

Helmreich, R., Spence, J., & Holahan, C. Psychological androgyny and sex role flexibility: A test of two hypotheses. *Journal of Personality and Social Psychology,* 1979, *37,* 1631–1644.

Helper, M. M., & Quinlivan, M. J. Age and reinforcement value of sex-role label in girls. *Developmental Psychology,* 1973, *8,* 142–147.

Heneman, H. G., III. Impact of test information and applicant sex on applicant evaluations in a selection simulation. *Journal of Applied Psychology*, 1977, *62*, 524–526.

Hoffman, L. W. Changes in family roles, socialization, and sex differences. *American Psychologist*, 1977, *32*, 644–657.

Horner, M. S. Toward an understanding of achievement related conflicts in women. *Journal of Social Issues*, 1972, *28* (2), 157–175.

Hunady, R. J., & Wahrman, J. Influence of sex-role stereotypes on personnel decisions made by business students. Paper presented at the meetings of the Academy of Management, Kissimmee, Fl., August, 1977.

Hunter, J. Images of woman, *Journal of Social Issues*, 1976, *32* (3), 7–17.

Huston-Stein, A., & Higgins-Trenk, A. The development of females: Career and feminine role aspirations. In P. B. Baltes (ed.), *Life-span development and behavior* (Vol. 1). New York: Academic Press, 1978.

Hyde, J. S., & Rosenberg, B. G. *Half the human experience: The psychology of women*. Lexington, Mass.: D. C. Health, 1976.

Jones, R. A. *Self-fulfilling prophecies: Social, psychological, and physiological effects of expectancies*. Hillsdale, N.J.: Erlbaum, 1977.

Jones, W., Chernovetz, M. E., & Hansson, R. O. The enigma of androgyny: Differential implications for males and females? *Journal of Consulting and Clinical Psychology*, 1978, *46*, 298–313.

Kagan, J. Acquisition and significance of sex typing and sex role identity. In M. L. Hoffman & L. W. Hoffman (eds.), *Review of child development research* (Vol. 2). New York: Russell Sage Foundation, 1964.

Katz, P. A. The development of female identity. *Sex Roles*, 1979, *5*, 155–178.

Kaye, H. E. *Male survival: Masculinity without myth*. New York: Grosset & Dunlap, 1974.

Keller, S. *Male and female: A sociological view*. Morristown, N.J.: General Learning Press, 1975.

Kelly, J. A., & Worell, J. New formulations of sex roles and androgyny: A critical review. *Journal of Consulting and Clinical Psychology*, 1977, *45*, 1101–1115.

Kohlberg, L. A cognitive-developmental analysis of children's sex-role concepts and attitudes. In E. E. Maccoby (ed.), *The development of sex differences*. Stanford, Calif.: Stanford University Press, 1966.

Kohlberg, L., & Ullian, D. Z. Stages in the development of psychosexual concepts and attitudes. In R. C. Friedman, R. M. Richart, & R. L. Vande Wiele (eds.), *Sex differences in behavior*. New York: Wiley, 1974.

Korman, A. K. Toward a hypothesis of work behavior. *Journal of Applied Psychology*, 1970, *54*, 31–41.

Kravetz, D. F. Sex role concepts of women. *Journal of Consulting and Clinical Psychology*, 1976, *44*, 437–443.

Krefting, L. A., Berger, P. K., & Wallace, M. J., Jr. The contribution of sex distribution, job content, and occupational classification to job sex typing: Two studies. *Journal of Vocational Behavior*, 1978, *13*, 181–191.

Kristal, J., Sanders, D., Spence, J. T., & Helmreich, R. Inferences about the femininity of competent women and their implications for likability. *Sex Roles*, 1975, *1*, 33–41.

Lamb, M. E., & Urberg, K. A. The development of gender role and gender identity. In M. E. Lamb (ed.), *Social and personality development*. New York: Holt, Rinehart, & Winston, 1978.

Levitin, T. E., Quinn, R. P., & Staines, G. L. A woman is 58% of a man. *Psychology Today*, 1973, *6* (10), 89–91.

Lewis, M., & Weinraub, M. Origins of early sex-role development. *Sex Roles*, 1979, *5*, 135–154.

Liebert, R. M., McCall, R. B., & Hanratty, M. A. Effects of sex-typed information on children's toy preferences. *Journal of Genetic Psychology*, 1971, *119*, 133–136.

Lockheed, M. E., & Hall, K. P. Conceptualizing sex as a status characteristic: Applications to leadership training strategies. *Journal of Social Issues*, 1976, *32* (3), 111–124.

Locksley, A., & Colten, M. E. Psychological androgyny: A case of mistaken identity? *Journal of Personality and Social Psychology*, 1979, *37*, 1017–1031.

Loeb, R. C., & Horst, L. Sex differences in self and teachers' reports of self-esteem in preadolescents. *Sex Roles*, 1978, *4*, 779–788.

Lubinski, D., Tellegen, A., & Butcher, J. N. The relationship between androgyny and subjective indicators of emotional well-being. *Journal of Personality and Social Psychology*, 1981, *40*, 722–730.

Lyle, J., & Hoffman, H. R. Explorations of patterns of television viewing by preschool-age children. In F. A. Rubenstein, G. A. Cornstock, & J. P. Murray (eds.), *Television and social behavior* (Vol. 4). Washington, D.C.: U.S. Government Printing Office, 1972. Pp. 257–273.

Maccoby, E. E., & Jacklin, C. N. *The psychology of sex differences*. Stanford, Calif.: Stanford University Press, 1974.

Maccoby, E. E., & Wilson, W. C. Identification and observational learning from films. *Journal of Abnormal and Social Psychology*, 1957, *55*, 76–87.

Maccoby, E. E., Wilson, W. C., & Burton, R. V. Differential movie-viewing behavior of male and female viewers. *Journal of Personality*, 1958, *26*, 259–267.

Major, B., Carnevale, P.J.D., & Deaux, K. A different perspective on androgyny: Evaluations of masculine and feminine personality characteristics. *Journal of Personality and Social Psychology*, in press.

Manes, A. L., & Melnyk, P. Televised models of female achievement. *Journal of Applied Social Psychology*, 1974, *4*, 365–374.

Marcus, D. E., & Overton, W. F. The development of cognitive gender constancy and sex role preferences. *Child Development*, 1978, *49*, 434–444.

Mason, K. O., Czajka, J. L., & Arber, S. Change in U.S. women's sex-role attitudes, 1964-1974. *American Sociological Review*, 1976, *41*, 573–596.

Massengill, D., & Di Marco, N. Sex-role stereotypes and requisite management characteristics: A current replication. *Sex Roles*, 1979, *5*, 561–570.

Masters, J. C., & Wilkinson, A. Consensual and discriminative stereotypes of sex-type judgments by parents and children. *Child Development*, 1976, *47*, 208–217.

McArthur, L. Z., & Eisen, S. V. Achievements of male and female storybook characters as determinants of achievement behavior by boys and girls. *Journal of Personality and Social Psychology*, 1976, *33*, 467–473.

McKee, J. P., & Sherriffs, A. C. The differential evaluation of males and females. *Journal of Personality*, 1957, *25*, 356–371.

Meyer, J. W., & Sobieszek, B. I. Effect of a child's sex on adult interpretations of its behavior. *Developmental Psychology*, 1972, *6*, 42–48.

Miles, C. Sex in social psychology. In C. Murchinson (ed.), *Handbook of Social*

Psychology. Worcester, Mass.: Clark University Press, 1935. Pp. 699–704.

Miller, M. M., & Reeves, B. B. Children's occupational sex-role stereotypes: The linkage between television content and perception. *Journal of Broadcasting*, 1976, *20*, 35–50.

Mills, K. Fighting sexism on the air waves. *Journal of Communication*, 1974, *24*, 150–156.

Mischel, H. Sex bias in the evaluation of professional achievements. *Journal of Educational Psychology*, 1974, *66*, 157–166.

Mischel, W. A social learning view of sex differences in behavior. In E. E. Maccoby (ed.), *The development of sex differences*. Stanford, Calif.: Stanford University Press, 1966.

Mischel, W. Sex-typing and socialization. In P. H. Mussen (ed.), *Carmichael's manual of child psychology*. New York: Wiley, 1970.

Money, J., Hampson, J. G., & Hampson, J. L. Imprinting and the establishment of gender role. *Archives of Neurology and Psychiatry*, 1957, *77*, 333–336.

Montemayor, R. Children's performance in a game and their attraction to it as a function of sex-typed labels. *Child Development*, 1974, *45*, 152–156.

Morgan, Robin. *Sisterhood is powerful: An anthology of writings from the women's liberation movement*. New York: Vintage Books, 1970.

Muchinsky, P. M., & Harris, S. L. The effect of applicant sex and scholastic standing on the evaluation of job applicant resumes in sex-typed occupations. *Journal of Vocational Behavior*, 1977, *11*, 95–108.

Mussen, P. H. Early sex-role development. In D. A. Goslin (ed.), *Handbook of socialization theory and research*. Chicago: Rand McNally, 1969.

Nadelman, L. Sex identity in London children: Memory, knowledge, and preference tests. *Human Development*, 1970, *13*, 28–42.

Nadelman, L. Sex identity in American children: Memory, knowledge, and preference tests. *Developmental Psychology*, 1974, *10*, 413–417.

Neufeld, E., Langmeyer, D., & Seeman, W. Some sex-role stereotypes and personal preferences, 1950 and 1970. *Journal of Personality Assessment*, 1974, *38*, 247–254.

Newland, K. *The sisterhood of man*. New York: Norton, 1979.

Newman, B. M., & Newman, P. R. *An introduction to the psychology of adolescence*. Homewood, Ill.: Dorsey, 1979.

O'Bryant, S. L., & Corder-Bolz, C. R. The effects of television on children's stereotyping of women's work roles. *Journal of Vocational Behavior*, 1978, *12*, 233–244.

Orlofsky, J. L. Sex-role orientation, identity formation, and self-esteem in college men and women. *Sex Roles*, 1977, *6*, 561–575.

Orlofsky, J. L., Aslin, A. L., & Ginsberg, S. D. Differential effectiveness of two classification procedures on the Bem Sex Role Inventory. *Journal of Personality Assessment*, 1977, *41*, 414–416.

Orlofsky, J. L., & Windle, M. T. Sex-role orientation, behavioral adaptability, and personal adjustment. *Sex Roles*, 1978, *4*, 801–811.

Osgood, C. E., Suci, J. G., & Tannenbaum, P. H. *The measurement of meaning*. Urbana: University of Illinois Press, 1957.

Papalia, D. E., & Tennent, S. S. Vocational aspirations in preschoolers: A manifestation of early sex role stereotyping. *Sex Roles*, 1975, *1*, 197–199.

Parish, T. S., & Bryant, W. T. Mapping sex group stereotypes of elementary and high school students. *Sex Roles*, 1978, *4*, 135–140.

Parlee, M. B. Conversational politics. *Psychology Today*, 1979, *12* (12), 48–56.

Parsons, J. E., Frieze, I. H., & Ruble, D. N. Intrapsychic factors influencing career aspirations in college women. *Sex Roles*, 1978, *4*, 337–348.

Parsons, J. E., & Ruble, D. N. The development of achievement related expectancies. *Child Development*, 1977, *48*, 1075–1079.

Parsons, J. E., Ruble, D. N., Hodges, K. L., & Small, A. W. Cognitive-developmental factors in emerging sex differences in achievement-related expectancies. *Journal of Social Issues*, 1976, *32*, 47–62.

Pedhazur, E. J., & Tetenbaum, T. J. Bem Sex Role Inventory: A theoretical and methodological critique. *Journal of Personality and Social Psychology*, 1979, *37*, 996–1016.

Perloff, R. M., Brown, J. D., & Miller, M. M. Mass media and sex-typing: Research perspectives and policy implications. Paper presented at American Psychological Association annual convention, Toronto, August, 1978.

Perry, D. G., & Bussey, K. The social learning theory of sex differences: Imitation is alive and well. *Journal of Personality and Social Psychology*, 1979, *37*, 1699–1712.

Petro, C. S., & Putnam, B. A. Sex-role stereotypes: Issues of attitudinal changes. *Sex Roles*, 1979, *5*, 29–39.

Pheterson, G. I., Kiesler, S. B., & Goldberg, P. A. Evaluation of the performance of women as a function of their sex, achievement, and personal history. *Journal of Personality and Social Psychology*, 1971, *19*, 114–118.

Pingree, S. The effects of non sexist television commercials and perceptions of reality on children's attitudes about women. *Psychology of Women Quarterly*, 1978, *2*, 262–277.

Pleck, J. H. Masculinity-femininity: Current and alternative paradigms. *Sex Roles*, 1975, *1*, 161–178.

Pleck, J. H. The male sex role: Definitions, problems, and sources of change. *Journal of Social Issues*, 1976, *32* (3), 155–164.

Pleck, J. H., & Brannon, R. (eds.). Male roles and the male experience. *Journal of Social Issues*, 1978, *34* (1).

Powell, G. N., & Butterfield, D. A. The "good manager": Masculine or androgynous? *Academy of Management Journal*, 1979, *22*, 395–403.

Putnam, L., & Heinen, J. S. Women in management: The fallacy of the trait approach. *MSU Business Topics*, 1976, Summer, 47–53.

Quattrone, G. A., & Jones, E. E. The perception of variability within ingroups and outgroups: Implications for the law of small numbers. *Journal of Personality and Social Psychology*, 1980, *38*, 141–152.

Rabban, M. Sex-role identification in young children in two diverse social groups. *Genetic Psychology Monographs*, 1950, *42*, 81–158.

Rebecca, M., Hefner, R., & Oleshansky, B. A model of sex-role transcendence. *Journal of Social Issues*, 1976, *32* (3), 197–206.

Renwick, P. A., & Tosi, H. The effects of sex, marital status, and educational background on selection decisions. *Academy of Management Journal*, 1978, *21*, 93–103.

Rheingold, H. L., & Cook, K. U. The content of boys' and girls' rooms as an index of parents' behavior. *Child Development*, 1975, *46*, 459–463.

Rose, G. L., Sex effects on effort attributions in managerial performance evaluation. *Organizational Behavior and Human Performance*, 1978, *21*, 367–378.

Rose, G. L., & Andiappan, P. Sex effects on managerial hiring decisions. *Academy of Management Journal*, 1978, *21*, 104–112.

Rose, G. L., & Stone, T. H. Why good job performance may (not) be rewarded: Sex factors and career development. *Journal of Vocational Behavior*, 1978, *12*, 197–207.

Rosen, Benson, & Jerdee, Thomas H. Effects of applicants' sex and difficulty of job on evaluations of candidates for managerial positions. *Journal of Applied Psychology*, 1974, *59*, 511–512. (a)

Rosen, Benson, & Jerdee, Thomas. Influence of sex role stereotypes on personnel decisions. *Journal of Applied Psychology*, 1974, *59*, 9–14. (b)

Rosenkrantz, P., Vogel, S., Bee, H., Broverman, I., & Broverman, D. M. Sex-role stereotypes and self-concepts in college students. *Journal of Consulting and Clinical Psychology*, 1968, *32*, 287–295.

Rubin, J. Z., Provenzano, F. J., & Luria, Z. The eye of the beholder: Parents' views on sex of newborns. *American Journal of Orthopsychiatry*, 1974, *44*, 512–519.

Ruble, D. N., Balaban, T., & Cooper, J. Gender constancy and the effects of sex-typed televised toy commercials. *Child Development*, 1981, *52*.

Ruble, D. N., & Brooks-Gunn, J. Menstrual symptoms: A social cognition analysis. *Journal of Behavioral Medicine*, 1979, *2*, 171–194.

Ruble, D. N., Croke, J. A., Frieze, I., & Parsons, J. E. A field study of sex-role attitude change in college women. *Journal of Applied Social Psychology*, 1975, *5*, 110–117.

Ruble, D. N., Frieze, I. H., & Parsons, J. E. (eds). Sex roles: Persistence and change. *Journal of Social Issues*, 1976, *32* (3).

Ruble, D. N., & Higgins, E. T. Effects of group sex composition on self-presentation and sex-typing. *Journal of Social Issues*, 1976, *32* (3), 125–132.

Ruble, T. L. Sex-role stereotypes and management potential: An exercise. *Journal of Experiential Learning and Simulation*, 1979, *1*, 283–292.

Ruble, T. L. Sex stereotypes: Issues of change in the 1970's. *Sex Roles*. In press.

Schein, V. E. The relationship between sex role stereotypes and requisite management characteristics. *Journal of Applied Psychology*, 1973, *57*, 95–100.

Schein, V. E. Relationships between sex role stereotypes and requisite management characteristics among female managers. *Journal of Applied Psychology*, 1975, *60*, 340–344.

Schlesinger, Y. Sex roles and social change in the family. *Journal of Marriage and the Family*, 1977, *39*, 771–780.

Seavey, C. A., Katz, P. A., & Zlak, S. R. Baby X: The effect of gender labels on adults' responses to infants. *Sex Roles*, 1975, *1*, 103–109.

Shaw, E. A. Differential impact of negative stereotyping in employee selection. *Personnel Psychology*, 1972, *25*, 333–338.

Sherman, J. A. Social values, femininity, and the development of female competence. *Journal of Social Issues*, 1976, *32* (3), 181–196.

Shields, S. A. Functionalism, Darwinism and the psychology of women: A study in social myth. *American Psychologist*, 1975, *30*, 739–754.

Shinar, E. H. Sexual stereotypes of occupations. *Journal of Vocational Behavior*, 1975, *7*, 99–111.

Shinar, E. H. Person perception as a function of occupation and sex. *Sex Roles*,

1978, *4*, 679–693.

Slaby, R. G., & Frey, K. S. Development of gender constancy and selective attention to same-sex models. *Child Development*, 1975, *46*, 849–856.

Smith, C., & Lloyd, B. Maternal behavior and perceived sex of infant: Revisited. *Child Development*, 1978, *49*, 1263–1265.

Smith, S. Age and sex differences in children's opinions concerning sex differences. *Journal of Genetic Psychology*, 1939, *54*, 17–25.

Spence, J. T., & Helmreich, R. L. *Masculinity and femininity*. Austin: University of Texas Press, 1978.

Spence, J. T., & Helmreich, R. L. The many faces of androgyny: A reply to Locksley and Colten. *Journal of Personality and Social Psychology*, 1979, *37*, 1032–1046.

Spence, J. T., Helmreich, R., & Stapp, J. The personal attributes questionnaire: A measure of sex-role stereotypes and masculinity-femininity. *JSAS Catalog of Selected Documents in Psychology*, 1974, *4*, 43. (MS no. 617)

Spence, J. T., Helmreich, R., & Stapp, J. Ratings of self and peers on sex role attributes and their relation to self-esteem and conceptions of masculinity and femininity. *Journal of Personality and Social Psychology*, 1975, *32*, 29–39.

Stein, A. H., & Bailey, M. M. The socialization of achievement orientation in females. *Psychological Bulletin*, 1973, *80*, 345–366.

Stein, A. H., & Friedrich, C. K. The impact of television on children and youth. In E. M. Hetherington (ed.), *Review of Child Development Research*. Chicago: University of Chicago Press, 1975.

Stein, A. H., & Smithells, J. Age and sex differences in children's sex role standards about achievement. *Developmental Psychology*, 1969, *1*, 252–259.

Sternglanz, S. H., & Serbin, L. A. Sex role stereotyping in children's television programs. *Developmental Psychology*, 1974, *10*, 710–715.

Stockard, J., & Johnson, M. M. The social origins of male dominance. *Sex Roles*, 1979, *5*, 199–218.

Strahan, R. F. Remarks on Bem's measurement of psychological androgyny: Alternative methods and a supplementary analysis. *Journal of Consulting and Clinical Psychology*, 1975, *43*, 568–571.

Streicher, H. W. The girls in the cartoons. *Journal of Communication*, 1974, *24*, 125–130.

Tavris, C. Who likes women's liberation and why: The case of the unliberated liberals. *Journal of Social Issues*, 1973, *29* (4), 175–194.

Tavris, C. Men and women report their views on masculinity. *Psychology Today*, January, 1977, pp. 34–38, 42, 82.

Tavris, C., & Offir, C. *The longest war*. New York: Harcourt, Brace, Jovanovich, 1977.

Taynor, J., & Deaux, K. When women are more deserving than men. *Journal of Personality and Social Psychology*, 1973, *28*, 360–367.

Taynor, J., & Deaux, K. Equity and perceived sex differences: Role behavior as defined by the task, the mode, and the actor. *Journal of Personality and Social Psychology*, 1975, *32*, 381–390.

Terborg, James R. Women in management: A research review. *Journal of Applied Psychology*, 1977, *62*, 647–664.

Terborg, J. R., & Ilgen, D. R. A theoretical approach to sex discrimination in traditionally masculine occupations. *Organizational Behavior and Human Performance*, 1975, *13*, 352–376.

Thompson, S. K. Gender labels and early sex role development. *Child Development*, 1975, *46*, 339–347.

Thompson, S. K., & Bentler, P. M. The priority of cues in sex discrimination by children and adults. *Developmental Psychology*, 1971, *5*, 181–185.

Tuchman, G. Women's depictions by the mass media. *Signs*, 1979, *4*, 528–542.

Tuddenham, R. D. Studies in reputation III: Correlates of popularity among elementary school children. *Journal of Educational Psychology*, 1951, *42*, 257–276.

Ullian, D. Z. The development of conceptions of masculinity and femininity. In B. Lloyd & J. Archer (eds.), *Exploring sex differences*. London: Academic Press, 1976.

Urberg, K. A. Sex role conceptualization in adolescents and adults. *Developmental Psychology*, 1979, *15*, 90–92. (a)

Urberg, K. A. The development of androgynous sex-role concepts in young children. Paper presented at the Society for Research in Child Development meetings, San Francisco, March 1979. (b)

Urberg, K. A., & Labouvie-Vief, G. Conceptualization of sex-roles: A life-span developmental study. *Developmental Psychology*, 1976, *12*, 15–23.

Van Dusen, R. A., & Sheldon, E. B. The changing status of American women: A life cycle perspective. *American Psychologist*, 1976, *31*, 106–116.

Van Maanen, J., & Schein, E. H. Career Development. In J. R. Hackman & J. L. Suttle (eds.), *Improving life at work*. Santa Monica, Calif.: Goodyear, 1977.

Vener, A., & Snyder, C. A. The preschool child's awareness and anticipation of adult sex-roles. *Sociometry*, 1966, *29*, 159–168.

Ward, W. D. Process of sex-role development. *Developmental Psychology*, 1969, *1*, 163–168.

Weitzman, L. J., Eifler, D., Hokada, E., & Ross, C. Sex-role socialization in picture books for preschool children. *American Journal of Sociology*, 1972, *27*, 1125–1150.

Wertheim, E. G., Widom, C. S., & Wortzel, L. H. Multivariate analysis of male and female professional career choice correlates. *Journal of Applied Psychology*, 1978, *63*, 234–242.

Wesley, F., & Wesley, C. *Sex role psychology*, New York: Human Sciences Press, 1977.

Whetton, C., & Swindells, T. A factor analysis of the Bem Sex-Role Inventory. *Journal of Clinical Psychology*, 1977, *33*, 150–153.

Whitbeck, C. Theories of sex differences. In C. C. Gould and M. W. Wartofsky (eds.), *Women and philosophy: Toward a theory of liberation*. New York: G. P. Putnam, 1976.

White, D. G. Effects of sex-typed labels and their source on the imitative performance of young children. *Child Development*, 1978, *49*, 1266–1269.

Will, J. A., Self, P. A., & Datan, N. Maternal behavior and perceived sex of infant. *American Journal of Orthopsychiatry*, 1976, *46*, 135–139.

Williams, J. E., Bennett, S., & Best, D. Awareness and expression of sex stereotypes in young children. *Developmental Psychology*, 1975, *11*, 635–642.

Williams, J. H. *Psychology of women. Behavior in a biosocial context*. New York: Norton, 1977.

Wolf, T. M. Effects of live modeled sex-inappropriate play behavior in a naturalistic setting. *Developmental Psychology*, 1973, *9*, 120–123.

Wolf, T. M. Influence of age and sex of model on sex-inappropriate play. *Psychological Reports*, 1975, *36*, 99–105.

Wolff, L., & Taylor, S. E. Sex, sex-role identification and awareness of sex-role stereotypes. *Journal of Personality*, 1979, *47*, 177–184.

Wood, J. P. *Magazines in the United States*. New York: Ronald Press, 1971.

Yanico, B. J., Hardin, S. I., & McLaughlin, K. B. Androgyny and traditional versus nontraditional major choice among college freshmen. *Journal of Vocational Behavior*, 1978, *12*, 261–269.

Yorburg, B. *Sexual identity, sex roles and social change*. New York: Wiley, 1974.

Zanna, M. P., & Pack, S. J. On the self-fulfilling nature of apparent sex differences in behavior. *Journal of Experimental Social Psychology*, 1975, *11*, 583–591.

Zellman, G. L. The role of structural factors in limiting women's institutional participation. *Journal of Social Issues*, 1976, *32* (3), 33–46.

Zikmund, W. G., Hitt, M. A., & Pickens, B. A. Influence of sex and scholastic performance on reactions to job applicant resumes. *Journal of Applied Psychology*, 1978, *63*, 252–254.

ADDITIONAL READINGS

Brooks-Gunn, J., & Matthews, W. S. *He and she: How children develop their sex-role identity*. Englewood Cliffs, N.J.: Prentice-Hall, 1979.

Through an examination of relevant research, the authors investigate how children acquire sex-typed behavior. The book is aimed at undergraduates and parents. The developing child is the focus as the authors discuss evidence for sex differences and consider how children acquire sex-typed behavior (from the socializing influence of family, school, and the media to the child's changing awareness of sex roles). Theories of sex-role acquisition—identification, social learning, and cognitive-developmental—are compared. The book is readable, with enjoyable anecdotes complementing empirical results.

Frieze, I. H., Parsons, J. E., Johnson, P. B., Ruble, D. N., & Zellman, G. L. *Women and sex roles: A social psychological perspective*. New York: W. W. Norton, 1978.

The authors pose several questions that they attempt to answer throughout the book: What are the effects of sexism upon women and men, and how are their options limited by it? Can biology explain any sex differences that exist, or are cultural beliefs and expectations a better explanation? Are traditional sex roles changing—and if not, what factors maintain them?

The book, suitable as a college text, covers material ranging from theories of feminine personality, origins of sex differences, and theories of sex-role acquisition, to women's roles and adult development, their psychological disorders, prejudice and discrimination against them, their power and use of it and their lives today. It is readable, and includes an extensive bibliography.

Pleck, J. H., & Brannon, R. (eds.). Male roles and the male experience. *Journal of Social Issues*, 1978, *34* (1).

This issue furnishes a necessary perspective upon growing up male—the demands and expectations of the male sex role. Articles address the issues from several different perspectives describing the male role and results of deviation from it; biological correlations between the male role and mortality and physique; male roles and behaviors in specific contexts (with women, as parents, in the military and sports); the black male sex role and the changed perceptions of it historically.

Ruble, D. N., Frieze, I. H., & Parsons, J. E. (eds.). Sex roles: Persistence and change. *Journal of Social Issues*, 1976, *33* (3).

The journal issue examines societal and psychological factors that interact to contribute to the persistence of traditional sex roles in spite of all that has been said by the women's movement. These factors range from specific institutional shortcomings, such as inadequate or nonexistent child care, to societal beliefs that value maternity (and not competence) for women—all of which affect individual role behavior. The need and possibility for changes in traditional sex roles are considered. Articles cover topics such as images of woman, the motherhood mandate, sex differences in achievement-related expectancies, the dilemmas that dual roles pose for women, effects upon behavior of the sex composition of a group, the development of female competence, nonverbal behavior and traditional sex roles, male sex roles, and stability and change in sex-role norms and behavior.

Spence, J. T., & Helmreich, R. L. *Masculinity & femininity. Their psychological dimensions, correlates & antecedents*. Austin: University of Texas Press, 1978.

Using the Personal Attributes Questionnaire (PAQ), Spence and Helmreich found that masculinity and femininity are not bipolar, but independent, dimensions. They collected data from a wide socioeconomic and geographic base with both college and adolescent populations, and explored correlates of masculinity and femininity, such as achievement motivation and parental behaviors and attributes.

Chapters describe the measuring instruments and sample populations, as well as the interrelationships among personal attributes, self-esteem, and attitudes toward women. Other chapters examine achievement motivation and achievement factors and their correlates. Parental variables—their femininity and masculinity, behavior and attitudes, and child-rearing practices—are examined. The extensive appendix contains the measuring instruments, demographic characteristics of samples, and several subsidiary analyses of relationships with achievement scales, parental attributes, and parental behavior.

Tavris, C., & Offir, C. *The longest war*. New York: Harcourt, Brace, Jovanovich, 1977.

Geared as a text for undergraduates, the book tries to answer the questions of why male supremacy, rather than equality of status between the sexes, has been the case historically and cross-culturally, and why sex differences rather than similarities have been stressed. It uses an interdisciplinary approach to consider the nature of sex differences and their origins—biological or learned—from psychological, sociological, and cross-cultural viewpoints. The authors conclude by seeking examples of equality between the sexes in belief and in practice in China, Sweden, the Soviet Union, and Israel, but find equality more a myth, in spite of each society's prevailing ideology.

6

PHYSICAL ATTRACTIVENESS

Gerald R. Adams

It may be true that beauty is only skin deep, but the fact remains that the world judges you on appearance a great deal of the time.

(Korda, 1977, p. 133)

While many of us can escape being stereotyped on the basis of membership in a specific religious, minority, or poverty group, it is less likely that individuals who are extreme in their appearance will escape stereotyping associated with physical appearance. For the most part, we are trapped inside our bodies. While certain cosmetic or surgical modifications can be undertaken to change body image, it is difficult to create major transformations of facial structure or body type, or to correct disfigurement associated with a major disability. Therefore, for many, regardless of social role or group membership, there is a strong probability that at some point in their lives, social interactions will be strongly influenced by physical attractiveness or appearance.

Physical attractiveness stereotypes appear in various forms. For example, shortness in children and adults is commonly seen as an indication of weak competitive drive and delayed social maturity (Stabler, Whitt, Moreault, D'Ercole, & Underwood, undated). Obesity is viewed as being associated with lack of self-control (Rodin, 1977). Tallness, for males, is thought to be associated with strength and success (G. Wilson & Nias, 1976). There is a norm which dictates that in romantically involved couples, the male should be taller than the female (Gillis & Avis, 1980). Evidence also suggests that girls are willing to undergo controversial biochemical treatments to reduce their height for purely "psychosocial" reasons (Wettenhall, Cahill, & Roche, 1975). Blondes are expected to have more fun, while redheads are expected to act like Bozos (Clayson & Maugham, 1976). Such stereotypes seem to emerge even in the absence of immediate confirming evidence. Indeed, their presence is hard to understand. It would appear that physical attractiveness may lead to stereotyping because of the ease in visually identifying extremes in bodily or facial attractiveness. Indeed, there is a common-sense notion that real beauty may be as unusual as real ugliness. Once observed, neither of those two states of appearance is likely to be confused with average looks.

HISTORICAL ROOTS

The origins of physical attractiveness stereotypes are unknown. Most of us are aware of the physical allure of Eve, reported in Genesis. Others recall the magnificent beauty of Helen of Troy, or the power of Delilah in captivating Samson. History abounds with the recognition of the impact of beauty. To paraphrase Edgar Allan Poe, if God were to send a messenger, surely it would be a woman of beauty, loftiness, and purity. But what factors account for this continuing interest in physical beauty?

Research on the philosophical study of aesthetics suggests that we are inclined to treat each other as aesthetic objects. That is, through visual examination of each other, we come to recognize what is visually pleasant and what is not. Experimental evidence suggests that as early as four months of age, infants can express their appreciation or displeasure for visually pleasing or displeasing human forms (Kagan, Henker, Hen-Tov, Levine, & Lewis, 1966). These investigators presented faces that were in either a normal-appearing figuration or a distorted, grotesque one. Infants who viewed the normal face were content to stare at it; infants who viewed the distorted face responded with apprehension, anxiety, fear, and crying. Thus, humans may be born with a genetically determined mechanism that influences judgments about the quality of perceptual sets.

It appears that in both childhood and adulthood there is a ready expression of aesthetic preferences (Valentine, 1962). Given that evidence suggests a common developmental sequence in the maturity of aesthetic judgment, it is possible that the origin of an attractiveness stereotype lies in a biogenetic determinacy. That is, we may all be born with a genetically determined cognitive structure to make aesthetic judgments, and with increasing experience we develop more mature cognitive processes that allow us to expand our emotional expression of aesthetic preference. Hence, judgments about body types and characteristics may reflect the individual expression of a biogenetic foundation of aesthetic judgment. However, the form in which aesthetic preference manifests itself is highly influenced by cultural standards unique to each society. For example, in several African tribes body tattooing is thought to enhance physical appearance, while industrial nations are inclined to view it as body disfigurement. Indeed, modern medicine is exploring ways to remove a tattoo with laser equipment (Van Leer, 1980).

In Western society the "medium is the massage" (McLuhan, 1964).

Magazine advertisements and television commercials carry stron
sonal communications about appropriate standards of beauty. It
that anyone can escape the influences of these media messages a
from internalizing some of the media-based assumptions about ~~y..~al
appearance in his or her aesthetic preference behavior. Whimsically, a
colleague and I (Adams & Crossman, 1978) wrote a summary of how
television commercials portray their image of beauty:

> Masculinity is judged by overall appearance and impression. The
> commercials on television will suggest the main attributes a man needs
> to be considered attractive and desirable. "The dry look" is important.
> "Reaching for the gusto" is absolutely essential. Using Right Guard and
> smelling of Brut, English Leather, Old Spice, Musk or one of a half
> dozen other men's colognes are also necessary. And depending upon the
> "type," he will drive a certain make and model of car, smoke a certain
> brand of tobacco, and above all, read *Playboy* magazine. He doesn't
> have to have a face like Paul Newman or Robert Redford, or a physique
> like Adonis, though it won't hurt if he does. Primarily, he must be trim,
> rugged but not too rugged, manly, and have a nice smile. Femininity, on
> the other hand, is characterized by perfection in every detail. Unlike
> masculinity, femininity cannot be acquired merely by using the right
> deodorant and applying a number of external props. A woman must
> have hair with body and fullness that is marvelously highlighted. Each
> feature must be an equal contributor to her pretty face. She must have
> eternally young and blemish-free skin. Her figure must not only be trim,
> but meet certain "idealized" standards to be considered beautiful. Her
> hands must be silky soft and not too large. Her nails must be long and
> perfectly trimmed. Her legs must be shapely, firm, and preferably long.
> To attain all this, she must "enter the garden of earthly delights" and use
> "Herbal Essence Shampoo"—hair conditioners scented with lemon,
> strawberry or apricot, which give marvelous body, . . . and rinse or dye,
> which will make her the "girl with the hair." Her skin must be nurtured
> with moisturizers and emollients so she can look eternally young. Her
> figure should surpass that of a Greek goddess by being amply bosomed
> and slim waisted, but rounded in the hips. As for her legs, "gentlemen
> prefer Hanes." For finishing touches, she should use "sex appeal
> toothpaste" and put her "money where her mouth is." She should know
> that "Blondes have more fun" and Lady Clairol blondes have the most
> fun of all. For a foundation, she should wear the "cross your heart bra"
> and never be without her "18-hour girdle." Finally, above all else, her
> beauty must look natural. (pp. 21–22; reprinted by permission of Libra
> Publishing)

As the quotation implies, there are economic aspects to the attractiveness stereotype. That is, advertisements, whether viewed as causing attractiveness stereotypes or reflecting them, seem to exploit beauty for profit.
Indeed, there is a growing body of marketing research directed at the study

of physical attractiveness on promotional effectiveness of advertisement campaigns. For example, Smith and Engel (1968) examined the effects of the degree of attractiveness of a female model on males' perceptions of automobiles. While post-experimental interviews revealed that male subjects denied any influence of the female model on their perceptions and preferences, experimental data indicated that an attractive female model increased perceptions of automobile appeal (its youthful and lively appearance), and improved perceptions of design. Further, the attractiveness of the model increased perceptions associated with price, power and speed, and limited safety.

Another investigation, by Baker and Churchill (1977), suggests that attractive female models may increase perceptions of appeal and attractiveness while enhancing attentiveness to an advertised product, but it remains unclear whether beauty actually increases purchases of advertised products. Indeed, there was some evidence in this investigation to suggest that for nonromantic products (such as coffee), an unattractive woman may be more effective in influencing males' purchasing behavior. However, for romance-related products (such as perfume or cologne) there was a tendency for men to be swayed in their purchasing interests by an attractive female model.

Perhaps the advertising agencies also capitalize on yet another important dimension of physical appearance. It is not only important in our culture to be beautiful but, at least for females, it is equally important to be young or youthful appearing (Sontag, 1972). Most advertising campaigns readily illustrate the connection between youth and beauty. The "youth" culture, in which vigor and youthfulness are perceived in conjunction with idealized appearance, portrays for many the truly prized period of life. The Oil of Olay advertisement and commercial series illustrate the connection between youth and beauty; the emphasis is placed not only upon having beautiful skin, but also upon displaying "young-looking skin." While it is true that wrinkles may be hard to glorify aesthetically, it is equally true that beauty (and ugliness) can be observed at many ages in the life cycle. Nonetheless, there is an obvious attempt at economic exploitation of purchasing power associated with beauty and youthfulness.

Susan Sontag, in a popular article on the subject, summarized the problems associated with the "beauty syndrome" quite succinctly:

> The privileges of beauty are immense. . . . To be sure, beauty is a form of power. And deservedly so. What is lamentable is that it is the only form of power that most women are encouraged to seek. This power is always conceived in relation to men; it is not the power to do but the power to attract. For this power is not one that can be chosen freely—at least, not by women—or renounced without social censure. (1975, p. 119)

Thus, verbal and nonverbal messages abound. These messages indicate that beauty is good and ugliness is bad.

In summary, the historical origins of the physical attractiveness stereotype are unclear. The tendency to make aesthetic judgments about the human body, however, is pervasive. Whether this is biogenetically determined may be questionable, but media influences clearly reinforce physical appearance stereotypes. If consistent and repeated social experiences have effects upon individual perceptions, it is logical to assume that the "media message" has a pervasive effect on the manner in which the physical attractiveness stereotype emerges in everyday social interaction.

EARLY THEORETICAL PERSPECTIVES

It can be argued that the theoretical origin of the physical attractiveness stereotype has its foundation in "constitutional psychology." Early constitutionalists assumed that body characteristics such as physical build or facial features were associated with specific hereditary factors. Using elements of this perspective, three early scientists stand out in historical accounts of the early efforts directed toward the study of physical appearance: Lombroso (1891), Kretschmer (1925), and Sheldon (1940).

Lombroso, in the late 1800s, attempted to identify certain body types that were thought to be associated with specific criminal behaviors. However, because of his pre-experimental and subjective form of methodology, these early efforts have not been accepted by any scientific community. It was not until Ernst Kretschmer's publication of *Physique and Character* that any wide recognition was given to the study of physical appearance. Of particular historical importance was the identification of three basic body types that were thought to relate to personality and social behavior. Kretschmer focused on the pyknic, or fat, person; the athletic, or muscular, person; and the asthenic, or skinny, person.

William Sheldon, in *The Varieties of Human Physique* (1940), identified three parallel body types, but gave them different names. Many readers may be familiar with Sheldon's labels for fat (endomorph), muscular (mesomorph), and thin (ectomorph) persons. In their research both Kretschmer and Sheldon attempted to identify personality profiles that were constitutionally associated with the three different body types. They both assumed that the fat person would be jolly, fun-loving, and inclined toward depressive psychosis. The thin person, on the other extreme of body mass, was expected to be shy, withdrawn, and somewhat disorganized (referred to as acute schizophrenia today). The muscular person was expected to display active, aggressive behavior, with tendencies toward paranoia.

Although constitutional psychology has never been well received in social science, it did set the stage for more recent research approaches. Erving Goffman, in his influential text *Stigma: Notes on the Management of Spoiled Identity* (1963), has argued for a social rather than a constitutional perspective to the study of body characteristics. He maintains that the relationship between body attributes and individual character is mediated through a social interactional process. According to Goffman, when an individual has unique characteristics that are different from the average, this uniqueness promotes undesirable social impressions and the individual is discredited or assumed to have a spoiled identity. Thus, certain types of uniqueness are viewed as stigmata that trigger a social process that confirms the attributions surrounding the stigmata. For example, if we view a beggar as unique, and assume this indeed must be a wretched human being, our stigmatization of this individual may well help him or her to confirm his or her spoiled identity by acting in wretched ways. This person was not born to be a wretched beggar, but social circumstances place him or her in a unique status—a status that is viewed in undesirable ways. We communicate to the beggar, through subtle means, how he or she *ought* to behave.

In referring to stigmata associated with physical appearance, which Goffman has labeled "abominations of the body," visibility plays an extremely crucial role in the social interaction process. The more obtrusive the body stigma, the more it intrudes into the social interaction process. This body stigma turns attention from the words and actions of the person to the stigma—which, through certain attributions, expectations, and anticipations, may call for social confirmation. Hence, the more obtrusive the physical stigma, the less likely it is that others will attend to an individual's positive social features, and the higher the probability that individual attention will be directed toward social interaction that confirms the attributions associated with physical stigmatization.

EARLY SEMINAL EFFORTS

Prior to the publication of Goffman's book, there was recognition of the stigma associated with physical disability or disfigurement. Early person-perception research had noted the potential consequences of physical disability for the social relations of the handicapped. It was generally accepted that a person's physical characteristics might have biasing influences upon others' reactions, but empirical support for such a statement was not widely documented. An investigation by Stephen Richardson and his associates (Richardson, Goodman, Hastorf, & Dornbusch, 1961) had an influential effect upon later research addressing the effects of physical disability upon perceived interpersonal attraction. In their investigation, children in public schools or summer camps in the states of New York, Montana, and California were shown a standard set of drawings of children who differed in their physical characteristics and appearance. It was hypothesized that when asked which stimulus child was liked best, there would be a culturally uniform order of preference for the physical characteristics associated with the various children. It was hypothesized that the nonhandicapped child would be liked most, followed in preferential order by the child with crutches and a brace, a child in a wheelchair, a child with a hand missing, a facially disfigured child, and an obese child. The hypothesis was supported in six samples from three geographic regions. These data support a cultural uniformity among children in their deprecatory evaluation of persons with physical disabilities. Furthermore, as the authors conclude, "The data indicate that increased liking is shown for the child whose disability is more distant from his face" (p. 246). Both disfigured *and* obese children were the least preferred. Thus, facial features and body attributes (paralleling an endomorphic body form) are given even lower preferences than what are typically thought of as physical handicaps. These data clearly indicated that facial attractiveness and body morphology are likely to be potent factors in interpersonal attraction.

Two important investigations by Walker (1962; 1963) concerned the relationship between body build and social behavior in young children. Their impact was best shown in an influential study by Robert Staffieri (1967). Recognizing the work of Walker, Staffieri examined children's expectations of the association between body image and behavioral attributions. Given silhouettes exemplifying extreme endomorphic, mesomorphic, and ectomorphic body types, elementary school children were asked to assign various behavioral or personality traits to each of the stimuli. A summary of the traits assigned to a given body type is found in Table 6.1. A clear body-image stereotype was associated with each silhouette. All traits or

TABLE 6.1

Summary of Traits Differentially Assigned to Endomorphic, Mesomorphic, and Ectomorphic Body Silhouettes by School-Age Children

Endomorph	Mesomorph	Ectomorph
Cheats	Strong	Quiet
Nervous	Best friend	Seldom fights
Argues	Clean	Worries
Gets teased	Lots of friends	Lonely
Forgets	Happy	Sneaky
Lazy	Helps others	Afraid
Lies	Polite	Sad
Sloppy	Seldom sick	Weak
Naughty	Healthy	
Mean	Honest	
Ugly	Brave	
Dirty	Good-looking	
Stupid	Smart	
	Seldom tired	
	Neat	

Source: Staffieri (1967), Table 1, p. 102. Copyright 1967 by the American Psychological Association. Reprinted by permission.

behaviors associated with the mesomorphic body were favorable, while attributions associated with the endomorphic body type were unfavorable, suggesting a perceived image of social aggressiveness. Most of the traits or behaviors associated with the ectomorph were unfavorable, with a general image of social submission or passivity.

The early work of Richardson et al. suggested that nonhandicapped children were preferred to handicapped or obese youth, and social attribution research by Staffieri indicated that fat (endomorphic) and thin (ectomorphic) body types generate unfavorable social impressions. Although Richardson et al. have demonstrated that facial disfigurement has undesirable effects on social preference, few investigations can be found that examine this phenomenon. However, a series of case studies by Francis Cooke MacGregor and colleagues (MacGregor, Abel, Bryt, Lauer, & Weissmann, 1953; MacGregor, 1974; 1979) suggest that facial disfigurement has strong negative effects upon interpersonal impressions. Furthermore, studies on the effects of facial attractiveness in nonhandicapped population samples suggest that facial unattractiveness is associated with unfavorable impressions, while pretty or handsome faces are likely to generate favorable social perceptions.

One of the most seminal investigations suggesting an attractiveness stereotype was conducted by Karen Dion and her colleagues (Dion, Berscheid, & Walster, 1972). They hypothesized that physically attractive men and women generally are assumed by others to possess more socially desirable personality traits, and are expected to lead better personal lives than their less attractive counterparts. To test these hypotheses, college students were asked to judge attractive, average-looking, and unattractive pictures on different personality traits and life experiences. The primary results of this investigation are summarized in Table 6.2.

The reported significant differences between conditions are summarized in the right-hand column. For example, on the social desirability of the person's personality, L < M < H indicates that unattractive stimulus persons were judged to have less desirable personality characteristics than the average-looking person, while the average-looking individual was judged as less desirable than the attractive stimulus person. On all measures except parental competence, attractive stimulus persons were judged to be more socially desirable, to obtain more prestige or competence, and to live better lives than their less attractive counterparts. These data support the notion that a physical attractiveness stereotype exists with respect to normal, nonhandicapped populations. The Dion, Berscheid, and Walster study has been instrumental in stimulating a host of studies that have tested the "what-is-beautiful-is-good" hypothesis.

In summary, although Lombroso, Kretschmer, and Sheldon initially assumed that physical appearance influenced social behavior through a genetic or constitutional mechanism, Goffman brought theoretical relevance for social psychologists to the study of physical appearance. Several lines of

TABLE 6.2
Summary of Differential Traits Assigned to Unattractive,
Average, and Attractive College Students

Trait	Unattractive Stimulus	Average Stimulus	Attractive Stimulus	Significant Difference
Social desirability of the stimulus person's personality	L	M	H	L < M < H
Occupational status of the stimulus person	L	M	H	L = M < H
Marital competence of the stimulus person	L	L	H	L < H
Parental competence of the stimulus person	M	H	L	L < M = H
Social and professional happiness of the stimulus person	L	H	H	L < H
Total happiness of the stimulus person	L	H	H	L < H
Likelihood of marriage	L	M	H	L = M < H

L = low, M = medium, and H = high trait ascription scores.
Source: Dion, Berscheid, & Walster (1972), Table 1, p. 288. Copyright 1972 by the American Psychological Association. Reprinted by permission.

social psychological research have developed concerning the effects of physical appearance upon social attribution and behavior. Most of the early work focused upon person-perception or social attribution hypotheses that confirmed the existence of physical attractiveness social stereotypes. Before addressing contemporary research developments, it will be useful to examine why physical attractiveness is so important to most people, and to briefly identify the most common research strategies in the study of physical attractiveness.

THE VALUE OF PHYSICAL ATTRACTIVENESS

Why does physical appearance have such power in influencing social perceptions? As suggested earlier, it may simply be an aesthetic affinity for beauty. Perhaps through some neurological mechanism, a combination of finely tuned body lines, curves, and angles triggers some aspect of the pleasure center of the brain. Or could it be that the lure of beauty is actually a straightforward social process? In their classic overview of the attractiveness literature, Ellen Berscheid and Elaine Walster (1974) noted several social mechanisms that account for the impact of attractiveness. They were struck by the influence that attractiveness has on adolescent dating patterns. Recognizing that dating can be conceptually viewed as human interaction in a competitive marketplace, Berscheid and Walster summarized a series of investigations that addressed the "matching hypothesis" originally suggested by Erving Goffman. Goffman has written of the dating and mating experience: "A proposal of marriage in our society tends to be a way in which a man sums up his social attributes and suggests to a woman that hers are not so much better as to preclude a merger or a partnership in these matters" (1952, p. 456). Thus, individuals of comparable social desirability are thought to selectively seek each other out for marriage.

To test the matching hypothesis, a "computer dance" study was conducted in which physical attractiveness was assessed when students purchased their tickets (Walster, Aronson, Abrahams, & Rottman, 1966). During an intermission, a questionnaire was completed by the dating partners. The single most potent factor in determining likability of a date was physical attractiveness. The more attractive the date, the more the person was liked. But because the computer matching of dates may have minimized the possibility of potential rejection, another investigation was undertaken to test the matching hypothesis in a more natural environment. Berscheid, Dion, Walster, and Walster (1971) conducted two experiments in which the participants actually chose a dating partner rather than evaluating a partner already secured.

In these investigations the possibility of rejection was highlighted, reflecting a natural possibility in the dating marketplace. While attractive dates were preferred by all, the potential of being rejected by an attractive person appeared to lead individuals to select dates close to their own level of attractiveness. Another investigation in this series has shown that while males prefer to date the most attractive women available, they may not be confident that their request for a date will be accepted by beautiful women (Huston, 1973).

Berscheid and Walster (1974) have suggested several reasons why physical attractiveness may be valued in American society. Through social learning we come to view only physically attractive persons as appropriate targets for dating. Since most advertisements and commercials focus upon beautiful people, we may unconsciously internalize the assumption that only beautiful persons are desirable. In children's literature, beauty is often associated with goodness, while ugliness is paired with wickedness, evil, or badness (Adams & Crossman, 1978)—for example, the stepsisters of Cinderella or the witchlike creatures in Snow White, Rapunzel, and Hansel and Gretel.

In the dating marketplace, social prestige can be acquired through association with an attractive partner (for instance, Bar-Tal & Saxe, 1974; Sigall & Landy, 1973). A woman's beauty may actually radiate to her male partner's image, inflating the male's social status beyond what it would be if he were judged without his beautiful companion. Goffman (1963) has also proposed that being seen with a stigmatized or "discredited" person can make one discreditable. Being associated with an unattractive person may be perceived as discrediting, as much as association with beauty is socially elevating. Finally, physical attractiveness may be a rewarding value. Huston's study (1973) indicates that attractiveness is not perceived as easily obtainable. Hence, when we obtain a much-sought-after, but difficult to acquire, commodity, our personal esteem is raised.

Unfortunately, there is little systematic study of the perceived value of physical attractiveness. However, pilot data by Jay Schvaneveldt (summarized in Adams & Crossman, 1978) offer an initial step toward empirically identifying factors underlying the perceived value of physical attractiveness. Schvaneveldt asked college students to indicate what they judge to be the essential social and psychological attributes underlying the importance of physical attractiveness. As summarized in Table 6.3, physical attractiveness

TABLE 6.3
Selected Quotations from Students' Responses to a Question on Why Physical Attractiveness Is Such a Strong Determinant of Attraction

Dimension I: status, self-esteem, and success
   "Physical attractiveness is important and especially in the case of a businessman because his wife must accompany him to social gatherings, and a physically attractive wife would make a good impression."
   "The male ego is often bolstered by having an attractive female."
   "People want to be seen and associated with someone who others consider attractive. They envy this person for her beauty."

Dimension II: hereditary factors
   "The more attractive the other member, the more attractive the children will be—making them more socially acceptable."
   "For underlying biological reasons an attractive person is chosen because that person appears to be disease-free and capable of mating."

Dimension III: mass media influence
   "TV and books tell us that society gears females toward the need for physical attractiveness in order to attract males for marriage, status, and acceptability."

Dimension IV: good values
   "Persons of great physical attractiveness are often attributed with very desirable qualities."

Dimension V: complementary association
   "Physical attractiveness is a strong determinant of attraction because a person's body language—facial wrinkles, choice of clothes, and even body build and posture are all excellent indicators of personality and compatibility; we tend to pick what would be complementary to us."

Source: Adams & Crossman (1978) pp. 49–50, Table 1.

was thought to have a major influence upon a person's social status, elevation of self-esteem, and perceived interpersonal success. Also, many respondents described physical attractiveness as an important variable associated with hereditary influences. Particular attention was given to the implications for bearing offspring. Numerous students recognized the mass media influence associated with attractiveness. For many, beauty was thought to be associated with desirable social values and the satisfaction of personal needs through the compatible association with a beautiful person. Thus, beauty may be perceived as a valued possession for any number of significant social reasons beyond mere aesthetic appeal.

The importance of facial attractiveness goes beyond the social premium placed upon it by society. The face is intimately associated with communication. It is the center of attention in face-to-face communication, and has been recognized as the focal point of nonverbal and verbal expression (Allport, 1967). As MacGregor (1974) has remarked, "As a receptor of impressions as well as medium by which rejection, threat, or invitation may be expressed, it is a dominant aspect in the interaction of individuals, serving to qualify the interplay between them and to influence communication" (pp. 31–32). Thus, the importance of the face lies in its function as a social stimulus to provide important visual impressions that communicate a wide range of interpersonal messages (including attitudes, emotions, sentiments, and invitations).

MEASUREMENT OF PHYSICAL ATTRACTIVENESS

While "Beauty is in the eye of the beholder" is a familiar bit of folk wisdom, data from various studies suggest that certain common standards are used to judge a person's degree of physical attractiveness. One investigation has compared a U.S. and a South African sample, with the authors concluding that American men and women have a more consistent perception of the "meaning" attached to physical attractiveness judgments (Morse, Reis, Gruzen, & Wolff, 1974). In both cultures, physical attractiveness was thought to have strong sex-appeal implications. However, while both cultures shared a great deal of similarity, American men and women viewed good looks as being linked to perceptions of sex appeal for both self-evaluations and evaluations of others. That is, when judging themselves or others, it was believed that high physical attractiveness was associated with an appealing sexual image. In the South African sample, looks and sex appeal were associated for judgments made about women, but not about men. It is possible that the failure to find the same results for both men and women in South Africa may be due to an unusual or nonrepresentative sample. However, these data suggest that American men and women have very similar perceptions of who is judged to be physically attractive, and attach similar meaning to such judgments.

There appears to be a relatively common standard of beauty that is acquired early in life. For example, Cross and Cross (1971) had 7-, 12-, and 17-year-olds rate pictures that had previously been judged for degree of facial attractiveness by a sample of college students. Ratings were compared on degree of similarity in judgment. All four age groups were found to give approximately the same ratings for the pictures, suggesting that as early as seven years of age, children are using the equivalent of an adult standard of beauty. Other investigations, which have attempted to identify whether very young children can distinguish attractive from unattractive persons, have suggested that children as young as three years have internalized the culturally held standards of beauty (Dion, 1973; Adams & Crane, 1980).

Social psychologists measure the physical attractiveness of an individual to assess the degree to which beauty is associated with other perceptual or behavioral measures. These studies involve the "scaling" of stimuli on physical attractiveness. In this strategy the study of physical attractiveness is usually conducted in some naturally occurring social context. That is, there is no attempt to manipulate or change the attractiveness of individuals. For example, in the computer-dance methodology discussed earlier, Walster et al. (1966) rated the facial attractiveness of individuals as they obtained tickets for a dance. Later they correlated the ratings of attractiveness with personality assessments and interpersonal liking scores gathered during the dance. However, researchers frequently use experimental research designs rather than survey, naturalistic observation, or interview techniques. Here the researcher is more likely to manipulate degree of attractiveness, usually to extremes, and to study the effects of widely discrepant degrees of attractiveness on interpersonal behavior during a laboratory investigation.

PHYSICAL ATTRACTIVENESS STEREOTYPES: FROM PERCEPTIONS TO INDIVIDUAL DEVELOPMENT

In recent years the implications of physical attractiveness for social behavior have been examined in numerous contexts. Investigations have looked at the relationship between appearance and dating, job promotions, school success, singles-bar behavior, moral action, likes and dislikes, jury decisions, peer relations, self-satisfaction, attributions of responsibility, personality styles, social satisfaction, marriage, and marital adjustment. From this extensive research an important synthesis can be generated that gives both direction and meaning to the study of physical attractiveness stereotypes.

In Figure 6.1, I have attempted to synthesize the interrelationship among several lines of research in terms of a "developmental social psychological" perspective. It will be instrumental in examining the organizational scheme and reviewing some of the physical attractiveness research that supports its configuration. While our measurement scales remain somewhat

FIGURE 6.1.

A Conceptual Scheme for Understanding the Organizational Relationship of Varying Research Approaches to the Study of the Physical Attractiveness Stereotype

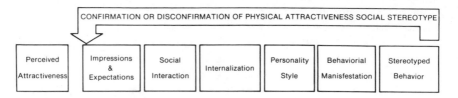

Source: Compiled by author.

impressionistic, raters can and do evaluate differences between various degrees of physical attractiveness. Further, there is strong evidence to indicate that attractive persons are expected to possess more socially desirable characteristics than unattractive individuals. Perhaps the most startling aspect of studying social stereotypes comes with the realization that stereotypes may actually evolve into social reality. It is possible that, as Erikson (1968) has noted, our anatomy is our destiny. However, it may be less due to biological characteristics associated with sex differences, and more a function of the social interactional styles, which create different social milieus for attractive and unattractive individuals. Thus, attractiveness stereotypes may begin as relatively benign social impressions, but end as channeling effects on personality and social development.

In the next section we shall examine some of the research evidence that supports the conceptual framework outlined in Figure 6.1. In particular, we will focus upon facial attractiveness and physical disability. The goal is to provide an overview of the research evidence and to focus upon illustrative research examples to document various methodologies employed in the study of physical attractiveness.

RESEARCH ON IMPRESSION FORMATION

In an address to the New York Symposium on Cosmetic Benefits, Thomas Cash (1979) argued that throughout history beauty has been linked with all that is good. For example, in ancient Greece, Eros was viewed as young and handsome, and was the god of love. Likewise, Aphrodite occupied the position of goddess of love and beauty. Perhaps one of the more compelling statements in Cash's address came from a work by Finck entitled *Romantic Love and Personal Beauty*. Finck (1887) has been quoted as writing: "Inasmuch as Personal Beauty is the flower and symbol of perfect health, it might be shown, by following out this argument, that ugliness is a sin, and man's first duty is the cultivation of beauty" (cited in Cash, 1979, p. 3). With such statements in both historical and contemporary literature, it is not too surprising that Dion et al. (1972) have been able to establish strong evidence for a "beauty-is-good" belief.

Expectations of Personality and Social Behavior

A wide range of investigations in person perception support the notion that most individuals expect attractive individuals to possess more desirable personalities and to engage in more successful social behavior than unattractive persons. Young children (for instance, Adams & Crane, 1980; Dion & Berscheid, 1974; Dion, 1973), college students (Dion, Berscheid, & Walster, 1972; Miller, 1970a; 1970b), and older adults (Adams & Huston, 1975) are influenced by the attractiveness of the person being judged. This research suggests that attractive individuals are viewed as possessing better character; are seen as more self-confident, poised, kind, and flexible; are expected to obtain more education and occupy higher-status employment; and are thought to be more sociable, outgoing, and likable than unattractive peer comparisons. In contrast, the research on physical disability and disfigurement suggests that handicapped individuals are often viewed in socially undesirable terms, and that the peer relations of these children are cold, distant, and interpersonally removed from what is considered normal social intercourse (cf. Richardson, 1976; Adams, 1979a).

Physical Attractiveness and Sex Stereotypes

Three investigations suggest that person perception is influenced by the interrelationship between physical attractiveness, sexism, and other stereotyping processes. In an early influential study, Miller (1970a) demonstrated that college males and females are inclined to rate attractive men and women as possessing more socially desirable personality dispositions (such as curious, complex, perceptive, confident, assertive, happy, active, amiable, humorous, pleasure-seeking, outspoken, and flexible) than unattractive men and women. However, these findings were qualified by an interaction between sex of the target subjects and their degree of attractiveness. Few differences were evident when contrasting ratings between attractive men and women, but for moderate or low attractive comparisons, consistent sex differences were noted. Miller stated: "It appears that as one departs from high physical attractiveness, a stimulus person's sex becomes a more influential impression determinant . . . a plausible hypothesis in this context might be that unattractive males are perceived more adept at compensating for their unattractiveness than are females, i.e., if one must be unattractive, it is a better fate to be male than female" (pp. 242–243).

Indeed, for some individuals (particularly unattractive women) social impressions may be influenced by an interaction between two social stereotypes—physical attractiveness and sex. Millman (1979) has, for example, suggested that obesity is a particular problem for women in the American culture. While a woman who weighs 25 pounds more than average is often perceived to be fat, a man may weigh as much as 50 pounds more than the norm and merely be viewed as "heavy." Millman views fat women as an unrecognized but particularly compelling category of victims of sex stereotypes. An investigation by Goldberg, Gottesdiener, and Abramson (1975) examined the relationship between "perceived" and "real" degree of physical attractiveness and support for the feminist movement. In the first of two studies, male and female subjects rated 30 women, who were either against or in favor of women's liberation, on a scale of facial attractiveness. Although a wide range of ratings was obtained, no significant differences were observed between the two groups for ratings completed by either male or female raters. In the second investigation another sample of college students was asked to examine the same pictures and place them into categories marked "support" or "not support" for women's liberation groups. Both male and female subjects placed the less attractive pictures into the category that was thought to support the feminist movement. In this investigation a sexist attitude was found to elicit a related unattractiveness stereotype. Thus, women who support the feminist movement may experience a "social put-down" in the sense that people may expect (or perceive) them to be less pretty or (typically) feminine.

It should be noted, however, that two investigations have failed to replicate Goldberg et al.'s (1975) findings. Johnson, Doiron, Brooks, and Dickinson (1978) found a sex-of-perceiver effect. As in the Goldberg et al. study, male undergraduates "put down" supporters of the women's liberation movement by attributing unattractive appearance to them. However, female undergraduates misperceived *in the opposite direction* by attributing attractive appearance to supporters of the movement. Johnson, Holborn, and Turcotte (1979) subsequently found that *both* females and males selected more attractive photographs as reflecting support for the feminist movement and less attractive photos as reflecting nonsupport for the movement. Johnson et al. (1979) include differences in geographical locality of the research (Goldberg et al. in the United States, Johnson et al., 1978, 1979, in Canada), and the time span between the investigations as possible explanations of the discrepancy in research findings. Clearly, the image or stereotype of supporters of women's liberation was far more positive among subjects in the Johnson et al. studies than in the Goldberg et al. investigation.

Additional evidence suggests that the use of the physical attractiveness stereotype may be strongly associated with a person's personal sex-role development. In an investigation of the relationship between sex-role stereotyping and liking for physically attractive individuals, Touhey (1979) had male and female college students complete a Macho Scale that assesses extremes in sex-role stereotyping. They were also provided with folders containing pictures of either an attractive or an unattractive person and a brief biographical information sheet. Subjects were asked to indicate their degree of liking for the individual, summarize (through recall) the bio-graphic information, and attribute personality traits to the target persons.

Males and females scoring high on the Macho Scale were found to report more liking for the physically attractive persons than low-stereotyped research subjects. Low sex-role-stereotyping subjects recalled more bio-graphic information than high-stereotyped persons. On ascribed personali-ty traits, high sex-role-stereotyping subjects expected the attractive stimulus persons to be respecters of authority, dutiful, religious, and good providers, while low sex-role-stereotyping subjects judged them to be more companion-able, involved, and emotionally open. Collectively, these investigations suggest that the effects of physical appearance can, at times, be mediated by other stereotype processes. Individuals who hold extreme views about sex differences or have a highly sex-role-stereotyped personality will be particu-larly likely to use physical attractiveness information in making judgments about others.

Physical Attractiveness and Age-ism

There is also evidence that the use of physical attractiveness informa-tion in social impressions is mediated by age of the research subject. Since aging stereotypes exist, it seems reasonable that aging and deterioration of physical attractiveness are linked in many persons' minds. To assess the relationship between age of rater and physical attractiveness effects, Adams and Huston (1975) had young adults and elderly retired persons ascribe personality traits to middle-aged men and women of high and low facial attractiveness.

Regardless of the age of the subject rating the stimuli, middle-aged attractive women and men were more likely than their unattractive stimulus comparisons to be viewed in socially desirable terms. Furthermore, females were more inclined than male research subjects to be influenced by a physical attractiveness stereotype in their person perception judgments. Also, regard-less of degree of attractiveness, elderly raters judged middle-aged men and women more favorably than did the younger raters. Finally, while both the young and old raters judged attractive persons more favorably, the elderly research sample was found to hold stronger physical attractiveness percep-tions than the younger group. This investigation suggests that future research directed at testing stereotype effects at different life stages might offer a rich source of new information on the effects of physical attractive-ness on person perception.

The Radiation of Beauty

Three different investigations using similar methodologies have examined the effects of being associated with an attractive partner (Sigall & Landy, 1973; Bar-Tal & Saxe, 1974; Hartnett & Elder, 1973). In all three studies, being associated with an attractive friend or partner stimulated more favorable social perceptions than association with an unattractive one. Also, when asked, research subjects reported that they expected others to view them in more favorable terms when associated with a beautiful or handsome person.

Evidence also suggests, however, that radiating effects may create a social problem. Kenrick and Gutierres (1980) have demonstrated that an average-appearing female may be judged as less attractive and desirable when a "contrast effect" is established with a highly attractive person. When males have been viewing highly attractive females on television or in advertisement information, a comparison standard can be temporarily established that influences the subsequent perception of physical attractiveness. While the effects of such a "contrast effect" may be short-lived, it may have certain undesirable influences on social impressions for average-appearing females who meet males immediately following media exposure. Also, it should be recognized that initial impressions can be difficult to change and, at times, are self-fulfilling.

Some Important Qualifiers

Dermer and Thiel (1975) have aptly stated, "All that glitters may not be gold." While recognizing all of the positive social attributes associated with beauty, these experimenters have shown that attractive individuals may also be viewed as egocentric, snobbish, and vain. Thus, physical attractiveness may generate a beauty-is-good impression with an auxiliary assumption that beauty is also self-centered (Wilson, Cash, & West, 1978). For example, in two experiments Dermer and Thiel (1975) had male and female subjects judge women of varying levels of attractiveness on socially desirable and undesirable attributions. Consistent with previous research (such as Dion, Berscheid, & Walster, 1972), a direct association between physical attractiveness and sexual responsiveness, social desirability of the target's personality, husband's occupational status, and social and professional happiness was observed. However, attractive women were also expected be be conceited, egotistical, vain, likely to engage in adultery, or likely to obtain a divorce.

Styczynski and Langlois (1977) have questioned the research implications of having subjects always rate unfamiliar target stimuli. In an investigation where children were asked to rate familiar and unfamiliar children on attractiveness and social attributions, it was observed that familiarity did not significantly affect attractiveness ratings, but did change popularity ratings and behavioral expectations. Thus, our impressions of others may be more seriously influenced by attractiveness during encounters of "the third kind" (initial contact with a stranger).

Stephen Richardson and colleague (Richardson & Friedman, 1972; Richardson, 1971) have demonstrated that the internalization of group norms is predictive of the use of the physical disability stereotype. That is, children who are in the mainstream of social communication and have friends who hold the handicap stereotype, were more likely than children removed from the social network to use stereotypic judgments in making decisions about handicapped persons. Familiarity is an important issue in person-perception research. If an individual has internalized group values and norms, it can have a significant influence upon characteristics attributed to attractive-unattractive or handicapped-nonhandicapped person comparisons.

Summary

Person-perception research has documented that individuals of all ages are influenced by a physical attractiveness stereotype in their expression of social impressions. Also, physical attractiveness and sex stereotypes may interact in their influence upon social expectations. The attractiveness stereotypes involve both desirable and undesirable impressions, although clearly the emphasis has been on the positive inferences drawn from high attractiveness (and vice versa). It is possible, however, that familiarity with individuals may attenuate physical attractiveness effects on social impressions and interpersonal expectations. There is also some evidence to suggest that social norms may influence the use of appearance stereotypes.

SOCIAL INTERACTION

Evidence from both observational and experimental studies indicates that the effects of a person's physical appearance generalize beyond social impressions to social interaction. Various studies indicate that the effects of attractiveness are evident from birth through adulthood, across a wide range of social settings.

Early Socialization Experiences

Early socialization experiences have been shown to be influenced by care givers' perceptions of an infant's or child's attractiveness (for instance, Corter, Trehub, Boukydis, Ford, Celhoffer, & Minde, 1978; Hildebrandt & Fitzgerald, 1978). In an extensive and systematic research effort, Hildebrandt and Fitzgerald demonstrated that adults are influenced in their social interaction with a child by its degree of facial attractiveness. Not only do adults look longer at cute infants (Hildebrandt & Fitzgerald, in press; Hildebrandt & Fitzgerald, 1978), but cuter infants are more likely to be labeled female (Hildebrandt & Fitzgerald, 1977; 1979a). Infants with facial features that include short and narrow facial lines, large eyes and pupils, and a large forehead have been judged the most likely to receive high cuteness ratings (Hildebrandt & Fitzgerald, 1979a). The implications of this series of investigations suggest that cute infants may be given more individual attention and may receive a more nurturing child-rearing environment.

Dion (1972) has shown that when college students were asked to play the role of an uninvolved evaluator, their socialization behavior was influenced by a child's degree of facial attractiveness. Specifically, when attractive and unattractive children were portrayed as breaking a well-established rule, attractive children were viewed as having an "off day," while unattractive children were viewed as having deep-seated antisocial characteristics. These data are similar to a survey that found attractive boys were more likely than their unattractive counterparts to receive inductive reasoning by adults during disciplinary actions (Adams & LaVoie, 1975).

In an investigation of children's attractiveness as a determinant of adult punitiveness, Dion (1974) had adult men and women observe a videotaped interaction between the experimenter and a physically attractive or unattractive boy or girl. On the basis of the child's performance on a picture-matching task, each subject was requested to administer penalties for incorrect responses. Women were more lenient toward an attractive than unattractive boy or attractive or unattractive girl. Men were unaffected in their punitive behavior by a child's level of attractiveness.

In an extension of the Dion study, Berkowitz and Frodi (1979) noted that aversive environmental stimuli might facilitate the display of involuntary aggressive reactions. Using a parallel experimental design, they found in two consecutive studies that unattractive children were inclined to receive more intense punishment than their attractive comparisons. In summarizing their conclusions, Berkowitz and Frodi stated:

> ...we believe the undesirable physical characteristics evoke the aggression-facilitating reactions because they are aversive to the potential agressors. This may well be one example of a fairly general phenomenon. Whatever their exact nature, we suggest, objects that are associated with aversive events (i.e., that arouse avoidance tendencies) theoretically also elicit aggression-facilitating responses. (pp. 424–425)

Thus, physical unattractiveness may function as an elicitor of undesirable social consequences through an aggression-facilitating reaction that unconsciously occurs in individuals. The implications are that unattractive children are inclined to be reared in relatively aggressive social conditions associated with harsh physical and verbal punishment that may lead to poor socialization.

Socialization Effects in School

Young children appear to experience stereotype-related teacher-student expectations and interactions. Several investigations have shown that attractive children experience higher teacher expectations for their school performance (see Adams & LaVoie, 1977, for a review of this research). Adams and Cohen (1974), for example, studied the teacher-student interactions in a kindergarten, a fourth-grade, and a seventh-grade classroom, and found that for older (but not younger) children, facial attractiveness was an important determinant of the frequency and quality of interaction with teachers. In this investigation student-teacher interactions were observed and recorded according to a simple rating system in which each interaction was judged to be either a verbal support, control, or neutral statement. After classroom observations were complete, each child was rated on a physical attractiveness scale. Interaction scores (frequency counts) were compared on the three types of statements, using a level of attractiveness x grade level factorial analysis. This study suggested that older children were more likely than the young to experience supportive teacher-student interactions as a function of physical attractiveness.

Felson (1980) examined the relationship between a number of variables related to academic performance (grade-point average, standardized test scores) and physical attractiveness in a national sample of over 2000 tenth-grade boys. The evidence suggested that teachers assign higher grades and attribute more ability to attractive children. Felson's results corroborate those of Clifford and Walster (1973) in suggesting that "stereotyping against unattractive children in the past may have resulted in less actual achievement on their part" (Felson, 1980, p. 70). It should be noted, however, that the relationship between physical attractiveness and *actual* (as contrasted with estimated) achievement is complex, and is likely to be influenced by a variety of contextual variables, age and school-history factors, and individual differences among teachers in their perceptions of attractiveness-ability linkage. It is therefore not surprising that at least two investigations have failed to document a significant relationship between physical attractiveness and academic performance (Clifford, 1975; Sparacino and Hansell, 1979).

Peer Relations

Attractive children and adolescents are generally perceived as more likable and desirable as a friend or playmate (see, for example, Dion, 1973;

Langlois & Stephan, 1977; Adams & Crane, 1980; Horai, Naccari, & Fatoullah, 1974). For example, Kleck, Richardson, and Ronald (1974) demonstrated in an observation study at a summer camp that popularity ratings and friendship choices are influenced by peer judgments of facial attractiveness. Using a sociometric device, these investigators identified five children who were judged by peers as having either high or low social acceptance. Their pictures were then shown to another group of children, who rated them on attractiveness and preference for becoming a friend. High social acceptance children were judged to be better-looking by children their own age, and to be preferred as a possible friend.

These same investigators also examined the social status of physically handicapped boys in a camp setting (Richardson, Ronald, & Kleck, 1974). Using a similar methodology, they investigated the effects of visible (such as amputations, cosmetic deformities) and nonvisible (such as asthma, hearing impairment) handicaps upon children's social status. On the basis of sociometric status information gathered from bunkmates and other boys in the camp, visibly handicapped boys clearly were viewed in negative terms. Thus, the unattractiveness associated with a visible handicap is associated with undesirable social images.

In an extension of the earlier camp studies (Richardson, Ronald, & Kleck, 1974; Kleck, Richardson, & Ronald, 1974), Kleck and Dejong (submitted) have demonstrated for both male and female children that physical appearance has compelling effects upon social status. Not only were able-bodied children better liked than their obviously handicapped peers, but when handicapped factors were partialed out, high physical attractiveness was again associated with high sociometric status. These investigators are the first to clearly demonstrate that children rate handicapped children lower in terms of physical attractiveness than able-bodied children.

Dating and Marriage

A review of the effects of physical attractiveness on dating and marriage (Adams, 1977a) concluded that physical appearance stereotypes have strong and consistent effects upon dating preferences (for instance, Walster et al., 1966; Brislin & Lewis, 1968; Byrne et al., 1970; Berscheid et al., 1971; Murstein, 1972; Curran, 1973; Curran & Lippold, 1975); attractiveness is related to sex appeal and sensations of love and emotional arousal (Cavior et al., 1974; Critelli, 1975; Peplau, 1976; Shea & Adams, 1979); and being associated with an attractive person has positive effects upon one's social status (for example, Bar-Tal & Saxe, 1974; Sigall & Landy, 1973).

If given a choice, most of us will choose "beauty" over "brains" when considering a mate (Meiners & Sheposh, 1976), with the matching hypothesis gathering little support in a dating context. Further, when dating, an attractive interloper is likely to stimulate strong reactions through a jealousy-evoking response. In particular, Shettel-Neuber, Bryson, and Young (1978) have found that male respondents report they would be inclined to start going out with others and become more sexually aggressive with other women if they found their dates showing evidence of interaction with another male who was highly attractive.

Several investigations directed toward examining the matching hypothesis with married couples (and same-sex friends; Cash & Derlega, 1978) indicate reasonable support for this hypothesis. Therefore, it appears that while early dating patterns are less influenced by the matching hypothesis, final mate selection involves individuals of generally similar levels of attractiveness marrying each other (for instance, Cavior & Boblett, 1972; Murstein & Christy, 1976). Further evidence suggests that attractive women may increase their social status through marriage (Elder, 1969; Taylor & Glenn, 1976). One might speculate that if the matching hypothesis is a consistent phenomenon, attractive women from the lower class might be able to use their beauty to attain a higher social status through marriage to a husband having a higher social rank.

Work Opportunities

Physical attractiveness has also been shown to influence work opportunities. For example, attractive job applicants have been shown to be more likely than their less attractive peers to receive an employment offer (Cash, Gillen, & Burns, 1977; Dipboye, Fromkin, & Wiback, 1975). When hired, attractive persons may be viewed as more competent and effective, even when their performance is poor (Landy & Sigall, 1974; Maruyama & Miller, 1980). To illustrate, Landy and Sigall had male college students read a poor or well-written essay supposedly prepared by either an unattractive or an attractive female. Evaluators were asked to make judgments about the quality of the writing and the writer's ability. A well-written essay was judged to be good regardless of the level of attractiveness of the female author. However, when the quality was poor, essays were evaluated more positively if their writers were attractive. Parallel results were observed for judgments of the writer's ability.

Further evidence suggests that sex-role stereotypes may interact with a physical attractiveness stereotype in a work setting. Assuming that attractive women are viewed as more feminine than unattractive women, and attractive men are viewed as more masculine than unattractive men (Cash et al., 1977), it has been proposed that attractive women may find it difficult to obtain positions in industry that have been historically viewed as "a man's job." To assess this possibility, Heilman and Saruwatari (1979) had male and female college students review files of applicants for jobs associated with clerical activities (nonmanagerial) and decision making (managerial). Folders included pictures of either an attractive or an unattractive man or woman.

In various personnel decisions completed by the research subjects, it was observed that overall, attractive applicants were viewed as more qualified than unattractive ones; for females only, attractiveness was a bonus in obtaining a nonmanagerial position, and a disadvantage in perceived qualifications for a managerial post; for males, attractiveness was positively associated with hiring decisions, while for females it was a benefit only in the nonmanagerial positions; and when females were being considered for a managerial job, the research subjects recommended that unattractive applicants get a higher starting salary than their attractive competitors. These data suggest that there are behavioral qualifiers to the "beauty-is-good" assumption, and that beauty can, depending upon the level of occupational interest, have disadvantageous effects upon work-related activities.

Interaction with the Legal System

When confronting the legal system, attractive individuals may receive unique attention. Various "mock" jury studies suggest that attractive defendants are treated more generously when found guilty of a crime (Efran, 1974; Stewart, 1980; Storck & Sigall, 1979; Leventhal & Krate, 1977; Solomon & Schopler, 1978). But there may also be conditions where attractive individuals may have their appearance work against them. For example, Sigall and Ostrove (1975) have shown in a mock jury study that when attractive persons are found guilty of using their looks to disarm the victim during a swindle or con game, the jury decision is likely to be harsher than if they had been caught in a burglary. For unattractive persons, however, being guilty of a swindle is less likely to result in harsh punishment than being guilty of burglary. Indeed, some jury members may recognize the potential bias associated with the sentencing of attractive and unattractive defendants and actually "lean over backwards" to avoid such bias in their final judgments. Friend and Vinson (1974) suggest this may lead to unattractive persons being treated more leniently and attractive individuals more harshly than might be expected.

The victim's level of attractiveness can also play an influential role. For example, Kerr (1978) has demonstrated that a defendant in a mock jury experiment is most likely to be convicted when the victim is portrayed by the plaintiff's attorney as both beautiful and blameless. Thus, extreme levels of attractiveness can have both beneficial and detrimental effects upon the outcome of the legal process, depending upon the circumstances. Further, these effects must be considered for both the defendant and the plaintiff.

Two investigations directed at the study of physical attractiveness of a plaintiff illustrate the potential importance of appearance in court settings. Seligman, Brickman, and Koulack (1977) had research subjects read an account of either an attractive or an unattractive woman who was described as the victim of either a rape, a mugging, or a robbery. Drawing upon attribution theory, these investigators proposed that only in the rape condition would subjects maintain that an unattractive woman (an unlikely victim) would be less responsible than an attractive woman (a likely victim). Findings indicated that while physically attractive women were judged to have been more likely victims of rape, the physically unattractive women were judged as being more responsible in provoking the rape incident. These investigators argue that although attractiveness can be a triggering mechanism of a rape, in the case of an unattractive woman (who is thought to be an unlikely victim) there must be behavioral indexes, such as flirtation, that incite the rapist to act.

Kulka and Kessler (1978) argued that tests of the impact of appearance on jury judgment could be potentially limited by the exclusive use of the short written synopsis as the means of trial presentation (such as that employed by Seligman et al.). Therefore, these investigators tested the impact of physical attractiveness on jurors' judgments in an automobile negligence trial. Subjects were presented with an audiovisual tape of either an attractive or an unattractive plaintiff and defendant. Subjects exposed to an attractive plaintiff and an unattractive defendant were more likely to judge in favor of the plaintiff and award more money in damages than students viewing an unattractive plaintiff and an attractive defendant. The effects of physical attractiveness appear to have been the result of differential perceptions of the seriousness of the accident.

Counseling Settings

While it might be expected that mental health professionals would readily see the potential pitfalls of a physical attractiveness stereotype, there is evidence to suggest that they also are influenced by physical attractiveness, and may influence others through their own physical appearance. Several investigations, for example, suggest that attractive people are judged as less disturbed and better adjusted during intake interviews, and generate an impression of better prognosis for recovery, than unattractive clients (Barocas & Vance, 1974; Cash & Salzbach, 1978; Cash, Kehr, Polyson, & Freeman, 1977; Hobfoll & Penner, 1978). Furthermore, physically attractive counselors are perceived to be more intelligent, friendly, assertive, trustworthy, competent, likable, and warm, and also as capable of eliciting more favorable counseling outcomes (Cash, Begley, McCown, & Weise, 1975). In contrast, unattractive counselors are viewed by clients in debilitative ways. In particular, an investigation by Cash and Kehr (1978) has demonstrated that unattractive counselors are viewed by clients as less committed, effective, and trustworthy, and elicit generally pessimistic views by their clients about counseling outcomes. (For research on the relationship between physical attractiveness and mental illness, refer to Farina's discussion in Chapter 7 of this volume).

A Portrait of the Social Exchange Process

Recognizing the wide variety of social contexts in which physical attractiveness plays a differential role in the quality of social exchange, let us turn to the actual social process experienced by attractive and unattractive persons. As we have seen, the general tendency is for attractive individuals to be viewed more positively than unattractive persons. However, the "power" of beauty has more far-ranging effects than perceived likability. Facial attractiveness captures our attention and serves as an important incentive in maintaining social contact and involvement (Dion, 1977; Fugita, Agle, Newman, & Walfish, 1977). The effects of interacting with an attractive person linger beyond face-to-face contact. While interacting with attractive persons, we are inclined to not only look at them, but to smile at them; when no longer in their presence, we remember more about them and continue to like them longer than unattractive persons (Kleck & Rubenstein, 1975). During social exchange we are more reinforcing of facially attractive persons (for instance, Davis, Rainey, & Brock, 1976), disclose more freely (Brundage, Derlega, & Cash, 1977; Cash & Soloway, 1975; Shea & Adams, 1979), and cooperate with and help them more often than unattractive persons (Kahn, Hottes, & Davis, 1971; Benson, Karabenick, & Lerner, 1976; West & Hodge, 1975; Sroufe, Chaikin, Cook, & Freeman, 1977).

However, when meeting strangers, those who are high in physical attractiveness may be judged as unapproachable. For example, Dabbs and Stokes (1975) have filmed attractive and unattractive individuals being approached by other pedestrians on public streets. Individuals were more inclined to maintain a greater distance between themselves and attractive strangers then unattractive strangers. Perhaps in situations where strangers mingle, attractive individuals are judged as more desirable but perceived as being less receptive to contact with unfamiliar persons. There is also evidence that people may be less inclined to seek help from a potential helper who is high in physical attractiveness (Nadler, 1980; Stokes & Bickman, 1974). These data suggest that beauty may at times be intimidating and more readily worshipped from afar.

The social environment and interpersonal interaction experienced by the physically disabled are in many ways the inverse of that experienced by the facially attractive. When normals interact with the handicapped, they are inclined to experience heightened emotional tension (as measured by galvanic skin response), to stare at the disability, to report being uncomfortable, and to place greater social and physical distance between themselves and the handicapped (Kleck, Ono, & Hastorf, 1966; Kleck, 1966; Langer, Fiske, Taylor, & Chanowitz, 1976; Kleck, 1969). Disabled individuals are unlikely to receive overt approval for appropriate behavior (McGarry & West, 1975), nor are they likely to receive help when in need (Piliavin, Piliavin, & Rodin, 1975).

Handicapped persons are more likely to receive inaccurate and less critical feedback for their performance. For example, Hastorf, Northcraft, and Picciotto (1979) created an experimental situation in which normal subjects were asked to provide feedback to either a handicapped or a normal student-confederate, on the basis of a predetermined script that was designed to produce a below-average performance. While the handicapped confederate elicited less critical feedback, there was no positive evidence that subjects expected him to perform less well. Rather, it appeared that the research subjects were attempting to be "kind" to the disadvantaged. However, when striving toward competence, "kindness can kill you." Constructive negative feedback is a necessary ingredient of improvement.

Not only are the social interactions between normal and handicapped persons strained, but there is also a strong tendency to avoid interaction with the handicapped. However, Snyder, Kleck, Strenta, and Mentzer (1979) have demonstrated that only when an individual's motivation is cloaked by ambiguous circumstances will an obvious avoidance pattern emerge. These investigators demonstrated that when the same movie was available in the location of either a handicapped or a nonhandicapped person, there was no significant difference in preference of college research subjects for watching the movie with one or the other individual. However, when given a plausible reason for choosing between two movies, one being viewed by a handicapped person and the other being watched by a nonhandicapped individual, there was an overwhelming tendency to choose the film being seen by a nonhandicapped person.

Therefore, in normal social exchange, where there are apparent justifications for choosing one activity over another, nonhandicapped persons may easily be able to find excuses for not interacting with the handicapped. Whether handicapped individuals perceive the avoidance as due to differing interest (such as liking a different type of movie) or an obvious escape route is yet to be determined. There is evidence that when interacting with another person, the possessor of a physically stigmatizing characteristic is very likely to perceive the stigma as the cause of various aspects of the other's behavior (Kleck & Strenta, 1980).

In summary, social interaction data clearly suggest that facially attractive persons experience social milieus consistent with the beauty-is-good hypothesis. Conversely, unattractive or disabled persons experience social interaction consistent with an unattractive-is-bad assumption. These interaction patterns appear to be consistent across a diversity of social settings.

INTERNALIZATION OF THE ATTRACTIVENESS STEREOTYPE PERSONALITY

Is there evidence suggesting that attractive and unattractive individuals internalize the social consequences of stereotypic impressions and attributions? Much less work has been directed at the question of internalization. However, given that parents, teachers, friends, strangers, and employers are inclined to interact with others according to stereotypic assumptions, it seems reasonable that differential patterns of social interaction may be internalized in the form of varying personality styles. According to symbolic interaction theory, the concept of self emerges from social interaction, in which, on the basis of a "looking glass self" hypothesis, an individual's personality develops out of others' expectations, feedback, and interpersonal appraisals. Thus, attractive individuals should internalize reflected appraisals of goodness, while unattractive or disabled persons should internalize undesirable social attributes.

In an imaginative field experiment, McDonald and Eilenfield (1980) observed students who were walking on a path adjacent to a wall of reflective windows (which functioned as a mirror). An experimenter, unseen by the students, recorded the amount of time each walker spent gazing toward the reflecting glass. Two independent observers subsequently categorized the students into one of three levels of attractiveness. The results indicated that both males and females spent more time gazing to the degree that they were more physically attractive. The results were interpreted as suggesting that persons higher in physical attractiveness are more likely to engage in behaviors which create objective self-awareness. In the context of the present discussion, the simple act of looking at one's self in a mirror may be viewed as an internalization of the positive features of the (high) attractiveness stereotype.

The Creation of a Social Reality

To test the assumption that stereotypes may actually create their own social reality, Snyder, Tanke, and Berscheid (1977) had college males conduct telephone conversations with females who, in fictitious photographs, were shown to be either attractive or unattractive. The actual female participants were randomly assigned to an unattractive or attractive condition, but were unaware of the photographs being given to the male participants. Once the conversations were taped and questionnaires were completed, these data were rated by research subjects unaware of the treatment condition. In questionnaire responses, males expected attractive female participants to be more sociable and interpersonally adept. Unattractive females were expected to be serious and interpersonally inept. The analyses of conversations indicated that females who were assigned to the attractive condition actually became more animated, confident, and adept than the females assigned to the unattractive condition. Thus, the attractiveness stereotype in the males actually channeled females into personality and behavioral manifestations of the stereotype.

Other personality studies have shown that attractive persons manifest

more positive personality characteristics than their unattractive counterparts. Attractiveness has been shown to be associated with positive self-
concept, sensation seeking, independence, academic inquisitiveness, and
positive emotional and mental health indexes (see Adams, 1977a, for a
review). For example, Lerner and Lerner (1977) demonstrated, using
elementary school children, that physical attractiveness is positively correlated with good peer relations, teachers' appraisals of academic ability, and
clinically assessed social adjustment. In my own research I have attempted to
document the relationship between attractiveness and personality style
(Adams, 1979b).

In an investigation I randomly sampled 301 men and women from a
total population of 75,000 persons living in a rural area of Utah. To my
surprise, little confirmation of the relationship between physical attractiveness and personality characteristics could be confirmed for the men in this
sample. However, attractive women were found to be more self-accepting,
likable, mentally stable, and less anxious or fearful than unattractive
women. Thus, it is possible that the consequences of the physical attractiveness stereotype may influence the social milieu of men and women, but,
given the perceived importance of beauty for females in our society, it may
be that only women experience personality development paralleling
stereotype-related social interaction patterns.

Handicapped and Disabled Individuals

Undesirable consequences are evident for disabled and handicapped
persons. In a summary of the relationship between a "stigmatized identity"
and personality development, Robert Kleck (1975) concluded that disabled
persons are inclined to internalize a personality profile reflecting "social
ineffectiveness." Other investigations suggest that disabled persons are prone
to develop a constrained personality style similar to that reported for facially
unattractive persons (Krebs & Adinolfi, 1975).

An excellent illustration of much-needed research on the effects of
physical disability upon personality development can be found in the work
of Frances MacGregor. In an early investigation of 46 patients who
experienced facial disfigurement, MacGregor et al. (1953) reported the
psychological consequences were withdrawal, tendencies toward extreme
aggressiveness, difficulty in coping with unsatisfied needs and feelings of
anxiety or insecurity, projection of blame to others for frustration associated
with failure to succeed, feelings of inadequacy, and frequent use of denial
about the degree of disfigurement. In a follow-up study of these facially
disfigured persons, MacGregor (1979) indicates that these individuals still
use high degrees of denial and that the primary means of confronting the
social barriers associated with their disfigurement "ranged from daring and
blatant defiance to alienation and complete withdrawal from any form of

social interaction" (p. 104). In many cases, feelings of impotence and anger surfaced readily.

THE MANIFESTATION OF ATTRACTIVENESS-RELATED BEHAVIORS

Research suggests that attractive persons are more socially skilled and adept than unattractive individuals. Facially attractive men and women are more self-confident and resistant to peer conformity influences (Adams, 1977b); they are more assertive in response to impolite behavior (Jackson & Huston, 1975); and they have greater interpersonal skills (Goldman & Lewis, 1977). When interacting with others, attractive persons are more influential in manipulating others (for instance, Singer, 1964), and possess unique but effective interpersonal influence styles. Dion and Stein (1978) have demonstrated that attractive boys and girls are more influential than less attractive children in their persuasion effects upon peers. In attempts to persuade opposite-sex peers, attractive boys are more assertive than attractive girls, but both sexes are equally effective in persuasion.

In contrast, the social behavior of disabled persons is both constrained and unskilled. Kleck and DeJong (submitted) have, for example, shown that handicapped children are much less effective in friendship-making skills than able-bodied children. Comer and Piliavin (1972) have observed that disabled persons are likely to terminate social interaction as soon as possible, demonstrate social inhibitions, smile infrequently, maintain poor eye contact, and admit discomfort when interacting with normals. They appear more comfortable when in the presence of other disabled persons. The disfigurement research would suggest a strong manifestation of asocial behavior leading to withdrawn behavior (MacGregor, 1979).

A Field Study

To assess behavioral indexes of attractiveness, Chaiken (1979) designed a procedure to investigate the relationship between attractiveness and persuasiveness in a nonlaboratory setting. Prior to a field participation experience, male and female college students were trained in the delivery of a persuasive message. These communicators were also evaluated on degree of physical attractiveness. Attractive and unattractive men and women were then placed in the university setting where they were assigned to acquire signatures on a petition. After providing signatures, the target persons were given a confidential questionnaire that assessed the communicator's behaviors. In the course of their persuasive attempts, attractive adults were viewed as more friendly and verbally fluent, and were seen as more optimistic, interesting, and persuasive than unattractive communicators. Further, attractive communicators were able to acquire more frequent agreement by target subjects than were the unattractive confederates. Given that both attractive and unattractive individuals were equally trained but were differentially effective, Chaiken's investigation suggests that unattractive persons are less effective in their ability to influence others.

A Journal Record Study

Using a different methodological approach, Reis, Nezlek, and Wheeler (1980) addressed the relationship between attractiveness and everyday social behavior. Subjects were trained to maintain records of their social experiences over a 40-day period. Further, their degree of physical attractiveness was judged through ratings of photographs obtained at the close of the data-collection period. An overall summary of this study indicates that attractive men and women are more socially involved than their unattractive counterparts. More specifically, attractive males were found to socialize more often, for longer periods of time, and for a greater proportion of their total social participation, with females. They also engaged in mixed-sex groups more often and for longer periods of time. However, their interaction with males was infrequent. Surprisingly, there were no discernible relationships between attractiveness and interaction frequency for women. For both sexes, however, attractiveness was strongly associated with satisfaction in social relations. As to the nature of their interactions, both attractive men and women were more likely to spend their interaction time in conversations or social activities.

MECHANISMS SUPPORTING SOCIAL STEREOTYPING

There is no simple, single mechanism that accounts for the "why" and "how" of social stereotyping. We have reviewed several lines of research that support a developmental framework—that is, a chain of events initiated by the attractiveness stereotype. However, there are other theoretical perspectives that provide additional clarification regarding the social-psychological processes associated with the physical attractiveness stereotype. In particular, we shall briefly examine the violation of expectation and novelty hypothesis, implicit personality theory, and self-fulfilling prophecy as research perspectives that offer additional support to the process outlined in Figure 6.1.

Violation of Expectations and Novelty Hypothesis

In working with physically handicapped persons, Stephen Richardson (1976) has proposed that when we encounter someone whose appearance exceeds the variability of our normal expectation, we experience emotional arousal, fear, or anxiety. During our early socialization experience we internalize a complex set of expectations about our social environment that includes expectations about how others look, speak, move, and behave. When we are confronted by individuals who depart from these internalized expectations of normality, we must adjust or explain such occurrences. Generally, we are unaware of our reactions, and only through conscious awareness of them can we reduce the impact of violation of expectations. Further, the more extreme the violation, the more frequent the social interaction needed with the violator before diminution of anxiety and fear will occur. Transposing this assumption to appearance in general, it might be that when interacting with either beautiful or unattractive persons, we are captivated by their appearance through the violation of expectations associated with normal appearance. Captivated by another's appearance, we are inclined to stare at the individual in the process of reacting to the violation.

But most individuals report being uncomfortable staring at another because of his or her physical deviance. Langer, Fiske, Taylor, and Chanowitz (1976) propose that a novelty hypothesis accounts for staring behavior. Because of social norms, individuals would rather avoid a unique-appearing person than interact with him or her. Thus, discomfort in interacting with a handicapped person, for example, may be less influenced by attitudes toward the handicapped than by the self-perceived discomfort associated with staring at another person's physical deviance. In their experiment Langer et al. discovered that having visual access to a handicapped person prior to an exchange experience led to longer social interaction than when research subjects were surprised to find they were to interact with a handicapped individual.

In understanding the mechanisms for the physical attractiveness social stereotype, novelty may be one aspect that triggers stereotypic behavior. Novelty also creates a violation of expectations. Thus, novelty and violation of expectations highlight physical characteristics, which become the focus of attention.

Implicit Personality Theory

Once we are attuned to another's physical appearance, what accounts for the use of stereotypic assumptions? One determinant relates to a central concept in social perception (see Chapter 2 of this book), the "implicit personality theory." From this theoretical perspective it is argued that we have a natural tendency to believe that when individuals possess certain central characteristics, other peripheral characteristics are assumed to covary around the central attributes. Thus, one central trait can be used to infer several peripheral characteristics. When one is viewed as ugly, one may be automatically viewed as aggressive, unkind, undisciplined, and so on. In this case the central trait or attribute is ugliness, while peripheral traits are aggressiveness, unkindness, and so on. In a review of research on implicit personality theory, Schneider (1973) has argued that there is little reason for us not to expect facial features, emotional expression, or physical attractiveness as a central attribute. As we have argued elsewhere, "From this psychological perspective, stereotypes might be viewed as culturally, or subculturally, shared implicit personality theories" (Adams & Crossman, 1978, p. 51).

Therefore, when novelty triggers the "violation" of expectations, a psychological process could be stimulated that compels the individual to draw upon implicit personality theorizing. Physical characteristics as potential central attributes create expectations of peripheral characteristics that are stereotypic in nature. Thus, a chain of psychological processes might be hypothesized wherein the more focused the social condition is upon physical attractiveness, the greater the likelihood that physical characteristics will serve as central attributes in an implicit personality attribution process.

Self-Fulfilling Prophecy

In Figure 6.1 I proposed that a self-fulfilling prophecy may lead to the internalization of stereotype-based personality and social behavior. How might this process work? Mark Snyder (1981) has reviewed attempts to answer this question. Research indicates that when a person views a target person as being attractive, there is a corresponding search for stereotypic confirming information. Through cognitive reconstruction of past information, an individual can selectively reinterpret past behavior of the attractive person to give meaning and confirmation to stereotypic beliefs. Thus, previous social experiences will be selectively recalled to confirm the beauty-is-good stereotype. When memory fails, or information is missing, the perceiver is inclined to fill in the gaps with clues generated from stereotypic beliefs. In searching for interpretations for previous behavior, stereotyped beliefs will create a cognitive set that will enhance congruence between the stereotype and current perceptions. Thus, one way of leading to a self-convincing process that beauty is good is through a selective reconstruction of the past to fit current stereotypic beliefs.

Once an individual has completed a self-convincing process, Snyder argues, there are stereotype-produced behavioral confirmations of social stereotypes. For example, Snyder, Tanke, and Berscheid (1977) illustrated that stereotypes can have channeling effects upon social interaction that lead to confirmation of the stereotype. In an extensive discussion of the implication of these data and others for the internalization and perseverance of social stereotypes, Snyder (1981) has concluded:

If the "new" behaviors displayed by the target as a result of behavioral confirmation are not overly discrepant from his or her own self-image, then these new behaviors may be internalized and incorporated into the target's self-conceptions. If internalization occurs . . . then both the target and the perceiver will share stereotyped conceptions of the target. The target then may be prepared to act on his or her new stereotyped self-conception in contexts beyond those that include the original perceiver who first initiated the behavioral confirmation process. (p. 198.)

BREAKING THROUGH: ON OVERCOMING STEREOTYPE EFFECTS

Since the commitment to confirmatory hypothesis testing strategies is a pervasive one, how might individuals dispel the tendency to preferentially solicit feedback from others that confirms a physical attractiveness stereotype? Perhaps one of the best strategies might be to dispel the "erroneous" assumptions from the beginning. For example, we can recognize that nonhandicapped and handicapped persons are uncomfortable interacting with each other. Both types of individuals are not inclined to know what kind of behavior is expected or clearly appropriate. This establishes a state of interpersonal ambiguity. What is the appropriate conduct? Research by Hastorf, Wildfogel, and Cassman (1979) suggests that the mere acknowledgment of the handicap can function as an important tactic in "breaking through" to normal social discourse. In three investigations research subjects preferred to interact with handicapped persons who acknowledged their handicap rather than with others who disclosed personal matters not associated with being handicapped. Thus, recognition of the handicap appears to remove some of the ambiguity associated in interacting with a deviant individual and discharges the social attention given to the handicap, allowing more normal social processes to emerge.

There is another manner in which stereotyped individuals might unknowingly "break through." In our own research we have, for example, noted the influence that social responsiveness can have on social exchange (LaVoie & Adams, 1978). Thus, personality attributes may assist an individual in overcoming the physical attractiveness stereotype. To test such a hypothesis, Eugene Mathes (1975) arranged to have high and low anxious individuals, who were judged as being either attractive or unattractive, interact with a randomly assigned "Coke date" over a five-session dating period. Contrary to expectations, attractiveness maintained an effect over these sessions, with no evidence that its effects were diminished by potentially overriding personality characteristics. However, given the importance of appearance in the dating market, it may be impossible to minimize its influence within the dating and courtship setting.

But it is possible that in other contexts, the "power" of looks may be dispelled by other personality or interpersonal factors. For example, Sigall and Aronson (1969) attempted to identify certain mediating factors associated with physical attractiveness effects. In their investigation subjects interacted with either an attractive or an unattractive female research confederate who gave negative or positive evaluations of their performance on an experimental task. When the attractive female confederate was positive in her evaluations, she was liked the best. But when this same attractive woman gave negative evaluations, she was liked least. Unattractive women who were positive were liked better than those who were negative, and the ratings of unattractive women as a whole fell between those of the attractive women who were positive and negative. These latter findings suggest that, apart from appearance, certain interpersonal factors may mediate liking. Attractive women who are negative may not be liked or experience a beauty-is-good social milieu; unattractive women who are positive may be liked considerably more than negative but highly attractive women.

There is some possibility that there is also a process that can limit the impact of unusual praise and/or attention given to extremely attractive women. Sigall and Michela (1976), for example, demonstrated that attractive women may be suspicious of the sincerity of praise in face-to-face encounters. These investigators had an evaluator provide positive feedback to attractive and unattractive women under two experimental conditions. Essays were completed under a condition where the evaluator either had "seen" the women or was not present to see the writer (unseen condition). Evaluation (always of a positive nature) was given through an intercom mechanism, and each female subject was asked to rate the evaluator on a set of adjectives. In a comparison of the attractive seen and attractive-unseen conditions, the latter conditions resulted in the evaluator being judged as significantly more sincere, frank, genuine, and trustworthy. Furthermore, in the unattractive-seen versus unattractive-unseen condition, the evaluator was, likewise, judged as more sincere, genuine, and trustworthy. Subjects in the attractive-seen (versus attractive-unseen) condition judged the evaluator as more deceitful and manipulative, while subjects in the unattractive-unseen condition (versus unattractive-seen) rated the evaluator higher in manipulativeness.

There data suggest a social mechanism indicating that both attractive and unattractive women may be suspicious of praise when their performance is evaluated directly—that is, by people who may be influenced by their looks. Therefore, both attractive and unattractive women may hesitate to internalize praise under certain social conditions. Further, it may be difficult for these women to be sure when their actions are truly worthy of praise.

It would seem that certain interpersonal tactics might alleviate stereotype effects, or certain interpersonal styles might be used to override stereotyping consequences. But it must be recognized that much is yet to be learned about such possibilities, and that we are more at the stage of possibility than of actuality.

SOCIAL TRANSMISSION

In an earlier section of this chapter, the work of Stephen Richardson was cited as indicating that peers may act as an important transmission agent of stereotypes associated with physical handicaps and disability. If a child was observed to be in the mainstream of social communication, and if his or her peers held stereotypic assumptions about handicapped children, it was very likely that that child would show stereotypic attitudes, too. Thus, peer groups may function as transmission agents of certain social stereotypes. But how do they acquire the stereotype to begin with? I suspect there is a cross-generation mechanism that precedes peer group reinforcement of the physical attractiveness stereotype. Indeed, in two related studies a student colleague and I have been able to demonstrate that the stereotype associated with facial attractiveness may begin with the socialization practice of parents and preschool teachers (Adams & Crane, 1980).

Using photographs of white and black children who were judged to be either attractive or unattractive, we began by having preschool-age children assess which child of an attractive-unattractive comparison was judged to be the "nicer" person. Further, we asked the research subjects to indicate which of the two children they would prefer to play with, if given a chance. Next, we had the parents and preschool teachers of these same children indicate how they expected their children to respond to the same task.

In their perception responses children clearly indicated that they thought the attractive persons were nicer than the unattractive ones. However, on the play preference measure, unattractive children were chosen as frequently as attractive children. Thus, attributions, but not social preference, were operating in preschool children's use of the attractiveness information. In contrast, parents and teachers expected the children to use the stereotype in both perception and play preference situations. These data suggest that parents and teachers may be the first agents in the social transmission of the stereotype.

To gather further evidence of this possibility, in the second investigation we repeated the same research methodology, but were interested in looking at the correlation between parents' expectations and children's actual use of the stereotype. While fathers expected their children to use the stereotype in this study, the correlation between their expectations and the children's actual behavior was not significant. However, mothers' and female preschool teachers' expectations were strongly associated with the children's actual use of the physical attractiveness stereotype. Thus, women, who in some instances are more strongly affected by physical attractiveness stereotypes, may function as one of the major transmitters of the stereotype.

SPECIAL ISSUES IN ATTRACTIVENESS RESEARCH

Mediational Factors

Although measurement issues have been addressed in the research literature, there has been no attempt to develop a comprehensive model of physical attractiveness evaluations. Little is known about factors that might influence evaluations of physical appearance. However, some fascinating work offers certain hints about individual factors that are likely to mediate perceptions of beauty and interpersonal evaluations. In Figure 6.2 I have attempted to outline what might be the foundation for understanding adult judgments of aesthetic appeal. Dotted lines suggest a social psychological process, while solid lines imply a sociocultural factor.

If we can begin with the assumption that we have a reasonably universal standard of attractiveness that is learned at a relatively early age (as several studies suggest), the central foundation for the suggested model in Figure 6.2 is established. Next, it is assumed that the cultural standard of beauty has direct influences upon what is judged to be attractive, while also stimulating individuals to modify their appearance (when possible) to conform to this standard. In attempting to conform to the standard, individuals reinforce this cultural preference. Hence, when heavy individuals diet, unattractive persons learn how to use cosmetics to accentuate their desirable features, or short men purchase elevator shoes, they are accepting the standard and reinforcing its social reality. As the cultural standard of beauty is internalized into our perceptual/psychological system, it is mediated by characteristics of the individual. That is, when perceiving another and making judgments about his or her physical attractiveness, certain mediational factors can potentially moderate the cultural standard of attractiveness.

FIGURE 6.2

A Proposed Model of Physical Attractiveness Rating

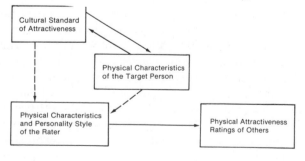

Physical Attractiveness of the Rater

What impact, if any, does an evaluator's level of physical attractiveness have upon attractiveness ratings of others? Is facial attractiveness, for example, so compelling that extremely attractive individuals are always judged as extremely attractive? Apparently the answer is no! When attractive raters evaluate others who are likewise attractive, beautiful individuals are judged as less attractive than when the raters are low in attractiveness. Indeed, there appears to be an inverse relationship between one's own attractiveness and ratings of highly attractive others. The more attractive the rater, the lower the rating given to extremely attractive persons (Paschall, 1975).

The most obvious implication is that physical attractiveness ratings are potentially mediated by self-evaluations. Thus, we need to know more about the beholder before we can understand the statement "Beauty is in the eye of the beholder." Further, what implications might this physical attractiveness mediating process have upon attribution research? At least one investigation suggests that the consequences might be extensive. Chitayat and Goodfriend (undated) summarize an investigation suggesting that the more closely subjects identify their own body build with a particular body type, the more positive the personality attributed to that body form. If an individual views himself or herself as closely identified with an ectomorph body form, for instance, the more likely he or she is to attribute socially desirable personality traits to other individuals with the same body type.

Body-ism or Face-ism?

According to the theoretical work of Erik Erikson (1968), anatomy is our destiny. That is, our bodies have unavoidable implications for our social behavior. Thus, women are incorporative and men are intrusive because of their respective anatomy. In common terms we frequently portray man as the hunter and woman as the enticer. Thus, the male uses body features to cause a physical effect, while women use their bodies to attract and captivate. Some sociological research suggests that the mass media reinforce this distinction between the sexes. Archer, Kimes, and Barrios (1978), in a study of body image in photographs found in popular magazines, demonstrated that commercial advertising clearly emphasizes faces of men and bodies of women. Furthermore, when male and female college students were asked to draw either a man or a woman, both groups emphasized faces of men and bodies of women. Also, more often than not, the female body was drawn in a sexy pose. These data suggest that when we evaluate another's degree of physical attractiveness, facial features may be emphasized for men and body type for women. Thus, an attractive woman with a poor physique may actually be rated as less attractive than an unattractive woman with a sexy body.

Personality Correlates

As factors associated with ratings of physical attractiveness, personality characteristics have generally been ignored as possible mediating variables. Yet there is clear evidence that among college students, preference (heterosexual attraction) for individual body parts is mediated by personality characteristics. For example, Wiggins, Wiggins, and Conger (1968) explored the relationship between males' personality characteristics and preference for such female body parts as breasts, buttocks, and legs. Some of the findings indicated that preference for large breasts was associated with a nonnurturant, independent, highly masculine personality profile; preference for large buttocks was characterized by orderliness, passivity, dependence, and guilt; and preference for large legs was associated with social inhibition, and preference for small legs was characterized by a need for social involvement and participation.

Further, a comparative study (Beck, Ward-Hull, & McLear, 1976) examining a female sample indicated that preference for a large-chested man was associated with social outgoingness and academic achievement; preference for large buttocks was characterized by a highly feminine, orderly, and neat personality style; and preference for large legs was associated with intraceptiveness (imaginative, subjective outlook), and preference for small legs was associated with an affiliative and socially introverted personality.

What's in a Name?

Schlenker, in his text on impression management (1980), noted that "All people control, more or less, through habit or conscious design, the ways they appear to themselves and others" (p. 7). First names are a case in point, for as Collin's (1978) has observed, the use of name *changes* in politics and show business reflects our sensitivity to the stereotyping aspect of names. Might our name influence how attractive we are seen by others? Garwood and his colleagues (1980) asked college students to select a beauty queen from among six photographs equivalent in physical attractiveness. Half of the photographs were paired with names which had been previously rated as relatively undesirable (Ethel, Harriet, and Gertrude), and half were paired with desirable names (Kathy, Jennifer, and Christine). Photographs with desirable names received 158 votes to 39 for those with undesirable names. Observers may have been indicating their preference for the names of a beauty-contest winner without implying that women with desirable names seemed more physically beautiful. Garwood and his colleagues interpret their findings, however, as suggesting that "when physical attractiveness is held constant, judgments of such attractiveness are influenced by first names" (p. 343). (On the issue of stereotypes associated with names, the references in Garwood et al. [1980] are recommended).

In conclusion, a number of factors are involved in the assessment of physical attractiveness. Attractiveness clearly has an objective basis in terms of the physical features of the target person. Yet, there is sufficient ambiguity in the judgment of attractiveness to permit other factors to exert influence, such as the attractiveness of the rater or the impact of other aspects of the target person (for example, their height or name). We are just beginning to appreciate the complex network of relationships involving attractiveness—both in terms of its impact *on* judgments and behavior and how attractiveness itself is influenced by other factors.

AN IMPORTANT RIVAL HYPOTHESIS: GOOD IS BEAUTIFUL

This chapter would be incomplete without recognizing an important line of research that questions whether beautiful persons are good or the good are beautiful. That is, might it be possible that personality characteristics are stronger determinants of perceived beauty than perceived beauty is predictive of personality? In one of the first tests of the good-is-beautiful hypothesis, Gross and Crofton (1977) found that research subjects perceived female students as more attractive if they had received a favorable description of their personality. Owens and Ford (1978) replicated these findings for females, but were unable to find the same relationship for males. In my doctoral dissertation I was able to identify a similar relationship. When comparing attractiveness ratings completed by oneself and others, self-ratings were found to be correlated with various socially desirable personality characteristics (Adams, 1977b). However, self-ratings were not strongly correlated with ratings provided by peer evaluations.

Therefore, all of these investigations may suffer from a confounding effect associated with social desirability tendencies. It is also unfortunate that although additional confirmation of the Gross and Crofton study continues to emerge (such as Felson & Bohrnstedt, 1979; Campbell, 1979), none of these investigations have used peer-evaluated attractiveness ratings or objective measures of personality or social behavior. Nonetheless, it remains possible that there is a chained association between ability and self-perceived attractiveness, whereby ability determines attractiveness and self-perceived attractiveness increases ability.

SUMMARY AND FUTURE PROSPECTS

The study of physical attractiveness stereotypes has broadened into various research contexts. The early efforts of constitutional psychologists brought attention to the importance of physical appearance. However, it was not until a social determinist perspective emerged that the study of physical appearance blossomed as a credible research field. Most of the contemporary study of appearance has focused upon physical attractiveness stereotypes. In this chapter particular attention has been given to facial attractiveness and the study of physical handicaps as a special example of unattractiveness.

Previous research has utilized measurement techniques that focus upon a global, subjective assessment of physical attractiveness, or manipulate attractiveness through cosmetic modification or unbecoming costumes. Correlational data assessing the relationship between individual attractiveness and social or personality characteristics have suggested that the beauty-is-good and ugliness-is-bad hypotheses have some element of truth. Furthermore, experimental studies assessing the effects of laboratory manipulations of physical appearance on social behavior that suggest behavioral correlates can be demonstrated for the physical attractiveness stereotype. This evidence has been integrated into what has been called a "developmental social psychological" perspective. That is, physical attractiveness stereotype effects begin with simple person-perception effects, but proceed to channel social interaction in ways that lead to a "self-fulfilling prophecy" effect. While much is yet to be learned through experimental studies, observational investigations, and social surveys, available data suggest that physical attractiveness stereotypes can influence perceptions, channel behavior, affect personality development, and predict social behavior of attractive and unattractive individuals.

Further research is, in particular, needed to understand how the physical attractiveness stereotype is transmitted from one generation to the next, and how unattractive individuals (normal or handicapped) can "break through" the channeling effects of a physical attractiveness stereotype into normal social interaction. Perhaps by identifying the major sources of transmission of the stereotype, efforts can be directed at mediating such influences. Also, research might focus directly upon how to diminish stereotyping effects in interpersonal contexts. Much is currently known about the stereotype, but continuing efforts need to be directed at understanding the "social dynamics" of the stereotype. In many ways the study of the physical attractiveness stereotype is "theory"-poor. With the exception of the "developmental social psychological" perspective, there has been little major attempt to develop an integrated series of theoretical propositions that are empirically testable. Therefore, both theory construction and hypothesis testing must be undertaken with the recognition that the social psychology of beauty has yet to find its foundation in an integrated theoretical perspective.

REFERENCES

Adams, G. R. Physical attractiveness: Toward a developmental social psychology of beauty. *Human Development*, 1977, *20*, 217–230. (a)

Adams, G. R. Physical attractiveness, personality, and social reactions to peer pressure. *Journal of Psychology*, 1977, *96*, 287–296. (b)

Adams, G. R. Social psychology of physical appearance: A dialectic-interactional perspective. Paper presented at the symposium "Conference on the Social Psychology of Physical Deviance," Dartmouth College, 1979. (a)

Adams, G. R. Beautiful is good: A test of the "kernel of truth" hypothesis. Submitted manuscript, 1979. (b)

Adams, G. R., & Cohen, A. S. Children's physical and interpersonal characteristics that affect student-teacher interactions. *Journal of Experimental Education*, 1974, *43*, 1–5.

Adams, G. R., & Crane, P. An assessment of parents' and teachers' expectations of preschool children's social preference for attractive or unattractive children and adults. *Child Development*, 1980, *51*, 224–231.

Adams, G. R., & Crossman, S. M. *Physical attractiveness: A cultural imperative.* Roslyn Heights, N.Y.: Libra, 1978.

Adams, G. R., & Huston, T. L. Social perception of middle-aged persons varying in physical attractiveness. *Developmental Psychology*, 1975, *11*, 657–658.

Adams, G. R., & LaVoie, J. C. Parental expectations of educational and personal-social performance and childrearing patterns as a function of attractiveness, sex, and conduct of child. *Child Study Journal*, 1975, *5*, 125–142.

Adams, G. R., & LaVoie, J. C. Teacher expectations: A review of the student characteristics used in expectancy formation. *Journal of Instructional Psychology*, 1977, *4*, 1–28.

Allport, F. H. *Social psychology.* New York: Johnson Reprint, 1967.

Archer, D., Kimes, D. D., & Barrios, M. Face-ism. *Psychology Today*, September 1978, pp. 65–66.

Baker, M. J., & Churchill, G. A. The impact of physically attractive models on advertising evaluations. *Journal of Marketing Research*, 1977, *14*, 538–555.

Barocas, R., & Vance, F. L. Physical appearance and personal adjustment. Paper presented at the Eastern Psychological Association convention, Philadelphia, 1974.

Bar-Tal, D., & Saxe, L. Effect of physical attractiveness on the perception of couples. Paper presented at the meeting of the American Psychological Association convention, New Orleans, August, 1974.

Beck, S. B., Ward-Hull, C. I., & McLear, P. M. Variables related to women's somatic preferences of the male and female body. *Journal of Personality and Social Psychology*, 1976, *34*, 1200–1210.

Benson, P. L., Karabenick, S. A., & Lerner, R. M. Pretty pleases: The effects of physical attractiveness, race, and sex on receiving help. *Journal of Experimental Social Psychology*, 1976, *12*, 409–415.

Berkowitz, L., & Frodi, A. Reactions to a child's mistakes as affected by her/his looks and speech. *Social Psychology Quarterly*, 1979, *42*, 420–425.

Berscheid, E., Dion, K., Walster, E., & Walster, G. W. Physical attractiveness and dating choice: A test of the matching hypothesis. *Journal of Experimental Social Psychology*, 1971, *7*, 173–180.

Berscheid, E., & Walster, E. Physical attractiveness. In L. Berkowitz (ed.), *Advances in experimental social psychology* (Vol. 7). New York: Academic Press, 1974.

Brislin, R. W., & Lewis, S. A. Dating and physical attractiveness: Replication. *Psychological Reports*, 1968, *22*, 976.

Brundage, L. E., Derlega, V. J., & Cash, T. F. The effects of physical attractiveness and need for approval on self-disclosure. *Personality and Social Psychology Bulletin*, 1977, *3*, 63–66.

Byrne, D., Ervin, C., & Lamberth, J. Continuity between the experimental study of attraction and real-life computer dating. *Journal of Personality and Social Psychology*, 1970, *16*, 157–165.

Campbell, R. T. The relationship between children's perceptions of ability and perception of physical attractiveness: Comment on Felson and Bohrnstedt's "Are the good beautiful or the beautiful good?" *Social Psychology Quarterly*, 1979, *42*, 393–398.

Cash, T. F. Behavioral science and the benefits of beauty. Invited address at the New York Symposium on Cosmetic Benefits, November 16, 1979.

Cash, T. F., Begley, P. J., McCown, D. A., & Weise, B. C. When counselors are heard but not seen: Initial impact of physical attractiveness. *Journal of Counseling Psychology*, 1975, *22*, 273–279.

Cash, T. F., & Derlega, V. J. The matching hypothesis: Physical attractiveness among same-sexed friends. *Personality and Social Psychology Bulletin*, 1978, *4*, 240–243.

Cash, T. F., Gillen, B., & Burns, D. S. Sexism and "beautyism" in personnel consultant decision making. *Journal of Applied Psychology*, 1977, *62*, 301–310.

Cash, T. F., & Kehr, J. Influence of nonprofessional counselors' physical attractiveness and sex on perceptions of counselor behavior. *Journal of Counseling Psychology*, 1978, *25*, 336–342.

Cash, T. F., Kehr, J., Polyson, J., & Freeman, V. Role of physical attractiveness in peer attribution of psychological disturbance. *Journal of Consulting and Clinical Psychology*, 1977, *45*, 987–993.

Cash, T. F., & Salzbach, R. F. The beauty of counseling: Effects of counselor physical attractiveness and self-disclosure on perceptions of counselor behavior. *Journal of Counseling Psychology*, 1978, *25*, 283–291.

Cash, T. F., & Soloway, D. Self-disclosure correlates of physical attractiveness: An exploratory study. *Psychological Reports*, 1975, *36*, 579–586.

Cavior, N., & Boblett, P. J. *Physical attractiveness of dating versus married couples.* Proceedings of the 80th Annual Convention of the American Psychological Association, 1972, *1*, 175–176.

Cavior, N., Jacobs, A., & Jacobs, M. The stability and correlation of physical attractiveness and sex appeal ratings. Unpublished manuscript, West Virginia University, 1974.

Chaiken, S. Communicator physical attractiveness and persuasion. *Journal of Personality and Social Psychology*, 1979, *37*, 1387–1397.

Chitayat, D., & Goodfriend, R. Self-perception in body type stereotyping. Unpublished manuscript. CASE Institute for Research and Development, Graduate School and University Center, City University of New York.

Clayson, D. E., & Maugham, M. Blond is beautiful: Status and preference by hair color. Paper presented at the Rocky Mountain Psychological Association convention, Phoenix, Arizona, 1976.

Clifford, M. M. Physical attractiveness and academic performance. *Child Study Journal*, 1975, *5*, 201–209.

Clifford, M. M., & Walster, E. The effect of physical attractiveness on teacher expectations. *Sociology of Education*, 1973, *46*, 248–258.

Collins, L. A name to conjure with. *European Journal of Marketing*, 1978, *11*, 339–363.

Comer, R. J. & Piliavin. J. A. The effects of physical deviance upon face-to-face interaction: The other side. *Journal of Personality and Social Psychology*, 1972, *23*, 33–39.

Corter, C., Trehub, S., Boukydis, C., Ford, L., Celhoffer, L., & Minde, K. Nurses' judgments of the attractiveness of premature infants. *Infant Behavior and Development*, 1978, *1*, 373–380.

Critelli, J. W. Physical attractiveness of dating couples. Paper presented at the meeting of the American Psychological Association, Chicago, September, 1975.

Cross, J. F., & Cross, J. Age, sex, race, and the perception of facial beauty. *Developmental Psychology*, 1971, *5*, 433–439.

Curran, J. P. Correlates of physical attractiveness and interpersonal attraction in the dating situation. *Social Behavior and Personality*, 1973, *1*, 153–157.

Curran, J. P., & Lippold, S. The effects of physical attraction and attitude similarity on attraction in dating dyads. *Journal of Personality*, 1975, *43*, 528–539.

Dabbs, J. M., & Stokes, N. A. Beauty is power: The use of space on the sidewalk. *Sociometry*, 1975, *38*, 551–557.

Davis, D., Rainey, H. G., & Brock, T. C. Interpersonal physical pleasuring: Effects of sex combinations, recipient attributes, and anticipated future interaction. *Journal of Personality and Social Psychology*, 1976, *33*, 89–106.

Dermer, M., & Thiel, D. L. When beauty may fail. *Journal of Personality and Social Psychology*, 1975, *31*, 1168–1176.

Dion, K. Physical attractiveness and evaluation of children's transgressions. *Journal of Personality and Social Psychology*, 1972, *24*, 207–213.

Dion, K. K. Young children's stereotyping of facial attractiveness. *Developmental Psychology*, 1973, *9*, 183–188.

Dion, K. K. Children's physical attractiveness and sex as a determinant of adult punitiveness. *Developmental Psychology*, 1974, *10*, 772–778.

Dion, K. K. The incentive value of physical attractiveness for young children. *Personality and Social Psychology Bulletin*, 1977, *3*, 67–70.

Dion, K. K., & Berscheid, E. Physical attractiveness and peer perception among children. *Sociometry*, 1974, *37*, 1–12.

Dion, K., Berscheid, E., & Walster, E. What is beautiful is good. *Journal of Personality and Social Psychology*, 1972, *24*, 285–290.

Dion, K. K., & Stein, S. Physical attractiveness and interpersonal influence. *Journal of Experimental Social Psychology*, 1978, *14*, 97–108.

Dipboye, R. L., Fromkin, H. L., & Wiback, K. Relative importance of applicant sex, attractiveness, and scholastic standing in evaluation of job applicant resumes. *Journal of Applied Psychology*, 1975, *60*, 39–43.

Efran, M. G. The effect of physical appearance on the judgment of guilt, interpersonal attraction, and severity of recommended punishment in a simulated jury task. *Journal of Research in Personality*, 1974, *8*, 45–54.

Elder, G. H. Appearance and education in marriage mobility. *American Sociological Review*, 1969, *35*, 519–533.

Erikson, E. H. *Identity: Youth and crisis.* New York: Norton, 1968.

Felson, R. B. Physical attractiveness, grades and teachers' attributions of ability. *Representative Research in Social Psychology*, 1980, *11*, 64–71.

Felson, R. B., & Bohrnstedt, G. W. "Are the good beautiful or the beautiful good?" The relationship between children's perceptions of ability and perceptions of physical attractiveness. *Social Psychology Quarterly*, 1979, *42*, 386–392.

Friend, R., & Vinson, M. Leaning over backwards: Jurors' responses to defendants' attractiveness. *Journal of Communication*, 1974, *3*, 124–129.

Fugita, S. S., Agle, T. A., Newman, I., & Walfish, N. Attractiveness, self-concept, and a methodological note about gaze behavior. *Personality and Social Psychology Bulletin*, 1977, *3*, 240–243.

Garwood, S. G., Cox, L, Kaplan, V., Wasserman, N., & Zulzer, J. L. Beauty is only "name" deep: The effect of first-name on ratings of physical attraction. *Journal of Applied Social Psychology*, 1980, *10*, 431–435.

Gillis, J. S., & Avis, W. E. The male-taller norm in mate selection. *Personality and Social Psychology Bulletin*, 1980, *6*, 396–401.

Goffman, E. On cooling the mark out: Some aspects of adaptation to failure. *Psychiatry*, 1952, *15*, 451–463.

Goffman, E. *Stigma: Notes on the management of spoiled identity.* Englewood Cliffs, N.J.: Prentice-Hall, 1963.

Goldberg, P. A., Gottesdiener, M., & Abramson, P. R. Another put-down of women? Perceived attractiveness as a function of support for the feminist movement. *Journal of Personality and Social Psychology*, 1975, *32*, 113–115.

Goldman, W., & Lewis, P. Beautiful is good: Evidence that the physically attractive are more socially skillful. *Journal of Experimental Social Psychology*, 1977, *13*, 125–130.

Gross, A., & Crofton, C. What is good is beautiful. *Sociometry*, 1977, *40*, 85–90.

Hartnett, J., & Elder, D. The princess and the nice frog: Study in person perception. *Perceptual and Motor Skills*, 1973, *37*, 863–866.

Hastorf, A. H., Northcraft, G. B., & Picciotto, S. R. Helping the handicapped: How realistic is the performance feedback received by the physically handicapped? *Personality and Social Psychology Bulletin*, 1979, *5*, 373–376.

Hastorf, A. H., Wildfogel, J., & Cassman, T. Acknowledgment of handicap as a tactic in social interaction. *Journal of Personality and Social Psychology*, 1979, *37*, 1790–1798.

Heilman, M. E., & Saruwatari, L. R. When beauty is beastly: The effects of appearance and sex on evaluations of job applicants for managerial and nonmanagerial jobs. *Organizational Behavior and Human Performance*, 1979, *23*, 360–372.

Hildebrandt, K. A., & Fitzgerald, H. E. Gender bias in observers' perception of infants' sex: Boys most of the time. *Perceptual and Motor Skills*, 1977, *45*, 472–474.

Hildebrandt, K. A., & Fitzgerald, H. E. Adults' responses to infants varying in perceived cuteness. *Behavioral Processes*, 1978, *3*, 159–172.

Hildebrandt, K. A., & Fitzgerald, H. E. Adults' perceptions of infant sex and cuteness. *Sex Roles*, 1979, *5*, 471–481. (a)

Hildebrandt, K. A., & Fitzgerald, H. E. Facial feature determinants of perceived infant attractiveness. *Infant Behavior and Development*, 1979, *2*, 329–339. (b)

Hildebrandt, K. A., & Fitzgerald, H. E. Mothers' responses to infant physical appearance. *Infant Mental Health Journal*, in press.

Hobfoll, S. E., & Penner, L. A. Effect of physical attractiveness on therapists' initial judgments of a person's self-concept. *Journal of Consulting and Clinical Psychology*, 1978, *46*, 200–201.

Horai, J., Naccari, N., & Fatoullah, E. The effects of expertise and physical attractiveness upon opinion agreement and liking. *Sociometry*, 1974, *37*, 601–606.

Huston, T. L. Ambiguity of acceptance, social desirability, and dating choice. *Journal of Experimental Social Psychology*, 1973, *9*, 32–42.

Jackson, D., & Huston, T. L. Physical attractiveness and assertiveness. *Journal of Social Psychology*, 1975, *96*, 79–84.

Johnson, R. W., Doiron, D., Brooks, G., & Dickinson, J. Perceived attractiveness as a function of support for the feminist movement: Not necessarily a put-down of women. *Canadian Journal of Behavioral Science*, 1978, *10*, 214–221.

Johnson, R. W., Holborn, S. W., & Turcotte, S. Perceived attractiveness as a function of active vs. passive support for the feminist movement. *Personality and Social Psychology Bulletin*, 1979, *5*, 227–230.

Kagan, J., Henker, B. A., Hen-Tov, A., Levine, J., & Lewis, M. Infants' differential reactions to familiar and distorted faces. *Child Development*, 1966, *37*, 519–532.

Kahn, A., Hottes, J., & Davis, W. L. Cooperation and optimal responding in the prisoner's dilemma game: Effects of sex and physical attractiveness. *Journal of Personality and Social Psychology*, 1971, *17*, 267–279.

Kenrick, D. T., & Gutierres, S. E. Contrast effects and judgments of physical attractiveness: When beauty becomes a social problem. *Journal of Personality and Social Psychology*, 1980, *38*, 131–140.

Kerr, N. L. Beautiful and blameless: Effects of victim attractiveness and responsibility on mock jurors' verdicts. *Personality and Social Psychology Bulletin*, 1978, *4*, 479–482.

Kleck, R. Emotional arousal in interactions with stigmatized persons. *Psychological Reports*, 1966, *19*, 1126.

Kleck, R. Physical stigma and task oriented interactions. *Human Relations*, 1969, *22*, 53–60.

Kleck, R. E. Issues in social effectiveness: The case of the mentally retarded. In J. J. Begab & S. A. Richardson (eds.), *The mentally retarded and society: A social science perspective*. Baltimore: University Park Press, 1975.

Kleck, R., & DeJong, W. Physical attractiveness, deviant physical characteristics, and sociometric status in children. Submitted manuscript.

Kleck, R., Ono, H., & Hastorf, A. H. The effects of physical deviance upon face-to-face interaction. *Human Relations*, 1966, *19*, 425–436.

Kleck, R. E., Richardson, S. A., & Ronald, L. Physical appearance cues and interpersonal attraction in children. *Child Development*, 1974, *45*, 305–310.

Kleck, R. E., & Rubenstein, C. Physical attractiveness, perceived attitude similarity, and interpersonal attraction in an opposite-sex encounter. *Journal of Personality and Social Psychology*, 1975, *31*, 107–114.

Kleck, R. E., & Strenta, A. Perceptions of the impact of negatively valued physical characteristics on social interaction. *Journal of Personality and Social Psychology*, 1980, *39*, 861–873.

Korda, M. *Success!* New York: Random House, 1977.

Krebs, D., & Adinolfi, A. A. Physical attractiveness, social relations, and personality style. *Journal of Personality and Social Psychology*, 1975, *31*, 245–253.

Kretschmer, E. *Physique and character*. New York: Harcourt, 1925.

Kulka, R. A., & Kessler, J. B. Is justice really blind?—The influence of litigant physical attractiveness on juridical judgment. *Journal of Applied Social Psychology*, 1978, *8*, 366–381.

Landy, D., & Sigall, H. Beauty is talent: Task evaluation as a function of the performer's physical attractiveness. *Journal of Personality and Social Psychology*, 1974, *29*, 299–304.

Langer, E. J., Fiske, S., Taylor, S. E., & Chanowitz, B. Stigma, staring, and discomfort: A novel-stimulus hypothesis. *Journal of Experimental Social Psychology*, 1976, *12*, 451–463.

Langlois, J. H., & Stephan, C. The effects of physical attractiveness and ethnicity on children's behavioral attributions and peer preferences. *Child Development*, 1977, *48*, 1694–1698.

LaVoie, J. C., & Adams, G. R. Physical and interpersonal attractiveness of the model and imitation in adults. *Journal of Social Psychology*, 1978, *106*, 191–202.

Lerner, R. M., & Lerner, J. V. Effects of age, sex, and physical attractiveness on child-peer relations, academic performance, and elementary school adjustment. *Developmental Psychology*, 1977, *13*, 585–590.

Leventhal, G., & Krate, R. Physical attractiveness and severity of sentencing. *Psychological Reports*, 1977, *40*, 315–318.

Lombroso, C. *The man of genius*. London: Scott, 1891.

MacGregor, F. C. *Transformation and identity: The face and plastic surgery*. New York: Quadrangle, 1974.

MacGregor, F. C. *After plastic surgery: Adaptation and adjustment*. New York: J. F. Bergin, 1979.

MacGregor, F. M. C., Abel, T. M., Bryt, A., Lauer, E., & Weissmann, S. *Facial deformities and plastic surgery: A psychological study*. Springfield, Ill.: Charles Thomas, 1953.

Maruyama, G., & Miller, N. Physical attractiveness, race, and essay evaluation. *Personality and Social Psychology Bulletin*, 1980, *6*, 384–390.

Mathes, E. W. The effects of physical attractiveness and anxiety on heterosexual attraction over a series of five encounters. *Journal of Marriage and the Family*, 1975, *37*, 769–774.

McDonald, P. J., & Eilenfield, V. C. Physical attractiveness and the approach/avoidance of self-awareness. *Personality and Social Psychology Bulletin*, 1980, *6*, 391–395.

McGarry, M. S., & West, S. G. Stigma among the stigmatized: Resident mobility, communication ability, and physical appearance as predictors of staff-resident interaction. *Journal of Abnormal Psychology*, 1975, *84*, 399–405.

McLuhan, M. *Understanding media*. New York: McGraw-Hill, 1964.

Meiners, M. L., & Sheposh, J. P. Beauty or brains: Which image for your mate? Paper presented at annual convention of the American Psychological Association, Washington, D.C., 1976.

Miller, A. G. Social perception of internal-external control. *Perceptual and Motor Skills*, 1970, *30*, 103–106. (a)

Miller, A. G. Role of physical attractiveness in impression formation. *Psychonomic Science*, 1970, *19*, 241–243. (b)

Millman, M. *Such a pretty face: Being fat in America*. New York: Norton, 1979.

Morse, S. J., Reis, H. T., Gruzen, J., & Wolff, E. The "eye of the beholder": Determinants of physical attractiveness judgments in the U.S. and South Africa. *Journal of Personality*, 1974, *42*, 528–542.

Murstein, B. I. Physical attractiveness and marital choice. *Journal of Personality and Social Psychology*, 1972, *22*, 8–12.

Murstein, B. I., & Christy, P. Physical attractiveness and marriage adjustment in middle-aged couples. *Journal of Personality and Social Psychology*, 1976, *34*, 537–542.

Nadler, A. "Good looks do not help": Effects of helper's physical attractiveness, and expectations for future interaction on help-seeking behavior. *Personality and Social Psychology Bulletin*, 1980, *6*, 378–383.

Owens, G., & Ford, J. G. Further consideration of the "What is Good is Beautiful" finding. *Social Psychology Quarterly*, 1978, *41*, 73–75.

Paschall, N. C. Effects of raters' own physical attractiveness on rating others' attractiveness. Paper presented at the meeting of the American Psychological Association, Chicago, 1975.

Peplau, L. A. Sex, love, and the double standard. Paper presented at the meeting of the American Psychological Association, Washington, D.C., 1976.

Piliavin, I. M., Piliavin, J. A., & Rodin, J. Costs, diffusion, and the stigmatized victim. *Journal of Personality and Social Psychology*, 1975, *32*, 429–438.

Reis, H. T., Nezlek, J., & Wheeler, L. Physical attractiveness in social interaction. *Journal of Personality and Social Psychology*, 1980, *38*, 604–617.

Richardson, S. A. Children's values and friendships: A study of physical disability. *Journal of Health and Social Behavior*, 1971, *12*, 253–258.

Richardson, S. A. Attitudes and behavior toward the physically handicapped. *Birth Defects: Original Articles Series*, 1976, *12*, 15–34.

Richardson, S. A., & Friedman, M. J. Social factors related to children's accuracy in learning peer group values towards handicaps. *Human Relations*, 1972, *26*, 77–87.

Richardson, S. A., Goodman, N., Hastorf, A. H., & Dornbusch, S. M. Cultural uniformity in reaction to physical disabilities. *American Sociological Review*, 1961, *26*, 241–247.

Richardson, S. A., Ronald, L., & Kleck, R. E. The social status of handicapped and nonhandicapped boys in a camp setting. *Journal of Special Education*, 1974, *8*, 143–152.

Rodin, J. Research on eating behavior and obesity: Where does it fit in personality and social psychology? *Personality and Social Psychology Bulletin,* 1977, *3,* 333–354.

Schlenker, B. R. *Impression management.* Monterey, Calif.: Brooks/Cole, 1980.

Schneider, D. Implicit personality theory: A review. *Psychological Bulletin,* 1973, *79,* 294–309.

Seligman, C., Brickman, J., & Koulack, D. Rape and physical attractiveness: Assigning responsibility to victims. *Journal of Personality,* 1977, *45,* 554–563.

Shea, J. A., & Adams, G. R. Correlates of male and female romantic attachments: A path analysis study. Submitted manuscript, 1979.

Sheldon, W. H. *The varieties of human physique: An introduction to constitutional psychology.* New York: Harper, 1940.

Shettel-Neuber, J., Bryson, J. B., & Young, L. E. Physical attractiveness of the "other person" and jealousy. *Personality and Social Psychology Bulletin,* 1978, *4,* 612–615.

Sigall, H., & Aronson, E. Liking for an evaluator as a function of her physical attractiveness and nature of the evaluations. *Journal of Experimental Social Psychology,* 1969, *5,* 93–100.

Sigall, H., & Landy, D. Radiating beauty: The effects of having a physically attractive partner on person perception. *Journal of Personality and Social Psychology,* 1973, *28,* 218–224.

Sigall, H., & Michela, J. I'll bet you say that to all the girls: Physical attractiveness and reactions to praise. *Journal of Personality,* 1976, *44,* 611–626.

Sigall, H., & Ostrove, N. Beautiful but dangerous: Effects of offender attractiveness and nature of the crime on juridic judgment. *Journal of Personality and Social Psychology,* 1975, *31,* 410–414.

Singer, J. E. The use of manipulative strategies: Machiavellianism and attractiveness. *Sociometry,* 1964, *27,* 128–150.

Smith, G., & Engel, R. Influence of a female model on perceived characteristics of an automobile. Paper presented at the meeting of the American Psychological Association, San Francisco, 1968.

Snyder, M. On the self-perpetuating nature of social stereotypes. In D. L. Hamilton (ed.), *Cognitive processes in stereotyping and intergroup behavior.* Hillsdale, N.J.: Erlbaum, 1981.

Snyder, M., Kleck, R., Strenta, A., & Mentzer, S. J. Avoidance of the handicapped: An attributional ambiguity analysis. *Journal of Personality and Social Psychology,* 1979, *37,* 2297–2306.

Snyder, M., Tanke, E. D., & Berscheid, E. Social perception and interpersonal behavior: On the self-fulfilling nature of social stereotypes. *Journal of Personality and Social Psychology,* 1977, *35,* 656–666.

Solomon, M. R., & Schopler, J. The relationship of physical attractiveness and punitiveness: Is the linearity assumption out of line? *Personality and Social Psychology Bulletin,* 1978, *4,* 483–486.

Sontag, S. The double standard of aging. *Saturday Review,* September 29, 1972, p. 38.

Sontag, S. A woman's beauty: Put down or power source? *Vogue,* 1975, *165,* 118–119.

Sparacino, J., & Hansell, S. Physical attractiveness and academic performance: Beauty is not always talent. *Journal of Personality,* 1979, *47,* 449–469.

Sroufe, R., Chaikin, A., Cook, R., & Freeman, V. The effects of physical attractiveness on honesty: A socially desirable response. *Personality and Social Psychology Bulletin*, 1977, *3*, 59–62.

Stabler, B., Whitt, J. K., Moreault, D. M., D'Ercole, A. J., & Underwood, L. E. Social alertness in short stature children. Unpublished manuscript, University of North Carolina School of Medicine, undated.

Staffieri, J. R. A study of social stereotype of body image in children. *Journal of Personality and Social Psychology*, 1967, *7*, 101–104.

Stewart, J. E. Defendant's attractiveness as a factor in the outcome of criminal trials: An observational study. *Journal of Applied Social Psychology*, 1980, *10*, 348–361.

Stokes, S. J., & Bickman, L. The effect of the physical attractiveness and role of the helper on help seeking. *Journal of Applied Social Psychology*, 1974, *4*, 286–294.

Storck, J. T., & Sigall, H. Effect of a harm-doer's attractiveness and the victim's history of prior victimization on punishment of the harm-doer. *Personality and Social Psychology Bulletin*, 1979, *5*, 344–347.

Styczynski, L. E., & Langlois, J. H. The effects of familiarity on behavioral stereotypes associated with physical attractiveness in young children. *Child Development*, 1977, *48*, 1137–1141.

Taylor, P. A., & Glenn, N. D. The utility of education and attractiveness for females' status attainment through marriage. *American Sociological Review*, 1976, *41*, 484–498.

Touhey, J. C. Sex-role stereotyping and individual differences in liking for the physically attractive. *Social Psychology Quarterly*, 1979, *42*, 285–289.

Valentine, C. W. *The experimental psychology of beauty*. London: Methuen, 1962.

Van Leer, T. University doctors wield a sword of healing light. *Deseret News* (Salt Lake City), January 12, 1980, p.1.

Walker, R. M. Body build and behavior in young children: I. Body build and nursery school teachers' ratings. *Monographs of the Society for Research in Child Development*, 1962, *27*, no. 84, entire issue.

Walker, R. M. Body build and behavior in young children. II. Body build and parents' ratings. *Child Development*, 1963, *34*, 1–23.

Walster, E., Aronson, V., Abrahams, D., & Rottman, L. Importance of physical attractiveness in dating behavior. *Journal of Personality and Social Psychology*, 1966, *4*, 508–516.

West, S. G., & Hodge, P. G. Physical attractiveness, blindness (dependency), and helping. Paper presented at the Southeastern Psychological Association, Atlanta, 1975.

Wettenhall, H. W. B., Cahill, C., & Roche, A. F. Tall girls: A survey of 15 years of management and treatment. *Journal of Pediatrics*, 1975, *86*, 602–610.

Wiggins, J. S., Wiggins, N., & Conger, J. C. Correlates of heterosexual somatic preference. *Journal of Personality and Social Psychology*, 1968, *10*, 82–90.

Wilson, G., & Nias, D. Beauty can't be beat. *Psychology Today*, September, 1976, pp. 96–98.

Wilson, M., Cash, T. F., & West, S. G. Divergent effects of physical attractiveness on impression formation as a function of the situational context. Paper presented at the Eastern Psychological Association convention, Washington, D.C., April, 1978.

ADDITIONAL READINGS

Adams, G. R., & Crossman, S. M. *Physical attractiveness: A cultural imperative.* Roslyn Heights, N.Y.: Libra, 1978.

As a text written for popular consumption, or to be used as a supplemental text for a course in interpersonal attraction, this book provides an interface between social psychological research and public commentary. The effects of social stereotypes in several contexts are reviewed. Potential sex differences in the meaning of physical attractiveness are explored. The reality of channeling effects upon nonverbal behavior, social reinforcement, and interpersonal exchange are highlighted. A whimsical examination of the relationship between contemporary advertising and various dimensions of physical attractiveness is included.

Berscheid, E., & Walster, E. Physical attractiveness. In L. Berkowitz (ed.), *Advances in experimental social psychology* (Vol. 7). New York: Academic Press, 1974.

The first major review of physical attractiveness research, this offers an excellent overview of psychological research directed at the study of physical attractiveness. In particular, in relationship to this chapter, it offers a sense of continuity in research both prior to and after 1974. The authors provide a number of very stimulating suggestions for future research and examine several minitheories of psychology as they apply to the study of physical attractiveness.

Friedman, M. *Buried alive: The biography of Janis Joplin.* New York: William Morrow, 1973.

An examination of the life of a contemporary rock star, this volume provides an insightful illustration of the effect that self perceptions of physical attractiveness can have upon social behavior. In particular, it provides an important example of the potential destructiveness of a physical attractiveness stereotype upon an individual in the "limelight" and always "upfront." The biographic material provides information about self-perceptions associated with body image during childhood, adolescence, and adulthood.

Huston, T. L., & Levinger, G. Interpersonal attraction and relationships. In M. R. Rosenzweig & L. W. Porter (eds.), *Annual review of psychology.* Palo Alto, Calif.: Annual Reviews, Inc., 1978.

Within the broader framework of interpersonal attraction, this reading offers an overview of the physical attractiveness research within the context of heterosexual involvement. Particular attention is given to the relationship between physical attractiveness and similarity as important influences of attraction.

Katz, I. Some thoughts about the stigma notion. *Personality and Social Psychology Bulletin*, 1979, 5, 447–460.

An extension of Goffman's notion of stigma is provided through an examination of three causal models of the stigmatization process. These models focus upon attribute-as-cause, labeling, and scapegoating. Illustrations from physical disability, mental illness, and other stereotyping research are used throughout to provide clarity and insight.

Sontag, S. The double standard of aging. *Saturday Review*, September 29, 1972, p. 38.
A pointed portrayal of the relationship between the beauty "syndrome" and aging effects is presented in both cutting and insightful ways. The author is quick to recognize the distinction between the power of beauty and the source from which this power is obtained. An excellent illustration of the potential "tyranny of looks" as it applies to the female.

7

THE STIGMA OF MENTAL DISORDERS

Amerigo Farina

PAST CONCEPTIONS OF MENTAL DISORDERS, AND THE CARE AND TREATMENT ACCORDED SUFFERERS

For nearly 3000 years the belief that devils and other supernatural creatures are responsible for mental disorders has prevailed in Western society. At the time of Homer it was supposed that gods had taken the sufferer's mind away (Zilboorg & Henry, 1941, p. 37). The popular name for the mentally disordered during classical Roman times was *larvatus* (full of phantoms). And during the years 1400 to 1750 it was widely believed that demons were everywhere, and caused people to become mad by possessing them. It was clergymen who thereafter faced the problem of driving those devils out. Exorcisms are still practiced by some religious denominations and are of great interest to people in general, as indicated by the popularity of *The Exorcist*, a movie released in the mid-1970s that featured such an event.

The mentally disturbed almost always have been viewed with extreme disfavor and have been treated badly. Typically the afflicted person was held to be unclean, mysterious, and not a part of the natural worldly processes. He—more frequently, she—was considered no longer human. For example, during certain periods "lunatics" were thought to be totally insensitive to cold, perhaps like a cold-blooded snake (Deutsch, 1965, p. 159). They were kept in unheated quarters, even in the winter.

At times this social disfavor expressed itself in more than malevolent neglect. The mentally ill were actively sought, persecuted, imprisoned, and tortured in the most imaginative and horrible ways. Even in the classical Hellenistic period they were at times driven away from healing temples with stones (Zilboorg & Henry, 1941, p. 38). Those who wandered the countryside were subject to beatings, both to be rid of them and for sheer amusement (Deutsch, 1965, p. 45). But especially during the sixteenth century their lot was ghastly, since the busy witch-hunters accepted the most common of the symptoms of mental disorder as proof of demonic possession. Once a sufferer was apprehended, he or she could expect torture, and often death by being burned alive.

The methods that have been employed over the years to treat the mentally disordered have two salient characteristics. The procedures have been exceedingly heterogeneous, and they have been most unpleasant (Deutsch, 1965; Zilboorg & Henry, 1941). It is as if society felt obligated to do something, but also felt that what was done should be in keeping with the demonic and inhuman nature of the deranged. These "therapies" have included physical assaults: beatings, whippings, blistering the shaved head, burning, and scarring fingers. Surgically the mentally disordered have had lengths of intestines removed and teeth pulled, they have been castrated, hysterectomies have been performed, the clitoris has been cauterized, they have had animal blood transfused into their veins, and their own blood has been removed in such prodigious quantities that patients not infrequently died as a result of the treatment (Zilboorg & Henry, 1941, pp. 261–262).

Fear was thought to be beneficial, and was induced by an appalling mixture of practices. Sufferers were led to believe they would be killed, they were held under water until they lost consciousness, and elaborate scenarios were staged to make them think they had seen ghosts. They were at times given enemas with debilitating frequency, and a profusion of substances were administered to induce vomiting and bowel movements. Magical procedures, such as calling the possessing demon evil names to dislodge it, were frequently used, and while these treatments were less noxious, they were not pleasant. Perhaps the most commonly used nonmagical and nontheological treatments were emetics to make them vomit, purgatives to thoroughly empty their bowels, and bloodletting (Zilboorg & Henry, 1941, p. 262).

Where did the mentally deranged eat and sleep during these past years? Quite surely a large but undeterminable proportion of people whom we would now label "mentally ill" wandered the countryside and had no certain home. The kind of life they led is indicated by a 1756 entry in the *Public Records of Connecticut* (Deutsch, 1965, p. 46): A woman who called herself Susannah Roberts and who said she was from Pennsylvania is described as wandering from town to town, unresponsive to laws and mores, in a chaotic mental state and totally naked. Sufferers sometimes begged for their food and used whatever shelter was available (such as animal barns). Others lived in various places.

An institution intended specifically to house the mentally disturbed existed as early as the fourth century in Byzantium (now Istanbul); it was called the "house of lunatics" (Zilboorg & Henry, 1941, p. 561). However, the number of mentally deranged people who were cared for in such specialized places was minuscule until after 1850. In general, the institutions that housed a meaningful number of them were those established for all kinds of people (including the mentally disturbed) who could not or would not function in society, or who were driven away from society. When monasteries existed in great numbers, many persons with mental problems lived there. Later, when jails, prisons, and workhouses were common institutions, they became receptacles for the mentally disordered. Even leper hospitals were used to house them (Zilboorg & Henry, 1941, p. 575).

If no institution was available, a one-person asylum would sometimes be built that might be no bigger than five by seven feet (Deutsch, 1965, p. 42). Perhaps the most astonishing practice for housing those with mental problems and unable to take care of themselves was the New England system, which was commonly used in nineteenth-century America (Deutsch, 1965, pp. 117–119). In essence, these outcasts were sold at auction. The successful bidder was the one willing to care for the "lunatic" at the lowest compensation from town funds. The sale was generally binding for one year, and it was understood the buyer would get all the work possible from the acquisition.

Perhaps we should inform ourselves about past events concerning mental disorders for their intrinsic value. But does this history also help us to understand the stigma that is now associated with this condition? I believe it does. I believe those disagreeable happenings in the past could very well color contemporary opinions about the mentally disordered. Learning about such former views and practices may negatively influence present conceptions and behaviors toward afflicted individuals. But this unceasing pattern of rejection and degradation in earlier years, together with present similarly unfavorable social views and comportment toward mental patients, indicates something very fundamental about mental disorders and stigma. What past and present events together suggest will be considered at the end of this chapter, after the contemporary situation is reviewed.

CONTEMPORARY SOCIAL ATTITUDES

Mental health professionals do not at present agree among themselves about how negative public attitudes are toward those afflicted by mental problems. Some students of this issue believe there is little evidence indicating that the public holds mental patients in low regard. Crocetti and his co-workers have been particularly emphatic in expressing this view (Crocetti & Lemkau, 1965; Crocetti, Spiro, & Siassi, 1974). They believe that while public attitudes may have been negative in the past, they have so improved that it is now time to ". . . write a belated epitaph . . ." to the theory that mental patients are rejected (Crocetti et al., 1974, p. 163). Halpert (1970) also concludes, on the basis of his review of studies, that tolerance or acceptance of the mentally disordered is clearly increasing. However, most investigators believe that mental patients, now as in the past, are viewed with great disfavor and are held in extremely low esteem (for instance, Lamy, 1966). Sarbin and Mancuso (1970) are among those who believe the public still harbors negative feelings. In addition, they also doubt the possibility of changing these feelings by means of procedures that Crocetti claims are the very ones that have led to improvements. The main aspect of these procedures entails informing the public that mental aberrations are illnesses like any other illness (Crocetti et al., 1974).

Perhaps we should not be surprised at this disagreement. It is more surprising that the disagreement is confined to a very few people saying attitudes are not negative (or are improving), while the rest of the experts seem to agree that public feelings are decidedly unfavorable. After all, attitudes are subject to potent influences from all sorts of extraneous variables and are notoriously tricky to measure. As long ago as 1934, LaPiere demonstrated, in a study that became widely known, that his subjects both expressed negative feelings toward Orientals and yet seemed to act in such a way as to indicate they harbored neutral or positive attitudes. Wicker's review of the research on attitudes (1969) indicates this pattern of results is common. It is easy to see, in view of this, how someone could conclude that research shows that attitudes toward mental patients are highly unfavorable while someone else, focusing on another facet of the research or on different studies, might deduce those feelings are neutral or even positive.

Furthermore, investigators have frequently failed to make a distinction between attitudes toward patients and beliefs about the nature of mental disorders. This failure may account for some seemingly inconsistent results. As generally used, the term "attitudes" refers to values and feelings, while "beliefs" involve objectively verifiable information. Consider the following attitudinal question, followed by one about beliefs. "Are you afraid of the mentally ill?" and "Do mental patients have glassy eyes?" Nunnally (1961) has very clearly demonstrated that different principles apply to these two types of variables, and that they are related to different factors. Nunnally also has demonstrated that people's beliefs about mental disorders can be easily and quickly changed. Let me give an example. If a mental health expert asserts that psychiatric patients do not have glassy eyes, people who formerly thought that patients' eyes were glassy will readily change their beliefs. However, efforts to alter attitudes, such as to view mental patients as nonthreatening and valuable, are not very effective.

These two types of variables may influence each other, of course. If someone has a change of mind and comes to believe the eyes of mental patients are not, after all, glassy, he or she may as a result become less fearful of mental patients. Moreover, it is not always clear whether a statement refers to beliefs or attitudes. But, obviously, to argue that mental patients are generally liked because people believe their eyes are not glassy involves a number of unwarranted assumptions. Asking subjects specifically about their likes and fears regarding mental patients is almost certain to prompt different conclusions about public attitudes in comparison with inferring such attitudes on the basis of beliefs. It is noteworthy that Halpert (1970) drew his conclusion about improving public acceptance of mental patients largely from studies of beliefs, not attitudes.

Another problem encountered in trying to assess public attitudes toward mental disorders probably represents the most common and important difficulty. At the center of this problem is a phenomenon similar to "social desirability," but it does not imply pretense, such as when a subject states that he or she likes neurotics because society expects this while he or she is well aware that he or she does not like neurotics. "Humane ethics" may be more descriptive of what is responsible for this serious problem faced by investigators of social stigma. To society, mental patients are possessed of something that is frightening and incomprehensible, and people are exceedingly uncomfortable in their presence. However, patients are also patently unfortunate people and, because of this, any decent person will not further injure or abuse them. Indeed, nice people should try to help them, and we all think we are nice people.

As a consequence of these conflicting motivations—fear and disdain on the one hand and an obligation to help those stricken by misfortune on the other—subtle differences in how research is done can produce dramatically different results.* Consider an illustration that, in order to serve the purpose, must be fairly unsubtle. Many times, subjects have been given questionnaires composed of items such as "Who is more valuable, a mental patient or a factory worker?" Routinely the results of such studies indicate that mental patients are severely stigmatized. But now look at an item like that used by Rayne (1969) in his study: "If you had to give an electric shock to a mental patient or to a factory worker, whom would you choose to shock?" Rayne found that subjects are favorably disposed and supportive of mental patients when such items are used to assess attitudes.

But in spite of these problems the nature of public attitudes toward mental disorders is quite clear. In toto the scores of studies indicate unequivocally that these attitudes are extremely negative. The results of a few studies will make the extremity of these feelings clear. In one of these, Gussow and Tracy (1968) had subjects evaluate various degrading conditions, and concluded that people believe the two most horrible things that can befall a person are leprosy and insanity. In another study public attitudes toward a "leper" and an "insane person" were measured (Nunnally, 1961, pp. 270–272). These attitudes were found to be much more negative toward the insane person, who was regarded as more dangerous, insecure, unpredictable, bad, tense, and foolish. A former convict, too, is viewed with

---

*This conflict is especially salient and obvious when someone is in a face-to-face interaction with a mental patient. That research will be reviewed under the headings "How People Perceive and Behave Toward Those with Mental Disorders" and "Sufferers from Mental Disorders are not Uniformly Treated Badly by Everyone."

greater favor than a former mental patient (Lamy, 1966). For example, people believe a mother would entrust her baby to the care of someone who has been convicted of a crime and jailed in preference to someone who has been a mental patient. These strongly unfavorable attitudes are quite uniformly held by members of society. Old and young, country and city dwellers, rich and poor, men and women, bright and dull, all regard people with mental disorders as fundamentally tainted and degraded (Nunnally, 1961, p. 47).

Let us look specifically at the attitudes of those members of society whose roles are particularly important in determining what happens to patients. These include employers, mental health workers, community medical practitioners (who generally have the legal power to commit someone to a mental hospital), innkeepers, families of patients, and other mental patients with whom prolonged periods of time may have to be spent. We have evidence showing that people in all those roles reject and look down upon mental patients (for instance, Cohen & Struening, 1962; Harrow, Fox, & Detre, 1969; Nunnally, 1961; Olshansky, Grob, & Malamud, 1958; Page, 1977). The degree of rejection and disdain encountered by someone with a mental disorder appears to be related to the severity of the mental disorder. For example, it seems clear from Nunnally's extensive research that psychotics are held in lower esteem than neurotics by the general public (Nunnally, 1961, p. 46). Lawner (1966) both confirmed the finding and showed that people with other mental problems were stigmatized in accordance with the degree of disturbance they showed. Thus a "person treated by a psychiatrist" was rated more favorably than a "neurotic." However, even mild interpersonal difficulties requiring no treatment elicit social stigma (Jones, Hester, Farina, & Davis, 1959).

Not only are public attitudes very negative but, as was stated, it is extremely difficult to change them. Such a conclusion was reached by Nunnally after doing a profusion of studies (1961, p. 220). Hence it cannot be expected that the effort mounted by mental health groups to promote better public attitudes will have much success. Can former mental patients themselves do something to improve their reception? Sherman (1967) sought an answer to this question. He found that an excellent performance on a task by a former mental patient readily changed the beliefs of observers regarding the ability of patients to do the task. These observers had initially thought that anyone who had suffered a nervous disorder would perform very incompetently. But although they came to believe the former patient was very skillful, their attitudes remained highly unfavorable.

In a related study some subjects learned that their co-worker, who was believed to have been in a mental hospital, had compelling reasons for his problems because he had experienced a very unhappy childhood (Farina, Holland, & Ring, 1966). Other subjects were led to believe that there were no mitigating circumstances in the co-worker's past. It was expected that the stigmatized individual would be viewed more favorably when he had an excuse for his failings. The excuse did lead subjects to be careful not to hurt the afflicted person but, instead of viewing him more positively, they held him in lower esteem. And what happens if someone with mental problems acts as society implies he or she should act, availing himself or herself of mental health services? At least one study has revealed that people become more intolerant and rejecting toward someone who undergoes treatment in comparison with an identically described individual who has no psychiatric care (Phillips, 1963).

It is apparent that highly unfavorable attitudes are engendered in all people toward someone whose adjustment is poor. These attitudes are very stable and resistant to change. Although people may be in conflict over looking down on someone they regard as stricken by misfortune, they nevertheless do so. We will now look at the major consequences of this state of affairs.

HOW PEOPLE PERCEIVE AND BEHAVE TOWARD THOSE WITH MENTAL DISORDERS

The unfavorable feelings the public harbors toward those blemished by mental disorders are frequently accompanied by negative behaviors. People also see, in afflicted individuals, personal shortcomings and dislikable conduct that do not objectively exist. These processes are made evident by a host of reports that range from anecdotal accounts to carefully controlled experiments.

Among the less rigorous and less formal sources of information are a number of articles by people who have pretended to be suffering from a mental problem in order to enter psychiatric institutions as patients. This is a technique that has long been used by newspaper reporters to investigate corruption and crime. Firsthand accounts by these pseudo patients are quite revealing. In institutions where we might expect to find the best care and most sympathetic understanding, we find neither. Mental health workers are observed treating very competent and rational patients as if they were little children. For example, Caudill reports foolish parties are given to entertain the patients, who find the parties patronizing and humiliating—they participate only to avoid further embarrassment (Caudill, Redlich, Gilmore, & Brody, 1952).

If a patient is asked a question, a truthful and reasonable response may not be believed because of the assumption that he or she really does not understand himself or herself—or anything else. Rosenhan (1973) found that when quite normal and able people in the role of a patient asked a relevant question of staff members, the most frequent reaction of the staff members was to ignore the supposed patient. He also found that physical abuse of patients by the staff was not uncommon. Page (1974) culled items from newspapers and television broadcasts that indicate society's disposition to perceive unfavorable characteristics in patients and to behave adversely toward them. In a syndicated column a dentist reassuringly states that mental patients do not often inflict bites. A labor spokesman denounces the inept staff of a particular railroad station, and asserts that the station could have been better managed by a mental patient. And an advertisement of babies available for adoption describes a baby who will make a delightful daughter for a family that would not be concerned over mental illness in her background.

Systematic experiments amply confirm these less formal observations. First of all, they make clear society's low opinion of mental patients' abilities. The belief prevails that stricken individuals are incompetent and inadequate in a broad and general way. Sherman (1967) had subjects meet and talk to a confederate and estimate how well he would do a certain task requiring motor skills. The results indicated that they expected the confederate to perform more poorly when he was presented as having a history of mental disorder as compared to a control condition.

A study by Farina and Ring (1965) focused upon the consequences of these beliefs. Pairs of male college students, strangers to each other, were asked to provide, in writing, some personal and revealing information for the other person to read. Previously prepared information sheets were substituted, one of them describing the writer as a typical student and the other revealing that he had been in a mental hospital. A clear and very strong effect was found. Not only did subjects want to avoid further contact with the supposed former patient, but they also perceived inadequacies in his behavior that, in fact, did not exist—as Sherman's study suggested would happen (see Table 7.1). Moreover, actual joint performance on a motor task was significantly affected by the belief that the partner had been hospitalized.

While the behavioral changes caused by the supposed mental disorder were obvious in this experiment, the interpersonal significance of the changes in task performance were ambiguous. Perhaps performance on the task employed in the experiment means nothing about being nasty or nice toward the former patient. Therefore, another study was done (Farina,

TABLE 7.1
Number of Subjects Perceiving Co-worker as Helping or Hindering Joint Performance as a Function of Believing He Was Normal or Had Been in a Mental Hospital

	Co-worker Perceived as	
	Helping	Hindering
Co-worker believed normal	27	3
Co-worker believed to have been hospitalized	18	12

Source: Adapted from Farina & Ring (1965), Table 2, p. 50. Copyright 1965 by the American Psychological Association. Reprinted by permission.

Holland, & Ring, 1966). In that study a confederate in the role of another subject portrayed himself as a typical student or as having a deviant history, including admission to a mental hospital. A naive subject was required to teach the confederate a pattern of button presses, using electric shock to direct the learner toward the correct pattern. (Of course, in these experiments no shocks were actually received by the confederate.) Thus, duration and intensity of each shock were controlled by the subject, and were the main dependent measures of the study. As expected, the "subject" with the abnormal history received more painful shocks. Unlike the earlier study, the meaning of that behavior is clear enough. People with a history of mental disorders are treated unfavorably, at least under some conditions. Moreover, in this study the task performance of the deviant person was perceived as less adequate than that of the control, although the performances were identical.

In a similar study, independent groups of male subjects met a male confederate presented as an average college student or as a resident of a state institution who had suffered a mental disorder (Farina, Thaw, Felner, & Hust, 1976). As in the Farina, Holland, and Ring study (1966), subjects had to teach the confederate a pattern of button presses by varying the duration and intensity of the shocks that they used to communicate. The confederate was given more painful shocks when he was thought to have suffered a mental disorder. The entire study was then replicated with new groups of naive subjects and a different male confederate (Farina, Thaw, Felner, & Hust, 1976). Again the confederate in the mental disorder condition was given more painful shocks (see Table 7.2). These studies provide convincing evidence that a history of mental disorder can induce people to behave unfavorably toward the sufferer. This applies to male subjects interacting with male "patients." Females behave differently. These sex differences will be considered in detail later in the chapter.

A very different type of negative consequence of mental disorder was studied by Lawner (1966). Lawner reasoned that if those whose past has been burdened with mental difficulties are held in low regard, not only can

TABLE 7.2
Mean Duration of Shock Administered to the Confederate as a Function of Believing He Was an Average College Student or Was Mentally Disordered (seconds)

	Confederate Perceived as	
	Normal	Mentally Disordered
Experiment 1	76.5	83.1
Experiment 2	54.5	73.9

Source: Adapted from Farina, Thaw, Felner, & Hust (1976), Table 3, p. 420. Reprinted by permission of AAMD.

we expect them generally to be viewed unfavorably and treated harshly, but the degree of influence they can exert upon others may be small. To test this, he had a subject meet a confederate in the role of a naive subject; both were informed that one was to communicate some newly learned information to the other. The confederate, always assigned the role of communicator, went to another room, where he allegedly read a pamphlet on a procedure for dating archaeological sites. The confederate then communicated verbally what he had supposedly read, and expressed strongly favorable opinions about the procedure. The degree of influence he exerted was measured by how favorably disposed the naive subject was toward the technique.

Beliefs about the past mental history of the confederate were manipulated by a message supposedly written by the confederate but, in fact, prepared earlier and its content unknown to the confederate. In this way some subjects learned the confederate was a typical and ordinary student, while others read that he had been "mentally ill" and in a mental hospital. The same spoken communication caused subjects in the "mentally ill" condition to be significantly less influenced than subjects in the control group. Evidently, a person who has suffered a mental disorder is less likely to be believed by other people and to have them accept his or her opinion about something. Such reactions can certainly constitute a serious impediment to the satisfactory interpersonal relationships of former patients.

Evidence of negative attitudes and behaviors toward victims of mental disorders is particularly clear and striking in relation to finding a job. Olshansky, Grob, and Malamud (1958) found that of 200 employers (whose workers constituted 14 percent of the labor force in the greater Boston area), 25 percent openly said they would not hire a former mental patient. Furthermore, 40 percent of those who were willing to hire such a person said they would restrict him or her to certain jobs they believed were not very demanding. Perhaps more revealing was the finding that only 13 percent of the employers had knowingly hired a former mental patient during the preceding three years, and only five of the 200 were willing to hire such a person at the time they were interviewed, even if he or she was otherwise qualified. In another study (Olshansky, Grob, & Ekdahl, 1960) it was found that a number of former patients who had revealed the fact of their psychiatric hospitalization to the potential employer had been denied jobs. They reported that when next they sought employment, they were careful to hide their history of hospitalization.

Using a more experimental procedure, Farina and Felner (1973) had an experimenter pose as a job applicant and obtain employment interviews at 32 manufacturing concerns. He presented himself in the same way and gave an identical work history in each case. However, at 16 of the places, selected at random, he revealed he had been in a mental hospital for the preceding nine months. In the remaining 16 places he indicated he had been traveling across the country for the prior nine months. More jobs were offered to the "traveler" than to the "the mental hospital patient," although in the depressed economy of that time so few were offered (four and two jobs, respectively) that the difference was not reliable. Other measures were taken from the conversation between the applicant and the interviewer, which was in all cases surreptitiously sound-recorded. Raters, blind to the purpose of the study, scored the tapes for friendliness of the employment interviewer and for the likelihood that the applicant would be hired. The interviewers were significantly less friendly and indicated a significantly lower probability of being hired in the "mental hospital" condition than in the control condition.

Thus, it seems there are special handicaps in finding a job faced by someone who has suffered a nervous disorder. Because of the sex differences alluded to above, we will here confine ourselves to the reactions of males. The sex differences will be discussed more fully and for now we need only note that, with regard to finding work, males behave in an unfavorable way toward former mental patients.

In addition to problems in finding a job, there is evidence indicating that should a male former mental patient be hired, his extra problems are by no means over if his history becomes known to his co-workers. In one study, male workers such as aides and kitchen helpers at a Veterans Administration (VA) hospital were the subjects (Farina, Felner, & Boudreau, 1973). They were told that since they knew their own job best, they would be asked to meet a job applicant, a former patient, and evaluate how well he would do if hired to work with them. All subjects actually met the same male confederate, but half were told he was a former mental patient and the rest that he was a former surgical patient. Relative to the surgical patient condition, they expected to get along less well with the former mental patient, they recommended him less strongly for the job, and they perceived him as possessing stereotypic mental patient characteristics, such as unpredictability. In a very similarly conducted study, male workers were asked to evaluate a female confederate posing as a job applicant (Farina, Murray, & Groh, 1978). She was presented to some as an ordinary job seeker and to others as a former mental patient. In this study, too, the workers responded less favorably to the confederate in the mental patient condition, but the rejection was much less decisive and severe than in the prior study, which had utilized a male confederate.

The problem of employment would appear to be an especially critical one for those who have endured psychiatric disorders, particularly for those who have been confined to a mental hospital for a period of time. There are, first of all, the related problems of self-esteem and social status. Clearly for a man, and increasingly for a woman, social prestige is largely determined by the job held. If the former patient can find no job, or finds only an undesirable one, his standing in society is marginal, and his view of himself cannot be very positive. Such conditions are hardly likely to promote a former patient's readjustment to the community. But there are more concrete and inescapable consequences of failing to find employment. The former patient cannot live in the community without income, and unless he receives help from some source, he may have to return to the hospital for food and shelter.

People also behave negatively toward former mental patients who are in need of housing when there is the possibility that they will become neighbors or tenants. Such individuals are not wanted nearby. One such incident occurred in Long Beach, New York, in 1974. The event was widely reported and attracted national attention. By 1974 this Long Island seaside community was no longer attracting tourists in large numbers and its many hotels remained unfilled. State mental institutions began housing discharged patients, who had no homes to go to, at those hotels, and the hotel owners were eager to cooperate. The community then passed a law banning anyone in need of continuous psychiatric care or medication from the facilities.

The strength of this inhospitable reaction toward former mental patients is amply demonstrated by several experiments carried out in the community. Most clearly, it can be seen from the results of a study by Page (1977). Telephone calls were made to 180 individuals from one city who were advertising furnished rooms or flats in the city's two major newspapers. The same female assistant asked if the room was still available in each instance. She said nothing unusual about herself in the control condition, while for other conditions she revealed she was about to leave a mental hospital. In still other conditions the caller stated she was inquiring for her brother, who was about to leave jail. Whereas she received 25 positive responses in 30 calls for the control condition, the largest number of positive responses received in any of the other conditions was 9 out of 30 calls. The control condition was highly and significantly different from all other conditions, while the mental hospital and jail conditions did not differ reliably from each other.

Page even made certain the refusals were not due to the unlikely occurrence of quick rental of rooms in the experimental conditions. Twenty advertisers were randomly selected from those who had asserted the room was no longer available to the caller when she indicated the prospective tenant had been in jail or a mental hospital. These 20 were then called a second time, but this time the caller followed the control condition procedure. Eighteen of the 20 advertisers, who had just stated their rooms were no longer available, revealed they could be rented on the second call.

Two studies concerned with this problem of finding housing by people known to have suffered a nervous disorder are very similar, and can be described simultaneously (Cutler, 1975; Farina, Thaw, Lovern, & Mangone, 1974). A male in his twenties called upon people in their own homes, announcing that he was investigating the problem of finding a place to live faced by individuals who had been hospitalized for a prolonged period. Half the subjects were told the patients had been hospitalized for medical reasons, and the rest that they had been admitted for nervous disorders. They were also asked to listen to a recorded interview between a patient and the investigator in order to have a better impression of what a particular patient was like. Subjects in the control and experimental conditions actually heard the same recording. After listening, they were asked a series of questions about how they and their neighbors would respond if that particular patient were to move into a house nearby.

The results of both studies show that a former mental patient is expected to encounter more difficulty in finding a job, it is foreseen that neighbors will not accept him, and he is expected to have greater difficulty in various areas of community functioning. Moreover, it was also found that subjects interviewed in the mental patient condition would be less willing to take part in similar future experiments than would subjects in the medical patient condition. The very important implication of this finding may be that people find it unpleasant to think that a former mental patient may move near them, even if they assert that they themselves—if not their neighbors— would welcome him.

Even when visiting a doctor engaged in private practice, former mental patients are treated differently. This was shown in a study by Farina, Hagelauer, and Holzberg (1976) in which 32 physicians were selected and an appointment was made with each by an investigator posing as a patient. During the visit the same symptoms, principally stomach pains, were described to each doctor. For 16 randomly selected practitioners the "patient" stated he had experienced the same symptoms nine months earlier while traveling; for the rest he reported having had the symptoms while confined to a mental hospital. All medical procedures used during the visit were carefully noted and were divided into those directly related to the symptoms, such as a rectal examination, and those peripheral to the symptoms, such as testing reflexes. It was found that significantly more ancillary and peripheral procedures were used for the former mental patient condition (12) than for the control condition (6). The finding suggests that the reports of people who have suffered a mental disorder are not fully trusted, and that physicians feel a need to personally determine how such individuals are functioning in various areas.

Thus we see numerous ways in which the community responds unfavorably toward someone who has suffered a psychiatric disorder. Sadly, it appears that those individuals who are least able to contend with personal problems, and therefore receive psychiatric help, find that, as a consequence of that help, their problems become magnified. Those identified as psychiatric patients are perceived as having nonexistent shortcomings, they are treated more harshly, they have greater difficulty finding work, they are not wanted as neighbors, and their reports seem not to be trusted. There are other aspects of life in the community, such as joining clubs and receiving credit, that can be investigated. It is highly likely that patients will find a similar unfavorable reception is given to them. Whatever future studies reveal, it is simply not true now that ". . . the mentally ill need not fear rejection in any of the most common social interactions, such as employment, housing, and social clubs," as Crocetti et al. (1974, p. 83) claim.

SUFFERERS FROM MENTAL DISORDERS ARE NOT UNIFORMLY TREATED BADLY BY EVERYONE

Much of the writing on stigmatizing conditions suggests their interpersonal significance is rather easily understood and simple: People hold strongly negative views toward those bearing stigmas, and behave unfavorably toward them. There is plenty of evidence supporting these conclusions, some of which we have reviewed. But even if we confine ourselves to one stigma, having experienced problems in adjustment, things are very much more complicated than the preceding conclusions suggest. Hints about these complications are contained in what has already been covered. For example, reference has been made several times to sex differences in favorability toward those stricken by mental problems. We will now systematically consider the evidence indicating that sufferers from mental disorders are not always treated badly by everyone. This evidence is presented below in three sections: humane ethics, sex differences, and personal experience with mental disorder.

Humane Ethics

The moral principle that one must help unfortunate others appears to prevail in all societies, and history indicates its presence from the earliest times. It is a central and salient theme in the major religions. We must help the poor, the sick, the victims of misfortune, and we must not harm someone who is suffering. It is a very important part of our personality, and determines our opinion of what kind of person we are. Passing a crippled beggar without giving alms makes most of us feel we have done something wrong. And it seems that those who beg sometimes fake being blind or crippled, which suggests that such adversities elicit a sympathetic and generous response from others.

We need not rely on anecdotes regarding this phenomenon, however, since careful experiments have made this supportive behavior very clear. In one pertinent study (Doob & Ecker, 1970), a female researcher went to people's houses and asked the residents to complete a questionnaire for her. Her appearance was not unusual for half the subjects, but for the remainder she wore an eyepatch and thus seemed to be missing an eye. A significantly greater proportion of people completed the questionnaire when they thought the requester was missing an eye than when she seemed quite normal. Kleck (1969) had subjects interact with a confederate who seemed normal for half the subjects but whose left leg appeared to be amputated for the rest. The illusion was created by placing the confederate in a special wheelchair that had a hidden compartment for the apparently missing leg. Significantly more positive feelings were expressed toward the confederate when the leg was missing than when she was normal. In a very similar study a confederate was given less painful shocks when his leg appeared to be missing than when he seemed normal (Farina, Sherman, & Allen, 1968).

Let us now focus upon the stigma of mental disorders. The motivation to be kind toward people stigmatized by this condition, while at the same time looking down upon them, is readily seen. It will be recalled that Rayne (1969) found no evidence of a disposition to behave unfavorably when subjects were asked if they would shock a former mental patient or an ordinary person. It appears that people will check their unfavorable attitudes and act supportively toward those who have suffered a mental disorder. Another part of Rayne's study indicates that these dispositions to act generously exist and that mental patients are aware of them. Two groups of hospitalized psychiatric patients were selected. One group believed society considered them degraded, while patients in the second group thought others viewed them as relatively normal. All patients then interacted with a confederate who, they were told, expected to administer electric shocks to them as a technique for teaching them a task. Each subject was asked how much pain he expected the confederate to inflict upon him. It was found that the more a patient believed himself to be stigmatized by others, the better he expected to be treated. Evidently those who have had personal experience with the stigma of mental disorder come to believe that the more unfortunate such a person is considered, the more favorable the treatment he will be accorded.

There are more direct studies of this tendency to be kind to those who have suffered mental problems. Some research has shown that while subjects expect others to behave in a nasty fashion toward afflicted individuals, they assert that they themselves would not act unfavorably (Farina & Ring, 1965). In the study by Farina, Felner, and Boudreau (1973), workers already on the job who met a confederate presented as a former mental patient expected to get along better with her than did other workers who thought she was an ordinary job applicant. And in the study of community response to discharged patients (Farina, Thaw, Lovern, & Mangone, 1974), the respondents in the "mental disorder" condition said they were more likely to invite the former mental patient to a party than those in the "surgical disorder" condition.

The beneficial consequences for mental patients, and perhaps for people degraded by other conditions as well, of what I am calling humane ethics are also indicated by several other studies. In the Farina, Holland, and Ring study (1966), subjects had to teach a pattern of button presses to a person who was in another room. They could communicate only by means of electrically connected panels; and the person in the other room, a confederate, at first apparently was required to guess the correct pattern. But the real subject could guide him to the correct solution by shocking him when he was wrong. He could choose any of ten intensities for each shock, and he could vary the duration by keeping a button pressed for as long as he wanted. In fact shocks were not really given, but the durations and intensities used were recorded. The confederate was shocked for a reliably longer period when he was perceived as stigmatized by a mental disorder, but the intensity of shock did not vary between conditions. These findings also seemed to reflect the conflict that people experience in interacting with a person who is in some manner deformed, and hence unfortunate. The subjects wanted to treat the stigmatized confederate fairly, and this they managed to do in their use of shock intensities. The intensities had to be consciously selected on every trial, and hence the subjects knew very well which levels they used. But they were much less aware of the durations used; here their unfavorable attitudes could be expressed less consciously, and therefore without arousing guilt.

A similar pattern of results was found in two other and quite different studies. One was the study in which a confederate appeared physically normal for half the subjects and seemed to have a leg amputated for the remainder (Farina, Sherman, & Allen, 1968). There were no intensity differences between conditions, but in the cripple condition the confederate was given significantly shorter shocks. Here, too, it seemed possible that subjects followed the salient ideal to be fair and to treat the amputee like anyone else. They were able to do this with intensity, but their underlying feelings of sympathy led them to act more favorably toward him when their own behavior could not be easily monitored. In the second study subjects' beliefs about their own emotional stability were manipulated (Ring & Farina, 1969) to evaluate the effect of similarity to a mentally disordered person on the treatment accorded that person. Degree of similarity made little difference in the intensities used, but once again highly significant duration differences were found. The more similar a subject was to the patient, the shorter the duration of the shocks administered.

Some studies were done to check the tenability of this explanation. The subjects of the Ring and Farina study (1969) were asked to estimate the mean shock intensity and duration they had used. The correlation between estimated and actual mean shock intensity was .92, which shows they were very well aware of the strength of the shocks they had just delivered. However, the correlation for actual and estimated shock duration was only .38, indicating a hazy and tenuous knowledge of how long the shocks were. The difference between the two correlations is highly significant ($p < .0001$), which indicates a greater awareness of the intensities of the shocks than of the durations.

In another study done to check this hypothesis, a female confederate revealed to some female college students that she was an ordinary undergraduate, while she told others she had often been paid by men for sexual favors (Mosher, Farina, & Gliha, 1970). The reasoning here is that people will not feel morally compelled to treat a prostitute supportively or even equitably. The same task and apparatus were used, and this time no duration differences were found; but in accord with theoretical expectations, the intensity scores were significantly higher in the prostitute condition.

In sum, the widely held belief that the stigma of mental disorder elicits uniformly low regard from others, together with unalloyed rejection and unfavorable behavior, is an overly simple one and is incorrect. This becomes apparent if we ask ourselves, "Would I behave that way? Do I reject mental patients and treat them badly?" The great majority of us are highly likely to deny it. We can more easily believe that other people are like that. But other people are much like us. Other people also will generally believe that those stricken by misfortunes are not suitable targets for maltreatment, just as we believe. How, then, does it happen that victims of mental disorder clearly encounter unfavorable social responses from people just like us, as the research indicates?

While much remains to be done, what we have learned indicates that former mental patients will be treated badly when such treatment does not produce guilt on the part of the actor. This can happen when someone feels his or her unfavorable behavior is justified. An employer can reason that he or she has nothing against former mental patients, but this particular one looks as if he cannot endure the pressures of the job, and hence it would be no favor to hire him. Or a former patient can be treated badly when the actor is not fully conscious of his behavior. And so, while subjects will state that should a former mental patient become a neighbor, they would invite him to a party, they, more often than subjects in the medical-surgical condition, decline to participate as subjects in similar future experiments. The latter action is a much less obvious form of personal distantiation or rejection than declining to invite the new neighbor to a social gathering.*

Sex Differences in Response to Mental Disorders

Earlier some studies were described that examined the reaction of workers to a job applicant with a psychiatric history. It will be recalled that male workers responded unfavorably to the applicant who was thought to have been in a mental hospital (Farina, Felner, & Boudreau, 1973; Farina & Hagelauer, 1975; Farina, Murray, & Groh, 1978). This had been expected, in view of what the attitude research had revealed. However, there were also findings from this series of studies that were unprecedented and wholly

---

*Obviously, the results described in this section could be given quite different theoretical interpretations. For example, it might be argued that greater pain is inflicted upon mental patients because they are perceived as less responsive than normal people. The present explanation in terms of unfavorable attitudes and guilt arousal is offered because it seems to fit best the facts currently available.

unexpected. In the first of these studies, female department store clerks met a female confederate presented to half the clerks as an ordinary applicant and to the rest as someone about to be discharged from a mental hospital. In addition, the confederate acted in a relaxed fashion with half the clerks in each condition but behaved in a tense and nervous way with the rest. It was found that the confederate's history of mental disorder made no difference whatever. The clerks indicated equal willingness to work with the confederate and saw her as equally competent, whether they thought she was an ordinary job seeker or someone who had suffered a severe mental disorder (see Table 7.3).

Of course, it had been expected that the workers, being generally humane and benign people, would be reluctant to be unkind to the mental patient. Therefore, measures varying in how clearly they indicated personal favorability were included. For example, each clerk was asked how the applicant would get along with other workers in the subject's department. It would seem easier for the clerk to believe that other people would behave in an unkind and prejudiced way than for her to think that of herself. No evidence of an unfavorable reaction was found. We can assume that, in addition to a deeply felt sense of generosity toward afflicted others, the workers also were influenced by social pressure to say nice things about the patient regardless of how they really felt. But we would not expect such pressure to make them advocate that the store hire her and place her on the job and in close contact for an indefinite period if they felt a basic dislike for the patient and viewed her as greatly degraded. And the workers clearly did not feel compelled to be charitable to everyone. In the nervous condition the applicant was unequivocally disliked and rejected, even though a worried and tense person can also be considered as unfortunate and in need of support (see Table 7.3).

The findings were so unexpected that the study was replicated with males. The results revealed that males thoroughly rejected and disliked the

TABLE 7.3
Rating of Female Applicant by Female Clerks Regarding How They Expected to Get Along with Her and Whether She Should Be Hired

Applicant Described as	Expectation of "Getting Along"		Recommendation for Hiring	
	Applicant's Behavior			
	Calm	Tense	Calm	Tense
Normal	1.3	1.5	1.2	1.7
From a mental hospital	1.0	1.2	1.3	1.8

Note: Smaller number means more favorable rating.

Source: Adapted from Farina, Felner, & Boudreau (1973), Table 1, p. 365. Copyright 1973 by the American Psychological Association. Reprinted by permission.

confederate in the mental patient condition, in total contrast with female subjects. The males did act like the females in that they also responded very negatively to the nervous applicant. But the different reaction of the two sexes to the former mental patient was puzzling. The attitude studies then available indicated no attitude difference of any sort between men and women (Nunnally, 1961). However, there were dissimilarities between the two studies that might have produced contrasting findings. The most obvious was that the female subjects were clerks in a department store while the males worked in a VA hospital that had a ward for psychiatric patients. Perhaps the attitudes toward mental patients prevailing in the two settings were quite different. Also, the work at the two places of employment was certainly not the same. A former patient may be an acceptable co-worker to a sales clerk whose interactions are predominantly with customers. But the VA workers had to cooperate with other workers in the preparation of meals, cleaning, and maintaining the hospital, and hence may have been more selective about who would work with them. A third study was done to assess the role of such differences between settings.

The third study was done at the VA hospital, the site of the second study. However, the subjects were all females with various jobs, such as aide, clerk, and laundry worker. There was a new female confederate, but the procedure used was the same as that in the earlier studies. The results were identical to those of the first study. The female workers rejected the nervous applicant, but the former mental patient was fully accepted. Hence, the variable that accounts for the difference in rejection of people with a psychiatric history must be gender. But in the above studies, male subjects met a male confederate while female subjects encountered only a female confederate. Consequently, it is impossible to know if men reject former mental patients more than women, if female former mental patients are more fully accepted than comparable males, or both.

Therefore, a fourth study was done in the department store where the first study in the series was carried out. The same procedure was used with a new group of female clerks, and this time the "applicant" was a new male confederate. The results were identical to the two earlier studies of female subjects. The confederate was fully accepted whether the clerks thought he was an average job applicant or had been in a mental hospital. Once again nervousness had a clear impact, the confederate being rejected and disliked in the nervous condition.

The only question that remained was how male workers would respond to a female former mental patient. To answer this question, males employed in the physical plant division of a state university were selected as subjects. A new female confederate was used to play the role of job seeker, and the procedure used in the prior studies was followed once again. For the fifth time, and with the fifth confederate, nervousness produced rejection and dislike. The workers were also more rejecting of the applicant when she was thought to have been in a mental hospital. However, the negative reaction was milder than that of males toward the male confederate with a psychiatric history found in the study done at the VA hospital.

Another series of studies provides results in close agreement with the five just reviewed (Farina, Thaw, Felner, & Hust, 1976). The studies were carried out at an institution for the mentally retarded, and the subjects were college students. Each was told the institution wanted to find out what kind of student worked best with what kind of resident. Hence, they would meet a resident and teach him or her a series of button presses by administering shocks to guide the learner to the correct solution. This procedure is the same as that used in the Farina, Holland, and Ring study (1966). Male subjects then met a male confederate. One-third were told he was mentally disordered but of average intelligence, one-third that he was well-adjusted but mentally retarded, and the rest, in a control condition, were told that the confederate was a normal volunteer worker. The confederate was kept blind as to condition. After that, female subjects met a female confederate and the same procedure was followed. Then the study was repeated with a new group of male subjects who met a different male confederate. And finally a new group of female subjects met a still different female confederate. Males administered significantly longer shocks to the confederate in the "mentally disordered" condition in comparison with the control condition. Females did not administer longer shocks; they actually gave shocks of briefer duration in the "mentally disordered" condition relative to the control condition.

In conclusion, there is a clear sex difference in the response accorded to those who have been afflicted with a mental disorder. At least under certain conditions, males behave in a harsher and more punishing manner than females. A second conclusion can also be drawn, although this must be stated more tentatively. Female former mental patients are treated better than males, at least by men. How can we explain these findings? A comparison of attitudes toward the mentally disordered manifested by men and women certainly does not clarify things. Indeed, it is these attitude studies that make the findings so surprising. Nunnally (1961) found no difference between the sexes in any of his many studies. Coie, Pennington, and Buckley (1974) also discovered little difference between men and women. Even worse, both Farina, Felner, and Boudreau (1973) and LaTorre (1975) report that males express more benign and supportive attitudes toward former mental patients than women do.

However, while the attitude studies may leave us perplexed, there are sex differences that make these findings more comprehensible. Parsons and Bales (1955) have long held that women are more concerned with the immediate ongoing interpersonal interaction, while men focus on the more intangible and abstract goals in the future. Other studies have substantiated these generalizations and have added information that also helps to clarify these differences in behavior between men and women. One experiment led Hoffman (1975) to conclude that consideration for others is a more salient value for women than for men, and that women feel more guilty than men when they do something bad to others.

And, quite in keeping with the beliefs of Parsons, Bales, and Hoffman, Diggens (1974) obtained data that indicate women are more sensitive and responsive to interpersonal situations than men are. And so it appears that women, in interaction with one of our confederates, would be more influenced by and more responsive to the behavior and personal characteristics of that confederate than men would. The presence or absence of psychiatric problems in the background of the confederate changes neither the confederate's behavior nor the confederate's personal characteristics, and so women respond in the same way regardless of the history of mental disorder. But men are relatively more influenced by abstract factors, such as learning that a potential co-worker has been in a mental hospital, that could affect their job in the future, and so they respond to that knowledge. The report that they feel less guilty than women when they hurt another person is also consistent with the finding that they inflict more painful shocks when they believe the applicant has had a mental disorder.

Let us now consider the findings that suggest that a female who has suffered a mental breakdown will be treated differently from and more favorably than a comparable male. Here, also, attitude research is inconsistent with these results. Thus, Coie, Pennington, and Buckley (1974), Farina, Felner, and Boudreau (1973), and Nunnally (1961) all find essentially no difference in attitude expressed toward male and female mental patients. However, some attitude studies are congruent with the behavioral findings that have been reviewed. Phillips (1964) reports that his subjects, all women, rejected male mental patients more strongly than comparable female mental patients. And Hammen and Peters (1977) found that subjects of both sexes were less favorable toward a male with mental health problems than toward a comparably described female. Moreover, there is an abundance of other questionnaire studies, not specifically focused on attitudes, that suggest that male and female mental patients will be treated differently.

Differences in the conceptions held by people of mentally disordered men in comparison with women, and of mentally healthy men in comparison with women, have been reported by Broverman, Broverman, Clarkson, Rosenkrantz, and Vogel (1970); Chevron, Quinlan, and Blatt (1978); Coie, Pennington, and Buckley (1974); and Nowacki and Poe (1973). The Coie, Pennington, and Buckley study revealed that men are expected to react more violently than women under conditions of stress, which may account for some of the greater disfavor expressed toward men. That is, people are afraid that males will become violent, and therefore reject them. Research by Derlega and Chaikin (1976) suggests an additional pertinent factor. A woman who reveals intimate things about herself is regarded as better-adjusted than a male who discloses comparable information. In the studies we are considering, subjects learn that the confederate has been in a mental hospital. Such information is probably regarded as quite personal, and may cause the male to be judged as more maladjusted than the female, and hence to be treated less favorably.

Obviously we remain less than certain as to why these sex differences exist. However, they seem to be substantial, and very likely they say something important about the nature of mental disorders. For example, they hint that guilt and concern for other people felt by members of a society play a crucial part in determining who is designated as psychopathological and in how the society responds to the afflicted individual. Further research is surely merited.

Finally, we must briefly concern ourselves with the results of the nervousness manipulation. In five experiments, using the same procedure, virtually identical results were obtained. Whether male or female, former mental patient or average person, a nervous and tense individual is unequivocally and strongly rejected by others. The consistency and strength of the findings are noteworthy, and have both theoretical and practical implications. At a more theoretical level they raise the question of why tense people are responded to so negatively. Perhaps this reaction occurs only in the context of evaluating someone as a potential co-worker and the results have limited significance, such as that anxious people are expected to do a poor job. But it is more probable that the reaction is a very general one, and could occur for various possible reasons.

We can speculate that anyone who has been exposed to traumatic events was in the presence of people who were made nervous by those events, and so nervous people evoke memories of traumatic experiences. Or perhaps people have found from past interactions that tense people are gloomy and unpleasant companions, and therefore reject them. Whatever is responsible, it seems quite clear that tense people are less readily accepted than calm individuals, and it seems likely that we can improve the social relationships of nervous persons by reducing the visibility of their tension. If former mental patients are especially tense, as is widely believed, it may be particularly important to their readjustment at home if they can be helped to look more calm. Conceivably, nervousness displayed by former mental patients is an important factor in creating the social rejection they encounter. Here, also, further research seems merited.

Personal Experience with Mental Disorder

Quite a lot of research has been done to determine the effect of personal contact with those who have suffered a mental problem. These investigations are unusual in that the ubiquitous college sophomore, studied in the confines of a college laboratory, is almost never the subject. The research has generally been done in applied settings and with subjects whose occupation entails interacting with mental patients. Perhaps this state of affairs indicates the very practical and clinical motives for doing this research. However, Nunnally (1961) did use students as subjects in one of the early studies on this topic, and he reported that contact with mental patients could improve attitudes toward mental disorders in general. Other research has made it very clear that, given certain conditions, contact with patients does make people's feelings toward mental disorders more favorable.*

The subjects of the Nunnally study were given a talk intended to improve attitudes toward mental disorders. Target attitudes were measured three days later by someone the subjects were led to believe had nothing to do with the talk. To assess the impact of personal contact, some of the students were informed at the end of the talk that the speaker was a former mental patient, while other students were told nothing about the speaker. It was found that those subjects who believed the speaker was a former patient expressed more favorable attitudes toward mental disorders than subjects in the group having no contact with mental patients.

Gelfand and Ullmann did two studies that substantiate the Nunnally experiment. In one of these studies, 36 nursing students had their views toward psychopathology measured before and after exposure to mental patients (Gelfand & Ullmann, 1961b). Another group of 23 students, not exposed to mental patients, also had their attitudes measured twice over a comparable period. Relative to the control group, the attitudes of the student nurses exposed to patients became more accepting and benign. The second study was essentially the same as the first one, but this time the subjects were medical students (Gelfand and Ullmann, 1961a). Again they found that the subjects exposed to mental patients expressed more favorable attitudes toward mental disorder than did a control group of medical students. A very similar study of the effect on attitudes of nursing students produced by exposure to psychiatric patients was done by Altrocchi (1960). And, like Gelfand and Ullmann, Altrocchi found that the contact changed the attitudes of the subjects in a more favorable direction.

Nonprofessional hospital employees have also been the focus of this type of research. In one such study, Wright and Klein (1965) found the attitude of psychiatric hospital workers toward mental disorders was more favorable than that of community residents, presumably because the hospital workers were exposed to mental patients. A more interesting result that tends to confirm this reasoning was additionally reported. The nonprofessional treatment employees (such as nursing assistants), who had a lot of contact with patients, had more favorable attitudes than nonprofessional, nontreatment employees (such as laundry workers), who had relatively little such contact.

Smith (1969) studied three groups of subjects (hospital employees, student nurses, and mental patients themselves) to see what personal

---

*It does not follow that this process will make people with extensive exposure to mental patients (such as mental health professionals) free of any dislike of patients. Obviously their attitudes can improve and, after improvement, still remain negative.

experience with mental patients in a psychiatric hospital did to their attitudes toward mental disorders. Relative to a control group having no contact, all three groups were found to have more favorable attitudes after they had personal experience with psychiatric patients.

Several investigators have availed themselves of the opportunity provided by companion programs to learn about this process. Companion programs are attempts to improve the mental condition of patients by assigning a person to interact with the patient regularly and in a friendly and supportive way. These companions are generally unpaid volunteers, and while the main intent of the programs is to help patients, the volunteers have extensive and close contact with patients in the process. Therefore, they become excellent subjects for studying the effect of this contact. Both Chinsky and Rappaport (1970) and Holzberg and Knapp (1965) systematically studied students enrolled in such programs, and found that the experience led to significant increases in favorability of attitudes toward mental patients. Subjects were more approving and accepting of patients, and viewed them as being more like other people after having served as companions. Even a much more limited and casual experience with mental patients evidently can serve to ameliorate feelings toward them. Phillips (1967) measured the attitudes of two groups of subjects, a group who had personal experience with a mental patient and a group who had never known anyone who had suffered an emotional disorder. He found that those who had had personal contact were less rejecting of someone who was suffering from a mental disorder.

There is also reasonably good evidence that those who personally experience a severe mental problem and are consequently hospitalized improve their attitudes toward mental disorders. The study by Smith (1969) indicates this, since the attitudes of patients became more favorable as a result of exposure to a psychiatric hospital. And Gynther, Reznikoff, and Fishman (1963) found some suggestive differences between first-admission and readmission patients. Although they did not measure attitudes toward mental disorders per se, they found that readmitted patients had more approving attitudes toward psychiatric facilities and operations, which might have resulted from favorable experiences during earlier admissions. In another pertinent study, all the patients in a small mental hospital had their attitudes toward psychiatric disorders assessed (Jones, Kahn, & McDonald, 1963). The attitudes were found to be strongly favorable, and even though these researchers used no control group, it is arguable that the patients' feelings were shifted in a positive direction by the exposure to the environment of the psychiatric hospital.

And, finally, a study by Harrow, Fox, and Detre (1969) is also relevant. The subjects were a group of psychiatric patients and their spouses. For both husband and wife the favorability of perception of self and marital partner was measured one week after hospitalization, and it was found that the afflicted partner was viewed less favorably by each member of the pair than the nonafflicted partner. On a second measurement seven weeks later, the patient's concept of himself or herself was found to be significantly more favorable, presumably as a result of personal experience with sufferers from psychiatric problems. While it is possible that the patients' improvement of attitude was limited to themselves, it seems likely they felt more positively toward mental patients in general.

The question raised by these studies is why people generally view mental patients more positively after having contact with them. Two possible explanations, which are not mutually exclusive, seem reasonable. One is that people have distorted beliefs about mental patients—for example, that they look exceedingly strange and vacant, and that their behavior is altogether unpredictable and frightening. And it is because of these beliefs that people's attitudes are highly negative. However, after having personal experience with patients, they come to see that afflicted persons are not very strange-looking and do not behave very oddly. As a result, their distorted beliefs are modified, which causes their attitudes to improve.

The second explanation is similar, but rests less on logical processes and focuses on the prevailing view of insanity as a mysterious and threatening alien force that must be kept at a distance at all costs. By looking at the afflicted as very different from themselves (somewhat like the earlier view that they were possessed by demons), people may feel it is less likely that they themselves will become insane. So this distantiation, alienation, and dislike of the mentally disordered serves as an ego-protecting mechanism. However, personal experience makes it apparent to most people that mental patients are really very much like themselves. As a result, they feel more vulnerable and frightened. This awareness—the realization that they, too, could become insane—makes them feel closer to and more understanding of mental patients, and hence more sympathetic and kindly.

Some studies support the last explanation. One is the study by Ring and Farina (1969), which involved inducing some subjects to believe they were emotionally very stable, others that they were somewhat unstable, and others that they were highly unstable. They were then required to administer electric shocks to someone who was alleged to be a mental patient. The alleged patient remained in another room, and subjects never saw him. With increasing emotional instability, increasingly less painful shocks were delivered to the mental patient. (As in other experiments, no shocks were actually given.) In this study, beliefs about mental patients probably were not changed, since the subject never encountered the patient (and so such belief changes cannot be responsible for the changed behavior). It appears that being made to feel similar to patients is what induced the more benign behavior. Some findings reported by Milgram (1965) also support this identification explanation. Milgram showed that decreasing psychological distance between teacher and victim in his obedience experiment resulted in a decrease in willingness to shock the victim, as well as a decrease in the intensity of the most intense shock that the teachers administered.

Whatever is the most reasonable explanation, it is quite certain that we can improve people's attitudes toward mental patients by having them interact with afflicted individuals. However, it also seems certain that simply exposing people to anyone with mental problems may not lead to improvement. We have by now collected sufficient information to know there are factors that inhibit the generally favorable effect of interpersonal contact. Indeed, certain kinds of personal experiences with mental patients will cause feelings about them to become more negative than they were prior to the contact.

One such experience is a disagreeable encounter with a patient that can make attitudes toward mental disorders in general more negative, as seems intuitively obvious. Given that we do not know very much about a class of individuals, if we meet a member of that class whose behavior is unexpectedly dislikable, we will subsequently feel more negatively about all members of that class. A relevant study was done by Schwartz, Myers, and Astrachan (1974), whose subjects were relatives of patients who had returned home after hospitalization in a psychiatric facility. The mental status of the returning patient was assessed, and we can assume that the poorer the mental status of the patient, the more upsetting and disagreeable was the behavior he or she displayed. They found that the more disturbed the patient, the more negative were the attitudes of the relatives toward mental disorders in general.

This may also explain the results reported by Harrow, Fox, and Detre (1969). The attitudes of a husband or wife toward a hospitalized mate were found by those researchers not to improve. As in the Schwartz, Myers, and Astrachan study, the personal experience with a mentally disordered individual is a painful one. Although not all the patients may behave obnoxiously, the mental disorder brings the loss of companionship and sex and help in running the household. It also brings degradation in the eyes of others for having a "crazy" husband or wife, and perhaps financial losses.

Another condition that may make personal experience with mental patients a negative one occurs when people believe they are similar to the afflicted individual, even though similarity can lead to supportive behavior (Ring & Farina, 1969). Novak and Lerner (1968) led some subjects to think they were very similar to a confederate who was presented as having suffered a mental breakdown, while other subjects were induced to think they were quite different. Those who thought they were similar rejected the confederate decisively more than those who believed they were different. In keeping with one of the hypotheses discussed earlier, people probably feel threatened by insanity when they see themselves as similar to victims of that condition, and they respond to the threat by increased repudiation and distantiation of the patient.

A facet of the Nunnally (1961) experiment indicates still another condition that may lead to worsening of attitudes. Subjects were given a talk intended to improve attitudes toward the mentally disordered. When the speaker revealed, after her talk, that she had suffered a mental disorder, attitudes were more favorable than when she said nothing. However, when she identified herself as a former patient before the talk, the attitudes were significantly more unfavorable than for either of the other two conditions. Evidently the students expected incompetent and disagreeable behavior from the mental patient, perceived it even though objectively it was not there, and came to have a lower opinion of mental patients in general. This suggests that if we want to improve attitudes, we should not reveal to people that they are interacting with a former mental patient until they have had an opportunity to evaluate the individual without prejudice.

In summary, then, we have seen in this section that the mentally disordered are not always treated poorly and evaluated unfavorably by everyone, although their social reception is generally negative. A widely felt need to help unfortunate people seems to be responsible for the fact that sometimes we find mental patients treated better just because of their affliction. It may be that they are treated poorly only if people do not feel guilt, as when they are not aware of their unfavorable behavior or they feel it is justified. Victims of mental disorders are also treated much better by women than by men. In fact, women treat them quite equitably, under some conditions at least, in spite of expressing attitudes that are just as negative as those of men. Finally, those with mental problems are treated better by persons who have had contact with psychiatric patients and facilities than by those who have not. However, exposure to patients does not always improve behavior and feelings, since certain experiences with patients (such as unpleasant encounters) may make people more negative.

CHANGING PUBLIC BELIEFS ABOUT MENTAL DISORDERS

Over the years dramatic changes have occurred in what the public believes to be the nature of mental disorders. Radical alterations have taken place even over relatively short periods of time. For example, in seventeenth-century Europe and America, mental problems were commonly thought to be caused by demons, and sufferers were feared and despised by a society that literally considered them not human. These beliefs were not limited to the ignorant and superstitious. We have accounts, from that period, of people being tried in courts of law and executed for being in league with the devil. Their only crime was behaving in a way that now would lead to a diagnosis of schizophrenia (Deutsch, 1965, p. 33). Yet, less than 200 years later, insanity was viewed as a simple medical problem that could easily be remedied if the patient was taken to the proper institution. The afflicted were treated, and quickly and routinely "cured." Of course, we should note that the medical authorities of that day seemed strangely unimpressed by the fact that patients had to be "cured" over and over again. We have documented instances of people dying in insane asylums after being declared cured as many as 46 times (Deutsch, 1965, p. 156). These marked variations suggest that public beliefs are unstable and easily changed, something we now know to be true.

Another fact suggesting that public beliefs are easily influenced is the lack of crystallization and structure that characterizes them. People are very uncertain about what mental disorders are, and appear quite open to information about this phenomenon. Nunnally (1961, pp. 21–22) administered 240 statements about causes, symptoms, prognosis, treatments, and social significance of mental health problems to a sample of 349 persons. They were asked to indicate their views about the truth or falsity of each statement. The answers were factor-analyzed and only weak item clusters were found, the first ten factors accounting for only 25 percent of the variance. People agreed with inconsistent statements and disagreed with seemingly consistent ones. For example, an individual might agree with both a statement that women have more nervous breakdowns than men and one that men and women experience comparable frequency of emotional problems.

The results of factor analyses done on responses to a different questionnaire (Farina, Fisher, Getter, & Fischer, 1978) were in accord with Nunnally's findings. That was true even when the questionnaire used was composed only of items selected by a group of clinical psychologists for their clear portrayal of mental disorders as either a disease or a problem in interpersonal relationships. Hence we see that people are unsure and confused regarding the nature of mental disorders, and we would expect them to readily accept authoritative information—which, as we will see, they do.

What the public believes about mental disorders is certainly complex and multifaceted. Included in this array are beliefs about causes, cures, appearance, and behavior of the sufferers, how vulnerable people are, and whether insanity develops in an acute or an insidious fashion. However, there is a group of related beliefs that, for several reasons, seems more important and in need of our attention than other clusters. These related views are ranged along a continuum that has mental problems conceived as diseases at one extreme and as manifestations of social and interpersonal difficulties at the other.

These beliefs seem particularly important, first, because they appear to have a central position within the total constellation of beliefs. They appear to determine and to inform us about many other beliefs. For example, if a given person is of the opinion that mental problems are essentially diseases like diabetes, he or she is likely to think that drugs can provide effective treatment and that the victim's interpersonal experiences did not play an important role in causing the problem. Second, a great deal of research has been done on views along this dimension, and apparently we know much more about these than about other kinds of beliefs about mental health. And, third and most important, a nationwide effort has been under way for a number of years to convince the public that mental health problems and alcoholism are medical problems. It seems important to know, for both theoretical and practical reasons, what the consequences of this effort are. We will return to the issue of consequences after considering the process of changing beliefs.

Beliefs about the nature of mental disorders can be altered quite easily. In 1961, Nunnally concluded from the results of his studies that ". . . people will readily accept new mental health information and foresake their old ideas." Much other research leads to the same conclusion. For example, Costin and Kerr (1962; 1966) showed that attending a class where mental disorders are discussed produces very big changes in people's views of those disorders. More pertinent for the present topic are the studies that have focused on the continuum having mental problems conceived as a disease at one extreme and as products of social learning at the other.

Much of this research has been done by Morrison and his colleagues, who think there are distinct advantages to viewing mental health problems as social difficulties rather than as diseases. They have conducted seminars that openly try to convince the subjects enrolled in them to accept this view. Samples of community residents (Morrison & Teta, 1977), mental health professionals (Morrison & Becker, 1975), family caretakers (Morrison & Nevid, 1976a), and psychiatric outpatients (Morrison, 1976; 1977; Morrison & Nevid, 1976b) have all had their beliefs significantly shifted in the desired direction as compared with control subjects. These effects were still present when measured as long as eight months after the seminar.

Using entirely different procedures, we too have obtained very similar results (Farina, Fisher, Getter, & Fischer, 1978; Fisher & Farina, 1979). However, in our experiments we also attempted to shift the beliefs of some subjects toward viewing difficulties in adjustment as due to a disease. Four experiments were carried out. In two, randomly divided groups of college students were given some descriptive information about a mental health clinic. The only difference in the treatments was that for one group two sentences embedded in the message described mental problems as diseases, while for the other group two different sentences stated they were a manifestation of interpersonal difficulties. In the third study subjects read a pamphlet alleged to be a press release from an association of mental health professionals. One version of the pamphlet described mental disorders as a disease, while the other version presented them as products of social difficulties. Students enrolled in two abnormal psychology classes, whose beliefs about mental problems were initially comparable, were the subjects of the last study. The instructor in one of the classes strongly favored a social learning conception of mental disorders, while the other instructor thought biological factors played a role in such conditions. In each of the four studies, beliefs were significantly shifted in the expected direction (see Table 7.4).

Thus, beliefs about the nature of mental health problems can easily be altered. Various types of messages can be used to induce people to view such problems as more like a disease or as more similar to a pattern of learned behaviors than they formerly thought. There are two critical questions regarding such changes that should now be explicitly considered. One is "Does it make any difference?" As has already been suggested, there is evidence indicating that such changes have important consequences for both the "normals" and those suffering from emotional problems. This evidence will be reviewed after considering the second question: "Do changes in people's beliefs about mental health problems take place only within the confines of psychological experiments?" If that were true, the issue of beliefs about the nature of psychopathology might be deemed unimportant. But it is evident that such changes are occurring in everyday contexts outside the laboratory, and are widespread.

There are massive, nationwide efforts to alter beliefs about the nature of mental disorders. A major goal of groups like Alcoholics Anonymous and mental health associations is to convince the public that those displaying problems in adjustment are suffering from a disease. Consider, as an example, an article that appeared on January 21, 1979, in a major Connecticut newspaper, the *Hartford Courant*. The article (pp. 8–9) concerned the Glastonbury Mental Health Group. The group's president stated, "Mental illness is not something to be ashamed of. It's really no different from, say, an attack of appendicitis or other illnesses." Just about everyone in our

TABLE 7.4
Belief About Mental Disorders Expressed by Subjects in Four Studies, as a Function of Message They Received

| | Message Describing Mental Disorder as a | |
Study	Disease	Result of Learning
1	3.33	4.11
2	3.27	3.60
3	3.7	5.1
4	3.65	4.19

Note: The smaller the number, the more like a disease mental disorders are thought to be.

Sources: Adapted from Farina, Fisher, Getter, & Fischer (1978), Table 1, p. 275, and Fisher & Farina (1979), Table 1, p. 324. Copyright 1978 and 1979 by the American Psychological Association. Reprinted by permission.

society has heard or read that mental disorders are diseases like any other disease. Similarly, we are instructed to look upon alcoholics *not* as self-indulgent and culpable persons who should be punished for their excesses, but as innocent victims of a common sickness. The research reviewed indicates that these efforts are probably very successful in changing what people believe about these problems.

But there seems to be another avenue through which public beliefs are altered. The mental health field is clearly dominated by the medical profession, which determines how patients are cared for and treated. Mental institutions are usually managed by physicians, and medical procedures such as blood pressure measurement and X rays are routinely used. Less severe and more prevalent adjustment difficulties are likely to lead to contact with a medically trained person, and prescriptions for tranquilizers are extremely common. For example, on CBS's "Sixty Minutes" program, broadcast July 30, 1978, it was reported that Valium is the most frequently prescribed drug in America. A total of 44 million prescriptions for it were filled during the preceding year in America alone, according to the September 10, 1979, "CBS Evening News" broadcast. And Valium is just one tranquilizer in one of a number of classes of tranquilizers. These seem to be powerful cues implying that sufferers from mental problems have something physically wrong with them, and these may influence beliefs about the nature of mental disorders. There is research that suggests this is just what happens.

Whitman and Duffey (1961) measured what a group of mental patients believed to be wrong with them as well as what they thought was wrong with other mental patients. These beliefs were then coded as functional or nonfunctional, the latter category including the belief that the mental problem was due to a disease. Prior to treatment, 20 to 30 percent of the patients expressed the view that both their own and other patients' problems were nonfunctional in nature. The patients were then treated exclusively with drugs and, one month after the start of treatment, their beliefs were measured again. The subjects did not change their beliefs about other patients' problems. However, 73 percent of them now felt their own condition was nonfunctional in nature, a statistically reliable change. On the basis of the preceding data and other data that were consistent with them, the authors conclude as follows: "Chemotherapy can result in strong denial of interpersonal difficulties . . ." (Whitman & Duffey, 1961, p. 292). It is surely possible that it is not only the millions of people who actually receive treatment whose beliefs are changed. Others who learn about these practices may be similarly affected.

We will now consider the all-important question of the consequences of believing mental disorders are diseases or are the products of interpersonal problems. We will examine separately the consequences for the public, for the patient, and for the mental health worker.

As far as the public is concerned, believing the sufferer's problems are biologically based leads to a poorer opinion of him or her than thinking they are the end results of a learning process. One of the earliest studies showing this was done by Rothaus, Hanson, Cleveland, and Johnson (1963). They trained a group of hospitalized psychiatric patients to describe their condition as being like an illness or as stemming from interpersonal difficulties. Each patient was then seen by an employment interviewer who was unaware of any aspect of the study. The interviewers judged that it would be more difficult for the patients in the disease condition to find a job than for those in the social learning condition. The results of a study by Ommundsen and Ekeland (1978) are quite consistent with these findings. Three independent groups of subjects were given information about a driver who was involved in an auto accident. Subjects in the control group were additionally told that the driver had been hospitalized for an operation, those in the second group were told he had been hospitalized for a mental disorder that was presented as a disease, and those in the last group learned he had been hospitalized for a mental disorder that was described as due to problems in living. Subjects rated the surgical patient and the mental patient whose condition was attributed to social difficulties as equally culpable for the accident. However, when the driver's mental condition was presented as a disease, they blamed him more for the accident than they blamed the control driver.

While the preceding two studies seem to be the most pertinent ones, there are several others that confirm them. In the study by Farina, Fisher, Getter, and Fischer (1978), groups of college students were induced to view mental health problems either as diseases or as a set of learned behaviors. Those who thought of such conditions as diseases believed, in comparison with the other group, that there was little a sufferer could personally do to improve his or her condition. It seems that a view of mental health problems as learned entails a more hopeful and optimistic outlook on such conditions. Virtually identical results were obtained in an investigation by Morrison and Nevid (1976a). And so, contrary to the assumptions of the mental health associations, these studies indicate that telling people mental disorders are diseases may make the sufferers' problems in society more, rather than less, severe.

Perhaps the most important aim of the massive nationwide campaigns to convince people that mental disorders are a type of disease is to reduce the social stigma these conditions bring. Quite plainly, many of these messages ask us to be helpful and understanding toward mental patients *because* they are ill. The assumption seems to be that if someone's psychopathological behavior is viewed as caused by a bodily sickness, the afflicted person will not be held accountable for the behavior that ordinarily would bring degradation. However, the results of some experiments raise doubts about the wisdom of this strategy. First of all, a social learning view of mental disorders is, in some ways, preferred by people (Colson, 1970). Colson asked a group of students of both sexes if they would prefer to be treated by a professional who viewed mental health problems as emotional illnesses or a professional who viewed them as inadequacies in learning coping skills. Of

56 subjects, 85 percent preferred the professional with the social learning outlook. More important, in three separate studies, subjects with social learning views were as favorably disposed toward people with emotional problems as were subjects holding a disease conception of mental disorders (Farina, Fisher, Getter, & Fischer, 1978; Fisher & Farina, 1979).

The consequences for the patient personally of believing his or her affliction is the culmination of interpersonal difficulties versus a reflection of a pathological bodily condition seem quite obvious. Consider the plight of an individual who is fully convinced that his or her interpersonal problems are due to a disease, perhaps one with a biochemical basis. He or she cannot hope to get along better with others by thinking about frictions, failures, or rejections, nor can there be much hope of totally mastering personal behavior. If the behavior is controlled by a disease, thinking about it is fruitless and can only be painful. The only way to change things, if a disease is at the basis of the problem, is to attack the disease. This means turning to doctors or to drugs for improvement.

Matters are entirely different for the individual who is similarly afflicted but who believes the troubles are at least in part due to personal shortcomings in interacting with other people. Such a person can hope to improve matters by thinking about past experiences and considering possible changes in behavior. Certain behavioral patterns that lead to difficulties may be recognized and stopped. And the sufferer can experiment with talking less, paying more attention to others, and keeping his or her temper in check. If these beliefs really do have the effect described, then they will cause maladaptive behaviors in those with problems of adjustment if they accept a disease view of their condition. Since we all have problems in adjustment, the beliefs we hold would seem to have important consequences for everybody. But do the belief-behavior relationships outlined really exist? The following research indicates that they do.

Morrison, Bushell, Hanson, Fentiman, and Holdridge-Crane (1977) did a study to see whether individuals with a somatic view of emotional problems are more dependent on mental health professionals than people who conceive of such problems as reflecting faulty learning. If beliefs have the consequences described above, it follows logically that the more someone believes his or her troubles are biologically based, the more that person will believe he or she needs medical experts to help. Consistent with this expectation, Morrison et al. (1977) found a correlation of .60 between degree to which psychiatric outpatients believe their mental disorders are diseases and how dependent they feel on mental health experts.*

This may explain the results of another study by Morrison (1976), which entailed shifting the beliefs of a group of former mental patients

---

*Wehler (1979) replicated this study with psychiatric in-patients. He also found that those who saw their problems as biological felt more dependent on mental health workers. The correlation was not statistically significant, however.

toward viewing their problems as learned. Another group of patients served as controls. More patients were rehospitalized from the control than from the experimental group (although the numbers—four patients to one—were too small to be statistically significant). Conceivably, patients in the experimental group became less dependent on professionals, felt greater responsibility for their own welfare, and took actions beneficial to their personal adjustment.

Data from two of the studies we did provide good support for the foregoing interpretation. In the Fisher and Farina (1979) study, it will be recalled, students attending one abnormal psychology class became more biologically oriented than students in another class. Students in the biologically oriented class reported being less likely than members of the other class to seek help at a clinic, they thought medically based treatments were more effective in curing mental disorders, they judged it less valuable to identify the causes and solutions of their emotional problems, they believed self-reliance to be less important, and they reported using more drugs and/or alcohol to relieve emotional problems during the semester.

What may be a more definitive study about the impact on the individual of changing his or her beliefs was done with female college students. They were recruited to receive a therapy session that, they were told, was intended to help them with their own personal problems (Farina, Fisher, Getter, & Fischer, 1978). Their beliefs were then manipulated so that half viewed mental disorders as more like diseases and the rest viewed them as more like social problems. Following therapy, they were asked to note in a journal during the subsequent week each time they thought about a personal problem like the one discussed in the therapy session. The disease group thought about personal problems significantly less often than the social learning group. Evidently people with a disease view of disorders in adjustment believe there is little they can do about their problems, and they actually do little to improve their state.

Like the patient, the mental health worker plays a central role in the phenomenon of psychopathology. Let us now consider some systematic studies that have been concerned with the significance of beliefs about mental disorders held by mental health workers. Two of the studies have used a general questionnaire to assess beliefs that is called the Opinions about Mental Illness (OMI) questionnaire (Cohen & Struening, 1962). While some items composing this questionnaire seem to assess attitudes, most pertain to beliefs (as these two variables were defined earlier). One of the studies entailed giving the OMI to mental health workers at each of 12 mental hospitals (Cohen & Struening, 1964). The interest of the investigators was to see whether length of time spent in the community during the first year following admission could be predicted for the patients in these hospitals. The expected and logical significant relationship was found between the beliefs of mental health workers and how many days patients cared for by those workers spent in the community during the first year following admission. For hospitals where the staff believed mental patients to be different from and inferior to others, and to require restriction for the protection of society and the family, patients spent fewer days in the community than did patients in hospitals where the staff viewed patients as more like ordinary people. The researchers demonstrated that differences across hospitals in degree of emotional disturbance of patients housed there did not account for the relationship.

Ellsworth (1965) obtained results quite consistent with those of Cohen and Struening. The OMI and another questionnaire were given to nurses and aides while hospitalized psychiatric patients under their care were asked to describe those nurses and aides. The staff members were perceived by the patients to behave just as the beliefs of those staff members implied. Nurses and aides who believed psychiatric patients are dangerous and need to have limitations placed on their behavior were described by their patients as behaving in a controlling and restrictive way. Evidently the beliefs of mental health workers about the nature of mental disorders do have consequences that may be important. They certainly appear to play a role in the treatment and care that psychiatric patients receive.

Langer and Abelson (1974) also did a relevant study. One group of mental health professionals believed mental disorders to be products of social learning processes, while another group thought biological factors played an important role in such conditions. All were shown the same videotaped interview, but half the subjects in each group were told the interviewee was a job applicant, while the rest were informed he was a mental patient. The behaviorally oriented professionals described the interviewee in the two conditions comparably. However, those with a disease view of mental disorders described the "patient" as significantly more disturbed than the "job applicant." Once again we see that beliefs of mental health workers along the social-learning-to-disease continuum have a significant influence. And once again we see that a disease view of mental disorders has unfavorable effects. In this instance both the professional and the mental patient suffer the consequences. The patient is perceived as displaying disturbed behavior that is nonexistent, and he or she may encounter unneeded restriction and medication as a result. And the mental health worker's perception of reality is distorted, which may constitute a handicap in the satisfactory performance of his or her job.

It should not be concluded from the foregoing that the view espoused is that a social learning interpretation of behavioral problems is to be preferred under each and every circumstance. Sometimes behavioral difficulties do occur for somatic reasons. For example, brain tumors can cause emotional lability and produce memory lapses that will interfere with smooth interpersonal functioning. Certainly it seems better for individuals in such circumstances to believe that the problems are due to a disease than to try to improve things by changing their behavior. There may be other benefits of such a conception. For example, it cannot be ruled out, without further research, that a mental disorder is less of a disaster to patient and family when it is seen as a disease than when it is seen as an inability to cope with problems.

NOT ALL STIGMAS ARE ALIKE

The existence and very wide usage of the term "stigma" indicates the belief in the similarity of a multitude of conditions that have a common characteristic. They degrade the person afflicted with them. There certainly are many of these unwanted entities that plague the life of human beings, as we have already seen. There are problems in appearance and in abilities of all kinds, such as intellectual, athletic, and social; there are occupational and family blemishes; and so forth. In fact, any departure from the social ideals of physical appearance, mental adroitness, social position of both the self and the family, and past behavior may constitute a stigma. Yet it is widely supposed that all these varied conditions have important functions in common. Goffman (1963), one of the more compelling and influential spokesmen on this issue, believes all stigmas fall into one of three categories: bodily disfigurements, such as missing members or scars; personality deficiencies, such as dishonesty or unnatural passions; and membership in groups looked down upon by others, such as blacks and Jews. All these very different conditions, asserts Goffman, lead to the same social consequences: the possessor is discredited and rejected, and ". . . we believe the person with a stigma is not quite human" (Goffman, 1963, p. 5).

To be sure, there are similarities among stigmas that make them seem homogeneous and merely different manifestations of the same underlying entity. For example, under ordinary circumstances nobody would want a stigma. Moreover, there may be heuristic value to looking upon all blemishing characteristics as basically the same. It seems more appealing and exciting to investigate the social significance of all stigmas instead of only what the consequences of mental disorders are, for example. So perhaps this tendency to believe all degrading characteristics are the same has helped to motivate research that has yielded some intriguing results. However, no matter how eloquently one emphasizes the similarity of stigmas, it is starkly clear there are very important differences among them. A paraplegic, a homosexual, a former mental patient, and a shoplifter do not strike us as being very similar. And research on such conditions has made the differences among them, for both possessor and society, very clear.

A great deal of the research has relied on questionnaire reports. In essence, subjects have been asked to describe how they feel and how they would act toward people with various kinds of stigmatizing conditions. Such a procedure is not as satisfactory as directly measuring the behavior of interest. There are many possible sources of error when one uses self-reports, perhaps the most ubiquitous one being that caused by social desirability.

Subjects want to be viewed favorably by the experimenter, and they very frequently slant their answers for that reason rather than reporting what is true. Nevertheless, the research results are consistent. Moreover, there are studies that have measured behaviors and are in agreement with the research using questionnaires.

A number of the questionnaire studies have concentrated on degrading conditions other than emotional problems, these being primarily physical blemishes. Richardson, Hastorf, Goodman, and Dornbusch (1961) presented to groups of children pictures of children who had various physical blemishes, such as missing limbs, and they also showed a child whose only defect was obesity. Striking differences in preference were expressed by their subjects, and there was an unexpectedly high degree of similarity in choices made from one group of children to another. Furthermore, the preferences evidently were not determined by logical and intuitively comprehensible reasons, such as the degree to which the pictured child's defect interfered with functioning. For example, extremely strong dislike was expressed toward the fat child. Matthews and Westie (1966) did a very similar study and obtained essentially the same results. They concluded that there is a high degree of cultural uniformity in how much people dislike various kinds of degrading physical conditions.

In one study people's feelings toward blindness and physical handicaps were assessed (Whiteman & Lukoff, 1965). A clear differentiation was made by the subjects. And Siller, Ferguson, Vann, and Holland (1968) extensively investigated subjects' perception of three types of physical stigmas: amputation, blindness, and cosmetic conditions. They found that people responded rather comparably to amputation and blindness. However, both those handicaps were viewed in a way distinctly different from cosmetic conditions. This research, then, indicates that people do react differently to various kinds of blemishing conditions even if we restrict such conditions to physical defects.

The stigma of mental disorders has been studied in various ways, and it has been compared with the degradation produced by numerous other conditions. Here, also, self-report, paper-and-pencil measures have been predominant. Nunnally (1961) assessed public feelings toward numerous types and degrees of mental disorders, as well as feelings toward other conditions. For much of his research he used the Osgood Semantic Differential, which measures three attitude dimensions, including favorability toward such conditions. He found, first, that people clearly distinguish one mental disorder from another, and the more severe the disorder, the more they dislike the person afflicted. He also found that adjustment problems are distinguished from other stigmatized conditions, and that people experiencing such problems are disliked particularly strongly by the public. Even those unfortunate ones who are stricken with diseases that have a notoriously bad reputation, such as leprosy, are not so thoroughly rejected as those who are insane.

Lawner (1966) did a study of which a part was quite similar to the work of Nunnally. Subjects' favorability toward people suffering from 11 different kinds of mental disorders was determined. These disorders ranged from mild problems (a person who has been treated by a psychiatrist) to extremely severe ones (insane person). He also measured attitudes toward someone with tuberculosis, a former convict, and a person addicted to narcotics. Like Nunnally, Lawner found that people distinguish among mental disorders, and the more severe the problem, the more unfavorably they regard the person suffering from it. He also found that an insane person was the most unfavorably viewed of all the stigmatized people in his study.

Two other studies were done similarly, and obtained results very much like those of Nunnally and Lawner. Eisdorfer and Altrocchi (1961) used the Osgood Semantic Differential to rate both males and females when they were described as average, old, neurotic, and insane. No distinction was made between men and women, but they were clearly distinguished by their other characteristics; degree of favorability diminished in the order listed above. Kleck, Buck, Goller, London, Pfeiffer, and Vukcevic (1968) measured the distance from a silhouette of themselves at which subjects placed figures of a mental patient and four other stigmatized figures. A greater distance presumably indicated less willingness to be intimate with that kind of person. The order in which these blemished people were placed, from closest to most distant from the self, was someone who was blind, black, amputee, epileptic, and mental patient. Thus all these studies indicate that people with mental disorders are disliked strongly and to a greater extent than people who have other types of degrading characteristics. Clearly, not all stigmas have a comparable public impact.

Several investigators have wanted to learn more than that different stigmatizing conditions have different consequences. They have been concerned with the exact nature of some of these consequences. Lamy (1966) had subjects compare how much difficulty would be encountered in society by a former convict and a former mental patient. His subjects strongly preferred the role of former convict, and thought such a person would have fewer problems than a former mental patient. A former mental patient was perceived as permanently vulnerable and unable to forestall future hospitalizations, incompetent in emergencies, and, as an employee, less trustworthy and desirable than a former convict. MacDonald and Hall (1969) assessed how four disabling (and therefore stigmatizing) conditions would affect six dimensions of social functioning. The conditions were internal disorders, such as a heart or back condition; sensory disorders, such as deafness or blindness; cosmetic disorders, such as facial scars or obesity; and emotional disorders, such as being depressed or withdrawn. The dimensions of social functioning investigated were vocational, marital, social relationships with neighbors, interactions with offspring, interactions with family, and subjective feelings about the self.

They also found some conditions to be more detrimental than others to functioning in general. Cosmetic conditions were thought by their subjects to cause the most severe problems, followed by emotional disorders and internal disorders. But the pattern of dimensions where these conditions were thought to cause the greatest and least serious problems was unique to each stigmatizing condition. The most and least severely affected dimension of social functioning for the four conditions were as follows: cosmetic disorders, personal most and social least; emotional disorders, parental most and vocational least; internal disorders, vocational most and social least; and sensory disorders, personal most and marital least. Thus these studies indicate not only that there are quantitative differences between stigmas in severity of consequences, but also that there are qualitative differences among them. Some stigmas are most debilitating in certain areas of interpersonal relationships, while others negatively influence other kinds of interpersonal functioning.

Not many studies have been concerned with measuring differences in actual behaviors that are caused by different kinds of stigmatizing conditions. However, there are two studies, using the same procedure, one of which examined how a former mental patient is treated while the other investigated how people behave toward someone with an amputated leg. In the Farina, Holland, and Ring (1966) study, subjects had to steer a confederate toward the correct solution of a problem by administering shocks of which they could control the intensity and duration. The confederate was presented as normally adjusted to half the subjects and as having been in a mental hospital to the rest. In the second study (Farina, Sherman, & Allen, 1968) the same procedure was used, but while half the subjects saw the confederate limp slightly, to the rest he appeared to have had his leg amputated just below the knee. When the confederate was presented as having had a mental disorder, he was given more painful shocks than in the control condition. However, he was given less painful shocks when his leg was missing than in the control condition.

Another study of the behavioral consequences of different kinds of stigmas is Farina, Thaw, Felner, and Hust (1976). Male subjects met a male confederate in a state residential institution. The confederate was presented to some as a normal college student, to others as mentally disordered, and to still others as mentally retarded. The same procedure involving the bogus shocking apparatus was used. The confederate was given longer shocks in the mental patient condition than in the control condition, but when presented as mentally retarded, he was given much briefer shocks than in the control condition. The study was then replicated with a different male confederate and different male subjects. The results were identical. These studies of behavior are consistent with the questionnaire studies. Different stigmatizing conditions do not elicit the same social reaction. Even though such conditions are thoroughly degrading, society may respond to them in distinctly different ways.

Even when we confine ourselves to a single stigma, its consequences for both the victim and society will vary as a function of other factors that inevitably are involved. It seems intuitively obvious that the personal characteristics of the stigmatized person will play a role. If we meet a mentally disordered person who is small, thin, and elderly, we will feel quite differently about him than if he is 25 years old, big, and brawny. The role of the personal characteristics of the stigmatized person was very clearly shown in the Farina, Thaw, Felner, and Hust study (1976). In that study, four confederates, two of each sex, met independent groups of subjects of their own sex in the role of a normal, mentally disordered, or mentally retarded person. The subjects had to teach a task to the confederate that allegedly required them to shock him or her; the main dependent measure was shock duration. The effect of those stigmatizing conditions was a function of the specific personal characteristics of the confederate. One female confederate was treated better as retarded than as mentally disordered; the other female was treated more poorly. Also, in comparison with the control condition, one female confederate was treated more harshly when she was thought to be retarded, while the other three confederates were each treated more favorably.

A study using the same procedure (Ring & Farina, 1969) demonstrated the influence of another variable on the social consequences of a degrading condition. Subjects were tested and then randomly assigned to one of three groups. In one they were told the test showed that their adjustment was superior, in another that it was average, and in the last they were informed that their adjustment was very poor and a cause for alarm. They were then asked to teach the task described earlier to someone in the next room who was said to be a patient from a nearby mental hospital. All three groups were significantly different from each other in terms of the duration of the shocks they delivered. Those in the well-adjusted group delivered the longest shocks, while those in the poor adjustment group gave the shortest. From this study it appears that similarity to the stigmatized person influences the treatment the afflicted is accorded. Those who see themselves as similar to the degraded individual will evidently treat him or her better.

A study by Dohrenwend and Dohrenwend (1969) indicates another variable that influences how someone suffering from a mental disorder will be treated. People of the lower socioeconomic class are more tolerant of certain kinds of disorders, such as simple schizophrenia, than are people of higher classes. Here we see that social class membership is a determiner of one stigma's consequences. Lower-class people may respond differently and more favorably to individuals with such a personality disorganization. Finally, a study by MacDonald and Hall (1969) reveals a personality variable that may influence how an emotionally disturbed individual will be treated by those who interact with that individual. The variable is locus of control (Rotter, 1966), which is the disposition, at one extreme of this dimension, for individuals to believe they are fully in control of what is going to happen to them (they are called Internals), while those at the other extreme believe their destiny is determined by luck, fate, or other people (they are called Externals). MacDonald and Hall found that Internals regarded emotional disorders as more serious and debilitating than Externals did. The suggested explanation is that Internals view the loss of control implied by the disorder as a more serious and threatening matter than do Externals, who believe they have little control over events to begin with. Whatever the explanation for the difference between Externals and Internals, these results suggest that Internals will view mental problems as more degrading and will treat people afflicted with such problems less favorably.

Clearly, then, not all stigmas are alike. (This conclusion is supported by research reviewed in the following section when we focus on the possessor of the stigma.) As attractive as it may appear to engage in the study of the common role of all stigmas, it does not seem that such a plan is feasible. What we discover about one stigma is unlikely to apply exactly to another. For the immediate future it appears likely that each type of affliction degrading the social status of human beings will require separate and independent investigation. Only when much more is known will we be able to discern what patterns exist and what generalizations are possible.

THE IMPACT OF STIGMA UPON THE STIGMATIZED

It seems intuitively obvious that the interaction between two people will not go smoothly when one of them has a deeply degrading stigma, such as having suffered a mental disorder. We have already seen that the "normal" contributes to the difficulties in such interpersonal interactions by basically disliking the blemished other, perceiving nonexisting shortcomings, and treating him or her badly. But the "normal" is not the only one involved in the interaction, of course, and he or she may not be the only one responsible for the problems encountered by stigmatized people. It seems likely that the stigma is more important and salient to the afflicted than to the observer, and the blemished person's perception and actions may be strongly influenced by the stigma independently of the behavior of others. Research makes it clear that that is precisely what happens.

Farina, Allen, and Saul (1968) told one member of pairs of male students who were unacquainted with each other to reveal some intimate, personal information to the other member, and he was taken to another room to write it. When alone with the experimenter, he was told the study was really to see how the other subject would treat someone he believed to have something wrong with him. Then one-third were asked to copy a typed statement saying they had suffered a mental disorder, one-third copied a statement revealing they were homosexuals, and the rest were assigned to the control group that copied an innocuous and unrevealing statement. The experimenter then departed with the statement, saying the other subject would read it. Actually, the bland control statement was always given to the other subject, regardless of what had been copied. Thus, only the belief of the subject that he was perceived as normal or stigmatized was varied. The results unambiguously showed that believing he was viewed as stigmatized influenced the believer's behavior, and caused the other subject to reject him. Thus, the study suggests not only that social attitudes and beliefs about stigmas influence the behavior of the stigmatized, but also that the social rejection blemished people encounter is, in part, caused by themselves. However, the subjects were ordinary college students, and it remained to be determined if truly stigmatized people behave this way.

A study by Farina, Gliha, Boudreau, Allen, and Sherman (1971) was done to find out about this. Males who had been mental patients in a VA hospital that also treats medical and surgical patients were the subjects of the experiment. They were asked to participate in a study that, it was alleged, was to find out whether employers discriminate against former mental patients in their hiring practices. Hence, it was explained, they would meet one of a group of employment interviewers brought to the hospital to talk to them and to judge how good a worker each patient was. To find out about a possible bias, some of the employment interviewers would know the subjects were former mental patients, while others would be told they were meeting a former medical patient. Half the subjects were then told the interviewer knew they had been mental patients, while the rest were assured they were thought to be former medical patients. Actually, all subjects met the same confederate, who was unaware of what they had been told, and all underwent an identical experimental procedure. This included having the subject do a task, explain it to the "employment interviewer," and complete a questionnaire measuring his feelings and perceptions. The confederate also made ratings of the subject's behavior.

A very consistent and comprehensible pattern of results was found. When the subjects believed the interviewer was aware of their status as former mental patients, they felt less appreciated, they found the task more difficult, and their task performance was poorer than in the control condition. Subjects in the mental patient condition were also rated by the confederate as more tense, anxious, and poorly adjusted than those in the control condition, although the rater was unaware of the group assignments. Together, the two experiments indicate that both the feelings and the behaviors of former mental patients are adversely affected simply because they think other people know they have had a mental disorder. But these studies also indicate something that is surprising and perhaps even startling. Consider what happened when the subjects thought they were viewed as former mental patients. Their levels of tension and anxiety increased, and their adjustment became poorer. They felt more unappreciated by others, somehow they alienated others, and their task performance became less adequate.

These are central components of the syndrome of behaviors that indicates a mental disorder. And it is generally agreed by both the experts and the public that the mental disorder, whether due to faulty upbringing or an erroneous biochemical process, is somewhere in the physical and mental composition of the afflicted. Yet, here we see that such behaviors are produced by the immediate social situation, evidently because of prevailing beliefs and attitudes toward mental disorders. These results have numerous implications. One is that we will not fully understand the behavior of mental patients if we concentrate our efforts on their past history or present bodily functioning, and neglect the ongoing social situation. This is not to deny the role of other factors (such as an individual's history) in psychopathology. It has been well established that a number of factors are important in determining adjustment. But ultimately the contribution of social beliefs and attitudes must be taken into account.

People who have been mental patients are not the only ones who show an adverse reaction as a result of having their condition become known to others. This response is also shown by people with other conditions that are viewed as unsavory or degrading by society. Homosexuality, at least for males, appears to be one such condition. In the Farina, Allen, and Saul (1968) study, male students induced to believe they were viewed as homosexuals showed both behavioral and subjective changes as a result. Of course, those subjects were not truly homosexuals, but there is another study in which the subjects *were* male homosexuals; the results were consistent with those of the Farina, Allen, and Saul experiment. Pollack, Huntley, Allen, and Schwartz (1976) had members of a Gay Lib group do a cognitive task and provide self-descriptions of their mood under two conditions. In one of the conditions the subjects thought their homosexuality had been revealed to the examiner, whereas in the other they believed he was unaware of it. Actually, the examiner was always ignorant of the subjects' sexual orientation. Nevertheless, thinking their sexual orientation was known significantly influenced both the mood and the task performance of the subjects.

There is a final pertinent study in which male college students were led to believe another male student thought they were homosexuals (Farina, Thaw, & Boudreau, 1970). The procedure used to create this belief was the same as that used in the Farina, Allen, and Saul study: the subject was asked to write the unfavorable information about himself and was told the other person would read it. In fact, the other student did not read this information. The results of that study also showed that the revelation caused changes in both behavior and subjective feelings of the subjects. A different stigmatizing condition was also investigated in the Farina, Thaw, and Boudreau experiment. Some subjects thought the other student learned they were stupid, unable to do the college work, and about to leave school. Their behaviors and feelings were also significantly influenced by the belief of the revelation.

Thus, we see that three very different kinds of socially degrading conditions—mental disorder, homosexuality, and low intelligence—each appear to have an effect on the possessor merely as a result of his thinking others have become aware of it. Now if we are to understand the behavior of the stigmatized person when he or she thinks he or she has been found out, we must distinguish between voluntary and involuntary behavior. It may be that for any degrading condition, the involuntary behaviors will be very much like those shown in the case of mental disorders. The person will show anxiety, feel rejected and unappreciated, alienate others, and display behavioral deficits in task performance. And there seems to be a similarity in voluntary behavior, too, insofar as we can tell from data presently available. That is, the blemished individual does whatever the circumstances allow to convince the observer that he or she really does not possess all the unfavorable characteristics that the stereotype of the condition attributes to him or her. But these unfavorable characteristics differ from one degrading condition to another. Thus, former mental patients are thought to be nervous and incompetent at doing tasks, homosexuals have effeminate interests and are weak, and stupid people are slow to understand and have an oxlike insensitivity. And so, when a victim seeks to demonstrate personal worth, what he or she does varies according to the stigma possessed.

A stereotypic societal belief about mental disorders is that the afflicted are very inept at tasks requiring motor skills (Farina & Ring, 1965; Sherman, 1967). When the subjects in the Farina and Ring study were led to believe they were viewed as former mental patients, they performed a motor task significantly better than subjects in the control condition. We reasoned in that 1965 report that, by demonstrating they were not like former mental patients, subjects in that condition were proving that they should be regarded with greater favor than would generally be accorded people of their status.

The results of a study by Thaw (1969), the subjects of which were hospitalized mental patients, are in close agreement with that reasoning. In Thaw's study patients met a confederate who interviewed them and asked them to do various tasks ranging from extremely simple to quite difficult. However, half the patients, selected at random, were told the confederate thought mental patients were incompetent at even the simplest tasks, while the rest were led to believe he thought they had difficulty doing only very hard tasks. Highly significant differences in task performance were found between the groups as a function of the manipulation. Patients in the former group did better on the very simple tasks, while those in the latter group did better on the difficult ones. Evidently the patients, like the students in the Farina and Ring study, wanted to prove they were not as incompetent as the interviewer believed them to be.

But if a male believes he is viewed as a homosexual, he cannot prove he does not possess the attendant stereotypes by showing excellent performance on a psychomotor task. Being good at motor tasks seems quite compatible with homosexuality in the views of our society. Consequently, subjects in the homosexual condition did not perform better than the controls in the Farina and Ring study. What can someone who is viewed as a homosexual or as stupid do to remove some of the stigma associated with those conditions? That was what the Farina, Thaw, and Boudreau (1970) study sought to determine.

It will be recalled that in that study, some subjects believed the other student viewed them as homosexuals while others thought they were considered stupid. And in the experiment an opportunity was given the subjects to prove they possessed characteristics incompatible with the uncomfortable role in which they were placed. For example, they had to squeeze a hand dynamometer, so they could demonstrate strength of hand grip, and they were asked to discuss several topics, which gave them an opportunity of displaying intellect and sensitivity. Not all results were consistent with expectations, but in the main the findings did confirm the theory. For instance, students in the stupid condition talked longer and more pretentiously than those in the other conditions, while those in the homosexual condition were more persistent in their efforts to show strength and masculinity (see Table 7.5). This study seems to support the belief that when people think they are viewed as possessing stigmatizing characteristics, they will do whatever they can to dispel such beliefs. It also shows that people will react very differently when they think one type of stigma is attributed to them in comparison with another. This finding supports the conclusion of the preceding section, which was that not all stigmas are alike.

MENTAL DISORDERS IN OTHER CULTURES

The topic of how mental disorders are manifested, treated, and viewed in other cultures is a major one, and to review it in any detail is well beyond the scope of this chapter. The limited component of the topic that we will briefly consider is the favorability of attitudes toward mental problems across cultures. Much has been written about mental disorders in other societies, mostly emphasizing the differences from culture to culture (for instance, Farina, 1976, pp. 137–140). Sociologists and anthropologists have

TABLE 7.5
Discussion Time and Time Taken to Squeeze a Hand Dynamometer by Subjects in Each Experimental Condition
(in seconds)

Condition	Discussion Time	Time Taken to Squeeze Dynamometer
Control	86.3	8.4
Homosexual	101.9	12.8
Stupid	174.2	9.9

Source: Adapted from Farina, Thaw, & Boudreau (1970), Table 1, p. 21.

argued that there are no generally unstable and disorganized individuals who would be recognized as suffering from mental problems no matter in which culture they were placed. Allegedly, a set of behaviors that would cause an individual to be judged psychotic by one society might be valued in another society, and the person displaying them might even be revered. Moreover, it is asserted that the person in question would be able to perform competently in the honored role. For example, a reclusive and withdrawn man who might be designated as schizophrenic in American society could be regarded as a holy man if placed among certain people of India, and there he would behave as a holy man should behave.

These speculations suggest great variability from society to society in the characteristics of the mentally disordered members and the social attitudes toward them. But let us consider one cross-cultural study. Lawner (1966) did a study measuring the favorability of American college students' attitudes toward 11 different kinds of mental disorders as well as toward a normal individual, someone with tuberculosis, a former convict, and a person addicted to narcotics. That study was later replicated with comparable samples of Mexican students and Italian students. The correlation between the attitudes of the Americans and the Mexicans was found to be .91, while the Americans and the Italians correlated .82. The Mexicans and Italians correlated .75 with each other.

While there certainly are many differences from society to society in regard to mental disorders, we see from the Lawner study that there also are strong similarities. In all of these three quite different societies, people with mental problems are viewed in very much the same way. Relative to a normal individual, such people are held in extremely low regard. Also, in all three societies, the more severe the mental disorder, the greater the disfavor in which the afflicted is held. True, the subjects are all students, and one might argue that it is the high socioeconomic status of the subjects that produces the similarity. However, it must be remembered that Nunnally (1961) found no relationship between socioeconomic status and attitudes toward mental disorders. It seems likely that the study reflects a similarity in people of different cultures. If a person is recognized to have a mental disorder, he or she is apparently rejected and held in disfavor in all societies. This is an important matter, in view of some of the conclusions to be drawn in the next section.

WHY ARE THE MENTALLY DISORDERED DISLIKED?

Scheff (1963) attempted to answer the question of why people with mental disorders are looked upon with so much disfavor. He felt that the unfavorable stereotypes associated with mental patients are constantly encountered in our society, while a more realistic portrayal of mental disorders is seldom seen. The language is replete with terms, such as "running like mad" and "it's a madhouse," that make mental patients seem out of control and dangerous, he argues. And newspapers seem determined to find a history of mental problems in the background of people who commit sensational crimes. Even if such a history does not exist, a police-man may be quoted as saying that it looks like the work of a "mental case." And so, says Scheff, we find, on the one hand, a society that appears disposed to believe mental patients are violent and likely to commit terrible crimes, while, on the other hand, the evidence shows the incidence of any kind of crime is lower among mental patients than in the general population. He goes on to conclude that a society may retain such a concept of mental disorders, although it is stereotypic and untrue, because it maintains the ". . . customary moral and cognitive world" (p. 467).

To be sure, what the public may hold to be typically true for mental patients may be true for only a small percentage of people in this category. But is it the case that all or most of what the public believes is unfounded in fact, and that the unfavorable attitudes related to those beliefs are also totally unjustified? That is emphatically not the case. There *is* a realistic basis for the public's beliefs, although this is certainly not to say that the extremely low esteem in which people with mental problems are held is therefore excusable. An objective consideration of the facts indicates that the public is not being completely arbitrary in selecting those with psychiatric problems for special disapproval and dislike. Mental patients are not a randomly selected sample of the population. They have, as a group, a number of characteristics that make them unpleasant as companions and undesirable as friends. And even why some of them are shunned or held in contempt becomes comprehensible, although we may still think such a reaction is not defensible.

First of all, some things are so obvious they require no documentation. People who become mental patients ordinarily do so because their behavior is deviant and unacceptable to those around them, or their subjective feelings are so distressing to themselves as to be unbearable.* In either case, interaction with them is likely to be difficult, tense, and disagreeable. Paranoid ideation is a very common symptom of mental disorder. And who can enjoy the company of people who may accuse us of complicity in a plot against them or who may make totally unexpected, cryptic, and disconcert-ing remarks like "Don't play dumb with me. You know what I mean."? Depression is perhaps the most common symptom of mental disorders, and it seems very obvious that it is upsetting and unpleasant to be with depressed people. In the case of depression, systematic and convincing research has revealed what happens to people who interact with depressed patients.

---

*Of course, it is possible to find some people who have never been mental patients but whose behaviors and subjective state are more deviant than those of some patients. But the mental patient population certainly differs from the nonpatient population in the ways indicated.

Coyne (1976) paired female undergraduates with either a depressed psychiatric patient, a nondepressed psychiatric patient, or a nonpatient control subject. They were required to talk by telephone for 20 minutes, ostensibly to get acquainted, but they were not to reveal their identity or location. It was found that those who had talked with the depressed patient were significantly more depressed, anxious, hostile, and rejecting than the subjects in the other groups. Also, the depressed patients were evaluated very much more negatively. Here we see that it is the *behavior* that is characteristic of mental disorders, and not the recognition of someone's role as a patient (which was unknown in the Coyne study), that makes people with mental disorders noxious and disliked.

Furthermore, the mentally disordered as a group appear to possess numerous other primarily behavioral, but also personal, characteristics that make them disliked or at least deprive them of social status. It has been very well established that they are disproportionally drawn from the lower socioeconomic classes. It was noted over a century ago that the "pauper class" furnished insane people at many times the rate of the "independent class" (Farina, 1976, p. 67). Since that time the same association has been repeatedly reported for people formally recognized as mental patients. Among the best of these studies is the one done in New Haven, Connecticut, by Hollingshead and Redlich (1958). They found that only 1 percent of the patients came from the highest social class, although that class made up 3.1 percent of the normal population. In striking contrast, 36.8 percent of the patients came from the lowest class, which made up only 17.8 percent of the normal population. This pattern was also reported for untreated and undiagnosed subjects (Srole, Langer, Michael, Opler, & Rennie, 1962).

The lower the social class of the subject, the more likely he or she was to be rated maladjusted on the basis of a systematic psychiatric interview. Although there is disagreement about the reasons for this association, it almost certainly means mental patients will have the socially degrading characteristics of low socioeconomic class individuals. That is, they will be poor, they will have held jobs of low prestige, their education will be limited, and their speech and manners will be held in low regard by people of the higher classes.

It is also very well established that, as a group, those who suffer from a mental disorder achieve a relatively low level of personality integration and maturity, and they lack the social skills to participate in smooth and pleasant interpersonal relationships. Consistent with this, the history of their social relationships is characterized by an absence of close friendships and an aloofness and detachment from other people that long precede the mental disorder (Zigler & Phillips, 1962). Moreover, the more severe the mental disorder, the more strongly they show this alienation from others in the premorbid period. For example, Barthell and Holmes (1968) examined high school yearbooks to determine how extensive the social relationships were for three groups of subjects. One group had later been diagnosed as schizophrenic, another group had later been diagnosed as neurotic, and the third had not been hospitalized and served as a control. They found the controls had shown the most extensive social participation, the neurotics were intermediate, and those later diagnosed as schizophrenic had been the least involved with others.

A direct test of the relationship between social skill and adequacy of adjustment was made by Kelly, Farina, and Mosher (1971). Hospitalized female mental patients were first divided into two groups, one consisting of those whose mental disorder was relatively mild and the other of those who were more severely afflicted. They were then interviewed by a female researcher who was blind to all conditions. Half of each group was told to make the interviewer like them, while the rest were told to make her dislike them. The more severely afflicted patients were less skillful both at making the interviewer like them and at making her dislike them. These inadequacies in interpersonal interaction would also make the public dislike and avoid mental patients.

Finally, research indicates that mental patients may be physically less attractive than control subjects (Farina, Fischer, Sherman, Smith, Groh, & Mermin, 1977). In that study female mental patients and two groups of nonmentally disordered females were observed and independently rated for physical attractiveness by two raters. The interrater agreement was found to be .93, indicating a high degree of objectivity for the procedure. It was found that the patients were rated as significantly less attractive than either of the control groups, while the two control groups did not differ from each other. Photographs of the faces of the patients and of the women in one of the control groups were taken. These were given to a group of "blind" judges to rate for attractiveness. The photos of the patients were rated as significantly less attractive (see Table 7.6).

Moreover, a replication and extension of this study indicates that the patients' unattractiveness was not due to their unwillingness or inability to

TABLE 7.6
Means of Attractiveness Ratings Received by Female Mental Patients and Two Control Groups

		Control Group	
	Mental Patients	1	2
Rating based on	Mean	Mean	Mean
Observation	2.3	3.3	3.2
Photographs	2.5	3.7	—

Note: High scores indicate greater beauty.
Source: Adapted from Farina, Fischer, Sherman, Smith, Groh, & Mermin (1977), Table 1, p. 513. Copyright 1977 by the American Psychological Association. Reprinted by permission.

groom and care for themselves (Napoleon, Chassin, & Young, 1980). Their high school yearbook photographs, taken before the mental disorder, were also judged less attractive than those of their peers. Thus it appears that maladjusted people are physically unattractive, and the voluminous research has made it very clear that unattractiveness is a disliked characteristic of people that leads to rejection. (Refer to Chapter 6 in this volume.)

We should remember the research showing that the mentally disordered are evaluated and treated negatively when only their psychiatric history is known and there is no objective basis for such a reaction. We have also seen that the maladjusted person's own knowledge of being socially degraded has an influence. These factors combine with their objective socially disliked characteristics to produce a probably very complicated effect on society and on the patient. A part of this effect is certainly due to such characteristics possessed by the mentally disordered as annoying behaviors, unattractiveness, and social incompetence.

Bearing in mind these characteristics of the mentally disordered, let us now reconsider how they have been viewed and received by society both in the past and at the present time. In the past they were held in extremely low regard and treated badly. At times society explicitly justified the status and treatment that was the lot of the mentally disordered. For example, when they were thought to be witches, it was considered quite justifiable to burn them. A list of the methods used to "cure" them is a catalog of ways to torture human beings. This history does not appear to be peculiar to Western culture. Tseng (1973) reviewed how the mentally disordered were evaluated and treated in China from the earliest times to the present, and reported the pattern to be remarkably similar to that of the West in spite of the absence of contact between the two cultures until relatively recently. When we consider the situation now and in the recent past, we also see that afflicted individuals are rejected and treated unfavorably. And our "enlightened" methods for curing mental problems are in some particulars strikingly similar to past practices. Consider electric, insulin, and carbon dioxide shock, surgical destruction of brain tissues, and a seemingly endless variety of chemicals that tend to be judged therapeutic when they make patients less troublesome.

The specific behaviors and personal characteristics that lead a society to view a given individual as being mentally disordered may vary somewhat over time. There is one invariant component, however, about what causes a man or a woman to be labeled as "possessed," "a lunatic," or "a schizophrenic." Their behaviors are held to be foolish, unacceptable, embarrassing, or threatening. The people who display these behaviors are judged queer, unpredictable, and disagreeable. So mental disorders seem, at least in part, to be the result of a social reaction to unacceptable behavior rather than being medical problems. Trying to eradicate the stigma associated with such conditions cannot be wholly successful. Stigma was an important factor in creating them.

PROSPECTS FOR FURTHER RESEARCH

The following research is being carried out now or has been completed. When interpretable results have been obtained, they are reported and references are given to allow readers to obtain more information when such is available. The research done is in three areas covered in this chapter.

The Reactions of Boys and Girls to Children with Problems in Adjustment

Mary Luckhardt (1979) wanted to determine how children in school would react to other children who were known to receive help for problems in adjustment. The main results were surprising, since receiving treatment from a mental health professional made rather little difference. Janet Gillmore did both her M.A. and Ph.D. studies (1980a; 1980b) on the consequences of sending mentally retarded and emotionally disturbed children to a regular classroom. This practice, called "mainstreaming," is widely used in the early 1980s. The M.A. thesis was a questionnaire study that entailed asking children how an afflicted child would be responded to in their school. The Ph.D. study entailed having subjects actually meet children who were confederates but were presented as retarded, normal, or emotionally disturbed. In both studies the afflicted children were decisively rejected. The different results in the Luckhardt and the Gillmore studies may be due to the difference between a child's being treated for a problem and one described as having a problem.

Physical Attractiveness and Level of Adjustment of Mental Patients and Their Consequences

A. Farina, E. Fischer, and J. Council are currently (1981) studying the role played by a patient's physical attractiveness and adequacy of adjustment in finding a job. Female patients varying in these characteristics are being videotaped, and the tapes are subsequently shown to employment interviewers. The dependent measures are evaluations of how good the patients would be as workers.

Studies of Beliefs About the Nature of Mental Disorders

Dana Christensen, Neil Facchinetti, Amerigo Farina, Jeffrey Fisher, and Michael Pisano are carrying out studies on the relationship between drugs and beliefs and the influence of beliefs on behavior. Several strategies have been followed to devise a questionnaire to measure beliefs, and questionnaires have been used to carry out several preliminary studies. One study entails giving questionnaires to patients filling prescriptions at a pharmacy. The patients are selected to fall into two groups: those who are being prescribed tranquilizers for mental problems, and those who are filling prescriptions for strictly medical problems. If our theorizing is correct, the belief of the mental problems group, relative to the other group, ought to shift over time toward viewing mental disorders as diseases.

SUMMARY

The present chapter began with a summary of the way the mentally disordered were viewed and treated in the past. Until about the 1880s they were commonly regarded as not really human beings at all, but as creatures akin to demons and witches. The methods used to cure them were often theological and magical, and almost always these procedures were quite unpleasant. While there have been some radical changes over time in conceptions about the nature of these afflictions, contemporary attitudes continue to be extremely unfavorable, just as they were in the past. The mentally disordered are held in very low regard by all segments of society, and even mild problems in adjustment bring social rejection.

These unfavorable attitudes suggest that the mentally disordered will be treated badly in society, and research reveals that is often true. They are refused jobs, they are not wanted as neighbors, and under some conditions they are treated more harshly because of their problems. Moreover, the perceptions of onlookers are distorted, and they see the mentally disordered as displaying shortcomings that objectively do not exist. However, the mentally disordered are not always treated badly by everyone, and sometimes they are actually treated better *because of* their problems. The available research suggests that people are unkind to them when they can avoid feeling guilty as a result. They can avoid guilt when they are unaware they are being unkind, for example. A totally unexpected research finding regarding how the mentally disordered are treated is that females are much more accepting and supportive of such afflicted individuals than are males.

An issue that has been the focus of practical as well as theoretical interest is that of changing beliefs about the nature of psychopathology. In particular, mental health associations and other social action groups have been making a concerted effort to convince the general public that problems in adjustment and with alcohol are diseases. Research suggests such efforts will be successful, since beliefs about these phenomena are very malleable. Unfortunately, studies also reveal that the changed beliefs will not make those affected more socially acceptable. On the contrary, the social consequences for a mental patient of being viewed as sick, and thinking this of him or herself, seem wholly negative.

Also considered in the chapter was the uniformity of social reaction to the many different kinds of socially degrading conditions (stigmas) that can affect a human being. While there are certain similarities, there are also very important differences in public reaction to such stigmas as being crippled, mentally disordered, and mentally retarded. There may be similarities in how the victims respond to believing they are viewed as degraded by others. Under such conditions only the belief of the stigmatized person that his or her condition is known adversely affects his or her behavior independently of how others act. Even so, each stigma elicits particular kinds of behavior from the stigmatized.

Finally, the question was raised as to whether there are objective grounds that explain the persistent state of social degradation that has been the lot of the mentally disordered over the ages. It seems quite apparent that persons suffering from such problems are possessed of socially unacceptable characteristics, although this is by no means to say that their treatment at the hands of society is justified. It may be possible that it is not being classed as a mental patient that brings social stigma. Rather, people who behave in a deviant way and have other defacing attributes are socially stigmatized, and hence are classed as lunatics or mental patients.

REFERENCES

Altrocchi, J. Changes in favorableness of attitudes toward concepts of mental illness. *American Psychologist*, 1960, *15*, 461. (abstract)

Barthell, C. N., & Holmes, D. S. High school yearbooks: A nonreactive measure of social isolation in graduates who later became schizophrenic. *Journal of Abnormal Psychology*, 1968, *73*, 313–316.

Broverman, I. K., Broverman, D. M., Clarkson, F. E., Rosenkrantz, P. S., & Vogel, S. R. Sex-role stereotypes and clinical judgments of mental health. *Journal of Consulting and Clinical Psychology*, 1970, *34*, 1–7.

Caudill, W., Redlich, F. C., Gilmore, H. R., & Brody, E. B. Social structure and interaction processes on a psychiatric ward. *American Journal of Orthopsychiatry*, 1952, *22*, 314–334.

Chevron, E. S., Quinlan, D. M., & Blatt, S. J. Sex roles and gender differences in the experience of depression. *Journal of Abnormal Psychology*, 1978, *87*, 680–683.

Chinsky, J. M., & Rappaport, J. Attitude change in college students and chronic patients: A dual perspective. *Journal of Consulting and Clinical Psychology*, 1970, *35*, 388–394.

Cohen, J., & Struening, E. L. Opinions about mental illness in the personnel of two large mental hospitals. *Journal of Abnormal and Social Psychology*, 1962, *64*, 349–360.

Cohen, J., & Struening, E. L. Opinions about mental illness: Hospital social atmosphere profiles and their relevance to effectiveness. *Journal of Consulting Psychology*, 1964, *28*, 291–298.

Coie, J. D., Pennington, B. F., & Buckley, H. H. Effects of situational stress and sex roles on the attribution of psychological disorder. *Journal of Consulting and Clinical Psychology*, 1974, *42*, 559–568.

Colson, C. E. Effects of different explanations of disordered behavior on treatment referrals. *Journal of Consulting and Clinical Psychology*, 1970, *34*, 432–435.

Costin, F., & Kerr, W. D. Effects of an abnormal psychology course on students' attitudes toward mental illness. *Journal of Educational Psychology*, 1962, *53*, 214–218.

Costin, F., & Kerr, W. D. Effects of a mental hygiene course on graduate education students' attitudes and opinions concerning mental illness. *Journal of Educational Research*, 1966, *60*, 35–40.

Coyne, J. C. Depression and the response of others. *Journal of Abnormal Psychology*, 1976, *85*, 186–193.

Crocetti, G. M., & Lemkau, P. V. On rejection of the mentally ill. *American Sociological Review*, 1965, *30*, 577–588.

Crocetti, G. M., Spiro, H. R., & Siassi, I. *Contemporary attitudes toward mental illness.* Pittsburgh: University of Pittsburgh Press, 1974.

Cutler, W. D. The relationship of subjects' sex to attitudes and behaviors toward male mental patients. Ph.D. dissertation, University of Connecticut, 1975.

Derlega, V. J., & Chaikin, A. L. Norms affecting self-disclosure in men and women. *Journal of Consulting and Clinical Psychology*, 1976, *44*, 376–380.

Deutsch, A. *The mentally ill in America* (2nd ed.). New York: Columbia University Press, 1965.

Diggens, D. The role of social and nonsocial traits in interpersonal attraction. *Journal of Personality*, 1974, *42*, 345–359.

Dohrenwend, B. P., & Dohrenwend, B. S. *Social status and psychological disorder: A causal inquiry.* New York: Wiley-Interscience, 1969.

Doob, A. N., & Ecker, B. P. Stigma and compliance. *Journal of Personality and Social Psychology*, 1970, *14*, 302–304.

Eisdorfer, C., & Altrocchi, J. A comparison of attitudes toward old age and mental illness. *Journal of Gerontology*, 1961, *16*, 340–343.

Ellsworth, R. B. A behavioral study of staff attitudes toward mental illness. *Journal of Abnormal Psychology*, 1965, *70*, 194–200.

Farina, A. *Abnormal psychology.* Englewood Cliffs, N.J.: Prentice-Hall, 1976.

Farina, A., Allen, J. G., & Saul, B. B. The role of the stigmatized in affecting social relationships. *Journal of Personality*, 1968, *36*, 169–182.

Farina, A., & Felner, R. D. Employment interviewer reactions to former mental patients. *Journal of Abnormal Psychology*, 1973, *82*, 268–272.

Farina, A., Felner, R. D., & Boudreau, L. A. Reactions of workers to male and female mental patient job applicants. *Journal of Consulting and Clinical Psychology*, 1973, *41*, 363–372.

Farina, A., Fischer, E. H., Sherman, S., Smith, W. T., Groh, T., & Mermin, P. Physical attractiveness and mental illness. *Journal of Abnormal Psychology*, 1977, *86*, 510–517.

Farina, A., Fisher, J. D., Getter, H., & Fischer, E. H. Some consequences of changing people's views regarding the nature of mental illness. *Journal of Abnormal Psychology*, 1978, *87*, 272–279.

Farina, A., Gliha, D., Boudreau, L. A., Allen, J. G., & Sherman, M. Mental illness and the impact of believing others know about it. *Journal of Abnormal Psychology*, 1971, *77*, 1–5.

Farina, A., & Hagelauer, H. D. Sex and mental illness: The generosity of females. *Journal of Consulting and Clinical Psychology*, 1975, *43*, 122.

Farina, A., Hagelauer, H. D., & Holzberg, J. D. Influence of psychiatric history on physicians' response to a new patient. *Journal of Consulting and Clinical Psychology*, 1976, *44*, 499.

Farina, A., Holland, C. H., & Ring, K. The role of stigma and set in interpersonal interaction. *Journal of Abnormal Psychology*, 1966, *71*, 421–428.

Farina, A., Murray, P. J., & Groh, T. Sex and worker acceptance of a former mental patient. *Journal of Consulting and Clinical Psychology*, 1978, *46*, 887–891.

Farina, A., & Ring, K. The influence of perceived mental illness on interpersonal relations. *Journal of Abnormal Psychology*, 1965, *70*, 47–51.

Farina, A., Sherman, M., & Allen, J. G. Role of physical abnormalities in interpersonal perception and behavior. *Journal of Abnormal Psychology*, 1968, *73*, 590–593.

Farina, A., Thaw, J., & Boudreau, L. A. People's reaction to being viewed as blemished and degraded. Unpublished manuscript, University of Connecticut, 1970.

Farina, A., Thaw, J., Felner, R. D., & Hust, B. E. Some interpersonal consequences of being mentally ill or mentally retarded. *American Journal of Mental Deficiency*, 1976, *80*, 414–422.

Farina, A., Thaw, J., Lovern, J. D., & Mangone, D. People's reactions to a former mental patient moving to their neighborhood. *Journal of Community Psychology*, 1974, *2*, 108–112.

Fisher, J. D., & Farina, A. Consequences of beliefs about the nature of mental disorders. *Journal of Abnormal Psychology*, 1979, *88*, 320–327.

Gelfand, S., & Ullmann, L. P. Changes in attitudes about mental illness associated with psychiatric clerkship training. *International Journal of Social Psychiatry*, 1961, *8*, 292–298. (a)

Gelfand, S., & Ullmann, L. P. Attitude changes associated with psychiatric affiliation. *Nursing Research*, 1961, *10*, 200–204. (b)

Gillmore, J. L. Attitudes of boys and girls toward mainstreaming children. M. A. thesis, University of Connecticut, 1980. (a)

Gillmore, J. L. The social reception of mainstreamed children in the regular classroom. Ph.D. dissertation, University of Connecticut, 1980. (b)

Goffman, E. *Stigma. Notes on the management of spoiled identity.* Englewood Cliffs, N.J.: Prentice-Hall, 1963.

Gussow, Z., & Tracy, G. S. Status, ideology, and adaptation to stigmatized illness: A study of leprosy. *Human Organization*, 1968, *27*, 316–325.

Gynther, M. D., Reznikoff, M., & Fishman, M. The attitude of psychiatric patients toward treatment, psychiatrists and mental hospitals. *Journal of Nervous and Mental Disease*, 1963, *136*, 68–72.

Halpert, H. P. Public opinions and attitudes about mental health. In H. Wechsler, L. Solomon, & B. M. Kramer (eds.), *Social psychology and mental health*. New York: Holt, Rinehart, & Winston, 1970. Pp. 489–504.

Hammen, C. L., & Peters, S. D. Differential responses to male and female depressive reactions. *Journal of Consulting and Clinical Psychology*, 1977, *45*, 994–1001.

Harrow, M., Fox, D. A., & Detre, T. Self-concept of the married psychiatric patient and his mate's perception of him. *Journal of Consulting Psychology*, 1969, *33*, 235–239.

Hoffman, M. L. Sex differences in moral internalization and values. *Journal of Personality and Social Psychology*, 1975, *32*, 720–729.

Hollingshead, A. B., & Redlich, F. C. *Social class and mental illness: A community study*. New York: John Wiley, 1958.

Holzberg, J. D., & Knapp, R. H. The social interaction of college students and chronically ill mental patients. *American Journal of Orthopsychiatry*, 1965, *35*, 487–492.

Jones, E. E., Hester, S. L., Farina, A., & Davis, K. E. Reactions to unfavorable personal evaluations as a function of the evaluator's perceived adjustment. *Journal of Abnormal and Social Psychology*, 1959, *59*, 363–370.

Jones, N. F., Kahn, M. W., & McDonald, J. M. Psychiatric patients' views of mental illness, hospitalization, and treatment. *Journal of Nervous and Mental Disease*, 1963, *136*, 82–88.

Kelly, F. S., Farina, A., & Mosher, D. L. Ability of schizophrenic women to create a favorable or unfavorable impression on an interviewer. *Journal of Consulting and Clinical Psychology*, 1971, *36*, 404–409.

Kleck, R. Physical stigma and task oriented interactions. *Human Relations*, 1969, *22*, 53–60.

Kleck, R., Buck, P. L., Goller, W. L., London, R. S., Pfeiffer, J. R., & Vukcevic, D. P. Effect of stigmatizing conditions on the use of personal space. *Psychological Reports*, 1968, *23*, 111–118.

Lamy, R. E. Social consequences of mental illness. *Journal of Consulting and Clinical Psychology*, 1966, *30*, 450–454.

Langer, E. J., & Abelson, R. P. A patient by any other name. . .: Clinician group difference in labeling bias. *Journal of Consulting and Clinical Psychology*, 1974, *42*, 4–9.

LaPiere, R. T. Attitudes vs. actions. *Social Forces*, 1934, *13*, 230–237.

LaTorre, R. A. Gender and age as factors in the attitudes toward those stigmatized as mentally ill. *Journal of Consulting and Clinical Psychology*, 1975, *43*, 97–98.

Lawner, P. Unfavorable attitudes and behavior toward those bearing mental illness stigmas. M.A. thesis, University of Connecticut, 1966.

Luckhardt, M. Social responses of boys and girls to boys who receive treatment for adjustment problems. Ph.D. dissertation, University of Connecticut, 1979.

MacDonald, A. P., Jr., & Hall, J. Perception of disability by the nondisabled. *Journal of Consulting and Clinical Psychology*, 1969, *33*, 654–660.

Matthews, V., & Westie, V. A preferred method for obtaining ranking reactions to physical handicaps. *American Sociological Review*, 1966, *31*, 851–854.

Milgram, S. Some conditions of obedience and disobedience to authority. In I. Steiner & M. Fishbein (eds.), *Current studies in social psychology*. New York: Holt, Rinehart, & Winston, 1965.

Morrison, J. K. Demythologizing mental patients' attitudes toward mental illness: An empirical study. *Journal of Community Psychology*, 1976, *4*, 181–185.

Morrison, J. K. Changing negative attributions of mental patients by means of demythologizing seminars. *Journal of Clinical Psychology*, 1977, *33*, 549–551.

Morrison, J. K., & Becker, R. E. Seminar-induced change in a community psychiatric team's reported attitudes toward mental illness. *Journal of Community Psychology*, 1975, *3*, 281–284.

Morrison, J. K., Bushell, J. D., Hanson, G. D., Fentiman, J. R., & Holdridge-Crane, S. Relationship between psychiatric patients' attitudes toward mental illness and attitudes of dependence. *Psychological Reports*, 1977, *41*, 1194.

Morrison, J. K., & Nevid, J. S. Demythologizing the attitudes of family caretakers about "mental illness." *Journal of Family Counseling*, 1976, *4*, 43–49. (a)

Morrison, J. K., & Nevid, J. S. Demythologizing the service expectancies of psychiatric patients in the community. *Psychology*, 1976, *13*, 26–29. (b)

Morrison, J. K., & Teta, D. C. Increase of positive self-attributions by means of demythologizing seminars. *Journal of Clinical Psychology*, 1977, *33*, 1128–1131.

Mosher, D. L., Farina, A., & Gliha, D. F. Moral stigma, punishment, and guilt. Unpublished manuscript, University of Connecticut, 1970.

Napoleon, T., Chassin, L., & Young, R. D. A replication and extension of "Physical attractiveness and mental illness." *Journal of Abnormal Psychology*, 1980, *89*, 250–253.

Novack, P. W., & Lerner, M. J. Rejection as a consequence of perceived similarity. *Journal of Personality and Social Psychology*, 1968, *9*, 147–152.

Nowacki, C. M., & Poe, C. A. The concept of mental health as related to sex of person perceived. *Journal of Consulting and Clinical Psychology*, 1973, *40*, 160.

Nunnally, J. C. *Popular conceptions of mental health*. New York: Holt, Rinehart, & Winston, 1961.

Olshansky, S., Grob, S., & Ekdahl, M. Survey of employment experience of patients discharged from three mental hospitals during the period 1951–1953. *Mental Hygiene*, 1960, *44*, 510–521.

Olshansky, S., Grob, S., & Malamud, I. T. Employers' attitudes and practices in the hiring of ex-mental patients. *Mental Hygiene*, 1958, *42*, 391–401.

Ommundsen, R., & Ekeland, T.-J. Psychiatric labeling and social perception. *Scandinavian Journal of Psychology*, 1978, *19*, 193–197.

Page, S. The elusive character of psychiatric stigma. *Canada's Mental Health*, 1974, *22*, 15–20.

Page, S. Effects of the mental illness label in attempts to obtain accommodation. *Canadian Journal of Behavioral Science*, 1977, *9*, 84–90.

Parsons, T., & Bales, R. F. *Family socialization and interaction process*. Glencoe, Ill.: Free Press, 1955.

Phillips, D. Education, psychiatric sophistication, and the rejection of mentally ill help-seekers. *Sociological Quarterly*, 1967, *8*, 122–132.

Phillips, D. L. Rejection: A possible consequence of seeking help for mental disorders. *American Sociological Review*, 1963, *28*, 963–972.

Phillips, D. L. Rejection of the mentally ill: The influence of behavior and sex. *American Sociological Review*, 1964, *34*, 679–687.

Pollack, S., Huntley, D., Allen, J. G., & Schwartz, S. The dimensions of stigma: The social situation of the mentally ill person and the male homosexual. *Journal of Abnormal Psychology*, 1976, *85*, 105–112.

Rayne, J. T. The effect of perceived attitudes on expectancy for punishment by psychiatric patients. Ph.D. dissertation, University of Connecticut, 1969.

Richardson, S. A., Hastorf, A. H., Goodman, N., & Dornbusch, S. M. Cultural uniformity in reaction to physical disabilities. *American Sociological Review*, 1961, *26*, 241–247.

Ring, K., & Farina, A. Personal adjustment as a determinant of aggressive behavior toward the mentally ill. *Journal of Consulting and Clinical Psychology*, 1969, *33*, 683–690.

Rosenhan, D. L. On being sane in insane places. *Science*, 1973, *179*, 250–258.

Rothaus, P., Hanson, P. G., Cleveland, S. E., & Johnson, D. L. Describing psychiatric hospitalization: A dilemma. *American Psychologist*, 1963, *18*, 85–89.

Rotter, J. B. Generalized expectancies for internal versus external control of reinforcement. *Psychological Monographs*, 1966, *80* (1, whole no. 609).

Sarbin, T. R., & Mancuso, J. C. Failure of a moral enterprise: Attitudes of the public toward mental illness. *Journal of Consulting and Clinical Psychology*, 1970, *35*, 159–173.

Scheff, T. J. Social support for stereotypes of mental disorder. *Mental Hygiene*, 1963, *47*, 461–469.

Schwartz, C. C., Myers, J. K., & Astrachan, B. M. Psychiatric labeling and the rehabilitation of the mental patient. *Archives of General Psychiatry*, 1974, *31*, 329–334.

Sherman, M. The influence of perceived mental illness and competence of performance on interpersonal impressions. M.A. thesis, University of Connecticut, 1967.

Siller, J., Ferguson, L. T., Vann, D. H., & Holland, B. Structure of attitudes toward the physically disabled: The disability factor scales—amputation, blindness, cosmetic conditions. Paper presented at the meeting of the American Psychological Association, San Francisco, 1968.

Smith, J. J. Psychiatric hospital experience and attitudes toward mental illness. *Journal of Consulting and Clinical Psychology*, 1969, *33*, 302–306.

Srole, L., Langer, T. S., Michael, S. T., Opler, M. K., & Rennie, T. A. C. *Mental health in the metropolis: The Midtown Manhattan study* (Vol. 1). New York: McGraw-Hill, 1962.

Thaw, J. The reactions of schizophrenic patients to being patronized and to believing they are unfavorably viewed. Ph.D. dissertation, University of Connecticut, 1969.

Tseng, W. S. The development of psychiatric concepts in traditional Chinese medicine. *Archives of General Psychiatry*, 1973, *29*, 569–575.

Wehler, R. Attitudes toward mental illness and dependency among hospitalized psychiatric patients. *Psychological Reports*, 1979, 1979, *44*, 283–286.

Whiteman, M., & Lukoff, I. F. Attitudes toward blindness and other physical handicaps. *Journal of Social Psychology*, 1965, *66*, 135–145.

Whitman, J. R., & Duffey, R. F. The relationship between type of therapy received and a patient's perception of his illness. *Journal of Nervous and Mental Disorders*, 1961, *133*, 288–292.

Wicker, A. W. Attitudes versus actions: The relationship of verbal and overt behavioral responses to attitude objects. *Journal of Social Issues*, 1969, *25*, 41–78.

Wright, F. H., & Klein, R. A. Attitudes of various hospital personnel categories and the community regarding mental illness. Unpublished manuscript, VA Center, Biloxi, Miss., 1965.

Zigler, E., & Phillips, L. Social competence and the process-reactive distinction in psychopathology. *Journal of Abnormal and Social Psychology*, 1962, *65*, 215–222.

Zilboorg, S., & Henry, G. W. *A history of medical psychology*. New York: Norton, 1941.

ADDITIONAL READINGS

Caudill, W., Redlich, F. C., Gilmore, H. R., & Brady, E. B. Social structure and interaction process on a psychiatric ward. *American Journal of Orthopsychiatry*, 1952, *22*, 314–334.
An early "infiltration" experiment in which a normal person is admitted to a mental hospital. Detailed observations of staff misperception of patients are made and reported.

Deutsch, A. *The mentally ill in America* (2nd ed.). New York: Columbia University Press, 1965.
A well-written and objective history of the perception and treatment of the mentally disordered in America. Old documents are frequently cited, allowing the reader to get a good flavor of what occurred.

Goffman, E. *Stigma. Notes on the management of spoiled identity.* Englewood Cliffs, N.J.: Prentice-Hall, 1963.
A book that has had a great deal of influence on the field of stigma and stereotype. It is readable and convincing, but it is also more novelistic than scientific. A reader should be aware that many of its assertions remain to be tested.

Nunnally, J. C. *Popular conceptions of mental health.* New York: Holt, Rinehart, & Winston, 1961.
A clearly and simply written report of many years of research on public beliefs and attitudes toward mental disorders. This is basic reading for anyone who would know this area and, because public reaction toward all kinds of afflictions is measured and reported, it is an important reference book.

Rosenhan, D. L. On being sane in insane places. *Science*, 1973, *179*, 250–258.
Another "infiltration" study, but one done in a systematic and controlled way. The report is startling. Sane and insane appear to be indistinguishable to mental health experts. This report has generated a great deal of activity in the mental health field.

Reich, W. The force of diagnosis. *Harper's*, May, 1980, Pp. 20–33.
A highly readable, provocative essay on the functions of psychiatric diagnoses. Reich surveys the utility and apparent virtue of using psychiatric labels to explain the actions of others, but recognizes the stigmatization that lurks in applying such labels. Reich emphasizes the role of psychiatric terminology for people in general, not only as used by professionals.

Scheff, T. J. (ed.) *Labeling madness.* Englewood Cliffs, N.J.: Prentice-Hall, 1975.
A collection of articles dealing with the misuse of labels like "schizophrenia" and the harmful effects of institutionalization. This book illustrates the labeling theory of social deviance as applied to mental illness. A basic premise is the powerful role of preconceptions and stereotypes in directing societal reaction to rule breaking.

8

STEREOTYPING AND
THE LIFE CYCLE:
VIEWS OF AGING AND THE AGED

Kenneth J. Branco
John B. Williamson

> *We who are old* know that age is more than a disability. It is an intense
> and varied experience, almost beyond our capacity at times, but
> something to be carried high. If it is a long defeat it is also a victory,
> meaningful for the initiates of time, if not for those who have come less
> far. (Scott-Maxwell, 1968, p. 5)

INTRODUCTION

A few years ago a youth of 17 was fortunate enough to reach the finals
of his home-town tennis tournament. It was the summer after his high school
graduation, and he felt strong, quick, and confident, qualities he identified as
exclusively those of young people. His opponent was 58, and upon learning
of the competitor's "advanced age," the youth's confidence grew. The local
newspaper saw an opportunity for combining a human interest story with a
sports story, and headlined an article on the match "Age and Experience
Versus Youth and Ambition." Even though the older man was known to be
a good player, the youth was convinced that he would triumph rather easily.
"After all," he thought, "it's a hot summer afternoon and we're going to play
on a hard asphalt court." His strategy was clear: "Make the old man run."
He believed that all he had to do was keep hitting the ball first to one side of
the court and then to the other. The hot sun and the hard court would do the
rest. He was sure that no one of his opponent's age could continue that pace
through an entire match.

He was wrong. The older man ran continuously for the two hours they
were on the court. He also kept the youth running after shots that were so
well placed that it was all the youth could do just to hit the ball. He hit many
of them out of the court, into the net, or right back to the older man, who
won rather easily.

The youth learned an important lesson. As a result of this experience he became much more cautious when it came to making generalizations about older people. Many of our readers, no doubt, have had experiences with older persons that violated their conceptions of what it means to be old. Unfortunately, these experiences are often discounted or forgotten. We say, "That's an exception," and the stereotype lives on. One of our goals here is to explore some of the most prevalent contemporary stereotypes about the elderly in American culture. We also seek to offer an account of why these stereotypes persist. In so doing, it is our hope that the present analysis will contribute to an understanding of the phenomenon of stereotyping in more general contexts, including many of those considered in other chapters of the present volume. In any society there are "common sense" understandings of aging and what it means to be old. Here we are concerned with the discrepancy between these "common sense" understandings and the under-standings that are produced by gerontologists.* An objective of this analysis, as with the discipline of gerontology more generally, is the debunking of myths about aging and the aged.

"How old is he (or she)?" is one of the first questions we ask ourselves when we meet a new person. On the basis of our answer to this question, we decide, often without much thought, to categorize the person on other dimensions. We mistakenly assume that by knowing a person's age, we also know a great deal about his or her personality, intelligence, political orientation, athletic ability, and (even) sex life. We often decide who will be our friends, teachers, lovers, and acquaintances on the basis of the answer to this question. On a larger scale we decide who should attend school, who should work, and sometimes even who should live or die on the basis of the answer to the same question. In the present analysis we hope to demonstrate why this is not the first question we should be asking, and why the attention we give to the way in which the question is answered is problematic for both the elderly and society. Robert Butler (1980) has noted, "Since the attitudes of the members of a society shape the policies that govern it, bias, prejudice, and stereotypes can interfere with effective policy formulation. Through their effect on social policy, attitudes become institutionalized. This has been true with racism and sexism, and so it is with ageism as well" (p. 8).

STEREOTYPES ABOUT THE AGED IN HISTORICAL PERSPECTIVE

While it seems clear that in American society, within this historical period, old age is generally approached with some dread, it is also evident

---

*Gerontology is the scientific study of the aging process and those who are old. It includes the study of service programs and public policy dealing with the aged. Many gerontologists consider the biological, social, and psychological changes that take place across the entire span of the adult years.

that in other societies, within other historical epochs, the reverse was true. The pattern in hunting and gathering societies of prehistoric as well as recent times indicates a far different view of aging than that in present-day America. Fischer (1978) has outlined four characteristics of these societies. The first is that old people were quite rare. The average length of life was less than 25 years, and only a very few were fortunate enough to survive beyond age 50 (Cook, 1972). Second, in spite of the fact that very few persons survived to an age that would be considered old by our standards, all of these societies identified some of their members as old. These persons may have been only 40 or 50, but by the standards of their day they were old (Simmons, 1945). His third point is that those people who were seen as old were held in high esteem. In fact, one writer has commented that in primitive societies "Some degree of prestige for the aged seems to have been practically universal" (Simmons, 1945, p. 79). Finally, if these old people lived long enough for their mental and physical capacities to deteriorate to the point that they were a burden on the society, they were often disposed of. Abandonment or neglect was the usual means of removing the "overaged," but there were also instances of live burial and ritualized suicide (Fischer, 1978; de Beauvoir, 1972).

It may seem unusual that the very societies that venerated their elders also practiced senecide. However, both practices were crucial for the survival of those societies and their cultures. At a time when writing was unknown, the only way in which culture could be transmitted from one generation to another was through the memories and oral teachings of the elders. The norms, values, religious beliefs, technical knowledge, and all other aspects of culture might cease to exist if not passed on. Yet this veneration of elders was also the source of their doom if severe mental deterioration set in. Senility in a society that so depended on the wisdom of its elders was intolerable. In like fashion those who could no longer physically care for themselves were too great a burden on a society that could feed its members only when all but the youngest children participated in hunting and gathering activities. A case can be made that in primitive societies, being old was viewed as desirable, but being very old typically was not welcomed.

When we turn our attention to societies that were more developed economically, we find some important changes in the pattern of respect for elders. When societies shifted from hunting and gathering to agriculture and the domestication of animals, it became possible to accumulate an economic surplus. Some of these societies eventually went on to develop a written language. Both an economic surplus and literacy had important consequences for the status of at least some older members of these societies. An economic surplus meant that some of those older persons who could no longer care for themselves would be supported, for example, by those who had gained control of the surplus. Simultaneously, the development of literacy made the society less dependent on the oral transmission of culture by elders. Thus senility was no longer a great threat. We therefore see a shift in the social ethics of these societies. Senecide was now defined as immoral.

The book of Genesis contains some of the earliest writings on the nature of aging in agricultural and pastoral societies. In a time when the average length of life was 18 years, those who survived beyond 60 were both rare and venerated. It appears that the "common sense" understanding of old age in those times was that those who were granted a long life had been chosen by God for divine purposes. Adam, for example, who with Eve was selected to begin the human race, is reported to have lived for 930 years. Likewise, Noah, whose purpose was to reintroduce life to Earth after moral decay had required its destruction, is said to have lived for 950 years (Birren & Clayton, 1975).

The validity of such claims is not an issue of concern to us here. What is important is that these myths of creation and re-creation tell us something about the value placed on long life, and served to establish the high esteem in which the elderly were held. When the written word began to replace the spoken word, the elders lost little authority, since few were literate and elders controlled the latter medium, as they had the former. However, only a small minority of older persons were able to profit from these changes. It is likely that among the poor elderly in these societies, life remained harsh. But for a small elite group of elders, high status was supported by economic and moral sanction. This state of affairs appears to have predominated throughout the period of the Roman Empire and the Middle Ages (Haller, 1960; Coffman, 1934). Up to this point in history, there is little disagreement between scholars on the status of the elderly and the causes of that status. When we turn our attention to modern history, however, two competing theoretical perspectives emerge: modernization and idealism. Both perspectives represent attempts to explain the apparent shift from the high status of the elderly in the past to a much lower status in modern Western societies.

Modernization Theory

Modernization theory seeks to explain the reduction in status of the elderly by means of the coming of industrialization. There is a "before" and "after" emphasis in the theory, which asserts that "before" modernization, agricultural activity dominated the economy, while "after" modernization, industrial activity predominated. "Before" modernization the bulk of the population was located in rural areas; "after" modernization it was concentrated in urban environments. "Before" modernization the majority of the population was illiterate; "after" modernization public education created a majority capable of reading and writing. "Before" modernization persons were closely tied to an extended family system, while "after" modernization many ties were broken and a nuclear family structure became the norm. "Before" modernization, tradition was the basis of culture, while "after" modernization, innovation became a central cultural component.

Modernization theory asserts that just as the shift from hunting and gathering to agriculture led to important cultural changes that affected the status of the elderly, so the shift from agriculture to industry brought about a reorganization of social structures that in turn affected cultural norms concerning the status and treatment of the elderly. However, while the shift from hunting and gathering to agriculture was generally beneficial to the aged, the transformation that accompanied the shift from an agricultural to an industrial base tended to reduce the status of the elderly.

Donald Cowgill (1974), a leading proponent of the effect of modernization on the status of the elderly, has outlined four ways in which shifts in social structure affect the status of the elderly. First, improvements in health technology have led to great increases in the numbers of older persons, so that they no longer derive status through their rarity. The increasing number of older persons has led to the institutionalization of retirement. This arrangement has forced older persons out of the high-status roles in the society, and decreased their share of the society's most valued medium of status, money. Second, modern economic technology continuously creates new occupations and forces change in old ones, so that long experience in a position is not as valuable as being aware of the new ways of doing things. This also has led to loss of income and status for society's older members. Third, an industrial economy has pulled younger people to urban areas. This has led to the breakdown of the extended family and destroyed the basis of the high status of the older people who had controlled the agricultural property and economy. Finally, public mass education has led to widespread literacy, which has challenged the elders' position as the transmitters of cultural knowledge and wisdom (Cowgill, 1974; Cowgill and Holmes, 1972; Burgess, 1960).

As can be seen from this summary, the central causal factors in modernization theory are shifts in social structures. These structural factors dominate the "common sense" conception of what it means to be old. In this framework beliefs and values (ideas) are of little importance in and of themselves. They are but reflections of the dominant structural arrangements in a society. We shall now turn our attention to a second and competing view of age relations in modern society. As we shall see, in this alternative perspective ideas, in and of themselves, are assumed to shape "common sense" conceptions of what it means to be old.

The Perspective of Idealism

The perspective known as "idealism" offers an alternative to modernization theory. It seeks not to completely refute modernization theory, although in some areas it does just that, but to shift emphasis from social structural arrangements as causal factors in age relations. Industrialization, urbanization, and the modernization of cultural norms are not denied.

However, they are seen as the social setting in which age relations are played out rather than as the source of those relations. Idealism finds its causes in human thought, particularly in those thoughts that take on political significance, that lead people to question the social arrangements under which they live, and, more important, lead them to action that changes those arrangements. According to idealism, two such ideas—equality and liberty—are crucial to understanding modern history.

Modernization theory places the onset of changes in the status of the elderly at about 1850, to coincide with the period of industrialization. Idealism asserts that the shift in the status of the elderly began sooner, placing it between 1770 and 1840. That period saw two great political and social revolutions, the French and the American. In both the old order was based at least in part on what Fischer (1978) describes as "veneration" of the aged. The aged were regarded with deference, respect, reverence, and even awe. The new order demanded equality, and equality among the young and old was a central principle:

> . . . in the famous public Fetes of the French Revolution, where a symbolic harmony of youth and age was celebrated in elaborate rituals . . . the old men distributed gifts of figs and raisins to the youths; in turn, the young women presented baskets of bread and fruit to their elders. (Fischer, 1978, p. 78)

Similarly, in America the framers of the Declaration of Independence and the Constitution were very much concerned with the idea that "all men are created equal." As the idea of equality took hold, the previous "veneration" accorded to elders disappeared.

The idea of liberty also was subversive to the hierarchy of age relations that dominated the old order in both France and America. The authority of age had rested upon the notion that an individual was less important than the group. The claims made by family, community, or religion predominated over those of any individual member's right to control his or her own destiny. And the older members of those collectivities sat firmly in control of what was defined as right for the group. The idea of liberty, of individuals' possessing the right to pursue their own interests even against group demands, eliminated the basis of the moral authority that had been held by elders. Fischer tells us, in no uncertain terms, of the consequences of these facts for determining causes of change in the status of the aged:

> The timing of the revolutionary change tells us many things about its cause. First, it tells us what its cause was *not*. In America, at least, it was not industrialization, urbanization, and the growth of mass education— not "modernization" in the ordinary meaning of the term. We know that because there is one clear and simple law of causality which always operates in history: if event B happened after event A, it cannot have

been the cause of A. That is one of life's few certainties. The great transition in age relations began in America before urbanization, industrialization, and universal education could have had any effect. (Fischer, 1978, pp. 101–102)

At this point in Fischer's analysis we might be tempted to ask why the ideas of liberty and equality did not lead to an equality of age relations in modern society. How does idealism explain the fact that youth has gained an advantage over age? The answer is that here, too, causes are sought in the ideas of the time rather than in social structures. Idealism recognizes the growth in the numbers of older people in modern history, but sees no necessary reason for increases in number to be associated with decreases in status. Fischer points to the experience of Japan, where rapid modernization took place without a drop in the status of the old (Palmore, 1975).

Turning to American history, idealism finds the causes of the lowered status of the elderly and the advantages gained by youth again to be in the ideas that gained dominance in American culture. Fischer argues that the period between 1770 and 1970 in the United States saw the ever expanding growth of a "cult of youth." It was somewhat anticipated in the thought of Thomas Jefferson, who wrote:

It is reasonable we should drop off, and make room for another growth. When we have lived our generation out, we should not wish to encroach upon another. (Fischer, 1978, p. 77)

This idea of politely asking elders to step down so as to not interfere with the equality or liberty of the society's youth was quickly transformed into a demand by the early nineteenth-century Transcendentalists, among whom Henry David Thoreau was the strongest advocate of such as view:

I have lived some thirty years on this planet, and I have yet to hear the first syllable of valuable or even earnest advice from my seniors. They have told me nothing and probably cannot teach me anything. (Thoreau, 1942, p. 33)

Fischer (1978) argues that ideas such as this continued to expand throughout American history, reaching their peak in the youth culture of the 1960s. Thus, the cause of the present "common sense" view of the aged is seen, from the perspective of idealism, as being due to beliefs and values, and not the social structures of modern society. Further, Fischer argues against the view of modernization theory that all was good for the aged in the past, and all is bad in the present. The cult of youth certainly destroyed all remnants of veneration for the aged. However, he argues that as reverence and awe receded, the aged gained in the expression of love and affection, especially by family members. As individuals we may prefer one to the other, but idealism makes it clear that within any historical period, the aged are unlikely to receive both veneration and love.

An Assessment of Historical Perspectives

Fischer's work is a significant contribution to our understanding of age relations in historical perspective. In pointing out that veneration and love of the elderly are unlikely to coexist, he laid to rest the myth that there was ever a "golden age" for society's older members. He also helped to encourage a greater appreciation of the complexity of age relations in society.

Achenbaum (1978) has further stressed this complexity that views of the aged and aging cannot be understood through any unicausal theory. He believes that both modernization theory and idealism contain some truth. However, he argues that both perspectives lead us to overly simplified explanations that do not adequately represent the many causes of age stereotypes and relations in any historical period. He sharply disagrees with those who contend that significant changes and developments have neatly occurred in an inevitable and unidirectional manner (Achenbaum, 1978, p. 5). Nor is he convinced by notions that the development of ideas of the Transcendentalists, or any other set of cultural ideas, had an overriding influence on perceptions of the elderly in American history. Of Fischer's work he writes:

> I find neither sudden nor radical transformations in conceptions of old age or the elderly's condition during any specific decade(s) or period(s). Thus I seriously doubt [Fischer's statement (1978, p. 113)] that "from Thomas Jefferson's era to our own, the lines of change have been straight and stable." The historical record . . . is far more complex and complicated. (Achenbaum, 1978, p. 5)

Achenbaum stresses the distinction between ideas about the elderly and their actual status within the society. He argues that ideas evolved gradually, and that some remained even when they no longer accurately portrayed the circumstances of the aged. He cautions us to be aware that shifts in conceptions of older Americans' status have not always coincided with shifts in the actual situation of the aged in society. Nor are changes in older people's actual situation necessarily reflected by altered conceptions of their lives. This is an important insight, since it forces us to demonstrate, rather than assume, connections between the structure of age relations and ideas about the elderly.

It is our view that both modernization theory and idealism present important insights to those who wish to understand the processes leading to the present status of the aged and associated stereotypes. Each of these perspectives offers its own contribution to our efforts to account for the "common sense" stereotypes that pervade our society today. Keeping in mind this historical context, we now turn to an analysis of contemporary stereotypes about the aged and the process of aging. We shall first consider studies that have attempted to measure the "common sense" stereotypes of aging and the aged. Following that, we will turn our attention to a consideration of the discrepancy between existing stereotypes and the findings of gerontological research on these issues.

MEASURING STEREOTYPES OF AGING AND THE AGED

Our discussion of historical trends focused on social structural arrangements and ideas as the sources of stereotypes of aging and the aged in modern society. Another important line of research in gerontology has sought to sample populations within modern society in order to understand the typical view of aging and the aged. These studies have not so much concerned themselves with how people come to hold a particular view of older people as they have been designed to specify what that view is at any given moment in time.

Empirical research on attitudes toward aging and the aged began in earnest in the 1950s. In the early part of that decade, Tuckman and Lorge developed a questionnaire to measure attitudes toward old age that consisted of 137 statements about old people. These statements were classified into 13 categories: physical, financial, conservatism, family, attitude toward the future, insecurity, mental deterioration, activities and interests, personality traits, best time of life, sex, cleanliness, and interference. Table 8.1 presents each of these categories with a corresponding sample statement drawn from the Tuckman and Lorge Stereotype Scale.

Between 1952 and 1958, Tuckman and Lorge published a number of studies based on the administration of this questionnaire to samples of both young and old persons. Their goal was to gain knowledge of the nature and extent of negative stereotypes and misconceptions about the elderly. Their findings indicated that while the particular negative ideas about the aged differed between young and old groups, both groups saw the elderly in essentially negative terms. Declines in physical and mental capacities, poor health, poverty, unwillingness to change, and loneliness were all seen as typical characteristics of the elderly (Tuckman and Lorge, 1952a; 1952b; 1953a; 1953b; 1954; 1956).

A modified version of the Tuckman and Lorge Stereotype Scale was utilized by Axelrod and Eisdorfer (1961) to determine whether young people's negative stereotypes increased as the age of the groups they were asked to respond to increased. Groups of young people were instructed to complete the modified Tuckman and Lorge Stereotype Scale, applying the statements to people who were 35, 45, 55, 65, and 75 years old. Axelrod and Eisdorfer (1961) found that the mean number of negative stereotypes

TABLE 8.1
Categories and Sample Statements from the
Tuckman and Lorge Stereotype Scale

Category	Sample Statement
Physical	They spend much time in bed because of illness.
Financial	They are usually supported by their children or old-age pensions.
Conservatism	They are conservative.
Family	They usually live with their children.
Attitude toward the future	They are afraid of death.
Insecurity	They worry about unimportant things.
Mental deterioration	They are absent-minded.
Activities and interest	They like to play checkers or dominoes.
Personality traits	They are grouchy.
Best time of life	They never had it better.
Sex	They should not marry.
Cleanliness	They never take a bath.
Interference	They meddle in other people's affairs.

Source: Adapted from Tuckman & Lorge (1952b), Table 2, pp. 339–342.

increased as the age of the five stimulus groups increased. They thus concluded that their findings confirmed those of Tuckman and Lorge—that is, that old age is seen in essentially negative terms.

Beginning in the early 1960s, a series of studies by Kogan (1961a; 1961b) and Kogan and Shelton (1962a; 1962b) raised some new questions about stereotypes of the elderly. Kogan developed an Old People Scale and administered it to groups of both young and old persons, much as Tuckman and Lorge had done before him. However, while Tuckman and Lorge had worded the vast majority of their statements about the elderly in negative terms (see Table 8.1), Kogan was careful to include as many positive as negative items about the elderly in his questionnaire.* (See Table 8.2.)

---

*Kogan extended the research in terms of both scope and methodology. He was the first to use Likert scaling procedures so that an individual could be given an overall score on an Old People Scale. He was also the first to explore the relationship between these scores and personality dimensions of respondents, such as achievement, autonomy, narcissism, and nurturance, and their relationships to scales of attitudes toward other minority groups, such as the California F and the Anti-Negro scales (Adorno, Frenkel-Brunswik, Levinson, and Sanford, 1950), Srole's Antiminority and Anomie scales (Srole, 1956), a scale of attitudes toward mental illness, and a scale of attitudes toward blindness (Bennett & Eckman, 1973).

TABLE 8.2
Sample Statements From Kogan's Old People Scale

N	It would probably be better if most old people lived in residential units with people of their own age.
P	It would probably be better if most old people lived in residential units that also housed younger people.
N	Most old people get set in their ways and are unable to change.
P	Most old people are capable of new adjustments when the situation demands it.
N	It is foolish to claim that wisdom comes with old age.
P	People grow wiser with the coming of old age.
N	Most old people make one feel ill at ease.
P	Most old people are very relaxing to be with.
N	There are a few exceptions, but in general most old people are pretty much alike.
P	It is evident that most old people are very different from one another.
N	Most old people are irritable, grouchy, and unpleasant.
P	Most old people are cheerful, agreeable, and good-humored.

    N = Negative statement.
    P = Positive statement.
    Source: Kogan (1961a), Table 1, pp. 46–47. Copyright 1961 by the American Psychological Association. Reprinted by permission.

Kogan's results were somewhat inconsistent with the earlier findings of an essentially negative view of the elderly. He found that subjects often disagreed with the positive statements about old people. This is consistent with the findings of the research of Tuckman and Lorge, and of Axelrod and Eisdorfer. However, Kogan also found that subjects disagreed even more strongly with the negative statements about old people. This finding is clearly inconsistent with the earlier findings.

Further doubt concerning the existence of an essentially negative view of older people was raised by Bell and Stanfield (1973). They stated that much of the difficulty in the previous research was the result of utilizing a survey method. They argued that the issue could be clarified by employing an experimental, rather than a sample survey, method. Bell and Stanfield therefore conducted the following experiment.

Subjects were told that they would be listening to a recorded discussion on ecology by a journalist named John Cross. One group of subjects was told that Mr. Cross was 65 (experimental group 1), another group was told that Mr. Cross was 25 (experimental group 2), and a third group was given no information about Mr. Cross's age (control group). After listening to the recording, subjects were asked to give their impressions of Mr. Cross by rating him on 46 items from the Tuckman and Lorge Stereotype Scale in the categories of personality, insecurity, conservatism, and mental deterioration. Bell and Stanfield argued that this research design made it possible to assess the significance of age in determining attitudinal judgments: "If significant differences are found between experimental and control subjects, a stronger case can be made for the specific character of age-related attitudes" (Bell & Stanfield, 1973, p. 342).

Bell and Stanfield's findings in this experiment, as in the Kogan study, call into question the predominantly negative character of the responses reported by Tuckman and Lorge. Experimental group 1, which believed Mr. Cross was 65, rated him in essentially the same way as experimental group 2, which believed he was 25. Further, the control group, which had no information on his age, rated him in essentially the same way as the two experimental groups had. All three groups responded positively to Mr. Cross. Bell and Stanfield concluded that age, in and of itself, does not result in any characteristic response pattern. They therefore recommended that future research should discard the use of chronological age categories, and use real stimulus individuals. By using real individuals, they suggest, the effect of other factors, such as dress, white hair, or wrinkled skin, on subjects' appraisals of older people could be assessed.

It is difficult to compare the results of Bell and Stanfield directly with those of Tuckman and Lorge. In employing the survey method, Tuckman and Lorge asked subjects to complete their questionnaires in response to old people in general. In the Bell and Stanfield experiment the subjects were not asked to respond to old people in general, but to respond to one person, Mr. Cross. As we pointed out earlier, it is certainly possible for people to believe that a negative stereotype generally applies to old people, and at the same time to believe that there are exceptions to the rule. Mr. Cross may very well represent such an exception. He was described as a journalist and as a person interested in ecology. It is entirely possible that either of these factors operated as an independent variable affecting the subjects' evaluations of him. Since journalists and ecology are fairly popular among college students, Bell and Stanfield's subjects, their positive evaluations of those characteristics might have outweighed the effect of any negative age stereotypes on their overall evaluation of Mr. Cross.

While these issues have not yet been resolved, Bell and Stanfield's (1973) suggestion that other factors, such as dress, white hair, or wrinkled skin, affect subjects' appraisals of older people has been explored. Silverman and Townsend (1977) designed an experiment to test the effect of these factors on subjects' evaluation. The first experimental group was given a photograph of a man clad in a checked shirt, his hair parted in the middle, sitting at a checkerboard. Traditional pictures were in the background of this photograph. The second experimental group was given a photograph of the same man, clad in a turtleneck shirt, and with a modern hair style. The background in this photograph contained an easel, and contemporary prints were on the wall. Both groups were told that the man in the picture was 65 years old. The control group was given no photograph, but was asked to rate men who were approximately 65 years old. The ratings for all groups were made on 88 items adapted from the Tuckman and Lorge Stereotype Scale.

The experimental group that viewed the photograph of the man in contemporary dress and surroundings was significantly less likely to apply the negative stereotypes to him than was the experimental group that viewed the photograph of him in traditional dress and surroundings. The same type of significant differences was found between the contemporary photograph group and the control group that had viewed no photograph. Silverman and Townsend (1977) therefore concluded that neither age designation nor age-specific characteristics, such as wrinkles and gray hair, are sufficient to elicit negative stereotypes of aging. Apparently "dressing young" or being involved with modern art provides some insulation against negative stereotypes.

The results of this study lend further support to the notion that while a generally negative view of the aged exists, particular older persons are likely to be viewed as exceptional people to whom these negative stereotypes do not apply. There is certainly nothing revolutionary about that conclusion. In fact, the basic difficulty with the experimental studies that have been conducted to date is that they elicit responses to a single older person. Bell and Stanfield's (1973) conclusion that age designation is not sufficient to elicit negative stereotypes, or Silverman and Townsend's (1977) conclusion that age-specific characteristics (such as wrinkles and gray hair) are not sufficient to elicit negative stereotypes, therefore can be applied only to evaluations of particular individuals. Their findings cannot be taken to mean that either chronological age designation or specific age characteristics will not elicit negative stereotypes when applied to the older population in general.

The distinction between judgments about groups and about individual members of those groups is an important one. It is, of course, heartening to note research that suggests that individual members of the category *aged* are in fact reacted to as individuals. Connor and Walsh (1980) observed such a result in a study of attitudes toward job applicants. Subjects responded to a transcript of a job interview in which the interviewee was presented as 65 years of age or 25 years of age. Sex, competence, and success/failure in obtaining the job were also manipulated. Age had very little impact on a variety of judgment items, although it was used to account for failure more in the case of the older job applicant. Lack of effort was given greater importance in the case of a younger applicant not being hired. Connor and Walsh suggest that "examination of reactions to specific stimulus persons is probably most relevant to the day-to-day experience of the elderly" (p. 920). However, if we have negative images of the elderly, we may be inclined to avoid interacting with individual members of this group unless forced to do so by circumstances. As Jones points out in Chapter 2 of this volume, we may be subsequently biased in attending selectively to information which confirms our initial expectations about the elderly. Finally, there are a number of important settings (for example, legislation and policy-making in the federal government) in which the elderly *as a group* are the object of discussion.

A different research strategy was employed by Palmore (1977) to clarify the issues raised by the Tuckman and Lorge and the Kogan studies. He argued that the questionnaires used in these studies were too long, that they confused factual statements with attitudinal statements,* and that the factual statements are undocumented by research, so that there is no way to verify whether they are true or false. In order to remedy the deficiencies that he saw in the previous research, Palmore designed a short questionnaire consisting only of factual statements that could be documented by empirical research (see Table 8.3).

Palmore administered the questionnaire to samples of undergraduates, graduate students in human development, and faculty members in human development. His findings indicate that the most common incorrect stereotype among undergraduates was that over 15 percent of the population are 65 or over (86 percent). Three others tied for second place as the most common stereotypes of the aged; 74 percent of undergraduates were incorrect in their beliefs that a large proportion of the aged are living in institutions, that a majority of the aged are frequently bored, and that a majority of older people have incomes below the poverty level (Palmore, 1977). Palmore compared the mean percentages of correct answers for each group. Undergraduates answered 65 percent correctly, graduate students completed 80 percent correctly, and faculty members were correct on 90 percent of responses. Palmore interpreted these differences as evidence of the validity of the quiz as a measure of knowledge about the elderly. He proposed that the one important use of the quiz is to compare different groups' level of information about the aged. He suggests that it would be fruitful to understand differences in knowledge about the aged between age, sex, race, religious, regional, socioeconomic, and other groups.

Palmore's (1977) basic contention is that since the quiz is based on factual statements that can be documented by empirical research, it therefore represents a valid measure of knowledge about the elderly. This conclusion has been challenged by Klemmack (1978), who argues that the quiz measures respondents' biases against the aged rather than their level of

---

*Palmore argues: "For example, Kogan's statement 'Most old people would prefer to continue working just as long as they can, rather than be dependent on anybody' is probably false, depending on what is meant by 'most,' 'working,' and 'dependent.' Yet a 'disagree' response is scored as showing an unfavorable attitude toward the aged. Unfortunately some 'negative' stereotypes about the aged are generally true and some of the 'positive' statements are generally false" (Palmore, 1977, p. 315).

TABLE 8.3
Sample Statements from Palmore's Old Age Quiz

1.   The majority of old people (past age 65) are senile (that is, defective memory, disoriented, or demented).
2.   All five senses tend to decline in old age.
3.   Most old people have no interest in, or capacity for, sexual relations.
4.   Lung capacity tends to decline in old age.
5.   The majority of old people feel miserable most of the time.
6.   Physical strength tends to decline in old age.
7.   At least one-tenth of the aged are living in long-stay institutions (that is, nursing homes, mental hospitals, homes for the aged, and such).
8.   Aged drivers have fewer accidents per person than drivers under age 65.
9.   Most older workers cannot work as effectively as younger workers.
10.   About 80 percent of the aged are healthy enough to carry out their normal activities.

Note: All odd-numbered items are false; all even-numbered items are true.
Source: Adapted from Palmore (1977), pp. 315–316. Reprinted by permission of *The Gerontologist.*

knowledge about aging per se. Klemmack administered the quiz to a stratified random sample of 202 adults in a medium-size southern city. He found that individuals who gave a correct response to negative-bias items were more likely to give incorrect responses to the positive-bias items. For example, someone who responded correctly to the false statement "The majority of old people are senile" was more likely to respond incorrectly to the true statement "All five senses tend to decline in old age." This pattern of response indicates a positive bias, since denying that the five senses decline indicates a more favorable image of old age than scientific evidence would warrant. On the basis of these findings, Klemmack (1978) argued that a respondent's total score on the quiz is more a function of a negative or a positive image of older people than it is a function of factual knowledge about aging. This is a direct contradiction of Palmore's (1977) assertion that the quiz is a valid measure of knowledge about the aged.

Holtzman and Beck (1979) sought to clarify these issues through further research. They administered the Facts on Aging Quiz to over 500 health workers and health career students. Like Palmore (1977) they found significant differences, with better-educated groups answering fewer items incorrectly. They concluded that "Since better educated persons generally have more knowledge than less educated persons, this finding is evidence for the validity of the quiz as a measure of knowledge" (Holtzman & Beck, 1979). It is our view that in drawing this conclusion, Holtzman and Beck overlooked the possibility that different degrees of bias between these differently educated groups might also be operating as an independent variable. Better-educated persons not only tend to be more knowledgeable, they also tend to be less biased. Therefore, Holtzman and Beck's (1979) conclusion is unwarranted here, since they did not isolate the effects of bias from the effects of knowledge by comparing groups with different levels of education.

Some of Holtzman and Beck's other findings do shed more light on the question of whether the Facts on Aging Quiz measures bias or knowledge. Along with the Facts on Aging Quiz they also administered Rosencranz and McNevin's (1969) Aging Semantic Differential. The Aging Semantic Differential is a measure of attitudes toward the elderly. In order to assess the extent to which Palmore's quiz measures bias, Holtzman and Beck (1979) correlated the number of incorrect responses on the quiz with scores on the Aging Semantic Differential. They found a weak significant positive correlation between number wrong and negative attitudes toward the aged. This indicated that the more positive respondents' attitudes toward the aged, the fewer items they missed on the Facts on Aging Quiz.

Further analysis by Holtzman and Beck (1979) also indicated a weak-to-moderate association between attitude, as measured by the Aging Semantic Differential, and the kinds of errors made on the Facts on Aging Quiz. Since the association was weak to moderate, Holtzman and Beck conclude that Palmore's quiz is a relatively poor measure of the bias. They further conclude that, contrary to Klemmack's contentions, the test actually measures knowledge rather than bias. This interpretation is open to criticism. It seems to us that Palmore's quiz measures both knowledge and bias, and that further refinements of the instrument or of its analysis will have to be made before a legitimate claim can be made that the effect of bias has been separated from the effect of knowledge.

It should be obvious from this summary of research that has attempted to measure stereotypes of the aged and aging that there are a number of methodological issues that have not yet been resolved. Kogan's (1961a; 1961b) finding that including both positively and negatively worded items influenced the outcome has not been given serious attention in the studies done since then.

The experimental design, because of its inclusion of a control group, offers great hope of clarifying issues. However, the findings of experimental studies that have been reported to date are limited to stereotypes as they apply to one person, and cannot be applied to stereotypes of the aged in general. Finally, the validity of Palmore's (1977) attempts to avoid mixing measures of bias toward the elderly with measures of factual knowledge about the elderly has been challenged by Klemmack (1978). (For a reply, see Palmore, 1980.) Future research on stereotypes of the aged and aging will have to give serious consideration to the issues raised here.

We have seen in this and the preceding sections that the study of stereotypes of the aged is a complex undertaking. Historical analysis indicated that while the aged have lost veneration, they have gained affection. Similarly, a look at studies that have attempted to measure stereotypes of aging and the aged points to the fact that while there are often negative trends in the responses, it is dangerously simplistic to characterize the "common sense" view as completely negative or as applying to all older people. In the following section we turn our attention to the discrepancy between some common stereotypes and the findings of gerontological research on these issues. We then seek explanations of the persistence of stereotyped views of aging and the aged from different theoretical perspectives.

CONTEMPORARY IMAGES OF THE AGED

It is only since the 1920s that a serious and sustained effort has been made to scientifically study the aging process (Birren & Clayton, 1975). Much of this effort has been directed toward separating the myths from the realities of aging. Gerontology has had a strong tradition of debunking stereotypes (Oriol, 1981; Tibbitts, 1979). In this section we will review some of the most significant research in this tradition.

We have chosen to divide the stereotypes considered into three categories: biological, psychological, and social. While it is generally accepted that these three aspects of the aging process do not proceed independently of each other, the distinction among them is useful for heuristic purposes. To fully understand the relationship between aging and the quality of life people experience, it is crucial to take into consideration the various ways in which these different aspects of the aging process interact. For example, we cannot fully understand the meaning of social isolation without an understanding of the psychological experience of loneliness. Similarly, we cannot fully understand the biological changes that accompany aging without some understanding of the consequences of these changes for the social and psychological experiences of those involved. The ways in which these processes interact vary between people, and this in part accounts for the marked differences among individuals with respect to the biological, social, and psychological experiences of aging. One of the most important conclusions that we will reach is that the aged are a very heterogeneous group of people, and any generalization about the aged that does not take this into consideration runs the risk of being inaccurate.

Biological Stereotypes

Biological aging, often called senescence, refers to the time-related changes in the anatomy and physiology of the individual (Rockstein & Sussman, 1979). To say that these biological changes are time-related should not be taken to mean that there is a one-to-one relationship between chronological age and the biological aging process that has taken place. However, many people do make such an assumption, and this is the source of various stereotypes.

The Chronological Age Stereotype

> "Grown-ups love figures. When you tell them that you have made a new friend, they never ask you questions about essential matters. They never say to you, "What does his voice sound like? What games does he love best? Does he collect butterflies?" Instead, they demand: "How old is he? How many brothers has he? How much does he weigh? How much money does his father make?" Only from these figures do they think they have learned anything about him. (Saint-Exupéry, 1943, pp. 17–18)

The above passage from *The Little Prince* is a comment on our cultural preoccupation with numbers. Asking questions like "How old are you?" is so much a part of our taken-for-granted reality that we ask them without ever thinking about why we ask them. We just assume that it is important to know a person's age, and that people everywhere have always made similar assumptions. This is not the case. Clark and Anderson (1967) have discussed different ways in which other cultures have defined old age. In many, chronological age is much less important, and in some a person's chronological age is not even known. Rather, they attach significance to the person's functional capacities. What can the person do? Can the person hunt or fish? Can the person tend crops? Can the person care for livestock? Basically, then, the important questions in these societies have to do with a person's ability to continue to fulfill the tasks required of the adult role. When one cannot, then he or she is considered old. This is true of most societies where hunting and gathering, agriculture, or domesticated animals are the basis of the economic system.

However, in industrialized societies like our own, a person's chronological age becomes more important. Birth records are kept on everyone. These are used as a proof that a child is ready to enter school, that a worker is ready to enter the labor force, or that a worker is ready to retire.

In this culture we are very much tied to the idea that chronology determines biology (Butler, 1974). Ask anyone how long it takes from conception to birth, and the answer will be nine months. If the child is born after only eight and one-half months, we say the baby was "early." If the child is not yet born after nine and one-half months, we say the child is "late." Well, as any good obstetrician knows, it is not that the child is "early" or "late," but that the chronological system of counting off nine months provides only a rough estimate of when birth will occur. Some fetuses will be biologically developed and ready for birth after eight and one-half months. Others will take nine and one-half months. It is the system of counting that is inaccurate. Yet we tend to give secondary significance to biology, and place our faith in the chronological definition.

So it is with aging. Counting off years provides us with a poor estimate of a person's biological aging. As Rockstein and Sussman point out (1979, p. 11), using chronological age (whether age 65, 70, or even 80) as a magic dividing line between "old" and "not old" is at best a convenience for policy makers and social researchers; it is certainly not a valid biological criterion. Once we begin to seriously question this assumption that is so much a part of our taken-for-granted reality, we are ready to call into question a whole series of related misconceptions.

The Uniform Aging Rate Stereotype

Biological aging (senescence) is not one simple process that affects all parts of the human body in the same way. Rather, there are many aging processes that affect different parts of the body in different ways. The heart, lungs, stomach and intestines, brain, nervous system, sexual organs, muscles, skin, and bones of any older individual do not age at the same rate (Rockstein & Sussman, 1979). We are misled when we see a person with gray hair or dry, wrinkled skin and assume that the person also has poorly functioning lungs or a weak heart. We are also mistaken if we believe that in all humans the heart, or the arteries, or the brain, or any other single organ is usually "the first to go." We must discard our simple notions of aging and recognize that it is a complex, multifaceted process.

Strehler (1962) has outlined four basic criteria that can be used to distinguish the effects of biological aging from the effects of diseases, especially those that are common in later life. The first point is that in order to be considered a part of senescence, the process must be universal. It must be a process that goes on at some time in everyone. The general decline in the ability to resist infection and disease is such a process. Losing one's teeth, on the other hand, is not. Many older people lose their teeth because of poor diet and inadequate dental hygiene. It is neither universal nor inevitable.

Strehler's second point is that in order to be considered a part of senescence, the processes must be based mainly within the body, as opposed to processes that are mainly in reaction to the environment in which the person lives. Thus, the decrease in pulse rate with age and the heart's decreased ability to meet the body's requirements under strenuous exercise would be part of biological aging (Rockstein & Sussman, 1979). On the other hand, heart diseases and lung cancer, although they occur more frequently in older people, are often reactions to smoking or other environmental stresses to which the person has been exposed, and therefore cannot be considered part of biological aging.

Strehler's third point is that senescence occurs over a long period of time, as opposed to changes that take place quickly. While some diseases may give a person the appearance of having aged overnight, the effects of senescence show gradually. His fourth point is that senescence affects the performance of organs so that at some point, some organs will no longer be able to function well enough to sustain life. As we have seen, organs age at different rates in different individuals. Therefore, we cannot predict which organ will cease to function first. However, we can predict that even in the absence of disease, the aging process will eventually lower the functioning of some organ sufficiently to cause death. With these criteria in mind, we can begin to distinguish aging from disease.

The Poor Health Stereotype

Since the process of aging has been so confused with disease processes, many people have assumed that to be old is also to be unhealthy. Older people are usually thought to be in "poor" or "fair" health, sometimes in "good," but never in "excellent" health. This view comes through in studies of stereotypes. Riley and Foner (1968) found large percentages of people agreeing with statements such as "Older people have to expect a lot of aches and pains" and "No matter how careful people are, they have to expect a good deal of illness in their lifetimes." Demos and Jache (1981), in analyzing attitudes toward aging as expressed in birthday cards, noted that the most frequent theme linked aging with a decline in attractiveness, both physical and physiological. Humor in such messages often takes the form of suggesting the existence of a negative image of the elderly and then implying that the recipient of the birthday card is, fortunately, an exception to that rule: "Another year older, smile, it could be worse . . . You could look it!" (p. 212).

More recent studies have indicated that over 50 percent of those sampled believed that "poor health" is a problem for older people (Manion, 1972; Harris et al., 1975). The evidence suggests that while there is some basis for these beliefs, it would be incorrect to assume that all, or even a majority, of older people have health problems. In one study 21 percent of older people polled believed that health was a problem for them (Harris et al., 1975). Another study found 37 percent of persons over 65 reporting limitations in their major activity due to ill health (National Center for Health Statistics, 1972). Thus, while it is true that many chronic conditions, such as high blood pressure, arthritis, and rheumatism, are more frequently found in older than in younger persons, the Shakespearean notion of old age as a time "Sans teeth, sans eyes, sans taste, sans everything" is a misconception.

A study by Birren et al. (1963) sought to clarify the physical capabilities of older men. Three groups were compared. Those in the first group were very healthy older men, with no signs of disease. Those in the second group were older men who were relatively healthy, but did have one or more detectable diseases that were not perceived as interfering with their daily lives in any way. Those in the third group were very healthy younger men. Differences between very healthy old men (group 1) and relatively healthy old men (group 2) could thus be accounted for as the result of disease, not aging. Differences between very healthy old men (group 1) and very healthy young men (group 3) could be representative of the changes produced by biological aging. The results indicate as many differences between very healthy old men (group 1) and relatively healthy old men (group 2) as between very healthy old men (group 1) and very healthy young men (group 3).

This study has two important implications. First, observations of disease in older people should not be taken to be a part of normal aging. Disease can be treated in older persons as well as in younger persons, and the older person can regain a higher level of functioning. Second, unless the performance of a role requires unusual strength and endurance, such as that required of professional athletes, very healthy older people often are able to perform just as well as younger people.

We began our discussion of biological stereotypes by criticizing the view that chronological age determines biological age. We noted the evidence that in other cultures, definitions of old age are based on functional capacities rather than on chronological age. In the American culture we have put the chronological cart before the functional horse. We assume that people in their sixties, seventies, and eighties have biologically aged to a point where they can no longer function as well as people in their thirties, forties, and fifties. These cultural myths are institutionalized in laws such as mandatory retirement. One effect is age segregation. Older people are excluded from many roles that they are physically and mentally capable of performing.

Closely related to the biological stereotypes are the psychological stereotypes of aging. The basis for many of these is that biological aging produces changes in the brain that affect personality, intelligence, emotions, motivation, and even sexual drive. It is to these and related stereotypes that we now turn.

Psychological Stereotypes

Margaret Mead (1972), when in her seventies, remarked, "When I advocate some unpopular point of view, my age is used as a target and some fanatic is likely to denounce me as senile." Mead's comment rings with the anger of one unjustly accused. The accusation of a failing mind threatens one's continued participation in social life.

Long before Descartes wrote, "I think, therefore I am," the "mind" was assumed to be central to human existence. The capacity to think—that is, to carry on the dialogue with the self through which we make decisions about how to act in the situations that confront us daily—has been held as the single most important feature that distinguishes the human from all other animals. The capacity to experience and to give meaning to the emotional processes within us by attaching significant symbols such as love, hurt, and anger to these processes is also vital to our conception of what it means to be human. In view of this, the "common sense" view that assumes older people become increasingly incapable of "appropriate" emotional responses and rational dialogue with the self has profound implications for the way in which they are treated by others and for the conception they hold of themselves.

We might speculate about the consequences of such stereotypes as the belief that the elderly possess only limited capacity for dialogue with the self. What will this do to the prospects for dialogue between young and old? It is unlikely that the young will choose to share their thoughts with those regarded as incapable of understanding them. Similarly, the old person's presumed lack of ability to comprehend his or her own or another's emotional life would preclude the possibility of sharing affective thoughts. Basically, then, the view is that the young and old have little to talk about. The old person is simply not regarded as fully human and worthy of the effort required to make human contact. Fortunately, very few older people are stereotyped in this way by all those with whom they come in contact. We do not know with any precision what proportion of the aged are so stereotyped. One of the difficulties here is the lack of empirical studies that attempt to assess the quality of human relationships in later life. It is far easier to ask questions like "Are you married?" or "How often do your children visit you?" than to attempt to comprehend the extent to which older people have opportunities to express their intellectual and emotional potential, or to understand when and how that expression is blocked.

The Senility Stereotype

What is meant when an older person is referred to as senile? The term seems to be a catch-all label that people use to explain any action by an older person that violates their expectations of normal behavior. The label is likely to be applied to older people who talk to themselves in public, wander aimlessly, dress in unusual costumes, stand too close to someone when they talk, appear untidy and unwashed, stare into space, or in some other way fail to meet the social expectations for proper behavior in a given situation.

If a younger person is seen violating these expectations, they are not labeled "senile"; they are labeled "crazy." While being labeled "crazy" is certainly not a status to which we can aspire, it is in many ways an improvement over the label "senile." The most important distinction is that craziness is seen as something that can sometimes be changed, while senility is seen as something that can only get worse with the passage of time. The senility stereotype is the view that the unusual behavior of some older people is a normal part of the aging process, that everyone who lives long enough will experience deterioration of the brain that will lead to the performance of strange acts. Thus, senility has been conceived of as an aspect of senescence or biological aging (Atchley, 1977). However, even if "senility" is today seen as too imprecise a term for medical diagnosis, it still enjoys widespread usage in the "common sense" view of growing old. The view that aging necessarily leads to senility has been criticized by many gerontologists, including Alex Comfort:

In fact, rather fewer old people are crazy than at earlier years: about nine per thousand over 65 need psychiatric hospitalization, and that includes chronic brain disease, alcoholism, the lot. Old people become crazy for three reasons: because they were crazy when young, because they have an illness, or because we drive them crazy. (1977, p. 11)

The illnesses of which Comfort speaks are cerebral arteriosclerosis or hardening of the brain's arteries or other brain disease, none of which are a normal part of aging. Side effects of drugs (especially tranquilizers), malnutrition, or physical illness, such as congestive heart failure or pneumonia, can also result in unusual behavior by depriving the brain of the needed blood, food, and oxygen (Butler, 1974). Thus there is no justification for assuming that all older people are slowly going crazy and denying them the opportunity to share their emotional lives with others.

The Intellectual Decline Stereotype

We are all aware of certain individuals who did some of their most meaningful creative, intellectual work in their later years. For example:

At 100, Grandma Moses was painting.
At 93, George Bernard Shaw wrote the play, *Farfetched Fables*.
At 90, Pablo Picasso was producing drawings and paintings.
At 89, Mary Baker Eddy was director of the Christian Science Church.
At 81, Benjamin Franklin effected the compromise that led to the adoption of the U.S. Constitution.
At 81, Johann Wolfgang von Goethe finished *Faust*.

Although we are aware of these and other people's high level of intellectual functioning in their later years, we tend to think of them as exceptions to the general rule of intellectual decline with age. Sheppard (1981) has observed, in this context, that cartoons which feature the theme of *ineffectuality* in the elderly are rated as relatively high in humor content. Cartoons which suggest disparagement or isolation are judged to be less humorous. In an important review of aging and television, Kubey (1980) also notes, regarding elderly people, the prevalent images of ineffectiveness, unimportance, and low status or power. Many of the early studies comparing the IQs of young people, middle-aged people, and older people supported the maintenance of this stereotype. They were typically based on cross-sectional data—that is, data collected at one point in time for persons of different ages. The observed differences in intelligence test scores were assumed to be due to aging (Wechsler, 1958; Doppelt & Wallace, 1955; Jones, 1959). Such studies, often using the Wechsler Adult Intelligence Scale (WAIS) measure of IQ, typically found a pattern in which scores peaked in the late teens or early twenties, and then declined with age (Botwinick, 1977, p. 583). Cross-sectional results, such as those presented in Figure 8.1, are

FIGURE 8.1

**Full-scale Weschler Adult Intelligence
Scale Scores as a Function of Age**

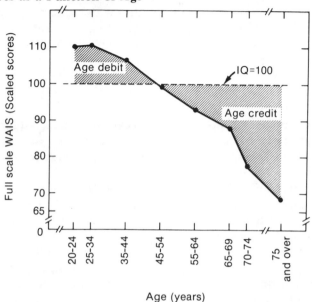

Age (years)

Source: Reprinted from Jack Botwinick, *Cognitive Processes in Maturity and Old age,* p. 3. Copyright © 1967 by Springer Publishing Company, Inc., New York. Used by permission.

entirely consistent with the stereotype of declining intelligence throughout the middle and later years.

In recent years it has become very evident that cross-sectional studies of the relationship between age and intelligence yield a very distorted picture. We get a much more accurate view if we test the same group of people several times as they age. In the ideal case we would test the same people at ages 10, 20, 30, 40, 50, 60, 70, and 80. However, such a study would take too long to be practical. An alternative to this is to study several age groups over a shorter period of time. For example, we might test a sample of persons in each of the above age categories and test them again ten years later. Thus, we would be able to estimate the change in intelligence between the ages of 20 and 30 from one subsample, the change from 30 to 40 from another, and so on.

Studies of this sort have been conducted, and they reach somewhat different conclusions. They tend to show less decline in intelligence with age and to find that the decline starts later in life (Botwinick, 1977; Nesselroade, Schaie, & Baltes, 1972). Another important finding that has come out of these longitudinal studies is that the relationship between age and intelligence varies according to which component of intelligence we are considering. For some there is evidence that intelligence continues to increase well into the seventies.

Figure 8.2 presents data on the longitudinal relationship between age and four dimensions of intelligence. The longitudinal trend is indicated by the broken line that connects the black dots with the corresponding white dots. For crystallized intelligence* it is clear that intelligence is increasing rather than decreasing during the later years. This has been a very common finding in studies of verbal ability. By following the trend in the black dots (or the trend in the white dots) for this dimension of intelligence, we can see a cross-sectional trend suggesting a decline in intelligence. However, the longitudinal trend is in the opposite direction.

Of the four components of intelligence considered—crystallized intelligence, cognitive flexibility, visuo-motor flexibility, and visualization, Nesselroade et al. (1972) found a decline over the seven-year span in only one component, visuo-motor flexibility. In what they considered the most important dimension, crystallized intelligence, they found an increase in scores, even for those over age 70. There was no statistically significant difference in the other two dimensions over time, but the trend for the visualization component certainly suggests an increase rather than a decrease. The investigators in this study concluded that the differences found in intelligence could not be attributed to chronological age. Rather, they believe that the differences are due to the differing educational and life experiences of people born at different times. Thus, the best scientific evidence presently available fails to support the stereotype of a sharp decline in intelligence with age. If we wish to know something of a person's intellectual functioning, we shall have to know a great deal more than the number of years that person has lived.

The Sexual Decline Stereotype

An 84-year-old college professor was delivering a lecture on human sexuality at a well-known university. After the talk the professor asked if there were any questions.

---

*Crystallized intelligence encompasses the sorts of skills one acquires through education and acculturation, such as verbal comprehension, numerical skills, and inductive reasoning. To a large degree it reflects the extent to which one has accumulated the collective intelligence of one's own culture. It is the dimension tapped by most traditional IQ tests. Cognitive flexibility measures the ability to shift from one way of thinking to another, within the content of familiar intellectual operations, as when one must provide either an antonym or synonym to a word, depending on whether the word appears in capital or lower-case letters. Visuo-motor flexibility measures a similar but independent skill, the one involved in shifting from familiar to unfamiliar patterns in tasks requiring coordination between visual and motor abilities, as when one must copy words but interchange capitals with lower-case letters. Visualization measures the ability to organize and process visual materials, and involves tasks such as finding a simple figure contained in a complex one or identifying a picture that is incomplete" (Baltes & Schaie, 1974, pp. 35–36).

FIGURE 8.2

Relationship Between Age and Four Components of Intelligence Based on Two Cross-Sectional (1956, 1963) and Eight Seven-Year (1956–1963) Longitudinal Studies

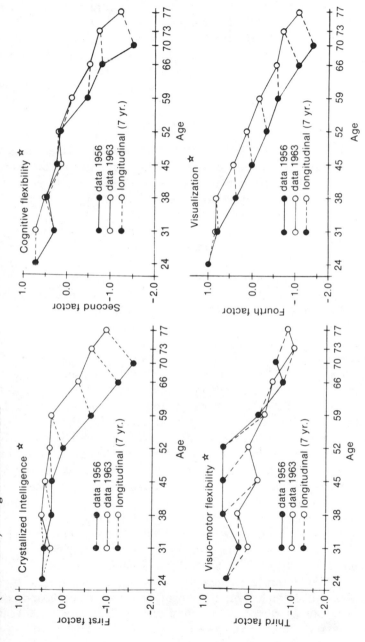

Source: Nesselroade, Schaie, and Baltes (1972), Figure 1, p. 225. Reprinted by permission of the Journal of Gerontology. Vol. 27, No. 2, April 1972.

"Yes," said one student from the rear of the lecture hall. "At what age do people lose interest in sex?"

The professor paused a moment, and then responded, "I'm not sure, but I know it's sometime after 84."

The fact that the above story is being told these days is some indication that the sexual stereotypes of old age may be beginning to break down. The fact that the story is told as a joke indicates that there is still some persistence of the "dirty old man" stereotype. We laugh at things that we see as incongruent: sneakers and tuxedos, a person standing on his head in a train station—and, unfortunately, old people making love.

As we noted earlier, the danger of psychological stereotypes is that they may deny older people opportunities for intellectual and emotional sharing with other human beings. This is certainly the case with sexual stereotypes, which threaten to deprive older persons of one of the most intimate types of human contact. How do the facts contrast with these stereotypes?

In their pioneering study, Masters and Johnson (1966) found that in older women hormonal imbalance after menopause sometimes leads to reduced vaginal lubrication and, therefore, painful intercourse. However, they found no evidence of a reduced sex drive among older women, and therefore concluded that with hormonal therapy there is no biological reason for reduced sexual activity in older women.

The results for men are also in opposition to the stereotype that the elderly are no longer interested in or capable of sexual relations. While men do show a slow, steady decline in sexual capacity throughout the adult years from a peak in the late teens, most are still biologically capable of sexual functioning (intercourse) well into their seventies and eighties. In sharp contrast with the evidence regarding biological capacity is the evidence of a marked reduction in the extent of sexual activity during the later years. They found, furthermore, that the extent of the reduction in sexual activity after age 60 can in large measure be attributed to social and psychological, as opposed to biological, factors. Monotony and boredom in the sexual relationship, preoccupation with career and economic pursuits, mental or physical fatigue, overindulgence in food or drink, physical and mental infirmities, and a fear of failure are all related to decreased sexual interest and activity (Masters & Johnson, 1966). Ludeman (1981) reports that although most people experience a decline in sexual behaviors with advancing age, older men are generally more active and interested in sexual activities than are older women.

There is nothing about these problems that makes them unique to old age; they can interfere with a sexual relationship between 30-year-olds as easily as they do between 60-year-olds. In the context of an intimate relationship there are no factors related to senescence that prevent sexual activity from continuing into the sixties, seventies, and beyond (Masters & Johnson, 1966). The social reasons, particularly loss of a spouse, and social norms about who is considered to be an age-appropriate sex partner for an older person are often harder on older women than older men. In 1970 more than 50 percent of women over 65 were widows. In the same year only 17 percent of men over age 65 were widowers (U.S. Bureau of the Census, 1970). The pool of available older men is small. There are only 72 men over age 65 for every 100 women over age 65 (U.S. Bureau of the Census, 1970). Sexual expression, like other forms of emotional or intellectual expression, is limited by decreased opportunities for older people.

We have chosen to be selective rather than exhaustive in our review of psychological stereotypes of aging and the aged. However, there are other psychological stereotypes that might also have been analyzed: rigidity increasing with age, older people being naturally grouchy, depression as a normal concomitant of later life, and old age as a time of peaceful serenity (see Butler, 1974; Saul, 1974). Our goal has been to give the reader a sense of the ways in which psychological stereotypes misrepresent the reality of the aging process and to point out the kinds of threats these stereotypes pose to older people. There are also a number of stereotypes about the social situation of older people in American society. These, like the biological and psychological stereotypes, sometimes lead people to believe that the majority of older people are worse off than they in fact are, while at other times lead us to ignore real problems of substantial segments of the elderly population.

Social Stereotypes

In this section we explore social stereotypes of aging and the aged. One reason they are so important is the potential impact they have on government social policy toward the aged. In recent years elected officials have been greatly influenced by public opinion dealing with the perceived needs of the elderly. It tends to be politically very safe to support new programs and increased spending for the elderly. However, if this effort is to be optimally effective, it ought not to be based on misconceptions about the elderly and their needs. Stereotypes about the elderly run the risk of contributing to ineffective programs and policies on their behalf.

The social conditions of older people are in some ways the most flexible and most susceptible to change. Unlike biological aging, in which most people believe that significant change would require technological breakthroughs, changes in the social situation of older people seem more within reach. Some would argue that it is simply a matter of getting the political system to work.

The Poverty Stereotype

I am 74 years old and live in a building seventy years old. I moved here six years ago and paid $90 a month for rent. Then the building was sold.

> The first two years my rent was raised $5 each year. Then I got a $10
> increase. Now $20 more. I get $141 Social Security. Rent is $130. Plus
> gas, plus utilities, plus telephone. How can I eat? (Percy, 1974, p. 73)

Many older people suffer the kind of poverty this person describes.
However, is it typical? Let's look at another example of older people in
retirement.

> We have some friends who have settled on two homes. They spend late
> spring and fall on Cape Cod and the colder months in a delightful and
> unique home in the old city of Antigua in Guatamala. Some years back
> they found a partially ruined old home in this once capital of Spanish
> colonial Guatamala, and they have gradually restored it for modern
> occupancy. Thus they alternate between the delights of mile-high winter
> tropics and seaside summer in New England. (Hersey & Hersey, 1969,
> p. 109)

Contrasts like these between the very rich and the very poor are not
hard to find in American society. Anyone who has ever taken a walking tour
of an American city knows that. Those distinctions do not end when people
grow old. The very rich continue to enjoy their privileges, and the very poor
continue to endure their misery.

One stereotype about the aged is that they experience less income
inequality than other segments of the population. It is generally assumed
that the reduction in income that typically accompanies retirement contributes to a leveling of incomes among the elderly, and thus to a reduction in
the extent of inequality in the distribution of income. But this view turns out
to be in error. There is actually more, rather than less, income inequality
among the aged than there is in other age groups (Riley & Foner, 1968). An
important factor contributing to this is the minority of the aged who remain
in the labor force, earning at the highest levels of their lives, while the
majority experience a substantial drop in income. This results in a dispro-
portionate number of persons at the income extremes, which leads to an
increase rather than a decrease in income inequality.

The most common stereotype about the economic status of the elderly
is that they are poor. It turns out that poverty rates are higher for the elderly
(14 percent in 1977) than they are for the general population (12 percent),
but the difference is more accurately described as moderate than as large
(Johnson & Williamson, 1980). However, we get a somewhat different
picture if we consider those who have near-poverty incomes as well as
poverty incomes. When this is done, it has been estimated that approximately one in four of the elderly lives on a poverty or near-poverty income
(Williamson, Evans, & Munley, 1980). Even when we use this more liberal
definition, we would have to conclude that at least 75 percent of the aged are
not poor. While almost 50 percent of black elderly females are poor, less

than 10 percent of elderly white males are poor (Williamson, 1979). Poverty rates among the 20 percent of elderly males still in the labor force are very low. In short, there is marked variation in economic status between various subgroups of the elderly. Any description that does not take this variation into consideration will be distorted (Williamson, 1979). Hellebrandt (1980), for example, analyzed self-reports from over 100 elderly people who were relatively advantaged in terms of socioeconomic status (for example, retired medical school professors, business leaders, school administrators). The replies were overwhelmingly positive on a variety of interpretive dimensions (such as, activity, attitudes toward death, social relations, lack of depression), leading Hellebrandt to conclude that "The image of the elderly needs to be linked more intimately to socioeconomic factors" (p. 404).

Another economic stereotype about the aged is that most are living on a fixed income, and thus are particularly vulnerable to the effects of inflation. However, since 1974, Social Security payments have been automatically adjusted each year for increases in the cost of living due to inflation. For this reason the elderly who have had little to live on except their Social Security have not been living on fixed incomes, and have not been vulnerable to the effects of inflation in recent years. However, we must qualify any such conclusion by pointing out that many of the aged have also been depending on income from earnings (20 percent of elderly males and about 8 percent of elderly females) and income from pensions that are not adjusted for inflation.* Thus, at least a substantial minority of the aged are exposed to some of the effects of inflation.

One of the most common economic stereotypes about the aged is that they are living on a much lower income than prior to retirement. This assessment does prove to be true for the majority of the elderly who have withdrawn from the labor force, but it is an inaccurate generalization when applied to the minority who remain at work. This stereotype has, no doubt, contributed to the increased attention to the economic problems of the aged that we have witnessed in the United States since the turn of the century (Lowy, 1979).

Paying one's own way is a basic value in the American economy. People who are unable to maintain financial independence are seen as somehow morally inferior. "They should have planned and saved for their old age" is an often-heard comment. This independence value has been institutionalized in a Social Security system that is designed to "help out," but not to provide full support for retired workers. Next we shall look at another stereotype that is also related to strong independence values: the stereotype of social isolation in old age.

---

*In 1972 some 39 percent of the aggregate income of the elderly came from earnings, 16 percent came from asset income, and 6 percent came from other pension income (Moon, 1977). These sources of income are not protected from erosion due to inflation in the way that Social Security income is.

The Social Isolation Stereotype

> When I was lonely as a girl or as a young woman . . . I could distract myself in a hundred ways. I'd call a friend on the spur of the moment and go out, or I'd clean the house, or go to a movie, or take a walk in the park, or share my loneliness with my husband. Now it is a terrible effort to fight loneliness. My husband is dead; most of my friends are dead; the friends I have left live so far away. It didn't seem so far away when I was young, but now it does. I haven't the strength to clean the house; I'm afraid to walk in the park. I feel hemmed in on all sides. (Gornick, 1976, p. 32)

Again we must ask whether this case is typical. Do we find that most older people are isolated, many of them, or relatively few? First, let us consider the various categories of the elderly that are considered most likely to experience social isolation. One category is the institutionalized elderly, many of whom do not have families. The experience of being institutionalized is very disruptive to a person's network of friendship ties. Those who have recently become widowed are also quite vulnerable to isolation. Elderly widows find themselves at a great disadvantage with respect to replacing a deceased spouse, as compared with elderly widowers. Another group that many would expect to be isolated is the never-married.

Empirical research suggests that the elderly are not as bothered by social isolation as many people think. In a study a national sample was asked to list the worst things about being over age 65. Among adults age 18 to 64, some 36 percent mentioned loneliness, but only 20 percent of those over age 50 mentioned it (Harris et al., 1975). Loneliness is a problem for the elderly, but it is a problem for a smaller minority of the aged than many people think.

Institutionalization does contribute to social isolation, but it is not as major a factor as the stereotypes about being old would have us believe. Only 4 or 5 percent of the elderly are in institutions (Siegel, 1976).* Of these, 80 percent are over age 75 (Murphy & Florio, 1978). We must take into consideration the social isolation that those who require institutionalization are likely to experience even if they remain in the community. They are often afflicted by serious physical and mental problems. The mistake is often made of contrasting the networks of such persons at a time prior to institutionalization, when they were younger and healthier, with their networks after institutionalization. At least part of the decrease is due to changes in health rather than to institutionalization. A case can be made that in some instances institutionalization increases the person's social network.

---

*This is an estimate based on cross-sectional data. When we consider the proportion of persons who spend at least some time in a nursing home prior to death, the estimate is somewhat higher—in the 20–25 percent range (Kastenbaum & Candy, 1973; Ingram & Barry, 1977).

Most of the elderly have been married at some time in their life, and more than 80 percent have living children (Troll, Miller, & Atchley, 1979). Contrary to the myth of social isolation of the elderly, 84 percent of the aged live within an hour of at least one of their children (Shanas, Townsend, Wedderburn, Friis, Milhhoj, & Stehouver, 1968). In addition, 52 percent have seen at least one of their children during the past 24 hours, and 78 percent have seen one during the past week (Shanas, 1973). There is no evidence to support the notion that children abandon their parents in their old age (Shanas, 1979). In fact, the evidence is all to the contrary, even when parents become bedfast and housebound. While only 5 percent of the elderly are institutionalized, another 8 percent are housebound or bedfast, and being taken care of by family (Shanas, 1962).

Widows are less likely to remarry than widowers. About 5 percent of women who become widows after age 55 ever remarry (Cleveland & Gianturco, 1976). In contrast, most widowers under age 70 remarry (Troll et al., 1979). However, it is important to make the distinction between living alone and feeling lonely. Many widows adjust quite quickly to the change. More than half of widows live by themselves rather than with children, and prefer to do so (Troll et al., 1979). One study reports higher rates of social interaction for widows than for older women who were still married (Atchley, Pignatiello, & Shaw, 1975).

About 5 percent of the elderly have never been married. We might expect this to be a particularly isolated group. However, Clark and Anderson (1967) did not find this to be the case. They report that most of the never-married had learned very early in life to get along by themselves and to be self-reliant. Gubrium (1975) argues that this experience in early life helps to protect a person against loneliness in late life.

The Elderly Voting Bloc Stereotype

One of the most prevalent political stereotypes about the aged is that there exists an "elderly vote." We can point to the great lengths to which big city mayors, congressmen, senators, and others running for public office go to point out how much they have done or plan to do for the elderly. It would seem that more is "promised" to this group than to any other major population subgroup. This certainly would suggest that the elderly vote is very important to most politicians. When we look at the data on voter participation, we find that the turnout rate is higher for those over age 65 than it is for those 21 to 45, even though it tends to be somewhat lower than for the group aged 45 to 64 (Ward, 1979).

However, as Robert Binstock (1974) points out, there is little evidence that the aged vote as a bloc today or that they are likely to do so at any time in the foreseeable future. Very few of the aged see themselves as members of an age group when it comes to voting. They are much more likely to vote on the basis of such sources of identity as ethnicity, social class, religion, or occupation.* These are sources of identity that the older person has had for a much longer period of time, and sources that are more highly valued.

If the aged do not vote as a bloc, can the case be made that they tend to support conservative issues and candidates? There is evidence that the aged are, in the aggregate, more conservative than are younger age groups (Hudson & Binstock, 1976; Ward, 1979). However, this observation must be qualified. The aged tend to be less tolerant of nonconformity and resistant to social change (Riley & Foner, 1968). They tend to oppose school busing, women's rights issues, and the legalization of marijuana (Cutler & Schmidhauser, 1975). However, they take a more liberal stand on other issues, such as government health care efforts (Bengtson & Cutler, 1976). The elderly also were more "dovish" on U.S. involvement in Vietnam during the 1960s and early 1970s (Campbell, 1971). A case can be made that it is more accurate to argue that the liberalizing of the aged has not kept pace with changes in the views of the general population than to argue that they have grown more conservative (Glenn, 1974; Hudson & Binstock, 1976).

Some have pointed to the Supreme Court and U.S. Senate to illustrate that the elderly are in positions of considerable power and political influence in America. However, as Binstock (1974) has pointed out, relatively few of these persons in positions of power identify with the elderly and the interests of the elderly. The older senator is as likely as not to be caught up in projecting a "young image," and there is no evidence that older senators and congressmen tend to be more favorable to the interests of the aged.

In this section we have contrasted a number of "common sense" stereotypes about the aged with the evidence from various empirical studies by social researchers. The "common sense" perspective tends to lead to the overgeneralization of characteristics that accurately describe only a minority of the aged. If there is any one conclusion that gerontologists can all agree upon, it is that the elderly are a very heterogeneous lot. Stereotypes about the aged tend to suggest that age has a leveling effect and that we will find less variation among those who are elderly than within other age groups. But gerontologists have time and again found that there is more variation among the aged than in any of the other age groups they have considered. This is true with respect to the distribution of income, with respect to health, and with respect to many other factors that we have considered.

THEORETICAL PERSPECTIVES ON THE MAINTENANCE OF STEREOTYPES

In the preceding section we presented some of the "common sense" stereotypes of aging and the aged, and contrasted them with the "facts" of aging as derived from scientific research. We have seen that while there is a

---

*See Rose (1965) for the argument that the elderly are in the process of forming a subculture that could become a major source of political strength at some time in the future.

"kernel of truth" in many of the stereotypes, there is a consistent tendency in the "common sense" view to overgeneralize the negative effects of aging to all older people. While a higher percentage of older than younger persons suffer from chronic diseases that cause them to be bedridden, housebound, or otherwise limited in their activity, there is a tendency to assume that all or most people suffer such limitations in old age. While there is a small percentage of older people who have diseases that affect the brain and psychological functioning, there is a tendency to assume that these conditions will affect almost everyone who lives to old age. And while many older persons suffer from poverty and social isolation, the tendency is to assume that a majority of older persons experience these conditions. Thus, the effects of aging are consistently seen as worse than they are.

In this section we shall address the question of why this tendency exists. Why is there not a more accurate perception of aging and the aged? One explanation of the disparity between "common sense" knowledge of aging and scientific knowledge of aging is the fact that most people are not aware of the gerontological literature. They are not scientists, and therefore have no reason to spend their time pondering the scientific accuracy of their views of aging and the aged. While this may be a partial explanation for the maintenance of negative stereotypes about older people, it does not adequately answer the question. It does not, for example, explain why the "common sense" view so rarely presents a positive perspective on aging. Yet we know from our review of historical literature that an overly positive view, one of "veneration," dominated the "common sense" perception of the aged in past times. To explain the present-day "common sense" view, we need a better understanding of the social influences on perception of aging and the aged. We shall approach this problem from two major theoretical perspectives in sociology: the functionalist perspective and the conflict perspective.

The Functionalist Perspective

The functionalist perspective in sociology sees society as a system of interrelated parts that work together to produce a working social system. The parts of a society are its social institutions. Examples of the interrelated parts, or social institutions, are the family, the educational system, the economic system, and the government. Each part has a certain function to perform that contributes to the operation of the whole. The function of the family is to produce and raise children, the function of the schools is to educate those children, the function of the economic system is to produce and distribute goods and services, and the function of the government is to make laws and provide for defense. Thus, if we try to understand the existence of any part (social institution) in a society from a functionalist perspective, we ask: What function does that part perform for the society as a whole?

When we take the functionalist perspective and apply it to the status of older people in modern society, we first look for a social institution that primarily affects the aged. One such institution is retirement. This institution, unique to modern industrialized societies, was unknown in the agricultural or hunting and gathering societies of the past. We can then ask what function the institution of retirement performs for the society as a whole.

The answer to this question can be found in what is called disengagement theory. Disengagement is a theory in social gerontology that derives its assumptions from the functionalist perspective. Disengagement is not directed at explaining negative stereotypes per se, but attempts to explain why people play less important roles in old age than they did in middle age. Its focus, then, is clearly on the institution of retirement. The theory holds that retiring from important social roles performs important functions both for the society as a whole and for the individual older members of the society. For the society retirement functions to provide an orderly system of replacing people in important social roles. Society is thus spared the potential chaos that would occur if persons remained in these roles until death. A leading proponent of disengagement theory has stated: "Very roughly, the depth and breadth of a man's engagement can be measured by the degree of potential disruption that would follow his sudden death" (Cumming, 1964, p. 4).

For the individual older person, retirement is seen as fulfilling the function of relieving him or her of the burdens of many important roles. That person is thus free to spend his or her last years with fewer pressures, and can conserve energy for the tasks found most meaningful.

Within the context of disengagement theory, the function of negative stereotypes of aging and the aged is clear. They bring order to the transition from full engagement in the middle years to disengagement in the later years. If the negative aspects of aging were not emphasized, if the old were seen as just as capable (or even more capable) of performing some important roles as younger persons, there would be resistance to the notion of retiring. An orderly transition in roles would be inhibited, and the society would suffer the disruption of sudden deaths and reduced productivity in important roles.

As we have pointed out, in their writings disengagement theorists do not explicitly deal with the role of negative stereotypes. Yet their emphasis on the potential disruption caused by death or the infirmities of old age would logically lead one to think of the negative, rather than the positive, aspects of aging. Disengagement theory has been soundly criticized in the gerontological literature for taking this emphasis. The theory itself has been attacked as supporting negative stereotypes of the elderly. Yet even if disengagement theory is guilty of what some people consider the worst sin of social science—simply rephrasing the "common sense" view in scientific terms—it can be useful for understanding why these negative stereotypes persist. The negative stereotypes do not just occur; they are functional for maintaining the status quo of age relations in modern society—a status quo that continuously sees younger people being phased into important social roles, and older people as being phased out.

Lest we make the mistake of concluding that all theories in the functionalist perspective are similarly supportive of the status quo, let us take a look at another, quite different application of this theoretical perspective. The functionalist perspective would also be useful in explaining recent shifts to more positive views of aging in some sectors of the society. For example, the changes in government policy, such as the raising of the age of mandatory retirement from 65 to 70, can also be accounted for by reasoning from a functionalist perspective.

Robert Merton (1968), a functionalist, has pointed out that not all parts of a social system are always functional. Some parts might be at least temporarily disruptive to the social order, and thus be dysfunctional. From this perspective it could be argued that a mandatory retirement age of 65 is dysfunctional because it forces a large number of older people out of the work force when they could have continued to work and support themselves. In a society where over 10 percent of the population is over 65, it is dysfunctional for the society as whole to force all those persons into a situation of economic dependence. For the next 50 years it is likely that our society will continue to age—that is, the proportion who are over age 65 will continue to increase. This will have obvious implications for the economic burden on those who are younger and in the labor force, paying for the Social Security benefits to those who have retired. In view of this trend, it is perhaps more functional for the society to allow those persons who wish to continue earning an income to do so until age 70, or even longer.

The growth of gerontology and the increased government support of gerontology's efforts to "debunk" negative stereotypes about aging can also be seen as an attempt to correct the dysfunctional aspects of those stereotypes. If these stereotypes serve to prevent 10 percent of the population from full participation, and thus make older people dependent, then such views are dysfunctional for the society as a whole. They create more problems than they solve, and gerontology can function to correct this situation.

Thus, we have considered several examples of the ways in which the functionalist perspective can be used to account for the persistence of stereotypes about the aged or to account for evidence of change. In functionalist theory, as in the modernization theory that we considered earlier in the chapter, the role of ideas is seen as secondary to the social structures of the society. Negative or positive stereotypes of the elderly are not seen as having a life of their own; rather, they are seen as reflections of the social institutions that dominate the society. In modernization theory the institutional arrangements that derive from the form of economic production (agriculture or industry) were seen as determining the ideas about the status of the elderly. In functionalist theory the same holds true. The society's need to have important positions in its social institutions filled by persons who will not die while in those positions is seen as most important.

Stereotypes of the elderly are viewed as reflective of this need to maintain social order within the society. Even shifts to more positive stereotypes are explained through needed changes in social arrangements, as in the case of society's recent reconsideration of mandatory retirement rules.

Next we shall consider another perspective that also gives precedence to social arrangements over the role of ideas in society: the conflict perspective. Yet while both the functionalist and the conflict perspectives see social structures and institutions as the source of ideas about the elderly, we shall see that the emphasis of the conflict perspective is quite different from that of the functionalist perspective.

The Conflict Perspective

The assumptions of, and the questions asked by, those using the conflict perspective are quite different from those of theorists using the functionalist perspective. The functionalist perspective assumed a system of parts working together to maintain a balanced, whole society. The basic question about any part of the system was "What function does it perform for the whole?" The conflict perspective begins from very different assumptions. The various parts of the society are not seen as working for the whole. Rather, the conflict perspective views society as composed of competing groups: blacks versus whites, rich versus poor, young versus old. When conflict theorists explain the existence of some part or social institution in the society, they do not ask "What function does this part perform for the whole society?" Rather, they ask questions like "Who benefits from the existence of this social institution?" "Whose interests are served?" "Who suffers as a result of the existing social arrangements?" Levine (1980) discusses these issues in terms of intergroup rivalry and competition.

When we apply this perspective to the situation of the aged, we find very different explanations for the existence of social institutions such as retirement. A conflict theorist would attempt to understand which social groups benefit or suffer from the existence of the retirement institution.

Let us first look at the relative benefits and the potential conflicts between the old and the young over this issue. There are obvious benefits to the old from retirement: they receive an income in their later years; they are able to leave jobs that they may not have enjoyed; there is a possibility of spending their later years free of the burdens of the work world. However, the institution of retirement also presents clear disadvantages for older people. The income they receive in retirement is often inadequate. They are forced to leave their jobs at a certain age even if they do not wish to. The freedom from the burdens of the work world is often replaced by the burdens of losing the status that came with their position in the labor force.

For our purposes it is this latter loss that is most significant. In American society the status accorded to people is very much tied to their work position. Persons who occupy lowly positions, or no work positions, are subject to a number of negative stereotypes. They are, for example, often assumed to be lazy, unintelligent, or incompetent. (For more elaboration on this point, see Chapter 9.) A retiree is often seen as "useless" in the economic sphere, and this perception carries over into other perceptions of the individual. Thus, from the conflict perspective the gains in status that the young derive by entering important positions in the work force are made at the expense of the older members of the society.

Let us next apply the conflict perspective to how retirement benefits two other conflicting groups, the rich and the poor. Here the conflict perspective is useful in explaining differences in status accorded to various older people. This view draws its original inspiration from the work of Karl Marx, who focused on conflict between social classes. Throughout this chapter we have emphasized the fact that older people are not all alike. This observation applies to differences in status, just as it did to other aspects. If we take a Marxist perspective, we will focus on differences in the status accorded to rich and poor older people. We will point to the fact that retired corporation presidents, generals, and senators often enjoy a high status that retired factory workers, secretaries, and cooks never experience. We might also look at the historical data that tell us that old age for the upper class has never been too bad—in fact, in many societies it has been a time of very special privilege (de Beauvoir, 1972; Fischer, 1978).

From a Marxist perspective the high status accorded to wealthy people in old age would be explained through an analysis of the capitalist system of production. In a capitalist society productivity is highly valued. The prestige accorded to a person is based to a large extent on what he or she produces in terms of goods and services. For the upper classes productivity comes through ownership of the means of production. Owning a railroad, steel mill, mine, factory, or other means of production brings prestige to the owner. This does not change when one grows old, since ownership is usually held until death. On the other hand, for the middle and lower classes productivity is not based on ownership, but on labor, on what one does while working. Labor ends at retirement, not at death; and therefore, unlike owners, workers lose their source of prestige when they retire.

From a conflict perspective there are other ways in which the upper classes benefit from the retirement institution. Retirement allows the owners of the means of production to remove older workers who are receiving relatively high wages and to replace them with younger workers who receive relatively low wages. The recent shift from a mandatory retirement age of 65 to one of 70 could also be explained in terms of the interests of the upper class. Now that the "baby boom" of the post-World War II period is over, fewer younger workers will be entering the labor force in the 1980s than entered in the 1960s and 1970s. It is in the interests of the upper class to maintain a labor pool that is larger than the number of available jobs. Otherwise, there would be a shortage of workers and owners would have to pay much higher wages in order to attract people to work for them. Increasing the age of retirement from 65 to 70 also increases the available labor pool, and this is very much in the interests of the upper class.

When we turn to "common sense" stereotypes of the elderly, we find that conflict theory, like functionalism, sees the social arrangements of the society as the source of ideas. However, while functionalism views the "common sense" ideas of the aged as good for the whole society, conflict theory sees those ideas as serving the interests of one group over another. Marx was quite explicit in his views about the source of ideas in a society. He wrote that "The ruling ideas of each age have ever been the ideas of its ruling class" (Marx & Engels, 1962, p. 52). By this he meant that in any historical period, the dominant ideas on any topic are the ideas of the upper class, and that these ideas serve the interests of that class at the expense of other classes.

From this perspective, stereotypes of the aged are seen as serving the interests of the upper class. When the labor force was large, the interests of the upper class were best served by retiring workers at 65, and negative stereotypes of the aged helped to support such policies. Now that older workers are becoming needed to keep the labor force large, the retirement age has been raised to 70 and negative stereotypes of the aged are being replaced by more positive views. From a conflict perspective the growth of gerontology and increased funding of gerontology's efforts to "debunk" the "common sense" negative view of aging and the aged would be seen as very much in keeping with the interests of the upper class.

Thus, we have two theoretical perspectives of the social influences on perception of aging and the aged. Both focus on social structures and institutions as greatly influencing the "common sense" view of aging. However, while functionalists see the dominant ideas about the aged as benefiting the whole society, the conflict theorists focus on the benefits of those ideas to particular groups within the society.

SUMMARY AND DIRECTIONS FOR FUTURE RESEARCH

In this chapter we have taken the view that stereotypes about aging and the aged can be explained in their historical and social context. Two theoretical perspectives dominate thought about the apparent shift from a positive view of old age in the past to a negative view of old age in the present. The first, modernization theory, seeks its explanation of the lowered status of the elderly in modern history by focusing on shifts in social structures. It sees the transformation from traditional, agricultural societies to modern, industrial societies as the source of negative stereotypes. Idealism presents a quite different explanation of historical shifts in views of the aged. Rather than focusing on social structures, it points to the role of two crucial ideas in modern history: equality and liberty. These are seen as fostering a

302

M 61
H 16

Say something
about earning
respect

continue to use "Great Britain."

of Germany, use "Germany (West)."
use "Germany (East)."

s Republic of Korea, use "Korea
use "Korea (South)."

"District of Columbia" as the head-
with "Washington (D.C.)" used only
try element for cross references

the heading

London" for items from the

"cult of youth" that dominated age relations in this country through the 1960s.

In assessing the impact of the historical perspective, we stressed the importance of demonstrating the relationship between ideas about the elderly and the actual situation of the elderly in society. It is our view that the value of historical research is that it provides us with a moving picture of how attitudes toward the elderly have been shaped through the decades. Since the historians have paid a great deal of attention to how stereotypes of the elderly are interrelated with social structures and other cultural ideas, we get a sense of the significance of their work. However, the drawback of this research is that the further back in time we go, the less sure we are of our statements. We have to infer our conclusions from whatever records are available. Thus, while the findings seem significant, we do not know whether they are valid.

After the historical analysis we turned our focus to studies that had attempted to measure stereotypes of aging and the aged. We saw that the first studies reported an essentially negative view. Later studies have called this finding into question either by varying the wording of statements positively and negatively or by changing the research design from sample survey to experimental. We questioned the generalizability of the experimental studies, since they solicit responses to particular individuals rather than to the elderly in general. We also discussed research that attempted to distinguish between attitudes toward and knowledge about the elderly. The complexity of measuring stereotypes was emphasized.

The value of this line of research is that it provides us with snapshots of a particular group's perceptions at a given point in time. Since these are smaller-scale studies than the historical works, if we are careful about our questionnaire design, sampling procedure, and other methodological concerns, we can be reasonably assured that our findings are valid. However, there is little effort to relate these findings to social structures, other cultural ideas, or the actual situation of the elderly in society. Thus, the drawback of these studies is that we cannot know the significance of our snapshots for the elderly in society.

The section on measuring stereotypes was followed by a presentation of some of the major stereotypes of aging and the aged in our time. These stereotypes were divided into three categories: biological, psychological, and social. Three biological stereotypes were discussed: the chronological age stereotype, the uniform aging rate stereotype, and the poor health stereotype. Three psychological stereotypes were discussed: the senility stereotype, the intellectual decline stereotype, and the sexual decline stereotype. Three categories of social stereotypes were discussed: the poverty stereotype, the social isolation stereotype, and the elderly voting bloc stereotype. We saw that while each stereotype contains some "kernel of truth," there is a consistency in the "common sense" view to overgeneralize that bit of truth to all or most older people. The major thrust of the scientific research on these issues has been to point out the marked diversity among those who share the one trait of being elderly.

Finally, two of the dominant theoretical perspectives in modern sociology were used to explain the maintenance of and shifts in the "common sense" view of aging and the aged. The functionalist perspective seeks its answers within the social institutions of the society and is particularly useful in accounting for retirement. From this perspective one is likely to view retirement or "disengagement" as functional for the whole society because it protects the society from the disruption of having people grow old and die while occupying important social positions. Negative stereotypes of aging and the aged are seen as supporting these social arrangements. Using the functionalist perspective, we were also able to account for the recent growth of gerontology and its debunking of negative stereotypes about aging and the aged.

Like the functionalist perspective, the conflict perspective seeks its explanation of stereotypes within the social institutions of society. However, rather than seeing the dominant social institutions and stereotypes as functional for the whole society, the conflict perspective focuses on the benefits that these social arrangements and stereotypes have for competing groups within the society. Here the benefits to the young and the rich were contrasted with the losses for those who are neither young nor rich.

We have outlined these two theoretical perspectives in sociology because we believe that a promising intersection between the path toward "what is valid" and the path toward "what is significant" lies in the integration of theory and data. Functionalism leads us to ask certain kinds of questions, and therefore to look at certain kinds of data, especially the interconnections between different types of social roles and institutions. Conflict theory leads us to ask a different set of questions, especially those that help us to understand who benefits from the existing ideas and social arrangements vis-à-vis the elderly.

We have not exhausted the theoretical perspectives in sociology that may bring new questions and answers to the study of stereotyping and the elderly. That would require a book. Nor have we even attempted to illustrate the application of theoretical perspectives in other social sciences to these issues; that would require volumes. Our hope, however, is that we have stimulated thought in the direction of bringing theory and data together. At that juncture we can better assess whether our findings are both valid and significant.

REFERENCES

Achenbaum, W. A. *Old age in the new land: The American experience since 1790.* Baltimore: Johns Hopkins University Press, 1978.

Adorno, T. W., Frenkel-Brunswik, E., Levinson, A. S., & Sanford, R. N. *The authoritarian personality*. New York: Harper, 1950.

Agello, T. J., Jr., Aging and the sense of political powerlessness. *Public Opinion Quarterly*, 1973, *37*, 251–259.

Atchley, R. C. *The social forces in later life* (2nd ed.). Belmont, Calif.: Wadsworth, 1977.

Atchley, R. C., Pignatiello, L., & Shaw, E. *The effect of marital status on social interaction patterns of older women*. Oxford, Ohio: Scripps Foundation, 1975.

Axelrod, S., & Eisdorfer, C., Attitudes toward old people: An empirical analysis of the stimulus group validity of the Tuckman-Lorge questionnaire. *Journal of Gerontology*, 1961, *16*, 75–80.

Baltes, P. B., & Shaie, K. W. Aging and IQ—the myth of the twilight years. *Psychology Today*, 1974, *7*, 35–40.

de Beauvoir, S. *The coming of age*. New York: Putnam's, 1972.

Bell, B. D., & Stanfield, G. G. The aging stereotype in experimental perspective. *Gerontologist*, 1973, *13*, 341–344.

Bengtson, V., and Cutler, N. Generations and intergeneration relations: perspectives on age groups and social change. In R. H. Binstock & E. Shanas (eds.), *Handbook of aging and the social sciences*. New York: Van Nostrand-Reinhold, 1976.

Bennett, R., & Eckman, J. Attitudes toward aging: A critical examination of literature and implications for future research. In C. Eisdorfer & M. P. Lawton (eds.), *The psychology of adult development and aging*. Washington, D.C.: American Psychological Association, 1973. Pp. 575–597.

Binstock, R. H. Aging and the future of American politics. *Annals of the American Academy of Political and Social Science*, 1974, *415*, 199–212.

Birren, J. E., Butler, R. N., Greenhouse, S. W., Sokoloff, L., & Yarrow, M. R. (eds.), *Human aging: A biological and behavioral study*. Bethesda, Md.: U.S. Public Health Service, 1963.

Birren, J. E., & Clayton, V. History of gerontology. In D. S. Woodrull & J. E. Birren (eds.), *Aging: Scientific perspectives and social issues*. New York: Van Nostrand, 1975. Pp. 15–27.

Botwinick, J. *Cognitive processes in maturity and old age*. New York: Springer, 1967.

Botwinick, J. Intellectual abilities. In J. Birren & K. W. Schaie (eds.), *Handbook of the psychology of aging*. New York: Van Nostrand-Reinhold, 1977.

Burgess, E. W. (ed.), *Aging in Western societies*. Chicago: University of Chicago Press, 1960.

Butler, R. N. Successful aging and the role of the life review. *Journal of the American Geriatric Society*, 1974, *22*, 529–535.

Butler, R. N. Ageism: A foreword. *Journal of Social Issues*, 1980, *36*, 8–11.

Campbell, A. Politics through the life cycle. *Gerontologist*, 1971, *11*, 112–117.

Clark, M., and Anderson, B. *Culture and aging*. Springfield, Ill.: Charles C. Thomas, 1967.

Cleveland, W. P., & Gianturco, D. T. Remarriage probability after widowhood: A retrospective method. *Journal of Gerontology*, 1976, *31*, 99–103.

Coffman, G. R. Old age from Horace to Chaucer: Some literary affinities and adventures of an idea. *Speculum*, 1934, *9*, 249–277.

Comfort, A. Age prejudice in America. In F. Riessman (ed.), *Older persons: Unused resources for unmet needs.* Beverly Hills, Calif.: Sage, 1977. Pp. 9–17.

Connor, C., & Walsh, R. P. Attitudes toward the older job applicant: Just as competent, but more likely to fail. *Journal of Gerontology,* 1980, *35,* 920–927.

Cook, S. Aging of and in populations. In P. S. Timiras (ed.), *Developmental physiology and aging.* New York: Macmillan, 1972.

Cowgill, D. O. The aging of populations and societies. *Annals of the American Academy of Political and Social Science,* 1974, *415,* 1–18.

Cowgill, D. O. A theory of aging in cross-cultural perspective. In D. O. Cowgill & L. Holmes (eds.), *Aging and modernization.* New York: Appleton-Century-Crofts, 1972. Pp. 1–14.

Cowgill, D. O., and Holmes, L. (eds.), *Aging and modernization.* New York: Appleton-Century-Crofts, 1972.

Cumming, E. New thoughts on the theory of disengagement. In Robert Kastenbaum (ed.), *New thoughts on old age.* New York: Springer, 1964.

Cutler, N., & Schmidhauser, J. Age and political behavior. In D. Woodruff & J. Birren (eds.), *Aging: Scientific perspectives and social issues.* New York: Van Nostrand, 1975.

Demos, V., & Jache, A. When you care enough: An analysis of attitudes toward aging in humorous birthday cards. *Gerontologist,* 1981, *21,* 209–215.

Doppelt, J. E., & Wallace, W. L. Standardization of the Wechsler Adult Intelligence Scale for older persons. *Journal of Abnormal and Social Psychology,* 1955, *51,* 312–330.

Fischer, D. H. *Growing old in America.* New York: Oxford University Press, 1978.

Foner, A. Age stratification and age conflict in political life. *American Sociological Review,* 1974, *39,* 187–196.

Glenn, N. D. Age and conservatism. In F. R. Eisele (ed.), *Political consequences of aging.* Philadelphia: American Academy of Political and Social Science, 1974. Pp. 176–186.

Glenn, N. Aging and conservatism. *Annals of the American Academy of Political and Social Science,* 1974, *415,* 176–186.

Gornick, V. For the rest of our days, things can only get worse. *The Village Voice,* May 24, 1976.

Gubrium, J. F. Being single in old age. *International Journal of Aging and Human Development,* 1975, *6,* 29–41.

Haller, R. S. *The old whore and medieval thought.* Ph.D. dissertation, Princeton University, 1960.

Harris, L., and Associates. *The myth and reality of aging in America.* Washington, D.C.: National Council on the Aging, 1975.

Hellebrandt, F. A. Aging among the advantaged: A new look at the stereotype of the elderly. *Gerontologist,* 1980, *20,* 404–417.

Hersey, J., and Hersey, R. *These rich years: A journal of retirement.* New York: Scribner's, 1969.

Holtzman, J. M., & Beck, J. D. Palmore's facts on aging quiz: A reappraisal. *Gerontologist,* 1979, *19,* 116–120.

Hudson, R. B., & Binstock, R. H. Political systems and aging. In R. H. Binstock & E. Shanas (eds.), *Handbook of aging and the social sciences.* New York: Van Nostrand-Reinhold, 1976. Pp. 369–400.

Ingram, D. K., & Barry, J. R. National statistics on deaths in nursing homes: Interpretations and implications. *Gerontologist*, 1977, *17*, 303–308.

Johnson, E. S., & Williamson, J. B. *Growing old: The social problems of aging*. New York: Holt, Rinehart, & Winston, 1980.

Jones, H. E. Intelligence and problem-solving. In J. E. Birren (ed.), *Handbook of aging and the individual*. Chicago: University of Chicago Press, 1959. Pp. 700–738.

Kastenbaum, R., & Candy, S. The four percent fallacy: A methodological and empirical critique of extended care facility program statistics. *International Journal of Aging and Human Development*, 1973, *4*, 15–21.

Klemmack, D. L. Comment: An examination of Palmore's facts on aging quiz. *Gerontologist*, 1978, *18*, 403–406.

Kogan, N. Attitudes toward old people: The development of a scale and examination of correlates. *Journal of Abnormal and Social Psychology*, 1961, *62*, 44–54. (a)

Kogan, N. Attitudes toward old people in an older sample. *Journal of Abnormal and Social Psychology*, 1961, *62*, 616–622. (b)

Kogan, N., & Shelton, F. Images of "old people" and "people in general" in an older sample. *Journal of Genetic Psychology*, 1962, *100*, 3–21. (a)

Kogan, N., & Shelton, F. Beliefs about "old people": A comparative study of older and younger samples. *Journal of Genetic Psychology*, 1962, *100*, 93–111. (b)

Kubey, R. W. Television and aging: Past, present, and future. *The Gerontologist*, 1980, *20*, 16–35.

Levine, M. Four models for age/work policy research. *The Gerontologist*, 1980, *20*, 561–574.

Lipset, S. M., & Ladd, E. C., Jr. The political future of activist generations. In P. G. Altbach & R. S. Laufer (eds.), *The new pilgrims: Youth protest in transition*. New York: David McKay, 1972. Pp. 63–84.

Lowy, L. *Social work with the aging*. New York: Harper & Row, 1979.

Ludeman, K. The sexuality of the older person: Review of the literature. *The Gerontologist*, 1981, *21*, 203–208.

Manion, O. V. *Aging: Old myths versus new facts*. Eugene, Ore.: Retirement Services, Inc., 1972.

Marx, K., and Engels, F. *Selected Works (Vol. 1)*. Moscow: Foreign Language Publishing House, 1962.

Masters, W. H., and Johnson, V. *Human sexual response*. Boston: Little, Brown, 1966.

Mead, M. *Blackberry winter*. New York: Simon & Schuster, 1972.

Merton, R. K. *Social theory and social structure* (2nd ed.). New York: Free Press, 1968.

Moon, M. *The measurement of economic welfare*. New York: Academic Press, 1977.

Morse, D. W. Aging in the ghetto. In R. Gross, B. Gross, & Sylvia Seidman (eds.), *The new old: Struggling for decent aging*. Garden City, N.Y.: Anchor Press, 1978. Pp. 16–27.

Murphy, J., & Florio, C. Older Americans: Facts and potential. In R. Gross, B. Gross, & Sylvia Seidman (eds.), *The new old: Struggling for decent aging*. Garden City, N.Y.: Anchor Press, 1978. Pp. 50–57.

National Center for Health Statistics. Acute conditions: Incidence and associated disability, United States, July, 1969–June, 1970. *Vital and Health Statistics*, series 10, no. 77. Washington, D.C.: U.S. Government Printing Office, 1972.

Nesselroade, J. R., Schaie, K. W., & Baltes, P. B. Ontogenetic and generational components of structural and quantitative change in adult cognitive behavior. *Journal of Gerontology*, 1972, *27*, 222–228.

Oriol, W. E. "Modern" age and public policy. *Gerontologist*, 1981, *21*, 35–45.

Palmore, E. *The honorable elders: A cross-cultural analysis of aging in Japan.* Durham, N. C.: Duke University Press, 1975.

Palmore, E. Facts on aging: A short quiz. *Gerontologist*, 1977, *17*, 315–320.

Palmore, E. The facts on aging quiz: A review of findings. *Gerontologist*, 1980, *20*, 669–679.

Percy, C. H. *Growing old in the country of the young.* New York: McGraw-Hill, 1974.

Riley, M. W., & Foner, A. *Aging and society* (Vol. 1). New York: Russell Sage Foundation, 1968.

Rockstein, M., & Sussman, M. *Biology of aging.* Belmont, Calif.: Wadsworth, 1979.

Rose, A. M. The subculture of aging: A framework for research in social gerontology. In A. M. Rose & W. A. Peterson (eds.), *Older people and their social world.* Philadelphia: F. A. Davis, 1965. Pp. 3–16.

Rosencranz, M. A., & McNevin, T. E. A factor analysis of attitudes toward the aged. *Gerontologist*, 1969, *9*, 55–59.

Saint-Exupéry, A. de *The little prince.* New York: Harcourt, Brace, & World, 1943.

Saul, S. *Aging: An album of people growing old.* New York: Wiley, 1974.

Scott-Maxwell, F. *The measure of my days.* New York: Alfred A. Knopf, 1968.

Shanas, E. *The health of older people: A social survey.* Cambridge, Mass.: Harvard University Press, 1962.

Shanas, E. Family-kin networks and aging in cross-cultural perspective. *Journal of Marriage and the Family*, 1973, *35*, 505–511.

Shanas, E. Social myth as hypothesis: The case of the family relations of old people. *Gerontologist*, 1979, *19*, 3–10.

Shanas, E., Townsend, P., Wedderburn, D., Friis, H., Milhhoj, P., & Stehouver, J. *Older people in three industrial societies.* New York: Atherton, 1968.

Sheppard, A. Response to cartoons and attitudes toward aging. *Journal of Gerontology*, 1981, *36*, 122–126.

Siegel, J. Demographic aspects of aging and the older population of the U.S. *Current Population Reports: Special Studies*, series P-23, no. 59. Washington, D.C.: U.S. Government Printing Office, 1976.

Silverman, M., & Townsend, J. C. Effects of implied attitude similarity on stereotype of aging: A pilot study. *Perceptual and Motor Skills*, 1977, *45*, 894.

Simmons, L. W. *The role of the aged in primitive society.* New Haven: Yale University Press, 1945.

Srole, L. Social integration and certain corollaries: An exploratory study. *American Sociological Review*, 1956, *21*, 709–716.

Strehler, B. L. *Time, cells and aging.* New York: Academic Press, 1962.

Thoreau, H. D. *Walden*, G. S. Haight (ed.). New York: Walter J. Black, 1942.

Tibbitts, C. Can we invalidate negative stereotypes of aging? *Gerontologist*, 1979, *19*, 10–20.

Troll, L. E., Miller, S. J., & Atchley, R. C. *Families in later life.* Belmont, Calif.: Wadsworth, 1979.

Tuckman, J., & Lorge, I. The best years of life: A study in ranking. *Journal of*

Psychology, 1952, *34*, 137–149. (a)

Tuckman, J., & Lorge, I. The effect of institutionalization on attitudes toward old people. *Journal of Abnormal and Social Psychology*, 1952, *47*, 337–344. (b)

Tuckman, J., & Lorge, I. Attitudes toward old people. *Journal of Social Psychology*, 1953, *37*, 249–260. (a)

Tuckman, J., & Lorge, I. *Retirement and the industrial worker*. New York: Columbia University Teacher's College, 1953. (b)

Tuckman, J., & Lorge, I. Old people's appraisal of adjustment over the life span. *Journal of Personality*, 1954, *22*, 417–422.

Tuckman, J., & Lorge, I. Perceptual stereotypes about life and adjustments. *Journal of Social Psychology*, 1956, *43*, 239–245.

United States Bureau of the Census. *Census of population: Characteristics of the population*. Washington, D.C.: U.S. Government Printing Office, 1970.

United States Bureau of the Census. *Census of population: 1970* (Vol. 1, pt. I, sec. 1). Washington, D.C.: U.S. Government Printing Office, 1973.

Ward, R. *The aging experience*. New York: Lippincott, 1979.

Wechsler, D. *The measurement and appraisal of adult intelligence* (4th ed.). Baltimore: Williams & Wilkins, 1958.

Williamson, J. B. The economic status of the elderly: Is the problem low income? *Journal of Sociology and Social Welfare*, 1979, *6*, 673–700.

Williamson, J. B., Evans, L., & Munley, A. *Aging and society*. New York: Holt, Rinehart, & Winston, 1980.

ADDITIONAL READINGS

de Beauvoir, S. *The coming of age*. New York: Putnam's, 1972.
   An excellent analysis of the condition of the aged from the conflict perspective. The book also contains a well-written historical section.

Butler, R. N. *Why survive?: Being old in America*. New York: Harper & Row, 1975.
   A well-documented exposé of the problems faced by many older people in the United States. Poverty, housing, health, senility, the politics of aging, and other important issues are eloquently and passionately discussed.

Cowgill, D. O. A theory of aging in cross-cultural perspective. In D. O. Cowgill and L. Holmes (eds.), *Aging and modernization*. New York: Appleton-Century-Crofts, 1972. Pp. 1–14.
   A presentation of modernization theory as applied to the change in status of the elderly in hunting and gathering, agricultural, and industrial societies.

Fischer, D. H. *Growing old in America*. New York: Oxford University Press, 1978.
   In this book Fischer gives a critique of modernization theory and presents the perspective of idealism. The book is well-written and well-documented.

Gerontologist.
   This journal publishes many articles on issues relevant to stereotyping of aging and the aged.

Green, B., Parham, I. A., Kleff, R., & Pilisuk, M. (eds.) Old age: Environmental complexity and policy interventions. *Journal of Social Issues*, 1980, *36*, No. 2 (whole).
A collection of empirical investigations dealing with diverse aspects of aging. Of particular interest are papers by Rodin and Langer on the relationship between aging labels and self-esteem, and by Schulz on the general discipline of experimental social gerontology.

Johnson, E. S., & Williamson, J. B. *Growing old: The social problems of aging.* New York: Holt, Rinehart, & Winston, 1980.
This book focuses on the difficulties of aging from a social-problems perspective. Major issues facing older persons are discussed within their social and political context.

Lutsky, N. S. Attitudes toward old age and elderly persons. In C. Eisdorfer (ed.), *Annual review of gerontology & geriatrics.* Vol. 1. New York: Springer, 1980. Pp. 287–336.
A comprehensive review of the literature concerning attitudes and beliefs about the elderly. The absence of a strong, negative stereotype of the aged is noted, although there are prevailing specific misconceptions and negative beliefs. Lutsky documents a considerable diversity in attitudes toward the elderly as a function of target and perceiver characteristics, and the method of attitude measurement.

Research on Aging: A Quarterly of Social Gerontology.
A new interdisciplinary journal that includes publications on issues of stereotyping of aging and the aged.

Rockstein, M., & Sussman, M. *Biology of aging.* Belmont, Calif.: Wadsworth, 1979.
A short book that explains important aspects of the biology of aging. Written for those with no special training in biological science.

Williamson, J. B., Evans, L., & Munley, A. *Aging and society.* New York: Holt, Rinehart, & Winston, 1980.
A text in the field of social gerontology. Many of the issues raised in this chapter are treated in greater depth within the text.

9

STEREOTYPES AND SOCIAL CLASS:
A FOCUS ON POVERTY

Michael Morris
John B. Williamson

> Let every man be sober, industrious, prudent, and wise, and bring up his children to be so likewise, and poverty will be abolished in a few generations.
>
> (William Graham Sumner, 1887)

INTRODUCTION

The above pronouncement of a noted American sociologist represents a particularly appropriate beginning for this chapter, given the relevance of the statement's basic premise to the issues of stereotyping we will be addressing. The premise is that one's psychological characteristics—in this case one's sobriety, industriousness, prudence, and wisdom—play an important role in determining one's economic position. To the extent that such an assumption is correct, those who are economically successful should be found to be psychologically "different" from those who are less well-to-do.*

It is precisely this process of attributing different characteristics to different economic groups that constitutes the stereotyping phenomenon with respect to social class. In this context we will want to address several key questions. Do people in fact make these differing attributions? To the extent that such attributions occur, how accurate are they? Insofar as these

Preparation of this chapter was supported in part by a grant to the first author from the University of New Haven Faculty Research Fund. The authors wish to thank Wendy Ahrens, Patricia Reed, and Valaré Moore for their valuable assistance, as well as Robert Hoffnung, Judith Gordon, and Lloyd Stires for their comments on an earlier draft of this chapter.

*Of course, this is not the only way in which psychological differences between social classes could come about. Economic stratification could be the cause, rather than the result, of whatever dissimilarities are observed.

perceptions are not accurate, what generates and sustains them? Finally, what are the consequences of these stereotypes?

In examining these and other questions relevant to social-class stereotyping in this chapter, special attention will be paid to stereotypes about the poor (that is, persons generally seen as residing in the lower class). This focus would seem to be warranted in light of the fact that poverty is viewed as a social problem in the United States (for instance, President's Commission on Income Maintenance Programs, 1969; Williamson, Evans, & Munley, 1981), as it is in most industrialized nations. A careful assessment of stereotypes of the poor may lead us to a more complete understanding of the dynamics that perpetuate the existence of a disadvantaged economic class in our society. These dynamics include the use of pejorative stereotypes to justify treating the poor in a negative fashion. To the extent that the perceptions underlying this treatment are erroneous, a critical analysis of them may provide a basis for more productive behaviors.

There are alternatives, of course, to explaining poverty solely in terms of the psychological characteristics of the poor. Indeed, analyses that emphasize environmental rather than personal causes of poverty are readily available (such as Ryan, 1976; Schiller, 1976). In this context Mandell (1975) has observed that "Throughout the history of industrialized societies, there have been basically two different views of poverty and of the poor. One blames the socioeconomic system; the other blames the poor" (p. 3). As we shall see, however, one of these perspectives has traditionally dominated the other.

STEREOTYPES ABOUT THE POOR IN HISTORICAL PERSPECTIVE

To more fully understand contemporary stereotypes about the poor, it is necessary to consider their historical origins. Such an examination reveals that in Western society, individualistic explanations of poverty have been more frequent than environmental ones for at least the last six centuries. As Betten (1973) observes in understated fashion, "Leaders of public opinion in Western civilization have almost always suspected the integrity of the poor" (p. 1). This suspicion has typically involved the perception of the poor as, among other things, "'immoral,' 'uncivilized,' 'promiscuous,' 'lazy,' 'obscene,' 'dirty,' and 'loud' " (Rodman, 1964, p. 59).

The European Background

The available evidence suggests that negative beliefs concerning the poor began to develop on a large scale in fourteenth-century Europe (Betten, 1973; Coll, 1969, p. 4; Waxman, 1977, p. 73). Prior to that time the poor were generally accorded a respectable moral status consistent with the "blessed are the poor" theology of the influential Catholic Church.* Indeed, during the medieval period the nonpoor were regarded as having the moral duty to come to the aid of the poor. While the guidelines for providing assistance accorded a lower priority to the able-bodied poor than to those in other categories (elderly, sick, widowed), the perception that an individual had unmet needs served as the ultimate criterion for rendering help (Coll, 1969, pp. 2–3).

While a number of developments were responsible for the transformation of the poor from a positively to a negatively valued segment of European society, the massive reduction of the population due to the bubonic plague (the "Black Death") in the fourteenth century is perhaps the most appropriate starting point for such an analysis. The severe scarcity of labor resulting from this reduction produced elevated wage rates, which in turn encouraged increasing numbers of the poor to become geographically mobile in the hope of improving their fortunes. The paradoxical consequence of this process was an increase in the number of individuals temporarily needing assistance because of their moving from place to place in search of higher wages and better working conditions. Inevitably accompanying this phenomenon were acts of theft and violence by a minority of this new migrant population. Being poor thus began to be associated in the public's mind with being criminal and vagrant on a scale that had previously been unknown (Coll, 1969, p. 4). In short, poverty was becoming "disreputable" (Matza, 1966a).

Large-scale developments over the next three centuries contributed to the growth and solidification of negative attitudes toward the poor, especially those seen as able-bodied. The decline of feudalism, coupled with rapid population growth, generated an expanding class of poor, mobile laborers, which was seen by the nonpoor as posing an ever-growing threat to societal stability. A market economy was also emerging during this period, bringing with it the phenomenon of employment cycles and regular dislocations of large segments of the new labor force. The potential for civil disorder was thus increased even more, and with it came increased hostility toward the poor.

While it was perhaps inevitable that antagonism toward the poor would be generated by these developments, a cohesive ideology that could justify such hostility on a basis other than that of material self-interest awaited the emergence of the Protestant Reformation and Calvinism in the

---

*Going back even further historically, one would find that in primitive societies there was no segment of the population that was identified as being poor. This was due to the absence of marked material stratification in such societies. It was only with the emergence of traditional agrarian societies that inequality in the distribution of resources developed to the point where the poor began to be delineated as a vague category within the population (Eames & Goode, 1973, pp. 55, 69).

sixteenth and seventeenth centuries. Traditional Catholic views of the poor were challenged by the Protestant ethic, which presented an individualistic explanation of poverty and placed it within the context of religious dogma. The foundation for this ethic was laid by Martin Luther, who posited that individuals could serve God best by working at their vocations as conscientiously as possible, regardless of the material rewards received. To be idle was to be sinful, while hard work was associated with virtue. The motivational relevance of material rewards was further downplayed by John Calvin, even as he continued to stress the spiritual importance of industriousness. In his view the only legitimate motivation for working hard was the desire to do God's will and to help establish His kingdom on earth (Macarov, 1970, p. 71).

The implications of this conceptual framework for the way in which the poor and the nonpoor were perceived are simultaneously important and ironic. Although the asceticism of Calvin regarded financial rewards as inappropriate motivation for hard work, the possession of these rewards was considered a visible indication of the degree of one's industriousness. Thus, poverty was to be interpreted as a sign of defective character. The problematical nature of poverty now extended beyond the threat of societal disorder, venturing into the domain of personal morality (Feagin, 1975, p. 21).

It is important to emphasize that the Protestant ethic facilitated a more fine-grained stereotyping of those at differing economic levels in society than had previously been the case. Not only could the poor be distinguished from the nonpoor in terms of level of morality, but the nonpoor group could be seen as encompassing varying degrees of virtue that were indicated by the varying degrees of economic success attained by its members. The greater the material rewards received, the greater the extent to which the individual was doing God's will by being industrious.

It should also be noted that, theoretically, the Protestant ethic did not stigmatize all of the poor. Those who could not work, such as the elderly and the handicapped, were seen as "deserving" and were spared moral disapproval. To be sure, distinctions among subgroups of the poor had been made prior to the Reformation, resulting (in 1572) in the first clear-cut definitions differentiating the deserving and undeserving poor for the purposes of relief in England (Waxman, 1977, p. 76). Nevertheless, the views of Luther and Calvin provided an ideological buttress for repressive policies toward the undeserving poor ("rogues and vagabonds," in the language of the 1572 legislation) that drew from theological rather than secular sources.

Developments in America

It should not be surprising that settlers of the American colonies brought with them the same negative attitudes toward the poor that existed in Europe, a view that Bird (1973) calls "the poor as vagrant" conceptualization. In this perspective the poor represent a group "sometimes dangerous or degenerate, at times vicious, and ordinarily irresponsible" (p. 22). While the deserving poor were not made the target of such attributions, they were seen as forming only a small segment of the destitute population in the colonies (Betten, 1973).

By the nineteenth century it was clear that periods of high unemployment were associated with a significant reduction in the degree to which poverty was blamed on the personal faults of the poor (Betten, 1973). Such a relationship is to be expected, given that in times of economic crisis, the role of environmental factors in accounting for poverty becomes increasingly difficult to ignore. Thus, during these periods the "disreputable poor" (those "who remain unemployed or casually and irregularly employed, even during periods approaching full employment and prosperity" [Matza, 1966a, p. 289]) are seen as representing a smaller fraction of the total poverty population than they normally do.

In the last half of the nineteenth century, several major developments that contributed to a popular image of the social-class system that persists, with some modification, converged in the United States. At the core of these changes was the industrialization of America in the decades following the Civil War, a process that took place within the context of a capitalist economic system. While those who amassed great fortunes during this period were relatively few, there were many more who experienced some upward economic mobility. These circumstances helped to solidify in the public consciousness what Bird (1973) has described as "the poor as apprentices" view of poverty, which he regards as "the single most salient way of understanding poverty in American history" (p. 31). In this conceptualization poverty represents

> ... a temporary condition which poor persons in time would overcome as they developed themselves and their talents. Poverty exists, from this perspective, as a temporary condition, disciplining the poor, until the poor, through education, training, and self-discipline, develop themselves and learn to capitalize on the ample opportunities available in this land of opportunity. (p. 30)

The potential for exaggeration inherent in this outlook can be seen in the public's reaction to the stories of upward mobility penned by the Reverend Horatio Alger, Jr., which became enormously popular in the late nineteenth and early twentieth centuries (Wohl, 1966). A close examination of these stories reveals that their heroes typically achieved a modest degree of upward mobility following a specific altruistic act on their part, combined with a bit of good luck. The popular image of these tales, however, generally pictured a poor boy who attained great wealth and high status through hard work and the manifestation of a "laundry list" of virtuous personal characteristics, such as honesty, cleverness, temperance, ambition, and a willing-ness to learn (Bird, 1973, pp. 71–73). Thus, in the stereotyped perceptions of the Horatio Alger stories there can be discerned a more general set of beliefs that are most frequently described in America by the phrase "equality of opportunity" (Williams, 1970, p. 497). At the core of these beliefs is the perception of an open rather than a closed stratification system, a system in which an individual's motivation to succeed can result in significant econ-omic mobility for him or her.

The attributions of immorality and slothfulness, so much a part of the "poor as vagrants" model, receive much less attention in the apprentice concept, at least in the short run. To the extent that the poor remain poor, however, they become subject to disparaging perceptions that in many ways resemble those associated with the Protestant ethic. These negative views received a great deal of support from the evolving Social Darwinist doctrine of the period, a doctrine that envisioned the social and economic life of society as a "survival of the fittest" struggle among individual competitors (Bannister, 1979; Hofstadter, 1955). Economic stratification was considered one of the inevitable consequences of such competition. Thus, over time there would accumulate in the lower classes a group of individuals whose psychological characteristics indicated weakness and a lack of ambition, while in the upper classes the opposite characteristics would predominate.

The historical significance of Social Darwinism lies less in the content of its stereotypes, which are often very similar to those implied by the Protestant ethic, than in the fact that it was presented by social theorists and other influentials as a scientific justification for strongly held positive and negative views of the rich and poor, respectively. While the "science" involved was pseudoscience at best, an important precedent had been established. Stereotyping of the rich and the poor (and those in between), even in crude form, could be presented in a fashion that was compatible with a "value-free" mode of analysis. It could now be argued that social-class stereotyping was ultimately grounded neither in material self-interest nor in religious faith, but in the logical conclusions generated by a systematic analysis of reality. As we shall see, such analyses would recur in increasingly sophisticated forms as the social sciences refined their theoretical and methodological tools.

While individualistic explanations of poverty remained influential in the public imagination at least until the Great Depression, by the early 1900s a more environmentally based perspective was being developed in America and being disseminated by activists in the "scientific charity" movement, a movement originally characterized by a strong individualistic orientation. These early social workers, later joined by some social scientists, journalists, and political theorists providing complementary analyses, had come to the conclusion that pauperism and poverty could be eliminated only if greater attention was paid to their roots in the basic social and economic structure of society (Bremner, 1956, p. 124). In Europe, of course, Karl Marx had already engaged in a much more comprehensive attempt to conceptualize poverty—and, indeed, the entire stratification system throughout history—in structural terms (Marx & Engels, n.d.).*

In this context it is important to understand the significance of the more sympathetic view of the poor that developed among the population at large during the Depression. It was based less in the analyses provided by the commentators than in the perception that the deserving poor had increased in numbers because of unemployment. As the Depression subsided, a predictable increase in negative attitudes toward the poor recurred, even as more detailed environmental explanations of poverty continued to be developed by a segment of the academic community (Betten, 1973). Indeed, a growing awareness of these conflicting perceptions has been one factor prompting contemporary researchers to investigate social-class stereotypes in a systematic fashion.

CONTEMPORARY IMAGES OF THE POOR

Systematically gathered data on social-class stereotypes relevant to poverty come from three major sources: surveys of how people account for the existence of poverty and wealth, studies of community status systems, and investigations employing the adjective checklist technique.

Survey Studies

The explanations that people offer for various aspects of economic stratification have been the subject of considerable research. In a typical study of this genre, respondents are asked to indicate their beliefs as to the causes of poverty and/or wealth. One of the earliest of these investigations is reported by Centers (1948), in which a 1945 national sample of adult white males was asked, "Why do you think some of the population are always poor?" (More than one answer could be given.) The internal attribution of "poor management" was by far the most frequent response, given by 26 percent of the sample. Of the other five reasons cited by more than 10 percent of the sample, four were internal (laziness, lack of ambition, lack of ability, lack of thrift) and only one was external (lack of opportunity). Overall, internal attributions outnumbered external attributions by more than two to one. Centers aptly summarizes these results with his observation that "people seem to believe that poverty is something one brings on oneself more often than not" (p. 171).

---

*This is not to say that Marx viewed all of the poor in a positive light. He used the term "lumpenproletariat" to describe a stratum of society whose life-style resembled that associated with the "undeserving" and "disreputable" poor. Marx did not, however, argue that this life-style was the source of the lumpenproletariat's poverty.

Much the same message emerged from a national survey of adults conducted nearly a quarter of a century later by Feagin (1975). Respondents were asked to assess the importance of 11 reasons that might be invoked to explain the existence of poor people in America (see Table 9.1). Five of these reasons (items 6–10) were dubbed structural explanations by Feagin, since they focused on social and economic forces. Individualistic explanations were represented by three items (1, 2, and 4) that placed the cause of poverty in the poor themselves. The distinctiveness of Feagin's fatalistic explanations lay in the fact that they were either internal attributions involving factors beyond the control of the individual (items 3 and 5) or external attributions involving factors beyond the control of society (item 11). Examination of the percentages of the sample judging each reason to be "very important" reveals that in every instance individualistic factors are seen by more respondents as having high relevance to explaining poverty than are structural factors. This difference persists when the two fatalistic factors emphasizing internal attributions are considered. Both of them generate more responses of "very important" than any of the structural reasons.

It is interesting to compare these findings with those obtained by Feather (1974), who used the same list of 11 reasons in surveying an Australian sample. He found, as did Feagin, that structural factors were generally seen as having less importance for explaining poverty than individualistic or internal fatalistic attributions. Item-by-item comparisons of the two samples, however, indicated that the American group emphasized internal factors to a greater extent, and structural ones to a lesser extent, than did the Australians. The Americans attributed significantly more importance than the Australians to lack of effort, lack of ability and talent, and loose morals and drunkenness as causes of poverty. On the other hand, Americans viewed lack of good schools and exploitation of the poor by the rich as playing a less important role in poverty than did Feather's sample. The only exception to this pattern involved the "sickness and physical handicaps" factor, an internal (but "deserving") attribution that Feagin's respondents saw as being less important than did the Australian sample.* These results suggest that while explaining poverty in terms of the negative traits of the poor is a pervasive phenomenon in both countries, it is particularly characteristic of Americans.

That Americans are more prone than other nationalities to view poverty in individualistic terms is also suggested by the results of Gallup polls and comparative studies conducted in the United States and Great Britain. Explaining poverty in terms of lack of effort rather than "circumstances beyond his control" (or some other nonpejorative response) is more prevalent among U.S. respondents than British ones, though the differences

---

*Because Feather reworded item 8 to read "poor people" rather than "Negroes," the greater importance assigned to that factor by the American sample is not readily interpretable.

TABLE 9.1
Reasons for Poverty (percent)

Reason for Poverty	Very Important	Somewhat Important	Not Important	Uncertain	Total
1. Lack of thrift and proper money management by poor people	58	30	11	2	101
2. Lack of effort by the poor themselves	55	33	9	3	100
3. Lack of ability and talent among poor people	52	33	12	3	100
4. Loose morals and drunkenness	48	31	17	4	100
5. Sickness and physical handicaps	46	39	14	2	101
6. Low wages in some businesses and industries	42	35	20	3	100
7. Failure of society to provide good schools for many Americans	36	25	34	5	100
8. Prejudice and discrimination against Negroes	33	37	26	5	101
9. Failure of private industry to provide enough jobs	27	36	31	6	100
10. Being taken advantage of by rich people	18	30	45	7	100
11. Just bad luck	8	27	60	5	100

Note: Some totals do not add to exactly 100 percent because of statistical rounding procedures.
Source: Feagin (1975), Table 1, p. 97. Copyright 1975 by Prentice-Hall. Reprinted by permission.

TABLE 9.2
Ability versus Luck as Determinant
of Success (percent)

	1939 [a]	1942 [b]	1970 [a]
Luck	15	12	8
Ability	79	70	86
Pull	—	23	—
No opinion	6	5	6

[a]Actual question: "Do you think people who are successful get ahead largely because of their luck or largely because of their ability?"

[b]Actual question: "Do you think success is dependent mostly on luck, on ability, or on pull?" (More than one response was given by some respondents.)

Source: Adapted from Devine (1972), Table IV.59, p. 217. Reprinted by permission.

are usually modest (Free & Cantril, 1967, p. 28; *Gallup Political Index*, 1977, p. 8; 1970, p. 190; 1968, p. 152; 1964, p. 66; Reasons for poverty, 1967; Schiltz, 1970, p. 160; Stern & Searing, 1976).*

The tendency of Americans to attribute poverty more frequently to internal rather than external factors has been demonstrated in other investigations as well (Goudy, 1970, p. 170; Huber & Form, 1973, p. 101; Johnson & Sanday, 1971; Lane, 1962, p. 72; Lauer, 1971). While there have been studies in which the majority of respondents agreed that "most poor people are poor because of circumstances beyond their control," such findings are rare (for instance, Ogren, 1973).

Research that has focused on explanations of success and/or wealth also reveals popular images that are heavily laden with internal attributions, as might be expected. Respondents in these studies are typically asked to choose between ability and one or more external factors, such as luck or "pull," in accounting for success. (More than one choice is sometimes allowed.) Several national surveys spanning over three decades have found that Americans overwhelmingly select ability as the key variable that distinguishes the successful from the unsuccessful.† (See Table 9.2.)

Somewhat less dramatic results were obtained by Centers (1948), though ability was still chosen by more individuals in his national sample than any of the external factors presented (luck, "pull," better opportunities). This was the case regardless of whether respondents were being asked to explain success (45 percent choosing ability) or riches (41 percent).

---

*Interestingly, a 1977 European survey cited by Coughlin (1979, p. 26) indicates that the British are more likely to attribute poverty to "individual laziness and lack of willpower" than are the French, West Germans, or Danish.

†In a more recent nationwide survey Schlozman and Verba (1979) asked respondents to choose among hard work, family background, and luck in accounting for "who gets ahead in America." Hard work was selected by 68 percent of the sample, with family background and luck being chosen by 24 percent and 8 percent, respectively.

Studies employing more restricted samples also have obtained results indicating the perceived primacy of internal factors for explaining success (such as Bell & Robinson, 1980; A. Kornhauser, 1965, p. 210; Long & Long, 1974; Mizruchi, 1964, p. 82; Stern & Searing, 1976).

Even findings that might be interpreted as inconsistent with this pattern are not unambiguously so. An example is the 1964 national survey reported by Free and Cantril (1967, pp. 113-114). When respondents were asked to select the three things, from a list of eight, that they regarded as chiefly responsible for success, "good education and training" was the most popular choice, being selected by 71 percent of the sample.* Is this an internal or an external factor? Insofar as the quality of education and training a person receives is beyond his or her control, it makes sense to think of it as external. However, the results of a large-scale study of social-class imagery among Boston and Kansas City residents (Coleman, Rainwater, & McClelland, 1978) suggest that individuals are held at least partially responsible for the nature of their educational experiences. Respondents believed that one of the reasons that "people at the bottom of the ladder" lacked education was that they were not interested in it (pp. 198-199). This finding calls into question the status of education and training as an external factor uncontaminated by individualistic perceptions.

It is interesting to note in this context that in the Free and Cantril study (1967) the only other factors chosen by more than half the sample were both individualistic (initiative and effort, hard work: 66 percent; character, will power: 59 percent). External reasons such as "pull," good luck, and good family background were endorsed as being important by less than a quarter of the sample.

Even if education and training were regarded as purely external in nature, other findings from the Coleman et al. investigation suggest that these two factors are seen by most individuals as "necessary but not sufficient" conditions with respect to accounting for success. Consequently, they are not the variables that ultimately are viewed as separating the successful from the unsuccessful. The researchers asked a subsample an open-ended question: "From all that you've read or heard or seen, what do you think is the most effective way for a person to improve his social standing in America?" (p. 239). The responses indicated that four ingredients were seen as playing key roles in mobility: parental encouragement, education, ambition, and hard work. With respect to the interrelationships of these last three factors, Coleman et al. observe:

> [The respondents] acknowledged that in the final analysis education's role is only as an entry ticket to the contest for higher status, that it is no guarantee of winnings. In the crucible of adult life competition, they said, ambition and hard work count for more. (p. 240)

---

*Free and Cantril also found, as did Long and Long (1974), that "lack of education and training" was the factor most frequently cited by respondents in accounting for failure.

It should be noted that ability is not cited by these respondents as an important factor in mobility. Indeed, Coleman et al. suggest that the stratification system depicted by these individuals is much more of an "effortocracy" than it is a "meritocracy" (p. 241). To the extent that the open-ended responses obtained in this investigation more accurately reflect perceptions of mobility processes than do replies to the more structured items already discussed, popular images of success and wealth take on a new meaning. While both ability and effort represent internal factors, the latter is typically seen as being more under the control of individuals than the former. Thus, the demonstration of great effort is more likely to be regarded as indicating the possession of high moral character than is the demonstration of great ability.

It would seem, then, that not only are the successful stereotyped as a psychologically distinctive group, but their distinctiveness is such that positive judgments of their moral worth are encouraged, at least with respect to the dimension in question. A certain symmetry in moral perceptions of those at the top and the bottom of the stratification system can thus be discerned, given the immorality that is implied by the lack of effort so often attributed to the poor.

Community Studies

The way in which social scientists have conceptualized the phenomenon of social stratification frequently has facilitated the gathering of data relevant to social-class stereotypes. The work of Warner and his associates (such as Warner & Lunt, 1941) is usually regarded as particularly influential in this regard. In the course of his studies of "Yankee City" (Newburyport, Massachusetts), Warner concluded that classes should not be thought of as economic categories, but as "two or more orders of people who are believed to be, and are accordingly ranked by members of the community, in socially superior and inferior positions" (Warner & Lunt, 1941, p. 82). In Warner's model of the stratification system, the perceptions that community members hold of one another's personal characteristics, behavior, and life-style are of crucial importance in assigning individuals to a given social class.

As critics have noted, however, it was the views of Warner's upper- and upper-middle-class respondents that were accorded the most weight in his delineation of the social-class composition of the community (R. Kornhauser, 1953). Indeed, Warner's approach to studying stratification has been severely criticized on a number of grounds, not the least of which was his taking of one component of stratification (status) and treating it as if it were the ultimate criterion to be used in assembling a picture of the stratification system. In doing this, Warner absorbed into his concept of class other important components (such as economic position and power) in an undetermined way, thus rendering the whole notion of class imprecise and of dubious scientific value (Mills, 1942).

The validity of these criticisms notwithstanding, Warner's conceptualization of social class informed some of the classic community studies of his era (such as Davis, Gardner, & Gardner, 1941; Dollard, 1937), and has continued to influence studies of social-status perceptions (Coleman & Neugarten, 1971; Coleman et al., 1978). These studies provide a wealth of information pertaining to how people at different levels of society are stereotyped. There is a problem here, of course. To the extent that individuals are assigned to a given social class on the basis of their stereotyped personal characteristics rather than their incomes, stereotypes about the "lower class" are not necessarily stereotypes about low-income people.

There are at least two reasons, however, to believe that the lower-class stereotypes found in these studies do in fact refer to low-income persons. First, we shall see that the content of these stereotypes is quite consistent with what we already know about perceptions of poverty based on the previously reviewed survey research. Second, economic considerations appear to exert a major influence on Americans' views of what social class is all about (Bell & Robinson, 1980).

On the basis of their interviews, for example, Coleman et al. (1978, p. 29) concluded that "Money, far more than anything else, is what Americans associate with the idea of social class." One-third of their respondents mentioned money and nothing else when asked, "What does social class mean to you?" The investigators imply that, alone and in combination with other factors such as occupation, income was by far the variable that was most likely to be referred to when respondents answered this question. They also found that when individuals were asked to estimate numerically "the general standing as most people would see it" of families representing various combinations of income, occupation, and education, almost two-thirds of the variation in the resulting ratings could be accounted for by variation in income. Educational level and occupational status shared the remainder of the variation about equally (Coleman et al., 1978, pp. 219–220).

When community-based studies spanning nearly 40 years are compared, the stereotyped images that have been found of different class groups are striking in their consistency. Of particular relevance is the recurrent finding that respondents tend to divide the lower class into deserving and undeserving subgroups (Coleman et al., 1978, ch. 10; Davis, Gardner, & Gardner, 1941, ch. 3; Warner, Meeker, & Eells, 1960, ch. 1; West, 1945, ch. 3). Descriptions of the undeserving subgroup are generally so similar from study to study that they are virtually interchangeable. Consider the following two accounts from investigations separated by more than 35 years:

[Evaluations of the lower-lower class in Yankee City by those above them] include beliefs that they are lazy, shiftless, and won't work, all opposite of the good middle-class virtues belonging to the essence of the Protestant ethic. They are thought to be improvident and unwilling or unable to save their money for a rainy day and, therefore, often dependent on the philanthropy of the private or public agency and on poor relief. They are sometimes said to "live like animals" because it is believed that their sexual mores are not too exacting. (Warner et al., 1960, p. 15)

[People at the bottom of the ladder are seen as] indifferent to their condition. Or, if not truly indifferent . . . they do not mind it enough to put out the effort required to escape it. They are "just lazy"; they "lack ambition," "don't care about anything," "don't want to work hard," "have a nonchalant attitude—no purpose in life," and "just wait for things to happen." . . . [Theirs is a world of] social and behavioral pathology; of sexual misbehavior; of unstable, squabbling, and broken families. It is a world of people who have no standards at all. (Coleman et al., 1978, pp. 197–198)

This undeserving subgroup has been identified with increasing frequency in recent years as the "welfare class," in reference to their alleged long-term dependence on certain forms of public assistance. Indeed, several commentators have suggested that this dependent role occupied by many of the poor is an inherently stigmatizing one that lays the foundation for more general negative stereotyping of this subgroup (Beck, 1967; Coser, 1965; Matza, 1966b; Williamson, 1974c). In this context Feagin (1975, pp. 102–115) and Williamson (1974b) have documented the existence of major misconceptions in the public's mind concerning the characteristics and behavior of individuals on welfare. Williamson, for example, found that his sample of Boston residents significantly overestimated the percentage of able-bodied males on welfare, the percentage of dishonest welfare recipients, and the average number of children under 18 years old in welfare families.

When their views on the issue are reported, most of those respondents who would be judged by others to be members of the undeserving subgroup of the lower class appear to reject as inaccurate the views of their morals and motivations described in the quotations above (Coleman et al., 1978, ch. 10; Davis, Gardner, & Gardner, 1941, ch. 3; West, 1945, ch. 3). Instead, they attribute to themselves the orientations that the majority of respondents associate with the deserving subgroup of the lower class. This deserving subgroup is typically distinguished from the undeserving by the perception that "they're working and trying" (that is, they're employed or seeking employment) and "they're usually not on welfare" (Coleman et al., 1978, p. 199).

Interestingly, Coleman et al. found that the factors of effort and ambition were also used by most respondents to draw invidious comparisons between the deserving lower-class subgroup and the subgroup immediately above them in the status hierarchy ("Middle Americans who aren't lower class but are having a real hard time"). The deserving lower class, while being perceived as more motivated than those right below them in the status system, was seen as less motivated than those just above them.

This finding takes on added significance in view of the fact that respondents' moral judgments relevant to economic mobility decreased sharply in frequency as the subject of discussion became any subgroup above the lowest rung of the Middle America strata. Rather, respondents' descriptions of the higher classes tended to be more exclusively focused on the material life-styles and social networks associated with the more privileged strata. This suggests a certain asymmetry in individuals' perceptions of the stratification system that is not revealed by their answers to questions that simply focus on explanations of poverty, wealth, and mobility.

This asymmetry involves the qualitatively different dimensions that appear to be most salient to the nonpoor when they think of social classes at opposite ends of the stratification system. When they focus on people at the bottom, their imagery is suffused with stereotypes of deficient character and motivation. While we have seen that individuals of high rank (the "successful") are viewed more positively on these dimensions, the more crucial point is that these dimensions take a back seat to those involving such things as standards of living and social contacts. That the most prominent stereotypes concerning the lower classes are so clearly tied to justifications of their position in society, while views of those higher up are not, is an occurrence of sufficient significance to warrant its being discussed further when we address theories of social-class stereotyping.

Checklist Studies

Few studies of social-class stereotypes have employed the adjective checklist technique of Katz and Braly (1933). Those that have been done, however, have generated results fully supportive of the previously reviewed research. In the earliest such study Bayton, McAlister, and Hamer (1956) asked white and black college students to select, from a list of 85 adjectives, those they believed were descriptive of each of the following groups: upper-class white Americans, upper-class blacks, lower-class white Americans, and lower-class blacks. The study's most striking finding was that the social class of the group to be described influenced the adjective choices much more than the race of the group.

When the 10 (or 11 in case of a tie) most frequently cited adjectives for each target group were examined, the upper-class groups (regardless of race) were described by both black and white students as intelligent, ambitious, industrious, neat, and progressive. Lower-class groups, on the other hand, were seen as ignorant, lazy, loud, and dirty. There were no traits that the sample as a whole saw as describing blacks of both classes or whites of both classes. Even when the responses of black and white students were considered separately, the number of traits assigned on the basis of the target's race (that is, attributed to whites of both classes or blacks of both classes) were far outnumbered by those assigned on the basis of class (4 versus 12 for white students, 1 versus 12 for blacks).

In a similar study conducted in 1976, Smedley and Bayton (1978) found that class (middle class versus lower class) was once again more salient than race (white versus black) in the stereotypes of white students, but that the reverse was true for black students. Black students perceived both middle- and lower-class blacks more positively than they did middle-class whites, who in turn were perceived more favorably than lower-class whites.

Finally, investigations that have employed the Katz and Braly technique (or modifications thereof) in studying occupational stereotypes would seem to have implications for social-class stereotyping. It has been found fairly consistently that the personality of a target identified with a label such as "factory worker," "janitor," "carpenter," or "working class" is generally described in less favorable terms than one that is a "physician," "civil engineer," "professional," or "middle class" (Davidson, Riessman, & Meyers, 1962; Feldman, 1972; More & Suchner, 1976; Rim & Aloni, 1969; see Thielbar and Feldman [1969] for a partial exception to this pattern of results).

That the entire occupational status hierarchy tends to be viewed in terms of a continuum reflecting differences in certain individual characteristics is suggested by Villemez's (1974) study. Twenty occupations ranging from garbageman to bookkeeper to physician were rated for prestige by college students and, three weeks later, rated by the same students with respect to how much ability was required to enter and perform effectively in each of them, and how much effort was required in each. The ability/prestige and effort/prestige correlations were .99 and .98, respectively.

Given that, in general, an occupation's prestige is positively associated with its financial rewards, these findings suggest that individuals perceive economic stratification as "sorting people out" with respect to their psychological characteristics, at least where ability and effort are concerned. Recognition of this view helps to put into proper perspective the poverty stereotypes we have been discussing. To a great extent these stereotypes simply represent the tip of a perceptual iceberg. While our individualistic images of the poor may be our most salient social-class stereotypes, they apparently form just one part of a much more comprehensive—and stereotyped—view of the stratification system that we possess.

Who Stereotypes the Most?

To this point the evidence we have reviewed suggests that in American society stereotypes are widely held that, explicitly or implicitly, stress individualistic interpretations of poverty. However, we have not yet checked in any systematic way for differences between various population subgroups with respect to the extent to which these stereotypes are endorsed. These differences are important not only in their own right, but also for the light they may shed on the relative merits of different theories that attempt to explain social-class stereotyping.

One of the most frequently examined influences on such stereotyping is, understandably, the respondent's social class. Typically underlying this analysis is a set of assumptions that Williamson (1974a, p. 635) refers to as the "economic self-interest thesis," which he describes as follows:

> Those at higher socioeconomic levels benefit more than do those at lower levels from the existing distribution of resources and opportunities. *Beliefs that can be used to justify the existing distribution are thus likely to be most favorably received by those at high socioeconomic levels and least favorably received by those at low levels.* Beliefs which blame the poor for their poverty fall into this category. One such belief is that failure to escape poverty is in large measure due to lack of sufficient effort and motivation. (p. 635, emphasis added)

According to this logic, negative stereotypes concerning the poor should be positively associated with the respondent's social class. Given that income is the social-class component most directly implied by an argument stressing economic self-interest, the results reported in the first column of Table 9.3 provide the most straightforward test of the self-interest thesis. Of the 11 relevant studies, seven provide support for the notion that a person's income is positively associated with endorsement of individualistic explanations of poverty.* Most of the supporting studies find the relationship between the two variables to be moderate-to-weak rather than strong, however. One of the most impressive sets of findings comes from a study of

---

*The failures of Feagin (1975), Feather (1974), Johnson and Sanday (1971), and S. Stack (1978) to find such a relationship deserve comment. Feagin classified respondents as high, low, or medium in individualism on the basis of their summed responses to the three individualistic items in his poverty scale. The same procedure was followed with respect to the structural and fatalistic items. He found that middle-income respondents were more likely to be high on the individualistic-factors index than were those with low or high incomes, though the differences were small and no test of significance is reported. It is important to note that a respondent who was high on the individualistic-factors index could also be high on the structural and/or fatalistic indexes. A more valid test of the self-interest thesis would have entailed examining the proportion of each income group that ranked high only on the individualistic-factors index.

In Feather's study the categories into which respondents' incomes were grouped for the purpose of statistical analysis were such that only $2,001 separated the low-income category (below $4,000 per year) from the high-income group (above $6,000 per year). With such a narrow range, it should not be surprising that the self-interest thesis was not confirmed.

In the Johnson and Sanday investigation all respondents came from low-income neighborhoods, thus making it unlikely that significant income differences would be found. Finally, the results of Stack's study are based on a 35 percent return rate for a mailed questionnaire. Given the implications of such a low rate for the representativeness of the sample, interpretation of the study's findings becomes highly problematical.

TABLE 9.3

Relationship of Social-Class Components to Individualistic Explanations of Poverty

	Component		
Study	Income	Education	Occupation
Alston & Dean (1972)	—	Yes	No
Centers (1948)	—	—	No
Feagin (1975)	No	No	—
Feather (1974)	No	No	No
Free & Cantril (1967)	Yes	—	—
Gallup (1972, pp. 1910–1911)	Yes	—	—
Goudy (1970)	Yes	No	No
Huber & Form (1973)	Yes	—	—
Johnson & Sanday (1971)	No	—	—
R.W. Miller, Zeller, & Blaine (1968)	Yes	Yes	Yes
Reasons for poverty (1967)	Yes	Yes	No
Stack (1978)	No	No	—
Williamson (1974a)	Yes	No	Yes
Wooster (1972)	—	No	No

"Yes" indicates that a positive linear relationship was found between the variable and individualistic explanations of poverty.

"No" indicates that a positive linear relationship was not found between the variable and individualistic explanations of poverty.

"—" indicates that the variable was not examined.

Michigan residents by Huber and Form (1973, p. 100). The percentage of their white subsample that explained poverty solely in terms of unfavorable personal traits ranged from 30 percent of those with total family incomes (adjusted) under $4,000 annually to 62 percent of those with incomes of $25,000 and more. In contrast, in his study of white Boston women, Williamson (1974a) obtained a weak but significant Pearson coefficient of −.13 when he correlated respondents' total family incomes with scores on a four-item scale designed to measure the perceived strength of the poor's work motivation.

The point that needs to be stressed in this context is that even though negative stereotypes about the poor are more frequent among the nonpoor than among the poor, these disparaging views are by no means confined to the nonpoor group. Indeed, these beliefs have been found even among a significant percentage of welfare recipients (Kerbo, 1976).

In contrast with the findings for income, the majority of studies examining the influence of educational level do not support the self-interest thesis. R. W. Miller, Zeller, and Blaine (1968), for example, found a positive relationship between education and disparaging views of the poor in their study of residents of six Ohio cities. Wooster (1972), on the other hand, found exactly the opposite relationship in his study of residents of a rural

Colorado county. Curvilinear relationships have even been obtained between education and negative views of the poor, with respondents having the most and least schooling being less likely to hold such perceptions (Feagin, 1975, p. 99; Williamson, 1974a).

The findings for occupational status also do not present a clear picture. Studies that uncover weak-to-moderate positive relationships between this variable and negative stereotypes of the poor (Williamson, 1974a; R. W. Miller et al., 1968) coexist with investigations finding no significant differences or unsystematic differences across occupational categories (Alston & Dean, 1972; Centers, 1948; Feather, 1974; Reasons for poverty, 1967). Rounding out the picture are studies in which the findings for one occupational category are glaringly inconsistent with the more general pattern that both occurs and is expected (on the basis of the self-interest thesis) in the data (Goudy, 1970, p. 170).

Taken as a whole, the data on social-class differences indicate that the self-interest thesis is in need of revision. Included here would be a critical analysis of the assumptions that suggest that a respondent's occupation and education should affect social-class stereotyping independently of the influence these factors share with income. Of equal importance is the task of providing a more general theoretical framework that would account for the less-than-powerful role that even income plays with respect to negative perceptions of the poor.* Some preliminary efforts in this direction will be made in the section "Stereotyping the Poor: Theoretical Perspectives."

Social-class components are not the only variables that researchers have examined for their relationship to stereotypes about low-income people. The available evidence shows that negative views of the poor are associated with being white (Feagin, 1975, p. 99; Huber & Form, 1973, p. 101; Johnson & Sanday, 1971)† and being politically conservative (Free & Cantril, 1967, pp. 115–116; Gallup, 1972, pp. 1910–1911; Williamson, 1974a). They also are associated with scoring high on scales designed to measure commitment to the Protestant Ethic (MacDonald, 1972; Williamson, 1974a; Wooster, 1972).**

---

*It is interesting to note that when individuals are asked to predict how members of a given social class would explain poverty and wealth, their responses indicate that they believe the self-interest thesis to be accurate (Huber & Form, 1973, pp. 106–107; MacDonald & Majumder, 1972).

†Relevant to this result is a reanalysis of 1972 national survey data by Gurin, Miller, and Gurin (1980). They found that black respondents who closely identified with blacks as a group were less likely to explain poverty in individualistic terms than were respondents who closely identified themselves with the following groups: women, older people, workingmen, middle-class people, or whites.

**In evaluating the significance of this finding, it should be noted that Protestant ethic scales typically include several items (such as "Most people who don't succeed in life are just plain lazy.") that address issues conceptually similar to those dealt with in instruments designed to measure attitudes toward the poor (such as "Do you think poor people try harder, less hard, or try about the same as everyone else to get ahead?"). Such an occurrence should not be

Attempts to relate negative stereotypes of the poor to sex, religion, and age have yielded less consistent results. While some studies find males to be more negative than females in their attitudes (Alston & Dean, 1972; MacDonald & Majumder, 1972; Reasons for poverty, 1967), others find no difference (Feather, 1974; Wooster, 1972, p. 75). In no instance, however, have females been found to engage in negative stereotyping of the poor to a significantly greater extent than males.

A similar picture emerges when the role of Protestantism is examined. Studies that find that Protestants are more likely than members of other religious denominations to blame poverty on the poor (Feather, 1974; Williamson, 1974a) coexist with investigations finding no strong evidence of such a trend (Feagin, 1975, pp. 99–100; Huber & Form, 1973, p. 113; Reasons for poverty, 1967). There have been no cases, however, in which Protestants have been significantly less likely than members of other religious groups to negatively stereotype the poor.

Finally, while several investigations have found that older respondents perceive the poor more negatively (Feagin, 1975, p. 99; Feather, 1974; Grimm & Orten, 1973; Kerbo, 1976; Majumder, MacDonald, & Greever, 1977), others have obtained exactly the opposite relationship (Alston & Dean, 1972; Reasons for poverty, 1967), and still others have found no significant linear relationship (Williamson, 1974a; Wooster, 1972, p. 76).

Viewed in their entirety, the findings we have discussed can be assembled to produce a thumbnail portrait of the individual who is likely to engage in social-class stereotyping to the greatest degree, at least where the poor are concerned. This portrait depicts a white, financially secure person who is politically conservative and cherishes the work ethic. Moreover, there is some reason to believe that a Protestant man with these characteristics will view the poor more negatively than will a non-Protestant woman.

THE "CULTURE OF POVERTY" THESIS

Our focus thus far has been on stereotyping behavior in the general population. We have all but neglected stereotyping by those who design and administer the various social programs for the poor, as well as those who conduct the research that often justifies these programs and policies. While systematic data concerning the attitudes of these two groups are not presently available, we do know that these individuals have directed a great deal of their attention to what has come to be known as the "culture of poverty" thesis (for example; Ball, 1968; Banfield, 1974; O. Lewis, 1969; W. B. Miller, 1958). Whether this thesis has in fact had a major impact on

---

surprising, given that most formulations of the Protestant ethic include as a major component the belief that one's economic position is largely determined by one's effort (for instance, Feagin, 1975, pp. 91–92).

poverty policy has been a subject of disagreement (for instance, Aaron, 1978; Gladwin, 1967; Moynihan, 1969; C. Valentine, 1968). Whatever the outcome of this debate, the "culture of poverty" perspective deserves close examination. Insofar as this thesis represents an attempt to explain the persistence of poverty, it encompasses—in more formalized fashion—many of the stereotyped views of the poor discussed in the section "Contemporary Images of the Poor." Thus, an assessment of the validity of the thesis has major implications for evaluating the size of the "kernel of truth" contained in stereotypes about the poor.

Nature of the Thesis

The "culture of poverty" perspective is most closely associated with the work of anthropologist Oscar Lewis (1959; 1966; 1969). On the basis of his studies of families and communities in Latin America, Lewis concluded that in class-stratified, highly individuated, capitalistic societies a segment of the poor population was likely to develop a "culture of poverty." This culture represented an obstacle to upward economic mobility and was characterized by an interrelated network of approximately 70 social, economic, and psychological traits. A major reason for Lewis's application of the term "culture" to this trait network was his belief that this way of life was transmitted from one generation of poor people to another through the socialization process. In this regard he states:

> Once it [the culture of poverty] comes into existence, it tends to perpetuate itself from generation to generation because of its effect on the children. By the time slum children are age six or seven, they have usually absorbed the basic values and attitudes of their subculture and are not psychologically geared to take full advantage of the changing conditions or increased opportunities that may occur in their life-time. (1969, p. 188)

The overall thrust of Lewis's analysis can be seen in his delineation of "culture of poverty" traits at the psychological level. He includes strong feelings of marginality, helplessness, dependence, and inferiority; lack of impulse control; difficulty in deferring gratification and planning for the future; confusion of sexual identity; a sense of resignation and fatalism; widespread belief in male superiority; high tolerance for psychological pathology; weak ego structure; and a high incidence of maternal deprivation (1969, p. 188).

Lest this collection of negative characteristics leave the reader reeling, it should be noted that at the heart of the "culture of poverty" thesis is the contention that "the values of the [culture of poverty] poor differ substantially from those of the mainstream of American society" (Della Fave,

1974a, p. 609). These distinctive values supposedly form a self-maintaining system in which "the dominant norms and aspirations are accepted by members of the [poor] group, are interrelated in such a way as to sustain one another in an individual's internal organization of values, and are reinforced through social pressure upon deviants in the value setting institutions of the group (for example, family, streetcorner group)" (Spilerman & Elesh, 1971, p. 364).

Viewed in all its complexity, the "culture of poverty" thesis is clearly a more sophisticated analysis than the perceptions that summarily condemn the poor for their alleged slothfulness and immorality. Moreover, Lewis takes pains to indicate that in his view only about 20 percent of the poor in the United States can be accurately described as living in a culture of poverty (1969, p. 196). Unfortunately, both supporters and critics of Lewis's thesis sometimes fail to take this latter point into account when applying or evaluating the cultural perspective (Harrington, 1962; Spilerman & Elesh, 1971). This omission is particularly distressing in view of the fact that—the sophistication of Lewis's analysis notwithstanding—the cultural approach is one that stereotypes a segment of the poor as having distinctive psychological characteristics that perpetuate their poverty.

Thus, regardless of whether or not these stereotypes are accurate, the cultural perspective is functionally equivalent in this crucial respect to less refined perceptions of the undeserving poor. Indeed, the very fact that some commentators have extended the "culture of poverty" thesis beyond the domain intended by Lewis might be regarded as an instance of stereotyping in its own right, given the tendency of stereotyping to involve unwarranted generalizations beyond the data.

Lewis was certainly not the first social scientist to systematically link poverty to such factors as culture, value systems, and clusters of psychological traits (see, for example, Davis, 1946; Hyman, 1953; Knupfer, 1947). However, the fact that Harrington (1962) adopted Lewis's approach in his influential analysis of American poverty just prior to the War on Poverty in the 1960s helped to insure that the "culture of poverty" perspective would receive significantly more attention than its less comprehensive predecessors. Given the individualistic attributions inherent in Lewis's thesis, it was inevitable that critiques of the "culture of poverty" concept would be forthcoming from those in the academic community who held a more environmentally based view of the persistence of poverty.

The ensuing debate has taken place at both theoretical and empirical levels. While the theoretical discussions have been undeniably important in assessing the adequacy of the conceptual foundations of the "culture of poverty" thesis (Gans, 1969; Leacock, 1971; Massey, 1975; Rainwater, 1969; Roach & Gursslin, 1967; Spilerman & Elesh, 1971; C. Valentine, 1968; Waxman, 1977), the data emerging at the empirical level are more directly relevant to "kernel of truth" questions concerning poverty stereotypes, and thus we will focus our attention on them.

Relevant Research

Simply put, the available evidence offers relatively little support for the "culture of poverty" thesis as formulated by Lewis. One of the most methodologically sophisticated attempts to assess its validity was undertaken by Kriesberg (1970) in his study of poor and nonpoor mothers living in or near public housing projects in Syracuse, New York. Among the many variables he examined were values, beliefs, and conduct relevant to child rearing, educational achievement, receiving public assistance, and housing preferences.

While some differences were found between the two groups of mothers that were consistent with the "culture of poverty" thesis, there was little support for the notion that the distinctiveness of the poor group was due to an intergenerational transmission of traits associated with a subculture. Current situational factors in the lives of the mothers were typically found to play a much more important role in influencing their orientations and behavior than were factors associated with their families of origin. Moreover, even when significant differences were found between the poor and the nonpoor, such as with respect to certain child-rearing attitudes, these differences were frequently quite modest in size. Consequently, in contrast with what Lewis would predict, there was little reason to believe that the two groups had fundamentally different orientations with respect to the dimensions in question.

A similar lack of convincing support for the "culture of poverty" thesis was found by Coward, Feagin, and Williams (1974) in their study of a black sample in a large southwestern city. They compared poor and nonpoor subsamples on the four major dimensions on which, according to Lewis, those living in a culture of poverty should manifest their distinctiveness: attitudes, values, and character structure; nature of the family; nature of the slum community; and the relationship between the culture of poverty and the larger society. Of the 18 variables in these categories that were examined, some measure of support for the cultural thesis was found in less than half the cases. Of greater import, however, was the fact that the thesis was most consistently upheld for variables that might more appropriately be regarded as alternative indicators of poverty, rather than as representations of a cultural life-style or a distinctive psychological orientation.

Thus, it should not be too surprising that the poor were found to have poorer housing conditions than the nonpoor, as well as being more crowded, being more racially segregated in their work places, and having fewer material resources than the nonpoor. In contrast, when the data for five variables of a more psychological nature were examined (powerlessness, self-esteem, social isolation, normlessness, psychopathology), it was only with respect to feelings of social isolation that the poor emerged as significantly more deprived than the nonpoor. It is interesting to note that Kutner (1975), employing a similar methodology, found much the same pattern of results in her study of women living in six widely separated parts of the country.

Other attempts to document the complex network of "culture of poverty" traits posited by Lewis have fared little better than the ones just reviewed. Johnson and Sanday (1971), for example, found that racial differences were far more important than income (that is, poor/nonpoor) differences in accounting for variation in life-styles and attitudes among a sample of Pittsburgh residents drawn from low-income neighborhoods. Irelan, Moles, and O'Shea (1969) found that male public assistance recipients in California expressed more feelings of dependency, fatalism, and alienation than did nonrecipients who were almost as poor. (This was true for black and white, but not Spanish-speaking, respondents.)

Of primary significance to the researchers, however, was the finding that the three ethnic groups studied (white, black, Spanish-speaking) differed significantly from one another on 14 of the 16 attitude measures employed. They assert that this result is inconsistent with the part of Lewis's thesis that implies that the cross-cultural nature of the culture of poverty should minimize ethnic group variation in the manifestation of "culture of poverty" traits. Research has even called into question the appropriateness of Lewis's perspective for understanding the attitudes of Appalachian residents (Billings, 1974).

This overall pattern of unimpressive results changes little when studies extending beyond North America are considered. Researchers either find the poor not exhibiting the network of psychological traits attributed to them by Lewis (Leeds, 1971; Perlman, 1976; Safa, 1970; Schwartz, 1975) or use alternative explanatory models in accounting for the distinctive behaviors they do observe (Eames & Goode, 1973; Rodman, 1971).

Additional evidence relevant to "kernel of truth" issues can be found in more narrowly focused studies dealing with popular stereotypes implied by the "culture of poverty" thesis. Two of the most important stereotypes in this context are that the aspiration level of the poor is very low, and there is an undeserving segment of the poor that does not endorse the work ethic. These stereotypes are related but distinct. The first involves the perception that low-income people are relatively content with their lot in life and are not particularly interested in improving their socioeconomic status. The second is more of a comment about how a segment of the poor wishes to maintain itself in its current state (that is, by not working very hard). Indeed, the research reviewed in the section "Contemporary Images of the Poor" suggests that these two stereotypes are among the most pervasive and persistently held about the poor (for instance, Coleman et al., 1978, ch. 10).

When the relevant studies are examined, both stereotypes are found to be seriously deficient. Recent investigations of aspiration for success have frequently been guided by Rodman's (1965) concept of the "lower-class value stretch." Rodman explains this notion as follows:

By the value stretch I mean that the . . . lower-class person, without abandoning the general values of the society, develops an alternative set of values. Without abandoning the values placed upon success, such as high income and high educational and occupational attainment, he stretches the values so that lesser degrees of success also become desirable. (p. 277)

Implicit in Rodman's analysis is the contention that lower-class individuals have a wider range of aspirations than do middle- and upper-class persons, a range that includes aspirations as high as those held by the latter two groups. While studies designed to test this proposition have not consistently supported it (Della Fave, 1974b; Della Fave, 1977; Della Fave & Klobus, 1976; Dillingham, 1980; Rodman & Voydanoff, 1978; Rodman, Voydanoff, & Lovejoy, 1974; Young & Cochrane, 1977), the results obtained are nevertheless inconsistent with the aspirational stereotype previously described.

It is true that the highest occupational, educational, and economic aspirations of lower-class respondents tend to be lower than those expressed by middle- and upper-class persons. However, when we consider the fact that the real-life position of poor families on these dimensions is very low, the evidence indicates that the mobility aspirations of low-income respondents are actually quite lofty. Put another way, the studies clearly demonstrate that the overwhelming majority of lower-class individuals wish to move out of the lower class. In this context it is regrettable that researchers have not used as one indicator of aspiration level a measure that takes into account the respondent's social-class origin. Such an approach would almost certainly reveal a considerable amount of aspiration on the part of low-income respondents and would render the results of such studies less vulnerable to unwarranted stereotyping of the poor's motivation.*

The very fact that lower-class individuals desire significant upward mobility would seem to call into question the veracity of a stereotype that suggests that a significant segment of the poor are lazy and wish to avoid work. A consideration of the evidence bearing more directly on work orientations and behavior of the poor confirms this suspicion.

Goodwin (1972a) conducted what is perhaps the most detailed study comparing work attitudes of the poor and nonpoor. The fact that his poor respondents were welfare recipients makes this a particularly important investigation, since this group is usually perceived as being near the core of

---

*It is interesting to note that in studies where respondents are asked to rank-order sets of values in terms of their perceived importance or personal relevance, no significant differences have been found between income groups in the average ranking they assign to "ambition" or "achievement" (Christenson & Yang, 1976; Feather, 1975; Rokeach & Parker, 1970). This is the case even when numerous income-related differences are found for other values (Feather, 1975; Rokeach & Parker, 1970).

disreputable poverty (Matza, 1966b). This study is also distinctive for the meticulousness with which Goodwin assessed and analyzed the work-related attitudes of his respondents. He found no significant differences between welfare recipients and the nonpoor in commitment to the work ethic, where this ethic was represented by items dealing with three basic dimensions: positive attitudes toward work, self-development as an occupational goal, and the belief that one's efforts control success. Other attitudinal indicators of a positive orientation toward work also revealed no significant differences between the poor and nonpoor.

These findings are all the more impressive in view of the fact that the nonpoor comparison groups were composed of middle- and upper-middle-class respondents (Goodwin, 1972a; 1972b; 1973). Goodwin (1972a) succinctly summarizes his results thus:

> Evidence from this study unambiguously supports the following conclusion: poor people—males and females, blacks and whites, youths and adults—identify their self-esteem with work as strongly as do the nonpoor. They express as much willingness to take job training if unable to earn a living and to work even if they were to have an adequate income. They have, moreover, as high life aspirations as do the nonpoor and want the same things, among them a good education and a nice place to live. This study reveals no differences between poor and nonpoor when it comes to life goals and wanting to work. (p. 112)

Goodwin is by no means the only investigator to document strong endorsement of the work ethic among the poor. Similar findings emerge from studies by Kaplan and Tausky (1972; 1974) and Davidson and Gaitz (1974).

With respect to stereotyping, it is interesting to note that Goodwin's nonpoor respondents misperceived both the attitudes of the poor sample and the relationships between these attitudes. The nonpoor predicted that welfare recipients would have both a weaker commitment to the work ethic and lower life aspirations than was in fact the case (1972b; 1973). Moreover, it was the expectation of the nonpoor that, among welfare recipients, endorsement of the work ethic would be negatively associated with seeing welfare as an acceptable means of support. The actual results, however, revealed no significant correlation between the two orientations among recipients (1973).

In evaluating Goodwin's research, a skeptic might assert that the expression of attitudes that indicate a willingness to work is not the same, or as important, as actually working. O. Lewis (1969) claims, for example, that "People with a culture of poverty are aware of middle-class values; they talk about them and even claim some of them as their own, but on the whole they do not live by them" (p. 190). An obvious problem with such a perspective is that the behavior of "not working" can have many causes, only one of which is the lack of a "true" commitment to the work ethic. Even so, data on the relationship of the poor to the labor market deserve consideration.

Particularly instructive in this context is a national survey of 56,000 households conducted by the U.S. Bureau of the Census (1980). Of the poor males in the sample who were from 22 to 64 years old, almost two-thirds (65 percent) were employed for all or part of 1978, with members of the employed group working an average of 36 weeks. Of those who did not work at all during the year, 86 percent cited illness, disability, inability to find work, school attendance, or retirement as the main reason (p. 62).* Earlier studies by Van Til (1973) and Davidson and Gaitz (1974) also found the majority of poor males to be employed.

These results take on added significance when one considers the fact that approximately half (49.7 percent) of the poor families in the United States are headed by males (U.S. Bureau of the Census, 1980, p. 2).

Finally, the results of the much-publicized New Jersey Negative Income Tax Experiment offered little support for the contention that providing a poverty-level income to low-income families would cause the male heads of such families to stop working in large numbers (Rees, 1977). In this government-sponsored study of 1,357 families, experimental subgroups were guaranteed incomes for three years ranging from 50 percent to 125 percent of the poverty line regardless of whether anyone in the family worked. The results for male heads of households indicated a significant decrease in the hours worked per week by whites, a significant increase in the unemployment rate of Spanish-speaking individuals, and no negative effects on the work behavior of blacks.

Neither of the significant changes that occurred was large in absolute terms, however, prompting Rees (1977) to observe that "The burden of proof now appears to be on those who assert that income-maintenance programs for intact families will have very large effects on labor supply" (p. 31). The results (some of them preliminary) of negative income-tax experiments in other parts of the country also suggest that income-maintenance plans would not have a major disincentive effect on males' work behavior (Moffitt, 1979, 1981; Stanford Research Institute, 1978; R. E. Miller, 1979).

It might be objected, of course, that whatever decrease there was in work behavior in these studies was due to the manifestation of "culture of

---

*The proportion of poor females in this age group who worked was much smaller (39 percent). However, a substantial percentage of these women lived with their spouses (approximately 31 percent) and/or had children to care for. Of the poor females in the sample who were between 14 and 54 years old, 28 percent had children under 6 (U.S. Bureau of the Census, 1980, pp. 62, 101, 136). A strong expectation that women should work under these circumstances has not traditionally existed in our society.

poverty" traits among a segment of the sample. The evidence from the New Jersey experiment is simply not consistent with such an interpretation, however. Wright (1977) examined the impact on work behavior of responses to measures tapping eight different psychological dimensions: anomie, self-esteem, personal inefficacy, time orientation, work involvement, occupational flexibility, job satisfaction, and perception of financial need. In the overwhelming majority of cases, these variables were found to have no significant effect on the male family head's employment status (employed/ unemployed), total earnings, or total hours worked during the experiment. In those isolated instances where statistically significant effects were found, the impact of the psychological variables was minor in comparison with the effects associated with economic and sociological variables such as education, age, family structure, and family size. This pattern of results persisted even when subgroups of respondents exhibiting "culture of poverty" attitudes on several dimensions were analyzed.

Wright's findings bring into focus a crucial "kernel of truth" issue that has yet to be addressed: What evidence is there that the alleged motivational deficiencies of the poor represent dimensions that are highly relevant to economic mobility to begin with? This is an extremely important question because it bears directly on stereotyped explanations of poverty and wealth. One might ask why this question is relevant to the present discussion, given the previously reviewed research indicating that the poor are not nearly as distinctive a group as the "culture of poverty" thesis would make them out to be.

It is relevant because more comprehensive reviews of the social-class literature indicate significant associations between socioeconomic status and individual characteristics in various areas, although the strengths of the observed relationships generally fall far short of what would be required to justify the use of "culture of poverty" terminology in describing them (for instance, Blum & Rossi, 1969; Inkeles, 1960; Kerckhoff, 1972; Lundberg, 1974). This point is perhaps put most succinctly by Rossi and Blum, who reviewed several hundred studies in an attempt to assess the adequacy of the "culture of poverty" thesis. They concluded that

> The poor *are* different, but the difference appears mainly to be one of *degree* rather than kind.
>
> Those traits used to define the culture of poverty are manifested by the extreme poor with only somewhat greater frequency than is true of those immediately above them in socioeconomic status. (1969, pp. 39, 42)

Thus, even though the "culture of poverty" thesis was not upheld by their review, the poor did emerge as a group possessing various negative characteristics in somewhat greater abundance than the nonpoor.

While this finding makes the mobility question raised in the preceding paragraph worth asking, the cross-sectional research examined by Rossi and Blum (1969) cannot answer it. Longitudinal studies are necessary in order to evaluate the claim that certain motivations cause poverty rather than simply describe it. Unfortunately, few investigations have examined the relationship of motivational factors to economic achievement in this fashion. Of those that exist, the majority have found that aspirations and work orientations (as tapped by attitudinal measures) are, at best, very weak predictors of later economic status (Featherman, 1972; Morgan, Dickinson, Dickinson, Benus, & Duncan, 1974; Otto & Haller, 1979; Sewell & Hauser, 1975).

Morgan et al., for example, studied a national sample of 5,060 families over a five-year period. Attitudes of family heads relevant to aspiration-ambition, trust-hostility, sense of personal efficacy, and perceived propensity to plan ahead were measured each year. For the most part these attitudes were found to have no significant relationship to changes in the families' economic well-being, as indicated by numerous measures, that took place over the five-year period. This lack of relevance persisted when analyses were repeated for subsamples that were thought to be particularly likely to show attitudinal effects. While achievement motivation, which was assessed in the fifth year only, was found to have somewhat greater relevance to economic change, its impact was neither systematic nor powerful on most of the measures examined. Even behavior patterns such as planning ahead, avoiding risks, and economizing in the use of resources had only inconsistent relationships to changes in financial status. Many times more important than any of the variables discussed thus far in affecting the economic situation of the families were changes in family composition (sex and marital status of family head, number of children, and such) and labor force participation (number of wage earners in the family).

A partial exception to the pattern of results emerging from these studies is the work of Jencks, Bartlett, Corcoran, Crouse, Eaglesfield, Jackson, McClelland, Mueser, Olneck, Schwartz, Ward, and Williams (1979). They conclude, on the basis of their analysis of two longitudinal studies, that the role of "noncognitive traits" (as measured by teacher ratings, self-assessments, behavioral reports, and attitudinal instruments) in accounting for economic success is greater than that suggested by previous research. This category of traits includes, but is not limited to, aspirations and work orientations. Jencks et al. also point out, however, that it is "Only when the effects of numerous measures of personality are considered together . . . [that] they explain even a moderate portion of the variation in individual achievements" (p. 157). The notion, then, that a major source of economic success is one's standing on a discrete motivational variable such as "desire to succeed" or "willingness to work hard" is left unsupported even by their data.

These findings strongly suggest that even if stereotypes of the motivational characteristics of the poor were highly accurate (which they are not), they would still be erroneous insofar as they depict these characteristics as holding the causal key to understanding why the poor are poor. More attention should, perhaps, be paid to economically based analyses of poverty that stress the importance of labor-market and related forces in accounting for existence and persistence of poverty (for example, Gordon, 1972; Schiller, 1976; Thurow, 1975). In this context one of the recommendations of a committee requested by the U.S. Department of Health, Education, and Welfare to assess the state of poverty research is instructive. The committee concluded that there was a "need for a shift of emphasis away from study of the situation and characteristics of people who are in poverty at a particular time . . . toward study of the social circumstances and systematic social forces that produce and perpetuate poverty itself" (Committee on Evaluation of Poverty Research, 1979, p. 11).

Indeed, to the extent that poverty in the United States is the "result of the normal functioning of societal institutions in a capitalist economy" (Wachtel, 1975, p. 181), stereotyped explanations of poverty that focus on the characteristics of the poor would be incorrect even if researchers found motivational factors to be highly relevant to economic success. Such a finding would simply show that if the economic system is such that someone has to be poor, then possessing certain psychological characteristics increases one's chances of being in that bottom group. That such a bottom group exists at all, however, would not be an occurrence explainable by reference to the psychological characteristics of the poor.

STEREOTYPING THE POOR: THEORETICAL PERSPECTIVES

The research reviewed to this point would seem to justify at least two major conclusions. First, negative stereotypes concerning the poor are widespread in American society. Second, the "kernels of truth" contained in these stereotypes tend to be very small. An obvious question is raised by this state of affairs: With so meager a foundation in reality, how and why do these stereotypes persist? Attempts to answer this question can be categorized according to the variables they emphasize: psychological self-interest, material self-interest, cognitive processes, and/or societal ideology.

Psychological Self-Interest

An example of an approach stressing psychological self-interest is Michael Lewis's (1978) examination of America's "culture of inequality." He suggests that the sense of self-esteem and personal worth of most Americans is continually jeopardized by a societal ideology that implies that the failure to reach one's high aspirations is a result of personal deficiencies. Negative stereotyping of the poor represents one way of handling this psychological threat. It allows individuals to see themselves as having personal strengths, in terms of motivation and character, that distinguish them from the ne'er-do-wells at the bottom of society. Given Lewis's analysis, it is not surprising that he believes a despised lower class is a necessary component of American society.

Lewis's perspective provides one interpretation for the previously reported finding from American community studies that the most salient stereotypes concerning the lower class tend to be personality-oriented, while those of the higher classes involve other dimensions. Emphasis on the motivational characteristics of the privileged would, in Lewis's view, only intensify the threat to self-esteem represented by one's failure to achieve a high class position.

The "culture of inequality" formulation is not without major problems, however. At the empirical level the finding that negative views of the poor are most prevalent in the upper economic classes is not readily derivable from Lewis's argument. Is it plausible to assume that the self-esteem of the affluent is more endangered by achievement failures than is the self-esteem of the less well-to-do? Indeed, it would seem that the relationship should be the other way around. At a conceptual level it can be argued that Lewis has formulated a solution to a problem that does not exist. He contends that we need to disparage the poor because we fail to achieve our high aspirations in a society that personalizes success and failure. A society that personalizes success and failure, however, is already one in which the poor are disparaged. In positing the existence of such a societal ideology, Lewis is in fact offering an explanation for the negative stereotyping he observes. Within this context the details of his analysis, as they involve the concept of self-esteem, become largely superfluous.

In contrast with Lewis's theory, at the core of most explanations of social-class stereotyping that stress psychological self-interest is the contention that poverty represents a direct challenge to people's views about the way society should operate and/or how individuals can live. Beyond this assertion some analyses go further than others in attempting to account for the specific forms taken by stereotypes of the poor. Rainwater (1970), for example, claims that the nonpoor are perplexed and made anxious by their perception that the poor have a way of life that they, the nonpoor, believe is "unlivable." In order to resolve this "highly unstable cognitive situation," individuals either deny the validity of their initial perceptions of how the poor live or stereotype the poor in ways suggesting that the poor are "not quite human."

Rainwater identifies five perspectives on the poor that frequently result from the processes outlined above. With one exception they portray the poor in terms of dichotomies of virtuous/evil and weak/potent (for instance, the moralizing perspective views the poor as evil and potent). While the typology is a provocative one, Rainwater provides little evidence to indicate the extent to which significant segments of the population endorse each of the perspectives. A more basic theoretical problem, however, is that the question of what prompts individuals to resolve their perplexity through the adoption of one perspective rather than another is not systematically addressed by Rainwater. Consequently, little understanding is gained of the dynamics leading to endorsement of negative stereotypes of the poor.

A more refined conceptual framework may be found in the "just world" hypothesis (Heider, 1958; Lerner & Miller, 1978). Though not formulated to account for negative stereotypes of the poor per se, Lerner and others (Lerner, 1971; MacDonald, 1973) have suggested that this hypothesis might help to explain such stereotyping. Briefly stated, the "just world" hypothesis contends that individuals have a need to believe in a world where people generally get what they deserve. Without such a belief in a stable and orderly environment, "it would be difficult for the individual to commit himself to the pursuit of long-range goals or even to the socially regulated behavior of day-to-day life" (Lerner & Miller, 1978, p. 1030). The hypothesis predicts that when individuals see someone suffering unjustly, they will be motivated to restore justice by compensating or helping the victim (Lerner, 1971). When this is not possible, however, another way to restore justice is to persuade oneself that the victim deserved to suffer because of his or her bad character or bad behavior (Lerner & Miller, 1978).

The "just world" hypothesis is certainly consistent with the overall finding of pervasive stereotypes that disparage the character and motivation of the poor. For people to be living in poverty through no fault of their own is a circumstance that most individuals would perceive as patently unjust. Thus, blaming the poor for their poverty serves to maintain one's faith in a just society.

As was the case with Lewis's theory, however, the finding that the affluent are more prone to derogate the poor is problematical for the "just world" hypothesis. Lerner and Miller state:

> To witness and admit to injustices in other environments does not threaten people very much because these events have very little relevance for their own fates. As events become closer to their world, however, the concern over injustices increases greatly, as does the need to explain or make sense of the events. (1978, p. 1031)

Such an analysis would appear to suggest that if there were any relationship among the nonpoor between economic status and maligning the poor, it would be a negative one. This is because the affluent should be the group least likely to be worried by the prospect that "this [poverty] could happen to me."*

---

*It might be objected here that the "just world" hypothesis would not make such a prediction, given Lerner and Miller's conclusion, based on their litrature review, that deroga-

Additional evidence suggesting that negative stereotypes of the poor are not adequately accounted for by the "just world" hypothesis comes from a study by Rubin and Peplau (1973). Using a 20-item scale to measure belief in a just world among college undergraduates, they found no significant correlation between scores on this instrument and scores on a scale tapping negative attitudes toward the poor. In contrast, scores on the "just world" scale were significantly related to negative attitudes toward both blacks and women.

The psychological self-interest perspective on stereotyping that is perhaps most applicable to the case of the poor is the one formulated by Campbell (1967). In his analysis the process leading to stereotyping begins with the ingroup member feeling hostility toward an outgroup. This hostility, however, does not stem from the outgroup's manifestation of stereotyped traits, but from some other source. Within the defensive psychological context of denying the real source of hostility, the individual comes to believe that the outgroup possesses objectionable characteristics that are responsible for the animosity he or she feels.

Where poverty is concerned, the taxes that the nonpoor must pay to provide welfare and social services for the poor could represent one source of the nonpoor's hostility. The nonpoor might also resent the poor for the feelings of guilt that their presence in society engenders in the nonpoor. Campbell's model would predict that the nonpoor will rationalize this resentment by attributing it to the stereotyped characteristics of the poor (laziness, immorality, and so on) that we have previously described.

This conceptualization of the stereotyping process would not appear to provide a strong a priori basis for predicting that nonpoor individuals from one economic level will dislike the poor more or less than those from another. Consequently, the finding that economic status is positively associated with deprecating the poor is not inherently problematical for it. What such a finding does suggest, however, is that by itself Campbell's analysis cannot be expected to account for all of the dynamics involved in stereotyping of the poor.

Material Self-Interest

The logic underlying analyses of social-class stereotyping that stress material rather than psychological self-interest has been described in the section "Contemporary Images of the Poor." Given the economic referent of such stereotypes, the fact that the self-interest thesis has been most consistently supported for the economic component of social class should not be

---

tion of the victim does not occur when observers believe they could be in the same situation as the victim in the future (1978, p. 1041). While this conclusion is certainly inconsistent with the expectation of a negative relationship between income level and pejorative stereotyping of the poor, it would also seem to be inconsistent with the quotation from Lerner and Miller describing the "just world" hypothesis.

surprising. However, we have noted that even this relationship between income level and negative stereotyping of the poor is not a particularly strong one.

It may be that one of the basic assumptions underlying the material self-interest argument is erroneous. It is the assumption that the perceived benefits one derives from the distribution of income are highly correlated with the actual benefits. For example, to the extent that the more affluent classes do not see themselves being as well-off as their objective circumstances would suggest they are, attempts to verify the self-interest thesis solely through the use of objective income measures are likely to have unimpressive results. Thus, in order to adequately evaluate the material self-interest perspective, studies in which subjective measures of economic well-being supplement more standard indexes would seem to be called for.

It should also be kept in mind that a number of convincing analyses are available that assert or imply that the persistence of a disadvantaged lower class in America contributes to the "normal" functioning of our socioeconomic system (for instance, Gans, 1973, ch. 4; Piven & Cloward, 1971). In this regard it might be argued that all segments of the nonpoor have something material to gain from the continued existence of poverty, and thus have an incentive for negatively stereotyping the poor. Formulating the issue in these terms emphasizes commonality of interests among the non-poor rather than difference, and suggests that the finding of less-than-striking social-class differences in stereotyping need not be problematical for all forms of a self-interest thesis.

One of the most cited versions of the material self-interest approach is Ryan's (1976) analysis of the "blaming the victim" process. With respect to poverty Ryan is less interested in accounting for traditional stereotypes that portray low-income people as shiftless and immoral than he is in explaining the alleged popularity of the "culture of poverty" view among the liberal middle class. For our purposes, then, blaming the victim may be regarded as synonymous with endorsing the portrait of the poor presented by Oscar Lewis.

Ryan contends that when it comes to thinking about the poor, middle-class people must reconcile their humanitarian concerns with their material self-interest. They sincerely wish to help the poor, but they do not want to do so in a way that might threaten their middle-class standard of living (a threat that a major redistribution of income might pose). In this context perceiving the poor as inherently lazy and unprincipled is problematical for the liberal middle class on at least two counts: it is inconsistent with their basic political orientation, and it implies that any attempts to aid the poor will probably be fruitless. Against this background acceptance of the "culture of poverty" view of the poor represents a compromise subconsciously reached. It allows the middle class to protect its self-interest (the solution to poverty does not lie in changing the economic structure of society) while demonstrating liberal social concern (the poor, who are not inherently defective, will benefit from our efforts to change their culture).

Ryan's delineation of the functional equivalence between the "culture of poverty" thesis and less sophisticated moral evaluations of the poor is unquestionably powerful. For all its popularity, however, his account of the "blaming the victim" process has not been explicitly tested in any published research on attitudes toward the poor. Such a test would require that respondents' explanations of poverty that emphasize a "culture of poverty" interpretation be distinguished from those that employ more traditional and simplistic stereotyping of the poor. This distinction has not been focused upon in previous investigations of poverty attitudes among the general population. If such studies were done, one would predict, on the basis of Ryan's analysis, that political liberals and the middle class would be the groups most likely to give "culture of poverty" responses. Results consistent with this expectation, however, would not necessarily prove the existence of a subconscious compromise process posited by Ryan, since the same results could occur through the more mundane mechanism of differential exposure to information pertaining to "culture of poverty" views.

Cognitive Processes

Insofar as a material incentive exists for negatively stereotyping the poor, it should be seen as building upon fundamental cognitive processes that contribute to stereotyping in general, such as those discussed by Hamilton (1979) and by Jones in Chapter 2 of this volume. While Jones raises numerous issues that have implications for perceptions of the poor, what has been called the "fundamental attribution error" (Ross, 1977) would appear to be particularly relevant. This error, which has been extensively documented in laboratory studies (such as Jones, 1979; Jones & Nisbett, 1971; Ross, 1977), can be summarized as follows: Observers tend to overestimate the extent to which an individual's behavior is due to his or her personal characteristics and to underestimate the extent to which it is influenced by the situation surrounding the person.

While poverty is not, strictly speaking, a behavior, it is nevertheless a condition closely tied to behaviors about which we customarily make attributions (working at a low-paying job, not working at all, applying for welfare, and so on). Consequently, when people attempt to explain poverty, they are in a sense trying to explain the behavior of poor people. In this context the fundamental attribution error is likely to contribute in a major way to negative stereotyping of the poor. It predisposes us to view the poverty-relevant behaviors of the poor as being due to their personal desires, regardless of how appropriate this interpretation might be.

The resulting judgments we render have the ring of individualistic certainty: If poor youths drop out of school, it's because they don't value education; if poor women are on welfare, they must simply be too lazy to do anything else; if poor men have low-paying jobs, lack of ambition must be a major reason. And, as suggested above, the psychological steps that lead from these stereotyped perceptions of the poor's behavior to person-centered explanations of poverty itself are short ones indeed. Thus, when conceptualized in terms of the fundamental attribution error, blaming poverty on the poor represents, at least in part, simply one manifestation of an attributional bias that characterizes our perceptions in a variety of contexts.

This bias is likely to be exacerbated by the "kernels of truth," however small, associated with stereotypes of the poor. Research reviewed by Ross (1977) indicates that when subjects are asked to predict the level of Variable A, which they have been told is weakly correlated with Variable B, the resulting estimates suggest that the subjects believe the A-B correlation is much higher than it actually is. The implications of this phenomenon for perceptions of the poor are straightforward. What are, in reality, weak relationships between social class and psychological characteristics are likely to be perceived as being much larger.

These inaccurate perceptions, once formed, are likely to be perpetuated by distortions in the way in which individuals attend to, and evaluate the quality of, incoming information relevant to the stereotypes. For example, experiments summarized by Hamilton (1979, pp. 73–75) show that individuals overestimate the amount of incoming information which is consistent with their stereotypes and underestimate the amount which is inconsistent. Thus, the occasional media account of welfare fraud is likely to have more of an impact on the individual than it should, while reports of low fraud rates will tend to be overlooked. Moreover, insofar as the inconsistent information is noticed, it is likely to be evaluated more critically than the consistent data (such as, "The only reason the reported fraud rates are low is because most fraud goes undetected!").

In this context Allen (1970) offers a particularly telling observation. Having concluded on the basis of his literature review that "most of the demonstrated relationships between personality and poverty are quite weak" (p. 259), he remarks:

> Apparently a process of leveling and sharpening occurs with respect to research data. Many findings [that suggest that the poor have distinctive personalities] are still widely accepted as valid in the face of data that are ambiguous at best and overwhelmingly contradictory at worst. There seems to be a psychological tendency—perhaps not unique to social scientists nor to data in this area—to sharpen the findings supporting one's preconceptions and to ignore or forget findings that are discrepant. (p. 259)

Finally, in considering how we react to discrepant data, it is important not to overestimate the amount of exposure that the nonpoor have to information inconsistent with negative stereotypes of the poor.* This point is concisely made by Goodwin (1972b):

> In a stratified social system . . . power and communication primarily flow downward. There is little opportunity for middle-class persons to be confronted with data challenging their projections about the psychology of the poor, much less to be confronted with poor people who can indicate how institutionalized blockages are preventing them from fulfilling their positive orientations. (p. 347)

Societal Ideology

In evaluating the role of cognitive processes in social-class stereotyping, we should recognize that in the United States this role takes place within the context of a cultural tradition that encourages misperceptions. The concept of equality of opportunity, a value stipulating that "Everyone should have a chance to go as far [economically and otherwise] as his abilities and desires will take him" (Rainwater, 1974, pp. 171–172), is at the core of America's ideological heritage (for instance, Chinoy, 1955; Huber & Form, 1973, ch. 1; Lipset & Bendix, 1959, ch. 3; Morris, 1978; Thio, 1972; Williams, 1970, p. 477).

Closely intertwined with this value is the belief that American society comes closer to achieving equality of opportunity than do other societies (Lipset & Bendix, 1959, p. 76). It should be evident that such a belief has direct implications for perceiving the stratification system in terms of social-class stereotypes. Indeed, it might even be argued that the "equality of opportunity" belief is virtually synonymous with the holding of such stereotypes.

What, then, can be concluded from the fact that the notion of equality of opportunity, both as value and as belief, forms part of the cultural context into which societal members are socialized? It is that social-class stereotyping, or at least a conceptual framework facilitating such stereotyping, is to a great extent learned by individuals in much the same fashion that they learn other components of their cultural heritage (through their families, the educational system, mass media, and so on). Indeed, the fact that this ideological message is so widely disseminated throughout society may be one reason why the relationship between economic status and negative stereotyping of the poor, though significant, is not stronger than it is.

That an "equality of opportunity" ideology is intimately associated with certain stereotypes of the poor is vividly illustrated when a society without such an ideology is used as a comparison. India, for example, has for much of its history been characterized by a caste system of stratification built on the premise that an individual born into a given caste remains in that caste for life. Studies of stereotyping in India indicate that the lower

---

*For a rare example of such exposure, see "Welfare Allotment" (1981).

castes are not perceived as being slothful (for example, Natraj, 1962; Sinha & Sinha, 1967), a trait that is very salient in public imagery of the lower class in the United States. On the contrary, "industrious" and "hard-working" are adjectives frequently used to describe the lower castes in India.

To the extent that social-class stereotyping develops within the framework of cultural socialization patterns building upon basic cognitive processes, the roles of psychological and material self-interest in accounting for such stereotyping would appear to be more supplemental than fundamental.* Such a possibility underscores the necessity for commentators on social-class stereotyping to forsake single-factor explanations of the phenomenon and to begin developing models that incorporate the multiple influences that contribute to stereotyping.

A possible starting point for such an approach is the analysis of American poverty provided by Pettigrew (1980). Using the concept of labeled deviance to organize his discussion, he attempts to trace, step by step, the process by which the poor are negatively stereotyped. In the course of this analysis a wide range of social-psychological concepts—from relative deprivation to role theory—are examined for their relevance. While analyses of this type are complex and difficult, the effort must be made if a more sophisticated understanding of the dynamics involved in stereotyping the poor is to emerge.

CONSEQUENCES OF STEREOTYPING

That many people have erroneous perceptions of poverty and the poor is, in and of itself, an interesting but not particularly consequential state of affairs. To the extent that conduct toward the poor is influenced by these views, however, it is likely that damage will be done to human lives. Unfortunately, the relevant research is consistent with this expectation.

Behavior Toward the Poor

Investigators have found that viewing the poor as motivationally deficient is associated with believing that too much is being spent on welfare and relief programs (Alston & Dean, 1972), opposing increased welfare payments (Williamson, 1974b), opposing greater government efforts to aid the poor (Williamson, 1974a), and rejecting proposals that would establish guaranteed jobs, a guaranteed minimum income, or equality of incomes in the United States (Feagin, 1975, p. 141).

---

*In a Marxist analysis, of course, cultural socialization patterns are seen as being largely determined by the economic structure of society. Thus, in America the material interests of the capitalist class would be regarded as contributing to the cultural fabric of society. From this perspective, then, it is not necessary to deemphasize the importance of material self-interest as a cause of social-class stereotyping in order to assert the relevance of cultural factors (see Afanasyev, n.d.).

The implications of these findings have been documented by Wohlenberg (1976) and Piliavin, Masters, and Corbett (1979). Using national survey data to rank different regions of the country with respect to how much their residents blamed poverty on the lack of effort of the poor, Wohlenberg correlated the results with several indicators of the support levels and eligibility restrictiveness of the welfare programs in these regions. For three of the four welfare indicators employed, over half of the regional variation in program characteristics could be accounted for by regional variation in attitudes toward the poor, with the least generous/most restrictive regions being the most negative in their attitudes. Focusing on the dynamics of the welfare office itself, Piliavin et al. found that case aides in Milwaukee who had negative attitudes toward the poor committed greater underpayment errors in their decisions regarding Aid to Families with Dependent Children (AFDC) recipients than did aides with more positive attitudes.

At a more general level the welfare system as a whole embodies many of the most persistently held stereotypes concerning the poor. This is particularly the case where programs serving the "undeserving" poor are concerned, such as AFDC and general relief. Assistance levels vary from state to state, but are typically very low, in order that the principle of less eligibility not be violated. This principle, dating from the 1830s, holds that persons receiving assistance should not have a standard of living equal to that of the lowest-paid full-time workers not receiving assistance (Waxman, 1977, p. 80). The objective here is to make welfare unattractive, so as to avoid undercutting the meager motivation to work that the poor allegedly have.

To receive these scant benefits, potential recipients must usually undergo a stigmatizing inquiry process to prove their eligibility. This process is heavily laden with moral judgments, not the least of which is the assumption that applicants are dishonest (Handler, 1972, p. 29; Matza, 1976, pp. 669–671). Once assistance is granted, the recipient's life becomes subject to the ongoing scrutiny of welfare and social workers.

One purpose of monitoring the recipient's conduct is to protect against fraud, an occurrence that the American public apparently grossly overestimates (Williamson, 1974b). A second purpose is to link recipients with a range of social services that might help them overcome the individualistically oriented problems that supposedly contributed to their need for welfare in the first place. This latter focus, dubbed "reformation through rehabilitation" by Handler, dates back at least to the nineteenth century and the early stages of the scientific charity movement (Speizman, 1965). Indeed, the overall plight of the recipient is perhaps best summarized by Coser's (1965) observation that "The very granting of relief . . . is forthcoming only at the price of a degradation of the person" (p. 144).*

---

*We should keep in mind that poverty stereotypes are not the only, or even the major, forces shaping public assistance in the United States. Convincing analyses are available that

There are other areas in which the behavior of the nonpoor toward the poor reveals negative stereotyping. On numerous occasions it has been found that elementary school teachers and teacher candidates have lower academic (and related) expectations for lower-class pupils than for middle-class ones (for example, Becker, 1952; Harvey & Slatin, 1975; Jensen & Rosenfeld, 1974; Long & Long, 1974; C. K. Miller, McLaughlin, Haddon, & Chansky, 1968; H. L. Miller, 1973; Schwarzwald, Shoham, Waysman, & Sterner, 1979). That such expectations can be manifested in differential behaviors toward these two groups has been vividly demonstrated by M. R. Harvey (1972, 1980), Rist (1970; 1973), Leacock (1969), and, to a lesser extent, Hoehn (1954).

Harvey (1972), for example, conducted an intensive observational study of eight second-grade classrooms in schools serving high- or low-income populations in the "Target City" school district. (There were three high-income schools and five low-income schools.) Although children in the low-income classrooms differed very little in their social behaviors from those in the high-income classrooms, low-income pupils were seen by their teachers as more physically active and aggressive, less cooperative with one another, less attentive, less mature, and generally less socialized than the high-income children (as the latter were ranked by their teachers). Consistent with these differing perceptions, the behaviors of teachers in the high- and low-income classrooms differed in numerous and important ways, with low-income children receiving

> . . . less praise than criticism, feedback which is incongruent with the appropriateness of their behavior, less teacher attentiveness and non-directive informality during Small Group activities, and great encouragement for dependency upon their teachers while [supposedly] working independently as well as for quiet, mannered, and passive behaviors whatever their nature. (1972, p. 117)

Children in the high-income classrooms benefited from exactly the opposite set of teacher behaviors. These results could not be accounted for by differences in the teachers' background characteristics or by any features of the schools themselves (such as class size or facilities).

There is reason to believe that the processes described above occur to some degree in economically integrated classrooms as well. In his longitudinal study of a kindergarten class, Rist (1970; 1973) found that a formal hierarchy was established by the teacher on the eighth day of school. While the hierarchy was supposedly based upon learning ability, it actually was a reflection of the differences in socioeconomic status among the children. (No

---

depict the welfare system as an essential societal mechanism for insuring the availability of a low-wage labor force. Within the context of achieving this goal, the stigmatizing and punitive nature of welfare policies is seen as instrumental (Piven & Cloward, 1971).

objective data concerning the abilities of the children were available at the time the hierarchy was established.) The social and academic impact of this initial hierarchy was still evident at the end of the study more than two years later (when the children were in the second grade).

Self-Fulfilling Prophecies

The ultimate significance of these educational studies goes beyond the documentation of negative behaviors directed toward poor children by their teachers. Even more disturbing is the researchers' suggestion that the teachers' stereotyped expectations and behaviors with respect to these pupils contribute to a self-fulfilling prophecy taking place in the school setting. Rist (1970), for example, notes that "the high degree of control-oriented behavior directed toward the [lower class] 'slow' learner, the lack of verbal interaction and encouragement, the disproportionately small amount of teaching time given to him, and the ridicule and hostility" (p. 446), all of which he observed in his study, prompt the lower-class child to withdraw from classroom participation. Poor academic performance is almost certain to follow such withdrawal, thus confirming the teacher's initial low expectations. Moreover, internalization by these children of negative stereotypes concerning their academic potential is likely to increase the probability of such a self-fulfilling prophecy occurring.

At a more general level, to the extent that even a very small segment of the poor is persuaded to see itself in negatively stereotyped terms, the problematical consequences of such stereotypes are magnified and perpetuated. This acceptance is likely to promote the manifestation of precisely those behaviors that are the subject of the stereotypes, thus contributing to the small "kernels of truth" that are more than sufficient to sustain the stereotyping process.

In this context there is even evidence to suggest that endorsement of these stereotypes by the poor is associated with passively accepting the demeaning roles offered them by society. In a study of midwestern welfare mothers, Kerbo (1976) found that respondents who agreed that poverty was the fault of the poor felt more stigmatized as welfare recipients than did those who disagreed. Feeling stigmatized was in turn negatively associated with expressing support for assertive methods of interacting with the welfare system as a recipient.

Conclusion

When confronting a negative and unwarranted stereotype of a particular group, the socially approved response is to recommend the elimination of the stereotype in question. Whatever problems there may be in achieving this goal with stereotypes of other groups, with respect to the poor in the United States this task would appear to be impossible on any long-term basis. The distinction between the deserving and undeserving poor notwithstanding, the poor are a population whose very existence signifies deviance in a society characterized by an "equality of opportunity" interpretation of economic stratification (Pettigrew, 1980, pp. 200–202). Matza (1966b) underscores this point clearly when he observes that "a certain element of disrepute attaches even to the poor who are deemed deserving and above reproach. Poverty in itself is slightly disreputable" (p. 620).

The conclusion suggested by this line of reasoning is that the only way to eliminate negative stereotypes of the poor is to eliminate the conditions that generate the target group—that is, to eliminate poverty itself. Paradoxically, however, strategies to accomplish this latter task are constrained by these very same stereotypes. To the extent that these characterizations of the poor and explanations of poverty are erroneous, any programs formulated on the basis of them are likely to be ineffective. Indeed, numerous commentators have raised exactly this point with respect to the anti-poverty programs of the 1960s (for instance, Bird, 1973; Feagin, 1975; M. Lewis, 1978).

With respect to the problems facing the poor, it is hard to deny the pessimistic implications of the preceding discussion. Indeed, it is ironic that the evidence we have reviewed suggests that the culture of "equality of opportunity" may contribute more to stereotypes of the poor and the perpetuation of poverty than any "culture of poverty" the poor might possess. The irony of this observation only heightens its importance, however. Insofar as future social research and, more important, social action are based upon it, today's pessimism may be less justified tomorrow.

FUTURE PROSPECTS FOR RESEARCH

It is unlikely that the next few years will see a great deal of research on stereotypes of the poor and related issues, given the rather low priority currently assigned to poverty in popular discussions of social problems.* Investigators who pursue this topic, however, would do well to employ more precise measures of stereotyping than have been used in the past. In a quantitative sense, for example, we actually know very little about the demographic and other characteristics that people associate with poverty. What percentage of the poor is perceived to be elderly? On welfare? Female? White? Employed? Poor because of lack of motivation? Poor because of lack of ability? This list could certainly be extended. Answers to these questions are needed if we are to move beyond the crude dichotomy of deserving and

---

*For a more comprehensive set of research recommendations complementing the ones presented in this section, see Pettigrew (1980, pp. 219–225).

undeserving poor in analyzing poverty stereotypes. In this context tools such as the "diagnostic ratio" measure of stereotyping developed by McCauley and Stitt (1978) should prove of great value.

There is also a need to examine more systematically the images of poverty and the poor transmitted by major societal institutions, such as the educational system and the mass media. For example, the study conducted by the U.S. Commission on Civil Rights (1977) of how women and minorities are portrayed on television might serve as a useful model for poverty researchers.* The treatment accorded the poor and the stratification system as a whole in elementary school texts in history and related areas represents another potentially fruitful area of investigation. From studies such as these, there should emerge a more firmly grounded and detailed knowledge of the cultural processes that contribute to the stereotyping of the poor.

SUMMARY

Social-class stereotyping can be understood as the process of attributing different psychological and behavioral characteristics to members of different class groups. Stereotypes focusing on the poor have been the subject of considerable research, at least in part because of the status of poverty as a social problem in American society. In this context explanations of poverty have major implications for social-class stereotyping, given that individualistic rather than environmental causes are often stressed.

Negative stereotyping of the poor on a large scale dates back at least to fourteenth-century Europe, with social, economic, and religious developments interacting to contribute to the process. In America a philosophy of Social Darwinism, building upon a foundation of the Protestant ethic and industrialization-related mobility patterns, helped to produce a view of the stratification system that was strongly individualistic in nature.

Systematically gathered data on social-class stereotyping come from at least three major sources: surveys of people's explanations of poverty and wealth, studies of community status systems, and research employing the adjective checklist format. The negative images of the poor revealed by these investigations are quite consistent with one another, with a major segment of the lower class (the "undeserving poor") being seen as lazy, immoral, and improvident, among other things. While the psychological characteristics of the rich are seen in a much more positive light, the most salient images of this group appear to involve material standards of living and social networks.

---

*It is interesting to note that in the six-year sample (1969–1974) of television programs examined by the Commission, only 1.1 percent of all major characters were depicted as being very poor (1977, p. 33).

The economic status of the respondent is positively associated with explaining poverty in individualistic terms. This relationship has generally been found to be of weak to moderate strength, however, indicating that a significant percentage of the poor hold negative stereotypes about themselves. Using internal attributions to account for poverty is also associated with being white, politically conservative, an endorser of the work ethic, and, less consistently, with being male and Protestant.

The social-class stereotypes inherent in Oscar Lewis's "culture of poverty" thesis have prompted considerable research. Relatively little support for his framework has been obtained, a finding that suggests that the "kernels of truth" associated with negative stereotypes of the poor are quite small. Moreover, longitudinal studies indicate that the psychological dimensions prominent in stereotyped explanations of poverty have, at best, only modest relevance to economic mobility.

Attempts to account for negative stereotyping of the poor are frequently based on notions of either psychological or material self-interest. While these factors undoubtedly contribute to the phenomena in question, the foundations of such stereotyping would appear to involve basic cognitive processes (such as the fundamental attribution error) and socialization of societal members into a cultural ideology emphasizing equality of opportunity. Theories of social-class stereotyping that incorporate multiple perspectives are clearly called for.

Research suggests that negative stereotypes of the poor are associated with such negative behaviors toward them as inadequate and stigmatizing welfare policies and discriminatory conduct by classroom teachers. Self-fulfilling prophecies are likely to be generated by such behaviors, especially when the relevant stereotypes have been internalized by low-income persons.

It is highly doubtful that negative stereotypes of the poor can be changed except through the elimination of poverty itself. Achievement of this latter goal, however, is seriously hindered by the misperceptions inherent in these very same stereotypes.

It is unlikely that the next few years will see a great deal of research on poverty stereotypes. Nevertheless, there is a need for researchers to assess with greater precision people's views of the demographic and motivational subgroups that make up the poor population. Experimental studies would also be valuable, as would investigations focusing on the images of the poor transmitted by major societal institutions.

REFERENCES

Aaron, H. J. *Politics and the professors: The Great Society in perspective.* Washington, D.C.: Brookings Institution, 1978.

Afanasyev, V. *Marxist philosophy: A popular outline* (L. Lempert, trans., & J. Riordan, ed.). Moscow: Foreign Language Publishing House, n.d.

Allen, V. L. Personality correlates of poverty. In V. L. Allen (ed.), *Psychological factors in poverty*. Chicago: Markham, 1970.

Alston, J. P., & Dean, K. I. Socioeconomic factors associated with attitudes toward welfare recipients and the causes of poverty. *Social Service Review*, 1972, *46*, 13–23.

Ball, R. A poverty case: The analgesic subculture of the southern Appalachians. *American Sociological Review*, 1968, *33*, 885–895.

Banfield, E. C. *The unheavenly city revisited*. Boston: Little, Brown, 1974.

Bannister, R. C. *Social Darwinism: Science and myth in Anglo-American social thought*. Philadelphia: Temple University Press, 1979.

Bayton, J. A., McAlister, L. B., & Hamer, J. R. Race-class stereotypes. *Journal of Negro Education*, 1956, *Winter*, 75–78.

Beck, B. Welfare as a moral category. *Social Problems*, 1967, *14*, 258–277.

Becker, H. S. Social-class variations in the teacher-pupil relationship. *Journal of Educational Sociology*, 1952, *25*, 451–465.

Bell, W., & Robinson, R. V. Cognitive maps of class and racial inequalities in England and the United States. *American Journal of Sociology*, 1980, *86*, 320–349.

Betten, N. American attitudes toward the poor: A historical overview. *Current History*, 1973, *65* (383), 1–5.

Billings, D. Culture and poverty in Appalachia: A theoretical discussion and empirical analysis. *Social Forces*, 1974, *53*, 315–323.

Bird, F. B. The poor be damned: An analysis of how Americans have perceived and responded to the problems of poverty, 1885–1970. Ph.D. dissertation, Graduate Theological Union, 1973. *Dissertation Abstracts International*, 1973, *34*, 2038A–2039A. (University Microfilm no. 72–23, 131, 652)

Blum, Z. D., & Rossi, P. H. Social class research and images of the poor: A bibliographic review. In D. P. Moynihan (ed.), *On understanding poverty: Perspectives from the social sciences*. New York: Basic Books, 1969.

Bremner, R. H. *From the depths: The discovery of poverty in the United States*. New York: New York University Press, 1956.

Campbell, D. T. Stereotypes and the perception of group differences. *American Psychologist*, 1967, *22*, 817–829.

Centers, R. Attitude and belief in relation to occupational stratification. *Journal of Social Psychology*, 1948, *27*, 159–185.

Chinoy, E. *Automobile workers and the American dream*. New York: Random House, 1955.

Christenson, J. A., & Yang, C. Dominant values in American society: An exploratory analysis. *Sociology and Social Research*, 1967, *60*, 461–473.

Coleman, R. P., & Neugarten, B. L. *Social status in the city*. San Francisco: Jossey-Bass, 1971.

Coleman, R. P., Rainwater, L., & McClelland, K. A. *Social standing in America: New dimensions of class*. New York: Basic Books, 1978.

Coll, B. D. *Perspectives in public welfare: A history*. Washington, D.C.: U.S. Government Printing Office, 1969.

Committee on Evaluation of Poverty Research. *Evaluating federal support for poverty research*. Washington, D.C.: National Academy of Sciences, 1979.

Coser, L. A. The sociology of poverty. *Social Problems*, 1965, *13*, 140–148.

Coughlin, R. M. Social policy and ideology: Public opinion in eight rich nations. In

R. F. Tomasson (ed.), *Comparative social research* (Vol. 2). Greenwich, Conn.: JAI Press, 1979.

Coward, B. E., Feagin, J. R., & Williams, J. A., Jr. The culture of poverty debate: Some additional data. *Social Problems*, 1974, *21*, 621–634.

Davidson, C., & Gaitz, C. M. "Are the poor different?" A comparison of work behavior and attitudes among the urban poor and nonpoor. *Social Problems*, 1974, *22*, 229–245.

Davidson, H. H., Riessman, F., & Meyers, E. Personality characteristics attributed to the worker. *Journal of Social Psychology*, 1962, *57*, 155–160.

Davis, A. The motivation of the underprivileged worker. In W. F. Whyte (ed.), *Industry and Society*. New York: McGraw-Hill, 1946.

Davis, A., Gardner, B. B., & Gardner, M. R. *Deep South: A social anthropological study of caste and class*. Chicago: University of Chicago Press, 1941.

Della Fave, L. R. The culture of poverty revisited: A strategy for research. *Social Problems*, 1974, *21*, 609–621. (a)

Della Fave, L. R. Success values: Are they universal or class-differentiated? *American Journal of Sociology*, 1974, *80*, 153–169. (b)

Della Fave, L. R. Aspirations through four years of high school: An inquiry into the value stretching process. *Pacific Sociological Review*, 1977, *20*, 371–388.

Della Fave, L. R., & Klobus, P. A. Success values and the value stretch: A biracial comparison. *Sociological Quarterly*, 1976, *17*, 491–502.

Devine, D. J. *The political culture of the United States: The influence of member values on regime maintenance*. Boston: Little, Brown, 1972.

Dillingham, C. L. The value stretch: An empirical test. *Sociology and Social Research*, 1980, *64*, 249–262.

Dollard, J. *Caste and class in a southern town*. New Haven: Yale University Press, 1937.

Eames, E., & Goode, J. G. *Urban poverty in a cross-cultural context*. New York: Free Press, 1973.

Feagin, J. R. *Subordinating the poor: Welfare and American beliefs*. Englewood Cliffs, N.J.: Prentice-Hall, 1975.

Feather, N. T. Explanations of poverty in Australian and American samples: The person, society, or fate? *Australian Journal of Psychology*, 1974, *26*, 199–216.

Feather, N. T. Values and income level. *Australian Journal of Psychology*, 1975, *27*, 23–29.

Featherman, D. L. Achievement orientations and socioeconomic career attainments. *American Sociological Review*, 1972, *37*, 131–143.

Feldman, J. M. Stimulus characteristics and subject prejudice as determinants of stereotype attribution. *Journal of Personality and Social Psychology*, 1972, *21*, 333–340.

Free, L. A., & Cantril, H. *The political beliefs of Americans: A study of public opinion*. New Brunswick, N.J.: Rutgers University Press, 1967.

Gallup, G. H. *The Gallup poll: Public opinion 1935–1971* (Vol. 3: 1959–1971). New York: Random House, 1972.

Gallup Political Index, June 1964, p. 66.

Gallup Political Index, October 1968, p. 152.

Gallup Political Index, December 1970, p. 190.

Gallup Political Index, November 1971, p. 201.

Gallup Political Index, February 1977, p. 8.

Gans, H. J. Culture and class in the study of poverty: An approach to anti-poverty research. In D. P. Moynihan (ed.), *On understanding poverty: Perspectives from the social sciences*. New York: Basic Books, 1969.

Gans, H. J. *More equality*. New York: Pantheon Books, 1973.

Gladwin, T. *Poverty U.S.A.* Boston: Little, Brown, 1967.

Goodwin, L. *Do the poor want to work? A social-psychological study of work orientations*. Washington, D.C.: Brookings Institution, 1972. (a)

Goodwin, L. How suburban families view the work orientations of the welfare poor: Problems in social stratification and social policy. *Social Problems*, 1972, *19*, 337–348. (b)

Goodwin, L. Middle-class misperceptions of the high life aspirations and strong work ethic held by the welfare poor. *American Journal of Orthopsychiatry*, 1973, *43*, 554–564.

Gordon, D. M. *Theories of poverty and underemployment: Orthodox, radical, and dual labor market perspectives*. Lexington, Mass.: D. C. Heath, 1972.

Goudy, W. J. "Shoot them if they won't work": A study of socioeconomic status, economic aspirations, and attitudes toward poverty, the poor, and public dependence. Ph.D. dissertation, Purdue University, 1970. *Dissertation Abstracts International*, 1971, *31*, 5530A–5531A. (University Microfilm no. 71-9396,350)

Grimm, J. W., & Orten, J. D. Student attitudes toward the poor. *Social Work*, 1973, *18* (1), 94–100.

Gurin, P., Miller, A. H., & Gurin, G. Stratum identification and consciousness. *Social Psychology Quarterly*, 1980, *43*, 30–47.

Hamilton, D. L. A cognitive-attributional analysis of stereotyping. In L. Berkowitz (ed.), *Advances in experimental social psychology* (Vol. 12). New York: Academic Press, 1979.

Handler, J. F. *Reforming the poor: Welfare policy, federalism, and morality*. New York: Basic Books, 1972.

Harrington, M. *The other America: Poverty in the United States*. New York: Macmillan, 1962.

Harvey, D. G., & Slatin, G. T. The relationship between child's SES and teacher expectations: A test of the middle-class bias hypothesis. *Social Forces*, 1975, *54*, 140–159.

Harvey, M. R. Differential treatment of upper-income and lower-income children by the public schools. Ph.D. dissertation, University of Oregon, 1972. *Dissertation Abstracts International*, 1973, *33*, 4488B. (University Microfilm no. 73-7900)

Harvey, M. R. School treatment of low-income children: Education for passivity. *Urban Education*, 1980, *15*, 279–323.

Heider, F. *The psychology of interpersonal relations*. New York: Wiley, 1958.

Hoehn, A. J. A study of social status differentiation in the classroom behavior of 19 third grade teachers. *Journal of Social Psychology*, 1954, *39*, 269–292.

Hofstadter, R. *Social Darwinism in American thought* (rev. ed.). Boston: Beacon Press, 1955.

Huber, J., & Form, W. H. *Income and ideology: An analysis of the American political formula*. New York: Free Press, 1973.

Hyman, H. The value systems of different classes. In R. Bendix & S. M. Lipset (eds.), *Class, status, and power: A reader in social stratification.* Glencoe, Ill.: Free Press, 1953.

Inkeles, A. Industrial man: The relation of status to experience, perception, and value. *American Journal of Sociology,* 1960, *66,* 1–31.

Irelan, L. M., Moles, O. C., & O'Shea, R. Ethnicity, poverty, and selected attitudes: A test of the "Culture of Poverty" hypothesis. *Social Forces,* 1969, *47,* 405–413.

Jackman, M. R., & Senter, M. S. Images of social groups: Categorical or qualified? *Public Opinion Quarterly,* 1980, *44,* 341–361.

Jencks, C., Bartlett, S., Corcoran, M., Crouse, J., Eaglesfield, D., Jackson, G., McClelland, K., Mueser, P., Olneck, M., Schwartz, J., Ward, S., & Williams, J. *Who gets ahead?: The determinants of economic success in America.* New York: Basic Books, 1979.

Jensen, M., & Rosenfeld, L. B. Influence of mode of presentation, ethnicity, and social class on teachers' expectations of students. *Journal of Educational Psychology,* 1974, *66,* 540–547.

Johnson, N. J., & Sanday, P. R. Subcultural variations in an urban poor population. *American Anthropologist,* 1971, *73,* 128–143.

Jones, E. E. The rocky road from acts to dispositions. *American Psychologist,* 1979, *34,* 107–117.

Jones, E. E., & Nisbett, R. E. *The actor and the observer: Divergent perceptions of the causes of behavior.* Morristown, N.J.: General Learning Press, 1971.

Kaplan, H. R., & Tausky, C. Work and the welfare Cadillac: The function of and commitment to work among the hard-core unemployed. *Social Problems,* 1972, *19,* 469–483.

Kaplan, H. R., & Tausky, C. The meaning of work among the hard-core unemployed. *Pacific Sociological Review,* 1974, *17,* 185–198.

Kasen, J. H. Whither the self-made man? Comic culture and the crisis of legitimation in the United States. *Social Problems,* 1980, *28,* 131–148.

Katz, D., & Braly, K. Racial stereotypes of 100 college students. *Journal of Abnormal and Social Psychology,* 1933, *28,* 280–290.

Kerbo, H. R. The stigma of welfare and a passive poor. *Sociology and Social Research,* 1976, *60,* 173–187.

Kerckhoff, A. C. *Socialization and social class.* Englewood Cliffs, N.J.: Prentice-Hall, 1972.

Knupfer, G. Portrait of the underdog. *Public Opinion Quarterly,* 1947, *11,* 103–114.

Kornhauser, A. *Mental health of the industrial worker: A Detroit study.* New York: Wiley, 1965.

Kornhauser, R. The Warner approach to social stratification. In R. Bendix & S. M. Lipset (eds.), *Class, status, and power: A reader in social stratification.* Glencoe, Ill.: Free Press, 1953.

Kriesberg, L. *Mothers in poverty: A study of fatherless families.* Chicago: Aldine, 1970.

Kutner, N. G. The poor vs. the non-poor: An ethnic and metropolitan-nonmetropolitan comparison. *Sociological Quarterly,* 1975, *16,* 250–263.

LaFrance, M., & Cicchetti, C. Perceived responsibility and blame for economic success and failure: Social class and employment status comparisons. *Journal of Applied Social Psychology*, 1979, *9*, 466–475.

Lane, R. E. *Political ideology: Why the American common man believes what he does*. New York: Free Press, 1962.

Lauer, R. H. The middle class looks at poverty. *Urban and Social Change Review*, 1971, *5* (Fall), 8–10.

Leacock, E. B. *Teaching and learning in city schools: A comparative study*. New York: Basic Books, 1969.

Leacock, E. B. Introduction. In E. B. Leacock (ed.), *The culture of poverty: A critique*. New York: Simon & Schuster, 1971.

Leeds, A. The concept of the "Culture of Poverty": Conceptual, logical, and empirical problems with perspectives from Brazil and Peru. In E. B. Leacock (ed.), *The culture of poverty: A critique*. New York: Simon & Schuster, 1971.

Lerner, M. J. All the world loathes a loser. *Psychology Today*, June 1971, pp. 51–54, 66.

Lerner, M. J., & Miller, D. J. Just world research and the attribution process: Looking back and ahead. *Psychological Bulletin*, 1978, *85*, 1030–1051.

Lewis, M. *The culture of inequality*. Amherst: University of Massachusetts Press, 1978.

Lewis, O. *Five families: Mexican case studies in the culture of poverty*. New York: Basic Books, 1959.

Lewis, O. *La vida: A Puerto Rican family in the culture of poverty*. New York: Random House, 1966.

Lewis, O. The culture of poverty. In D. P. Moynihan (ed.), *On understanding poverty: Perspectives from the social sciences*. New York: Basic Books, 1969.

Liebow, E. *Tally's Corner: A study of Negro streetcorner men*. Boston: Little, Brown, 1967.

Lipset, S. M., & Bendix, R. *Social mobility in industrial society*. Berkeley: University of California Press, 1959.

Long, S., & Long, R. Teacher-candidates' poverty perceptions. *Journal of Negro Education*, 1974, *43*, 494–505.

Lundberg, M. J. *The incomplete adult: Social class constraints on personality development*. Westport, Conn.: Greenwood Press, 1974.

Macarov, D. *Incentives to work*. San Francisco: Jossey-Bass, 1970.

MacDonald, A. P., Jr. More on the Protestant Ethic. *Journal of Clinical and Consulting Psychology*, 1972, *39*, 116–122.

MacDonald, A. P., Jr. A time for introspection. *Professional Psychology*, 1973, *4*, 35–42.

MacDonald, A. P., Jr., & Majumder, R. K. Do the poor know how we see them?: Preliminary study. *Perceptual and Motor Skills*, 1972, *34*, 47–49.

Majumder, R. K., MacDonald, A. P., Jr., & Greever, K. B. A study of rehabilitation counselors: Locus of control and attitudes toward the poor. *Journal of Counseling Psychology*, 1977, *24*, 137–141.

Mandell, B. R. (ed.). *Welfare in America: Controlling the "dangerous classes."* Englewood Cliffs, N.J.: Prentice-Hall, 1975.

Marx, K., & Engels, F. *Manifesto of the Communist party*. Moscow: Progress Publishers, n.d.

Massey, G. Studying social class: The case of embourgeoisement and the culture of poverty. *Social Problems*, 1975, *22*, 595–608.

Matza, D. The disreputable poor. In R. Bendix & S. M. Lipset (eds.), *Class, status, and power: Social stratification in comparative perspective* (2nd ed.). New York: Free Press, 1966. (a)

Matza, D. Poverty and disrepute. In R. K. Merton & R. Nisbet (eds.), *Contemporary social problems* (2nd ed.). New York: Harcourt, Brace, & World, 1966. (b)

Matza, D. Poverty and proletariat. In R. K. Merton & R. Nisbet (eds.), *Contemporary social problems* (4th ed.). New York: Harcourt Brace Jovanovich, 1976.

McCauley, C., & Stitt, C. L. An individual and quantitative measure of stereotypes. *Journal of Personality and Social Psychology*, 1978, *36*, 929–940.

Miller, C. K., McLaughlin, J. A., Haddon, J., & Chansky, N. M. Socioeconomic class and teacher bias. *Psychological Reports*, 1968, *23* (pt. 1), 806.

Miller, H. L. Race vs. class in teachers' expectations. *Psychological Reports*, 1973, *32*, 105–106.

Miller, R. W., Zeller, F. A., & Blaine, H. R. *Implications of social class differences in beliefs concerning causes of unemployment*. Morgantown: Office of Research and Development, Appalachian Center, West Virginia University, 1968.

Miller, R. E. *Job change behavior in the rural income maintenance experiment*. Discussion Paper #555-79. Madison, Wis.: Institute for Research on Poverty, September, 1979.

Miller, W. B. Lower class culture as a generating milieu of gang delinquency. *Journal of Social Issues*, 1958, *14* (3), 5–19.

Mills, C. W. Review of W. Lloyd Warner and Paul S. Lunt, "The Social Life of a Modern Community." *American Sociological Review*, 1942, *7*, 263–271.

Mizruchi, E. H. *Success and opportunity: A study of anomie*. New York: Free Press, 1964.

Moffitt, R. A. The labor supply response in the Gary experiment. *Journal of Human Resources*, 1979, *14*, 477–487.

Moffitt, R. A. The negative income tax: Would it discourage work? *Monthly Labor Review*, 1981, *104*(4), 23–27.

More, D. M., & Suchner, R. W. Occupational situs, prestige, and stereotypes. *Sociology of Work and Occupations*, 1976, *3*, 169–186.

Morgan, J. N., Dickinson, K., Dickinson, J., Benus, J., & Duncan, G. *Five thousand American families—Patterns of economic progress* (Vol. 1). Ann Arbor: Institute for Social Research, University of Michigan, 1974.

Morris, M. Psychological and social correlates of economic egalitarianism. Ph.D. dissertation, Boston College, 1978. *Dissertation Abstracts International*, 1978, *39*, 3052B. (University Microfilm no. 7824556)

Moynihan, D. P. (ed.). *On understanding poverty: Perspectives from the social sciences*. New York: Basic Books, 1969.

Natraj, P. Stereotypes of four Hindu castes about each other. *Journal of Psychological Researches*, 1962, *6*, 132–141.

Ogren, E. H. Public opinions about public welfare. *Social Work*, 1973, *18*(1), 101–107.

Otto, L. B., & Haller, A. O. Evidence for a social psychological view of the status attainment process: Four studies compared. *Social Forces*, 1979, *57*, 887–914.

Perlman, J. E. *The myth of marginality: Urban poverty and politics in Rio de Janeiro*. Berkeley: University of California Press, 1976.

Pettigrew, T. F. Social psychology's potential contributions to an understanding of poverty. In V. T. Covello (ed.), *Poverty and public policy: An evaluation of social science research*. Cambridge, Mass.: Schenkman, 1980.

Piliavin, I., Masters, S., & Corbett, T. *Administration and organizational influences on AFDC case decision errors: An empirical analysis*. Discussion Paper #542-79. Madison, Wis.: Institute for Research on Poverty, August, 1979.

Piven, F. F., & Cloward, R. A. *Regulating the poor: The functions of public welfare*. New York: Pantheon Books, 1971.

President's Commission on Income Maintenance Programs. *Poverty amid plenty: The American paradox*. Washington, D.C.: U.S. Government Printing Office, 1969.

Rainwater, L. The problem of lower-class culture and poverty-war strategy. In D. P. Moynihan (ed.), *On understanding poverty: Perspectives from the social sciences*. New York: Basic Books, 1969.

Rainwater, L. Neutralizing the disinherited: Some psychological aspects of understanding the poor. In V. L. Allen (ed.), *Psychological factors in poverty*. Chicago: Markham, 1970.

Rainwater, L. *What money buys: Inequality and the social meanings of income*. New York: Basic Books, 1974.

Reasons for poverty. *Gallup Opinion Index*, July 1967, p. 17.

Rees, A. The labor-supply results of the experiment: A summary. In H. W. Watts & A. Rees (eds.), *The New Jersey income-maintenance experiment, Volume II: Labor-supply responses*. New York: Academic Press, 1977.

Rim, Y., & Aloni, R. Stereotypes according to ethnic origin, social class, and sex. *Acta Psychologica*, 1969, *31*, 312–325.

Rist, R. C. Student social class and teacher expectations: The self-fulfilling prophecy in ghetto education. *Harvard Educational Review*, 1970, *40*, 411–451.

Rist, R. C. *The urban school: A factory for failure*. Cambridge, Mass.: MIT Press, 1973.

Roach, J. L., & Gursslin, O. R. An evaluation of the concept "Culture of Poverty." *Social Forces*, 1967, *45*, 383–392.

Rodman, H. Middle-class misconceptions about lower-class families. In A. B. Shostak & W. Gomberg (eds.), *Blue-collar world: Studies of the American worker*. Englewood Cliffs, N.J.: Prentice-Hall, 1964.

Rodman, H. The lower-class value stretch. In L. A. Ferman, J. L. Kornbluh, & A. Huber (eds.), *Poverty in America: A book of readings*. Ann Arbor: University of Michigan Press, 1965.

Rodman, H. *Lower-class families: The culture of poverty in Negro Trinidad*. New York: Oxford University Press, 1971.

Rodman, H., & Voydanoff, P. Social class and parents' range of aspirations for their children. *Social Problems*, 1978, *25*, 333–344.

Rodman, H., Voydanoff, P., & Lovejoy, A. E. The range of aspirations: A new approach. *Social Problems*, 1974, *22*, 184–198.

Rokeach, M., & Parker, S. Values as indicators of poverty and race relations in America. *Annals of the American Academy of Political and Social Science*, 1970, *388* (March), 97–111.

Ross, L. The intuitive psychologist and his shortcomings: Distortions in the attribution process. In L. Berkowitz (ed.), *Advances in experimental social psychology* (Vol. 10). New York: Academic Press, 1977.

Rossi, P. H., & Blum, Z. D. Class, status, and poverty. In D. P. Moynihan (ed.), *On understanding poverty: Perspectives from the social sciences.* New York: Basic Books, 1969.

Rubin, Z., & Peplau, A. Belief in a just world and reactions to another's lot: A study of participants in the national draft lottery. *Journal of Social Issues*, 1973, *29* (4), 73–93.

Ryan, W. *Blaming the victim* (rev. ed.). New York: Vintage Books, 1976.

Safa, H. I. The poor are like everyone else, Oscar. *Psychology Today*, September, 1970, pp. 26–32.

Schiller, B. R. *The economics of poverty and discrimination* (2nd ed.). Englewood Cliffs, N.J.: Prentice-Hall, 1976.

Schiltz, M. E. *Public attitudes toward social security 1935–1965*. Washington, D.C.: U.S. Government Printing Office, 1970.

Schlozman, K. L., & Verba, S. *Injury to insult: Unemployment, class, and political response.* Cambridge, Mass.: Harvard University Press, 1979.

Schwartz, A. J. A further look at "Culture of Poverty": Ten Caracas barrios. *Sociology and Social Research*, 1975, *59*, 362–386.

Schwarzwald, J., Shoham, M., Waysman, M., & Sterner, I. Israeli teachers' outlook on the necessity and feasibility of teaching values to advantaged and disadvantaged children. *Journal of Psychology*, 1979, *101*, 3–9.

Sewell, W. H., & Hauser, R. M. *Education, occupation, and earnings: Achievement in the early career.* New York: Academic Press, 1975.

Sinha, G. S., & Sinha, R. C. Exploration in caste stereotypes. *Social Forces*, 1967, *46*, 42–47.

Smedley, J. W., & Bayton, J. A. Evaluative race-class stereotypes by race and perceived class of subjects. *Journal of Personality and Social Psychology*, 1978, *36*, 530–535.

Speizman, M. D. Poverty, pauperism, and their causes: Some charity organization views. *Social Casework*, 1965, *46*, 142–149.

Spilerman, S., & Elesh, D. Alternative conceptions of poverty and their implications for income maintenance. *Social Problems*, 1971, *18*, 358–373.

Stack, C. B. *All our kin: Strategies for survival in a black community.* New York: Harper & Row, 1974.

Stack, S. Ideological beliefs on the American distribution of opportunity, power, and rewards. *Sociological Focus*, 1978, *11*, 221–233.

Stanford Research Institute and Mathematica Policy Research. The Seattle-Denver income maintenance experiment: Midexperimental labor supply results and a generalization to the national population. In T. D. Cook, M. L. Del Rosario, K. M. Hennigan, M. M. Mark, & W. M. K. Trochim (eds.), *Evaluation studies review annual* (Vol. 3). Beverly Hills, Calif.: Sage, 1978.

Stern, A. J., & Searing, D. D. The stratification beliefs of English and American adolescents. *British Journal of Political Science*, 1976, *6*, 177–201.

Thielbar, G., & Feldman, S. D. Occupational stereotypes and prestige. *Social Forces*, 1969, *48*, 64–72.

Thio, A. Toward a fuller view of the American success ideology. *Pacific Sociological Review*, 1972, *15*, 381–393.

Thurow, L. C. *Generating inequality: Mechanisms of distribution in the U.S. economy.* New York: Basic Books, 1975.

U.S. Bureau of the Census. *Characteristics of the population below the poverty level: 1978.* Current Population Reports, series P-60, no. 124. Washington, D.C.:

U.S. Government Printing Office, 1980.

U.S. Commission on Civil Rights. *Window dressing on the set: Women and minorities in television.* Washington, D.C.: U.S. Government Printing Office, 1977.

Valentine, B. *Hustling and other hard work: Life styles in the ghetto.* New York: Free Press, 1978.

Valentine, C. A. *Culture and poverty: Critique and counter-proposals.* Chicago: University of Chicago Press, 1968.

Van Til, S. B. Work and the culture of poverty: The labor force activity of poor men. Ph.D. dissertation, Bryn Mawr College, 1973. *Dissertation Abstracts International,* 1974, *34,* 6776A–6777A. (University Microfilm no. 74-8962,297)

Villemez, W. J. Ability vs. effort: Ideological correlates of occupational grading. *Social Forces,* 1974, *53,* 45–52.

Wachtel, H. M. Looking at poverty from radical, conservative, and liberal perspectives. In B. R. Mandell (ed.), *Welfare in America: Controlling the "dangerous classes."* Englewood Cliffs, N.J.: Prentice-Hall, 1975.

Warner, W. L., & Lunt, P. S. *The social life of a modern community.* New Haven: Yale University Press, 1941.

Warner, W. L., Meeker, M., & Eells, K. *Social class in America* (rev. ed.). New York: Harper & Row, 1960.

Waxman, C. I. *The stigma of poverty: A critique of poverty theories and policies.* New York: Pergamon Press, 1977.

Welfare allotment barely pays recipients' living expenses. *New Haven Register,* January 21, 1981, p. 15.

West, J. *Plainville, U.S.A.* New York: Columbia University Press, 1945.

Williams, R. M., Jr. *American society: A sociological interpretation* (3rd ed.). New York: Alfred A. Knopf, 1970.

Williamson, J. B. Beliefs about the motivation of the poor and attitudes toward poverty policy. *Social Problems,* 1974, *21,* 634–648. (a)

Williamson, J. B. Beliefs about the welfare poor. *Sociology and Social Research,* 1974, *58,* 163–175. (b)

Williamson, J. B. The stigma of public dependency: A comparison of alternative forms of public aid to the poor. *Social Problems,* 1974, *22,* 213–228. (c)

Williamson, J. B. *Strategies against poverty in America.* New York: Wiley, 1975.

Williamson, J. B. Beliefs about the rich, the poor, and the taxes they pay. *American Journal of Economics and Sociology,* 1976, *35,* 9–29.

Williamson, J. B., Evans, L. J., & Munley, A. *Social problems: The contemporary debates* (2nd ed.). Boston: Little, Brown, 1981.

Wohl, R. R. The "Rags to Riches Story": An episode of secular idealism. In R. Bendix & S. M. Lipset (eds.), *Class, status, and power: Social stratification in comparative perspective* (2nd ed.). New York: Free Press, 1966.

Wohlenberg, E. H. A regional approach to public attitudes and public assistance. *Social Service Review,* 1976, *50,* 491–505.

Wooster, J. H. Attitudes toward poverty, social services, and adherence to the Protestant Ethic in a rural Colorado community. Ph.D. dissertation, University of Northern Colorado, 1972. *Dissertation Abstracts International,* 1972, *33,* 1227A–1228A. (University Microfilm no. 72-23, 827,138)

Wright, S. Social psychological characteristics and labor-force response of male heads. In H. W. Watts & A. Rees (eds.), *The New Jersey income-maintenance experiment, Volume II: Labor-supply responses.* New York: Academic Press, 1977.

Young, P. A., & Cochrane, R. Success values and social class: A test of the value stretch hypothesis in Britain. *International Journal of Comparative Sociology*, 1977, *18*, 280–293.

ADDITIONAL READINGS

Banfield, E. C. *The unheavenly city revisited.* Boston: Little, Brown, 1974.
A revision of his controversial 1970 work in which he portrayed the American lower class as being psychologically incapable of, and largely uninterested in, significant upward mobility. This argument remains conspicuous in the revision.

Coleman, R. P., Rainwater, L., & McClelland, K. A. *Social standing in America: New dimensions of class.* New York: Basic Books, 1978.
A wide-ranging investigation of social-class imagery among Boston and Kansas City residents. Heavily influenced by the Warner approach to stratification, but methodologically more sophisticated.

Eames, E., & Goode, J. G. *Urban poverty in a cross-cultural context.* New York: Free Press, 1973.
An ambitious attempt to examine poverty from a historical and cross-cultural perspective. Of particular interest is the authors' extensive discussion of the historical processes responsible for transforming poverty into a stigmatized condition.

Feagin, J. R. *Subordinating the poor: Welfare and American beliefs.* Englewood Cliffs, N.J.: Prentice-Hall, 1975.
A frequently cited study of people's explanations of poverty and their implications for social policy. Current issues are put in historical context.

Goodwin, L. *Do the poor want to work? A social-psychological study of work orientations.* Washington, D.C.: Brookings Institution, 1972.
The answer suggested by this well-designed study of welfare recipients is an emphatic "yes."

Handler, J. F. *Reforming the poor: Welfare policy, federalism, and morality.* New York: Basic Books, 1972.
A well-reasoned analysis of the attributions concerning poverty and the poor inherent in America's welfare system.

Lewis, M. *The culture of inequality.* Amherst: University of Massachusetts Press, 1978.
A provocative attempt to account for the persistence of negative stereotyping of the poor in America. Pessimistic and powerful.

Lewis, O. The culture of poverty. In D. P. Moynihan (ed.), *On understanding poverty: Perspectives from the social sciences*. New York: Basic Books, 1969.
A detailed presentation of the theoretical framework underlying the "culture of poverty" thesis.

Matza, D. The disreputable poor. In R. Bendix & S. M. Lipset (eds.), *Class, status, and power: Social stratification in comparative perspective* (2nd ed.). New York: Free Press, 1966.
A broad-gauged analysis of the societal processes leading to the poor being stigmatized. The various subgroups that form the disreputable poor are delineated.

Ryan, W. *Blaming the victim* (rev. ed.). New York: Vintage Books, 1976.
The title of this book has become part of the jargon of social science. Ryan views the causes of poverty and related problems as basically environmental, and he severely criticizes the type of research that Banfield accepts unquestioningly. Reading Ryan and Banfield together is a fascinating exercise.

Spilerman, S., & Elesh, D. Alternative conceptions of poverty and their implications for income maintenance. *Social Problems*, 1971, *18*, 358–373.
A sophisticated comparison of cultural and situational explanations of poverty and their policy implications. The authors address important issues often overlooked in lengthier and better-known discussions. A definitive article.

10

STEREOTYPING:
FURTHER PERSPECTIVES
AND CONCLUSIONS

Arthur G. Miller

In this final chapter a number of additional matters bearing on stereotyping will be considered. First, we will examine the stereotypes about the physically disabled, and the role of stereotypes in group decisions. We will then consider the importance of stereotypes in relation to dehumanization and aggression, and the role of stereotypes in biasing judgments of responsibility. The chapter will conclude with a reconsideration of some basic themes presented in this book and some thoughts on issues that remain for future research.

STEREOTYPES ABOUT THE DISABLED

In an essay in the *New York Times*, Jose Fuentes, a disabled person, issued "a rallying cry for the physically disabled" (1979). His essay is about stereotypes, about the images that people have of the disabled. Acknowledging advances in environmental design for the disabled (such as ramps, elevators, water fountains, rest-room facilities), Fuentes is nevertheless critical. He asks, "But what of attitudes? What of opportunity? What laws can guarantee fairness in people's minds?" He describes handicapping as originating in the eye of the beholder:

> Unlike the popularized images of disabled people portrayed on television, we are not Ironsides or Longstreets. We are normal. We experience jubilation and depression, anxiety and anticipation . . . when our self-worth is challenged, we doubt. When our ability is questioned, we question. And like a self-fulfilling prophecy, we assume the symptoms of being "handicapped." I say unequivocally and without hesitation, that only society can handicap. (p. 25)

Fuentes's assertion that "we are normal," however, may be challenged. No analysis of the disabled and the difficulties they endure can proceed without candidly acknowledging their physical limitations—not necessarily in terms of abilities or capacities (where limitations *are* often perceived or expected rather than proved), but in terms of the novel, often unsettling reactions the disabled evoke in the nondisabled. In this sense the disabled are *not* normal. The wheelchair, the white cane, a missing limb, a burn scar— these are unusual, threatening images for many of us.

Physical disabilities and certain illnesses thus create ideal preconditions for stereotyping. We are forced to think about such misfortunes because we are likely to be affected by them at some time, because they may strike a relative or friend, or because we may currently be a victim. We wonder, perhaps with trepidation, what it is like to have such a problem, why someone might fall victim to such tragedy, and how we might be able to cope with—or better, avoid—such a fate. We do not have to invent answers to these questions, however, for our culture provides us with a wealth of stereotypes about maladies and impairments of all kinds. For most people the answers to questions about disabilities are not obtained through social interaction with the disabled themselves. Thus, the most authoritative sources of information are often the least likely to be consulted, and this is a fundamental component of the problem.

A number of theorists have drawn parallels between the disabled and other, more traditionally defined minority groups (Gliedman & Roth, 1980; Goffman, 1963; Wright, 1960). There are many similarities in terms of lowered social status and self-esteem. The disabled are the classic outgroup, often physically isolated from the nondisabled. Many people have never known or even encountered a seriously disabled individual. This lack of familiarity is not simply a function of the rarity of the diseases or conditions under discussion, but represents a strategy for avoiding the disabled—in our thoughts as well as in our interactions. One form of this avoidance is cognitive—we may blame innocent sufferers for their own victimization (Lerner & Miller, 1978; Ryan, 1976). It is consoling (to us) if we can somehow justify or make sense out of seemingly undeserved misery. Stereotyping, proceeding at a comfortable distance from the target, is one kind of effort to achieve an understanding about the disabled.

In reviewing Joseph Lash's *Helen and Teacher: The Story of Helen Keller and Ann Sullivan Macy*, Bruno Bettelheim (1980) speaks to our beliefs about the disabled. He addresses the illusion (or delusion) that most people had of Helen Keller. In contrast with the courage and cheerfulness that most people saw in Helen, the real Helen Keller may have been far less joyous. Bettelheim argues that people needed to perceive Helen through rose-colored glasses:

> We would like to believe that it is possible to transcend completely the
> most severe physical handicaps—even complete blindness and deafness

aggravated by partial mutism—when there is a will and a devoted helper. (p. 85)

Bettelheim notes the paradox—typical of reactions to the stigmatized—of everyone adoring Helen Keller and yet avoiding her. Helen, on her own part, helped to sustain the false though comforting image that others held about her:

> It is our wish to delude ourselves that those who are severely handicapped are not excluded from living, that we therefore do not owe them a compassion much deeper than words, which would express itself in deeds. It was Ann's wish that Helen should have a full life through her, and she tried to fulfill this wish at the expense of her own life. It gave Helen the strength to pretend to have a full life of her own. This pretense freed us of our obligation to be our handicapped brother's keeper. . . . Her public performances, her clever repartee, her sense of humor— all permitted us to forget how terribly she suffered. (p. 89)

Thus, the public loved Helen Keller, but for the wrong reasons—"for making it possible for us to fool ourselves that those who are so terribly handicapped are not really suffering deeply every moment of their lives" (p. 90). Bettelheim criticizes this deception because it adds the despair of loneliness to the very real problems of the disabled, and provides the nondisabled with a distorted conception of what it is like to be disabled.

Perhaps the truth, as Bettelheim construes it, is a pill that not all could or would wish to swallow. He seems to minimize the emotionally comforting outcomes of the beliefs that are so divorced from the realities of disability. There may be unsuspected virtues in pretenses of normality, both for the observer and for the victim. Helen Keller's ability to cope with her disabilities was probably extraordinary, yet she became, for millions, the prototype of what a severely disabled person should be like. Bettelheim, in distinguishing between public image and private life, reminds us of the costs involved in holding stereotypes about the disabled.

The paradox of avoidance coupled with admiration emphasizes that we do care about the disabled. We feel sorry for them, donate to charities on their behalf, volunteer social services for them, and may devote careers—in teaching, research, health sciences—to understanding and helping them. For most of us, there is ambivalence in our reactions to the disabled—an impulse to flee and, simultaneously, feelings of compassion. Katz and Glass (1979) have formulated a theory that focuses upon people's reactions to stigmatized others. The basic premise is that the initial reaction of ambivalence produces a state of attitudinal conflict, which is resolved by reacting with unusual intensity or extremity toward stigmatized persons.

The ambivalence-response amplification theory suggests that people may react in either a more unfavorable or a more favorable manner to a stigmatized other. Katz, Glass, and Cohen (1973), for example, induced research subjects to deliver mild or painful shocks to a black or white partner (experimenter confederate). In comparison with preshock ratings of the partner's personality, there was more postshock denigration or negative personality ratings when the black rather than white partner received painful shocks. Katz, Glass, Lucido, and Farber (1977) obtained similar results when the partner was seated in a wheelchair (versus an apparently nondisabled partner). The general tendency to blame the victim or rationalize the shocks by perceiving deservingness (Lerner, 1970) in the partner seems to be exaggerated when the victim is a member of a stigmatized group.

The phenomenon also can work in the opposite direction. Katz, Glass, Lucido, and Farber (1979) induced subjects to voice rather neutral or highly critical remarks to a black or white partner about his personality. When later given the opportunity to help the partner by performing a tedious task, subjects who had insulted the black partner gave the greatest amount of aid. Katz et al. (1979) obtained similar, though not as powerful, findings with respect to a disabled partner.

Related to the ambivalence that Katz discusses is the distinction between public and private reactions to the stigmatized. Although one might wish to be consistent in one's thoughts and deeds toward others, there is evidence that we may think one way and act in another toward the disabled. Norms of politeness and etiquette stipulate that we be courteous toward the stigmatized, that we smile at them, perhaps consciously avoid staring at them—in short, anything that we think will make them more comfortable. Inwardly, however, we experience tension, anxiety, perhaps revulsion. This complexity of responses was illustrated in an experiment by Sigall and Page (1971).

Sigall and Page confronted female subjects with an obnoxious-acting male (experimenter confederate) who was presented as stigmatized (massive leg brace) or normal. When a phone in the waiting room rang, the confederate was extremely rude to the caller, who, it appeared, had dialed a wrong number. The experimenter then came into the waiting room, acting unaware of the phone call, and brought the subject and confederate into the experiment itself. After a number of diversionary judgments, the crucial phase occurred, in which the subjects were asked to rate each other's personality. In one condition a rating scale was used in which the partner was rated on such traits as "obnoxious," "pleasant," and "pushy." In another, subjects were attached to an alleged monitor of muscle activity (EMG) that was described as an infallible measure of true attitudes (the bogus pipeline; Jones & Sigall, 1971). In this latter condition subjects were asked to predict the ratings that the EMG would indicate regarding their opinions about their partner.

The results bear on the private-public distinction. Responses to the rating scale were on the positive side of a −3 to +3 scale. In the EMG condition ratings were negative. Subjects in the EMG condition believed that the experimenter would know their "true" opinions, and thus they predicted negative readouts—what Sigall and Page argued was more likely their true attitude toward the partner. These differences, bearing on the method of obtaining personality impressions used in the two conditions, were similar for both the normal and (apparently) stigmatized partner, although there was a trend for the stigmatized confederate to be more positively evaluated in the rating scale condition than was the nonstigmatized partner. Carver, Glass, and Katz (1978) also found a handicapped person to be more favorably evaluated than either a normal partner or a black partner. This was true under conditions of standard rating-scale judgments or the EMG (bogus pipeline) procedure. Ratings under EMG conditions for the black target were particularly negative, although under standard rating-scale procedures, ratings of the black target were as high as for the handicapped target person.

The results of these experiments suggest that stigmatized persons evoke diverse images in many people. There is strain in interacting with the stigmatized, partly because of features inherent in the disability per se, but also because of psychological adjustments constructed to cope with the novelty or threat expected to occur in the interaction. The awkwardness, embarrassment, and guilt that accompany our involvement with the disabled are potent stimulants to the activation of stereotypes, in that stereotypes represent strategies for reducing uncertainty and providing a measure of predictability or subjectively experienced control. This gain in apparent understanding may, however, work to the detriment of the target and undermine the viability of a genuine, developing relationship between nondisabled and disabled persons. The barriers to such authentic interaction have been described by the sociologist Robert Scott, who has conducted important research on one of the most dreaded of disabilities—blindness.

Scott (1969) conducted extensive interviews with various individuals involved in blindness—the blind, workers for the blind, administrators of agencies for the blind, clients of such agencies, and those not being treated in such agencies. His major argument is that those without sight learn to become blind, defining themselves in ways that extend far beyond the essential limitations of being unable to see. Who are the teachers for the prospective blind individual? Scott asserts that they are those sighted persons, and other blind persons as well, who hold images and theories about blind people and behave in accord with them. Unless the nature of these beliefs is made explicit—why they are held, who holds them, their many erroneous features—the debilitating aspects of social relations between the blind and nonblind will persist.

What are the stereotypes associated with blindness? Scott describes the imagery that, he argues, is consistently portrayed in the media, literature, and even in charity campaigns:

> This world, which is believed to be less gross and materialistic than our own, is said to be infused with a spirituality that gives its inhabitants a

peculiar purity and innocence of mind . . . this world is thought to be
filled with melancholy. . . . Such gloom is said to be cast upon the blind
because of their need to settle some great inner conflict. The blind are
assumed to be frustrated. . . . They are thought to be helpless, and their
abilities are questioned at every turn. Helplessness, dependency, melancholy, docility, gravity of inner thought, aestheticism—these are the
things commonsense views tell us to expect of the blind. (p. 4)

The impact of these stereotypes is heightened by the constancy of the
affliction. Every social context seems potentially disrupted—occupational,
recreational, sexual, and so on. Some sightless persons accept the stereotypes and become docile, grateful, and helpless. Others reject them. All must
react to the likely presence of the stereotypes in others. The blind person
may often be placed in a "no-win" situation:

Several blind people have told me that when they use public transporta-
tion, fellow passengers will occasionally put money into their hands.
When this occurs, a blind man cannot very well give a public lecture on
the truth about blindness; in fact, to do anything but acquiesce and
accept the gift will leave him open to charges of ingratitude and
bitterness. (p. 23)

Some blind individuals—for example, beggars—will actually cultivate the
acquiescent facade for profit, in effect charging the sighted for holding
stereotypes about the blind person's helplessness and lack of occupational
potential.

On the basis of his interviews, Scott notes that the blind are a highly
diverse group. In the minds of observers, however, they are homogeneous. A
substantial proportion of people termed blind actually have reduced but
useful vision, yet these individuals often acquire the self-perceptions and
behaviors found in totally blind people. To most people the world is divided
into the sighted and the sightless—an imprecise categorization that is,
unfortunately, accepted by many partially sighted persons.

There are, of course, genuine constraints in the interaction between
blind and sighted persons. Noting how simple it would be to invite a sighted
person into one's office for coffee, Scott describes the same interaction but
with a blind guest:

When he enters my office, I find I cannot simply invite him to take a seat
but must conduct him to it. As I approach him, I realize that I do not
know how to direct him easily, and he does not know if I can do so
either. Consequently we share an awkward moment as I try to lead him
to a chair and back him into it. He in turn tries to accept my assistance
gracefully while trying not to be impaled by the arms of the chair. After
he is seated, I offer him coffee. When it arrives, I realize that he may
want cream and sugar. It is unclear if he can manage this himself. If he
cannot, and he asks me to do it for him, I may place the coffee in front of

him only to find that he knocks it over when reaching for it. When lighting a cigarette, he may put a match to it yet fail to ignite it. If he continues to puff away, do I tell him or let him discover it for himself? . . . from its inception to its conclusion, the interaction is filled with uncertainty, awkwardness, and ambiguity, making such meetings frustrating, embarrassing, and tense. (pp. 28–29)

It is, of course, difficult to know whether the difficulties in such an encounter are actually intrinsic to it, or whether they reflect the fulfillment of expectations and hypotheses that are held "in waiting." As Snyder (1981b) has shown, there are powerful cognitive biases operating so as to confirm one's hypotheses or beliefs about social reality; thus, the distinction between anticipation and social reality may be a false one. Note that this analysis applies not only to the sighted but also to the blind, who may have an analogous set of expectations.

There are, then, very real interactional problems in social interchange between sighted and sightless persons. The blind person often presents aversive or disruptive cues to the sighted, such as turning the head in order to follow the conversation by careful listening—an action that could suggest to the naive person that the blind person is not paying attention. The blind person's eyes—their color, position, movements—may be aversive, as is the smile expression of the blind person, a common feature that may convey the impression that he or she is retarded. These gestures or cues derive in many instances from the blind person's failure to obtain visual feedback from his or her own body movements. The blind person is thus unaware of the cues he or she emits. Certainly they cannot be experienced directly, and for obvious reasons the blind are not likely to be told about them.

The sighted person, in turn, cannot use his or her diverse repertoire of nonverbal cues when interacting with a blind person. Everything has to be verbalized, at least among people who are relatively unacquainted. This, in itself, is atypical, and contributes to the ambiguity or hesitancy in the encounter. There are, then, special communication problems that are justifiable causes for apprehension in both parties. As Scott notes, however, such problems are rarely given their proper causal role. The sighted person is likely to attribute to the blind person a host of dispositions that seem to explain the awkwardness experienced in their encounter. The blind person, in turn, assumes that the sighted person's tense or unusual behaviors are caused by stereotypes and negative attitudes. (Further evidence bearing on this point is found in Kleck & Strenta, 1980). Both persons are, to a degree, in error and are operating in a closed system that perpetuates rather than resolves the errors.

Scott also speaks to the social dependency of the blind person that disrupts norms of equity or social exchange. The blind feel unable to repay the sighted helper—the sighted helper also resents the "charity" label cast upon his or her behavior toward the blind. The striking success of certain blind celebrities—Stevie Wonder, Ray Charles, George Shearing, Jose Feliciano—is of little consolation. As Scott contends, people with these special talents

> . . . can exchange prestige or money for the favors they must accept in order to function in daily life. They are unusual. A majority of blind people are elderly and poor, two traits that also have very low potential attractiveness to others. (p. 37)

Scott, rather unexpectedly, blames agencies for the blind for contributing to certain stereotypes about blind people. For a complex of historical and ideological reasons, agencies tend to regard blindness as extremely serious and incapacitating, and view their role as promoting in blind people the "proper" conception of blindness. Agencies have considerable leverage in influencing the attitudes and behaviors of their clients. Society is content to relegate treatment of the blind to the agencies. The agencies are isolated and powerful, taking on features of asylums (Goffman, 1961). Anything done in their behalf assumes, for the uninformed, an unquestioned nobleness of purpose and scientific validity. In fact, Scott contends, many of their activities are more mundane, designed to promote fund raising in a highly competitive interagency market. The agencies are thus motivated to exploit stereotypes about the blind for their emotional impact on potential donors and contributors. Scott's analysis is similar here to some issues raised by Farina in Chapter 7 of this volume concerning attitudes of mental health professionals toward their clients.

The least expected of all sources becomes a determinant—a major one—of the mythology of blindness:

> These campaigns exploit a number of cultural stereotypes in our society concerning blindness, youth, work, and hope. The agencies project an image of blind persons as either educable children or young, employable adults who can be helped to overcome a serious handicap and become materially productive. These appeals leave the unmistakable but erroneous impression that most blind people are young, educable, and employable. This view of the problem is highly acceptable to the public, since it masks distasteful truths about the real nature of the problem. (p. 97)

Scott argues that the vast majority of the blind population are multiply handicapped, unemployable, untrainable, and uneducable. In this sense the agencies present a more favorable or optimistic perspective on blindness than is warranted.

Scott elaborates on his critique of agencies, in particular the nature of their employees and the pressures to promote the values and ideologies of the agencies they serve. He contends that most treatment philosophies create undesirable definitions of self among countless blind clients. Because of historical factors, demographic changes among the blind population, and political/economic factors in agency funding, the system has not served its citizens, be they sighted or blind, well. He remains optimistic, however, that evaluation research will "re-examine and critically evaluate the scientific validity of blindness workers' assumptions about blindness and the blind" (p. 121).

Scott's analysis is instructive because it recognizes the diversity of influential factors. His description of communication difficulties and dependency aspects of interactions between blind and sighted persons is informative. He documents reasons why people develop stereotypic beliefs about the blind, and how the blind are susceptible to the debilitating influence of such perceptions. He views the blind as a diverse group who react in highly varied ways to their predicament, and who may contribute to the stereotypes about themselves by interpreting behaviors of sighted persons as reflecting their beliefs rather than an adjustment to a difficult situation.

STEREOTYPES OF THE OUTGROUP IN GROUP DECISIONS

Perhaps the majority of illustrations in this text have implied that stereotyping involves the cognitive and behavioral activities of individuals, rather than groups. In a limited sense, of course, this is true, but it would be a serious oversight to neglect those circumstances in which people quite literally share in the operation of stereotypes. This is seen in group decision contexts, such as juries, clinical case conferences, parole boards, and child adoption agencies—in short, in any setting where decisions are formally in the hands of more than one person, and where the decision is reached in the process of group discussion. It is also symptomatic of intergroup conflict (see Chapter 3 of this volume). Irving Janis, in his influential book *Victims of Groupthink* (1972), has described a number of celebrated decisions, primarily in foreign and military policy, that turned out to be disastrous and were characterized by a number of common features of group dynamics.

Janis's focus is upon such events as the landing at the Bay of Pigs, the decision to enter North Korea, and the escalation of the U.S. involvement in Vietnam. These decisions, and many others, were made by the "brightest and the best," high officials and experts from the military, academe, foreign affairs, and other fields. One might have expected the ultimate in critical planning, checks and counterchecks, and efficient information search and processing. What appears to have occurred in these decisions was something far different.

Janis centers on the issue of group cohesiveness and the manner in which the preservation of high morale interferes with effective group decisions. Groups seem to be controlled by an implicit or hidden agenda: the maintenance of high self-esteem and the conviction that "we are right."

Conducive to these values are powerful pressures of conformity that suppress the expression of individual points of view likely to be unpopular with the group leader or the majority. Because the issues under consideration may themselves be stressful—for example, whether to invade a foreign country or to release a new, potentially dangerous drug—group members are inclined to avoid the additional burdens of argumentation or the voicing of persistent doubts. Janis emphasizes three factors: cohesiveness, the positive attraction for one's own group members; consensus, the positive feeling generated by solidarity or unanimity; and insulation, the need to prevent destructive elements of dissident opinion, counterevidence, or bickering.

Stereotyping is given preeminence in Janis's analysis. Two of the eight symptoms of groupthink (the name for the general syndrome under discussion) explicitly refer to stereotyping. One points to "stereotyped views of enemy leaders as too evil to warrant genuine attempts to negotiate, or as too weak and stupid to counter whatever risky attempts are made to defeat their purposes." The second, referring to the consensus factor, features "direct pressure on any member who expresses strong arguments against any of the group's stereotypes, illusions, or commitments" (p. 198). In line with the concept of ethnocentrism discussed in Chapters 1 and 3 of this volume, Janis notes the pervasive "we are good and strong—they are stupid and weak" polarization that permeates group policy discussions. For example, in the Bay of Pigs fiasco, the fact that the invasion force consisted of 1,400 Cuban exiles and that Castro had a military force of 200,000 was somehow minimized:

> Castro was regarded as a weak "hysteric" leader whose army was ready to defect; he was considered so stupid that although warned by air strikes, he would do nothing to neutralize the Cuban underground. This is a stunning example of the classical stereotype of the enemy as weak and ineffectual. (p. 38)

Throughout his book Janis expresses amazement that such "low level" cognition could dominate the deliberations of President Kennedy's high-level policy board members—in the Bay of Pigs case, figures such as Robert Kennedy, McGeorge Bundy, Robert McNamara, Dean Rusk, Douglas Dillon, and others.

Janis gives particular emphasis to the consensus factor, specifically a kind of shared illusion of unanimity. For example, according to Arthur Schlesinger, Jr. (a member of the Kennedy administration), meetings took place in an atmosphere of assumed consensus. There was clear indication that group members personally endorsed divergent views, yet these were fused in White House group meetings, resulting in a highly consequential assumption that "silence gives consent" (p. 39). In attributional terms (see Chapter 2 of this volume), this kind of consensus among observers is often extremely compelling "proof" that the entity or target is, in fact, as described—that is, there must be something about that person or group that is evoking the same kind of impression in diverse observers.

In addition, there is evidence that unless otherwise informed, people have a strong tendency to think that others share their opinions and engage in behaviors similar to their own—that is, people think that their own beliefs represent the consensus (Ross, Greene, & House, 1977).

Janis's discussion clearly emphasizes the falseness of stereotypes. Groupthink is powerful and destructive because it gives an aura of legitimacy to stereotypes, compounding the errors of stereotypes and linking them to behavioral consequences. In the Korean War, for example, Truman's policy board members relied upon stereotypes of the Chinese as docile puppets of Moscow, as weak and under the general stereotype "communistic." This was an erroneous perception, and led to a poor decision:

> McClellan points out that all previous experience forewarned that Red China would not tolerate the presence of hostile U.S. forces in its backyard, but the pervasive ideological tendency shared by Acheson and his critics alike was to belittle China's position in the world. (p. 62)

Thus, a defective conception of China led to an overly risky course of military action based on the erroneous presumption that China would not intervene on behalf of its neighboring ally, North Korea.

Decisions bearing upon U.S. involvement in Vietnam received extensive analysis, in particular the operation of groupthink in Lyndon Johnson's "Tuesday lunch group" (Clark Clifford, Robert McNamara, Walt Rostow, Dean Rusk, Richard Helms, and others). Quoting from historian James Thompson, who was a member of McGeorge Bundy's staff in the White House, Janis notes the role of stereotypes in Vietnam policy:

> Thompson was shocked to realize the extent to which crudely propagandistic conceptions entered the group's plans and policy statements. . . . As for the Vietcong and the North Vietnamese, the dominant stereotypes made these "Communist enemies" into the embodiment of evil and thus legitimized the destruction of countless human lives and the burning of villages. (pp. 115–116)

Such perceptions were not initially held by all members of the group. With time and a developing esprit—perhaps facilitated by the growing counterforce of public opinion—there grew an increasing homogenization of perception. We see, in the above quotation, that stereotypes may lower restraints against committing harmful acts upon the target. This may be the single most significant consequence of stereotypes, and will be considered in more detail later in this chapter.

What about group decisions that turned out successfully? Not surprisingly, Janis notes the absence of the domination of stereotyping. A case in point is the Cuban missile crisis:

> Stereotypes of the enemy as evil, weak, and stupid—which were so much in evidence during the White House discussions of the Bay of Pigs decision—seldom, if ever, were voiced after the bitter anger of the opening session of the Executive Committee. Most members viewed their opposite numbers in the Kremlin as no less rational than themselves and assumed that their choice of action would be selected from a broad spectrum, ranging from conciliatory to belligerent, depending largely on the words and actions of the United States government. (p. 159)

The group thus did not settle for stereotypes as a major explanation of why the Russians had placed missiles on Cuban soil. A major effort was made to allow the Soviets to withdraw from Cuba and yet save face, a kind of subtlety that would have been unlikely had the group discussion been dominated by stereotypes.

In summary, Janis's conception of groupthink provides an intriguing "real world" illustration of stereotypes "in action." The central variable is the degree to which social consensus becomes dominant, a factor basic to both stereotyping and group dynamics. A potential antidote for groupthink is the concerted restructuring of group decisions so as to defuse consensus or, at least, the presumption of consensus. It would obviously be unwarranted to rule out the value of popular sentiment and group cohesion. What must be avoided, however, is the stifling of diverse opinions simply for the sake of maintaining an illusion of conviction and ingroup solidarity.

The most novel aspect of Janis's work is that he documents the importance of stereotyping and associated cognitive processes—such as self-serving perceptions and conflict avoidance—where we might least expect to find them. Indeed, we have seen in other settings that professionals—physicians, social-service workers, mental health personnel—are by no means immune to the operation of stereotypes that characterize people in general. Janis also challenges the intuitively compelling idea that the deficiencies involved in stereotyped thinking are automatically corrected by the public airing of such perceptions. Indeed, stereotypes may become even more potent in group contexts.

One should comment, at least, upon the fact that Janis's approach was to rely upon various historical clues—observer accounts of private conversations, participant memoirs, and such—that are susceptible to various biases and distortions. Inadvertently, he may have given too much weight to evidence that supported his hypotheses and too little weight to contradictory illustrations. There are more recent studies that bear directly on Janis's approach and generally corroborate his theory (such as Flowers, 1977; Tetlock, 1979). There is also a considerable amount of research that, bearing more generally on intergroup perception and conflict, supports the hypotheses that the perception of outgroup members is less finely graded or cognitively complex than is perception of ingroup members (for instance, Linville & Jones, 1980), and that the reduction of intergroup conflict is facilitated considerably by individuating or making one's perception of members of the outgroup more personalized (for example, Wilder, 1978; Wilder & Thompson, 1980). Research pertaining to intergroup perception is also discussed in Chapters 2 and 3 of the present volume.

STEREOTYPING: LINKAGES TO VIOLENCE AND DEHUMANIZATION

Efforts to explain "man's inhumanity toward man" have persisted in challenging the resources of social scientists. An extensive literature has developed, particularly concerning the Nazi extermination of European Jewry (such as Arendt, 1963; Dawidowicz, 1975; Fein, 1979). Other events or epochs of extreme social destructiveness—the bombing of Japan, atrocities in Vietnam—also have received intensive scholarly attention (for instance, Lifton, 1967; Sanford & Comstock, 1971). At first glance the study of aggression would seem to be the appropriate conceptual perspective, but this has not proved to be true. Conceptions of aggression—anger, frustration, catharsis, modeling—have not been of significant help in explaining phenomena of this magnitude. The enormity of the killing, the innocence of the victims, and the absence of self-defense or retaliatory aspects seem to require a more distinctive approach, one that is better able to come to terms with such words as "Holocaust," "genocide," "atrocity," "depersonalization," and "inhumanity."

A central question that must be addressed deals with what Herbert Kelman (1973) has termed "loss of restraint." How is it that factors that usually restrain individuals from harming others—fear, empathy, guilt, anxiety, identification—are either negated or greatly reduced in their controlling functions? How can we account for an individual's willingness or enthusiasm to inflict pain and death upon a nonattacking victim—a woman, a child, an elderly person—without experiencing inhibitions ordinarily assumed to prevent such acts? Many commentators have pointed to the role of social perception and stereotyping as critically important in the destructive behaviors with which we are concerned.

A basic hypothesis, bearing on the general concept of dehumanization, is that when members of one group think about members of another as intrinsically different—as categorically bad, unworthy, despicable—they are capable of inflicting great harm upon them. Stereotypes, in this view, constitute what Sanford and Comstock (1971) term "sanctions for evil." They may induce or justify acts that would be unthinkable to commit against members of one's own group. Neil Smelser (1971) detects, in various episodes of human destructiveness, a theme that is central to our discussion:

> The rumors that often preceded lynchings in the post-Restoration South were that a black had assaulted a white man or raped a white woman—thus confirming the general belief that the black was a dangerous, uncontrolled animal and thus making his destruction, in the mind of the whites, both legitimate and imperative. The stereotype of the Jew in Nazi ideology and the stereotype of the Japanese in America in World War II, although differing in content, legitimized destructive behavior which would have been regarded as evil under other circumstances. (p. 19)

In *Warrant for Genocide*, Norman Cohn (1967) proposes that the single most influential determinant of the policy to liquidate European Jews was perception of Jews as plotting to conquer the world, a myth that had been described in a forged document, the Protocols of the Elders of Zion. In Cohn's view the stereotypes contained in this document were a decisive precursor to the Holocaust. Dr. Lucy Dawidowicz (1975) has analyzed anti-Semitic stereotypes in German history, and specifically in the Third Reich. Quoting from Hitler's *Mein Kampf*—written some 20 years prior to the Holocaust—she documents the vividness of the imagery, which was hardly original with Hitler but received its most vitriolic expression in his writings and speeches:

> The vileness of the Jew . . . resided in the blood of the race and was evident in the Jew's physical, mental, cultural being. . . . Over and over again he [Hitler] kept describing the Jews in terms of filth and disease. "If the Jews were alone in this world, they would stifle in filth and offal." . . . The depiction of Jews as the carriers of filth and disease, hence of death and destruction, goes back in the history of anti-Semitism to the Middle Ages, when Jews were accused of spreading the plague and poisoning the wells. Hitler accused the Jews, in particular, of sexual defilement and even blamed them for the presence of syphilis in post-war Germany. . . . From the concept of the Jew as parasite, vampire, bloodsucker, contaminating the Aryan race, it was but a small step to the Jew as figurative bloodsucker in the financial and economic spheres. "The spider was slowly beginning to suck the blood out of the people's pores" through the war corporations. That image had its source in the leftist anti-Semitic stereotype of the mid- and late nineteenth century. (pp. 19–20)

One should not minimize the significance of this kind of imagery presented by a man destined to become the chancellor of Germany. Cohn (1967) argues that there was widespread acceptance of these stereotypes among the German people. For those most closely involved with the killing of Jews in concentration camps, the imagery of dehumanization was, of course, highly instrumental:

For many of the SS, the conspiracy-myth was in fact far more than an ideology or world-view—it was something which took possession of their psyches, so that they were able, for instance, to burn small children alive without any conscious feelings of compassion or guilt. (pp. 213–214)

Bettelheim, in his eyewitness account of existence in a Nazi concentration camp (1943), reported that the SS guards were genuinely convinced of anti-Semitic ideology:

Occasional talks with these guards revealed that they really believed in a Jewish-capitalistic world conspiracy against the German people, and whoever opposed the Nazis participated in it and was therefore to be destroyed, independent of his role in the conspiracy. So it can be understood why their behavior to the prisoners was that normally reserved for dealing with one's vilest enemy. (p. 78)

Kelman (1973) has noted that harming others may also result in dehumanized perceptions of them. Thus, stereotypes not only may be one of the important causes of genocide, but also may result from such behavior. Although our emphasis here is upon stereotypes and perception, it must be noted that these alone did not slaughter innocent victims in the Third Reich. Powerful forces of authority (Milgram, 1974) were also a crucial determinant of the Holocaust.

In his analysis of the My Lai massacre in Vietnam, Robert Lifton (1971) conceives of this atrocity in fundamentally perceptual terms:

Those they were shooting were not people at all, but were, as one GI put it, "like animals." Or, in Hammer's words, "some subhuman species who live only by the grace of the Americans [so that] to kill them is no more a crime than to spray DDT on an annoying insect." This dehumanizing of all Vietnamese is not merely racist, but a product of the degrading role Americans have constructed for the people of the South. (p. 41)

Lifton's analysis was based on personal interviews with soldiers who served in Vietnam, in addition to two books on the My Lai massacre (Hersh, 1970; Hammer, 1970).

James Parkes (1963), a theologian, has discussed the Holocaust in terms that emphasize the manner in which the victims are perceived:

It is said that of the Jewish victims a million were children and babies. Men and women like ourselves took these little ones, inflicted hideous suffering of hunger, thirst, and fear upon them, and then murdered them in cold blood. They did so because they were told to do so by their government. But it is still true that they could only do so because they had insulated themselves from feeling anything in common with their victims. These children did not, to them, appear identical with their own children. Something took the place of the innocence and defenselessness of childhood; and that something was, in some form or other, created by group prejudice. (p. 4)

In its theme of ethnocentrism, this passage is similar to Janis's *Groupthink*. Parkes interprets such acts as characterizing ordinary people (people like us) in highly extraordinary circumstances—people who, because of their perceptions of their victims, were capable of ultimate evil. Because we are all prone to engage in stereotyping—a major theme of this book—the participation in atrocities, to the extent that these are facilitated by stereotypes of the enemy or outgroup, is within the repertoire of many of us—as bystanders, at least, if not as perpetrators.

A particularly eloquent expression of the dehumanization thesis is that of Herbert Kelman (1973), who has integrated his personal involvement with genocide—as a survivor of the Holocaust—with his career as a social psychologist. He asks, first, what it means to perceive another person as fully human. His answer is, essentially, the opposite of stereotyping:

To perceive another as human we must accord him identity and community.... To accord a person identity is to perceive him as an individual, independent and distinguishable from others.... To accord a person community is to perceive him—along with one's self—as part of an interconnected network of individuals who care for each other, who recognize each other's individuality, and who respect each other's rights. (pp. 48–49)

Individuality and uniqueness are crucial. Dehumanization represents the loss of these:

When a group of people is defined entirely in terms of a category to which they belong, and when this category is excluded from the human family, then the moral restraints against killing them are more readily overcome. (p. 49)

Various factors are described by Kelman as promoting the categorical perceptions involved in dehumanization. These include historical legacies of exclusion, group-based stereotypes, the use of labels and diagnostic terms, and an emphasis upon statistical, nonpersonalistic aspects of social categories. Kelman's emphasis upon categorical thinking once again raises an issue that has proved to be central in conceptions of stereotyping.

What are the origins of depersonalization? Clearly, effects are easier to list than are causes. Yet we have seen, throughout this book, the importance of recognizing the historical dimension of stereotypes. Notice, for example, the complex, long-term perspectives featured in Dawidowicz's historical analysis of anti-Semitism:

> Generations of anti-Semitism had prepared the Germans to accept Hitler as their redeemer. Layer upon layer of anti-Semitism of all kinds—Christian church teachings about the Jews, Volkist anti-Semitism, doctrines of racial superiority, economic theory about the role of the Jews in capitalism and commerce, and a half-century of political anti-Semitism were joined with the solder of German nationalism, providing the structural foundation upon which Hitler and the National Socialist movement were built. (p. 164)

The prevention of sanctioned massacres will require a concerted monitoring of the cognitive processes involved in them. Kelman suggests that

> One type of corrective effort against the sanctioned definition of victim categories is to use every opportunity to individualize the targets of violence, at home or abroad. As long as they remain identityless and are described in terms of stereotyped categories, they can more readily be dehumanized. . . . No attempt to exclude from the human community a group, by whatever criteria that group may be defined, must remain unchallenged. (p. 56)

The concepts of insulation and social distance are important psychological effects of stereotyping. In David Rosenhan's well-known paper "On Being Sane in Insane Places" (1973), individuals disguised as mental patients would ask hospital staff members "When will I be eligible for grounds privileges?" or "When will I be presented at staff conference?" Rosenhan stated that in a majority of cases, these questions received either the most cursory response from a doctor or no response whatsoever. In contrast, when individuals, in the role of student, asked Stanford University professors similar questions (such as "Do you teach here?" and "Could you direct me to Encina Hall?"), they often received complete answers and help beyond that called for in the request itself.

Rosenhan interprets these results as consistent with his conception of depersonalization. In his view the setting of the mental hospital evokes a modal kind of social perception among the staff in which patients are viewed in predominantly categorical terms. Their individuality or uniqueness is minimized:

> What are the origins of depersonalization?. . . First are attitudes held by all of us toward the mentally ill—including those who treat them—attitudes characterized by fear, distrust, and horrible expectations on the one hand, and benevolent intentions on the other. Our ambivalence leads, in this instance as in others, to avoidance. (p. 256)

Other factors mentioned by Rosenhan include the hierarchical structure of the hospital, in which staff members with the most prestige or authority have the least contact with patients, as well as the heavy use of medication at psychiatric institutions, which may also be another avoidance strategy:

> If patients were powerful rather than powerless, if they were viewed as interesting individuals rather than diagnostic entities, if they were socially significant rather than social lepers, if their anguish truly and wholly compelled our sympathies and concerns, would we not *seek* contact with them, despite the availability of medications? Perhaps for the pleasure of it all? (p. 257)

Rosenhan's perspective has not been overlooked by his colleagues, many of whom take sharp exception (such as Spitzer, 1975; Millon, 1975; Weiner, 1975). Yet, in the context of this chapter, there is considerable plausibility to Rosenhan's argument in linking social perception to the maltreatment of those categorized as victims. As Farina has noted in Chapter 7 of this volume (and apropos of Scott's analysis of blindness professionals), it is both paradoxical and disconcerting to observe these phenomena in professionals "who should know better." Rosenhan does not accuse the mental health professionals of intentional malice; rather (and somewhat vaguely), he attributes the effects to a kind of depersonalizing tradition that captures all—professionals and patients—who enter the social structure of the mental hospital.

The issues raised in discussions of atrocity and genocide are difficult not only in terms of their substantive, emotionally taxing nature, but also because of their limited amenability to controlled, experimental research. There are, however, a number of experimental investigations that bear on the issues raised in this section. A relevant study is that by Bandura, Underwood, and Fromson (1975), which dealt with disinhibition of aggression, a process similar to Kelman's theory of "loss of restraint" (1973).

Bandura and his colleagues examined two factors that may lower a person's restraint against harming another person. The first hypothesis, diffusion of responsibility, predicts that harming will be increased if the harm-doer does not feel personally responsible for his or her actions. A considerable amount of research supports this general principle (for instance, Diener, 1980; Milgram, 1974; Zimbardo, 1970). The second hypothesis, of more direct concern to this discussion, predicts that harming will be increased if the victim is dehumanized. The rationale for this prediction, based on the "loss of restraint" model of Kelman (1973), is that dehumanization lessens guilt and anxiety, and may, in fact, imply that the victim is less sensitive to mistreatment.

Bandura et al. told their subjects that the experiment concerned the effects of punishment on the quality of decision making. They were to assume a supervisory role and observe a three-person group engaging in a series of bargaining problems. This group (the target) would select options and receive an "effective" or "ineffective" signal in the form of an amber or red light, respectively. On red-light signals, the subject was instructed to administer an electric shock on a graded series of shock levers (1 to 10) at any level thought appropriate. Various cover instructions were given to justify aspects of the procedure, such as that the subjects were in separate cubicles and could not actually see the target group. No shocks were actually administered. (The experimental study of aggression has often employed this shock-punishment paradigm.)

The "diffusion of responsibility" variable was manipulated by having subjects think that they, alone, were responsible for determining the level of punishment (nondiffused) or that there were other subjects, like themselves, in the same experiment, and that the level of shock actually given would be an average of the total amount of shock recommended by all the subjects in the supervisory role.

The labeling of the victim was enacted in a subtle, complicated procedure to increase its apparent naturalness. Subjects listened through earphones to the experimenter purporting to instruct the target group on their bargaining task. What occurred first was an exchange between the experimenter and his research assistant. It was apparent that the earphone/microphone connections were not supposed to be on, and the assistant, in an offhand manner, described the group in terms of various personal qualities. For subjects in the humanized condition, the target group was described "as a perceptive, understanding, and otherwise humanized group" (p. 258). In the dehumanized condition the decision makers were described "as an animalistic, rotten bunch" (p. 258). A neutral condition involved no evaluative references being made about the target.

The red light was signaled on 10 of 25 trials, giving the subject 10 opportunities to recommend shock levels. The results are shown in Figure 10.1. The effects of both variables were highly influential in determining the number of shocks administered to the target—greater punishment in the dehumanized condition than in the neutral or humanized condition, greater punishment in the group responsibility than individual responsibility condition. In addition, post-experimental personality ratings of the target group (their intelligence, rigidity, sensitivity, and so on) indicated substantially more desirable impressions in the humanized condition than in the other two labeling conditions. When asked to explain their reaction to punishing the targets, subjects in the dehumanized condition produced a high incidence of self-absolving justifications, rationales for their behavior that supported the use of physical punishment as a corrective strategy. There was general disapproval of this approach in the rationales of subjects in the humanized condition.

After replicating these findings in a second experiment, the authors concluded:

FIGURE 10.1

Mean Intensity of Shocks Administered by Subjects as a Function of Diffusion of Responsibility and Dehumanization of the Recipients of Punishment

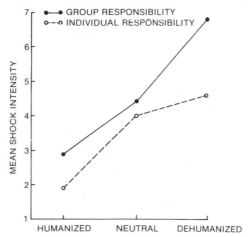

Source: Bandura et al. (1975), Figure 2, p. 259. Reprinted by permission of Academic Press.

> Dehumanized performers were treated more than twice as punitively as those invested with human qualities and considerably more severely than the neutral group.... The discussion thus far has focused on the disinhibiting power of labeling that divests people of human qualities. Of equal theoretical and social significance is the power of humanization in counteracting punitiveness.... These findings suggest that designations of others in terms that humanize them can serve as an effective corrective against aggression. (pp. 266–267)

The findings in this experiment support a number of concepts noted in this chapter. The experimental procedure in both the humanized and dehumanized conditions involved stereotyping the target group with trait adjectives, tagging the members as "good people" or "bad people." This is the only information subjects had about the target group. It strongly influenced their behavior, even though the target's performance, in terms of number of errors, was identical in all conditions.

There are a number of other experimental investigations that bear on the issues raised in this section. We have noted that stereotyping involves a loss of individual identity or uniqueness. In this respect stereotyping is conceptually linked to the term "deindividuation," which has received attention in the research of Philip Zimbardo (1970; Zimbardo, Haney,

Banks, & Jaffe, 1973). Zimbardo's conceptualization of deindividuation emphasizes factors that lower a person's restraints against committing acts of violence, aggression, or crime. His central concern is the psychological state of the person in terms of identifiability or self-control. Conditions inducing deindividuation are those in which the individual loses a sense of personal responsibility, identifiability, or self-monitoring. Being in a large group (versus alone), being anonymous (versus identifiable), and acting under various drugged or alcoholic states illustrate deindividuating preconditions. In a series of experiments, Zimbardo (1970) demonstrated that subjects, in experimentally manipulated conditions designed to induce anonymity, would administer significantly greater amounts of punishment to a victim.

While most of the research has viewed deindividuation as an internal state of the actor (for instance, Diener, 1980), it may also be conceived in terms of social perception. Thus, a perceiver may view another person or group as being more or less deindividuated. Such perceptions may readily influence the kind of behavior directed at other people. The link with stereotyping here is the conceptual analogy between deindividuation and categorization. In a widely cited investigation, Zimbardo, Haney, Banks, and Jaffe (1973) examined the interactions between persons randomly assigned to play "guard" and "prisoner" roles in a simulated prison. Those assigned to the guard role expressed unanticipated behaviors of extreme cruelty and abuse toward their prisoners.

A major emphasis in Zimbardo et al.'s account of the social destructiveness was the mental state of the guards and prisoners. The guards were deindividuated by making them all look alike—uniforms, reflector sunglasses, weapons. More important, perhaps, they tended to think and act alike because of the powerful imagery they shared regarding the role of prison guard. These conditions reduced the incidence of sympathy and helping—that is, behaviors incompatible with the stereotype of guard. More relevant for our concerns is the deindividuation of those in the prisoner role:

> We promoted anonymity by seeking to minimize each prisoner's sense of uniqueness and prior identity. The prisoners wore smocks and nylon stocking caps; they had to use their ID numbers; their personal effects were removed and they were housed in barren cells. All of this made them appear similar to each other and indistinguishable to observers. (p. 39)

As with the guards, those in the prisoner role, in addition to appearing similar physically, tended to behave in similar manners, in part as a function of the explicit orders imposed upon them by the guards, but also as a function of their acquired beliefs of what it means to be a prisoner. Thus, the social roles themselves induced a kind of homogeneity of behaviors. Self-reports by some of the "guards" suggest the powerful consequences of perceiving the prisoners as deindividuated human beings:

> Guard M: I was surprised at myself. . . . I made them call each other names and clean the toilets out with their bare hands. I practically considered the prisoners cattle. . . . (p. 42)

> Guard A: I watched them tear at each other on orders given by us. They didn't see it as an experiment. It was real and they were fighting to keep their identity. But we were always there to show them who was boss. (p. 42)

> Slowly the prisoners became resigned to their fate and even behaved in ways that actually helped to justify their dehumanizing treatment at the hands of the guards. Analysis of taperecorded private conversations between prisoners and of remarks made by them to interviewers revealed that fully half could be classified as nonsupportive of other prisoners. (p. 44)

The prison experiment shows the power of labels in influencing perceptions and behaviors. Individuals focus almost exclusively on their social roles and are guided in their actions by perceiving others in a role rather than individualized terms. What is intriguing about Zimbardo's approach is the momentum or force that seemed to be generated simply by assigning people arbitrarily to the role of prisoner or guard. The account of their subsequent behavior speaks strongly to the influence that perceptions of others can have on our behavior, particularly when those perceptions tend to categorize individuals. The acquired significance or meaning of the category is translated into seemingly "appropriate" behaviors. This is an essential theme of the stereotyping literature reviewed in this book.

Worchel and Andreoli (1978) conducted an experimental investigation on the relationship between deindividuated perceptions of others and behavior toward them. Their basic hypothesis was that people will shape their perceptions of others to be compatible with the type of interaction they expect to have with them. It was arranged that some of their subjects expected to aggress against another person, whereas others expected to encounter another person in a positive social action. All subjects had initially received a biographical sketch of the person with whom they would interact. This sketch contained numerous bits of individuating information (such as name, personality, physical characteristics, habits, background) and deindividuating information (such as age, home town, race, present address, religion, political party). A key measure was the subject's recall of this information. The results indicated that subjects expecting to aggress recalled significantly more deindividuating information, whereas those expecting to help the individual recalled significantly more individuating information.

The subject's mood also related to recall, with angry subjects deindividuating the target more than nonangry subjects.

This experiment is relevant in addressing the range of perceptions that individuals are capable of drawing upon to fit their specific social circumstances. The Worchel and Andreoli experiment is not a traditional study of stereotyping in terms of being concerned with established minority groups and social categories. However, it helps to clarify the relationship between social cognition and social behavior. It recognizes that there is a long-term perspective, in which people anticipate what kinds of interactions they will have with others, and align their mental images ahead of time to be consistent with these anticipated actions. This kind of anticipatory cognitive adjustment would seem to have important implications for shaping subsequent interactions, in the manner of a self-fulfilling prophecy.

STEREOTYPING IN JUDGMENTS OF RESPONSIBILITY

A basic feature of social perception, and one closely involved in stereotyping, is the attribution of causality—one person coming to some conclusion as to the "why" of another person's behavior (see Chapter 2 of this volume). Although this process occurs rather continuously with respect to all sorts of behaviors, of particular importance are judgments of causality involving social problems or antisocial acts. Consider, for example, decisions concerning responsibility for a crime, suitability for receiving welfare, requests for parole or release from a mental hospital, or a juvenile offender's plea for a second chance. There is often a sense of urgency or risk to such judgments, with implications not only for the individual but also for others, perhaps the community at large.

Stereotyping may play an important role in reaching decisions in such contexts. Judgments of responsibility (and related attributes, such as intent, guilt, sanity, and rehabilitation) are often difficult to make. The facts of the case may be less than clear. Consider the complex, often confusing testimony in the Chappaquiddick Island incident of Senator Edward Kennedy or the Patty Hearst trial. We have noted, in Chapters 1 and 2, a bias for observers to perceive personal causality in the behavior of others. Yet, situational factors are often compelling as well. An attorney may persuade a jury that the defendant's behavior was caused by circumstantial factors, thereby influencing the jury's verdict and penalty recommendation. The judgments themselves are obviously inferential, not only requiring estimates of the target person's current mental, emotional, or moral status, but also implying the importance of assessing the likelihood of future behaviors.

In the face of such ambiguity or uncertainty, the observer may rely upon stereotypic information about the target—social class, age, sex, race, or appearance. Such information, in principle irrelevant to the case at issue, aids the observer in reaching what seems to be an informed decision about the target, an opinion that appears rational and justified, and may be held with reasonable confidence. The stereotypes, consisting of expectancies and images generated by the target's social category (ies), lead the observer to (at least) think that he or she knows a great deal about the target. The observer, furthermore, is likely to be unaware of the informational gain supplied by the stereotypes (Nisbett & Bellows, 1977) and of the reasons for using them—namely, the uncertainties inherent in the judgment situation that have motivated him or her to resort to habitual ways of thinking about people of the kind represented by the target.

Another factor is the general attractiveness of the individuals being judged. The target person or object of judgment is likely to be quite different—lower, to be specific—from the judge in social status or power. Consider the reduced social status of mentally ill persons. Farina points out, in Chapter 7 of this volume, that these individuals are often disliked, not only by people in general but by the therapeutic community as well (also see Wills, 1978). Thus, there is often considerable social distance between the perceiver and the target person, a factor that may influence the judgments or verdicts rendered. The target person is, of course, in a vulnerable position to begin with, and is unlikely to be able to challenge the observer's biases.

Landy and Aronson (1969) asked subjects to read an account of an automobile homicide in which "John Sanders" killed a pedestrian, "Martin Lowe," after leaving an office Christmas party. The account left no doubt that Sanders was under the influence of alcohol or that he killed Lowe. There was ambiguity, however, in terms of situational factors, such as the Christmas party, norms about celebrating and overindulging on such an occasion, and the fact that it had been snowing, which made driving difficult and visibility poor.

Landy and Aronson varied the description of the character of both defendant and victim. The attractive victim was described as socially prominent, civically active, and a devoted family man; the unattractive victim was described as a gangster involved in underworld syndicate crime, currently out of jail on bond, having been charged with fraud and tax evasion. The attractive defendant was described as an elderly insurance adjuster, of high reputation, a widower on his way to spend Christmas Eve with his children; the unattractive defendant was described as a janitor, divorced, and with several misdemeanors on his record. A neutral defendant condition was also included, in which John Sanders was not described in any way other than in terms of the automobile case description.

Subjects were asked to consider the crime—negligent automobile homicide—as punishable from 1 to 25 years in prison, and to sentence the defendant according to their personal judgment. When John Sanders was described in attractive terms, subjects recommended substantially less severe sentences. The attractiveness of the victim also was influential—more punishment recommended if the victim was highly attractive. Thus, although the description of the automobile homicide was constant in all conditions, subjects used seemingly extraneous information about characteristics of both defendant and victim in producing their judgments. Why might this have occurred?

Landy and Aronson cite several reasons bearing on our discussion of stereotypes. Subjects may have been able to identify more easily with the attractive defendant, more able to imagine themselves in a similar predicament. In other words, in the attractive defendant condition vis-à-vis the unattractive defendant, subjects felt that they were judging a person more like themselves, and perhaps this factor—analogous to the role of ethnocentrism in intergroup perception (Campbell, 1967; Chapter 3 in this volume)—influenced their judgments in a sympathetic or lenient direction.

Although it was not assessed in their experiment, Landy and Aronson may also have been observing the impact of the subject-juror's liking for the defendant upon judgments of criminal responsibility. In Chapter 1 we noted the complex relationship between liking (affect) and stereotyping (beliefs, images). In this experiment, if the subject were asked "Do you like the attractive defendant more than the unattractive?" the answer would obviously bear on the qualities portrayed in the character description—qualities that, in the context of this analysis, locate the target in a particular social category and, hence, constitute a stereotyped image of him.

There is evidence supporting the general proposition that people may attribute responsibility in line with their liking or disliking of another person. Regan, Straus, and Fazio (1974) have shown, for example, that personal responsibility is attributed for positive outcomes or successful behaviors performed by a person we like, and for negative behaviors or failures performed by a person we dislike. The converse appears true, also, in that we attribute external or situational causality for actions that do not fit well with the attraction we have for the person, such as bad acts performed by people we like, or good deeds performed by people we dislike. In the Landy and Aronson study, therefore, the accident may have seemed inconsistent with the virtuous character of the attractive defendant. Subjects could not deny the "facts" of the case, but they were free to construct different interpretations of the case, and the data strongly suggest that this did occur.

What about the effect of the attractiveness of the victim? Landy and Aronson suggest that the crime itself may be perceived as more serious if the victim is a more desirable or "socially worthy" individual. An important study by Walster (1966) indicated that judgments of personal responsibility for an automobile accident were greater if the consequences of the accident were relatively severe. The serious accident or undeserved misfortune seems to demand "cognitive work" on the part of the observer, who attempts to restore a sense of control or understanding by imposing a judgment of causality (responsibility) that, while illogical, is nevertheless psychologically adaptive. One may also relate the findings relating to the unattractive victim condition to the previous discussion of dehumanization. The unattractive victim may have been perceived in dehumanized images, making his death by accident more tolerable to subjects.

Jones and Aronson (1973) conducted a research project concerning judgments about a rape incident. Their research centered on Lerner's "just world" theory, which emphasizes the need or motive for people to perceive fairness or justice in the outcomes of others. The image of undeserved or innocent suffering is a serious provocation to this motive, and Lerner and Miller document (1978) considerable research evidence bearing on the manner in which people resolve such a problem. A major strategy is to blame innocent victims for their misfortune. There are a number of reasons behind such an apparently cruel judgmental posture. There may be little, in fact, that the observer can do to help the victim, and the specific type of tragedy or injury may be threatening to the observer, as was noted in discussing reactions to the physically disabled. Again, the ambiguity of such concepts as "innocent suffering," "undeservingness," and "personal responsibility"—in conjunction with an attributional bias to perceive the behavior of others as caused by dispositional rather than situational factors—contributes to the likelihood of "blaming the victim."

Jones and Aronson's central question was the degree to which subjects would be influenced by information concerning the social status of the rape victim in determining her responsibility for being raped. The nonintuitive prediction was made that more fault would be attributed to the rape victim if she had relatively high status. Because such an incident would involve a relatively greater injustice, there would, ironically, be a greater pressure to restore perceived justice by allocating greater responsibility—vis-à-vis the case of a lower-status victim.

Subjects read about a rape that occurred on a college campus. The victim was described as either a married woman, a virgin, or a divorcee. In line with the prediction, subjects attributed significantly more fault to the victim if she was portrayed as a married woman or a virgin than as a divorcee. Jones and Aronson suggested that because of the virtuous character of the victim, subjects could not explain her victimization in terms of personal defects or traits. Thus, behavioral responsibility in terms of perceived fault was given greater weight. In this experiment stereotyping was directly related to the subjects' judgments of responsibility. The social category at issue was the victim's social respectability. The more respectable the victim, the more fault attributed to her. As in the study by Landy and Aronson (1969), more punishment was recommended for the attacker of the more respectable victim. The results are thus paradoxical—not only was the more respectable victim seen as more at fault, but the perpetrator of the rape was seen as more deserving of punishment if his victim was high in status.

In a quite unusual investigation, Ugwuegbu (1979) investigated the role of racial factors in the judgments of simulated jurors. He was able to study not only the effects of the race of the target person but also the race of the observer. He asked subjects to read a transcript of a rape incident on a college campus. The defendant was described as a 21-year-old male, black or white, who was charged with the rape of a 19-year-old woman, black or white. A central theoretical question in this study was the degree to which race information would influence judgments as a function of the quality of the evidence. In line with our previous discussion concerning the role of stereotypes in reducing uncertainty or ambiguity, Ugwuegbu hypothesized that the race variable would be most influential when the "facts" of the rape case were mixed or unclear; race information should exert minor influence if the evidence was clear, in either the guilty or the innocent direction, regarding the defendant's role in the rape.

The first of two experiments involved white research subjects in the role of simulated jurors. The key measure in this study was culpability, an index based on four judgments (intention to harm, perceived responsibility, verdict of guilty/not guilty, and recommended punishment). The results indicated that black defendants were judged more culpable than white defendants. If the rape victim was white, the defendant was judged more culpable than if the victim was black. This pattern relates to the social-distance dimension of stereotypes and to ethnocentrism. That is, a crime committed against someone similar to the juror (in race) was viewed as more blameworthy than the same crime committed against an outgroup member. As anticipated, the effects of the defendant's race were significant only when the evidence was marginal or ambiguous. Racial effects on judgments were not observed if the evidence was either extremely weak or overwhelmingly strong. These effects were in line with the predictions and are, of course, consistent with a pervasive antiblack stereotype.

Parallel data were obtained in a second study, in this instance from black subject-jurors. The results were essentially the mirror reverse of those from white subjects. The black defendant was rated as less culpable than the white defendant; when the victim was white, the defendant was rated as less culpable. As in the case of white subject-jurors, black subjects did not incorporate the race of the defendant into their judgments if the evidence regarding guilt was very weak. In both the mixed and strong evidence conditions, however, the white defendant was viewed as more culpable than the black. Ugwuegbu suggests that a partial explanation for the judgmental responses of the black subjects is based on black pride and awareness among college students. His results counter, in this context, earlier research findings suggesting self-rejection among black research subjects (for instance, Banks, 1970; Bayton, 1965).

The perception of justice is a vital concern of society. The research discussed in this section raises alarming issues concerning the ability of observers to render judgments that are uncontaminated by extraneous information. If such effects are observed in relatively uninvolving research settings, one suspects that the possibilities for biasing effects of stereotyping in the "natural" social world could be greater.

CONCLUSIONS

The purpose of this book has been to convey a sense of the diversity of stereotyping by examining its psychological foundations and its significance in interpersonal behavior. The issues featured in this volume were selected on the basis of the considerable research interest directed at them. A number of pertinent topic areas have not been covered, particularly stereotypes about certain American cultural minorities (such as Indians, Asians, and Latin Americans) and groups identified by behavioral or reputational stigma (such as homosexuals, former prisoners, and alcoholics). A collection edited by Atkinson, Morten, and Sue (1979) analyzes stereotypes about American minorities, with an emphasis upon cross-cultural factors.

A cynic might object that we have also neglected stereotypes about left-handed people, those who wear toupees or do not wear bras, and people who live in such places as Oxford, Ohio. For these sins of omission, we may be pardoned. A listing of this kind is virtually endless, for any discriminable feature of a person could conceivably provide the cognitive seeding for mental imagery about those sharing that characteristic.

Clearly, all stereotypes are not of similar concern or interest to people in general and to social scientists. Yet one probably should not be too quick to dismiss certain stereotypes as harmless. Consider that stereotypes about physical attractiveness have only recently received extensive research. These phenomena were long viewed as trivial or humorous, constituting folk wisdom with, perhaps, a measure of presumed validity. Who would deny that "Fat people are jolly," "You can't tell a book by its cover," or "Beauty is in the eye of the beholder" (or is it at least "skin deep?")? As Gerald Adams notes in Chapter 6, however, the effects of appearance are pervasive, and at times comparable with those of racial, sexual, and other (more traditional) stereotypes. A person's first name can even be a stimulant to stereotyping. Bruning and Husa (1972) have shown that stereotypes and behavioral expectancies exist for different first names, and that such differential perceptions occur as early as the third grade. Thus, what constitutes an important or relatively minor stereotype is not always clear. For the target or victim, things are rarely trivial.

In considering the diverse concerns of this book, one can point to a number of common themes. People clearly seem primed to engage in stereotyping of some kind. We are disposed to think in categorical terms, to differentiate among social groups, and to distinguish between others who appear similar to us or different from us. We are able to infer personality or character traits in others very readily, and to form expectations on the basis of limited, often extraneous information. In this fundamental perspective every instance of stereotyping represents our capacities as social perceivers, as observers with many "pictures in our heads," to use Lippmann's phrase. We are also prone to like or dislike other people, and to justify such evaluations and feelings. These affective or emotional responses—and the explanations we construct for having them—are also a pervasive element in the stereotyping process.

Differences in the ultimate form or substantive character of stereotypes are, however, glaring. Various historical, cultural, and contemporary social factors converge in unique patterns with respect to the targets of stereotyping reviewed in this book. Generalizations across topics are difficult to make. An "expert" on the stereotypes of physical attractiveness or social class might have virtually no precise knowledge of anti-Semitism or the stigma of mental illness. As Farina notes in Chapter 7, such categories as mental illness and physical disability are, themselves, only general headings that contain very distinct subcategories and conditions.

The chapter topics of this book present various dimensions or categories for the activation of stereotypes. Some of these are immediately visible, as in an individual's race and sex (although even here there may be occasional ambiguity); others are not directly apparent, as in a history of mental illness or a physical blemish covered by one's clothing. Certain categories are dichotomous—male or female, black or white; other dimensions seem more graduated or continuous, as in a person's attractiveness or age. Indeed, little is known about the precise factors that enter into our categorizing someone as old, as unattractive, or as upper-class, for example. At times there is confusion as to which category is responsible for the stereotype phenomenon itself. Stereotypes that at first suggest antiblack perceptions may often be based, more accurately, on stereotypes about lower social classes (Smedley & Bayton, 1978). Certain social targets of stereotyping have engaged in successful protest and collective liberation movements (blacks, women, and more recently, the physically handicapped, homosexuals, and the elderly); other victims have not done so (the mentally ill, the physically unattractive).

A related distinction is whether the object of a stereotype can readily be defined as a distinct social group. In social life, of course, people are generally not responded to as "book chapters," but as complex and multidimensional. A given individual may simultaneously be a member of many categories, any one of which could be the stimulant for stereotyping. A question worthy of future research concerns the determinants of an observer's decision to select a specific cue, from among many, for subsequent stereotyping. Sammy Davis, Jr., has pointed, with instructive humor, to the fact that people may respond to him as a black, a Jew, a physically handicapped person (sightless in one eye), and even as an entertainer!

Despite the complexity and breadth that characterize the various domains of stereotyping, we can point to a number of basic themes or problems that are common to the general concept. In some instances these represent important but as yet unanswered questions for the student of stereotyping.

The Relevance of Historical Factors

"Where did this stereotype come from?" This is an important and reasonable question to ask. It raises the possibility of adaptive or functional value to the stereotype under question. If one considers that at some time in the past, the stereotype did not exist, what factors were responsible for its initial appearance? Political and economic events may be involved, as noted in Chapter 3 of this volume. Chapters 8 and 9 in this book also reflect an emphasis upon historical issues. The difficulties of pursuing this kind of analysis—the tracing of historical documents, literature, and so on—should not mask the significance of understanding this dimension of stereotypes. Unquestionably, a major aspect of the many causes of stereotypes resides in history, whether it be the manner in which women (versus men) are depicted in the Old Testament or the change in racial stereotypes—from docility to aggressiveness—that accompanied the civil rights movement.

The Self-Fulfilling Prophecy

The concept of the self-fulfilling prophecy is one of the most valuable contributions of experimental social psychology to the understanding of stereotypes (Darley & Fazio, 1980; Rosenthal, 1974). Several chapters in this volume have noted the role of the self-fulfilling prophecy in perpetuating the existence of initially unwarranted perceptions or expectations (especially Chapters 2, 3, and 6). Evidence obtained by Snyder and his colleagues (Snyder, 1981b; Snyder & Swann, 1978) presents a convincing demonstration that individuals are "hell bent" on confirming their hypotheses about other people, and will selectively search for, and accept, information that corroborates their expectations. This places the individual who is the object of an initially false character description in an unenviable position. There may be strong pressures for such an individual to incorporate the perceiver's view into his or her own self-concept and "act out the part."

As discussed in Chapter 2 of this book, Synder and Uranowitz (1978) have shown that we tend to remember information selectively, in a manner that supports our "theories" about other people. In the opening chapter we cited the problems of the stability of stereotypes—why they tend to resist change—and the complexities involved in evaluating the accuracy or validity of stereotypes. Snyder's (1981b) research on the self-confirming nature of our hypotheses about others bears on these issues:

> Even if one were to develop sufficient doubt about the accuracy of these beliefs (i.e., stereotypes) to proceed to actively test them, one nevertheless might be likely to gather all the evidence one needs to confirm and retain these beliefs. And, in the end, one may be left with the secure (but

totally unwarranted) feeling that these beliefs must be correct because
they have survived (what may seem to the individual) perfectly appropriate and even rigorous procedures for assessing their accuracy. (p. 293)

In this passage, which is reminiscent of Lippmann's prophetic insights
into the nature of stereotyping (see Chapter 1 of this volume), one can
formulate an important problem for future research: What are the conditions under which individuals will recognize the uncertainties and potential
biases in their expectations, and proceed to acknowledge, and perhaps
even focus upon, the possibilities for disconfirming such beliefs? The answer
to this question will signify a significant advance in our understanding of the
social-cognitive bases of stereotyping.

The Measurement of Stereotyping

Despite periodic criticisms of the assessment of stereotypes (such as
Brigham, 1971), the Katz and Braly technique, described in Chapters 1 and 3
of this book, has prevailed. The general strategy—certainly that characterizing most of the research reported in this book—is to ask individuals to
describe the target group (or individual member) on various scales (trait
dimensions, behavioral descriptions, or others), as in the surveys featured in
the chapters on anti-Semitism (Chapter 4), social class and poverty (Chapter
9), and aging (Chapter 8). Research on attractiveness (Chapter 6) and sex
stereotypes (Chapter 5) has used a similar approach, in which individuals are
given a photograph or behavioral description that contains the variable of
interest (level of attractiveness, sex of the actor), and are asked to record
their impression of the person's personality, or perhaps to evaluate the target
person's performance.

With considerable variations in specific format, the basic method is to
assess the observer's impressions or images of the target person. The
popularity of this strategy, whatever its shortcomings, is such that it will
likely remain the measure of choice for most researchers in the near future.
As noted in Chapter 1 and throughout this book, the direct assessment of the
stereotype is often not obtained. In these instances the indication of a
specific social category—whether the target is described as a mental patient
or normal, stigmatized or not, old or young—is presumed to instigate the
covert operation of stereotypes and related attitudes, which in turn are
related to subsequent behaviors, be these judgments, evaluations, helping,
aggressing, and so on.

McCauley, Stitt, and Segal (1980) have called the measurement issue
into question again. Their primary concern is the need for an individual-
oriented measure of stereotyping, a technique that will enable the investigator to trace the antecedents and consequences of individual differences in
stereotyping. This is an issue that Brigham also raised (1971; cf. Chapter 1 of

this volume). In the present book the chapter on sex stereotypes best reflects an emphasis upon individual differences (and it is a minor emphasis). McCauley et al.'s conception of stereotyping is interesting and radically different from that presented in this book. Instead of viewing stereotypes as pictures or mental images, in the classic tradition of Lippmann and of Katz and Braly, McCauley et al. view stereotypes as predictions or probability estimates. A stereotype is defined as a differential trait attribution or "differential prediction based on group membership information" (1980, p. 197). Stereotypes are not all-or-none, but probabilistic. Thus, a person who believes that 40 percent of Germans are efficient, as opposed to, for example, 15 percent of "people in general" (or some other specified group) would be stereotyping the German people. It is irrelevant whether the estimate of the distribution of a given trait is high (90 percent or 100 percent) or relatively low (15 percent or 20 percent). What matters is the difference between the presumed incidence of a trait in a given group versus some other base line or comparison.

McCauley et al. (1978; 1980) describe a procedure for obtaining such probability estimates from research subjects. Like the Katz and Braly checklist, it requires the subject to make a large number of judgments. They are entered into a Bayesian statistical formula to yield the diagnostic ratio, which describes each respondent's degree of stereotyping with respect to whatever traits and social groups are at issue. This procedure represents an advance in terms of minimizing the ambiguity of instructions that ask subjects to describe "the typical" German, for example. It also recognizes that people may hold stereotypes about various social groups, and yet not behave toward individual members of such groups in a manner indicative of the stereotype.

Because it is inherent in the probability conception that not all members of a group will present the stereotype trait or feature in question, one may hold to a general belief about the group and, simultaneously, admit to many "exceptions to the rule" for individual acquaintances. Finally, the approach of McCauley et al. is neutral with respect to the social desirability of the stereotype. As probability estimates, stereotypes can be positive—"I think blacks are (significantly) more friendly than whites"—and they can be negative—"blacks are (relatively) more aggressive than whites." If there are available quantitative criteria (such as statistics on unemployment among blacks and whites), the accuracy of an individual's stereotypes may be readily assessed (McCauley & Stitt, 1978).

The McCauley et al. work is provocative. The need for a quantitatively rigorous approach to the measurement of stereotypes is a very real one. It would facilitate research on important questions, particularly those bearing on the early determinants or antecedent conditions of individual differences in stereotyping. A word of caution is in order, however. This book attests to the generality of stereotyping and to the fact that most people stereotype others, at least in certain settings or social interactions. This is not to negate the relevance of an individual-difference paradigm, but to place such an approach in perspective. As noted in Chapters 1 and 3, the psychodynamic model of prejudice and stereotyping was characteristic of an earlier period in social science research, highlighted by research on the authoritarian personality. This work was explicitly oriented toward the assessment of individual differences in ethnic intolerance and related phenomena. One reason for a decline of interest in this orientation has been the realization that people do not always behave in a manner that relates simply or directly to their responses on surveys, questionnaires, and similar items (for example, Crosby et al., 1980). This may ultimately present the McCauley et al. conception with its most glaring deficiency.

Stereotype measurement shares with attitude and personality measurement the problem of generalizing an individual's verbal or cognitive responses to social-behavioral responses. Often the generalization is not to be seen, not because people do not, in principle, link their beliefs to their behaviors, but because social behaviors reflect a great variety of influences, only some of which bear on stereotypes and related cognitive-affective processes. Stereotypes, as noted in the opening chapter, are also susceptible to measurement distortion because of the respondent's concern about making the socially appropriate judgment. It is obviously too early to assess the impact of McCauley et al.'s conception of stereotype measurement. It is likely, however, that the measurement of stereotyping will receive increasingly sophisticated attention. The development of new measurement techniques will not only suggest new issues for study, but will permit a new look at some older questions, for example the degree to which people perceive social groups in categorical versus qualified terms, the tendency for people to describe their own groups in favorable terms and outgroups in unfavorable terms, and the degree of homogeneity/heterogeneity which people perceive in their own groups versus outgroups (for example, Jackman and Senter, 1980).

Stereotypes About Groups and Individual Members of Those Groups

As McCauley et al. (1980) have pointed out, there are times when stereotyping seems minimized, when we relate to another person without attending to available stereotypic information about that individual. Why does this happen, and what are the implications for reducing the consequences of stereotyping? Research by Borgida, Locksley, and Brekke (1981) and Nisbett, Zukier, and Lemley (1979) suggests that the effects of stereotypes on judgments of individual members of the stereotyped group may be radically decreased by providing (to the perceiver or observer) additional information about the individual, information that individuates or describes in a personal way particular characteristics of the target.

Nisbett, Zukier, and Lemley (1979) utilized their subjects' stereotypes about college majors—for instance, that engineering majors would be able to tolerate more electric shock than would music majors, and that English majors would attend more movies than would premedical students. Such categorical information, when presented alone, clearly led to the expected, stereotypic predictions. However, when subjects were presented with both information about the college major and, in addition, target case information, such as the person's place of birth, grade average, and parents' occupations, the effects of the stereotype about the college major were substantially reduced.

Scheier and his colleagues (1978) also observed that providing personal information about an individual member of a stigmatized category—either handicapped or elderly—resulted in a more favorable impression rating of that person than a similarly portrayed normal target. Scheier et al. suggest that the observers may be more sympathetic in their judgment of a person who belongs to a social group that generally is negatively viewed if they have personal insight into the individual per se. The personal information may increase the observers' awareness of the difficulties experienced by the stigmatized person. In the Nisbett et al. research, the stereotypes did not involve stigmatization, but they also noted the powerful "dilution" effect of personalizing information:

> Stereotypes nevertheless may turn out to be less powerfully determinative of many kinds of social judgments than might be presumed. This supposition has the advantage of accounting in a satisfactory way for the "some of my best friends are . . ." phenomenon. People may believe that "blacks are lazy" without believing that any of the blacks whom they know personally are lazy. And one may speculate that the pernicious effects of social stereotypes may consist largely in the fact that they prevent the stereotype holder from exposure to the individuating information, that were it known, would serve to weaken or undermine the applicability of the stereotype. (1979, p. 37)

Certainly there are many instances in which individuals are victimized by being stereotyped by others who know them quite well. This is because the manner in which one individual responds to another is not simply a function of the amount of information known about the other, but also reflects social roles and various other factors. Thus, a sexist employer may respond to his female employees in a very sexist manner even if he knows them extremely well. Still, the point that there are potentially important differences between thinking about social groups and responding to individual members of such groups is of major interest. It obviously speaks to a basic strategy for reducing the effects of stereotypes. It also ties in with some of the ideas on dehumanization and violence considered earlier in this chapter. At first glance, at least, the "dilution effect," described by Nisbett et al., would seem inconsistent with the self-fulfilling nature of social stereotypes discussed by Snyder and others. The latter speak to the maintenance and strengthening of preconceptions, whereas the former emphasizes the deterioration or weakening of the influence of category-based expectations. Future research will be required to reconcile these contrasting arguments.

The Fundamental Attribution Error

As noted in the first two chapters of this book, there is abundant evidence that people are overly zealous in attributing personal causes or motives to the behavior of others. This is a particularly compelling issue in the analysis of stereotyping, because this kind of observer error or attributional bias can strongly exacerbate the extent and consequences of stereotyping. It can result in blaming the victim for his or her fate, whether it is a poor performance or being out of work or being physically disabled or the victim of atrocity. The error of finding others responsible for their condition in life, when there are convincing situational or contextual alternative explanations, is also likely to increase the distance between the observer and the observed. It is a judgmental stance that makes the perceiver feel that the target is somehow different, in an intrinsic or characterological way, from himself or herself—that "what is happening to *that* person could not happen to me." One important result of such a bias is that the observer either is unlikely to help the victim at all or is likely to recommend action and social policies that do not take into account situational factors responsible for the victimization in the first place (S. H. Jones & Cook, 1975; Ryan, 1976).

Walter Lippmann emphasized that the power of stereotypes resides, to a vital extent, in the unawareness that people have of their existence. We conclude with a similar thought. Unless people are sensitized to the constructive, highly active role that they, themselves, play in the perceptions and beliefs they hold about others, and are made conscious of the biases and errors that so readily take hold of such social judgments, the phenomena of stereotyping are unlikely to be profoundly altered.

REFERENCES

Arendt, H. *Eichmann in Jerusalem: A report on the banality of evil.* New York: Viking, 1963.

Atkinson, D. R., Morten, G., & Sue, D. W. (eds.). *Counseling American minorities.* Dubuque, Iowa: Wm. C. Brown, 1979.

Bandura, A., Underwood, B., & Fromson, M. E. Disinhibition of aggression through diffusion of responsibility and dehumanization of victims. *Journal of Research in Personality*, 1975, *9*, 253–269.

Banks, W. M. The changing attitudes of black students. *Personnel and Guidance Journal*, 1970, *48*, 739–745.

Bayton, J. Negro perception of Negro and white personality traits. *Journal of Personality and Social Psychology*, 1965, *1*, 250–253.

Bettelheim, B. Individual and mass behavior in extreme situations. *Journal of Abnormal and Social Psychology*, 1943, *38*, 417–452.

Bettelheim, B. Miracles: Review of Joseph P. Lash, *Helen and teacher: The story of Helen Keller and Anne Sullivan Macy. The New Yorker*, August 4, 1980, 85–90.

Borgida, E., Locksley, A., & Brekke, N. Social stereotypes and social judgment. In N. Cantor & J. Kihlstrom (eds.), *Personality, cognition, and social interaction.* Hillsdale, N.J.: Erlbaum, 1981.

Brigham, J. Ethnic stereotypes. *Psychological Bulletin*, 1971, *76*, 15–38.

Bruning, J. L., & Husa, F. T. Given names and stereotyping. *Developmental Psychology*, 1972, *7*, 91.

Campbell, D. T. Stereotypes and the perception of group differences. *American Psychologist*, 1967, *22*, 817–829.

Carver, C. S., Glass, D. C., & Katz, I. Favorable evaluations of blacks and the handicapped: Positive prejudice, unconscious denial, or social desirability? *Journal of Applied Social Psychology*, 1978, *8*, 97–106.

Cohn, N. *Warrant for genocide: The myth of the Jewish world-conspiracy and the Protocols of the Elders of Zion.* London: Eyre & Spottiswoode, 1967.

Crosby, F., Bromley, S., & Saxe, L. Recent unobtrusive studies of black and white discrimination and prejudice: A literature review. *Psychological Bulletin*, 1980, *87*, 546–563.

Darley, J. M., & Fazio, R. H. Expectancy confirmation processes arising in the social interaction sequence. *American Psychologist*, 1980, *35*, 867–881.

Dawidowicz, L. S. *The war against the Jews: 1933–1945.* New York: Holt, Rinehart, & Winston, 1975.

Diener, E. Deindividuation: The absence of self-awareness and self-regulation in group members. In P. B. Paulus (ed.), *Psychology of group influence.* Hillsdale, N.J.: Erlbaum, 1980.

Fein, H. *Accounting for genocide: Victims—and survivors—of the Holocaust.* New York: Free Press, 1979.

Flowers, M. A laboratory test of some implications of Janis' groupthink hypotheses. *Journal of Personality and Social Psychology*, 1977, *35*, 888–896.

Fuentes, J. L. A rallying cry for the physically disabled. *New York Times,* August 26, 1979, p. 25.

Gliedman, J., & Roth, W. *The unexpected minority: Handicapped children in America.* New York: Harcourt, Brace, Jovanovich, 1980.

Goffman, E. *Asylums: Essays on the social situation of mental patients and other inmates.* Garden City, N.Y.: Anchor Books, 1961.

Goffman, E. *Stigma: Notes on the management of spoiled identity.* Englewood Cliffs, N.J.: Prentice-Hall, 1963.

Hammer, R. *One morning in the war: The tragedy at Son My.* New York: Coward-McCann, 1970.

Hersh, S. M. *My Lai 4: A report on the massacre and its aftermath.* New York: Random House, 1970.

Jackman, M. R., & Senter, M. S. Images of social groups: Categorical or qualified? *Public Opinion Quarterly*, 1980, *44*, 341–361.

Janis, I. *Victims of groupthink.* Boston: Houghton-Mifflin, 1972.

Jones, C., & Aronson, E. Attribution of fault to a rape victim as a function of respectability of the victim. *Journal of Personality and Social Psychology*, 1973, *26*, 415–419.

Jones, E. E., & Sigall, H. The bogus pipeline: A new paradigm for measuring affect and attitude. *Psychological Bulletin*, 1971, *76*, 349–364.

Jones, S. H., & Cook, S. W. The influence of attitude on judgments of the effectiveness of alternative social policies. *Journal of Personality and Social Psychology*, 1975, *32*, 767–773.

Katz, I., & Glass, D. C. An ambivalence-amplification theory of behavior toward the stigmatized. In W. G. Austin & S. Worchel (eds.), *The social psychology of intergroup relations*. Monterey, Calif.: Brooks/Cole, 1979.

Katz, I., Glass, D. C., & Cohen, S. Ambivalence, guilt, and the scapegoating of minority group victims. *Journal of Experimental Social Psychology*, 1973, *9*, 423–436.

Katz, I., Glass, D. C., Lucido, D. J., & Farber, J. Ambivalence, guilt, and the denigration of a physically handicapped victim. *Journal of Personality*, 1977, *45*, 419–429.

Katz, I., Glass, D. C., Lucido, D. J., & Farber, J. Harm-doing and victim's racial or orthopedic stigma as determinants of helping behavior. *Journal of Personality*, 1979, *47*, 340–364.

Kelman, H. C. Violence without moral restraint: Reflections on the dehumanization of victims and victimizers. *Journal of Social Issues*, 1973, *29*, 25–62.

Kleck, R. E., & Strenta, A. Perceptions of the impact of negatively valued physical characteristics on social interaction. *Journal of Personality and Social Psychology*, 1980, *39*, 861–873.

Landy, D., & Aronson, E. The influence of the character of the criminal and his victim on the decisions of simulated jurors. *Journal of Experimental Social Psychology*, 1969, *5*, 141–152.

Lerner, M. J. The desire for justice and reactions to victims. In J. Macaulay & L. Berkowitz (eds.), *Altruism and helping behavior*. New York: Academic Press, 1970.

Lerner, M. J., & Miller, D. T. Just world research and the attribution process: Looking back and ahead. *Psychological Bulletin*, 1978, *85*, 1030–1051.

Lifton, R. J. *Death in life: Survivors of Hiroshima*. New York: Simon & Schuster, 1967.

Lifton, R. J. Existential evil. In N. Sanford & C. Comstock (eds.), *Sanctions for evil*. San Francisco: Jossey-Bass, 1971.

Linville, P. W., & Jones, E. E. Polarized appraisals of out-group members. *Journal of Personality and Social Psychology*, 1980, *38*, 689–703.

McCauley, C., & Stitt, C. L. An individual and quantitative measure of stereotypes. *Journal of Personality and Social Psychology*, 1978, *36*, 929–940.

McCauley, C., Stitt, C. L., & Segal, M. Stereotyping: From prejudice to prediction. *Psychological Bulletin*, 1980, *87*, 195–208.

Milgram, S. *Obedience to authority*. New York: Harper & Row, 1974.

Millon, T. Reflections on Rosenhan's "On being sane in insane places." *Journal of Abnormal Psychology*, 1975, *84*, 456–461.

Nisbett, R. E., & Bellows, N. Verbal reports about causal influences on social judgments: Private access versus public theories. *Journal of Personality and Social Psychology*, 1977, *35*, 613–624.

Nisbett, R., & Ross, L. *Human inference: Strategies and shortcomings of social judgment.* Englewood Cliffs, N.J.: Prentice-Hall, 1980.

Nisbett, R. E., Zukier, H., & Lemley, R. E. The dilution effect: Nondiagnostic information weakens the implications of diagnostic information. Unpublished manuscript, University of Michigan, 1979.

Parkes, J. *Antisemitism.* Chicago: Quadrangle Books, 1963.

Regan, D. T., Straus, E., & Fazio, R. Liking and the attribution process. *Journal of Experimental Social Psychology*, 1974, *10*, 385–397.

Rosenhan, D. L. On being sane in insane places. *Science*, 1973, *180*, 365–369.

Rosenthal, R. *On the self-fulfilling nature of social stereotypes.* New York: MSS Modular Publications, 1974. Module 53.

Ross, L., Greene, D., & House, P. The "false consensus effect": An egocentric bias in social perception and attribution processes. *Journal of Experimental Social Psychology*, 1977, *13*, 279–301.

Ryan, W. *Blaming the victim* (rev. ed.). New York: Vintage Books, 1976.

Sanford, N., & Comstock, C. (eds.). *Sanctions for evil.* San Francisco: Jossey-Bass, 1971.

Scheier, M. F., Carver, C. S., Schulz, R., Glass, D. C., & Katz, I. Sympathy, self-consciousness, and reactions to the stigmatized. *Journal of Applied Social Psychology*, 1978, *8*, 270–282.

Scott, R. A. *The making of blind men.* New York: Sage, 1969.

Sigall, H., & Page, R. Attenuation of the expression of affect. Cited in E. E. Jones & H. Sigall, The bogus pipeline: A new paradigm for measuring affect and attitude. *Psychological Bulletin*, 1971, *76*, 349–364.

Smedley, J. W., & Bayton, J. A. Evaluative, race-class stereotypes by race and perceived class of subjects. *Journal of Personality and Social Psychology*, 1978, *36*, 530–535.

Smelser, N. J. Some determinants of destructive behavior. In N. Sanford & C. Comstock (eds.), *Sanctions for evil.* San Francisco: Jossey-Bass, 1971.

Snyder, M. On the self-perpetuating nature of social stereotypes. In D. L. Hamilton (ed.), *Cognitive processes in stereotyping and intergroup behavior.* Hillsdale, N.J.: Erlbaum, 1981a.

Snyder, M. Seek, and ye shall find: Testing hypotheses about other people. In E. T. Higgins, C. P. Herman, & M. P. Zanna (eds.), *Social cognition: The Ontario symposium Vol. 1.* Hillsdale, N.J.: Erlbaum, 1981b.

Snyder, M., & Swann, W. B., Jr. Behavioral confirmation in social interaction: From social perception to social reality. *Journal of Experimental Social Psychology*, 1978, *14*, 148–162.

Snyder, M., & Uranowitz, S. Reconstructing the past: Some cognitive consequences of person perception. *Journal of Personality and Social Psychology*, 1978, *36*, 941–951.

Spitzer, R. L. On pseudoscience in science, logic in remission, and psychiatric diagnosis: A critique of Rosenhan's "On being sane in insane places." *Journal of Abnormal Psychology*, 1975, *84*, 442–452.

Tetlock, P. E. Identifying victims of groupthink from public statements of decision makers. *Journal of Personality and Social Psychology*, 1979, *37*, 1314–1324.

Ugwuegbu, D. C. Racial and evidential factors in juror attribution of legal responsibility. *Journal of Experimental Social Psychology*, 1979, *15*, 133–146.

Walster, E. Assignment of responsibility for an accident. *Journal of Personality and Social Psychology*, 1966, *3*, 73–79.

Weiner, B. "On being sane in insane places": A process (attributional) analysis and critique. *Journal of Abnormal and Social Psychology*, 1975, *84*, 433–441.

Wilder, D. A. Reduction of intergroup discrimination through individuation of the out-group. *Journal of Personality and Social Psychology*, 1978, *36*, 1361–1374.

Wilder, D. A., & Thompson, J. E. Intergroup contact with independent manipulations of in-group and out-group interaction. *Journal of Personality and Social Psychology*, 1980, *38*, 589–603.

Wills, T. A. Perceptions of clients by professional helpers. *Psychological Bulletin*, 1978, *85*, 968–1000.

Worchel, S., & Andreoli, V. Facilitation of social interaction through deindividuation of the target. *Journal of Personality and Social Psychology*, 1978, *36*, 549–556.

Wright, B. A. *Physical disability—a psychological approach*. New York: Harper & Row, 1960.

Zimbardo, P. G. The human choice: Individuation, reason and order versus deindividuation, impulse and chaos. In W. J. Arnold & D. Levine (eds.), *Nebraska symposium on motivation, 1969*. Lincoln: University of Nebraska Press, 1970.

Zimbardo, P. G., Haney, C., Banks, W. C., & Jaffe, D. The mind is a formidable jailer: A Pirandellian prison. *New York Times Magazine*, April 8, 1973, 38–60.

ADDITIONAL READINGS

Katz, I. *Stigma: A social psychological analysis*. Hillsdale, NJ.: Erlbaum, 1981.
A systematic, theoretical analysis of reactions to deviant and disadvantaged social groups. The central theme is the ambivalence or uncertainty that characterizes the nonstigmatized individual's perceptions of the stigmatized. The data are based on laboratory experiments conducted by Katz and his colleagues over the past ten years.

Nisbett, R., & Ross, L. *Human inference: Strategies and shortcomings of social judgment*. Englewood Cliffs, N.J.: Prentice-Hall, 1980.
A sophisticated, highly readable analysis of errors and biases in social perception and judgment. The writers examine in considerable detail the causes and consequences of the human judge's failure to use normative or relatively formal rules in forming impressions and making predictions.

Sanford, N., & Comstock, C. (eds.) *Sanctions for evil: Sources of social destructiveness*. San Francisco: Jossey-Bass, 1971.
An analysis of atrocities and related episodes of human destructiveness. A central premise is that evil is often performed by people who are doing what they consider to be proper and righteous—"I was following orders" being the

classic illustration. Linking a wide variety of historical episodes is the perception of the victim as less than human. It is this perspective on the victims of evil that is particularly informative for the student of stereotyping.

Schlenker, B.R. *Impression management: The self-concept, social identity, and interpersonal relations.* Monterey, Calif.: Brooks/Cole, 1980.
An analysis of how people attempt to control images in social interaction. Because the outcomes of social interaction are presumed to depend upon impressions and inferences held by others, people are motivated to present themselves strategically to increase the desired social goals. This volume, a thorough review of the vast literature in this area, is of particular value in terms of embedding issues of stereotypes and first-impressions in the context of interpersonal behavior.

NAME INDEX

Aaron, H.J., 431
Abate, M., 25
Abel, T.M., 260
Abelson, R.P., 339
Abrahams, D., 262
Abramson, P.R., 268
Achenbaum, W.A., 371
Adam, B.D., 104
Adams, G.R., 33, 34, 253–304, 255, 262, 263, 265, 267, 269, 272, 273, 274, 278, 281, 282, 285, 286, 288, 292, 493
Adelman, C., 124
Adinolfi, A.A., 281
Adorno, T.W., 7, 16, 137, 177, 373n.
Agle, T.A., 278
Ajzen, I., 79, 115
Alger, H., Jr., 415
Allen, J.G., 319, 320, 343, 345, 346, 347
Allen, V., 108, 109
Allen, V.L., 446
Allport, F.H., 264
Allport, G.W., 7, 8, 9, 16–19, 22, 28, 32–35, 103, 121, 137
Almquist, E.M., 229
Aloni, R., 426
Alston, J.P., 429, 430, 448
Altrocchi, J., 327, 342
Amabile, T., 62
Amir, Y., 121
Anderson, B., 381, 395
Andiappan, P., 205
Andreoli, V., 487, 488
Arber, S., 228
Archer, D., 290
Arendt, H., 478
Aronson, E., 2, 21, 122, 123, 125, 287, 489, 490, 491
Aronson, V., 262
Arvey, R.D., 205
Asch, S.E., 19, 20, 30, 53, 54
Asher, S., 108, 109
Ashmore, R.D., 15, 27, 30, 193, 194, 196, 201
Aslin, A.L., 235

Astrachan, B.M., 330
Atchley, R.C., 385, 395
Atkinson, D.R., 493
Austin, W.G., 10, 21
Avis, W.E., 253
Axelrod, S., 372, 374

Backman, C.W., 30
Bailey, M.M., 230
Baird, L., 209
Bakan, D., 199
Baker, M.J., 256
Balaban, T., 224
Bales, R.F., 324, 325
Ball, R.A., 430
Baltes, P.B., 387, 388n.
Bandura A., 214, 483
Banfield, E.C., 430
Banks, W.C., 110, 486
Banks, W.M., 492
Bannister, R.C., 416
Barkley, R.A., 223
Barocas, R., 277
Baron, R.A., 203
Barrios, M., 290
Bar-Tal, D., 262, 270, 274
Barthell, C.N., 352
Bartlett, F.C., 75
Bartlett, S., 439
Bayton, J.A., 25, 99, 425, 426, 492, 494
Bear, S., 228, 232
Beauvoir, S. de, 366, 401
Beck, B., 424
Beck, J.D., 378, 379
Beck, S.B., 291
Becker, H.S., 450
Becker, R.E., 333
Bee, H., 196
Begley, P.J., 277
Belkaoui, A., 228
Belkaoui, J.M., 228
Bell, B.D., 374, 375, 376
Bellows, N., 489
Bem, D.J., 2

SUBJECT INDEX

achievement orientation, 22
Adolescent Prejudice (Glock), 176–77
adolescents: dating of and attractiveness,
262, 274–75; and prejudice, 176–77
(*see also* children)
advertising: and physical appearance,
255–56
age, 54, 93; and anti-Semitism, 171–73;
and income, 391–95, 400; and
intelligence, 386–88; and marriage,
395 (*see also* aging/aged)
age-ism, 269
aggression, 28; and body type, 257, 260;
disinhibition of, 483; displacement of,
27; and expectations, 117, 118;
perception of, 82–83
aging/aged, 34–35, 364–404;
contemporary images of, 380–96
[biological stereotypes, 380–84;
psychological stereotypes, 384–91;
social stereotypes, 391–96]; historical
perspectives on, 365–72 [assessment
of, 371–72; and idealism, 367, 368–71;
and modernization, 367–68];
measurement of stereotypes of,
372–80; summary/future perspectives
on, 402–4; theory on stereotype
maintenance, 396–402 [conflict
perspective, 400–2, 404, functionalist
perspective, 397–400, 404]
Aging Semantic Differential, 379
agricultural societies, 366–68, 398, 402
Aid to Families with Dependent
Children (AFDC), 449 (*see also*
welfare)
Alcoholics Anonymous, 334
alienation and mental illness, 329
ambivalence-response amplification
theory, 468–69
American Jewish Committee (AJC), 16,
153
androgyny in behavior, 234–36
anticipatory thinking, 31

Anti-Defamation League of B'nai B'rith,
19
Anti-Negro scale, 373*n*.
anti-Semitism, 2, 22, 32, 33, 137–85,
481–82; and age, 171–73; and
attitudes, 150–52, 154–75; and
education, 169–70; and images of
Jews, contemporary, 139–53 [and
attitudes, 150–52, 154–75; and
feelings, 146–50; and Holocaust,
152–53; on loyalty, 142–43, 159, 163,
164–65; on power, 139–42; on
stereotypes, 143–45]; and income,
170–71; and occupation, 170–71; and
race, 174–75; and religion, 173–74,
180; theories of, 175–84 [and
authoritarianism, 175, 177–79; and
cognitive sophistication, 175, 181–83;
and contact, 175, 176–77; and values,
175, 179–81]; and values 175, 179–81
(*see also* Jews)
Anti-Semitism in America (Quinley and
Glock), 184
anxiety, 8, 178, 284
Aphrodite, 266
Armenians, 22
Aryans, 479
assimilation, 103, 115, 127–28; of tokens,
49
asthenic body type, 257
athletic body type, 257
attitudes, 31, 34, 93; and anti-Semitism,
150–52, 154–75; and discrimination,
150–52; on mental disorders, 307-11,
326-331, 356; and poverty, 439; and
prejudice, 150–52, 154–75; and sex
differences in mental patients, 321–26
attribution theory, 29, 58–64, 84–85;
fundamental attribution error, 28,
60–64, 445–46, 500; and legal
proceedings, 277
audiotapes, 277
Australia, 418

522

ABOUT THE EDITOR
AND CONTRIBUTORS

Arthur G. Miller received his Ph.D. from Indiana University (1967). He is Professor of Psychology at Miami University in Ohio, where he teaches courses in social psychology, prejudice, and interpersonal perception. He edited *The Social Psychology of Psychological Research* and wrote a chapter on ethical and methodological issues in research with human subjects for Seidenberg and Snadowsky's text *Social Psychology*. His research interests include attributional biases, stereotypes associated with appearance, and interpersonal attraction.

Gerald R. Adams received his Ph.D. in human development from Pennsylvania State University (1975). He is Associate Professor and Chair in the Department of Family and Human Development at Utah State University. He is a co-author of *Physical Attractiveness: A Cultural Imperative*, and maintains a research program on interpersonal attraction and physical attractiveness stereotyping.

Kenneth J. Branco received his M.S.W. from Boston College (1976) and is a doctoral candidate in sociology at Boston College. He is an instructor in sociology at St. Anselm College, where he pursues research on the effects of the new conservatism on the quality of life in later years. He is a contributing author of *Aging and Society*, a text in social gerontology.

Amerigo Farina received his Ph.D. from Duke University (1958). He has taught at Duke University, and is Professor of Psychology at the University of Connecticut. He is the author of *Abnormal Psychology* and a module entitled *Schizophrenia* (General Learning Press). His fields of specialization are clinical psychology and personality theory, and his research deals with societal factors in mental illness and stigma.

Russell A. Jones received his Ph.D. from Duke University (1969). He is Professor of Behavioral Science in the College of Medicine at the University of Kentucky, where he teaches courses on information processing and research design. He is the author of *Self-Fulfilling Prophecies* and is Editor-Elect of *Personality and Social Psychology Bulletin*. His research interests include implicit personality theories and the influence of expectations on health and illness behavior.

Michael Morris received his Ph.D. in community-social psychology from Boston College (1978). He is Assistant Professor of Psychology at the University of New Haven, and also serves as Field Placement Coordinator for its Master's Program in Community Psychology. His research interests include ideologies of economic stratification, community intervention strategies, and field training in community psychology. A recent seminar has dealt with the culture-of-poverty thesis.

David Rosenfield received his Ph.D. from the University of Texas (1976). He is Associate Professor of Psychology at Southern Methodist University. His research interests include intergroup relations in children, intrinsic motivation, and racial attitudes. He has co-authored, with Walter Stephan, a chapter on intergroup relations among children in Brehm, Kassin, and Gibbons' *Developmental Social Psychology.*

Diane N. Ruble received her Ph.D. from U.C.L.A. (1973). She taught at Princeton University and the University of Toronto, and is Associate Professor of Psychology at New York University. She teaches social and developmental psychology, and sex roles, and is a co-author of *Women and Sex Roles: A Social Psychological Perspective.* Her research deals with sex stereotyping, developmental aspects of social perception, and attribution processes.

Thomas L. Ruble received his Ph.D. in management from U.C.L.A. (1973). He has taught at Indiana University and is Associate Professor and Chair in the Department of Management at Rider College. He has authored a chapter on conflict processes for Hellriegel and Slocum's volume *Organizational Behavior.* His teaching specialization is organizational behavior and group dynamics, and his research concerns women in management and conflict-handling behavior.

Walter G. Stephan received his Ph.D. from the University of Minnesota (1971). He has taught at the University of Texas, and is Associate Professor of Psychology at New Mexico State University. He edited, with Joe Feagin, *School Desegregation: Past, Present, and Future.* His research interests include attribution processes and intergroup relations.

John B. Williamson received his Ph.D. from Harvard University (1969). He is Associate Professor of Sociology at Boston College, where he teaches courses in social gerontology and poverty. His books include *Strategies Against Poverty in America, Aging and Society, Growing Old,* and *The Politics of Aging.* His research interests include aging politics and policy, social control of the elderly, and the impact of technology on the elderly.

Robert Wuthnow received his Ph.D. from the University of California at Berkeley (1975). He is Associate Professor of Sociology at Princeton University. His books include *Adolescent Prejudice* (co-author), *The Consciousness Reformation,* and *Experimentation in American Religion.*